TWELFTH EDITION

REAL ESTATE

Jerome Dasso

H.T. Miner Chairholder in Real Estate
University of Oregon

James D. Shilling

Chairman and Professor of Real Estate
University of Wisconsin

Alfred A. Ring

Professor Emeritus
University of Florida

Prentice Hall
Englewood Cliffs, New Jersey 07632

Library of Congress Cataloging-in-Publication Data

Dasso, Jerome J.
    Real estate / Jerome Dasso, James D. Shilling, Alfred A. Ring—
12th ed.
      p. cm.
    Includes index.
    ISBN 0-13-766239-4
    1. Real estate business. 2. Real property.   3. Real estate
investment. I. Shilling, James D. II. Ring, Alfred A.
III. Title.
HD1375.R5   1995
346.7304'37—dc20
[347.306437]   94-39982
                                          CIP

Acquisitions Editor: Catherine Rossbach
Editorial/Production and Interior Design: Laura Cleveland, WordCrafters
Editorial Services, Inc.
Cover Design: Eileen Burke
Manufacturing Buyer: Ilene Sanford
Managing Editor: Mary Carnis
Director of Production and Manufacturing: Bruce Johnson

 ©1995, 1989, 1985, 1981, 1977, 1972, 1967, 1960, 1954, 1947, 1938, 1922
by Prentice Hall, Inc.
A Simon & Schuster Company
Englewood Cliffs, NJ 07632

Printed in the United States of America
10 9 8 7 6 5 4 3 2 1

ISBN 0-13-766239-4

Prentice-Hall International (UK) Limited, *London*
Prentice-Hall of Australia Pty. Limited, *Sydney*
Prentice-Hall Canada Inc., *Toronto*
Prentice-Hall Hispanoamericana, S.A., *Mexico*
Prentice-Hall of India Private Limited, *New Delhi*
Prentice-Hall Japan, Inc., *Tokyo*
Simon & Schuster Asia Pte. Ltd., *Singapore*
Editora Prentice-Hall do Brazil, Ltda., *Rio de Janeiro*

Dedicated to the reader's success
in the field of real estate
and to the wise use of our land resources.

BRIEF CONTENTS

PART FIVE   REAL ESTATE FINANCE   319

PART SIX   LAW AND BROKERAGE   441

CONTENTS

PART FOUR   SPATIAL ECONOMICS   265

Chapter 17   Spatial Economics and Urban Area Structure   265

Chapter 18   More About Urban Area Structure and Real Estate Markets   283

Chapter 21   Debt and Equity Financing of Real Estate   337

Chapter 22   Financing Homeownership   365

Chapter 23   Mortgage Underwriting   392

Chapter 24   Mortgage Securitization   418

Chapter 33   Title Closing   574

Appendix   Time Value of Money   594

Index   631

PREFACE

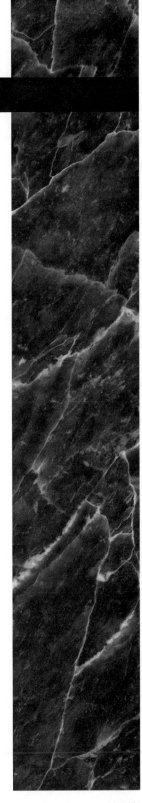

This book is written and designed for anyone seeking a clear understanding of the many decisions involved in the world of real estate. The intent is to create a mind set that will make it easier for the reader to understand how change and real estate values interact. The real estate ownership cycle—acquisition, administration, and alienation—used here provides an integrated, continuing frame of reference for the decision-making and implementation process. Using and administrating realty to maximize the self-interest of the investor, usually meaning maximizing wealth, is the assumed motivation or driving force of the cycle.

In this book you will learn about value analysis—market value and investment value—as well as development, finance, brokerage, and law with a balanced perspective. This approach provides a sound basis for further involvement in real estate. The format also provides an investor or practitioner with a continuing awareness of the decisions to be made in any particular situation or transaction.

As in the tenth and eleventh editions, the material is divided into major parts, each of which takes up important components of the decision-making process as it is applied to real estate. The parts are (1) value analysis, (2) market dynamics and property development, (3) finance, and (4) law and brokerage. Chapter sequences have been changed in several instances to improve the flow of presentation.

As in past editions, each chapter begins with a summary outline. Illustrations have been updated to make the content more easily understood. Key terms, discussion questions, and case problems continue to be provided.

Great effort has been made to provide accurate, up-to-date, authoritative content. Even so, the reader must recognize that this material is not meant to replace professional accounting, legal, real estate, and other expert advice.

Finally, we should add that there is over fifty years of experience behind the newest ideas in this edition of *Real Estate*. The first edition of *Real Estate* was published by Prentice Hall in 1922, with Nelson L. North and Philip A. Benson as the authors. Alfred A. Ring took over as the third author with the fifth edition and Jerome Dasso as the fourth author with the eighth edition. Now, James D. Shilling of the University of Wisconsin, with this edition becomes the fifth author of *Real Estate*, the longest continuously published book in real estate.

Reader comments have greatly helped improve past editions. As you use *Real Estate*, please note items that might improve the material and send them to the author as follows:

James D. Shilling
c/o Real Estate Editor
Prentice Hall
Englewood Cliffs, NJ 07632

Jerome Dasso
University of Oregon

James D. Shilling
University of Wisconsin

Alfred A. Ring
University of Florida

ACKNOWLEDGMENTS

A note of acknowledgment and grateful appreciation is extended to the following people who contributed to this revision. First, I would like to thank the reviewers: Professor Paul Asabere, Temple University, and Professor Dean Gatzlaff, Florida State University. Also, thanks go to Randy Guttery, University of North Texas at Dallas; Krisandra Guidry, Nicholls State University; and Jay Sa-Aadu and Ashish Tiwari, University of Iowa, who worked on the ancillary materials that go with this edition.

This revision also has benefitted substantially from the many insightful comments and suggestions of Professors David Ling, University of Florida, and Jay Sa-Aadu, University of Iowa, and from the comments of Professors Tony Ciochetti, University of North Carolina; Mark Eppli, George Washington University; and Elaine Worzalla, Colorado State University.

Students and colleagues at the University of Wisconsin-Madison also have been a constant source of inspiration and support. Greg Chun, Bob Liao, and Tom Ohlson helped with specific illustrations and end-of-chapter problems throughout the text.

Finally, my wife provided reassurance and understanding throughout the revision. For her moral support I am most grateful.

James D. Shilling

PART ONE
VALUE ANALYSIS

CHAPTER 1

INTRODUCTION

Chapter Outline

Our main ability is that we know how to win at this game of business. Society can make the rules it wants, as long as they are clear cut, the same for everyone. We can win at any game society can invent.

Michael Maccoby, *The Gamesman*

Many people consider real estate to be a market-oriented game, in the sense that there are players and rules, and a way to determine winners and losers. They have the same attitude as Michael Maccoby's gamesman, quoted at the beginning of this chapter. In fact, though, real estate is more than a game because it involves the very setting of life itself. Everyone must play because we all need space in which to live. After all, "under all is the land."

Success is not automatic, however. The world of real estate can be very risky and very illiquid. Just look at some of the more notable ventures in recent years—Olympia & York's Canary Wharf office complex in London, or some of the more prestigious addresses in Manhattan's financial district, like 40 Wall Street which is only steps away from the New York Stock Exchange, or 45 Wall Street, a 28-story building owned by Metropolitan Life Insurance Co.—which are currently sitting primarily vacant. Oversupply and a weakening demand have also brought woe to many smaller and midsize commercial and industrial properties, warehouses, and residential properties.

But it is possible to manage this risk. What is needed is a thorough understanding of basic real estate principles. With mastery of these principles, a reader should be able to make an informed decision as to whether to enter, and the best way to enter, real estate markets. To aid the reader, the "rules of play" are set forth throughout. This chapter takes up the several broad topics outlined. Subsequent chapters also begin with such an outline. Key concepts introduced in each chapter are defined at the end of the chapter.

REAL ESTATE AND THE ECONOMY

The activities and interaction of the people involved in buying, selling, exchanging, using, and improving realty make up the real estate market. The commodity involved in these transactions is rights in real property. The marketplace is the local community. Each market participant is motivated to maximize self-interest, whatever that may be. In economic and financial theory, maximizing self-interest is equated with wealth maximization. In life, however, self-interest can take other forms as well, such as protecting purchasing power, hedging against inflation, exhibiting power to control property, or helping others. The rules governing real estate investment come from several sources, including contract and real estate law, accounting and finance, management and marketing theory, licensure regulations, and professional and

MEANING OF REAL ESTATE

"Real estate" means different things to different people. It has three common meanings, which are interrelated. For clarification, consider the following definitions.

A Field of Study. Real estate as a field of study concerns the description and analysis of the occupational, physical, legal, and economic aspects of land and permanent improvements on or to land. The purpose of the study of real estate is greater knowledge and understanding for decisions and actions. Books, magazines, courses, and other educational activities focusing on real estate as a business or commodity fit into this definition. This entire book concerns real estate as a field of study.

A Form of Business Activity. People looking to real estate as their occupation, profession, or line of business activity are considered to be "in real estate." Appraisers, brokers, builders, lenders, planners, housing analysts, and inves-

tors are in real estate in this sense. In other words, real estate as a business activity focuses on human activities concerned with land and its use or improvement. This chapter explains the meaning further.

A Financial Asset. Real estate as a form of property or financial asset begins with the land and includes all "permanent" improvements on or to the land. As a financial asset, real estate is a national resource, whether publicly or privately owned. It accounts for nearly three-fourths of the tangible wealth of the United States. This asset or property concept is the most common meaning of real estate and is also the object or focus of all other meanings. The remainder of this book is devoted to real estate as a financial asset. And, unless otherwise indicated, the terms real estate, realty, and real property are used interchangeably in referring to real estate as an asset or commodity.

personal ethics. The setting for the community, in turn, is the United States and the world economy. So, a brief look at real estate and the economy seems an appropriate place to begin our discussion.

Land Ownership and Land Use

To begin with, just how much land is there in the United States? The answer is about 2.3 billion acres—2.265 billion to be exact. An acre contains 43,560 square feet, which is the equivalent of a square parcel about 209 feet on a side. A typical, single-family lot is about one-sixth of an acre. There are 640 acres in a square mile, which means that there are about 3.539 million square miles in the United States. A regional shopping center requires about 160 acres, or one-fourth of a square mile.

Who owns this land? Public lands account for 39.1 percent of the total, leaving 60.9 percent in private ownership (see Figures 1-1 and 1-2). The federal government controls almost one-third (32.1 percent) of our land area.

How do we use or employ our land? Of the total, 11.9 percent is employed for urban areas, transportation, recreation and wildlife, national defense, and industrial uses. The balance is devoted to agricultural purposes and other uses (see Figure 1-3). Somewhat less than 2 percent is devoted to urban uses.

FIGURE 1–1
U.S. Land Ownership
and Use

TYPE	LAND AREA (MILLION ACRES)	PERCENT DISTRIBUTION
LAND OWNERSHIP		
Private	1,380	60.93
Public	885	39.07
Federal	730	32.23
State and local	155	6.84
Total	2,265	100.00
LAND USE		
Cropland	469	20.71
Grassland	597	26.36
Forest	655	28.91
Special Uses[a]	270	11.92
Other	274	12.10
Total	2,265	100.00

SOURCE: Bureau of the Census, *Statistical Abstract of the United States 1989* (Washington, DC: U.S. Government Printing Office, 1989), Table 333.
[a] Urban, transportation, recreation, wildlife, national defense, and industrial areas.

In the overall, we really have no absolute shortage of land. We do often have a shortage of well-located urban land, however, just as we may have a shortage of highly productive agricultural land. Still, there is no shortage of land that legally may be farmed. Nor is there a shortage of land that legally may be developed for urban uses. How this land should be developed, if at all, is an entirely different question.

Real Estate as Wealth

Real estate occupies a dominant position in the United States insofar as real wealth is concerned. It accounts for nearly three-fourths of the fixed, tangible wealth of the United States (see Figures 1–4 and 1–5). Stocks, bonds, and mortgages are often obvious in investment portfolios, but a substantial portion of the worth of stocks and

FIGURE 1–2
Percentage Distribution
of Land Ownership in
the U.S.

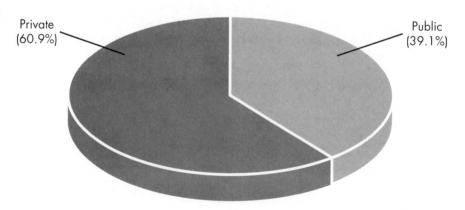

Private (60.9%)   Public (39.1%)

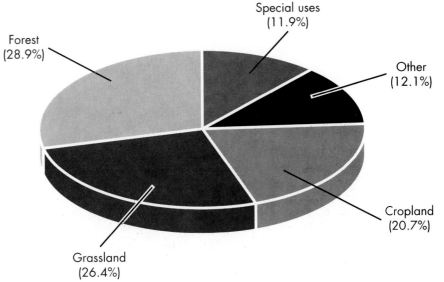

Forest
(28.9%)

Special uses
(11.9%)

Other
(12.1%)

Cropland
(20.7%)

Grassland
(26.4%)

FIGURE 1-3
Percentage Distribution
of Land Use in the U.S.

bonds actually reflects a claim on the earning power of business real estate. And, the total amount of mortgage loans outstanding, which represent a direct claim on real estate, approaches the national debt in size. As may be noted in the figures, slightly over 55 percent of total tangible wealth is residential real estate, and roughly 16 percent is nonresidential real estate.

Personal property was not taken into account as wealth by the data sources used. However, this omission is certainly more than offset by the worth of govern-

ASSET CLASS	AMOUNT (BILLIONS OF DOLLARS)	PERCENT DISTRIBUTION
NON-REAL ESTATE ASSETS		
Household Durables	1,806	11.56
Nonresidential Equipment		
Private	2,145	13.73
Public	540	3.46
Total Non-Real Estate Assets	4,491	28.75
REAL ESTATE ASSETS		
Nonresidential Real Estate	2,429	15.54
Retail	854	5.46
Office	958	6.13
Warehouse	292	1.87
Manufacturing	325	2.08
Residential Real Estate	8,703	55.71
Total Real Estate Assets	11,132	71.25
Total Fixed Tangible Wealth	15,623	100.00

FIGURE 1-4
Fixed Tangible Wealth
in the U.S. with
Percentage Distribution
by Type of Asset
(billions of dollars)

SOURCE: John C. Musgrave, "Fixed Reproducible Wealth in the U.S., 1986–1989," *Survey of Current Business,* U.S. Department of Commerce, Bureau of Economic Analysis, August 1990; David J. Hartzell, Robert Pittman, and David H. Downs, "An Updated Look at the Size of the U.S. Real Estate Market Portfolio," working paper, February 1992.

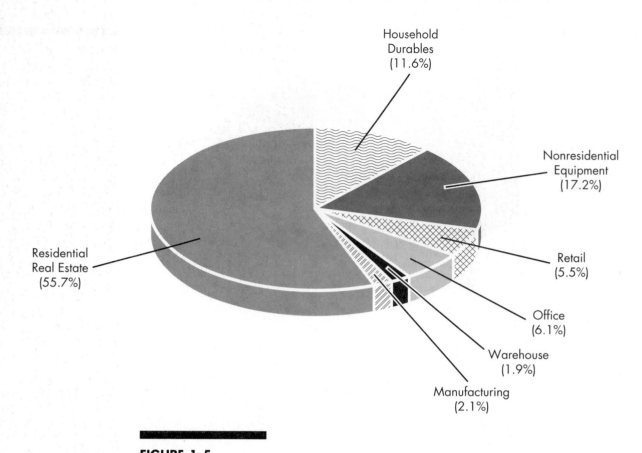

Household
Durables
(11.6%)

Nonresidential
Equipment
(17.2%)

Residential
Real Estate
(55.7%)

Retail
(5.5%)

Office
(6.1%)

Warehouse
(1.9%)

Manufacturing
(2.1%)

FIGURE 1–5
Percentage Distribution, by Type of Asset, of Fixed Tangible Wealth in the U.S.

ment land, the value of which tends to be under-represented because public property is not frequently sold or generally assessed for property tax purposes. Government land, as mentioned earlier, accounts for 39 percent of the total land area of the United States. A rough estimate of the value of government land (excluding mineral rights) is in excess of $175 billion.[1]

Real Estate Employment

Employment in real estate and construction typically accounts for about 5.5 to 7 percent of total employment in the United States (see Figure 1–6). The value of new construction approximates 10 percent of our gross national product each year. This construction includes from 1.0 to 3.0 million new dwelling units each year. The decline in the percent of total employment in real estate and construction between 1980 and 1990 reflects the shake-up that took place in the real estate industry during the 1980s. The decline in the percent of total employment in real estate and construction may

[1]Michael J. Boskin, Marc S. Robinson, Terrance O'Reilly, and Praveen Kumar, "New Estimates of the Value of Federal Mineral Rights and Land," *American Economic Review* (December 1985), 75: 923–936.

YEAR	EMPLOYMENT IN REAL ESTATE AND CONSTRUCTION	TOTAL EMPLOYMENT	PERCENTAGE OF TOTAL IN REAL ESTATE AND CONSTRUCTION
1940	2,517,155	44,888,083	5.61
1950	4,014,790	56,239,449	7.14
1960	4,415,057	64,639,256	6.83
1970	5,003,049	77,308,792	7.04
1980	7,249,000	102,315,000	7.05
1990	6,455,000	109,971,000	5.87

FIGURE 1–6
Employment in Real Estate and Construction, Compared to U.S. Total Employment, Selected Years, 1940–1990

SOURCE: Bureau of the Census, *U.S. Census of Population, 1940-1980;* Bureau of Labor Statistics, *Monthly Labor Report,* July 1991.

also reflect a change in the relative economic efficiency with which real estate can be produced. It is important to emphasize that the economic efficiency with which nations can produce various goods can and does change over time.

Real Estate as a Commodity

Real estate as a commodity is extremely complex. Each parcel has distinct physical characteristics. And, depending on the culture or society in which the parcel is located, specific institutional and economic characteristics apply. In addition, most urban real estate is man-made space that will be used over a long period of time. Builders and subdividers, investors and lenders, other professionals, local government officials, and users jointly create this space. Each parcel has a distinct space and time utility, benefit, or advantage. It is this distinct space–time utility that provides the basis for individual decisions and for differing values and, in the end, which drives the real estate market (see Figure 1–7). Professor James Graaskamp of the University of Wisconsin—Madison was the prime initiator of this space–time concept of real estate.[2]

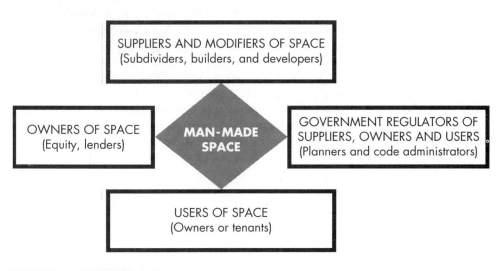

FIGURE 1–7
Real Estate as Man-Made Space and the Real Estate Market Participants

[2]See James A. Graaskamp, *Fundamentals of Real Estate Development.* Washington, D.C., Urban Land Institute, 1981.

REAL PROPERTY CHARACTERISTICS

As a market commodity, real property has distinct attributes or characteristics, which can be classified as physical, economic, and institutional. In practice, the distinction between the classes is sometimes uncertain. Figure 1–8 summarizes these attributes.

Physical Attributes

Immobility.   Land is physically immobile—that is, it is not movable in a geographic sense. Some of the substance of land—soil, minerals, oil—may be removed and transported, but the geographic location of a site remains fixed. An atomic bomb might destroy an entire city, but the geographic location of each parcel would be determinable by its latitude and longitude. It is *immobility* or *fixity* that causes land to be classed as real estate. Because of this immobility, the market for land tends to be local in character; demand must come to the site. Immobility results in the value of each parcel changing, for better or worse, in direct response to changes in its environment. Immobility also means that taxes may be levied against a parcel and collected, in one way or another; the parcel cannot escape.

Buildings and other realty improvements are not necessarily immobile. But considerable expense must be incurred to move a house or other structure. This means that if the value of a site becomes great enough to be no longer consistent with the site's improvements, the improvements may be moved. In turn, the value of the improvements in a different location must exceed the cost of moving them.

Indestructibility.   Land, as space, is *indestructible;* it cannot be destroyed; it goes on forever. The indestructibility of land tends to popularize it as an investment. A sophisticated investor, of course, distinguishes between physical indestructibility and economic (value) durability. Physically, land may go on forever, but its value may be destroyed by changing conditions. For example, the value of certain locations may disappear almost completely, as happened in "ghost towns." On the other hand, the permanence of land and space means that it may be used to support buildings and other improvements with extremely long lives. The buildings themselves, however, tend not to be indestructible, either in a physical or a value sense.

Heterogeneity.   No two parcels of land are exactly alike, an attribute called *heterogeneity,* nonhomogeneity, or unlikeness. At the very least, parcels have unique locations. Differences between parcels usually extend to size, shape, and topography. In addition, public *infrastructure* (roads and utilities) are location-specific and, not being uniform throughout a community, cause parcels to be unlike. Finally, external-

FIGURE 1–8

Physical, Economic, and Institutional Characteristics of Real Estate

PHYSICAL	ECONOMIC	INSTITUTIONAL
Immobility or fixity	Situs	Real property law
	Scarcity	Public regulation
Indestructibility	Interdependence	Local and regional custom
Heterogeneity	Durability or fixity of investment	Associations and organizations

CLASSES OF PROPERTY TRADED

Each class of real property represents stratified demand and constitutes a submarket that is often the basis of specialization by real estate practitioners.

Residential. Residential real estate is generally considered to include one-family and multifamily residences of up to six units, plus vacant land or lots that might be improved for anything up to six dwelling units, whether located in a city, a suburb, or a rural area. Technically, larger multifamily properties are also residential, but because of their higher value and greater complexity, they are more frequently classified as commercial-investment properties.

Commercial Investment. Large apartment buildings, stores, shopping centers, office buildings, theaters, hotels and motels, vacant commercial sites, and other business properties are termed commercial-investment real estate. Most commercial-investment properties are rental or income-producing and are usually located in urban areas.

Industrial. Industrial real estate includes factories, warehouses, utilities, mines, and vacant industrial sites. Large industrial properties are usually located in or near urban areas because of their dependence on an adequate labor supply. Industrial plants may sometimes be located and developed in rural areas if the availability of raw materials and power so dictates. Labor will be drawn to the plant and eventually an urban area will grow up around or near the plant.

Rural (Farm and Land). Farms and ranches make up the bulk of the rural properties that are bought and sold. Recreational properties are often included, but they seem likely eventually to become a distinct class. Raw, vacant land near urban areas, though ripe for conversion to residential, commercial, or industrial use, is also typically included in this category.

Special Purpose. Churches, colleges and other educational institutions, hospitals, cemeteries, nursing homes, and golf courses are collectively termed special-purpose properties. These properties are bought and sold infrequently, and no specialization has developed around them. They tend, for the most part, to be located in or near urban areas.

Public. Public agencies need real estate for highways, post offices, parks, administration buildings, schools, and numerous other public uses. Public properties are generally held for a long time and are sold only if considered excess property. For the most part, public properties are not considered as being bought and sold in a free market. Even so, public agencies do acquire and dispose of realty through the free market.

---

ities, positive and negative influences from other parcels, cause parcels to differ. An *externality* is an influence from outside the parcel. Zoning ordinances and title restrictions are efforts to limit negative external influences.

Heterogeneity has caused land to be legally declared a *nonfungible* (not substitutable) commodity requiring specific performance in contracts involving use or sale. In contrast, grain or IBM stock would be considered fungible or legally substitutable. *Specific performance* means that the terms of a contract must be exactly complied with; for example, a particular property must be conveyed and not a similar or substitute property.

Heterogeneity is the basis of problems in pricing or valuing realty because comparison of a site or property with similar but different properties is often a very complex undertaking. In an economic sense heterogeneity means that real estate is not homogeneous as a product, that the market is not perfectly competitive, and that the allocation of real estate resources may be less efficient than for other commodities.

Heterogeneity extends to buildings and other realty improvements. Structures usually differ in size, appearance, and complexity. Even if built to the same plan, workmanship and materials might differ slightly. At the very least, location and orientation are slightly different. In addition, differing owners and occupants lead to differing levels of use and maintenance.

Institutional Attributes

An *institution* is an accepted and established part of society; the term may be used to refer to an organization, a belief, a law, or a custom. Institutions shape the way we think and act, and in turn may exert a profound influence on values.

Real Property Law.   Real property has its own laws for the most part. Real estate is owned as real property rather than as personal property. This means that the laws affecting real estate ownership and financing differ from laws affecting the ownership and financing of personal property. This difference is so great that several subsequent chapters are devoted to real property law.

Public Regulation.   In a fashion similar to real property law, public regulation also affects real estate as a commodity or a product. Community plans and zoning ordinances, rent controls, subdivision regulations, laws pertaining to mortgage finance, and building codes all shape the development and use of our realty.

Local and Regional Custom.   Custom is the way of thinking or acting that is specific to a local area; it is similar to the habit of an individual. Custom results in Cape Cod-Style houses being prevalent in one community and almost nonexistent in another. New York City is relatively compact, whereas Los Angeles has been described as "seventeen suburbs in search of a city." Bicycles are an accepted mode of transportation in some areas and firmly rejected in others. Subtle, local attitudes and customs influence the nature, appearance, and use of real estate.

Associations and Organizations.   The National Association of Realtors (NAR), the National Association of Homebuilders (NAHB), and the Urban Land Institute (ULI) all greatly influence the nature of the real estate business and the development of our communities. Homebuilders change their methods of construction in response to manuals published by the NAHB. The Urban Land Institute did much of the pioneer work to get planned-unit developments, shopping centers, and curvilinear street systems accepted across the country. The National Association of Realtors emphasizes higher ethics and promotes multiple-listing systems to improve the real estate business. In another direction, the Federal National Mortgage Association (FNMA), often referred to as Fannie Mae, and the Federal Home Loan Mortgage Corporation (FHLMC), called Freddie Mac, cooperate with other organizations to create and maintain a secondary mortgage market, an institution developed specifically to benefit real estate.

Economic Attributes

Economic attributes are beyond the physical and institutional characteristics of real estate. Economic attributes may be a result of physical or institutional attributes. In any event, situs, relative scarcity, and interdependence all clearly affect real estate values.

Situs.   The location of a parcel relative to other external land-use activities is called *situs.* Both physical and economic location are involved, with the economic relationships being the more important. Situs is the result of choices and preferences of individuals and groups in selecting sites. Differences in situs cause otherwise similar parcels to have different uses and different values.

A major factor affecting locational choice is *accessibility*—the relative costs (in time, money, and effort) of getting to and from a property. When the relative costs of movement to and from are low, a property is said to have high accessibility. In turn, the property's value is likely to be high. Alternatively, poor or difficult accessibility generally leads to low values. The use of and the improvements or buildings added to a parcel are largely the result of its situs or relative accessibility. Other situs factors influencing locational decisions include direction of population growth, availability of services and utilities, shifts in centers of trade and manufacture, direction of prevailing winds, sun orientation, and changing life styles.

Scarcity.   Certain types of land may be in comparatively short supply, termed *scarcity.* The physical supply of land is fixed for all practical purposes. But scarcity of space, as such, is only relative. With money, time, and effort, the supply of man-made space can be increased in response to demand. Even so, the fear of an ever-increasing population outrunning a limited physical supply of land has caused periodic land booms and busts.

Interdependence.   The mutual interaction of uses, improvements, and values of parcels is called *interdependence.* The development of a shopping center across the street strongly influences how I use my site. Or, I may have a restaurant along a major highway that depends heavily on nearby motels for customers. Development of a by-pass route may severely cut the business both of the motels and my restaurant, with a consequent sharp drop in value of all the properties. Thus, the use and value of a given property is subject to modification by decisions and changes made about other properties. In net, the value relationship between properties tends to be synergistic, both positively and negatively.

Durability of Investment.   The long time required to recover costs of a site and its improvements is termed *durability of investment.* Once a site is purchased and labor and capital committed to build a structure, the investment is set or fixed for many years from the viewpoint of the community or of society. Drainage, sewage, electric, water and gas facilities, or buildings, as a rule, cannot be economically dismantled and shifted to locations in which they would be in greater demand. The investment is "sunk" in the realty and must be recovered during the economic life of the improvements. Further, the immobility and fixity of land and land improvements make real estate vulnerable to taxation and other social or political controls.

At the same time, fixity of investment does not preclude disposition of the property by one investor and acquisition by another. That is, the investment is not set or fixed for a specific owner.

Market Characteristics

The function of any market, by definition, is trade or exchange. Beyond trade, the market gives signals to change the quantity and quality of the product. Finally, markets provide price and value information to participants and others.

The real estate market appears disorganized and inefficient when compared to the stock and bond markets. This difference is partially due to greater government intervention in real estate markets, which takes the form of regulations, and several types of taxes (property, sales, and income) and tax incentives, such as depreciation allowances. Further, unit values tend to be high. In addition, differences flow from the physical and economic characteristics of real estate, discussed earlier, and from the classes of property traded. Thus, all things considered, real estate markets are undoubtedly less efficient than stock, bond, and commodities markets.

Market Attributes

The physical, institutional, and economic characteristics of real estate, along with its market attributes, all work in concert to make real estate markets relatively inefficient. Stated another way, the time and money costs of overcoming space constraints, and of collecting and analyzing data, all work to make real estate markets less efficient than most other markets. Let us look at these market attributes in more detail.

Localized Competition.   Immobility, heterogeneity, and durability cause competition for real estate to be area-specific. Inability to move real estate in response to changes in supply and demand conditions and lack of similarity and standardization means that a potential buyer must inspect each property of interest to understand fully its merits. Without easy means for buyers to compare one property with another, competition between properties is limited. Localized competition is more true of residential properties than of commercial and industrial investment properties. Commercial investors and industrialists are usually more knowledgeable and have greater reason to look around carefully before buying a property.

Stratified Demand.   People generally seek and use real estate for a specific purpose. For example, a family looking for a detached home limits its search to one-family houses. A merchant seeking a property from which to sell furniture looks only at store buildings. An investor for dollar income looks only at income properties. The market responds accordingly. The market for apartments may be very active, while the market for one-family residences may be very slow. Specializations develop and properties are classified according to this stratified demand; thus, brokers, appraisers, and managers may limit their activities to income or industrial real estate only.

Confidential Transactions.   Buyers and sellers usually meet in private, and, as a rule, their offering and agreed prices are not freely disseminated. Moreover, transactions are not made in a central marketplace but rather in homes, offices, restaurants, cars, planes, and dozens of other such locations. Decentralized and confidential transactions make market information difficult to collect and, therefore, costly.

WHY REAL ESTATE DECISIONS ARE DIFFERENT

High Value. Real estate has relatively high value. This high value tends to be a market-limiting factor; that is, the ability of most people to own real estate is limited because of their relatively low wealth or earning capacity.

Long Economic Life. Real estate has a long life. Land goes on forever; buildings last for decades. Real estate generates services and income over an extended time. And during this period, its services must be used as produced. They cannot be stored, to be used later, like toys, wheat, or cars. Each time period must stand on its own. If an apartment remains vacant during one month, the loss of rent cannot be made up in the next month.

Debt Financing. Debt financing for real estate purchases is usually necessary as well as desirable. It is (1) necessary because most people cannot afford to purchase real estate outright, and (2) desirable because the use of credit provides the opportunity for financial leverage and the possibility of a higher rate of return on the money invested. Leverage, or "trading on the equity," results from borrowing money on a property at an interest rate lower than the rate at which the property is expected to earn. Leverage is illustrated, by example, in the chapters on real estate finance and investment.

High Transaction Costs. In both time and money, costs of buying and selling real estate are high. At a minimum, several days are required to complete a simple closing and transfer of ownership. Several weeks is usual, and several months is not uncommon for large, expensive properties. A dollar transaction cost of 6 or 7 percent of the sale price of a property is also usual.

Relatively Uninformed Participants. Most buyers and sellers lack adequate price and value information in making their decisions, because collecting and analyzing information is costly. Business firms increasingly use real estate specialists—negotiators—to buy and sell properties in order to overcome information limitations. But owners and potential purchasers often make less than optimal decisions in their real property dealings. Only people closely associated with the market have relatively easy access to price and value information. Nevertheless, sellers and buyers increasingly seek, and pay for, price information to maximize self-interest. Of course, this means higher transaction costs.

Supply Fixed in Short Run. Supply in the real estate market is fixed, at least for periods of a few years. If demand falls, supply remains fixed. If demand increases, from several weeks to several months or longer are required to build new structures. Conversion of existing properties is no less time consuming. In any given year, the total supply of space is increased by only 2 to 3 percent.

Demand in a specific area or community can be quite volatile in the short run. Thus, demand could advance sharply. The consequence is a sharp price increase for space if demand runs too far ahead of supply. On the other hand, prices decrease only slowly if demand drops, because owners resist taking losses on high value, durable assets.

TOPICS COVERED IN THIS BOOK

This book covers the decision-making process involved in acquiring, administering, and eventually disposing of real estate. The material is presented in modules. The sequence followed is, first, investment decisions and value analysis, then appraisal, property development, spatial economics and urban area structure, real estate finance, and, finally, a series of modules on defining ownership and conveying ownership rights.

In Part One, we look at the basic valuation concepts essential to valuing real estate for investment purposes. Included in this discussion is a treatment of the risk and return on real estate. Certainly, by owning real estate, an equity investor is at risk for possible value decreases. Owning real estate also involves the possibility of new legislation that adversely affects the property, such as rent controls, rezoning, or increased taxes. Considerable attention is also given to identifying real estate investment opportunities and making investment decisions. Investing in real estate is certainly an appropriate place in which to spend extra time, money, and effort to reach the best decision.

In Part Two, we turn our attention to the real estate appraisal process. An appraisal is an estimate or opinion of value of a property, or some interest therein, rendered by an impartial person skilled in the analysis and valuation of real estate. Appraised values typically serve as a benchmark to both parties in buy–sell transactions. Appraised values also are important in property taxation or in determining compensation for property loss or damage.

Part Three is an overview of the property development process. Understanding the property development process is important to an investor for a variety of reasons. We will describe the property development process and provide a conceptual basis for making property development decisions.

Part Four covers spatial economics and urban area structures. Several theories exist as to why cities are established and how cities grow in response to the needs of people. A thorough understanding of these theories can help explain why certain land-use activities tend to locate at the point of greatest comparative advantage and how land is allocated among different users.

Part Five is devoted to real estate finance issues: the pros and cons of various types of mortgages, the key decisions relative to owning one's own home, what is involved in originating a mortgage loan, and how mortgage securitization is likely to affect the way in which real estate is financed in the future.

Part Six is comprised of nine chapters devoted to property descriptions and public records, real property rights and interests, leasing and lease analysis, government limitations to ownership, the investor–broker relationship, brokerage operations and practices, contracts for the purchase and sale of real estate, title assurances and title transfer, and title closings.

SUMMARY

Real estate accounts for nearly three-fourths of the tangible wealth of the United States. Real estate has relatively high value. It has a long life. Demand is stratified. Properties are immobile. Transactions are normally confidential. Supply is typically fixed in the short-run. And the costs of buying and selling real estate are high.

The task of the remaining chapters in Part One is to explain how investors make choices about owning, managing, and eventually disposing of real estate. In Chapter 2 we shall begin with a discussion of the real estate investment environment. Then in Chapter 3 we will discuss some basic valuation concepts. The major decision facing most participants in real estate is the investment decision. What house or income property to buy? How much to pay for the house or income property? And where the investment should be made?

After a brief discussion of the basic valuation concepts essential to valuing real estate for investment purposes, we will turn to a discussion of the potential risk involved in real estate investments. Risk analysis in real estate is critically important. Virtually all real estate financial decisions require that investors understand how the property stacks up as an investment before making a decision. Problems can be devastating, for example, if the economy enters into a slowdown and leaves you with a high vacancy rate and possible bankruptcy.

KEY CONCEPTS

Accessibility   The relative ease or difficulty of getting to and from a property; a property that is easy to get to has good accessibility or convenience of location.

Durability of investment   An economic characteristic of real estate; the long time required to recover outlays for improving realty—for example, for buildings.

Externality   Positive or negative influence from other parcels that affects the allocation of resources; examples are air or water pollution caused by neighboring parcels that have a negative effect on the value of a subject parcel.

Heterogeneity   A physical characteristic of real estate, meaning unlikeness from one property to another because of differences in location, size, shape, and topography.

Indestructibility   A physical characteristic of land or space. Land cannot be destroyed; it goes on forever.

Immobility   A physical characteristic of real estate, meaning a site is fixed as to location; also termed *fixity*.

Institution   An established organization, principle, law, belief, or custom.

Interdependence   An economic characteristic of real estate, wherein each parcel has an interaction of uses, improvements, and value that is shared mutually with surrounding parcels.

Scarcity   An economic characteristic of real estate; scarcity reflects the relative inadequacy of the supply of realty in a given use or a desired location.

Situs   An economic characteristic of real estate that refers to the locational aspects of a property (accessibility, exposure, and personal preference) relative to other properties.

Specific performance   A legal remedy compelling a defendant to carry out or live up to the terms of an agreement; often necessary in real estate because no other remedy would be adequate or appropriate because of a unique situs or location.

QUESTIONS FOR REVIEW AND DISCUSSION

1. List at least three physical attributes of realty and briefly give the implications of each.

2. What is situs and why is it important in real estate?

3. List at least two economic attributes of real estate, in addition to situs, and briefly give the implications of each.

4. Identify and explain briefly the implications of at least five characteristics of the real estate market.

5. Do the various classes of real estate (residential, commercial-investment, etc.) have different-sized areas of market influence? If so, why? Discuss.

6. State and explain briefly at least three ways in which real estate decisions tend to be unique.

7. In 150 words or less, write down your main objectives in studying real estate. Discuss your objectives with others and revise as desired. Then save it until your immediate study or term is completed, as an administrative check on yourself.

CHAPTER 2

INVESTMENT ENVIRONMENT

Chapter Outline

Never follow the crowd.

Bernard Baruch, *American financier and presidential advisor*

In real estate markets like those in the United States the level of investment spending is guided by the rate of net profit produced by the property. To the extent that the rate of net profit is high, the level of investment will be high. And if the rate of net profit is low, the level of investment will be low.

Note, too, that this rate of net profit is an expected rate of net profit. With respect to single-family residential properties, for example, the level of investment is based on the expected pleasures of owning and occupying a particular property. For office buildings and retail shopping centers, the level of investment is based on anticipated future income flows produced by the property.

Variability of expectations contributes to a high degree of instability in real estate investment spending. Changes in employment growth and therefore in anticipated market demand, changes in patterns of migration and population growth, changes in the cost of obtaining the money-capital required to negotiate the purchase of real estate, and a host of similar considerations may cause expectations to change and current real estate prices to fall or rise.

Optimism about the future also has a lot to do with the level of investment. Optimism may stimulate office tenants to upgrade their space or expand into new space. Optimism may also cause new households to purchase housing for the first time or existing households to purchase larger homes. These factors obviously mean a high level of investment.

There is also little doubt that taxes affect the level of real estate investment spending. Most real estate experts, for example, blame federal tax policy for the immense building boom in the U.S. during the 1980s. Federal tax laws during the 1980s permitted individual investors to shelter ordinary income with real estate deals, which led to an enormous amount of excess capacity. To illustrate, office vacancies nationwide increased fourfold between the 1970s and 1980s. At the same time, nationwide office rental rates fell from a peak of $30 per square foot in 1982 to $18 per square foot in 1990, causing property values to drop sharply. And if that were not enough, falling office rents and property values caused an increase in real estate bankruptcies.

In this chapter we will briefly examine some of the determinants of real estate investment spending. We begin with a discussion of the real estate decision-making cycle.

THE DECISION-MAKING CYCLE

The *decision-making cycle* of an investor making choices about owning, managing, and eventually disposing of real estate provides the framework for explaining real estate investment spending.

Real estate ownership decisions are best divided into three broad phases: (1) acquisition or purchase, (2) administration and management, and (3) alienation or disposition. The one commonality to all these decisions is the person making the choices. Almost every aspect of real estate is touched on in this decision-making cycle. Every investor goes through these phases. As one investor passes ownership on, another takes it up. The three phases may also be called the investment cycle. The cycle, with an indication of decisions to be made in each cycle, is shown in Figure 2–1.

The cycle is more easily understood if looked at in its entirety. Better investment decisions and results are likely if all aspects of ownership are looked at prior to actual acquisition, because the phases are interrelated. For example, understanding the property rights involved should precede any considerations of financing or investment analysis. Assuming a purchase contract, clear title has to be established at the same time that financing is obtained. Failure of an investor to give proper attention to any one of these areas may mean less than optimal results.

In looking at Figure 2–1, note that a major portion of the analysis and decision making connected with ownership takes place in the acquisition phase. Once a property is acquired (a contract signed, financing arranged, and title closed), an investor is locked in and may have a proverbial tiger by the tail. Even so, acquisition takes only a relatively short time, typically from 2 to 3 months. On the other hand, ownership administration requires only occasional major decisions, even though it may last for 5 to 10 years, or longer. Disposition may take several months or longer, measuring from the initial offering of the property to the closing of the sale. The main difference between acquisition and alienation decisions is that a specific investor is on the opposite side of the transaction.

What is not so readily apparent in Figure 2–1 is that a wide variety of specialists and professionals are involved in most real estate transactions. This includes real estate brokers, syndicators, equity investors and mortgage lenders, property developers, appraisers, architects, community planners, real estate counselors, property managers, and real estate lawyers.

MARKET PARTICIPANTS

Real Estate Brokers

Brokers act as catalysts or stimulants to the real estate market in that they earn fees or commissions by bringing buyers and sellers together. Together with investors and lenders, brokers are instrumental in carrying out the exchange function of the real estate market.

Brokerage is most generally thought of first when discussing careers in real estate because of its prominent image. The image comes about because brokers advertise widely and sales people move freely in search of listings and sales. With their extensive professional know-how and business contacts, brokerage personnel save clients much time, trouble, and money.

Arranging the sale and exchange of properties, such as apartment buildings, office buildings, stores, and warehouses is the essence of *commercial brokerage.* Current knowledge of population, income, other economic trends, finance, and tax law are all necessary to structure income-property transactions for greatest advantage to the parties involved. Commercial practitioners have considerable prestige, independence, and numerous opportunities for personal investing.

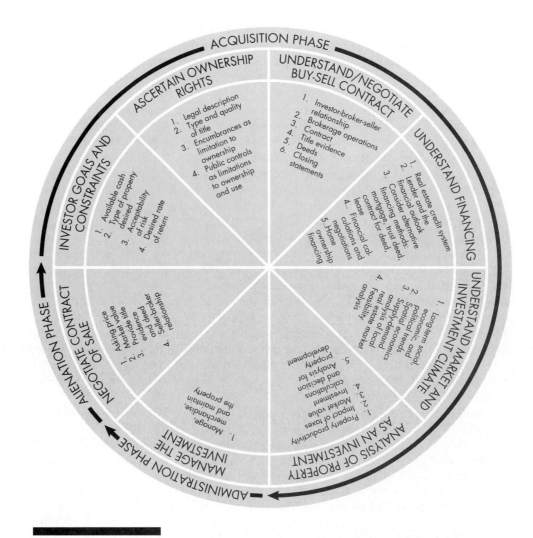

FIGURE 2-1
The Real Estate Decision-Making Cycle

Industrial brokers specialize in factories, warehouses, and vacant industrial sites. Knowledge of a community's economic base, transportation system, sources of raw materials, and factors of production, such as water, power, and labor, is very important for industrial brokers. An engineering or industrial management background is helpful because the work is frequently highly technical. The work is satisfying because complex problems are solved and prestige and high income may be gained.

Farm and land brokers specialize in the sale, leasing, and management of farms and ranches and in the sale and development of raw land. Properties handled may run from a 5-acre "ranchette" to a 160-acre farm to a 12,000-acre corporate spread. Obviously, a thorough knowledge of farming and ranching and a rural background are helpful. Specifically, a knowledge of soils, crops, seeds, fertilizers, seasons, machinery, government subsidies, and livestock is needed, and this, in turn, must be related to production costs and market prices of the products involved.

Syndicators

An outgrowth of commercial brokerage is the syndication of a real estate project. The work often requires changing the physical form (development) and the legal form (creating a corporation or limited partnership) of real estate to make a more marketable package and enhance value. Mainly, large, high-value properties are involved because they must absorb the overhead of the syndication process. Investors familiar with stock and bond investments invest in real estate primarily by buying shares in syndicated properties. The portion of all real estate that is syndicated is relatively small, however.

Equity Investors and Lenders

Equity investors and lenders are the primary decision makers in the real estate business. They put up the money and take the risks. They account for all major financial interests in the use and operation of real estate.

Most equity investors hold property for long-term benefits. Some even develop or improve property to realize these benefits. On the other hand, some real estate equity investors, termed *speculators,* specialize in holding property for short periods to seek quick gains.

Equity investors have many different modes of operation. Some investors regularly follow classified ads, visit brokerage offices, and maintain contacts with "cooperative" brokerage personnel in search of underpriced properties. Some investors develop properties for themselves. Others are particularly creative in adapting properties to changing local conditions to their own advantage.

The investment of most lenders is in the form of a loan to the owner, which is secured by the property. The lender's main concerns are that the property be kept operational and well maintained and that the loan be repaid on schedule. Banks, savings and loan associations, and insurance companies are the traditional lenders for real estate.

Property Developers

The property development team usually consists of a developer or subdivider, a land planner, an attorney, an architect, a contractor, and a lender.

The primary purpose of a *real estate developer* is to convert raw land into a complete operating property by adding roads, utilities, buildings, landscaping, financing, promotion, and other creative ingredients. The developer is the epitome of a risk taker. Considerable prestige and financial gain accrue to a successful developer; likewise, considerable risk is taken on if the project turns out to be less than successful.

Subdividers are drawn to a site for a number of reasons. For example, the market may have been extremely strong for commercial and residential development over the last few years. Or high future growth rates are anticipated. The main objective of the subdivider is to split a large parcel of land into lots for sale to builders or the general public.

The construction phase is the most visible stage of the development process. At this point, the developer selects a contractor and the contractor begins to create all site improvements, construct the buildings, and landscape the site.

Other Market Participants

Other real estate market participants include the following:

Appraisers are used to estimate market value. An appraisal is usually required when real estate is sold, financed, condemned, taxed, insured, or partitioned. A formal appraisal report contains an estimate of value, the date of the valuation, and qualifying conditions. Also included in all appraisal reports are the factual data and an analysis and interpretation of the data.

Architects are used to design and oversee the construction of improvements to land. The services of an architect are most often used for complex and expensive buildings that must meet both aesthetic and economic standards. Considerable desire and talent is necessary to become an architect.

Community planners relate development and land use to a community's economic and social needs. Planners usually work as consultants for local governments, civic groups, corporations, or developers. Planners coordinate the use of land and water resources needed for new streets and highways, schools, parks, and libraries, as well as for residential, commercial, and industrial neighborhoods.

Real estate counselors give expert advice on real estate problems, based on broad knowledge and considerable experience in the areas of brokerage, appraisal, development, financing, leasing, and investment. Counseling is usually combined with some other specialty, such as appraising, research, education, or market analysis.

A property manager supervises real estate for an owner, usually to achieve the maximum financial return. Rents are collected, space is leased, and the property must be repaired and maintained. Many corporations have a vice president for real estate asset management, recognizing that real estate constitutes nearly one-half, or more, of the firm's total assets.

Real estate attorneys perform a wide variety of duties, from negotiating leases to conducting title searches and examinations. Title search and examination and title insurance are involved in almost every real estate transaction. The purpose is to help investors achieve secure ownership. A *title search* is an examination of the public records to determine what, if any, defects there are in the chain of title. A title search will also reveal liens and encumbrances against the property. *Title insurance* is a contract in which the insurer promises to pay for losses arising from any defects in the title to the property.

DETERMINANTS OF REAL ESTATE INVESTMENT SPENDING

People invest in real estate only when it is profitable to do so. And only when the expected rate of net profits exceeds the cost of obtaining money-capital to finance the purchase of real estate.

As an example, suppose you are a large institutional investor and you pay $5,000,000 for an investment property. Further suppose that after all expenses have been paid, you expect to earn $500,000 in year 1 (see Figure 2–2). This, of course, is not bad. The ratio of income earned to equity investment, expressed as a percentage, is ($500,000 ÷ $5,000,000) × 100 = 10 percent. This means that you are earning a 10 percent *cash-on-cash rate of return.*[1]

A word about the calculations in Figure 2–2. Rents are self-explanatory. They consist of the rental payments made by the tenant or tenants. The total rent a property should earn in a year, based on market rents, constitutes its *potential gross income.*

Vacancy and collection losses are also self-explanatory. No income is earned if a subunit of space, such as an apartment, is not rented for a month or if it is rented but the tenant fails to pay. Vacancy and collection losses reduce the amount of income realized from the property.

The difference between potential gross income and vacancy and collection losses is termed *effective gross income.* Effective gross income is the amount of money the manager or owner actually collects from the property.

Operating expenses are out-of-pocket costs necessary to generate and maintain the income stream. These costs fall into two general categories: fixed expenses and variable expenses. A third general category, reserves for replacements, is sometimes added.

Property taxes and hazard insurance are the two main fixed costs. *Fixed costs,* as the name implies, are outlays that remain at the same level, regardless of the intensity of use of the property—for example, property taxes. Property taxes are levied on an annual basis and do not increase if occupancy climbs to 100 percent, nor do they decrease if occupancy drops to 65 percent.

Variable expenses, on the other hand, fluctuate with occupancy; more gas, electricity, and supplies are used with full occupancy than with 75 percent occupancy. Variable expenses also include such items as management fees and repairs, miscellaneous services, and reserves for replacement.

Replacement reserves, if and when deducted, reflect the fact that building parts and many items of equipment have lives longer than one year but much shorter than the expected life of the building. For residential income-producing properties, stoves, refrigerators, elevators, roofs, boilers, washers, dryers, carpeting, and air conditioning are examples of items that must be replaced as periodic out-of-pocket expenses. Accountants used to believe that the annual deduction for replacement of equipment and building parts should be placed in a special account called reserves for replacement. But, until the expense is incurred, it is not recognized by the Internal Revenue Service. For this reason, if reserves for replacement are deducted when computing net profits, the amounts must be added back in for calculating taxes.

The amount left over after total operating expenses have been deducted from effective gross income is called *net operating income.* Net operating income is the bottom line amount a property earns in competition with other properties that offer similar services.

---

[1] The astute reader will note that this 10 percent cash-on-cash rate of return is a pretax rate of return. This 10 percent cash-on-cash rate of return also ignores any appreciation or depreciation in the value of the property. Thus, the actual pretax return on this property may be significantly higher or lower than 10 percent, depending on whether property values are expected to increase or decrease over time. We will have more to say on the measurement of the rate of return on real estate in subsequent chapters.

FIGURE 2-2
Expected Net Profit on
a $5 Million Office
Building

Potential gross income	$925,926
Less: Vacancy and collection losses	$ 92,593
Effective gross income	$833,333
Less: Operating expenses	$333,333
Net Operating income	$500,000

In Figure 2–2, net operating income is $500,000. This is based on a potential gross income of $925,926, a vacancy and collection loss of $92,593 (or 10 percent of potential gross income), and operating expenses of $333,333 (or 40 percent of effective gross income).

Now for the determinants of the expected rate of net profit which investors hope to realize from real estate spending.

1. *Population and Population Movements.* Several factors determine the expected rate of profit on real estate. Foremost among these factors is population and population movements. Patterns of migration and growth, such as between the Northeast and the Sun Belt, or between urban and rural areas, can have a dramatic effect on the local demand for real estate services. Household income, age of households, type of households—couples with children, couples without children, so-called empty nesters, nontraditional families, and so forth—also tell us something about the demand for real estate.

2. *Economic Activity.* Just as population and population movements affect the demand for real estate services, so too does the level of economic activity influence the demand for real estate. To the extent that the level of economic activity in the local economy is weak, real estate investment in that market will be retarded. The reason is obvious: Real estate investment demand is a derived demand, derived from the wants, desires, and preferences of consumers or users. With a lower demand for real estate services, real estate investment spending will fall.

3. *Acquisition, Maintenance, and Operating Costs.* We also know that the initial construction costs, along with the estimated costs of operating and maintaining the property, are important considerations in the expected rate of profit on real estate. To the extent that these costs are high, the expected rate of net profit on real estate will be low.

4. *Vacancies.* Supply considerations are also important. If a local market has enough, or even excessive, inventories of vacant or unlet space, the expected rate of profit from further real estate investment will be low, and therefore little or no investment will occur.

5. *Variability of Expectations.* Real estate investment spending is based on expected profits. And one thing we have learned about expected profits is that expectations are sometimes subject to radical revisions when events change. Changes in patterns of migration and population growth, changes in employment growth and therefore in anticipated market demand, changes in the cost of obtaining the money-capital required to negotiate the purchase of real estate, and a host of similar considerations may give rise to a change in expected profits. Some investors earn superior returns on real estate because they are able to

buy properties at prices that are less than their real productivity, or they are able to put properties to new, higher-valued uses than anyone had formerly perceived, or because they were lucky, which is another way of saying that actual profits turned out to be much higher than expected profits.

6. *Optimism.* Optimism can have a lot to do with real estate investment spending. Just think of Japan's real estate market during the 1980s. After dizzying increases during the so-called bubble economy of the late 1980s, property prices in Japan's major cities are hurtling back to earth. In the nation's three largest metropolitan areas, Tokyo, Osaka and Nagoya, commercial property values have fallen around 13 to 18 percent from their peak, and residential values have fallen around 12 to 35 percent.[2]

7. *Tax Policy.* Tax policy has a way of encouraging or hindering real estate investment spending. For example, compared with other countries, few Britons rent private housing. In 1991, only 8 percent of Britons rented. In comparison, approximately 32 percent of all households in the United States rented private housing. In Sweden, roughly 24 percent of all households rented, and about 20 percent of all households in France rented. Why is the percentage so low in the United Kingdom? It has not always been that way. Back in the 1940s, approximately 90 percent of Britons rented. The explanation for such a low percentage of current renters in the United Kingdom is tax policy. Owning a house in the United Kingdom and renting private housing no longer compete on equal terms. Britons who buy their homes clearly enjoy favorable tax treatment.

MICRO DEMAND FOR REAL ESTATE

At the micro level, the demand for real estate depends on whether the site use is reasonably probable and appropriately supported by the market, and whether the proposed use is physically possible and maximally productive. A no answer to any of these questions means that the project may not be the highest and best use for the land. Should this occur, instead of forging ahead with the project as planned, the equity investor may want to regroup and redesign the project.

Consider the case of buying a house. Just as with any other real estate investment, you begin by looking at the physical characteristics of the site. Is the property well located in a good neighborhood? Is the property conveniently located with respect to shopping areas, churches, schools, transportation, and even recreational areas? Is the house a well-planned house? What are the neighborhood trends? Neighborhood changes from a higher to a lower level of use can bring about economic obsolescence and falling house values.

What we should expect to observe is that the choice of location for both residential and commercial real estate is extremely important. A homeowner choosing the right location can expect relative increases in property value. The same is true for commercial real estate investors. The decision as to where to locate can greatly influence the overall return on commercial real estate. The main reason is that commercial tenants like the prestige of a good location—whether it is in the downtown business district or on the outskirts of town.

[2]Commercial market prices in Japan are nearly impossible to measure because there have been almost no significant commercial property sales in Tokyo or Osaka in more than a year.

We should also point out that real estate values have a tendency to change over time and that not all investors value real estate similarly. Differences arise because investors have different investment goals or have different capacities to pay for an investment. That different investors value real estate differently may help explain why real estate is traded frequently, some properties more than others, and why we observe real estate being traded from the lower-valuing investor to the higher-valuing investor.

SUMMARY

The real estate investment process consists of three distinct decision-making phases: (1) acquisition or purchase, (2) administration and management, and (3) alienation or disposition. The one commonality to all these decisions is the person making the choices.

Success in the acquisition or purchase phase depends on whether the investor is able to negotiate the purchase of the property at a price less than its real productivity, or whether the investor is able to put the property to a new higher-valued use than anyone had formerly perceived.

In the administration and management phase, success depends on how well the property serves the consumer, who uses or consumes the space provided. Think of it in this way: Without the consumer or consumers, the real estate investment is worth very little. The space would sit empty, generating little, if any, net return.

In the disposition or alienation phase, the important considerations are the asking price, market value, and whether the property is owned free-and-clear of any defects. Note too that the trading of real estate will go from the lower-valuing investor to the higher-valuing investor.

Because the phases are interrelated, the best investment decisions and results are likely to eventuate if all aspects of ownership are looked at prior to actual acquisition. It is also important to focus on the expected rate of net profit produced by the property. People invest in real estate only when it is profitable to do so.

Population and population movements, economic activity, acquisition, maintenance and operating costs, vacancies, variability of expectations, optimism, and tax policy all contribute to the expected rate of net profit on real estate. At the micro level, whether the site use is reasonably probable, whether the proposed use is physically possible, whether the site use is appropriately supported by the market, and whether the proposed use is maximally productive are the basic determinants of profitability.

KEY CONCEPTS

Cash-on-cash rate of return   Usually either before-tax cash flow divided by equity investment, or net operating income as a proportion of total investment.

Decision-making cycle   The three broad phases regarding choices as an investor goes into and out of real estate ownership: (1) acquisition or purchase, (2) administration and management, and (3) alienation or disposition.

Effective gross income   Revenues actually collected in operating an income property; potential gross income less vacancy and collection losses.

Fixed cost   Outlays that remain at the same level, regardless of the intensity of use of a property.

Net operating income Earnings of an income property after operating expenses and maintenance have been deducted from effective gross income.

Operating expenses Expenses necessary to generate revenues on a sustained basis by an income property; examples are management, water, electricity, taxes, insurance, and maintenance.

Potential gross income The total rents a property should earn in a year, based on market rents.

Vacancy and collection losses Income not received, either because space is not rented or the tenant fails to pay.

Variable expenses Operating costs that fluctuate with occupancy; for example, more gas, water, electricity, and supplies are used with full occupancy than with partial occupancy.

QUESTIONS FOR REVIEW AND DISCUSSION

1. What contributes to a high degree of instability in real estate investment spending? What causes changes in expectations?

2. What are the three broad phases of real estate ownership? What occurs during each one of these phases?

3. List the different market participants in real estate? What do they do?

4. Which participants take most of the risk in real estate investment?

5. What are some different scenarios which may require appraisal of a property?

6. What is a title search? Why should one be done prior to the purchase of a real estate asset?

7. Discuss the major classifications of cash flows found in an annual pro forma operating statement for an income-producing property. What is the major distinction between potential gross income and effective gross income?

8. What are some examples of variable expenses for an office building?

9. What are some different factors that may affect the expected rate of net profit on real estate assets?

10. What factors determine the demand for real estate at the micro level?

PROBLEMS

1. If the effective gross income of a 45,000 square foot office building is $730,000 with a vacancy rate of 12 percent, what is the PGI? What are the gross rents per square foot, assuming all tenants pay the same constant amount?

2. Assume operating expenses are 30 percent of potential gross income for a 200,000 square foot office building. Gross rents are $18.00 per square foot and vacancy and collection losses amount to 15 percent. What is the net operating income on the property? What happens to net operating income if the vacancy and collection losses are 20 percent?

3. Organize the following items into a pro forma annual operating statement. All quantities are on an annual basis.

Gross income	$240,000
Miscellaneous expenses	$2,000
Property maintenance expense	$10,000
Supplies	$8,000
Property taxes	$20,000
Hazard insurance	$6,000
Salaries: maintenance and operating	$20,000
Vacancy and collection losses, as a percent of PGI	5%
Management, as percent of EGI	5%

4. New Plan Realty Trust, New York, recently acquired Factory Merchants Mall in Osage Beach, Missouri. With 90 factory-operated stores occupying 325,000 square feet of retail space, the center covers 41 acres. Opened in 1987, the center is fully leased. Average rental rates are $7 per square foot triple net. (Triple net means that in addition to the stipulated rent, the lessees assume payment of all expenses associated with the property, including fixed expenses, such as taxes and insurance, and operating expenses, such as maintenance and repair.) Determine first year net operating income for Factory Merchants Mall.

5. New Millennium Estate Ltd., acting on behalf of a European pension fund, recently acquired a 350,000 square foot office building at 10 East 53rd Street in New York City. The property was sold for $55 million. Terms of the sale are all cash. Built in 1972, the building is approximately 80 percent occupied. Rent per square foot is $27.68. Fixed and variable expenses are roughly $8 per square foot.

   Required: (a) Determine first year net operating income. (b) Compute the cash-on-cash rate of return to the European pension fund. Is this return attractive?

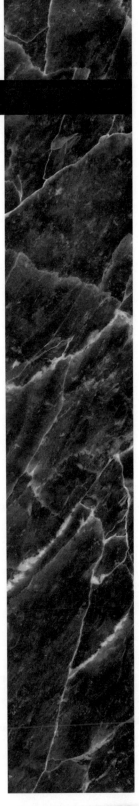

CHAPTER 3

BASIC VALUATION CONCEPTS

Chapter Outline

In this chapter basic valuation concepts essential to finding the worth of real estate for investment purposes are presented. The analysis occurs in three phases. First, the chapter takes up the problem of measuring the flow of services and income produced by a real estate investment. Included in this analysis is a discussion of what constitutes income from a real estate investment, the typical costs incurred in operating real estate, the distinction between fixed and variable expenses, and an assessment of some important financial ratios.

The second phase of the analysis is concerned with measuring the cash proceeds due on sale of the property. To the extent that the property appreciates over time, the investor will realize a capital gain upon disposition of it. This capital gain can be substantial, depending on when the investor purchased the property and what has happened to local real estate markets since acquisition. Capital gains are by no means guaranteed, however. An unexpected regional downturn in economic conditions, for example, can easily send real estate prices plummeting. Key financial decisions on how to value real estate often hinge on the forecast of price appreciation. Like any other asset, if real estate investors act rationally, expectations of future price appreciation should be embedded in current real estate prices. Thus, any real estate assets that were "good deals" will have already been bid up to the point where they are no better than previous "bad deals" whose prices have been allowed to fall until they are equally good deals. This means that you should accept the existing market price of real estate as an unbiased reflection of the worth of the property, unless you can better evaluate the local real estate market.

The third phase of the analysis deals with discounting the flow of services or income to the investor. *Discounting* in this context means to value the flow of income payments and cash proceeds at disposition at less than their apparent worth. Investors discount future payments to reflect their opportunity cost of funds and the uncertainty associated with the payment. Reversing the process can yield an estimate of the compounded or future value of the property.

MEASURING CASH RETURN ON INVESTMENT

The gross annual income a property earns serves as an initial index or measure of the cash return on investment. For refined estimates of cash return on investments, business executives, property managers, investors, and others use a pro forma annual operating statement. The statement shows both gross and net operating income, plus operating expenses.

The annual operating statement of Douglas Manor Apartments for years 1 through 4 is shown in Figure 3-1. The statement provides a series of income and expense projections over an assumed four-year holding period. Normally, however, holding periods for apartments, office buildings, and other commercial real estate are much longer. The statement should reflect actual market behavior, because realistic estimates of income and expense must be used to obtain a useful estimate of investment or market value.

Potential Gross Income

Potential gross income is tantamount to the total rents a property should earn in a year. The use of *should* here is important. *Market rent* rather than contract rent must be used in estimating potential gross income. *Contract rent* is the number of dollars that is paid in rent for a property based on a specific rental agreement. *Market rent* is the rent a property would command if exposed to the market, for a reasonable time. Contract rent is likely to be equal to market rent at the time a lease for the property is negotiated. Later, contract rent may exceed or fall below market rent, owing to changing economic conditions that are not accommodated in the lease. If the premises are leased for less than their market rent, then potential gross income is not an accurate reflection of the earning power of the property. Too low a potential gross income might be reported because of a long-term lease or because of ignorance or incompetence on the part of the owner or manager.

ITEM	YEAR			
	1	2	3	4
Potential Gross Income	$108,000	$113,400	$119,070	$125,024
Less: Vacancy and				
collection losses @ 4%	4,320	4,536	4,763	5,001
Effective Gross Income	$103,680	$108,864	$114,307	$120,023
Less: Operating expenses				
Fixed				
Property taxes	$20,908	$21,953	$23,051	$24,204
Hazard insurance	1,460	1,533	1,610	1,690
Licenses and permits	250	262	275	289
Variable				
Gas, water, and electricity	$2,800	2,940	3,087	3,241
Supplies	1,350	1,418	1,488	1,563
Advertising	730	767	805	845
Payroll	3,988	4,187	4,397	4,617
Management, 5% of				
effective gross income	5,184	5,443	5,715	6,001
Miscellaneous services	1,160	1,218	1,279	1,343
Property maintenance	1,850	1,943	2,040	2,142
Net Operating Income (NOI)	$64,000	$67,200	$70,560	$74,088

FIGURE 3-1
Pro Forma Annual Operating Statement: Douglas Manor Apartments

LEASEHOLD INTERESTS

It is an interesting sidelight that lease terms frequently create what is called a *leasehold interest* that benefits the lessee, or tenant. A leasehold interest is the right to use and occupy a property. A leasehold interest acquires value when contract rent is less than market rent. When contract rent exceeds market rent, a leasehold interest has no value.

Many examples exist of the dramatic benefits associated with leaseholds. Able tenants often are able to capitalize on leasehold interests by subleasing all or part of the property. Sapolin Paints, Inc. in 1980, for example, sold one-half of a 25-year lease for a manufacturing plant (with a 10-year renewal option) for $230,000 as part of a bankruptcy filing. The rent of $0.81 per square foot was $2 per square foot less than market. The sale resulted in a "$1 million asset" for the acquirer.

The shoe is on the other foot when contract rent exceeds market rent. Here, instead of creating a leasehold interest which is to the detriment of the *lessor,* or landlord, the difference between contract rent and market rent can actually benefit the lessor. In this case the landlord will earn a higher rent than the rent the real estate can command in the market. This rent premium tends to be short-lived, however. Normally, in such circumstances tenants will want to renegotiate their leases, often agreeing to extend the term of the lease in exchange for a lower rental rate.

Owners frequently rent subunits of space on a month-to-month basis, as with apartments. Office buildings, shopping centers, and even warehouses are also operated on this basis. By way of example, our sample property, Douglas Manor Apartments, contains 16 apartments: eight one-bedroom units and eight two-bedroom units. The current rents are $525 and $600 per month, respectively. With no adjustments in these rents during the first year, gross scheduled income in year 1 can be calculated as follows:

	ONE-BEDROOM UNITS	TWO-BEDROOM UNITS
Monthly market rental per unit	$525	$600
Multiplied by number of months	× 12	× 12
Annual market rental per unit	$6,300	$7,200
Multiplied by number of units	× 8	× 8
Gross scheduled income from units	$50,400	$57,600

The total potential gross income in year 1 is $108,000 ($50,400 plus $57,600).

In subsequent years, potential gross income may be higher or lower, depending on supply and demand conditions in the marketplace. For our sample property, market rents are expected to increase at 5 percent per year over the four-year holding period. Thus, beginning in year 2, the monthly market rent per unit for a one-bedroom unit is projected to be $551 ($525, plus .05 times $525). Likewise, the monthly market rent per unit for a two-bedroom unit is expected to be $630 in year 2 ($600, plus .05 times $600). During the year, the scheduled rents are expected to remain constant. This assumption implies that the potential gross income in year 2 will be

$52,920 for the one-bedroom units ($551 times 12 to convert monthly into annual rent per unit, and then times 8 to convert rent per unit into potential gross rent) and $60,480 for the two-bedroom units ($630 times 12 to convert into annual rent per unit, and then times 8 to convert into potential gross rent), so that the total potential gross income in year 2 equals $113,400 ($52,920 + $60,480). Total potential gross scheduled income in years 3 and 4 is calculated in a similar fashion.[1]

Vacancy and Collection Losses

In the sample operating statement, Douglas Manor Apartments is expected not to collect 4 percent of potential gross income because of vacancy and collection losses, based on experience in the area. These vacancy and collection losses are expected to remain constant at 4 percent over the four-year holding period.

Effective Gross Income

Effective gross income for Douglas Manor Apartments is projected to be $103,680 in year 1 ($108,000 in potential gross income, minus $4,320 in vacancy and collection losses). In years 2 through 4, effective gross income is estimated to be $108,864, $114,307, and $120,023, respectively. The increase in effective gross income over the four-year holding period is attributable to the fact that market rents per unit for Douglas Manor Apartments are assumed to be rising over time, while vacancy and collection losses are projected to remain constant. Clearly, one would want to revise these estimates of annual effective gross income downward if vacancy and collection losses were expected to increase over time, and raise the estimates of effective gross income if vacancy and collection losses were expected to decline over time.

Operating Expenses

For Douglas Manor Apartments, total operating expenses in year 1 are estimated to be $39,680. This figure is arrived at by taking the total fixed expenses for year 1, $22,618, and adding the total variable expenses, $17,062. Reserves for replacements are not taken into account as out-of-pocket property maintenance expenses in these calculations. Over time, both fixed and variable expenses are expected to increase by 5 percent per year. Thus, in year 2, total fixed expenses are projected to be $23,749 ($22,618, plus .05 times $22,618) and total variable expenses are estimated to be $17,915 ($17,062, plus .05 times $17,062), so that total operating costs are $41,664 ($23,749 plus $17,915). By year 4, total operating expenses are projected to be $45,935.

---

[1] Total potential gross income in year 3 is equal to $119,070 ($55,566 plus $63,504.36), while total potential gross income in year 4 is $125,024 ($58,344 plus $66,680). These figures reflect an increase in monthly market rents per unit on one-bedroom units from $551 in year 2 to $579 in year 3 ($551, plus .05 times $551) and to $608 in year 4 ($579, plus .05 times $579). Monthly market rents per unit on two-bedroom units are projected to be $662 in year 3 ($630, plus .05 times $630) and $695 in year 4 ($662, plus .05 times $662).

Net Operating Income

For Douglas Manor Apartments, net operating income (NOI) in year 1 is estimated to be $64,000 (effective gross income of $103,680, minus total operating expenses of $39,680). Projected annual increases in NOI over the four-year holding period are $3,200, $3,360, and $3,528, respectively. Thus, at the end of year 4, NOI for Douglas Manor Apartments will have increased to $74,088.

NOI is preferred to gross income as a measure of cash return on investment because it is a standardized concept. Differences in costs of operation or leasing terms are taken into account in reaching NOI. Thus, NOI allows comparison of the cash return on the subject property with that of other properties. A prestige office building that generates high rents but also has extremely high operating costs can thus be more fairly compared with a more modest office building on a long-term net (of operating costs) lease.

NOI is supposed to indicate what a property can do on its own. Thus, some items often considered by an owner-investor in analyzing an income property are not included in calculating NOI. For example, financing costs, owner's income taxes, depreciation, and corporation taxes are excluded. These items, though important to an investor, have no effect on the ability of a property to generate net revenue.

Debt financing does not increase or decrease the market rents a property is likely to earn. Likewise, the owner's income taxes on money earned from the property reflect the owner's tax situation and not the rent-generating ability of the property. Corporate ownership is an aside, so corporate taxes do not constitute an operating expense. Other items to be excluded are outlays for capital improvements and personal property taxes of an owner.

Building depreciation is not deductible as an operating expense because it is really a recovery of capital; it does not affect productivity and is not necessary to produce gross income. Depreciation is simply a loss in value that may be taken as an income tax deduction.

ANALYZING CASH RETURNS

Calculation of important ratios and an income forecast are both necessary prerequisites to finding investment value.

Productivity Ratios

The standardized accounting format of the pro forma operating statement provides an excellent basis for the calculation of useful operating ratios. The best operating data are available for apartment buildings, shopping centers, and hotels and motels. Thus, excellent norms for interpreting ratios for these property types are also available. Some caution is needed in interpreting the ratios, but still their potential usefulness is great.

The Institute of Real Estate Management publishes *Apartment House Income-Expense Experience* annually. The Urban Land Institute publishes *Dollars and Cents of Shopping Centers* every third year. The Building Owner's and Manager's Association and specialized accounting firms periodically publish operating information on hotels and motels, office buildings, and other specialized property types.

PRODUCTIVITY RATIOS

Names of the various productivity ratios, their manner of calculation, and their meaning are provided below. Deviations from industry norms indicate that the property may be poorly managed, or that income or property expense items have been left out.

RATIO	HOW CALCULATED	WHAT RATIO SHOWS
Income ratio	Net operating income/ Potential gross income	A high income ratio might be the result of good management—keeping the property fully rented while keeping control of operating expenses—or reflective of high-quality construction that minimizes costs of repairs and maintenance.
Operating expense	Operating expense/ Potential gross income	Important that this ratio be realistic before calculating other financial ratios. Deviations from industry norm may reflect a poorly managed property or indicate that certain expense items have been left out.
Vacancy and collection loss	Vacancy and collection loss/ Potential gross income	Reflects supply-demand conditions; signals when new supply needed, as well as when saturation or oversupply point has been reached. Highly sensitive to local economic conditions. Should have close relationship to vacancy rates reported by managers of similar properties.

Two of the more useful ratios for evaluating property productivity are the income and operating expense ratios. The *income ratio* is net operating income as a percentage of potential gross income.

$$\text{Income ratio} = \frac{\text{Net operating income}}{\text{Potential gross income}}$$

For Douglas Manor Apartments, the income ratio for year 1 equals

$$\text{Income ratio} = \frac{\$64,000}{\$108,000} = 0.593 = 59.3\%$$

where potential gross income for year 1 is $108,000 and net operating income for year 1 is $64,000 (see Figure 3–1).

The higher the income ratio, the greater the productivity of the property. This might be the result of good management—keeping the property fully rented while keeping control of operating expense. It might also be the result of high-quality construction that minimizes costs of repairs and maintenance.

An alternative ratio emphasizing control of expenses is necessary for cost-control purposes. An *operating expense ratio* reflects operating expenses as a percentage of potential gross income. For Douglas Manor Apartments, the operating expense ratio in year 1 is:

$$\text{Operating expense ratio} = \frac{\text{Operating expense}}{\text{Potential gross income}}$$

$$= \frac{\$39,680}{\$108,000} = 0.367 = 36.7\%$$

An operating expense ratio might be used as follows. New apartment buildings typically have an operating expense ratio between 35 and 40 percent. As the building ages, costs of repairs and maintenance go up. The ratio gradually increases toward 50 percent, and eventually toward 60 percent. The ratio tells the experienced investor or lender if an operating statement is realistic. A ratio of 32 percent for a new apartment building would indicate that perhaps not all expenses were reported, or that expenses have been understated. Operating ratios vary from property type to property type—that is, from apartment house to office building to hotel, and so on.

There is also a third useful ratio: the vacancy and collection loss ratio, which equals total vacancy and collection losses divided by potential gross income. A normal allowance of 4 to 10 percent is frequently set up for vacancy and collection losses, but different types of buildings (e.g., rent-controlled apartments located in good areas, where the rental level is considerably below the market level versus apartment buildings located in an area of transition or decline) and different market conditions (e.g., tight market conditions versus oversupplied market conditions) may demand greater or lesser percentages.

The sum of the vacancy and collection loss ratio plus the operating expense ratio and the income ratio total 100 percent. Thus, the three ratios give a complete accounting of potential gross income.

Forecasting Income and Expenses

An investor's central task is to forecast and evaluate expected benefits before investing, because expected benefits are the basis of value. The forecast depends on the location of the property, on its physical and functional capability, and on local market conditions.

Current revenues, expenses, and net operating income provide a take-off point of some certainty for forecasting. Unless secured by a lease with a strong tenant, a forecast is only a secular trend or tendency. Short-term influences will cause fluctuations above and below a projected trend. One can assume, however, that over time, up and down movements will offset each other, and the average will reflect the underlying long-term forces.

MEASURING CASH PROCEEDS DUE ON SALE

The net cash proceeds due on sale of a property represent the *reversion* or future value of the equity investment after all expenses associated with the sale have been paid. While some of this reversion value may, of course, be only a return of the investor's initial cash investment, part of the reversion may very well represent a return on investment, especially if the property appreciates significantly over the holding period. Forecasts of any price appreciation or depreciation over time are therefore extremely critical in the valuation of real estate.

For exposition purposes, the expected cash proceeds due on the disposition of the Douglas Manor Apartments are shown in Figure 3–2. To understand how the expected cash proceeds due on sale are measured, we begin with the definition of *gross sales price.*

Gross Sales Price.   *Gross sales price* represents the most probable selling price, in cash, to the investor at the end of the investor's holding period. For Douglas Manor Apartments, the most probable selling price at the end of four years is expected to be $777,924. This figure is our best estimate of the market value of the property at the end of the investor's holding period. From this amount, all expenses associated with arranging and negotiating the sale must be subtracted.

Selling Expenses.   Because it is costly in both time and money to arrange and negotiate the sale of real estate, selling expenses in a real estate transaction tend to be high. For instance, a dollar transaction cost of 6 to 7 percent of the sales price is not atypical for income-producing property. This is not to say, however, that all real estate transactions will involve a 6 to 7 percent selling expense; complex transactions obviously may end up costing more, while less-sophisticated transactions may end up costing less. For Douglas Manor Apartments, selling expenses are assumed to be 7 percent of the gross sales proceeds, or $54,454.

Net Sales Price.   The difference between the expected gross sales proceeds due on disposition and selling expenses is termed the *net sales price.* Net sales price is a measure of the amount of money the investor actually receives from the sale of a property after all selling expenses are paid. For Douglas Manor Apartments, the net sales price, or reversion value, is estimated to be $723,470 (see Figure 3–2).

PRICE APPRECIATION AND EFFICIENT REAL ESTATE MARKETS: A DIGRESSION

In measuring the cash proceeds due on sale of a property, there is a tendency to view the expected price appreciation, if any, as if it were "manna from heaven." Yet, if investors anticipate that property values will appreciate over time, they are apt to pay higher prices today in order to acquire the right to receive higher future payments.

ITEM	AMOUNT
Gross Sales Price	$777,924
Less: Selling expenses, 7% of sales price	54,454
Net Sales Price	$723,470

FIGURE 3–2
Expected Cash Proceeds Due on Sale: Douglas Manor Apartments[a]

[a] Cash proceeds due on sale of Douglas Manor Apartments represent the expected reversion or future value of the property at the end of year 4 after all expenses associated with the sale have been paid.

Similarly, if investors expect real estate prices to fall over time, they are prone to pay a lower price today in order to compensate for the loss in value over time. To the extent that investors act rationally, expectations of future price appreciation are, therefore, likely to be embedded in current real estate prices. If these expectations of future price appreciation are quickly reflected in current selling prices and values, then real estate markets are termed *efficient.*

Just how quickly information about the price outlook for real estate gets reflected into the probable selling price of a property has important implications for real estate investors. If, for example, changes in public and private information are reflected fully and instantaneously in current selling prices and values, investors will, on average, be unable to use either public or private information on, say, the relocation of a major thoroughfare or the announcement of a plant opening or information about other similar events to earn excess returns in real estate. Instead, current prices will adjust instantaneously to reflect the location decision and, hence, the best subsequent investors can hope for is to earn a normal return on their investment.

In inefficient markets, participants with greater knowledge or skill can exploit other participants and thereby rapidly increase their wealth because price information in inefficient markets is captured and disseminated rather slowly. Once information is known, however, the value expectations of participants is influenced. This suggests relative inefficiency in that those able to gain the greatest knowledge are also able to gain the greatest advantage in the market. This conclusion provides an extremely strong reason to study and follow cause-and-effect market indicators in investment real estate.

PRESENT WORTH OR DISCOUNTED VALUE

We use the term *discounting* quite frequently. For example, we are sometimes told to discount a statement or a rumor circulated by a commonly known gossip or liar—that is, to take the statement at less than face value. Merchants run sales at discounted prices, meaning reductions from regular or list price. Discounting, therefore, means to value a statement, an item, or a series of income payments at less than its apparent worth; this concept carries over when determining the present worth of real estate.

Investors discount future income payments on real estate and the cash proceeds due at disposition, in part because of the timing of the payments and in part because of the uncertainty surrounding the payments. Waiting to receive a future income payment or the cash proceeds due at disposition is costly, because a dollar today can be invested to start earning interest immediately. The cost is referred to as the *time value of money* and it compensates the investor for investing in the project rather than investing in securities with certain payoffs. Thus, the longer the investor must wait to receive the payment, the higher the cost. Therefore, when discounting a future income payment or the cash proceeds due at disposition, you need to ask yourself, "What is the value today of the future payoff, and does this discount adequately reward the investor for accepting delayed payment?"

Uncertainty adds to the time value of money by making future payments more risky. Here we note that an uncertain future payoff is worth less than a certain payment as long as the real estate investor is *risk averse*—that is, as long as the investor prefers to avoid risk without sacrificing return. Thus, to calculate how much an uncertain future income payment or an uncertain expected payoff at disposition is worth, an investor must assess whether the project is risky. The riskier the project, the greater the discount.

Adjusting present values for both time and uncertainty is complicated because not all real estate investments are equally risky and not all real estate projects promise similar payoffs each period. In the following pages we therefore take up the two effects separately. For the remainder of this chapter, we will sidestep the problem of how risk is defined or measured and assume that investors will discount expected future payoffs by the rate of return offered by comparable investment alternatives. This *discount rate* is often termed the *opportunity cost of capital.* The opportunity cost of capital is the return forgone by investing in a comparable project of equal risk. Our discussion of risk is postponed until Chapter 4.

Present Value of Lump-Sum Payments

For our sample problem, Douglas Manor Apartments, we suppose that the typical investor in the marketplace, after considering the riskiness of the projected cash flows, will discount the future income payments shown in Figure 3–1 and the cash proceeds due at disposition in Figure 3–2 by a 20 percent pretax discount rate. Convention is to discount the payments to equity as received at year-end. Convention is also to discount the payments to equity with annual factors.

Since the income payment of $64,000 is received at the end of year 1, this implies that the present worth of the payment is approximately $53,333. To calculate this value, we divide $64,000 by $(1 + .20)$, yielding $53,333. Thus, the discount associated with this expected future value is $10,667 ($64,000 − $53,333). We can interpret the $10,667 as the amount of interest on profit being earned by the investor during year 1.[2]

To find the present worth of the future income payment at the end of year 2, we discount the $67,200 payment at rate r according to the formula:

$$\text{Present value} = \frac{\text{Expected future payment}}{(1 + r)(1 + r)}$$

$$= \frac{\text{Expected future payment}}{(1 + r)^2}$$

$$= \frac{\$67,200}{(1 + .20)^2} = \$46,667$$

Thus, at a 20 percent discount rate, the $67,200 income payment to be received at the end of year 2 is worth only $46,667 to a potential investor in Douglas Manor

---

[2] You might check for yourself that $10,667 represents the amount of interest earned on $53,333 over a one-year period. By placing $53,333 into an investment earning 20 percent interest compounded annually, the investor would earn interest of 0.20 times $53,333, or $10,667, during the first year. The future value of this investment at the end of year 1 would be $64,000, made up of the initial principal, $53,333, plus accrued interest of $10,667.

Apartments. The difference between the future value of $67,200 and the present worth of $46,667, or $20,533, represents the amount of interest earned by the investor over a two-year holding period.[3]

The general formula for finding the present value of a future payment to be received at the end of year n, discounted at rate r, is, therefore

$$\text{Present value, } BOY_1 = \frac{\text{Future payment, } EOY_n}{(1 + r)^n}$$

where BOY_1 is shorthand notation for the beginning of year 1 and EOY_n means end of year n (i.e., if n equals 4, then future payment, EOY_4 means the payment to be received at the end of year 4).

Figure 3–3 shows the present value of the future income payments to be received from Douglas Manor Apartments over a four-year holding period and the present value of the cash proceeds due at disposition, each discounted at 20 percent. Also shown is the present value of $1 ($PV1$) factor, which is discussed below. Notice that each future payoff should be worth less today (i.e., at the beginning of year 1) because of the discounting. This is clearly so in our example. The net sales price (NSP), or reversion value, or $723,470 to be received at the end of year 4 is worth $348,895. Here the $723,470 payoff would be worth exactly that if the property could be sold instantaneously at a net (of expenses) sales price of $723,470. The four-year delay reduces the present value of the net sales price to $348,895.

FIGURE 3–3
Present Worth of Douglas Manor Apartments

YEAR	(1) NOI[a]	(2) NSP[b]	(3) PV1 FACTORS[c]	(4) = (1) × (3) PRESENT VALUE
1	$64,000		0.833333	$53,333
2	$67,200		0.694444	$46,667
3	$70,560		0.578704	$40,833
4	$74,080	$777,924	0.482253	$384,624[d]
			Present Worth =	$525,457[e]

[a] See Figure 3–1 for forecasts of future income payments.
[b] Taken from Figure 3–2.
[c] Calculated assuming an opportunity cost of capital, or discount rate, of 20 percent compounded annually (see TVM tables in the appendix at the end of the book).
[d] = $74,000 × 0.482253 + $777,924 × 0.482253 = $35,729 + $348,895.
[e] = $53,333 + $46,667 + $40,833 + $384,624.

[3] The amount of compound interest earned on $46,667 during the first year is 0.20 times $46,667, or $9,333. Thus, the future value of this investment at the end of year 1 would be $56,000 ($46,667, the initial principal, plus $9,333, the accrued interest). During the second year, the investor will earn interest on $56,000 at a 20 percent annual rate, or $11,200. Thus, the total interest earned over the two-year holding period is $9,333 plus $11,200, or $20,533, and the future value of this investment is $67,200 ($56,000 principal amount at the end of year 1 or the beginning of year 2, plus the $11,200 interest earned during year 2).

Present Value of 1 Factor

In present value terminology, the *present value of 1 (PV1) factor* for year 1 with $r = 0.20$ is expressed as the reciprocal of 1, plus the rate of return:

$$PV1 \text{ factor, year } 1 = \frac{1}{(1 + r)} = \frac{1}{1.20} = 0.833333$$

The $PV1$ factor converts a single payment to be received in the future into a present, lump-sum value. For Douglas Manor Apartments, multiplying the future income payment of $64,000 to be received at EOY_1 by the $PV1$ factor for year 1 at 20 percent interest, 0.833333, yields a present worth of $53,333 (see Figure 3–3). The $PV1$ factor is less than 1 since a dollar today is worth more than a dollar tomorrow.

For year 2, $n = 2$, the factor is 0.694444, calculated as follows:

$$PV1 \text{ factor, year } 2 = \frac{1}{(1 + r)^2} = \frac{1}{1.20^2} = 0.694444$$

and the present worth of the income payment at EOY_2 from Douglas Manor Apartments is $67,200 times 0.694444, or $46,667.

For year 3, $n = 3$, the factor is calculated by:

$$PV1 \text{ factor, year } 3 = \frac{1}{(1 + r)^3} = \frac{1}{1.20^3} = 0.578704$$

while for year 4, $n = 4$, and the factor is 0.482253:

$$PV1 \text{ factor, year } 4 = \frac{1}{(1 + r)^4} = \frac{1}{1.20^4} = 0.482253$$

The factors we have just calculated are shown in the $PV1$ column of the 20 percent annual time-value-of-money (TVM) table in the appendix. Tables of precalculated $PV1$ factors are also presented in the appendix for interest rates ranging from 6 to 50 percent. In making up these TVM tables, $(1 + r)$ is termed the base. Thus, for a 6 percent table, 1.06 is the base. For a 10 percent table, 1.10 is the base. Each of these $PV1$ factors can be used to convert a lump-sum future payment to a present value (see Figure 3–4).

Present Worth of Real Estate

Let us assume you own Douglas Manor Apartments. How much could you sell it for? Given the calculations presented in Figure 3–3, that is an easy question. Since the property produces future cash payments of $53,333, $46,667, $40,833, and $35,729, and cash proceeds due at disposition of $348,895, as measured in terms of a dollar today (see column 3), investors would be willing to pay $525,457 for it. The $525,457 present value is the sum of the present worth of the future cash payments (i.e., $53,333 + $46,667 + $40,833 + $35,729 = $176,562) and the present value of the cash proceeds due at disposition $348,895. That is what it would cost investors to get

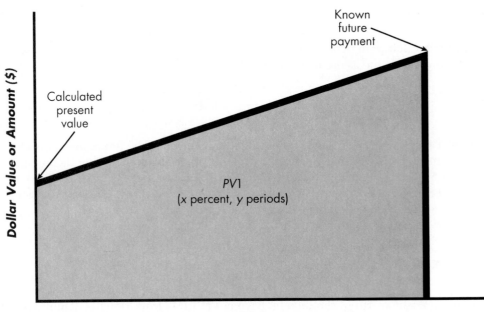

Known future payment

Calculated present value

Dollar Value or Amount ($)

*PV*1
(*x* percent, *y* periods)

Time

the same expected payoffs over the next four years from investing in a comparable property earning 20 percent interest.

The general formula for finding the present worth of a property is:

$$\text{Present worth of property} = \frac{NOI_1}{(1 + r)} + \frac{NOI_2}{(1 + r)^2} + \frac{NOI_3}{(1 + r)^3} + \cdots$$

$$+ \frac{NOI_n}{(1 + r)^n} + \frac{NSP}{(1 + r)^n}$$

remembering that NOI_1 denotes the expected income payment at the end of time period 1 (one year hence), NOI_2 denotes the expected income payment at the end of time period 2 (two years hence), and so on. In our Douglas Manor Apartments example, $n = 4$, and $NOI_1 = \$64,000$, $NOI_2 = \$67,200$, $NOI_3 = \$70,560$, $NOI_4 = \$74,080$, and $NSP = \$723,470$. We also made the assumption that the appropriate opportunity cost of capital is $r = 20$ percent. The present value formula then tells us that

$$\text{Present worth of property} = \frac{\$64,000}{1.20} + \frac{\$67,200}{1.20^2} + \frac{\$70,560}{1.20^3}$$

$$+ \frac{\$74,080}{1.20^4} + \frac{\$723,470}{1.20^4}$$

We can simplify this formula by recalling the definition of $PV1 = 1/(1 + r)^n$ for n years. This implies that

$$\text{Present worth} = \$64,000 \frac{1}{1.20} + \$67,200 \frac{1}{1.20^2} + \$70,560 \frac{1}{1.20^3}$$

$$+ \$74,080 \frac{1}{1.20^4} + \$723,470 \frac{1}{1.20^4}$$

or

$$\text{Present worth} = \$64{,}000 \times PV1_1 + \$67{,}200 \times PV1_2 + \$70{,}560 \times PV1_3$$
$$+ \$74{,}080 \times PV1_4 + \$723{,}470 \times PV1_4$$

where $PV1_1$ is the present value of 1 factor for year 1, $n = 1$, at 20 percent interest, $PV1_2$ is the present value of 1 factor for year 2, $n = 2$, at 20 percent interest, etc.

By looking the $PV1$ factors up in the TVM tables in the appendix at the end of the book, we obtain

$$\text{Present worth} = \$64{,}000 \times 0.833333 + \quad \$67{,}200 \times 0.694444$$
$$+ \quad \$70{,}560 \times 0.578704$$
$$+ \quad \$74{,}080 \times 0.482253$$
$$+ \$723{,}470 \times 0.482253$$

Multiply the future income payments and the cash proceeds due at sale by the $PV1$ factors, and we have our answer:

$$\text{Present worth} = \$53{,}333 + \$46{,}667 + \$40{,}833 + \$35{,}729 + \$348{,}895$$
$$= \$525{,}457$$

In this case the calculations are made easier by using the $PV1$ factors given in the TVM tables in the appendix.

Using Financial Calculators

All the calculations in the chapter can be performed on financial calculators, which can often be purchased for less than $50. Only four or five keystrokes are required to solve simpler problems. Complex problems must be broken down into subproblems, each of which can then be solved with four or five keystrokes. Using financial calculators is faster and more accurate than using TVM tables. Also, interest rates not provided in the TVM tables are easily taken account of with calculators.

The basic approach is the same, whatever the calculator. However, the keystrokes required vary from calculator to calculator. To begin with, financial calculators have a row of five financial keys, as shown:

n i PV PMT FV

The inputs for the keys are

n = number of periods
i = periodic interest rate
PMT = periodic level payment, as in an annuity (which is discussed in Chapter 19)
PV = present value (of a single future payment or a stream of payments)
FV = future value (of a single present-value payment or a stream of payments)

In most applications, known information for three variables must be fed in by pushing the appropriate keys. Each calculator has its own operating instructions and procedures, but generally pressing "2nd" or "CPT" (for compute) and the key representing the unknown information causes the desired answer to be displayed. These applications use the Douglas Manor Apartments example so that the emphasis is on developing facility in using your calculator.

Calculating Present Value of Future Income Payments and Cash Proceeds

What is the present value of the $64,000 income payment to be received at EOY_1 assuming a 20 percent rate of return? The $64,000 goes into the FV cell, $n = 1$ is the number of periods, and $r = 20$ percent is the interest rate. Compute PV.

Now for a similar problem. What is the present value of the $723,470 cash proceeds due on disposition at EOY_4 assuming a 20 percent rate of return? The $723,470 is FV, $n = 4$ is the number of periods, and $r = 20$ percent is the interest rate.

Calculating a PV1 Factor

What is the $PV1$ factor for 2 years with a 20 percent discount rate? Note that 1 goes into the FV cell, $n = 2$ goes into the number of periods cell, and $r = 20$ percent is the interest rate. What is the $PV1$ factor for 4 years with a 20 percent discount factor? Which factor is larger? $PV1$ for 2 years or $PV1$ for 4 years? Why?

How Real Estate Is Valued

What is the present worth of the following payoffs assuming a 20 percent opportunity cost of capital:

YEAR	NOI	NSP
1	$64,000	
2	$67,200	
3	$70,560	
4	$74,080	$723,470

Break the problem down into subproblems, and calculate the present value of each future income payment and the cash proceeds due at disposition. Then add the resulting present values to determine the present worth of the property.

FUTURE PROPERTY VALUES

Let us consider the Douglas Manor Apartment example, assuming for the moment that the present worth of the property is $525,457. Suppose you also know that Douglas Manor Apartments will appreciate in value by 10.31 percent per year compounded annually.[4] What is the future value of Douglas Manor Apartments at the end of year 1, end of year 2? end of year 3? end of year 4? A simple calculation gives us an answer.

At EOY_1, $n = 1$, the future value of Douglas Manor Apartments is

$$
\begin{aligned}
EOY_1 \text{ future value of property} &= \text{present value } (1 + \text{growth rate}) \\
&= \text{present value } (1 + r) \\
&= \$525{,}457 \, (1 + .1031) \\
&= \$579{,}632
\end{aligned}
$$

Therefore, at EOY_1, the value of Douglas Manor Apartments is \$579,632. At the end of two years, the value of the property totals \$639,392. This means that at the end of year 2, the value of Douglas Manor Apartments is given by:

$$
\begin{aligned}
EOY_2 \text{ future value of property} &= \text{present value } (1 + r)(1 + r) \\
&= \text{present value } (1 + r)^2 \\
&= \$525{,}457 \, (1 + .1031)^2 \\
&= \$639{,}392
\end{aligned}
$$

Generalizing, the future building values at the end of n years may be calculated by the formula

$$
EOY_n \text{ future value of property} = \text{present value } (1 + r)^n
$$

where n is the number of years and r equals the rate of property appreciation.

The compounding of appreciation for Douglas Manor Apartments at 10.31 percent interest for four years is shown in Figure 3–5. Compounding effects show up clearly in the equity build-up column. Note that the property value will grow much faster at 15 percent inflation than at 10.31 percent. Likewise, the property value will increase less rapidly at 6 percent than at 10.31 percent.

Looking for Shortcuts—How to Compute Future Value Factors

Tables of the precalculated *future value of \$1 (FV1) factors,* $(1 + r)^n$, have traditionally been used to speed future value calculations. For example, to determine the future value at the end of year 2 of a \$1,000,000 office building that is appreciating at 6 percent per year compounded annually, we can look up *FV1* in the TVM table in the

---

[4] Property values increase over time for a variety of reasons: The location of the property may become more desirable for some economic purpose; the transportation system may open up the property to development; the existing use of the reality may be modified to yield a higher income; a large, new development may be created near the property; general business conditions may improve; new financing and market conditions may provide buyers who accept lower returns on their investment; or general inflationary pressures may exist. Investors attempt to take these factors into consideration when forecasting whether property values will increase over time. Obviously, most investors hope that their investments will prove so advantageous that in the short run they will be able to sell at a large profit.

FIGURE 3–5
Four Years of Price
Appreciation at 10.31
Percent Compounded
Annually: Douglas
Manor Apartments

YEAR	(1) BEGINNING VALUE	(2) EQUITY BUILDUP[a]	(3) ENDING VALUE[b]
1	$525,457	$54,154	$579,611
2	579,632	59,716	639,348
3	639,348	65,892	705,240
4	705,240	72,684	777,924

[a] Equity buildup equals (3) − (1), i.e., equals the amount by which the property appreciates over time; compounding of price appreciation shows up clearly in this column.

[b] Ending value equals present worth of property × FV1 at 10.3062 percent interest (rounded to 10.31 percent in the text).

appendix at the end of the book. The table gives the future value of a dollar invested today. In our office building example $n = 2$ and $r = 6$ percent, and therefore we look at the second number from the top in the FV1 column at 6 percent interest. It is 1.123600. Multiply 1.123600 by $1,000,000, and we have the value of the office building at the end of year 2, $1,123,600.

Computing Future Values Using Financial Calculators

Future property values can be found even more easily with financial calculators. For example, the future value of the $1,000,000 office building at the end of year 2 can be determined by letting the interest rate $r = 6$ percent, the number of periods $n = 2$, and solving for FV. The $1,000,000 goes into the PV cell.

You can also compute the FV1 factors for appreciation rates or interest rates not provided in the TVM tables. For instance, suppose you invest $1 in real estate. If the property appreciates at an interest rate of r, you will have by year n an investment worth $\$1(1 + r)^n$. Letting $n = 2$ and $r = 6.5$ percent, you can find the future value of this investment by letting $PV = 1$ and computing FV. The answer would be 1.134225, which gives you the FV1 factor for two years at a 6.5 percent rate of compounding. Subtracting 1 from the FV1 factor tells you that your investment will increase by 13.42 percent over the two-year holding period.

SUMMARY

To value real estate for investment purposes, you must investigate each property carefully. Once you have done that, you must be able to forecast the expected income payments that the property will generate and the cash proceeds due at disposition. In estimating the future income payments from operations, the convention is to begin with forecasts of potential gross income and to work your way down to net operating income by subtracting both the variable and fixed costs of operations. Net operating income is the best indication of what a property can earn on its own. Net sales price, on the other hand, is the best measure of the reversion or future value of the property on a pretax basis.

Two of the more useful ratios for evaluating property productivity are the income and operating expense ratios. The higher the income ratio, the greater the productivity of the property. This might be the result of good management—keeping the property fully rented while keeping control of operating expense. It might also be the result of high-quality construction that minimizes costs of repairs and maintenance. An operating expense ratio tells the experienced investor or lender if an operating statement is realistic. Operating ratios vary from property type to property type—that is, from apartment house to office building to hotel, and so on.

The basic present value formula for a real estate asset that pays off in several periods is:

$$\text{Present worth of property} = \frac{NOI_1}{(1+r)} + \frac{NOI_2}{(1+r)^2} + \frac{NOI_3}{(1+r)^3} + \cdots$$
$$+ \frac{NOI_n}{(1+r)^n} + \frac{NSP}{(1+r)^n}$$

This expression implies that the present worth of a property is equal to its discounted future income payments and cash proceeds due at disposition. Remember that NOI_n is the pro forma net operating income at the end of year n, NSP is the expected cash proceeds due at disposition, and r is the opportunity cost of capital, or the discount rate.

While you can estimate the present worth of, say, an office building, shopping center, or apartment building by plugging into the above formula and manually calculating the numbers, it is often easier to use either the $PV1$ factors that appear in the time value of money tables in the appendix at the end of the book or financial calculators. The $PV1$ factors give the values of $1/(1+r)^n$ for various values of r and n. Financial calculators can solve for present values, future values, r, and n.

Our next step was to show that future building values can be calculated by

$$EOY_n \text{ future value of property} = \text{Present value } (1+r)^n$$

When someone tells us the current market value of the property, we can use the above formula to calculate the expected value of the property in the future given reasonable values for r and n. $FV1$ tables and financial calculators can help to perform these calculations. Comparing $PV1$ and $FV1$ factors, one should find that the $PV1$ factor is simply the reciprocal of the $FV1$ factor and vice versa.

KEY CONCEPTS

Contract rent   Agreed payments for the use of land or realty.

Discount rate   The annual percentage rate that reflects the competitive rate of return on an investment.

Discounting   Process of converting a future cash payment into a present value.

Efficient market   Market wherein changes in information about the outlook for a given commodity, such as a property, are quickly reflected in its probable selling price and value.

Future value of $1 factor   Future price of $1 invested today at a specific interest rate.

Gross sales price   Total amount of cash paid by the purchaser to the seller for the property.

Income ratio   Net operating income divided by potential gross income; a measure of the efficiency of an income property.

Leasehold interest   Right to use and occupy a property; a leasehold interest often acquires value when contract rent is less than market rent.

Market rent   Amount of rent a property would command if exposed to the market for a reasonable time and rented by a reasonably knowledgeable tenant; analogous to market value.

Net sales price   Amount realized from the sale of the property minus selling expenses.

Operating expense ratio   Operating expenses divided by potential gross income; a measure of a property's operating efficiency.

Opportunity cost of capital   Value of best choice [opportunity] that is given up in selecting or deciding among several alternatives. To maximize benefits, a decision-maker minimizes opportunity costs.

Present value of $1 factor   A time-value-of-money multiplier used to convert a single future payment into a lump-sum present value.

Reversion value   The net cash proceeds due on sale of a property.

Risk averse investor   An investor who requires a higher rate of return to compensate for a given amount of risk.

Time value of money   The opportunity cost of having to wait to receive a future income payment or the cash proceeds due at disposition.

QUESTIONS FOR REVIEW AND DISCUSSION

1. What is a leasehold interest? When does it acquire value?

2. What is an income ratio? Why is it a useful measurement tool?

3. What is the difference between a gross sales price and a net sales price?

4. Is one dollar today worth more than one dollar tomorrow? How does risk enter into the evaluation of this concept?

5. How does debt affect the net operating income of a property?

6. Does depreciation have an effect on the net operating income of a property?

7. Should an uncertain future payoff have a higher or lower discount rate than a more certain future payoff? Why?

PROBLEMS

1. A 60-unit apartment complex has rented out three different types of units based on the following rental schedule:

1 bedroom	$600/mo.	(30 units)
2 bedroom	$850/mo.	(15 units)
Efficiency	$450/mo.	(15 units)

If the operating expense ratio on the complex is 30 percent, how much are the annual operating expenses?

2. What is the *PV*1 factor for calculating the present value of $10,000 received three years from today with a discount rate of 6 percent? What is the present value?

3. What is the *FV*1 factor for calculating the future value of $5,000 four years from today at 12 percent interest? What is the future value?

4. What is the present worth of an income-producing property which receives a net operating income of $30,000 during year 1, $32,000 during year 2, $40,000 during year 3, and $43,000 during year 4? Assume the property is sold at the end of year 4 for $50,000 net of selling expenses and the discount rate is 15 percent.

5. Recalculate Problem 4 using a discount rate of 12 percent. Does the present worth of the property increase or decrease?

6. Forest City Enterprises Inc. has acquired the Pavilion, a 1,127-unit, upscale rental apartment complex in northwest Chicago. The $31.9 million purchase was completed through a partnership with The Harris Group, Chicago. The seller was New York-based Chemical Bank. The Pavilion is the fourth largest apartment rental complex in the Chicago area. It is comprised of five 15-story buildings near O'Hare International Airport. Assume that the property will appreciate in nominal terms by 2 percent per year during the next five years. Determine the future building value at the end of year 5.

7. A partnership led by the principals of The Continental Cos. has recently completed the purchase of the 504-room Bonaventure Resort in Fort Lauderdale, Florida. The Bonaventure is a combination hotel, health fitness spa, and convention facility overlooking two golf courses in the 1,250-acre Bonaventure residential community. The Bonaventure's 83,000 square-foot World Conference Center comprises 25 conference rooms, 3 ballrooms, and a 160-seat amphitheater. You are attempting to value the Bonaventure Resort. Assume that

Conference Center room rates	$60 per room per day
Occupancy rates	35%
Food and beverage income in year 1	$1,900,000
Rental income from Conference Center in year 1	$1,529,000
Other income	$153,000
Operating expenses (including a normal return to operate the resort)	$5,300,000

Conference Center room rates are expected to rise 2 percent during each succeeding year. Food and beverage income, rental income from the Conference Center, and other income are expected to increase 3 percent during each succeeding year. No change in the occupancy rate is expected. Operating expenses are anticipated to increase at 4 percent per year.

Because of your knowledge of the market, you expect the sales price at the end of year 5 to be $21.5 million. Disposition costs are expected to be 5 percent of the selling price. The expected holding period is 5 years.

a. Compute the NOI for the expected holding period.

b. Assume that the required before-tax rate of return on the Bonaventure Resort is 15 percent. What is the market value of the resort?

8. Two retail/office properties totaling 137,000 square feet in downtown San Francisco have been purchased by HCV Pacific Investors V. The following assumptions apply:

   Estimated average rents are $12 per square foot with rental increases of 2 percent per year.

   Estimated vacancy and collection losses are 5 percent per year.

   The operating expenses are estimated at $617,150 in year 1; increases are estimated at a rate of 2 percent per year.

   The project is expected to sell for $15.2 million in the fifth year; selling expenses are 5 percent.

   The holding period is 5 years.

   How much would you be willing to pay for the property, assuming a before-tax required rate of return of 13 percent?

9. In 1961 the Empire State Building Associates, a group formed by New York attorney Lawrence A. Wien, sold the 102-story Empire State Building to Prudential Insurance Company of America, which leased it back to the Empire State Building Associates for a 114-year term. (Prudential actually purchased the land under the Empire State Building in 1951.) Empire State Building Associates agreed to pay Prudential an annual rent of $3,220,000 for the first 30 years, $1,840,000 per year for the next 21 years, and $1,610,000 per year for the next 63 years. In turn, Empire State Building Associates planned to sublease the 2 million square feet of office space to various corporate tenants. If discounted at a before-tax rate of return of 7 percent, determine the value of the Empire State Building to Prudential.

CHAPTER 4

RISK AND RETURN
IN REAL ESTATE

Chapter Outline

Fortune is like the market, where many times, if you can stay a little, the price will fall.

Francis Bacon, English philosopher, statesman, and jurist

Real estate investors lay out money today for uncertain payments to be received in the future. They usually borrow to help finance the purchase of the investment properties and in the process realize positive financial leverage. The *equity* investor owns the property but is responsible for keeping the property operational, for debt-service payments, and for any other risks and obligations that may develop.

Certainly, by owning real estate an equity investor is susceptible to the possibility of value decreases. Asset values may fall because of lags in economic activity or extremely high interest rates. Further, expected revenues may fluctuate owing to variability in economic activity. Equity investors also run the risk of having managers who are unable to operate the property efficiently or are not capable of adapting quickly to a changing environment. Owning real estate also involves the possibility of new legislation, such as rent controls, rezoning, or increased taxes, that adversely affects the property.

Investors in real estate need to take these types of risks into account prior to making any investment decision. Generally, if the expected return on real estate is high enough to compensate for the risk involved, then the project is a "go," and the investment is undertaken. Otherwise, unless the equity investor who is putting together the deal has control over certain variables and is able to alter one of the parameters, the investment should not be undertaken.

In this regard, it is extremely important to understand how to analyze risk before moving on to real estate ownership decisions.

NATURE OF THE PROBLEM

Risk is the chance of unfavorable events or outcomes. Risk comes from a number of sources, such as a downturn in the economy that reduces the demand for all real estate, or is the result of something intrinsic either to the local market or the property itself. One of the problems of investing in real estate is the need to lock tenants into a long-term lease, in the hope that the investment will be returned by the end of the lease. Over time, however, buildings age and tenants tend to move to newer buildings. If tenants move, the investor can be left with a building that is only partially occupied.

Real estate investments have additional risks because they are fixed in location. Changes in the relative attractiveness of a particular location or changes in the local economy may adversely affect the use of real estate *idiosyncratically*—that is, the risk is peculiar to a single property. Thus, absent a reduction in demand for all real estate throughout the United States causing the general level of rents to fall, a downturn in the regional economy may raise uncertainty about the cash flow that the property can generate.

So-called specialty buildings, in which doctors, dentists, and lawyers are likely to be the tenants, create added concern. Investors view these buildings as *single-purpose buildings* and they are extremely wary about the possibility of a relatively high vacancy rate. The same is true for properties in a local market or trade area in which there is a single dominant employer. If that employer shuts down, investors are in trouble. All risk arises because of the possibility that a succession of unplanned outcomes will leave the real estate investor unable to meet outstanding commitments as they fall due.

Risk can also be defined in terms of *total risk,* which focuses on an individual property and how deviations from expected outcomes will affect the expected return on that property, and *systematic or market risk,* which focuses on a real estate portfolio. If an investor has only a single real estate asset, total risk is obviously very important. But with a portfolio of real estate properties, systematic or market risk is the only worry. By holding a well-diversified real estate portfolio an investor can potentially eliminate the unique risk that surrounds an individual property. Diversification works because prices of different property types or prices of real estate assets in different geographic regions do not move exactly together. In this case the risk that can potentially be eliminated by holding a well-diversified real estate portfolio is called *unsystematic* or *specific risk.*

One immediate implication may be noted. How risk is treated depends on the investor's unique perspective. For a reasonably well-diversified real estate investor, the predominant source of risk is whether the economy will rise or plummet. Alternatively, for the individual investor with all of his or her eggs in just one basket, dealing with risk can be very troubling. Such investors must not only worry about the economy-wide perils that endanger all real estate properties, but also must worry about the unique risks surrounding an individual property.

Individuals must also worry about personal constraints or limitations. Age, analytical ability, executive ability, energy level, work preferences, and available time all act as constraints on an investor. A young person can, for example, afford a longer time horizon than can an elderly investor. A person with limited time or energy is probably best advised to invest in a medium requiring little administrative or management effort. Likewise, a person with limited ability to analyze and administer investments may be better off avoiding active investments, meaning most real estate investments. Locational preferences are self-explanatory as personal constraints.

SPECIFIC TYPES OF RISKS

Most risk associated with real estate investment is either business risk or financial risk, but other risks do exist. *Business risk* is the probability that projected or predicted levels of income will not be realized or will not be adequate to meet operating expenses. Income is dependent on a property's physical capability, functional capability, and location. Each of these factors is subject to fluctuation and misinterpretation. *Financial risk* is the extra uncertainty created when money is borrowed to help finance a property. An investor who does not borrow has no financial risk. At the same time, no leverage is realized, and the return on the investment may be quite low. Financial risk might be rather slight for a wealthy owner with strong financial carrying capacity.

There are other risks involved in owning real estate: One is *purchasing power risk,* and another is *legislative risk.* Purchasing power risk is the chance of a drop in value in real terms. While real estate tends to ride with inflation, market values sometimes drop sharply, such as when a major business closes a plant or when the local economy takes a nose-dive because of changing economic conditions. Legislative risk is the chance that government influences, such as zoning, land-use controls, rent controls, taxes, and a host of other rules and regulations, may change. Legislative risk tends to be area-specific, but must still be recognized.

Liquidity risk and management risk are also important in real estate. Investment liquidity is measured by the ease with which a real estate asset can be converted into cash. A real estate asset is considered to have high liquidity when it can readily be sold for cash at or near its market value. High-value real estate is generally considered to have low liquidity risk. *Liquidity risk* is the risk of incurring a loss of market value in the process of having to convert the property to cash.

Lack of liquidity has traditionally been the economic Achilles heel of real estate. A well-informed, capable investor, therefore, balances his or her investment portfolio so as to weather impending and generally short-range economic fluctuations. With a balanced portfolio approach, the relative nonliquidity of real estate need not be a serious handicap to garnering its long-term benefits of net return and capital safety. Also, in situations where an investor may need cash, he or she has the option to raise cash by refinancing, giving a second mortgage, or entering into joint ownership by making a partial sale of the equity position.

Management risk is a necessary part of the job of adjusting the property to changing economic conditions and environments. There is always the chance of a miscalculation when conditions change and a poor decision is made.

These different types of risk can be classified as either systematic or unsystematic, or both, depending on whether all properties are affected simultaneously by the particular risk factor, as might happen if the economy were to go into a recession, or whether bad events in one property are offset by good events in another property, as might be the case if a large, new development is created near one property and a large military base is closed down near another property.

HOW RISK AFFECTS INDIVIDUAL PROPERTIES

Risk is the variance between one's expectations and realizations, between the expected return on the project and the actual return. Risk exists because the future is uncertain. We refer to risk, then, as the probability that some unfavorable event will occur. To illustrate how to calculate the risk associated with an individual property, suppose an investor has $2 million to invest in real estate. Three hypothetical investments, as shown in Figure 4–1, are being considered:

1. A strip shopping center with a discount department store as the anchor. The center is located in an inner-city neighborhood.

2. An upscale office building with an ornate interior. The venture is expected to do well in a boom economy.

3. A moderate-income, multifamily housing development project. The project is expected to take between 6 and 18 months to rent.

| RATE OF RETURN OF INVESTMENT UNDER ALTERNATIVE STATES OF NATURE (%) | | | | | FIGURE 4–1 |
STATE OF NATURE	PROBABILITY OF OCCURRENCE	SHOPPING CENTER	OFFICE BUILDING	APARTMENTS	Alternative Real Estate Investments
Pessimistic Outlook	0.25	4.0	−2.0	8.0	
Normal Outlook	0.50	20.0	22.0	18.0	
Optimistic Outlook	0.25	35.0	40.0	30.0	
Total	1.00				
Expected Rate of Return		19.75	20.5	18.5	

A subjective probability distribution is assigned to each of the three investment alternatives. In this case the probability distribution for all three investments is approximately normal. This means that the probability distributions resemble a bell-shaped curve—fat in the middle and small in the tails. It also means that we can judge the three alternative investments by simply comparing variances and expected rates of return. When the returns are *negatively skewed,* or skewed to the left, this rule no longer holds. Most investors would consider negative skewness as more risky because of the greater chance of a very bad outcome, holding all else constant. Likewise, most investors would consider *positive skewness,* or skewed to the right, as more desirable because of the greater chance of a very good outcome.

Given a light demand for the project, the rate of return on the strip shopping center is expected to be 4 percent. Assuming a most-probable outcome, however, the return on the strip shopping center is expected to be 20 percent. And, given an optimistic outlook, the return on the strip shopping center is expected to be 35 percent. Estimated rates of return on the other two investments range from −2 to 40 percent for the office building, and from 8 to 30 percent for the multifamily housing development project.

Expected Rate of Return

The *expected rate of return* for these investments can be calculated by multiplying each possible outcome by its probability of occurrence and then summing the products. The expected return can be expressed in equation form as:

$$\text{Expected rate of return} = \sum_{i=1}^{n} r_i P_i$$

where

r_i = rate of return corresponding to the ith outcome
P_i = the probability that the ith outcome will occur, and
n = number of possible outcomes

We can now calculate the expected rate of return on each of the three alternative investments. To illustrate, the expected rate of return on the strip shopping center is:

$$\text{Expected return} = \sum_{i=1}^{n} r_i P_i$$
$$= r_1 P_1 + r_2 P_2 + r_3 P_3$$
$$= 4\% \, (0.25) + 20\% \, (0.50) + 35\% \, (0.25)$$
$$= 19.75\%$$

Thus, on average, the expected return on the strip shopping center is 19.75 percent. The expected rates of return on the other two investments are calculated in a similar fashion.

Measuring Total Risk

The conventional measures of risk are *variance* and *standard deviation*. The variance of a return is the expected squared deviation from the expected return. To calculate the variance, we use the formula

$$\text{Variance} = \sigma^2 = \sum_{i=1}^{n} (r_i - \bar{r})^2 P_i$$

where $\bar{r}$ is the expected rate of return. The standard deviation is simply the square root of the variance:

$$\text{Standard deviation} = \sigma = \sqrt{\sigma^2} = \sqrt{\sum_{i=1}^{n} (r_i - \bar{r})^2 P_i}$$

The variance of the percentage return on the strip shopping center in Figure 4-1 is calculated as follows:

$$\sigma^2 = \sum_{i=1}^{6} (r_i - \bar{r})^2 P_i$$
$$= (4 - 19.75)^2 (0.25) + (20 - 19.75)^2 (0.50) + (35 - 19.75)^2 (0.25)$$
$$= 62.01 + 0.03 + 58.14$$
$$= 120.18$$

The standard deviation is the square root of 120.18, or 10.96. The standard deviation is expressed in the same units as the rate of return. This means that the variability in the rate of return on the strip shopping center is 10.96 percent. Assuming a normal distribution, we can further state that 95.5 percent of the outcomes will fall within two standard deviations of the expected rate of return. For the office building and multifamily housing development project, the standard deviations are 14.92 percent and 7.79 percent, respectively (see Figure 4-2).

FIGURE 4–2
Expected Rate of Return
and Risk Measures for
Alternative Investments
in Figure 4–1

EXPECTED RATE OF RETURN OR RISK MEASURE	SHOPPING CENTER	OFFICE BUILDING	APARTMENTS
Expected Rate of Return	19.75%	20.5%	18.5%
Variance	120.18	3.0	7.79
Standard Deviation	10.96%	14.92%	7.79%

CHAPTER 4

Risk per Unit of Return

One way of ranking the alternative real estate investments in Figure 4–1 is to compute a *coefficient of variation*. The coefficient of variation is defined as the standard deviation divided by the expected return:

$$\text{Coefficient of variation} = CV = \frac{\sigma}{r}$$

Investments with lower risk per unit of expected return will be preferred to investments with higher risk per unit of expected return, other things equal.

To illustrate, consider the three real estate investment alternatives in Figure 4–1. The standard deviations are: shopping center, 10.96 percent; office building, 14.92 percent; and multifamily housing development, 7.79 percent. The corresponding expected rates of return are: shopping center, 19.75 percent; office building, 20.5 percent; and multifamily housing development, 18.5 percent. The coefficients of variation are:

$$\text{CV for shopping center} = \frac{10.96}{19.75} = 0.55$$

$$\text{CV for office building} = \frac{14.92}{20.5} = 0.73$$

$$\text{CV for multifamily development} = \frac{7.79}{18.5} = 0.42$$

Thus, one can see that the multifamily housing development project is indeed the least risky investment—its coefficient of variation is 0.42 units of risk per unit of expected return. By comparison, the coefficient of variation for the strip shopping center is 0.55 and the coefficient of variation for the office building is 0.73—roughly 1.3 to 1.7 times larger than the coefficient of variation for the multifamily housing development project. Wise investors obviously prefer less risk per unit of expected return to greater risk per unit of expected return.

HOW RISKY IS REAL ESTATE?

This question is difficult to answer. Real estate markets are not blessed with an enormous quantity of performance data. The best available historical evidence on real estate performance is the Frank Russell Company/National Council of Real Estate Investment Fiduciaries (FRC/NCREIF) return series. This return series measures the rate of return on income-producing properties owned by commingled funds on behalf of qualified pension and profit-sharing trusts or owned directly by these trusts and managed on a separate-account basis by life insurance companies or pension fund investment managers, like JMB Institutional Realty Corporation and Balcor Institutional Realty Advisor.

The FRC/NCREIF return series represents an aggregate of individual property returns, calculated quarterly. The returns include both income receipts and capital appreciation or depreciation realized during the year. One major drawback is that the capital appreciation or depreciation realized during the year is based on appraised market values rather than actual sales transactions.

The property base for the index includes more than 1,500 properties, and is valued in excess of $22 billion (as of June 1991). The properties are either 100 percent owned or held in joint-venture partnerships. Performance measures are reported as if all properties were wholly owned, however. Standardizing the reporting mechanism in this way eliminates potential distortions in the returns series that could arise as a result of the differing risk-sharing agreements found in joint-venture partnerships. The returns are measured before deduction of portfolio management fees.

The return series contains performance data on several major categories of properties, including office buildings, retail properties, and warehouses. The need to measure real estate performance on a local level has also led to a FRC/NCREIF index segmented by four geographic regions.

Figure 4-3 shows the marked difference between the first quarter 1978 to fourth quarter 1981 and and first quarter 1986 to second quarter 1991 periods in the

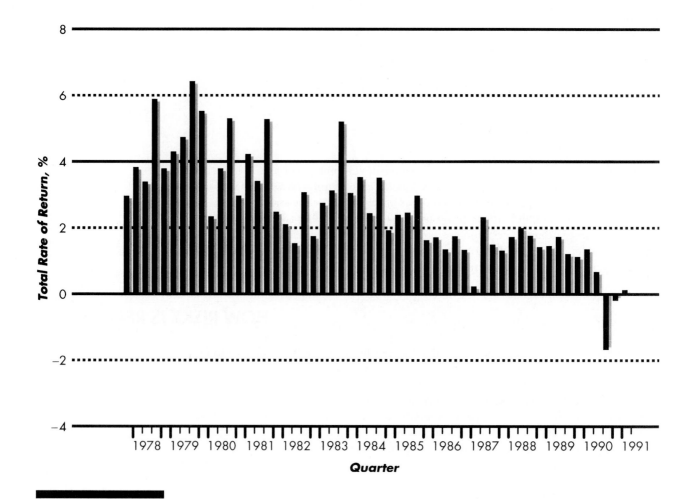

FIGURE 4-3
Plot of FRC/NCREIF Total Return Series

FRC/NCREIF total returns on real estate. In the former period, the FRC/NCREIF returns on real estate averaged 4.27 percent per quarter; in the latter period the rate of return averaged 1.15 percent per quarter. The downward drift in the FRC/NCREIF returns series begins around the first quarter of 1985 to the fourth quarter of 1986. This drop-off in performance can be attributed primarily to asset value declines.

During most of the 1980s the income component of the FRC/NCREIF returns series remained fairly stable, fluctuating between 1.5 and 2 percent per quarter. However, the capital appreciation component of the FRC/NCREIF returns series fluctuated widely. During the first half of the 1980s the capital appreciation component tended to be positive and significant. But, during the last half of the 1980s the capital appreciation component turned negative or, at best, slightly positive (see Figures 4-4 and 4-5).

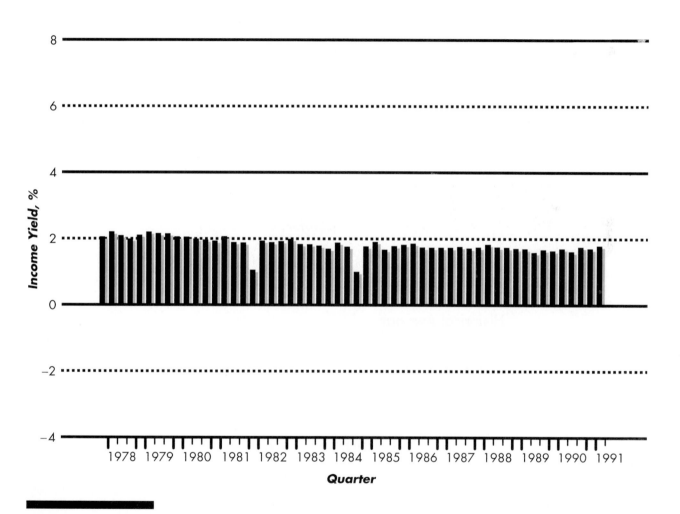

FIGURE 4–4
Plot of FRC/NCREIF Income Yield Series

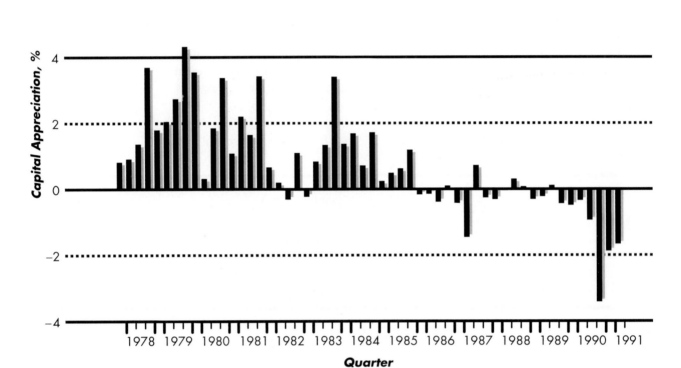

FIGURE 4–5
Plot of FRC/NCREIF Capital Appreciation Series

Historical Average

The average historical FRC/NCREIF return during the 1979–1991 period (years ending June 30) can be calculated as follows:

$$\text{Historical average} = \bar{r}_{avg} = \frac{\sum_{t=1}^{n} r_t}{n}$$

Since we have thirteen sample points, the calculation is:

$$\text{Historical average} = \bar{r}_{avg} = \frac{1}{13} (18.68 + 20.43 + 17.30 + 13.91 + 9.31 \\ + 15.66 + 10.60 + 8.96 + 4.66 + 8.99 \\ + 8.69 + 5.37 - 1.10)$$

$$= 10.88$$

Here the expected return is estimated by adding the observed returns and dividing by *n*.

Historical Variance

Figure 4-6 also shows the historical variance of the FRC/NCREIF returns series. The calculation is:

$$\text{Historical variance} = \sigma^2 = \frac{\sum\limits_{t-1}^{n}(r_t - \bar{r}_{\text{avg}})^2}{n - 1}$$

Note that when dealing with actual rather than estimated probabilities, the variance is estimated by adding the squared deviations and dividing by $n - 1$. In this case dividing by $n - 1$ corrects for what is called the loss of a degree of freedom. This is standard statistical methodology.

Let us illustrate the calculation. With thirteen sample points, the historical variance is:

$$\text{Historical variance} = \sigma^2 = \frac{\sum\limits_{t-1}^{n}(r_t - \bar{r}_{\text{avg}})^2}{n - 1}$$

$$= \frac{1}{13 - 1} [(18.68 - 10.88)^2 + (20.43 - 10.88)^2$$
$$+ (17.30 - 10.88)^2$$
$$+ (13.91 - 10.88)^2$$
$$+ (9.31 - 10.88)^2$$
$$+ (15.66 - 10.88)^2$$
$$+ (10.60 - 10.88)^2$$
$$+ (8.96 - 10.88)^2$$
$$+ (4.66 - 10.88)^2$$
$$+ (8.99 - 10.88)^2$$
$$+ (8.69 - 10.88)^2$$
$$+ (5.37 - 10.88)^2$$
$$+ (- 1.10 - 10.88)^2]$$

$$= 37.70$$

Now for the calculation of the historical standard deviation. The calculation is:

$$\text{Historical standard deviation} = \sigma = \sqrt{\frac{\sum\limits_{t-1}^{n}(r_t - \bar{r}_{\text{avg}})^2}{n - 1}}$$

$$= \sqrt{\text{historical variance}}$$
$$= \sqrt{37.70}$$
$$= 6.14$$

Our formula simply says that the historical standard deviation is the square root of the historical variance.

FIGURE 4-6

YEAR	ANNUAL RETURN (%)	DEVIATION FROM AVERAGE RETURN	SQUARED DEVIATION
1979	18.68	7.80	60.82
1980	20.43	9.55	91.17
1981	17.30	6.42	41.20
1982	13.91	3.03	9.17
1983	9.31	−1.57	2.47
1984	15.66	4.78	22.83
1985	10.60	−0.28	0.08
1986	8.96	−1.92	3.69
1987	4.66	−6.22	38.71
1988	8.99	−1.89	3.58
1989	8.69	−2.19	4.80
1990	5.37	−5.51	30.38
1991	−1.10	−11.98	143.56
Average return = 10.88		Historical variance = 37.70	
		Historical standard deviation = 6.14	

Implications for the Future

We are now in a position to draw some implications for the future. Historically, we know that the average return on real estate during the period 1979-1991 has been 10.88 percent and the standard deviation has been 6.14 percent. Thus, if past is prologue, real estate can be expected to yield an annual rate of return of 10.88 percent with a standard deviation of 6.14 percent.

Does this standard deviation look low to you? That is, do you think real estate returns are substantially more volatile? Many academicians believe they are. They believe that the use of appraisals, instead of actual sales or changes in value, tends to smooth a return series and therefore reduce the standard deviation. How much smoothing there is, is hard to say. Some contend that the true volatility of real estate returns can be as high as 2.5 times the historical FRC/NCREIF standard deviation.[1]

RELATIONSHIP BETWEEN RISK AND RETURN

To explain how real estate investors respond to risk requires a journey into microeconomics and utility theory. Utility theory in microeconomics is all about measuring the satisfaction derived from the ownership or use of some commodity. When dealing with the decision to invest, it is important to keep in mind that investors prefer more wealth to less—that is, they have positive utility of wealth. Thus, investors will always prefer a real estate investment with a large certain payoff to a real estate investment with a small certain payoff.

[1] For more on smoothing of return series, see David Geltner, "Bias in Appraisal-Based Returns," *AREUEA Journal* (1989), 17:338-352, and Michael Giliberto, "A Note on the Use of Appraisal Data in Indexes of Performance Measurement," *AREUEA Journal* (1988), 16: 77-83.

But how do investors rank various combinations of risky payoffs? The answer to this question depends on whether most investors are *risk averse, risk neutral,* or *risk takers.* For example, when faced with the choice of a certain $1,000 payoff versus a 50 percent chance of receiving $2,000 and a 50 percent chance of receiving nothing (which results in an actuarial value of $2,000 (0.50) + $0 (0.50) = $1,000), would the investor take the certain $1,000 or the gamble? If investors prefer the gamble, they are risk takers; if they are indifferent, they are risk neutral. Clearly, risk preferences are very personal; some may seek risk and opportunity, others avoid risk with a vengeance.

Evidence shows that most investors are indeed risk averse, which is to say that the risk of loss has a stronger impact on investors than a potential gain of the same amount. This means that most real estate investors would prefer to forego a certain amount to avoid taking on a risky investment. In utility theory parlance, the amount that investors would give up to avoid taking on a risky investment is called a *risk premium.*

In principle, then, faced with a riskier investment alternative, risk averse investors expect a higher risk premium to avoid taking on the investment. Or, flipping this statement around, the higher the riskiness of the investment, the higher its expected return must be to induce investors to hold the investment. Another way of describing the relationship between the level of risk and the required rate of return is

$$r = r_f + p$$

where

r = the required rate of return
r_f = the risk-free rate of return, and
p = a premium for risk

Generally, a risk premium is added to the risk-free rate for every real estate investment that involves additional risk. This risk premium compensates real estate investors for laying out money today for uncertain payments to be received in the future.

This relationship between the level of risk and the required rate of return on real estate is of fundamental importance. It means that anyone interested in real estate must weigh the risks against the expected rates of return. Here is an example that illustrates the risk–return tradeoff. Suppose you know the discount rate for safe projects—let us assume that it is 6 percent. Next, suppose San Francisco is on the verge of an important building boom and you are a Trammell Crow with the chance to develop the Embarcadero Center, the biggest deal Crow had undertaken to that time—$300 million, of which Crow would have an 8⅓ interest.

You acquire the land for $30 a square foot; you organize a team comprised of John Portman; David Rockefeller; James Caswell, an Atlanta developer who played a significant role in several of the projects Portman and Crow had put up in that City; and Cloyce Box, a contractor with the George A. Fuller Company. Portman is to provide the design, Rockefeller is to provide the equity financing, Box the construction, and Caswell is to be the chief operating officer. Metropolitan Life is the initial mortgage lender; Prudential Insurance is to provide debt financing for a hotel and the second and third office buildings, on the condition that it would be a 50 percent partner in both and that Hyatt be brought in as operator of the hotel.

How, then, do you go about evaluating the risk associated with this project? You start by asking the questions, What happens if large cost overruns develop as the project nears conclusion? Or what happens if in unsettled economic and financial conditions you are able to lease only about 10 percent of the third office building, leaving yourself strapped for cash? The answer, Prudential exercises its option to withdraw from the project and you are forced to sell your shares at a discount to Rockefeller to remain afloat.

From this, being a risk averter, you determine an expected risk premium, p, which, in the absence of cost overruns and economic hardships, you will earn on your investment. Suppose this premium is 4 percent. Then the required rate of return on this project is

$$r = r_f + p$$
$$= 6\% + 4\%, \text{ or } 10\%$$

Thus, in the absence of any unexpected events, you will do very well if the project earns a rate of return of 10 percent. And, when or if the project runs into hard times, you can take that 4 percent annual risk premium and help cover any losses—assuming, of course, you haven't yet spent the money.

Now suppose that investors on the whole become more risk averse over time. What would happen to the expected rate of return on a project like the Embarcadero Center? To answer this question, consider Figure 4-7. A safe-and-sure return justifies a relatively low rate of return. This is point A in Figure 4-7. At the same time, as risk

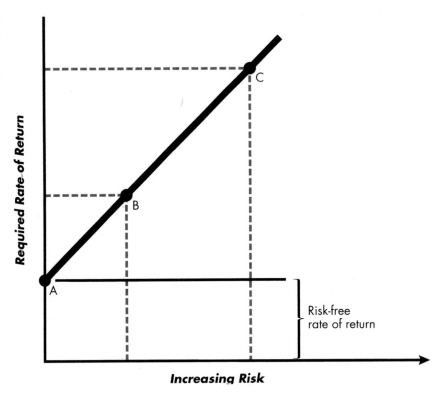

FIGURE 4-7
The Basic Risk-Return Relationship

and uncertainty increase, the required rate of return should also increase. Real estate investors who take on added risk expect higher rates of return. If the higher rate of return to compensate for the higher risk is not realized, a real estate investor would be better off investing in some other asset or some other security.

If investors on the whole become more risk averse this means that for each level of risk, the required return is now larger. Thus, the required rate of return on the Embarcadero Center might increase from 10 percent to, say, 12 percent—assuming a 6 percent risk premium. Likewise, if the risk-free rate were 10 percent instead of 6 percent, the expected rate of return on the Embarcadero Center would increase from 10 to 14 percent (10 percent risk-free rate plus a 4 percent normal risk premium). Finally, changes in investor attitudes toward risk plus an increase in the risk-free rate would cause the required return on the Embarcadero Center to increase from 10 to 16 percent.

HOW DIVERSIFICATION CAN REDUCE REAL ESTATE RISK

Diversification by property type and geographic region can help reduce risk without sacrificing return. Diversification involves choosing a set of properties whose returns do not move in tandem, so that as one set of returns decreases, another set rises. Indeed, it is theoretically possible to combine two real estate assets which are individually quite risky to form a portfolio which is completely riskless.

To illustrate, consider the two investment alternatives in Figure 4-8. These two assets are located in two different geographic markets. Plots of realized returns over time for these two assets are given in Figure 4-9A and 4-9B. Asset A has an average return of 14.5 percent, with a standard deviation of 6.06 percent. Asset B has an average return of 22.5 percent, with a standard deviation of 6.06 percent. Thus, in isolation, both assets would be considered quite risky. But in a portfolio context, the two assets can be combined to form a riskless portfolio.

YEAR	ASSET A $20 MILLION OFFICE BUILDING LOCATED IN CITY A r_A	ASSET B $20 MILLION OFFICE BUILDING LOCATED IN CITY B r_B	PORTFOLIO AB r_P
1986	9	28	18.5
1987	12	25	18.5
1988	16	21	18.5
1989	18	19	18.5
1990	24	13	18.5
1991	8	29	18.5
Average return =	14.5	22.5	18.5
Standard deviation =	6.06	6.06	0

FIGURE 4–8
Risk-and-Return Tradeoff for Two Perfectly Negatively Correlated Real Estate Assets

FIGURE 4–9(A)

Plot of Actual Returns on
Asset A

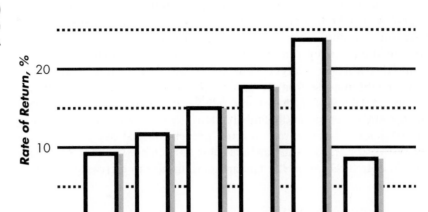

The return on this portfolio is simply a weighted average of the returns on the individual properties:

$$\text{Portfolio return} = r_p = \frac{A}{A + B}r_A + \frac{B}{A + B}r_B$$
$$= ar_A + br_B$$
$$= ar_A + (1 - a)r_B$$

FIGURE 4–9(B)

Plot of Actual Returns on
Asset B

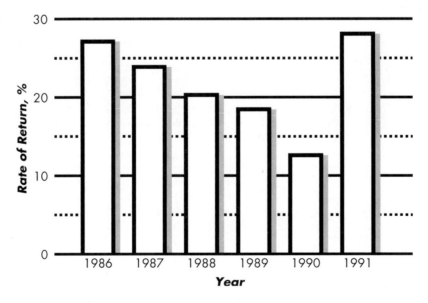

where

A = value of asset A
B = value of asset B
$A + B$ = combined value of portfolio A and B, and

$a = A/(A + B)$ is the percent invested in asset A, and $b = B/(A + B)$ is the percent invested in asset B. Given $a + b = 1$, it follows that $b = (1 - a)$.

The variance of this two-asset portfolio is

$$\text{Portfolio variance} = \sigma^2_p = a^2\sigma^2_A + (1 - a)^2\sigma^2_B + 2a(1 - a)\text{COV}(A, B)$$

where

σ_A^2 = variance of the return on asset A
σ_B^2 = variance of the return on asset B
σ_p = variance of the portfolio A and B, and
$\text{COV}(A, B)$ = covariance of the returns on A and B

The covariance term, COV (A, B), is a measure of the way in which the two returns move in relation to each other. If the covariance is positive, the returns move in the same direction—that is, if one return increases, the other also increases. If the covariance is negative, the returns move in opposite directions. If the two assets are unrelated, the covariance would be zero.

Often instead of talking about the covariance between A and B you will hear people talk about the correlation between A and B. The correlation between A and B is simply the covariance of A and B standardized by

$$\text{Correlation coefficient} = \rho_{AB} = \frac{\text{COV}(A, B)}{\sigma_A \sigma_B}$$

Possible values for ρ_{AB} range from -1 to $+1$. But diversification will reduce risk only when ρ_{AB} is less than 1. The greatest diversification benefits come when ρ_{AB} is negative. In fact, when $\rho_{AB} = -1$—that is, when there is perfect negative correlation—the portfolio of A and B will completely eliminate risk. This almost never occurs with real estate assets, except for illustration.

We now illustrate how to use these formulas to calculate a portfolio return and variance. Suppose you are considering investing in asset A and B. Your idea is to create a real estate venture for this purpose. The venture would own 100 percent of asset A outright and 100 percent of asset B outright. Thus, 50 percent of your portfolio would be in asset A and 50 percent of your portfolio would be in asset B.

The expected return on this portfolio is simply

$$
\begin{aligned}
\text{Portfolio return} &= r_p \\
&= ar_A + (1 - a)r_B \\
&= (0.50)\,14.5\% + (1 - 0.50)\,22.5\% \\
&= 18.5\%
\end{aligned}
$$

This calculation is the easy part.

Now let us try to calculate the portfolio variance. This is the hard part. The variance of return on asset A is 36.7, which can be calculated as follows:

$$\text{Historical variance on asset A} = \sigma^2 = \frac{\sum_{t-1}^{n}(r_t - \bar{r}_{\text{avg}})^2}{n-1}$$

$$= \frac{\begin{aligned}(9 - 14.5)^2 + (12 - 14.5)^2 + (16 - 14.5)^2 \\ + (18 - 14.5)^2 + (24 - 14.5)^2 \\ + (26 - 14.5)^2\end{aligned}}{5}$$

$$= 36.7$$

The standard deviation, of course, would be the square root of 36.7 or 6.06 percent.

It becomes a relatively simple matter to extend this framework to calculate the variance of return on asset B. The variance is:

$$\text{Historical variance on asset B} = \sigma^2 = \frac{\sum_{t-1}^{n}(r_t - \bar{r}_{\text{avg}})^2}{n-1}$$

$$= \frac{\begin{aligned}(28 - 22.5)^2 + (25 - 22.5)^2 + (21 - 22.5)^2 \\ + (19 - 22.5)^2 + (13 - 22.5)^2 \\ + (29 - 22.5)^2\end{aligned}}{5}$$

$$= 36.7$$

which means that the standard deviation of the return on asset B is also 6.06 percent.

Now for the calculation of the covariance. This calculation is set out in Figure 4-10. It involves multiplying the respective deviations for the two assets by each other, summing up the products, and then dividing by $n - 1$. The result is a measure of the way in which the two returns move in relation to each other. Going through this exercise, we find that the covariance is -36.7.

FIGURE 4–10
Calculation of
Covariance Between
Two Real Estate Assets

YEAR	ASSET A		ASSET B		
	(1) RETURN, %	(2) DEVIATION	(3) RETURN, %	(4) DEVIATION	(5) = (2) × (4) PRODUCT
1986	9	−5.5	28	5.5	−30.25
1987	12	−2.5	25	2.5	−6.25
1988	16	1.5	21	−1.5	−2.25
1989	18	3.5	19	−3.5	−12.25
1990	24	9.5	13	−9.5	−90.25
1991	8	−6.5	29	6.5	−42.25
Average return =	14.5		22.5	Sum =	−183.5
Standard deviation =	6.06		6.06	Covariance =	−36.7[a]
				Correlation =	−1[b]

[a]Covariance = sum of column (5) ÷ (n − 1), where n = 6.
[b]Correlation = covariance ÷ (standard deviation of A × standard deviation of B).

Now we can plug these figures into the portfolio variance equation. The result is:

$$\text{Portfolio variance} = \sigma^2_p$$
$$= a^2\sigma^2_A + (1 - a)^2\sigma^2_B + 2a(1 - a)\text{COV(A, B)}$$
$$= (0.5)^2 36.7 + (1 - 0.5)^2 36.7 + 2(0.5)(1 - 0.5)(-36.7)$$
$$= 9.175 + 9.175 - 18.35$$
$$= 0$$

Note that diversification in this case has completely eliminated the risk involved in real estate without sacrificing return; the two assets are perfectly negatively correlated—when the return on one asset goes up, the return on the other goes down.

In general, however, we are more concerned with the case of less-than-perfect negative correlation. With less-than-perfect negative correlation the benefits of diversification are not nearly as great. This is illustrated in Figure 4–11. With two real estate

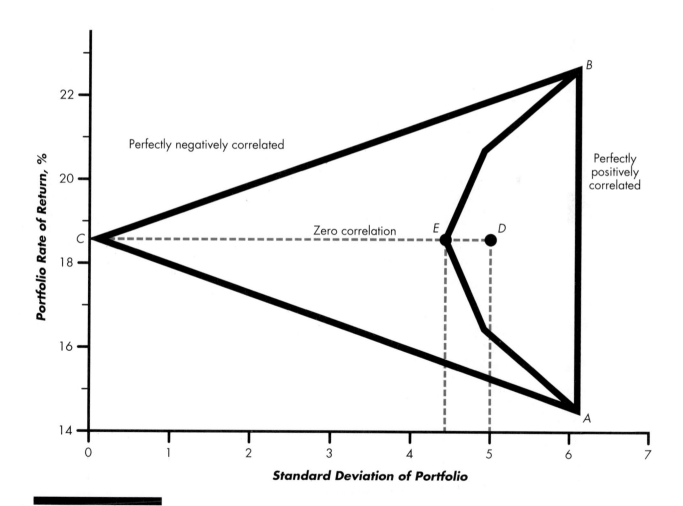

FIGURE 4–11
Plot of Portfolio Return and Standard Deviation

assets and perfect negative correlation, the efficient portfolio set is linear and includes points *A, B,* and *C*. Notice that asset B dominates asset A on a standalone basis because it offers a higher return for the same risk. But, as we saw above, both assets can be combined to eliminate the risk completely while producing a portfolio return of 18.5 percent.

With perfect positive correlation, diversification does no good whatsoever; as the return on one asset goes down, the return on the other asset goes down as well. The attainable set of returns in this case would be the line segment *AB*. But is this really a feasible opportunity set? Of course not. No rational real estate investor would hold a portfolio that lay on the line segment *AB* since, as we pointed out above, asset B offers a higher return for the same risk.

The last case to consider is when the correlation coefficient is between -1 and $+1$. This case produces an efficient set of portfolio returns that most closely resembles most real-world examples. Here it is possible to reduce the riskiness inherent in real estate but not completely eliminate it. To illustrate, assume that the returns on assets A and B were independent (zero correlation). This assumption produces a set of portfolio returns that lie on the curve between *A* and *B* in Figure 4-11. In general, any set of portfolio combinations formed by assets A and B which is less than perfectly correlated must lie inside the triangle *ABC*. Points along this curve can be calculated by plugging the respective portfolio weights, standard deviations, and covariance into the portfolio variance equation.

The curve *EB* is called the *efficient frontier* because all points below *EB* are dominated by a point found on the curve. To illustrate, suppose an investor wants to achieve a 18.5 percent return. The investor can achieve this return level with portfolio D or move to point *E* on the efficient frontier and achieve the same return with a lower level of risk. Portfolio E dominates portfolio D because it yields the same return at a lower risk or standard deviation. Extending this argument one can show that any point on the efficient frontier is preferable to any interior point. One can also show that the lower the correlation coefficient, the more curved the efficient frontier.

Point *E* on the efficient frontier has a unique interpretation: it is known as the *minimum variance portfolio*. The *maximum expected return portfolio* is at point *B*. Which portfolio is the best depends partly on your appetite for risk. If you want to stake all on getting rich quickly, choose portfolio B. However, if you want to minimize your risk, you should choose portfolio E.

CHOOSING A REAL ESTATE PORTFOLIO

How do you identify which assets to combine into an optimal real estate portfolio? A naive strategy is to categorize local markets into traditional North, South, East and West geographic regions. Then ask, What combination of assets will yield the minimum variance for a given rate of return?

The drawback with this naive diversification strategy is that you can potentially end up with investments in, say, Houston, which would be in the South, and Denver, which would be in the West. But both Houston and Denver are in the oil patch and, hence, are not economically independent locations. Accordingly, it is unclear how much diversification benefit one can achieve by traditional geographic diversification. A preferred strategy is to categorize individual metropolitan areas on the basis of their underlying economic performance. This approach focuses on the demand side of real estate markets.

Diversification benefits can also be obtained by investing in different types of real estate—office, retail, industrial, and residential. Some diversification may also be achieved within the real estate asset class itself. For example, it may be possible to diversify across lease terms, construction type, or tenant types—single tenants versus multiple tenants, high-tech tenants versus low-tech tenants, or business-service type tenants versus tenants involved in manufacturing operations.

Clearly, in setting up an optimal real estate portfolio one does not want to lose sight of the fact that excessive diversification can have certain disadvantages. For one thing, the transaction costs of buying and selling real estate can become extremely high. Further, the cost of time and information necessary to manage the additional properties also increases, and it may become virtually impossible for most individual investors to manage a large number of real estate properties.

SUMMARY

How real estate investors respond to risk varies; some seek risk and opportunity, while others avoid risk with a vengeance. Certainly, as risk and uncertainty increase, investors who are risk averse will generally require a higher rate of return. This higher expected return compensates investors for the risk of loss should one's expectations not be realized.

However, lest we expect too much of people in assessing risk, we might note some pitfalls facing decision-makers as described by William Clark in recasting and updating the fable, "The Lady and the Tiger." The story applies equally to homeowners or real estate investors in high value, commercial properties.

> The young man could open either door as he pleased. If he opened the one, there came out of it a hungry tiger, the fiercest and most cruel that could be procured, which would immediately tear him to pieces. But, if he opened the other door, there came forth from it a lady, the most suitable to his years and station that His Majesty could select among his fair subjects. So, I leave it to you, which door to open?
>
> The first man (investor) refused to take the chance. He lived safe and died chaste.
>
> The second man hired risk assessment consultants. He collected all the available data on lady and tiger populations. He brought in sophisticated technology to listen for growling and detect the faintest whiff of perfume. He completed checklists. He developed a utility function and assessed his risk averseness. Finally, sensing that in a few more years he would be in no condition to enjoy the lady anyway, he opened the optimal door. And was eaten by a low probability tiger.
>
> The third man took a course in tiger taming. He opened a door at random and was eaten by the lady.[2]

[2] William Clark, "Witches, Floods, and Wonder Drugs: Historical Perspectives on Risk Management," in Richard C. Schwing and Walter A. Albers, Jr., eds., *Societal Risk Assessment—How Safe Is Safe Enough?* New York: Plenum, 1980, p. 302.

Business risk   Chance that projected or predicted levels of income will not be realized, or will not be adequate to meet operating expenses.

Coefficient of variation   Standard deviation divided by the expected return.

Efficient frontier   A combination of portfolios that offers the lowest risk (standard deviation) for its expected return and the highest expected return for its level of risk.

Expected rate of return   A probability-weighted average of the rate of return in all scenarios.

Financial risk   Added uncertainty created when money is borrowed to help finance a property; chance of not meeting debt service, etc.

Legislative risk   Probability of loss in property value due to a "change in the rules of the game" through government action; an example is a city changing its zoning ordinance, initiating rent controls, or increasing property taxes; also known as political risk.

Liquidity risk   Chance of loss in converting an asset into cash within a short time.

Management risk   Chance of making a poor decision when adjusting a property to new conditions, such as a changing population mix or road system.

Market risk   Probability of loss in value due to changing economic conditions; an example is a major local business closing a plant.

Maximum expected return portfolio   The portfolio of risky assets with highest expected return and highest variance.

Minimum variance portfolio   The portfolio of risky assets with lowest variance.

Purchasing power risk   Chance of a drop in value of an asset, in real terms, due to inflation.

Required rate of return   Yield necessary to compensate for time and risk of an investment; also known as hurdle rate.

Risk premium   An expected return in excess of that on risk-free securities; provides compensation for the risk of an investment.

Standard deviation   A measure of variability; defined as the square root of the variance.

Systematic risk   Market risk.

Total risk   Chance of loss or unfavorable outcome relative to a specific property.

Unsystematic risk   Unique or specific risk; risk that can be reduced by diversification.

Variance   Mean squared deviation from the expected return.

QUESTIONS FOR REVIEW AND DISCUSSION

1. What is the difference between business risk and financial risk?
2. Define or explain the following risks involved in real estate investing. Give an example of each.

a. Liquidity

b. Management

c. Legislative

d. Market

e. Purchasing power

3. Is there any necessary relationship between risk and return in investing? Explain.

4. In comparing investments in real estate to investments in stocks and bonds, what major form of risk associated with real estate is much less significant in the latter case?

5. What are the conventional measures of risk? How is risk measured in tandem with the level of expected returns?

6. Which scenario provides for a more favorable investment—an asset with a 10 percent variance in expected returns and a 3.5 percent coefficient of variation, or an asset with a 5 percent variance in expected returns and a 2 percent coefficient of variation? Why?

7. Does a positive correlation between two assets indicate benefits of diversification? Why or why not?

8. What characteristics can be used to diversify a real estate portfolio? Which parameter would you consider the most effective (eg. geographic, etc . . .)?

PROBLEMS

1. Assume three different real estate assets are expected to provide the following levels of return under the different scenarios given:

	PROBABILITY OF OCCURRENCE	INDUSTRIAL	RETAIL	OFFICE
High demand	20%	30%	35%	40%
Medium demand	30%	20%	15%	25%
Low demand	50%	10%	−5%	−10%

Required: (a) Calculate the expected return for each product type. (b) What is the standard deviation for each asset class? (c) Based on the coefficient of variation, which asset class would be the most favorable for investment purposes?

2. a. What is the expected return of each product type based on the following historical returns:

YEAR	INDUSTRIAL	RETAIL	OFFICE
1986	10%	15%	20%
1987	6%	5%	10%
1988	4%	3%	5%
1989	3%	1%	2%
1990	2%	1%	−4%

b. Which of the investments is more risky?

c. Which investment offers the greatest return for the least amount of risk?

3. Consider a portfolio which contains 60 percent of asset A and 40 percent of asset B. Assume that the following historical returns have been received from each asset:

ASSET A		ASSET B	
YEAR	RETURN,%	YEAR	RETURN,%
1986	4	1986	0
1987	3	1987	2
1988	−1	1988	−1
1989	0	1989	1
1990	2	1990	0

a. What is the portfolio return on these assets?

b. What is the portfolio variance?

c. Does the correlation coefficient indicate any benefits of diversification?

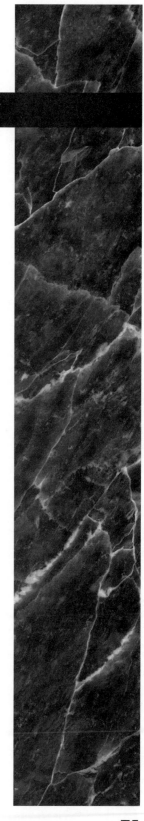

CHAPTER 5

FEDERAL TAXES
AFFECTING REAL ESTATE

Chapter Outline

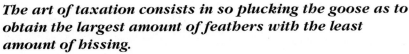

The art of taxation consists in so plucking the goose as to obtain the largest amount of feathers with the least amount of hissing.
Jean Baptiste Colbert

In this chapter we undertake a detailed analysis of the federal tax law affecting real estate. Our federal income tax law is administered and enforced by the Internal Revenue Service (IRS), which is a division of the U.S. Treasury Department. The tax law is very complex and sticky. Because of this it is sometimes called a bramble bush, implying that everyone working with it gets stuck at one time or another. Many books and manuals have been written to explain the subject. Millions of dollars are spent in tax litigation each year. No last word is possible because the law coming out of the tax courts changes on almost a daily basis. Decisions, therefore, should not be based solely on the material presented here; further checks should be made with competent accountants and attorneys, and other reliable sources.

TAX BASICS

Federal tax laws affect most real estate investment decisions as to income reported and taxes paid. Our discussion covers the federal tax regulations in generalized form. Basic concepts are taken up first to provide a framework, followed by applications in the three phases of the investment cycle: acquisition phase, administrative/operations phase, and alienation or disposition phase.

Taxable Income

Taxable income consists of two components: ordinary income and capital gains, each with its own tax treatment. It is important, therefore, that the distinction between ordinary income and capital gains not be confused.

Ordinary Income.   Ordinary income includes:

1. *Active income.* Wages, salaries, commissions, and fees for services earned make up active income. Income (net of expenses) from real estate activities also fits into this category, provided the taxpayer works at least half-time trading real estate—for example, as a real estate developer or broker—and materially participates in the endeavor. And, finally, active income also includes income (net of expenses) from the operation of a hotel or other transient lodging or a nursing home, regardless of whether or not the taxpayer works at least half-time trading real estate or materially participates in the endeavor.

2. *Passive income.* All other income (net of expenses) from real estate activities— including net income (or loss) from rental housing, office buildings, shopping centers, and other real estate activities in which the taxpayer is the landlord— is generally considered passive income.

3. *Portfolio income.* Portfolio income includes interest and dividend income from stocks, bonds, and some categories of real estate.[1]

These classifications are important because passive income or loss is treated substantially different from active income and portfolio income. First, profits and losses from passive activities, including rental activities, are netted against each other. Consider the following example. Suppose you own several passive investments in which you do not actively participate in the operations, nor do you work at least half-time trading real estate. Let us further suppose that one of your passive investments generates a $100,000 passive loss.

This $100,000 passive loss can be used only to offset other passive income. So, if you have $100,000 or more in other passive income, then the entire $100,000 passive loss can be used as a deduction to determine ordinary income. However, if you only have, say, $40,000 of other passive income, then any unused passive losses—in this case the $100,000 of passive losses less $40,000 of passive income, or $60,000—must be suspended and carried forward to offset passive income earned in future years.

Continuing with this example let us illustrate what happens to passive losses that are suspended. Suppose you earned $60,000 or more of passive income next year. In this case the entire $60,000 of suspended passive losses in the current year could be used to offset passive income earned next year. However, if you have only, say, $15,000 of passive income from other investments next year, then $45,000 of passive losses must be suspended and carried forward to future years. This process of carrying suspended passive losses forward continues until the passive losses are used up or the property is sold, at which time any suspended passive losses may be used to offset the capital gain due on sale.

Second, a special $25,000 exception for passive losses applies to rental real estate activities in which the investor actively participates in the operations of the property. The phrase *actively participates* in this case is taken to mean that the investor participates in making management decisions in a significant and bona fide way. Thus, by definition, this excludes certain types of real estate activities, like owning a limited partnership interest in a real estate limited partnership. Limited partners in real estate limited partnerships do not materially participate in the operations of the property. If they did, they would no longer be considered limited partners; rather, they would be considered general partners and lose their limited liability. Active participation also requires that the investor own at least a 10 percent interest in the activity.

---

[1] Included in this category is income or loss from real estate master limited partnerships (MLPs). A real estate MLP is a limited partnership that invests in mortgages or developed real estate. Real estate MLPs differ from ordinary limited partnership investments in that they are openly traded on major stock exchanges. This feature makes investments in real estate MLPs significantly more liquid than the ordinary limited partnership. Unfortunately, because all income or loss is treated as portfolio income rather than passive income, real estate MLPs have limited appeal to investors with significant passive losses in real estate. Also, beginning in 1997 real estate MLPs will be taxed as corporations rather than partnerships.

The special $25,000 exemption is phased out for individuals with adjusted gross incomes between $100,000 and $150,000. Thus, to be eligible for the entire $25,000 exemption means that an investor must not only actively participate in the operations of the property, but also that he or she must have an adjusted gross income of less than $100,000. For individuals with adjusted gross incomes in excess of $150,000, the special $25,000 exemption is phased out completely.

Example of Special $25,000 Exemption. To illustrate how the $25,000 exemption works, consider our example above. However, instead of assuming that the investor owns several passive investments in which he or she does not actively participate, let us now suppose that the investor actively participates in the operations of the property. In this case, the investor can use up to $25,000 of passive losses to offset other active income or portfolio income. Thus, as in our example above, if the investor has a $100,000 passive loss and no other passive income, $25,000 of this passive loss can be used to offset active income and/or portfolio income. The remaining $75,000 must be suspended and carried forward to offset passive income earned in the future.

Now, compare this situation with a case in which the taxpayer works at least half-time trading real estate and materially participates in the endeavor. Under these circumstances, the entire $100,000 loss is treated as active income or loss. Thus, all of the $100,000 can be used to offset the taxpayer's active income and/or portfolio income, and none of the $100,000 need be suspended and carried forward into the future.

Lastly, do not be confused by the different treatment of income from the operation of a hotel, other transient lodging, or a nursing home. For tax purposes hotels, other transient lodging, and nursing homes are considered businesses, as opposed to rental activities, and, hence, are taxed differently.

Capital Gains

A *capital gain* is a profit realized when a capital asset, such as real estate, is sold for more than its book value or adjusted basis. The *adjusted basis* for capital gains purposes (as described later on) is a value based on accounting calculations and events. For example, an investor pays $300,000 for an apartment property, on which $90,000 in accumulated tax depreciation is taken during a six-year ownership period. The investor then sells the property for $345,000. The capital gain or profit, is $135,000, calculated as follows:

Sales price, end of year 6		$345,000
Purchase price	$300,000	
Less: Accumulated tax depreciation	−90,000	
Adjusted basis of property[a]	$210,000	−210,000
Capital gain or profit		$135,000

[a] Alternately called the tax basis or book value of property.

The accumulated tax, or bookkeeping, depreciation accounts for $90,000 of the gain; market value appreciation accounts for the other $45,000.

The rationale for distinct tax treatment of capital gains and losses is that the gain or loss takes place over an extended period. With a progressive income tax, the impact would be magnified if all the gain or loss were attributed to the year of sale or exchange. Also, it is not practical to revalue each and every capital asset to determine possible gain or loss annually. So the tax code simply applied special rules to gains and losses realized from capital assets held for longer than a prescribed minimum period (12 months), termed long-term capital gains or losses.

A capital gain must be realized to be taxable. A *realized gain* means that cash, and/or boot, was obtained in the sale or exchange of the capital asset. *Boot* is cash, and/or the value of un-like personal property given or received to balance equities in the transaction. For example, an owner trades his hotel for an office building plus a 1992 Buick and $150,000 cash. The office building is *like-kind property;* the car and cash are boot. A known increase in the value of a capital asset that is not realized as boot or cash is termed *recognized gain,* which is not taxable until it is realized. That is, a recognized gain may be transferred from one capital asset or property to another without being subject to taxation; this is termed a *tax-deferred exchange.*

Tax Rates

Annual, net, taxable personal income is taxed at rates of either 15 percent, 28 percent, 31 percent, 36 percent, or 39.6 percent. Long-term capital gains are taxed at a maximum rate of 28 percent. Corporate tax rates graduate from 15 percent up to 35 percent (see Figure 5–1).

FIGURE 5–1
Marginal Income Tax Rates

SINGLE TAXPAYERS	
IF TAXABLE INCOME IS:	THE TAX RATE IS:
Less than $22,100	15%
Greater than $22,100 but not over $53,500	28%
Greater than $53,500 but not over $115,000	31%
Greater than $115,000 but not over $250,000	36%
Greater than $250,000	39.6%

MARRIED FILING JOINT RETURNS	
IF TAXABLE INCOME IS:	THE TAX RATE IS:
Less than $36,900	15%
Greater than $36,900 but not over $89,150	28%
Greater than $89,150 but not over $140,000	31%
Greater than $140,000 but not over $250,000	36%
Greater than $250,000	39.6%

CORPORATIONS	
IF TAXABLE INCOME IS:	THE TAX RATE IS:
$50,000 or less	15%
$50,001 to $ 75,000	25%
$75,001 to $10,000,000	34%
Greater than $10,000,000	35%

Tax Shelters

A *tax shelter* is a means of reducing taxes on income, generally obtained by deferring realization of the income. Realization is deferred by using a bookkeeping loss, an expense not involving an expenditure of cash, to avoid paying taxes on income as it is received. Such expenses are termed *artificial losses.*

Tax depreciation on buildings is an example of an artificial loss. The IRS recognizes buildings as wasting assets; therefore, an owner may take an annual depreciation allowance to recover an investment in a wasting asset, even though the building does not decline in value as judged by the market. The allowance is deducted as an expense from the income generated by the property. This deduction lowers the investor's reported taxable income and produces a tax savings without any cash outlay.

Tax depreciation deductions are limited to the cost of the improvements plus any installation (or acquisition) costs associated with placing the property into service. The IRS does not consider land to be a wasting asset and, therefore, no depreciation expense may be taken against it. To benefit from tax depreciation, market value must not, in fact, decline; if it does, the depreciation allowance is really a recovery of the investment and no advantage has been gained. In turn, no off-setting capital gain or profit will be realized upon sale of the property.

It is also social policy to encourage rehabilitation of older buildings and construction of low-income housing. Investment tax credits are used as incentives for these very worthy purposes. A *tax credit* is a dollar-for-dollar offset against taxes due and payable, which makes it a much more potent device than simply allowing costs incurred for these purposes to be expensed off in shorter periods. Tax credits produce a tax shelter cash flow without any expense.

Four Classes of Real Property

We are now ready to take up the four classes of real property recognized in the federal tax code. These are: (1) property held for sale, (2) property held for use in trade or business, (3) property held for investment, and (4) property held for personal use. Tax treatment differs from class to class.

Property Held for Sale.   The owner of property held for sale is termed a *dealer,* and such real estate is referred to as *dealer property.* Dealer property is considered merchant inventory and not a capital asset. Lots being held by a subdivider or condominiums being held by a developer are examples. The purpose is sale for profit as opposed to generation of income from rents or investment appreciation for capital gains.

Income or losses from dealer property receives the same tax treatment as income and losses on merchant inventory. To begin with, no tax depreciation is allowed. Further, all gains are treated as ordinary income and all losses as ordinary losses. Thus, houses held by a developer are the equivalent of cars held by an automobile dealer. Lastly, neither capital gains and losses nor a tax-deferred exchange is recognized.

Property Held for Use in Trade or Business.   A service station owned by an oil company, an industrial plant owned by a manufacturer, or a store owned by a merchant are examples of *trade* or *business property.* The real estate is considered a factor of production in much the same sense as equipment in a factory, rather than as merchandise held for sale. Tax treatment is according to Section 1231 of the tax code; hence, trade or business property is often termed *1231 property.*

Rental real estate qualifies as 1231 property, with the owner considered to be in the rental business—that is, in the business of owning and renting space. Owners of apartment houses, office buildings, stores, warehouses, shopping centers, and the like gain by taking the 1231 classification. The key tax implications are:

1. Tax depreciation may be taken on the wasting-asset portion of the property, along with other expenses of operating and maintaining the property.

2. The property may be traded for like-kind real estate in a tax-deferred exchange, making possible deferral of capital gains taxes in relocating or in trading up in property size.

3. Gains and losses on sale may be used as direct additions or offsets to ordinary income or expenses.

Property Held for Investment.   *Investment property* is held primarily for capital appreciation rather than the production of income; an investment motive must exist. Lots, unimproved land, or a condominium in a resort area fit into this class. Nominal income, such as grazing fees or rental of signboards is not sufficient to move property from this class to that of trade or business property.

Owners of investment property face the following tax implications:

1. Interest payments may be "expensed" only up to the amount of "nominal" income earned by the owner or owners from this and other property. Interest payments beyond nominal income must be capitalized, that is, added to the tax basis. All interest expense may be capitalized if the investor wishes.

2. A depreciation allowance cannot be taken because the property is regarded as not income-producing.

3. The property may be traded in a tax-deferred exchange for like-kind real estate.

Property Held for Personal Use.   A single-family house or a condominium used as a personal dwelling are examples of property held for personal use. Tax treatment of *personal residential property* is looked at in detail in the chapter on home ownership. Its tax treatment, in summary, is as follows.

1. Real property taxes and interest on a loan against the property may be taken as income tax deductions.

2. Depreciation may not be taken as an income tax deduction.

3. A sale or exchange may result in a taxable gain, but a loss is nondeductible for tax purposes. That is, if sold for less than the purchase price, the loss may not be used as an offset against other income. And a *rollover* privilege applies to the gain; if a replacement residence of equal or greater value is acquired within 24 months before or after the sale date, no tax need be paid on the gain.

4. A personal residence does not qualify as like-kind property in a tax-deferred exchange for other classes of real property.

At-Risk Limitations

Another tax rule that affects real estate is the *at-risk rule.* The at-risk rule limits the losses that are deductible for business or income-producing property. The at-risk rules are designed to prevent investors from deducting losses in excess of the investor's actual economic investment in an activity. Under the at-risk rule, deductible losses are generally limited to the sum of

1. Cash contribution, plus
2. Adjusted basis of property contributed in a like-kind exchange, and
3. Borrowed amounts for which the investor has personal liability or for which the investor has pledged property not used in the activity as security for repayment.

For real estate, item 3 effectively excludes seller financing of any kind.

Example of At-Risk Rule.   When the at-risk rule applies, the investor's cumulative allowable total deductions in connection with a property cannot exceed the amount for which the investor is at risk. To illustrate, suppose an investor purchases an office building for $10 million and obtains seller financing of $8 million. Because seller financing of any kind is not included in the amount that the investor has at risk, the investor's actual economic investment in the office building is:

Purchase price of office building	$10 million
Less: Seller financing	$ 8 million
Amount at-risk	$ 2 million

Thus, the investor can only deduct expenses up to $2 million. Once cumulative allowable total deductions in connection with the office building exceed $2 million, no further deductions are permissible.

In practice, restricting total allowable deductions to the investor's actual economic investment in an activity can have a big impact on the investment value of the property. If the at-risk rules become binding, the investor runs the risk of permanently losing all allowable tax deductions. The loss of allowable tax deductions lowers the investor's expected after-tax cash flows from the property, which in turn lower the price that the investor can afford to pay for the property.

ACQUISITION PHASE

When acquiring income-producing real estate, ownership form (i.e., the way ownership is held) and depreciable tax basis are the two crucial decisions.

Tax Implications of Ownership Forms

Selection of an appropriate ownership form (corporate, partnership, or sole) has definite implications for the amount of taxes payable on a real estate investment. Liability exposure and liquidity are also involved in selecting the ownership form. These concerns must be balanced one against the other in selecting the ownership form.

1. *Limit taxes payable.* Any taxes paid on income from an investment directly reduce the rate of return to be realized. Therefore, double taxation should be avoided; beyond this, opportunities to defer taxes are desirable.

2. *Limit liability.* Safety of principal is a primary concern; the less the chance of loss of principal, the better. Beyond this, for most investors, liability or chance of loss of more than the amount invested should be strictly avoided.

3. *Liquidity.* An investment that can readily be converted to cash is preferable to one that lacks liquidity.

Alternative forms of ownership include sole or individual proprietorships, general and limited partnerships, regular or C corporations, S corporations, and real estate investment trusts, REITs. These forms are compared briefly in Figure 5-2 relative to how they meet the above criteria.

Limited partnerships are the most commonly used form of business organization in which to own real estate. The limited partnership itself is not subject to tax, but instead serves as a conduit through which the tax consequences of a particular project are passed through to the individual partners. Limited partnerships are formed by one or more general partners and one or more limited partners. The general partner manages the affairs of the partnership and is personally responsible for the debts and obligations of the partnership. The limited partners are passive investors who are afforded limited liability.

The 1986 Tax Reform Act effectively puts limited partnerships, S corporations, and REITs on a par in that each allows avoidance of personal liability and double taxation. S corporations can be an advantageous form of investment for real estate. S corporations are organized like regular or C corporations. They issue stock which is freely transferable. They have a board of directors with clearly stated powers. And

CONCERNS OR CRITERIA
1. Double taxation
2. Personal liability
3. Liquidity of investment
4. Opportunity to maximize tax benefits

OWNERSHIP FORMS	
BENEFITS OR PLUSES (+)	LIMITATIONS OR MINUSES (−)
1. Sole proprietorship or general partnership	
Single taxation only	Personal liability
Maximum tax benefits	Liquidity is low
2. Limited partnership, S corporation, and REIT	
Single taxation only	Tax benefits not necessarily maximized
Limited personal liability	
Liquidity is high to moderate	
3. Regular or C corporation	
Limited personal liability	Double taxation of income
Liquidity is high to moderate	Tax benefits not necessarily maximized

FIGURE 5-2
Comparison of Ownership Forms for Real Estate Investments

shareholders have limited liability. The main difference between an S corporation and a C corporation is that C corporations first must pay a corporate income tax on their net income, and then shareholders must pay a personal income tax on all dividend income. In contrast, S corporations are not subject to double taxation. All profits and losses in an S corporation are passed through to the shareholders, just as in a partnership, and taxed only once.

One last point. Because limited partnerships, S corporations, REITs, and regular or C corporations are easier to sell or trade than equity positions, they often have better liquidity than sole ownership or general partnership interests. Also, sole ownership and general partnership interests have risks of loss and extended liability beyond the initial cash investment.

Adjusted Basis

Adjusted basis or *tax basis* is an expression of property value or cost for tax purposes that is determined at the time of acquisition. In an accounting sense, adjusted basis is *book value.* Adjusted basis is necessary to determine the amount of depreciation expense (tax shelter) that may be charged off for income tax purposes. Adjusted basis is also needed to determine the capital gain or loss on selling. Adjusted basis changes through time as a result of taking depreciation, making improvements, and exchanging property.

Acquisition and Adjusted Basis.   The purchase price or cost of land, plus improvements, is the initial basis of a property. The use of recourse mortgage credit by the new owner to help finance the purchase has no influence on the basis. Thus, a property purchased for $6.4 million has an initial basis of $6.4 million, even though a $5 million mortgage loan was used to help finance the purchase. Special rules, not discussed here, determine the basis to a new owner when property is acquired by other means, such as gift, inheritance, or exchange.

Allocation of Adjusted Basis.   Only the wasting-asset portion of a real asset may be depreciated for income tax purposes. Thus, a new owner must allocate the purchase price or basis between the land and improvements. The ratio of this allocation must be based on the fair market value of the land and the improvements at time of acquisition, according to the IRS. The two methods of making this allocation most often used are:

1. The ratio of land value and improvement value to total property value as determined by the local tax assessor.

2. An allocation of property value to land and improvements provided by an appraiser.

The allocation process is straightforward. For example, assume a property is purchased at its market value of $5 million. Its assessed value is $2.5 million, or 50 percent of market value. The assessor's records show an allocation of $500,000, or 20 percent, to the land, and $2 million, or 80 percent, to the improvements. In this case, $4 million, or 80 percent, of the purchase price may be depreciated by the new owner.

Changes in Adjusted Basis.   Adjusted basis changes through time. One common way of increasing adjusted basis is by making capital improvements, such as building an addition or installing an elevator. The purchase of adjacent property will also increase the basis. In addition, carrying expenses, property taxes, and loan interest may be capitalized to further increase basis for investment property. Taking depreciation, selling off a portion of a property, or an uninsured casualty loss, for instance, a fire, decreases the basis.

An example may be helpful here. An investor buys two vacant lots for $40,000. Each lot has an adjusted basis of $20,000. The investor adds $120,000 worth of improvements to lot 1, and sells the other for $60,000. Depreciation of $4,363 has been taken on lot 1. What is the current adjusted basis of the property still owned?

ACTION	AMOUNT	CHANGE IN BASIS	ADJUSTED BASIS
Purchase lots	$ 40,000	+ 40,000	$ 40,000
Add improvements	120,000	+ 120,000	160,000
Sell lot 2	60,000	− 20,000	140,000
Take depreciation on lot 1	4,363	− 4,363	135,637

The adjusted basis is $135,637. Note that in selling lot 2, only the basis attributed to lot 2 is deducted in making the adjustment to basis. The $40,000 profit on lot 2 (sale prices less cost, or $60,000 − $20,000) is reported as a capital gain.

ADMINISTRATIVE/OPERATIONS PHASE

A lot of wealthy investors hold real estate. Why? Primarily because of the tax benefits from operations. This includes the ability to subtract tax depreciation, which is a non-cash outlay, from net operating income to determine taxable income. As mentioned earlier, this generates what is called a *tax-sheltered cash flow*. Then there are tax credits. Tax credits effectively reduce the amount of equity investment in a property.

Depreciation or Cost Recovery

Federal tax laws allow the recovery of a wasting asset over its remaining useful life, which is consistent with economic principles. Prior to 1986, several methods of calculating depreciation or cost recovery were acceptable. The Tax Reform Act of 1986 reduced the methods to one—straight-line depreciation—thereby greatly simplifying tax depreciation calculations. Currently either 27.5 or 40 years is the period allowed for depreciating residential rental real estate, and either 39 or 40 years are allowed for nonresidential real estate.

The distinction between residential and nonresidential real estate for depreciation purposes has important social-policy implications. To be considered *residential real estate* for depreciation purposes, the property must derive at least 80 percent of its income from rentals, for example, from dwelling units for long-term tenants. Motels and hotels are not classified as residential property. With shorter cost-recovery times, real estate used for living units gets a faster write off. Theoretically, rents for a given amount of space should thus be slightly lower for families and low-income people. It follows that *nonresidential properties* are made up of commercial and industrial real estate—warehouses, stores, factories, office buildings, and motels and hotels.

Depreciation Expense and Taxable Income for Douglas Manor Apartments

The calculation of depreciation for Douglas Manor Apartments is as follows:

$$\text{Tax depreciation} = \frac{\text{Adjusted basis}}{\text{Useful life}}$$

$$= \frac{\$450,975}{27.5} = \$16,399$$

Here the adjusted tax basis is $450,975, or 85.9 percent of purchase price. The useful life for tax purposes is 27.5 years. This allowance is deducted as an expense from the income generated by the property. Thus, the NOI of $64,000 for the Douglas Manor Apartments may be reduced by $16,399 as a depreciation allowance or cost recovery. In addition, any interest on borrowed funds is deductible. The 27.5 year straight-line schedule for the Douglas Manor Apartments is shown in Figure 5–3.

The generalized format for calculating taxable income and income tax payable is shown in Figure 5–4. As can be seen, taxable income equals NOI less depreciation and mortgage interest. Taxable income for Douglas Manor Apartments in year 1 is $47,601. Assuming a 36 percent tax rate, this means a tax liability of $17,136 ($47,601 × 36%) in year 1. In each subsequent year, taxable income and income tax payable are calculated in a similar manner.

Tax Credits

Rehabilitation Tax Credits. Industrial, commercial, and other income-producing buildings (factories, office buildings, retail stores, hotels and motels) qualify for reha-

FIGURE 5–3
Douglas Manor Apartments: First Five Years Adjusted Basis and Depreciation Schedule

END OF YEAR	ADJUSTED BASIS OF SITE	ADJUSTED BASIS OF IMPROVEMENTS	ADJUSTED BASIS OF PROPERTY
1	$74,025	$450,975	$525,000
2	74,025	434,576	508,601
3	74,025	418,177	492,202
4	74,025	401,778	475,803
5	74,025	385,379	459,404

DEPRECIATION SCHEDULE

Purchase price and initial adjusted basis of property	$525,000
Less: Site value	−74,025
Initial adjusted basis of improvements	$450,975
Divided by: residential property depreciation term (years)	÷ 27.5
Annual depreciation allowance on straight-line basis	$ 16,399

	YEAR 1
Potential Gross Income	$108,000
Less: Vacancy and collection losses	4,320
Effective Gross Income	$103,680
Less: Operating expenses	39,680
Net Operating Income	$ 64,000
Less: Tax depreciation	16,399
Less: Interest on loan	0
Taxable Income	$ 47,601
Times: Tax rate	× 36%
Tax Payable	$ 17,136

FIGURE 5–4
Douglas Manor Apartments: Calculation of Taxable Income and Tax Payable

bilitation tax credits. However, residential rental structures do not qualify unless they are certified historical structures. Costs of acquisition or enlargement of residential rental properties are not recognized expenses.

The rehabilitation tax credit is limited solely to substantial rehabilitation. That is, the rehabilitation expenses must be at least $5,000 over a two-year period and exceed the adjusted basis of the property. In addition, there is the requirement that at least 75 percent of the existing exterior walls must be retained.

The amount of the allowable tax credit varies with the age and use of the building, according to the following schedule.

REHABILITATION EXPENDITURES FOR	INVESTMENT CREDIT
Nonresidential structures built before 1936	10%
Certified historical structure—residential or nonresidential	20%

In calculating the rehabilitation tax credit, the adjusted basis of the rehabilitated property is reduced by the amount of any such credit. The reduction in the adjusted basis cuts down on the allowable tax depreciation deduction and increases the capital gain due on sale (if sold prior to 39 years).

Example of Rehabilitation Tax Credit.   Alfa Romero buys a certified historic office building for $100,000 and spends $120,000 renovating it. The property qualifies for a 20 percent investment tax credit, which amounts to $24,000 ($120,000 × 20%). The land is worth $33,000.

The effect on taxes payable is easily determined as follows:

EFFECT ON ALFA'S TAXES FOLLOWING REHABILITATION	
Tax liability prior to investment credit	$60,000
Less: investment credit	− 24,000
Net taxes payable	$36,000

The adjusted basis of the property following rehabilitation is determined as follows:

Acquisition price	$100,000
Plus: Renovation costs	120,000
Total invested	$220,000
Less: Investment tax credit	24,000
Adjusted basis	$196,000

This means that the adjusted basis of the improvements following rehabilitation is $163,000 (= $196,000, which is the adjusted basis of the property, less $33,000, which is the value of the land).

Now let us look at the adjusted basis of the property and the improvements following rehabilitation had the property not qualified for a 20 percent investment tax credit. It is a simple calculation to show that the adjusted basis of the property in this case would have been $220,000 (= $100,000 acquisition cost plus $120,000 renovation costs), and that the adjusted basis of the improvements would have been $187,000 (= $220,000 adjusted basis of property minus $33,000 land cost).

The lower adjusted basis with the rehabilitation tax credit has two separate effects on Alfa's cash flows. First, the lower adjusted basis reduces the depreciation expense in any given year. The reduction in depreciation in any year is:

$$\text{Reduced depreciation expense} = \frac{\text{Reduction in adjusted basis}}{\text{Useful life}}$$

In our example this gives

$$\text{Reduced depreciation expense} = \frac{\$24,000}{39} = \$615$$

At a 36 percent marginal income tax rate, this means a foregone tax savings of $221 per year, which would have been available had the property not been eligible for the rehabilitation tax credit.

Second, with the rehabilitation tax credit, the adjusted basis of the property at the time of sale (say, in year 3) is $183,460, which is $22,155 less than without the rehabilitation tax credit (see below). Other things being equal, then, the lower adjusted basis of the property at the time of sale with the rehabilitation tax credit will increase the capital gain on sale by $22,155.[2] At a 28 percent capital gains tax rate, this means an additional capital gains tax of $6,203.

---

[2] This assumes that property values are either increasing over time or, at least, do not decrease. To illustrate the capital gain calculation, suppose that property values do not change over time. Then the capital gain due on sale at the end of year 3 without the rehabilitation tax credit is $220,000 − $205,615 = $14,385; when the rehabilitation tax credit is taken, the capital gain due on sale is $220,000 − $183,460 = $36,540, which is an increase of $22,155. The astute reader will realize that this differential gain due on sale will disappear over time; in fact, looking at the figures in the text you can actually see this happening. The differential capital gain due on sale declines over time owing to the reduced depreciation expense associated with the rehabilitation tax credit.

Depreciation Schedule With and Without Rehabilitation

	ADJUSTED BASIS OF PROPERTY		
END OF YEAR	WITHOUT REHAB TAX CREDIT	WITH REHAB TAX CREDIT	DIFFERENCE
1	$215,205	$191,820	$23,385
2	210,410	187,640	22,770
3	205,615	183,460	22,155
4	200,821	179,281	21,540
5	196,026	175,101	20,925

The rehabilitation tax credit is also subject to a *recapture* tax upon early sale of the rehabilitated property. The recapture percentages are as follows:

DISPOSITION IN 1ST YEAR	100% RECAPTURE
2nd year	80 %
3rd year	60 %
4th year	40 %
5th year	20 %

Thus, if Alfa sells the building in year 3, a $14,400 increase in tax liability is incurred ($24,000 × 60%) for the year.

When all of the cash flows are added up and discounted (assuming a required 10 percent after-tax rate of return), the net benefit of the rehabilitation tax credit is:

Present worth = Present value of investment tax credit
of tax credit   − present value of foregone depreciation tax savings
     − present value of increased capital gains tax
     − present value of recapture tax

$$= \$24,000 - \frac{\$221}{(1+.10)} - \frac{\$221}{(1+.10)^2} - \frac{\$221}{(1+.10)^3}$$

$$- \frac{\$6,203}{(1+.10)^3} - \frac{\$14,400}{(1+.10)^3}$$

$$= \$7,971$$

Looked at in this way, you can see that while the rehabilitation tax credit is advantageous, it is worth substantially less than it seems at first blush.

One easy way to increase the present worth of the tax credit is to hold the property for more than five years. By holding the property for more than five years, Alfa Romero can avoid the recapture penalty.

Remember also that there are substantial risks associated with rehabilitating a property. Cost overruns, for example, are much more likely in rehabilitations than in new construction. Often, rehabilitation projects are extremely small, too small for large developers, and the uncertainties are high. Small developers may lack the financial strength and experience to handle these risks. There is also a location risk associated with the rehabilitation tax credit; the tax credit is available for older properties, which often are located in marginal areas. Rehabilitation projects may also have atypical amenities that require special marketing. And financing may be difficult to obtain, especially if lenders require that the building be leased before committing permanent financing. Lastly, there are legal risks; the tax laws (as you have seen) are complex and there is no guarantee that the tax credit will be available when the building is completed.

Low-Income Housing Tax Credits.   Housing tax credits are allocated to specific low-income housing projects by state housing authorities.[3] The credit is used by investors to help finance the development or redevelopment of new or existing low-income housing projects.

The credit is earned over 15 years, but is taken by the investors over a 10-year period. The amount of the credit is calculated so that over a 10-year period the credit will have a present value equal to 70 percent of the investor's qualified basis in the project, where the present value is to be computed as of the last day of the first year.

To illustrate how the tax credit is calculated, consider the following hypothetical investment. A low-income housing project is constructed for a total cost of $312,500. The cost of the building is $250,000 and the value of the land is $62,500. We shall assume that the entire building is allocated to low-income housing. This assumption is crucial because the investor's qualified basis in the project depends on the number of low-income units in the building relative to the total number of residential units in the building (occupied or not). The smaller this unit fraction, the smaller the investor's qualified basis. The investor's qualified basis in the project also depends on the ratio of the total floor space of the low-income units in the building to the total floor space of residential units in the building (occupied or not).

We shall further assume that the project is financed entirely by unsubsidized funds. This assumption is equally critical because projects financed with federally subsidized funds (tax-exempt bonds and certain below-market loans) are eligible for only a 30 percent credit.

We can compute the present value of the tax credit as of the last day of the first year as follows:

$$
\begin{aligned}
\text{Present value of housing tax credit} \times PV1_{r,1} &= \text{annual credit} \times PV1_{r,1} + \\
&\quad \text{annual credit} \times PV1_{r,2} + \\
&\quad \text{annual credit} \times PV1_{r,3} + \cdots \\
&\quad + \text{annual credit} \times PV1_{r,10} \\
&= \text{annual credit} \times [PV1_{r,1} + PV1_{r,2} \\
&\quad + PV1_{r,3} + \cdots + PV1_{r,10}]
\end{aligned}
$$

which reduces to

$$
.70 \times \text{Qualified basis} \times PV1_{r,1} = \text{annual credit} \times [PV1_{r,1} + PV1_{r,2} + PV1_{r,3} + \cdots + PV1_{r,10}]
$$

[3] To qualify for the credit, the expenditure for construction or rehabilitation must exceed $2,000 per low-income unit and each project must meet either the "20/50" test or the "40/60" test. The 20/50 test is met if at least 20 percent of the housing units in the project are occupied by individuals whose incomes are 50 percent or less of the area median income. Similarly, the 40/60 test is met if at least 40 percent of the housing units in the project are occupied by individuals with incomes of 60 percent or less of area median income.

or

$$\text{annual credit} = \frac{.70 \times \text{Qualified basis} \times PV1_{r,1}}{[PV1_{r,1} + PV1_{r,2} + PV1_{r,3} + \cdots + PV1_{r,10}]}$$

$$= \frac{.70 \times \text{Qualified basis} \times PV1_{7.2\%,1}}{[PV1_{7.2\%,1} + PV1_{7.2\%,2} + PV1_{7.2\%,3} + \cdots PV1_{7.2\%,10}]}$$

$$= \frac{.70 \times \$250,000 \times 0.932836}{[0.932836 + 0.870183 + 0.811738 + \cdots + 0.498944]}$$

$$= \frac{.70 \times \$250,000 \times 0.932836}{6.959106} = \$23,458$$

Here the discount rate r is also determined as of the last day of the first year of the 10-year period. The value of r is the before-tax average annual long-term Treasury rate for the month, which in this example is assumed to be 10 percent, times 0.72. Multiplying by 0.72 in this case is intended to convert r from a before-tax rate to an after-tax rate (see Section 43 of IRS Code).

As can be seen, the credit is worth \$23,458 per year over the next ten years. So, the total tax credits taken will be \$234,580 (\$23,458 $\times$ 10). These credits are a dollar-for-dollar offset against taxes due and payable.

The main drawback with low-income housing tax credits is this: The credit is subject to full recapture with interest if the project (or more than a one-third interest in it) is sold before the end of the 15-year compliance period. The amount recaptured depends on when the project is sold. After ten years, for example, all the credits will have been taken, but only two-thirds will have been earned. Thus, in our example, if the project is sold after ten years, one-third of the tax credits, or \$78,193 (\$234,580 $\div$ 3), plus interest is subject to recapture.

ALIENATION OR DISPOSITION PHASE

After several years an owner often finds it advantageous to dispose of or get out of a specific property, mainly because the depreciation tax shelter has largely been used up. This change may be accomplished by a cash sale, an installment sale, or a tax-deferred exchange. Advantages vary with each of these techniques but are generally considered to be greatest with the exchange. In looking at these alternatives, the owner is assumed to have a capital gains tax rate of 28 percent.

Ordinary Sale

Cash sale means the owner/seller gets all of his or her equity out in cash in the year of sale. A cash sale is desirable when a taxpayer wishes to change the makeup of his or her investment portfolio. Also, a cash sale may be desirable if the taxpayer needs to release equity for personal reasons, such as to establish a retirement annuity.

Example of Ordinary Sale.   Ben Franklin sells a four-plex that he owned for four years for \$150,000 in December. He has used straight-line depreciation since buying the property and his present tax basis is $90,000. This means a profit of $60,000 and a potential tax of $16,800 on the sale.

Sale price	$150,000
Less: Adjusted tax basis	−90,000
Profit or gain	$ 60,000
Times: Capital gains tax rate	28%
Tax on gain	$ 16,800

With a tax bite as large as $16,800, deferring the tax as long as possible becomes important. Thus, installment sales and tax-deferred exchanges come into play in Ben's thinking.

Installment Sale

An *installment sale* is when the buyer makes payments over more than one year. The seller pays taxes on gains as they are received. An installment land contract and a first or second purchase-money mortgage are typical vehicles for deferring payments. To show the effect on Ben's taxes, let us restructure the previous cash sale to an installment sale, assuming no mortgage on the property. Including a mortgage greatly complicates the situation. Also considering properties that sold for more than $150,000 greatly complicates the calculations.[4]

Example of an Installment Sale. Assume Ben negotiates for equal payments of $30,000 plus 10 percent interest per year for each of five years. The initial payment would occur in the year of sale. What is the impact on taxes payable by Ben?

First, a brief restatement of the situation.

Sale price (contract price)	$150,000
Less: Present tax basis (3/5 of contract price)	−90,000
Long-term capital gain (2/5 of contract price)	$60,000

Ben will receive the full $150,000 over five years, of which $90,000 is a return of capital. The remaining $60,000 is the gain. Of every dollar received, three-fifths ($90,000 ÷ $150,000) is return of capital and two-fifths ($60,000 ÷ $150,000) is gain. Thus, in the year of sale and in each of the next four years, Ben's situation would look like this.

Payment received (1/5 of contract price)	$30,000
Less: Basis (3/5 of installment)	−18,000
Gain reported for year (2/5 of installment)	$12,000
Times: Ben's capital gains tax rate	28%
Tax payable on installment	$ 3,360

Ben's tax payable in the year of the sale is $3,360, or one-fifth of his payment in a cash sale. The calculation of tax is identical with the cash sale, except for the proration by installment.

[4] Properties sold for more than $150,000 are subject to certain limitations. These limitations require that the seller recognize *constructive payments* as well as the installment payments made by the buyer.

Comparable calculations would be made as payments are received in subsequent years. Thus, total taxes paid remain the same, but the timing of payment is deferred. And, if in later years Ben were in a 15 percent tax bracket, the total tax bill would be reduced. Also, Ben would expect to get interest on the unpaid balance with each installment received.

One final note regarding market-rate installment sales. By deferring the capital gains taxes that arise from the transfer of commercial real estate, an installment sale raises the value of the sale proceeds to the seller and causes property turnover rates to be higher than they would be in the absence of installment sales. The present worth of an installment sale is as follows:

Present worth of installment sale = Tax if sold outright for cash
$-PV$ of tax payments as each
installment is made

This point can be seen more clearly if we look at the present value of our hypothetical $150,000 installment sale. The present value of the installment sale to Ben is:

Present worth of installment sale = Tax if sold outright for cash
$- PV$ of tax payments as each
installment is made

$$= \frac{\$16,800}{(1 + .072)} - \frac{\$3,360}{(1 + .072)} - \frac{\$3,360}{(1 + .072)^2}$$

$$- \cdots - \frac{\$3,360}{(1 + .072)^5}$$

$$= \$1,969$$

The $16,800 is the tax due if the property were sold outright for cash (which we are assuming would be paid at the end of the year). The $3,360 is the actual capital gains tax payment each year (beginning at the end of the first year). One can think of the $16,800 as being akin to an interest-free loan from the Treasury, which Ben repays in equal installments of $3,360 per year in each of the next five years.

This assumes that Ben expects to earn 10 percent interest (before tax) on the unpaid balance with each installment payment (or 7.2 percent after tax) and that Ben's required before-tax rate of return is 10 percent, or 7.2 percent after tax.[5] Also implicit in this calculation is the assumption that Ben continues to be in a 28 percent capital gains tax bracket over the next five years.

Experience with respect to installment sales suggests that they were the rule rather than exception in the real estate partnership industry, especially in the early 1980s. Typical deal terms were 20 to 25 percent cash and 75 to 80 percent installment notes. The typical maturity of installment notes was ten years. Installment notes also typically bore below-market interest rates. This is significant because below-

---

[5] The problem becomes more complex should the seller offer the buyer a below-market interest rate on the installment note as an enducement to purchase the property. Clearly, in this case there is an opportunity cost associated with having to wait for each installment payment. This opportunity cost of having to wait for each installment payment lowers the value to the seller of selling the property. This opportunity cost may be offset in part or entirely if the quoted selling price of the property is above its fair-market value.

market interest rates will ordinarily increase the nominal sales price of real estate, resulting in a larger capital gain to the seller, which is postponable through the installment sale, and a larger step-up in depreciable property, deductible by the buyer against ordinary income.

Installment sales are not nearly as popular today owing to the dramatic shift in tax-oriented clientele. Whereas taxable investors used to dominate the holding of real estate, there has been a dramatic ownership shift to pension funds and other tax-exempt investors. Tax-exempt investors have little, if any, incentive to pursue installment sales because they do not have to pay capital gains taxes.

Tax-Deferred Exchange

In an exchange for like-kind property, the capital gains taxes that arise from the transfer, although realized in an economic sense, are not recognized for tax purposes. A transaction of this type is frequently referred to as a tax-free exchange; a more accurate statement is that it is a tax-deferred exchange. In a well-structured exchange, little or no gain is realized for tax purposes, and hence little or no tax must be paid.

Tax basis, market value, mortgages, and equities must all be taken into account in arranging an exchange; the actual structuring of an exchange tends to be very complex. For this reason, other than to stipulate elements of an exchange, the subject will not be pursued further here. The elements that must be present in an exchange to qualify it for nonrecognition of gain or loss are:

1. The transaction must be an exchange, as distinguished from a sale and a separate purchase.

2. The exchange must involve like-kinds or similar properties. Business and investment properties may be exchanged for each other. Likewise, city real estate may be exchanged for country property. A warehouse may be traded for a supermarket. Like-kind, therefore, refers to business or investment property that is exchanged for business or investment property.

On the other hand, a personal residence may not be exchanged for a business property. And a tax-deferred exchange of real property for personal property is not recognized. Finally, dealer real estate may not be exchanged for investment real estate.

Considerable planning is required to structure a tax-deferred exchange properly. Usually some un-like kinds of property (remember boot) must be added to balance the equities in the transaction. To the extent that boot is used and gain is recognized, taxes must be paid as a result of the transaction.

SUMMARY

The basic purpose of U.S. tax law is to raise revenue to operate the federal government; it is to be hoped that this is being done in an efficient and equitable manner. A second purpose is to promote and achieve socially and economically desirable ends.

In this chapter we have attempted to identify the key tax considerations that affect real estate investment decisions. Our discussion focused on the federal tax regulations in generalized form; including determining the appropriate marginal tax rate, rules for depreciating real property, tax credits available to real estate investors, and methods of disposing of real estate.

Active income   Wages, salaries, commissions, and fees for services earned plus income from the operation of a hotel or other transient lodging or a nursing home; also includes income from real estate activities provided the taxpayer works at least half-time trading real estate and materially participates in the endeavor.

Adjusted basis   Book value in an accounting sense; also referred to as tax basis.

Book value   Adjusted basis; tax basis.

Boot   Cash and/or the market value of personal property given or received in a tax-deferred exchange to balance equities; un-like property.

Capital gains   Profit from sale of a capital asset, such as real estate, held longer than one year, when net proceeds exceed adjusted or tax basis.

Dealer   Owner of property held for sale; for example, lots held by a subdivider.

Installment sale   Sale of property for two or more payments made over more than one year.

Like-kind property   Trading away for similar property, which results only in a recognized gain rather than a taxable realized gain.

Nonresidential property   Income property with less than 80 percent of its rents received from living units; for example, warehouses, stores, factories, office buildings, and motels and hotels.

Passive income   Income from real estate activities in which the taxpayer is the landlord.

Portfolio income   Includes interest and dividend income from stocks, bonds, and some categories of real estate.

Property held for use in trade or business   Real estate owned and operated for the purpose of deriving rental income; includes most real estate investments in office buildings, apartments, shopping centers, etc.

Property held for sale   Includes all properties held primarily for sale to customers in the ordinary course of trade or business; also referred to as dealer property.

Property held for investment   Includes property that is held primarily for capital appreciation rather than the production of income; examples include lots and unimproved land.

Property held for personal use   Includes all property held for owner-occupied housing.

Realized gain   A capital gain received as cash and/or boot, and therefore subject to taxation.

Recognized gain   A capital gain not subject to taxation because it was received in an exchange of like property.

Residential real estate   Income property that derives at least 80 percent of its income from rentals, for example, from dwelling units for long-term tenants.

Tax basis   Book value of property; see adjusted basis.

Tax credit   A dollar-for-dollar offset against taxes payable.

Tax-deferred exchange Exchange for like-kind property, with gain not recognized for tax purposes.

Tax depreciation Annual cost recovery allowed by the IRS on investment in a wasting asset, such as a building, even though there is no decline in its value as judged by the market.

Tax shelter Using a bookkeeping loss to avoid or defer paying taxes on income.

QUESTIONS FOR REVIEW AND DISCUSSION

1. What are the different classifications of ordinary income? Define each type and explain how they are treated when calculating taxes due.

2. What is the reasoning behind allowing for the depreciation of improvements but not the land on which the improvements are built?

3. What are the four different classes of real property according to the Federal Tax code? What are their distinguishing characteristics?

4. Does the initial tax basis of a property include the value of the land?

5. What type of depreciation is now used for real estate according to the Tax Reform Act of 1986? What are the different terms allowed for depreciation for different types of properties?

6. Why would an investor holding real estate assets prefer shorter periods of depreciation in the tax code?

7. What is a tax shelter? Give at least two examples.

8. Explain briefly the calculation of depreciation by the straight-line method.

9. Explain how investment value and market value of real estate are influenced by tax factors.

10. Is tax depreciation different from market depreciation? If so, must there always be a difference? Discuss.

PROBLEMS

1. An investor purchases a small office building for $320,000, which appreciates by 30 percent over five years. During that time, $25,000 per year is taken in depreciation allowances for tax purposes. What is the adjusted basis of the property at the end of year 5? What is the capital gain on sale, assuming no debt and no selling expenses?

2. Assume an office building is purchased for $2.3 million. Current tax assessor's records indicate an assessed value of $1.9 million with a 30 percent allocation of value to the land. How much depreciation may be taken over the life of the building?

3. If an apartment complex is worth $2 million and the land is valued at $180,000, how much annual depreciation can be taken by the owner for tax purposes?

4. What is the present worth of a rehabilitation tax credit taken on a nonresidential structure built in 1920 that is purchased for $200,000 and is then renovated at

a cost of $260,000? Assume that the land is worth $65,000 and the property is sold at the end of year 3; the tax rate is 28 percent and the after-tax required rate of return is 12 percent.

5. An apartment complex is sold by its owner for $500,000. At the time of sale, the adjusted basis of the property is $200,000. In order to defer the tax liability, the owner enters into an installment sale with equal payments from the purchaser over a four-year period. What is the annual tax liability of the original owner during each of the four years? What would the tax liability be for the original owner with an ordinary sale, with no debt, and no selling expenses? (assume a 28 percent tax rate in both cases)

6. Determine the value of an additional $2,000 of tax depreciation. Assume that the investor is in a 28 percent marginal income tax bracket.

7. Jennie purchased a vacant lot for $100,000 and added a $600,000 building to create a residential income property. Rentals started as of January 1. Determine the cost recovery allowance, using the 27.5-year straight-line method, for each of the first four years of ownership and for the total period.

8. Jennie sells the property in problem 7 above at the end of year 4. The sales price is $900,000. What is the tax liability from the sale, assuming a 28 percent marginal tax bracket?

9. If the property above were an office building and 39-year depreciation were used, what is the tax liability for Jennie on sale at the end of year 4? How much is the difference from the residential income property above?

10. David sells a property for $300,000 on an installment sale, with $50,000 down and the balance scheduled for equal payments over the next five years. His present tax basis is $200,000. What is the tax in the year of sale? What is the tax in subsequent years?

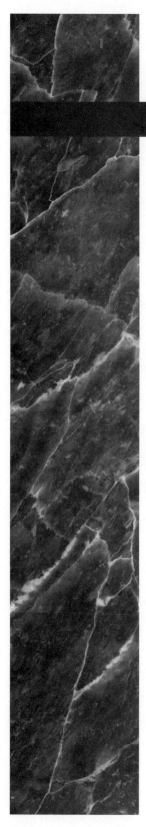

CHAPTER 6

INVESTMENT ANALYSIS

Chapter Outline

Buy land. They ain't making any more of the stuff.
Will Rogers, American humorist

Investors have varying goals depending on available resources (mainly money), age, and decision-making horizon. A recent college graduate with $5,000 to invest differs from an established family with investment experience and $100,000 to invest. An elderly person with $500,000 looking for an investment opportunity would be in still another class.

Some investors may want the comfort and convenience of owning a personal residence free-and-clear of any debt. Others may seek to own real estate as protection against inflation. Still others may enter real estate as a way of building prestige and maximizing wealth.

Investors also operate subject to constraints or limitations. Age, analytical ability, executive ability, energy level, work preferences, and time availability all act as constraints on an investor. A young person can afford a longer time horizon than can an elderly person. A person with limited time or energy is probably best advised to invest in a medium requiring little effort. Likewise, a person with limited ability to analyze and administer investments is better off avoiding active investments, meaning most real estate investments. Locational preferences as personal constraints are self-explanatory.

Note that we make simple, everyday decisions about what to eat or wear or do, about whom to see or where to go, by feel, habit, hunch, or intuition. Actions generally flow out of the decisions in a very natural manner. As situations become more complex, it becomes worthwhile to devote more time to identifying alternatives and their implications prior to making a decision and taking action. It also becomes worthwhile to devote more time to administering or implementing the decision. The benefits of a good decision or the costs of a bad decision become great enough at some point to warrant spending extra time, money, and effort to reach the best choice.

Real estate decisions clearly warrant spending extra time, money, and effort to reach the best choice. On a long-term basis, the investment must be reviewed periodically to determine if past choices and actions are working out. Often this means comparing the risks and rates of return from stocks and bonds with the risks and rates of return from real estate; it is a portfolio management concern. Additional or larger real estate investments may eventually be desirable. Investment in different types of properties may also become advantageous.

In this chapter we devote considerable attention to identifying real estate investment opportunities and making investment decisions. Here we will assume that the property to be acquired is 100 percent equity-financed, meaning that the property is purchased for all cash. Debt financing will be discussed in Chapter 21.

WHY INVEST IN REAL ESTATE?

Many of the advantages of real estate as an investment are in its surrounding traditions and institutions.

Leverage.   *Leverage* is the use of borrowed money to increase the rate of return earned from an equity real estate investment. Traditionally, real estate investors have been able to borrow up to 90 percent of the value of any property owned or acquired. Nowadays, because of the tightening of the credit markets for any new development, even the best financiers of real estate are rarely able to borrow more than 60 to 75 percent of the value of the property acquired. Nonetheless, leverage can be advantageous when the investment earns a higher rate of return than the interest on the borrowed money.

Leverage also enables an investor to control more property with a given amount of money. An investor can leverage by stretching out the repayment schedule or by refinancing. By maintaining high leverage an investor may pyramid investments more quickly. *Pyramiding* is controlling ever more property through reinvestment, refinancing, and exchanging. The objective is to control the maximum value in property with the least resources. Needless to say, pyramiding carries a high risk of a total wipe-out during a recession.

Tax Shelter.   Tax depreciation, installment sales, and tax-deferred exchanges all enable a real estate investor to minimize or defer income taxes.

Purchasing Power Protection.   Real estate usually offers protection against inflation. Whereas most capital assets tend to lose value in terms of purchasing power or constant dollars in inflationary periods, adequately improved realty, especially apartments, shopping centers, and selected commercial properties, tend to gain value as measured in constant dollars. In the absence of rent and price controls, real property, like a ship upon ocean waters, floats above its purchasing power–constant dollar line irrespective of depth or rise in the level of prices. For this real-value holding power to be true of a specific parcel of income real estate, the property must be well located, have rentals that can be adjusted periodically, and not be subject to sudden sharp increases in operating costs.

Pride of Ownership.   Many real estate investors gain identity by being "in the game" or by being "shrewd operators." Some investors also realize great satisfaction from owning something tangible that can be touched, felt, and shown to friends and relatives.

Control.   The immediate and direct control of an owner over realty enables the owner or an agent to make continuing decisions about the property as a financial asset and as a productive property. This control enables the investor to manage property to meet personal goals, whether they are to maintain the property as a showpiece for pride of ownership or to operate the property for maximum rate of return. Many owners experience a great sense of power and independence in this control.

Entrepreneurial Profit.   A last important advantage is that added value may be realized by building or rehabilitating a property, and the added value is immediately invested in the property without being taxed. Thus, many investors also develop property. Other investors combine real estate investing with brokerage or property management.

RATIONAL INVESTOR VERSUS ECONOMIC-BEING ASSUMPTION

The person making the real estate investment decision is assumed to be a rational investor. The assumptions about this rational investor are generally consistent with the economic person theory commonly found in economics. Each acts in self-interest. Each is strongly influenced by the institutional environment. But there are differences.

An *economic person* is defined in economic literature as a primary decision-maker motivated to maximize his or her economic return. The economic person has an uncanny knowledge of the alternatives and of what to expect under varying production, cost, and pricing strategies. In this sense, the economic person looks at the use of land resources from the viewpoint of the typical investor.

A *rational investor* operates under slightly different assumptions than does the economic person. Knowledge is less than total, which means that risk and uncertainty are present. Also, institutional considerations (laws and taxes, mainly) affect investors individually and specifically. These differences are the major reasons why the viewpoint of an individual, rational investor is preferred in making decisions about real estate as a financial asset.

The goal of maximizing self-interest (wealth) is an important assumption for our rational investor. The concept of a rational investor was developed shortly after World War II by Herbert Simon, who won a Nobel Prize for his work in economic and decision theory in 1978. Acting in self-interest, a rational investor always selects the choice or alternative within his or her range of knowledge that gives the greatest personal advantage. A rational investor will also anticipate the future and incorporate any expected changes into the current market price of real estate.

Note that self-interest is neither good nor bad, desirable nor undesirable, per se. In a sense, self-interest is to people as gravity is to the earth. Gravity may keep us from flying at will and require us to exert energy to conquer distance or elevation, but gravity also works to our advantage. It causes rain to fall and rivers to flow downhill. We turn gravity to our advantage in our work and play when we irrigate gardens, ski, skydive, or play ball.

Self-interest is a force or motivation that causes us to try to maximize our satisfactions in life. We seek leisure, self-expression, travel, company of loved ones, thrills from skydiving, or social changes out of self-interest. Most of us seek money only as an intermediate goal. In our complex society, an investor seeking profits may be making a contribution to society as great as or even greater than a doctor seeking fees or a politician seeking power.

Self-interest acts to push real estate to its highest-and-best use. *Highest-and-best use* is that legal and possible land use that gives it its greatest present value while preserving its utility. A *land use* is that activity by which a parcel of real estate is made productive—that is, it generates services of value—as a residential, commercial, or industrial property.

Highest-and-best use of a parcel to one investor in the market may well differ from the highest-and-best use of another investor because of differences in what each is seeking to maximize. This difference is the major reason why a financial approach rather than an economic approach to real estate investment is needed. Using a financial approach provides us with a highly useful model for numerous investment decisions about real estate as an asset. A more in-depth treatment of highest-and-best use concepts is covered in Chapter 12.

HOW DO DIFFERENT PROPERTY TYPES STACK UP?

Differing property types offer distinct advantages to specific investors. Figure 6–1 summarizes these comments.

PROPERTY TYPE	MAIN VALUE DETERMINANTS	INVESTMENT CHARACTERISTICS	PRINCIPAL RISKS	MOST LIKELY INVESTOR TYPE
Vacant or Raw Land	Expansion of demand Convenient location Travel patterns Planning/zoning/highest and best use	Passive Illiquid Limited leverage Rate of return by value appreciation No tax depreciation Capital gains taxation Expenses capitalized	Carrying costs: "alligator" Distress sale possible Value appreciation uncertain	Speculator Developer Estate as store of value
Residential Rentals (Apartments)	Expanding population Rising incomes Location: convenience, favorable exposure Prestige, sometimes	Moderately active Moderately liquid High leverage (loan-to-value ratio) Rate of return by periodic income and value appreciation Accelerated tax depreciation possible Ordinary and capital gains taxation	Start up when new Management: probably necessary to hire professional for larger projects	High income: benefiting from tax shelter Suitable for anyone but must be able to put up initial equity investment
Office Buildings	Expanding local economy Location linkages Prestige/status sometimes important Tenant-mix compatibility	Active, unless leased to one firm Moderately liquid Rate of return by periodic income and value appreciation Tax depreciation Ordinary and capital gains taxation	Start up when new Management: high level of service required Competitive facilities Obsolescence Shift in location of business activity	High income: needing tax shelter Suitable for anyone if professional management hired and able to put up initial equity investment
Warehouses	Commercial/industrial activity Location for ease of movement	Mostly passive: often on long-term lease Moderately liquid Moderate leverage	Obsolescence due to changes in materials handling equipment and techniques	Retired: desiring high cash flow and limited management

(continued)

PROPERTY TYPE	MAIN VALUE DETERMINANTS	INVESTMENT CHARACTERISTICS	PRINCIPAL RISKS	MOST LIKELY INVESTOR TYPE
	Structural design to endure change	Rate of Return mainly by periodic income Tax depreciation Ordinary and capital gains taxation		Anyone desiring tax shelter who has adequate initial equity capital
Neighborhood Shopping Centers	Community growth Effective demand: population, income Convenient location relative to competition Adequate parking Tenant mix relative to spending patterns Effective lease negotiation	Moderately active Liquidity limited Moderate leverage Rate of Return by periodic income and value appreciation Tax depreciation Ordinary and capital gains taxation	Start up: getting proper tenant mix Management: need to provide adequate level of service Vacancies Competitive facilities Obsolescence	Reasonably wealthy: need to make large equity investment Anyone able to use tax shelter plus other benefits
Hotels/motels	Location: linkages and convenience Demand: conference, tourist, resort, business Mix of facilities and services	Active Moderately liquid Moderate to poor leverage Rate of return by periodic income and value appreciation Tax depreciation Ordinary and capital gains taxation	Management: high tenant turnover (professional management almost a necessity) Competing facilities	Anyone able to use tax shelter and with adequate initial equity capital Smaller properties suitable for investors also willing to manage and maintain

FIGURE 6–1
Generalized characteristics of real property investment types

Vacant or Raw Land

Land is only one of several alternatives open to an investor. Supply is limited; demand is growing; therefore, investing in land is a sure thing. While generally valid, this argument is also limited.

The return from land must be realized through value appreciation, which depends on supply and demand. The supply of land is limited. But the supply of urban land may be increased simply by extending roads, water and sewer lines, and electrical services. Demand for land depends on expansion of demand in the specific community. Location relative to local road and travel patterns goes far to determine the demand for a specific parcel of realty. Finally, planning, zoning, and probable highest and best use greatly determine chances for value enhancement.

Land is passive and illiquid as an investment medium. Low loan-to-value ratios make it difficult to leverage land highly. Owning land gives no tax depreciation, and carrying costs must be capitalized. In that land earns little or no income, an investor must pay carrying costs from other income. Such an investment is sometimes called an "alligator" because it has to be fed. If the owner suffers reduced income, a distress sale may be necessary. The rate and amount of value appreciation likely to occur over a period adds additional uncertainty to investment in land.

The most likely investors in land are speculators for short-term gains and developers for long-term operating needs. Estates and others seeking a store of value and an easily managed hedge against inflation are also likely investor types for land.

Apartments

The number of households and income levels are the primary determinants of value for residential real estate. Some apartment buildings also realize value based on prestige considerations. Location, convenience, and environment also greatly influence value.

Apartments require moderately active attention as an investment. Apartments are more liquid than most realty investments because investors are more knowledgeable about residential properties than other types of property. Thus, with more investors, the market is broader. Also, high leverage is possible; up to 90 percent, and sometimes higher, loan-to-value ratios are possible. The rate of return may be enhanced both by periodic receipt of income and increase in value.

The major risks in apartment investment are during the start-up period of new properties and in obtaining or providing quality management on a continuing basis. For large complexes, professional management is almost a must because of the considerable know-how required and the need to avoid harassment from tenants and others. Smaller properties, roughly 12 units or less, may be managed and maintained by an owner with adequate time. Personal management gives the owner closer control, in addition to "psychological payment" for the services rendered.

Office Buildings

The value of office buildings depends heavily on the business health of the area. A convenient location, a compatible tenant mix, and a prestigious image also add to value.

Office buildings generally require active participation of an owner unless leased to a single party, because tenant demands must be dealt with. Liquidity and leverage are generally moderate. The rate of return is produced both by periodic receipt of income and value appreciation.

The main risks with an office property are during start-up, maintaining high-quality management, and obsolescence, most of which are within the control of the owner. Shifts in location of business activity and development of competitive facilities are risks outside the direct influence of the owner.

Likely owners of large office buildings are wealthy or high-income investors who are likely to have the high initial equity investment required, as is implied by the moderate leverage. Syndicates are sometimes organized to own office buildings, thereby opening the investment opportunity to persons of more moderate means.

Warehouses

Warehouses obviously depend heavily on the level of commercial and industrial activity for value. To maintain value, warehouses must be designed and built to accommodate changes in methods of handling materials. Ceilings too low and aisles too narrow to accommodate forklift trucks caused many warehouses to become obsolete in the 1950s and 1960s, for example. Warehouse value also depends on a location that allows easy movement through a community.

A warehouse on long-term lease to one firm tends to be a passive investment. Leverage and liquidity are moderate. Cash flow tends to be somewhat higher as a proportion of value than with some other improved properties because less value appreciation is expected. In turn, people desiring high cash flow and limited management requirements find warehouses an excellent investment. In most other respects, warehouses are similar to apartment and office buildings.

Small Shopping Centers

The value of shopping centers depends heavily on adequate purchasing power, meaning people and incomes, in their tributary area. The location must be convenient for the population and parking must be plentiful. Finally, the tenant mix must be suited to the demands of the population in the tributary area. Supermarkets, small variety and discount stores, restaurants, and gasoline stations are typical tenants.

Active management is required to establish and maintain a center. Effective lease negotiation is important. Liquidity is limited because few investors have the broad knowledge needed to manage a center; also, leverage is moderate. The tax treatment of shopping center investment is similar to that of other commercial properties. Vacancies and lease negotiation, obsolescence, and development of competitive facilities are the main risks of center ownership. Also, as with office buildings, a reasonably large equity investment is required. In other respects, any investor seeking periodic income and capital gains would find shopping center investment inviting.

Hotels and Motels

Hotels and motels depend primarily on tourist and business travelers for their demand. In recent years it has been in vogue to hold business conferences in motels and hotels. Having a location and the facilities to satisfy this demand with ease is a large determinant of value.

Hotels and motels are active investments with limited liquidity and offer moderate-to-poor leverage. They receive tax treatment as business property.

Major risks in hotel and motel investment are maintaining adequate size and competent management. Economies of scale apply. And high tenant turnover means that management must be effective. Obsolescence and the development of more adequate competing facilities are also major risks.

Large hotels and motels require considerable equity investment and, therefore, are limited to syndicates or wealthy investors. Smaller properties are suitable for less affluent investors who are also willing to manage and maintain the property.

HOW SPECIFIC INVESTMENTS ARE ANALYZED

Why are buildings like the Bank of America building in San Francisco or New York's towering World Trade Center eagerly sought by investors? The answer seems clear: they are the best in their markets. They are the most attractive, rentable, and efficient. Also, they generally yield a handsome rate of return.

By way of contrast, why, then, are no-frills older buildings, with mixed or low tenant prestige, poor design, inferior locations, and below-average workmanship and materials often sought by investors? The answer: even the worst properties in a market can yield an attractive rate of return if priced appropriately.

The point to note is that, after all things considered, most decisions to invest in real estate are undertaken to earn a profit. One widely used criterion for measuring whether a specific project is likely to earn a profit over and above a normal required rate of return is known as the *net present value rule.*

Let us look more closely at the net present value (NPV) criterion. Net present value is simply the difference between the present value of benefits and the market value or cost of the investment. If we define $ATCF_t$ as the expected after-tax cash flow generated by the property in period t and $ATER$ as the after-tax equity reversion due on sale, we may write

net present value = present worth of property − market value

$$= \frac{ATCF_1}{(1 + r_a)} + \frac{ATCF_2}{(1 + r_a)^2} + \cdots + \frac{ATCF_n}{(1 + r_a)^n} + \frac{ATER}{(1 + r_a)^n} - MV$$

where r_a denotes the required after-tax rate of return on the property and MV is the cost of the investment.[1] The NPV formula tells us if NPV > 0 or if NPV = 0, then buy. In either of these circumstances, the investors goals will be realized or exceeded.

But, if investment value is less than the cost of the investment, and market value is paid, the buyer's investment goals will not be realized.

The rationale for rejecting the investment when NPV is less than 0 is straightforward. A positive NPV means that the present worth of the property is greater than the cost of the investment; hence, the position of the equity investor is improved by undertaking the investment. A zero NPV means that the wealth of the equity investor is unaffected. Projects with zero NPV are a matter of indifference and, consequently, should be undertaken. A negative NPV means that the investment is not expected to earn the required rate of return if purchased at the market value.

NET PRESENT VALUE ANALYSIS FOR DOUGLAS MANOR APARTMENTS—AN EXAMPLE

Our case property, Douglas Manor Apartments, will be used to illustrate the elements and techniques of NPV analysis, with cash flows on an after-tax basis. The viewpoint is that of the equity investor.

---

[1]For ease of exposition, we have assumed that the project's discount rate, r_a, is constant across all periods. It is a simple matter, however, to allow r_a to vary from period to period.

The data or information needed to determine investment value have been discussed in earlier chapters. These data, plus any additional assumptions or inputs for Douglas Manor Apartments, are restated here in summary form for easy reference. Figure 6–2 provides a summary of projected cash flows and market value levels for the Douglas Manor Apartments. What follows is summary data:

1. Net operating income is $64,000, as presented in the pro forma operating statement shown in Figure 3–1.

2. The purchase price of Douglas Manor Apartments is taken to be $525,000 (rounded).

3. Improvements are assumed to make up 85.9 percent of the $525,000 purchase price, or $451,000. Using a 27.5-year life, with straight-line cost recovery as required by the Tax Reform Act of 1986, gives $16,399 per year of tax depreciation.

4. The property is to be purchased with 100 percent cash.

5. The investors are assumed to have a 36 percent marginal income tax rate. The investors' capital gains tax rate is 28 percent.

6. The investors have a minimum of 12 percent per year after-tax required rate of return on any equity investment.

7. The property is assumed to be held for four years, during which time its net operating income is expected to increase at 5 percent per year. The end-of-year 4 market value, which is also the disposition price, is expected to be $777,924.

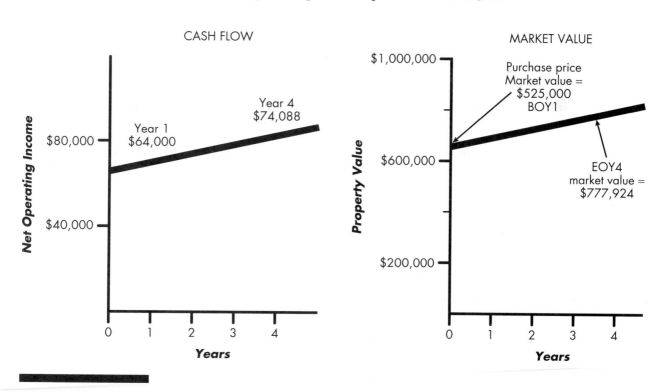

FIGURE 6–2
Douglas Manor Apartments: Projected Cash Flows and Market Value Levels

Disposition or selling costs at the end of year 4 are assumed to be 7 percent of the sales price.

8. Annual compounding is used for the equity time-value-of-money calculations.

We begin by calculating the investment value of Douglas Manor Apartments. Investment value equals the present value of the cash flow from operations, plus the present value of the reversion upon sale at the end of the holding period, discounted at the investor's required rate of return.

Note that with circumstances unique to an individual investor, such as being in a favorable tax position or having access to available financing at a below-market interest rate, the investment value of the property can conceivably exceed the market value of the property. This can also happen when individual investors are motivated by reasons other than wealth maximization for investing in a specific real estate project. In many instances real estate investors are willing to accept a lower rate of return on their investment in return for certain other intangible or subjective benefits, which are often difficult to quantify.

PROCESS USED TO DETERMINE AFTER-TAX CASH FLOW AND AFTER-TAX EQUITY REVERSION

The process used to calculate the after-tax cash flow (ATCF) from operations and the after-tax equity reversion (ATER) is illustrated below and in Figure 6–3.

Step 1: Determining Tax Payable

Generally speaking, taxable income from real estate equals net operating income less the depreciation expense and less interest paid on money borrowed to finance the property. However, with 100 percent equity used to finance the property, taxable income is simply net operating income less the depreciation expense.

Depreciation expense, you may recall, is a tax-deductible allowance to account for the decline in value or useful life of the real estate resulting from wear, tear, ob-

FIGURE 6–3
Process for Calculating Tax Payable and After-Tax Cash Flow

CALCULATION OF TAX PAYABLE		CALCULATION OF AFTER-TAX CASH FLOW	
Potential Gross Income	$		
Less: Vacancy and collection losses	_____		
Effective Gross Income	$		
Less: Operating expenses	_____		
Net Operating Income	$	Net Operating Income	$
Less: Tax depreciation		Less: Annual debt service	_____
Less: Interest on loan	_____	Before-Tax Cash Flow	$
Taxable Income	$	Less: Tax payable	_____
Multiplied by Tax Rate	_____	After-Tax Cash Flow	$_____
Tax Payable	$_____		

solescence, or actions of the elements. Depreciation expense can be taken regardless of whether the equity investor is leveraged. Interest expense, on the other hand, can be taken only if you borrow money to finance the purchase, which explains why in our 100 percent equity analysis the interest expense is zero. Multiplying the taxable income by the tax rate gives the tax payable on income from the property.

Figures 6–4 and 6–5 give a detailed cash-flow projection for the Douglas Manor Apartments, including the calculation of the income tax payable by an owner in a 36 percent tax bracket.

For year 1, taxable income is $47,601 and income tax payable is $17,136:

Net Operating Income	$64,000
Less: Depreciation	16,399
Less: Interest paid	0
Taxable income	$47,601
Times: Income tax rate	× 0.36
Income tax payable (tax savings)	$17,136

By year 4 in Figure 6–4, NOI has increased so that the Douglas Manor Apartments has taxes payable of $20,768.

	YEAR			
	1	2	3	4
Net Operating Income	$64,000	$67,200	$70,560	$74,088
Less: Straight-line tax depreciation	16,399	16,399	16,399	16,399
Less: Interest paid	0	0	0	0
Taxable income	$47,601	$50,801	$54,161	$57,689
Times: Investor's tax rate	× 0.36	× 0.36	× 0.36	× 0.36
Income tax payable	$17,136	$18,288	$19,498	$20,768

FIGURE 6–4
Douglas Manor Apartments: Calculation of Annual Tax on Income for an Equity Owner in 36 Percent Tax Bracket

Step 2: Determining After-Tax Cash Flow

The next step in the analysis is to determine ATCF from the property for each year of ownership. Generally speaking, *before-tax cash flow* (BTCF) equals NOI less annual debt service. Subtracting the tax payable on income from operations yields the ATCF that can be pocketed.

	YEAR			
	1	2	3	4
Net Operating Income	$64,000	$67,200	$70,560	$74,088
Less: Annual debt service	0	0	0	0
Before-Tax Cash Flow	$64,000	$67,200	70,560	$74,088
Less: Tax payable	17,136	18,288	19,498	20,768
After-Tax Cash Flow	$46,864	$48,912	$51,062	$53,320

FIGURE 6–5
Douglas Manor Apartments: Calculation of After-Tax Cash Flows from Operations

Obviously, with 100 percent equity used to finance the property, the required annual debt service payment to the lender will be zero, so BTCF will simply equal NOI. Confused? Think of it in this way: NOI is the income available to meet the investor's minimum acceptable return after all operating expenses have been paid. With no annual debt service payment, all the operating income will accrue entirely to the equity investor.

For year 1, BTCF-to-equity equals NOI, or $64,000, less the annual mortgage debt service, which equals zero since the property is 100 percent equity financed. Deducting the income tax payable from BTCF gives an ATCF of $46,864:

Net operating income	$64,000
Less: Annual debt service	0
Before-tax cash flow	$64,000
Less: Income tax payable	17,136
After-tax cash flow	$46,864

By year 4, ATCF has increased to $53,320.

Step 3: After-Tax Equity Reversion

After-tax equity reversion equals sale price less disposition costs, less the amortized mortgage balance, if any, and less capital gains taxes.

Let us look now at the projected disposition or sale of Douglas Manor Apartments. The calculations are summarized in Figure 6–6. Douglas Manor Apartments is projected to have increased in value by more than 48 percent, so a disposition sale price of $777,924 is realized. This figure is arrived at by taking the expected NOI for year 5, $77,792, and dividing by a 10 percent overall capitalization rate.

Since the property is 100 percent equity financed, the mortgage balance at the end of four years is zero. The long-term capital gain equals $264,066, all of which

FIGURE 6–6
Douglas Manor Apartments: Calculation of End of Year 4 Taxes Due on Sale and After-Tax Equity Reversion

Sales Price, End-of-Year 4		$777,924
Less: Selling expenses @ 7%		54,455
Net Sales Price		$723,469
Less: Adjusted basis		
Purchase price	$525,000	
Less: Accumulated depreciation	65,596	459,404
Taxable Capital Gain		$264,066
Times: Capital gains tax rate		× 0.28
Taxes Due on Sale		$73,938
Sales Price, End-of-Year 4		$777,924
Less: Selling expenses @ 7%		54,455
Net Sales Price		$723,469
Less: Mortgage balance outstanding		0
Before-Tax Equity Reversion		$723,469
Less: Taxes due on sale		73,938
After-Tax Equity Reversion		$649,531

is subject to the 28 percent tax rate. Thus, total taxes payable are $73,938. Total payments deducted from the sales price amount to $128,393 (selling expense of $54,455 plus taxes payable of $73,938), which leaves a net after-tax equity reversion of $649,531.

NET PRESENT VALUE

At a 12 percent required rate of return, the net present value of Douglas Manor Apartments is $38,855:

$$NPV = \frac{\$46,864}{(1 + 0.12)} + \frac{\$48,912}{(1 + 0.12)^2} + \frac{\$51,062}{(1 + 0.12)^3} + \frac{\$53,320}{(1 + 0.12)^4}$$

$$+ \frac{\$649,531}{(1 + 0.12)^4} - \$525,000$$

$$= \$38,855$$

For decision purposes, the rule is that NPV must be zero or positive for a go decision to invest. Thus, in this case the *decision rule* says invest.

At an 18 percent required rate of return, we get a present value for the cash flows of $468,444. In turn, NPV of the investment is a negative $56,556.

$$NPV = \frac{\$46,864}{(1 + 0.18)} + \frac{\$48,912}{(1 + 0.18)^2} + \frac{\$51,062}{(1 + 0.18)^3} + \frac{\$53,320}{(1 + 0.18)^4}$$

$$+ \frac{\$649,531}{(1 + 0.18)^4} - \$525,000$$

$$= (\$56,556)$$

In this case, the decision rule says "do not invest."

INTERNAL RATE OF RETURN

The internal rate of return is sometimes used as an alternative to NPV in making financial decisions. The *internal rate of return* (IRR) is that rate of return that discounts future cash flows to the exact amount of the investment. Stated another way, if used in NPV analysis, IRR would result in a NPV of zero.

Let us calculate IRR for Douglas Manor Apartments. We already have enough information to approximate it. The present value of the cash flows at 12 percent is $563,855, and at 18 percent it is $468,444. The investment cost is $525,000; therefore, NPV of the cash flows at 12 percent is $38,855, and it is ($56,556) at 18 percent. Thus, we know that IRR is somewhere between 12 and 18 percent. By trial and error, we find that IRR is:

$$NPV = \frac{\$46,864}{(1 + 0.1426)} + \frac{\$48,912}{(1 + 0.1426)^2} + \frac{\$51,062}{(1 + 0.1426)^3} + \frac{\$53,320}{(1 + 0.1426)^4}$$

$$+ \frac{\$649,531}{(1 + 0.1426)^4} - \$525,000$$

$$= 0$$

or 14.26 percent after tax. The same result could be obtained either through the use of a financial calculator or by interpolation.[2]

The decision rule for IRR is that if IRR is greater than or equal to the required rate of return, the investment should be made. Since the IRR of 14.26 percent exceeds 12 percent, the investment should be made.

NEGOTIATION AND RATE OF RETURN

What options are available when IRR is less than the investor's required rate of return? The decision rule for IRR would say "do not invest." Possible alternatives are to renegotiate a lower purchase price or shift some of the risk.

Much going back and forth between buyer and seller is likely when the IRR is less than the investor's required rate of return. It is a fair assumption that the owner will want to sell for as much as possible and is unlikely to accept less than market value. In turn, the investor will want to buy for as little as possible.

Successful negotiating involves the following four steps:

1. An investor must understand his or her personal goals and negotiating style. What are the relative priorities of the goals? What negotiating style best achieves the goals?

2. The property must be understood. What is its highest investment value to me as a buyer-investor? What is the lowest price at which as an owner, I will sell (market value, unless in distress)? What influence will terms have on these prices?

3. The investor must know the opponent and his or her goals. When buying, look in the public records to find out how much the seller paid for the property and how long it has been owned. Is the owner's tax depreciation about used up? Also, estimate the owner's mortgage balance and terms, if not included in the listing. Are there other liens against the property? Under how much pressure to sell is the owner?

4. When negotiating, remain objective. Losing one's temper or getting highly emotional leads to mistakes and to failure to achieve goals. Have high expectations

---

[2] The target NPV value equals $38,855 at 12 percent and ($56,556) at 18 percent. By interpolation, then, the approximate IRR is calculated as follows:

The difference between NPV at 12 percent and 18 percent is

$$\text{Difference between } NPVs = \$38,855 - (\$56,556) = \$95,411$$

The difference between NPV at 12 percent and x% is

$$\text{Difference between } NPVs = \$38,855 - 0 = \$38,855$$

This implies an approximate IRR of

$$x\% = 12\% + (18\% - 12\%) \frac{\$38,855}{\$95,4110} = 14.44\%$$

By calculator, the IRR is 14.26% after tax.

in the negotiations, be determined while pursuing them, but also be courteous. Recognize that no transaction occurs unless both parties expect to benefit. In buying, the property must have as high or a higher value to you than it does to the seller. The owner is selling because the value in exchange exceeds the value in use. Once a bargain is struck, look for ways in which to improve it by modifying terms. Cooperative negotiations are better for both parties in the long run.

Clearly, undue pressure on a buyer or seller, differences in negotiating ability, or lack of adequate information might result in an agreed price being above or below market value.

A CAUTION ABOUT BEING TOO OPTIMISTIC

Being overly optimistic in your forecasts can lead to artificially inflated NPVs. Thus, when in doubt, always look first to the marketplace for objective information about market rents and expenses, and a market-derived discount rate. A positive NPV may simply be an indication that either something has been left out of normal operating expenses, like reserves and replacements for a new roof or new fixtures, or market rents have been overstated. Of course, a positive NPV may be indicative of monopoly profits, but don't expect these monopoly profits to last forever. Whenever there are positive excess profits to be made, supply will usually increase, thereby exerting downward pressure on market rents and profit levels.

If your development project is large enough, you will also have to worry about how the increased supply of new space will affect market rents. In such circumstances it will not be good enough simply to look at market rents in forecasting expected revenues; instead, one must estimate ex post market rents—that is, market rents after the new supply has been added to the market. Only in instances where you are reasonably protected by local zoning or, say, in the case of a regional shopping center, by a natural monopoly, do you not have to worry about increased competition exerting downward pressure on rents and profit levels.

A CAUTION ALSO ABOUT RELYING TOO HEAVILY ON INTERNAL RATE OF RETURN ANALYSIS

IRR analysis is fraught with potential problems when the cash flows from investment start out positive and then become negative. In this case IRR may have multiple roots—one positive and one negative. IRR analysis may also be misleading when comparing investments of different size or varying durations. Some examples follow.

Multiple Solutions

Most real estate projects will have a unique rate of return, which implies the NPV function crosses the horizontal axis once, and only once. To illustrate, consider the following real estate project:

Project A
$2 million Office Building

YEAR	ATCF ($000'S)	ATER ($000'S)
0	($2,000)	
1	$400	
2	$400	$2,000

If the required rate of return is 10 percent after tax, what is NPV? The calculation of NPV is:

$$NPV = \frac{ATCF_1}{(1 + r_a)} + \frac{ATCF_2}{(1 + r_a)^2} + \frac{ATER}{(1 + r_a)^2} - MV$$

$$= \frac{\$400,000}{(1 + .10)} + \frac{\$400,000}{(1 + .10)^2} + \frac{\$2,000,000}{(1 + .10)^2} - \$2,000,000$$

$$= \$347,107$$

If you plot a graph like Figure 6-7, you will find that NPV decreases as the discount rate increases. You can also see in Figure 6-7 that IRR is 20 percent after tax.

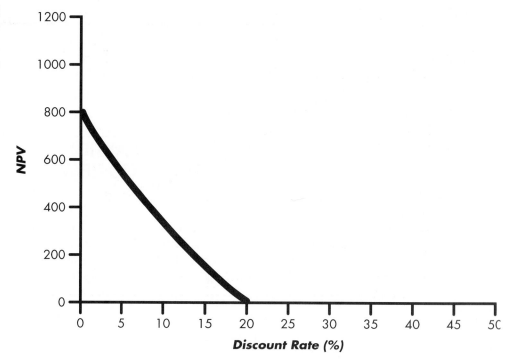

FIGURE 6–7
Relationship Between NPV and Required Rate of Return for $4 million Office Building

Now compare this investment to a $2 million coal mine, with the following cash flows:

Project B
$4 million Coal Mine

YEAR	ATCF ($000'S)	ATER ($000'S)
0	($2,000)	
1	$12,000	
2	$0	($11,000)

This project has an IRR of both 13 and 387 percent (see Figure 6-8). The two IRRs come about because the project generates $12 million in year 1 and then requires the investor to pay out $11 million in year 2.

Different Scales of Investment

NPV and IRR analysis will rank mutually exclusive projects differently when the scale of investment is different. To illustrate, consider the following mutually exclusive real estate investments.

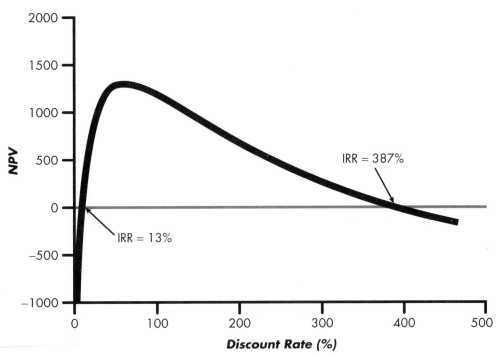

FIGURE 6-8
Relationship Between NPV and Required Rate of Return for $4 Million Coal Mine

**Two Mutually Exclusive Real Estate Projects
with Different Scales of Investment**

	GARDEN APARTMENTS		OFFICE BUILDING	
YEAR	ATCF ($000'S)	ATER ($000'S)	ATCF ($000'S)	ATER ($000'S)
0	($1,000)		($11,000)	
1	$505		$5,000	
2	$505		$5,000	
3	$505	$0	$5,000	$0
IRR	24%		17%	
NPV @ 10%	$256		$1,434	

Here the IRR decision rule ranks the $1 million garden apartments (the smaller project) higher; its IRR is 24 percent, while the IRR for the $11 million office building is 17 percent. In comparison, the NPV decision rule favors the $11 million office building (the larger project); its NPV is $1.434 million, while the NPV for the garden apartments is $0.256 million.

Given this conflict, which project should be accepted? Is it better to go with the garden apartments or the office building? Clearly, the answer depends on how much money the investor has. The answer also depends on the investor's discount rate.

Let us assume that the equity investor has sufficient cash to undertake either investment. We shall also assume that the investor's required rate of return on both projects is 10 percent after tax. Next, to show why the office building investment (the larger project) should be accepted, let us look at the differential cash flows between the two projects.

**Differential Cash Flows
Between Garden Apartments and Office
Building**

YEAR	OFFICE BUILDING LESS GARDEN APARTMENTS ($000'S)
0	($10,000)
1	$4,495
2	$4,495
3	$4,495
IRR	16.58%
NPV @ 10%	$1,178

This hypothetical investment has a cost of $10 million (the added cost of undertaking the office building). The NPV on this incremental investment is $1.178 million and generates your required 10 percent after-tax return; therefore, you should prefer the office buildings to the garden apartments.

Timing of Cash Flows Is Different

Even if the initial cash outlays are the same, the NPV and IRR ranking may vary if the cash flow patterns are very different.

Two Mutually Exclusive Retail Shopping Centers with Different Timing of the Cash Flows

YEAR	CENTER A		CENTER B	
	ATCF (MILLIONS)	ATER (MILLIONS)	ATCF (MILLIONS)	ATER (MILLIONS)
0	($100)		($100)	
1	$20		$100	
2	$20	$100	$0	$31.25
IRR	20%		25%	
NPV @ 10%	$17.3		$16.7	

As can be seen, center A has a higher NPV, but center B has a higher IRR. Again, there is a conflict between NPV and IRR.

So which project should be selected? To answer this question, we start with the differential cash flows between the two projects.

Differential Cash Flows for Retail Shopping Center

YEAR	CENTER A LESS CENTER B (MILLIONS)
0	$0
1	($80)
2	$88.75
NPV @ 10%	$0.62

The NPV of the incremental cash flows is $620,000; therefore, you should undertake center A rather than center B.

On a long-term basis, the investment must be reviewed periodically to determine if the past choices and actions are working out. This means comparing risks and rates of return from stocks and bonds with the risks and rates of return from real estate which is a portfolio-management strategy concern.

SUMMARY

Investment analysis attempts to ascertain the NPV of a property to a specific investor, based on available financing, desired rate of return, tax position, and other assumptions unique to the investor. NPV is the difference between the cost of an investment and the present value of the cash flows from the investment, discounted at the investor's required rate of return:

$$NPV = \frac{ATCF_1}{(1 + r_a)} + \frac{ATCF_2}{(1 + r_a)^2} + \cdots + \frac{ATCF_n}{(1 + r_a)^n} + \frac{ATER}{(1 + r_a)^n} - MV$$

The decision rule is that NPV must be zero or positive in order for the investment to be undertaken; otherwise, the investment should be rejected.

IRR is sometimes used as an alternative to NPV analysis. The IRR of an investment is that rate of return that discounts future cash flows to the exact amount of the investment or, stated another way, it is the return on the property. The decision rule for IRR is that if IRR is greater than or equal to the required rate of return, the investment should be made; otherwise, the investment should be rejected.

KEY CONCEPTS

After-tax cash flow (ATCF)   Net operating income less debt service and less taxes payable on income from operations.

After-tax equity reversion (ATER)   Sales price less disposition costs, amortized mortgage loan balance, and capital gains taxes.

Before-tax cash flow   A measure of the expected annual cash flow from the operation of a real estate investment after all expenses but before taxes.

Internal rate of return (IRR)   Rate of return that discounts future cash flows from an investment to the exact amount of the investment.

Net present value (NPV)   Present value of the cash flows from an investment minus the cost of the investment.

Pyramiding   Controlling ever more property through reinvestment, refinancing, and exchanging.

QUESTIONS FOR REVIEW AND DISCUSSION

1. List and explain briefly at least four advantages of real estate as compared with most other investment media.

2. What are the major disadvantages (not necessarily risks) of investing in real estate?

3. What are the drawbacks of investing in raw land as opposed to other types of real estate?

4. Should an investor purchase a real estate asset that provides for a net present value equal to zero? Why or why not?

5. If the net present value of a project equals zero, what does the internal rate of return equal?

6. Do NPV and IRR calculations always lead to the same decision? If not, when do the results vary?

7. What are the major weaknesses of the internal rate of return as a measurement tool for investments in real estate?

8. Compare vacant or raw land with an office building as an investment. On what bases or criteria should the comparison be made?

9. In real estate, only a small number of properties is available for investment at any one time. Given this situation, is it possible to analyze a single property and make an investment decision? Explain.

PROBLEMS

1. A retail shopping center was purchased for $2.1 million in cash in 1986. During the next four years, the property appreciated at 4 percent per year. Annual depreciation allowance is $16,000 per year. At the end of year 4, the property is sold; selling expenses are 8 percent. What is the after-tax equity reversion for an investor with an income tax rate of 28 percent?

2. An office building is purchased with the following projected cash flows:
   NOI is expected to be $130,000 at the end of year 1, with 5 percent annual increases thereafter
   The purchase price of the property is $720,000; 80 percent of the value is in the improvements
   100 percent equity financing is used to purchase the property
   The property is sold at the end of year 4 for $860,000; selling costs are 4 percent
   The after-tax required rate of return is 14 percent

   Based on the net present value of the project, should an investor undertake this investment? What if the after-tax required rate of return is changed to 18 percent?

3. With a purchase price of $350,000, a warehouse provides an initial after-tax cash flow of $30,000, which grows by 6 percent per year. If an initial equity investment of $75,000 is required and the after-tax equity reversion after four years equals $90,000, what is the IRR on the project? If the after-tax required rate of return on the project is 10 percent, should the project be undertaken?

4. XYZ Realty Group is considering the purchase of Lincoln Towers, an office building, for $6,200,000, of which $1,160,000 is attributable to the land. XYZ Realty Group expects to use a 39-year straight-line cost recovery schedule. Terms of the purchase are 100 percent equity.

   a. What is the cost recovery allowance each year?

   b. NOI is $640,000 in year 1 and $680,000 in year 2. At the end of year 2, XYZ Realty Group projects that the selling price of Lincoln Towers will be $7,200,000. Selling expenses are 4 percent. XYZ Realty Group has a 14 percent after-tax required rate of return on any real estate investment. Income from the investment will be taxed at the 28 percent rate. What is ATCF for the two years of ownership and operation?

   c. What is ATER from disposition at the end of year 2?

   d. What is the maximum amount that XYZ Realty Group can bid for Lincoln Towers and still expect to realize a 14 percent after-tax rate of return?

   e. If XYZ Realty Group were to buy Lincoln Towers for $6,200,000, what would be the internal rate of return to equity?

5. You, a developer, just completed Case Center, an apartment complex. The land cost $2,000,000 and the improvements cost $8,000,000, making total develop-

ment costs $10,000,000. The project was financed with 100 percent equity. You expect to take 27.5-year straight-line cost recovery. In year 1 of operations, NOI is $900,000 and in year 2, it is $1,200,000. At the end of year 2, you receive an offer you cannot refuse and sell Case Center for $12 million net after transaction costs. You are in a 28 percent tax bracket.

   a. Determine ATCF for both years of the investment.

   b. Determine the tax payable upon disposition at the end of year 2.

   c. Determine the ATER from sale at the end of year 2.

   d. Assuming that you have a 15 percent after-tax required rate of return, what is the investment value of the equity position?

   e. Given the $10,000,000 total development cost, what after-tax internal rate of return was earned on equity?

6. Suppose you are the Prudential Insurance Company of America. Further suppose that you agreed to purchase the 102-story Empire State Building in 1961 from the Empire State Building Associates for $29 million. You had already bought the land underneath the Empire State Building for $17 million. Now you own both the building and the land for $46 million. You also get an annual rent of $3,220,000 for the first 30 years, $1,840,000 per year for the next 21 years, and $1,610,000 per year for the next 63 years (see Problem 8 in Chapter 3). Determine your before-tax internal rate of return on investment.

7. The proposed development is a 150,000 square-foot neighborhood shopping center. Construction costs are $65 per square foot. The site is 10 acres, with a cost of $4 per square foot. The anchor tenant is a local grocery store, which signed a $5.25 per square foot per year rent on 55,000 gross square feet of space. Specialty tenants are expected to lease the remaining 95,000 square feet of space at $14.50 per square foot per year. Neighborhood center vacancy rates are 4 percent. Operating costs are $1.85 per square foot per year. Property taxes are $28 per one thousand dollars of assessed value (which is based initially on the cost of the project). In addition,

Rents are expected to rise 2 percent per year.

Operating costs are expected to rise 4 percent annually during each of the next five years.

Depreciation is 39 years, straight-line.

Real estate taxes are expected to rise 4 percent per year.

Marginal tax rate is 28 percent.

Holding period is five years.

Answer the following questions.

   a. Prepare a realistic after-tax cash flow statement for the next five years.

   b. Determine ATER from sale if the selling price at the end of year 5 is $14.4 million. Selling expenses will be 4 percent.

   c. What is the after-tax internal rate of return on equity?

   d. If the investor's required after-tax rate of return is 10 percent, would the proposed development be accepted?

8. Horatio Alger Inc. owns a vacant parcel of land and is trying to determine whether to build an office building or a retail shopping center. Using the following information, make a recommendation to Horatio Alger Inc.

	OFFICE BUILDING	RETAIL SHOPPING CENTER
Building size	160,000 net leasable square feet	125,000 net leasable square feet
Land cost	$1,500,000	$1,500,000
Construction cost per square foot	$75	$43
Rent per square foot of leasable area	$15 per square foot of leasable area in year 1, increasing at 2 percent per annum thereafter	$9.50 per square foot of leasable area in year 1, increasing at 6 percent thereafter
Common-area maintenance charges	None	Each tenant pays 85 percent of the prorata share of all expenses and taxes incurred, based on the proportion of net leasable square footage to all rentable area
Real estate taxes	$1.45 per square foot of leasable area in year 1, growing at 4 percent annually thereafter	$1.29 per square foot of leasable area, increasing at 5.5 percent annually thereafter
Vacancy	20 percent in year 1, 15 percent in year 2, 12 percent in year 3, and 10 percent in year 4	12 percent in year 1, 15 percent in year 2, 13 percent in year 3, and 85 percent in year 4
Operating expenses	$3 per square foot of leasable area in year 1, growing at 6 percent annually	$3.25 per square foot of leasable area in year 1, growing at 6 percent annually
Depreciation	39 years	39 years
Mortgage information	70 percent loan-to-value ratio, 9.5 percent interest for 25 years, annual payments	75 percent loan-to-value ratio, 8.5 percent interest for 25 years, annual payments
Sales information	Property will be sold at the end of year 4 for nine times NOI	Property will be sold at the end of year 4 for ten times NOI
Selling expenses	4 percent	4 percent
Before-tax required rate of return	15 percent	12 percent

a. Estimate the before-tax NPV and IRR for each project. Which project should Horatio Alger Inc. pursue?

b. For each project, what proportion of the IRR is from the cash flows and what proportion is from the reversion?

c. What would the rates of return have to be for you to be indifferent between the two projects?

CHAPTER 7

ADMINISTRATIVE AND PROPERTY MANAGEMENT ISSUES

Chapter Outline

Labor can do nothing without capital, capital can do nothing without labor; and neither can do anything without the guiding genius of management; and management, however wise its genius may be, can do nothing without the privileges which the community affords.

W.L. MacKenzie King, former prime minister of Canada

Three major issues face an owner when administrating a property to maximize its rate of return as a long-term investment. The first issue is maintaining leverage and disinvesting. Analysis for possible refinancing or reinvestment should be undertaken periodically to assure that the owner is getting the best possible rate of return on equity, on a risk-adjusted, after-tax rate-of-return basis.

The second issue is adapting to change. Periodically, a property's productivity relative to changing market and environmental conditions must be probed to determine if past choices and actions are working out. This means comparing the risks and rates of return from stocks and bonds with the risks and rates of return from real estate. The possibility of investing additional capital to change the use, such as modernizing the building or making an addition to the property, is always present. Investment in different types of properties may also be a possibility.

The third issue is routine administration. An owner must arrange for a competent manager to maintain the property's cash flow and value. The objective is to have routine details attended to by the manager and to have necessary financial concerns brought to the owner's attention through periodic reports.

Attention in this chapter is essentially on routine administrative concerns. First, we discuss ordinary management issues, like merchandising space to secure suitable tenants at the best rents obtainable, maintaining favorable tenant relations, collecting rents, purchasing supplies and authorizing wages, maintaining favorable employee relations, maintaining the property, and maintaining records and rendering reports. Then we discuss property tax and hazard insurance considerations.

MANAGEMENT CONSIDERATIONS

To help lease and monitor the performance of the property most owners hire a *property manager.* The property manager assumes all executive functions involved in the operation and physical care of the property, thereby relieving the investor or asset manager of all details associated with day-to-day operation of the property. The functions of the property manager are several.

Merchandising Space

Merchandising space is more difficult than outright selling in some ways. After a sale, a broker can go on to seek other prospects or listings. But in merchandising space the investor, or the property manager, seek to secure suitable tenants at the best rents obtainable. And after renting the space, the manager must keep the tenant satisfied in preparation for extending the rental period or renewing the lease.

In the short run, rent levels are a result of supply and demand and must first be established on a market-comparison basis. That is, a manager must set a rental schedule in line with market rentals for similar properties. On a longer term basis, rent levels must be high enough to pay all property operating costs, in addition to providing for a fair return on the investment in the property.

Rental schedules for the various units of space offered are most realistically established on a market-comparison basis. This is done by rating the subject property in relation to like properties in similar neighborhoods for which accurate rental data is available. The comparison approach, though simple in application, relies on sound judgment for effective application.

Comparison is generally made with a number of typical space units, and price adjustments for the subject property are based on quantitative and qualitative differences. For example, in the price of an apartment unit, consideration should be given to the following: amount of floor space, number of bathrooms, quality of construction, decorative features, floor location, type and quality of elevator service, nature and quality of janitorial services, reputation of building and characteristics of tenants, location of building in relation to public conveniences, and quality rating of neighborhood and neighborhood trends. Assuming that a standard unit in an ideal neighborhood rents for $500 per month and the comparative rating for the subject property, after due consideration of the factors enumerated above, is 90 percent, then the estimated fair rental is judged to be $450 per month. If a detailed comparison is made for each space with six or more comparable units, a fairly accurate and competitive rental schedule can be established and submitted for the owner's approval.[1]

Advertising is usually necessary to fill vacant space. Tenants react, as a whole, to a congenial atmosphere and amenities for living, both of which are important to a feeling of belonging and a pride of occupancy. Efforts should be made to attract qualified tenants who are relatively homogeneous in their requirements. Thus, some building managers cater to young couples; others cater to older, retired people who cherish an atmosphere of quiet restfulness.

Here is a related example. Suppose you are the owner of a 100-unit, one-bedroom apartment building in the State College, Pennsylvania, area. The apartment building is leased entirely to college students attending Penn State University. All leases are for a one-year period. Further suppose you must choose between two options:

Option 1: Offer students free rent for the first month, but charge $525 per month in months 2 through 12.

Option 2: Charge students a fixed, monthly rent of $450 for a one-year period.

---

[1] Students of management and those seeking to perfect their judgment in rental schedule preparation should study the rental formula developed by Leo J. Sheridan and William Karkow, two well-known Chicago building managers. Copies of the Sheridan-Karkow formula are available through the National Association of Building Owners and Managers Association, Chicago.

Which option should you choose? Clearly, you should choose the option that will maximize the present worth of the property. In this case, the present value of option 1 at a 12 percent annual before-tax required rate of return, or 1 percent per month, is:

$$PV \text{ of option } 1 = \frac{\$0}{(1 + .01)^1} + \frac{\$525}{(1 + .01)^2} + \cdots + \frac{\$525}{(1 + .01)^{12}}$$

$$= \$5,389$$

Likewise, the present value of option 2 at 10 percent per annum before tax, or 0.83 percent per month, is:

$$PV \text{ of option } 2 = \frac{\$450}{(1 + .0083)^1} + \cdots + \frac{\$450}{(1 + .0083)^{12}}$$

$$= \$5,119$$

So, you can see that you would be better off by offering the rental contract with the free rent. The difference in present values is $5,389 minus $5,119, or $270. And this analysis ignores any potential differences in operating costs and the time it would take to lease the property under the two different options. This simplifying assumption was made purely for ease of exposition.

Obviously, in practice, one might reasonably offer tenants free rent as a marketing tool in order to speed up the time it would take to lease the property which, in turn, should minimize net carrying costs. Offering free rent might also impact upon the total advertising budget. This would occur if the marketing strategy eliminated the need to advertise the property over an extended period of time.

At the other extreme, offering tenants free rent might also increase tenant turnover; some students who choose option 1 might default, or simply walk away, if they were required to pay a higher-than-average rental once the free rent period expired. This possible negative side effect explains why we have discounted the two rental streams at different rates. The higher discount rate in option 1 compensates the owner for any loss due to default and/or tenant turnover.

And now comes the important lesson. Offering free rent for the first month, but charging $525 per month in months 2 through 12, is equivalent to an *effective rent* of $474 per month. You can compute that by dividing $5,389 by 11.3745084, which is the present value of a 12-month annuity of $1 per month at 10 percent interest before tax, or 0.83 percent per month. The calculation is as follows:

PV of free rent, then $525 per month for 11 months = *PV* of effective rent
   through 12

$$\frac{\$0}{(1 + .01)^1} + \frac{\$525}{(1 + .01)^2} + \cdots + \frac{\$525}{(1 + .01)^{12}} = PV \text{ of effective rent}$$

$$\$5,389 = PV \text{ of effective rent}$$

$$\$5,389 = \frac{\text{Effective rent}}{(1 + 0.0083)^1} + \cdots + $$

$$\frac{\text{Effective rent}}{(1 + 0.0083)^{12}}$$

Thus, the effective rent per month is equal to

$$\text{Effective rent} = \$5{,}389 \left[\frac{1}{\dfrac{1}{(1 + 0.0083)^1} + \cdots + \dfrac{1}{(1 + 0.0083)^{12}}} \right]$$

$$= \$5{,}389 \times \frac{1}{11.3745084}$$

$$= \$474$$

This is a handy calculation. Once you know the effective rent, it is easy to determine what action to take. Owners will want to choose the highest effective rent possible. Tenants, on the other hand, will want to choose the lowest effective rent.

Note, too, that it really makes no difference whether we work with present values or effective rents. The two methods should give identical answers. Our example clearly illustrates this principle. The difference in effective rents, $24 per month ($474 − $450), is what would be earned if you were to choose option 1.

Maintaining Tenant Relations

Clear communications and an open manner go far toward establishing and maintaining cordial tenant relations. And cordial relations with tenants go far toward obtaining tenant cooperation in general and, specifically, toward making rent collections easier and avoiding organization of tenant unions. Prompt and courteous attention to tenant requests is important, although all requests do not have to be met. If a request cannot be met, the tenant should be so informed immediately.

Every effort should be made to attract qualified tenants who appear homogeneous in living characteristics. Tenants reactions to each other can add or detract from the amenities of living and the congenial atmosphere that is conducive to pride of occupancy and a feeling of belonging. Some buildings may be deemed best-suited for young couples with children; others may be best for older and retired people who cherish an atmosphere of quiet restfulness. The fact that an attempt is being made to suit the facilities of the building to the housing needs and requirements of the tenants makes a favorable impression upon prospects, and generally contributes importantly to the development of tenant goodwill and to the furtherance of good public relations. If the rental schedule is properly prepared and the building space effectively advertised, as a rule, one out of every five eligible prospects calling at the property should become a building tenant.[2] If the ratio of tenants to prospects is greater or smaller, the space units may be underpriced or overpriced.

Collecting Rents

Tenants expect to pay rent, and most do so without coercion. However, some do not. Therefore, a firm and clear rent collection policy is needed; the existence of

---

[2] See James C. Downs, Jr., "Merchandising Residential Space," *Principles of Real Estate Management,* 11th ed., Chicago, Institute of Real Estate Management, 1975.

such a policy is the mark of a good manager. Upon moving in, tenants should be impressed with the importance of making payments on time. A follow-up notice should be sent promptly when rents are past-due. After a second notice, say about ten days later, legal proceedings may be initiated to collect the unpaid rent or to obtain possession of the space. Prompt action in a few cases quickly "educates" marginal tenants as to what is expected of them.[3]

The collection of rents need not pose a problem if the credit rating of each tenant, before his or her acceptance, is checked carefully and if the collection policy is clearly explained and firmly adhered to. There are credit bureaus in most communities with a population of 10,000 or over, and it is possible to secure from them a credit record of the prospective tenant at a nominal cost. As a rule, credit reports are an excellent safeguard against acceptance of tenants who have demonstrated financial instability. It is also wise policy to require references and to check with property owners from whom the applicant has rented in the immediate past. If, for instance, the applicant has not given a proper vacate notice at a previous place of residence or failed to pay the rent, the application should be rejected or an advance deposit of an extra month's rent be required.

A firm collection policy is basic to successful management. Tenants should understand the importance of making payments on time as specified in the lease agreement. Tenants may also be informed that periodic statements will not be sent and that it is their obligation to submit payment on the due date to the manager's office. In many cases, however, notices are sent. For record purposes, it is deemed good policy to issue rental receipts even though payments are received by check. Such receipts permit uniform rental auditing and provide a ready reference for bookkeeping purposes.

Purchasing Supplies and Authorizing Wages

Costs must be incurred to operate and maintain a property. Many costs, such as for employee wages and utility bills, are recurring and payment becomes routine.[4] On the other hand, in ordering or arranging for nonroutine services, such as repairs, remodeling, pest control, etc., close monitoring and inspection become necessary to insure that value is received prior to any payment. Because a manager deals with the latter issues on a continuing basis, it is likely that he or she will obtain the services at a much lower cost and with better quality than an individual owner might. It is in these matters that managers justify their fees.

In meeting expenditures for repairs, the manager may refer all work to a general contractor who assumes the responsibility for carrying out the needed work, or the manager may purchase and stock required materials and hire skilled workers to attend to the repairs under his or her general supervision. The former practice is rec-

---

[3] A procedure for follow-up of past-due rentals should be rigidly and uniformly adhered to. A statement for past-due rents should be sent to delinquent tenants within five to ten days after the rental due date. This due notice may be followed with a final notice a week or ten days later. If this notice is ignored or not satisfactorily acted upon, legal proceedings are then in order to obtain possession or to collect the unpaid rent.

[4] Even in meeting these routine expenditures, operational practices can be reviewed and economy practiced.

ommended when buildings under one management are small in size and number. With large buildings and extensive scope of managerial functions, the latter practice may prove more economical. Also, service can be restored and repairs attended to more promptly if workers and technicians are subject to direct control. Where the practice of attending directly to repairs is followed, a repair voucher order should be issued for each job and an accurate record kept of labor and materials used. The owner is then billed for actual expenditures plus a nominal overhead service charge (5 to 10 percent) for job superintendence. The direct control of purchases, wages, and expenditures for repairs, provided the size and number of buildings managed warrant it, should prove more economical and more efficient in the maintenance and restoration of building service.

Maintaining Employee Relations

Much of a manager's success depends on arranging for technically competent people for specialized tasks. Thus, the selection and training of personnel is a major management function. Clear communications and fair treatment are also necessary for satisfactory long-term management/employee relations.

It is of utmost importance that the selection and training of personnel be given special care and consideration. Employees, although not vested with agency responsibility, indirectly represent the owner, and their conduct and ability to provide service affect public relations and tenant goodwill.

In selecting personnel, consideration should be given to the following:

1. Is the applicant technically qualified?

2. Is the person sufficiently interested in the work to make it a career?

3. Is the compensation offered at least as high as that earned for similar work in the applicant's prior position?

4. Is the applicant congenial, emotionally adjusted, and worthy of becoming a member of the firm's family?

5. Does the applicant display an interest in growing with the firm?

These questions, of course, cannot be answered satisfactorily solely by the facts disclosed during the initial interview. A follow-up of the applicant's experience and personnel records and direct interviews with prior employers may supply the needed information. The initial care and trouble assumed in the hiring of employees is more than repaid in the economy that flows from the effective teamwork of competent and well-adjusted personnel. Proper personnel selection, too, reduces employee turnover and minimizes organizational inefficiency.[5]

The careful selection of an employee should be followed with a well thought-out and effective training program. The employee should be given an opportunity to meet coworkers, to feel a sense of pride in his or her work, and to acquire a feeling of belonging to an organization that cares. Where the executive is unable to instruct

---

[5] The important fact that should be kept in mind is that it takes weeks and even months to effectively train an employee and, as a consequence, changes in personnel will prove expensive. Initial care in hiring employees should receive the due attention it merits.

the new employee, a manual, in which the overall objectives of the organization are clearly stated, should be prepared.

Maintaining the Property

A thorough knowledge of property service and maintenance requirements is required to be a competent manager. Certainly the premises should be kept clean and attractive at all times. Periodic inspections should be made to ascertain that halls are well lighted, janitorial duties are being performed, and elevators, heating and other building systems are property functioning. Flaws and hazards should be checked for and removed from sidewalks, stairs, roofs, wiring, plumbing, or anywhere else they might cause an accident. In some leases, tenants contract to perform these functions; inspections are still necessary to ascertain compliance.

In the effective accomplishment of property service and maintenance, the interests of the owner and those of the tenants must be properly balanced. It is in the physical care of the property that the service interests of the owner and those of the tenants merge. The owner is interested in having the manager give the structure constant care and attention in order that the property investment may yield the highest possible net return over the life of the building. The tenants, on the other hand, are entitled to reasonable building service performance. The manager's pride and concern about good service generally invites tenant cooperation and stimulates proper building use rather than abuse.

Tenants, by and large, are reasonable in their demands, and voiced complaints should be attended to promptly. No matter how small the request, good managerial policy calls for attending to it at once. Never should a request for service be ignored. Prompt action is essential in building goodwill not only with the tenants but also with the property owner, whose interests are at stake.

The building should be kept clean and attractive at all times. Inspection of the property should be made at regular intervals. It should be seen to that the janitor is on the job and carrying out janitorial duties. Halls should be kept lighted and elevators running. Heating systems and building service utilities must be kept in proper order. Constant watch should be kept for possible defects around the property. The maintenance problems and repairs referred to above apply only to buildings that are rented to numbers of tenants and where the landlord controls portions of the building. In some cases, the tenant agrees to attend to all repairs, and consequently the owner is not liable for damages. The question of liability for damages is more fully discussed in Chapter 27.

Keeping Records and Rendering Reports

A professional manager must keep an adequate system of accounts, as records are necessary for historical data on occupancy and serve as a basis for management policy. Managers also are usually charged with maintaining records and filing governmental reports such as those for tax withholding and Social Security purposes. Finally, monthly and annual statements for owners must be provided in a format similar to that shown in Figure 7-1.

FIGURE 7-1 Investment Alternatives	ALTERNATIVE	AFTER-TAX EQUITY INVESTMENT	NPV	AFTER-TAX IRR	CASH RELEASED FOR INVESTMENT ELSEWHERE
	Continue without change	$162,725	$21,910	19.16%	None
	Refinance Douglas Manor	82,725	36,436	27.36%	$80,000
	Sell and reinvest in Swift Office Building	125,000	9,549	17.43%	37,725

MANAGEMENT REQUIREMENTS BY PROPERTY TYPE

Apartment buildings are the most commonly managed property types, so they serve as the standard in our society. Even so, each property type has management requirements unique to itself. Here, we seek only to highlight the differences. Professional management requires a much deeper look. Excellent sources of in-depth information on property management are the Institute for Real Estate Management (IREM), the Building Owners and Managers Association (BOMA), the Urban Land Institute (ULI), and the International Council of Shopping Centers (ICSC).

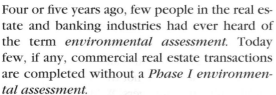

ENVIRONMENTAL REVIEW

Four or five years ago, few people in the real estate and banking industries had ever heard of the term *environmental assessment*. Today few, if any, commercial real estate transactions are completed without a *Phase I environmental assessment*.

A Phase I environmental assessment of the property can be performed at a moderate cost to identify and delineate the potential for environmental problems (e.g., contaminated groundwater, hazardous waste, radon, asbestos, and so on) on the site. The Phase I environmental assessment may or may not lead to a Phase II environmental assessment. In a Phase II environmental assessment, samples of soil, groundwater, and air are collected and analyzed for the contaminants suspected. This involves drill rigs, subsurface soil and groundwater samples, and chemical and/or physical analysis of the samples.

Driving the need for an environmental review is the potential liability, or fear of liability, for cleanup costs at a contaminated site. If the contamination at the site endangers public health, the federal or state government can require the landowner to clean up the problem. This situation can cost millions of dollars and force the landowner into bankruptcy, leaving the lending institution with the responsibility and the cost of cleaning up the contamination—particularly if the lender has foreclosed.

Specific environmental concerns include, but are not limited to, underground and aboveground storage tanks, superfund sites, landfills, and hazardous waste sites, pesticides and herbicides, polychlorinated biphenyls (PCBs), asbestos, radon, indoor air quality, lead-based paints, lead pipes and lead-containing pesticides, wetlands, threatened and endangered species, and archaeologic, historic, and cultural sites.

Residential

Apartments usually lease on a month-to-month basis, although one- to three-year leases are used. Awareness of changing environmental and market conditions is necessary, in any event. For example, in recent years, many apartment buildings have been converted to condominiums because of the strong demand for ownership in multifamily structures.

What are the management requirements for residential properties? Whether apartments or condominiums, physical maintenance and security are necessary to retain value. A full set of accounting records must be maintained. In condominium properties, tenant-owners are served rather than absentee owners. The main differences between managing rental property versus condominiums is that in a condominium the interior of each unit must be maintained by its owner and the manager need not be concerned with maintaining full occupancy.

Commercial

Commercial space rents in units of size varying from a small cubicle for a newsstand to an office to a multistory building. Leases are usually complex and long term, and therefore require considerable negotiation; they often contain *escalation clauses,* which call for an automatic increase in rents as taxes, insurance, and operating costs go up; sometimes the increase is based instead on an index of costs. Appearance, cleanliness, and efficiency must be carefully monitored to maintain prestige, and occupancy and rent levels. Retail outlets, stores, shops, and shopping centers are likely to be rented on percentage leases. Administrative reports to owners are often more involved because of the wide variety of spaces rented and different tenant-occupants.

Industrial

Industrial properties often require a large capital investment and tend to be special-purpose and built to user specifications. In turn, most are owner-occupied. Value is therefore tied closely to the success and financial capability of the firm, if not the industry. Thus, most industrial properties do not require professional managers. Warehouses, an exception to this statement, tend to be rented out for several years at a time, through contracts similar to commercial leases.

PROPERTY TAX APPEAL

The property taxation process breaks down into four phases for our purposes: (1) property valuation and assessment, (2) budget and tax levy, (3) tax billing and collection, and (4) property tax appeals.

In the valuation and assessment phase, all real estate in a tax jurisdiction (township, school district, park district, city, or county) is appraised at market value. Each parcel is then assigned an assessed value, which typically is a legally required proportion of market value. *Assessed value* is, therefore, the worth of a property for tax purposes. Nationally, the ratio of assessed value to market value averages about

40 percent, though in some states it is set at 100 percent. The assessed values of all properties in a tax district, when added together, make up the *tax base* of the district.

In the budget and tax levy phase, the tax district makes up a budget summarizing its financial needs for the coming fiscal year. The proportion of the budget to be financed by property taxes is then decided upon and the dollar amount of taxes to be collected is calculated. This amount is divided by the tax base of the district to arrive at the *tax levy rate,* or the amount of tax to be paid per $1,000 of assessed value. The *tax levy,* the actual amount in dollars payable by each property, is then determined by multiplying the assessed value of each property by the tax levy rate. Levying the tax on each property completes this phase.

A tax roll is then made up, listing taxes levied against each property, as a basis for easy determination of the claim against each property. At this point, the claim becomes a lien against the property. Owners are then billed for the taxes due. Failure to pay would eventually result in a tax foreclosure sale of the property.

Uniformity of Assessment

Uniformity of assessment is important for the property tax to be fair. Too low an assessment means other owners must pay greater amounts to meet the budget requirements. Too high an assessment means that a property owner is bearing more than his or her equitable share of the tax load.

As a matter of social policy exemptions from taxes are given in some states for homesteads, elderly persons, and veterans. Typically, the exemption serves to lower the overall tax base.

Each tax district establishes its own levy rate, often stated in *mills;* a mill is one-one thousandth of a dollar. Several different tax districts, such as the city, county, school district, park district, etc., may levy taxes against a given property. Typically the assessor is also the tax collector.

Figure 7–2 gives an overview of the entire assessment and taxation process, which begins with an appraised property value of $112,000. In this state, the assessed value is set at 50 percent of market value, or $56,000. The owners qualify for homestead and elderly exemptions totaling $6,000. Thus, taxable assessed value is $50,000. The total millage, or levy rate, is $30.00 per $1,000 (3.00 percent) of taxable assessed value. The total tax levy on this property, therefore, calculates to $1,500 ($50,000 × 3.00 percent).

Challenging Property Tax Assessments

Each assessing district, usually a county, has a board of review to consider protests from any owner that considers his or her property to be assessed at too high a value. This board considers all information available and makes a decision. Owners frequently hire appraisers to present evidence of value. If relief is denied, an owner may then petition the court for a judicial review.

Many large real estate advisory firms, like JMB Institutional Realty Corporation, have recently set up tax appeal groups with expertise in law and accounting. The reason: During the 1980s, the assessed values of U.S. commercial properties rose rapidly.

Determination of Taxable Assessed Value			
Land value		$20,000	
Building value	$104,000		
Less: depreciation	−12,000		
Depreciated building value	$92,000	92,000	
Total property value		$112,000	
Times: assessed value (percent of total value)		×50.00%	
Assessed value		$56,000	
Less: exemptions			
Homestead	$5,000		
Elderly	1,000		
Total exemptions	$6,000	$6,000	
Taxable assessed value		$50,000	$50,000
Determination of Total Millage Rate			
County rate	5.40		
City rate	8.60		
School district rate	14.20		
Park district rate	1.80		
Total millage rate	30.00		.30
Total Property Tax Levy (taxable assessed value × levy rate per $1,000) =			$1,500

Today, real estate market conditions have shifted, and the reality of the marketplace is that many properties are over-assessed.

The benefits of property tax appeals are quite easy to determine. Consider, for example, a West Coast office building. Let us suppose that its true market value is $12 million, while its current assessed value is $16 million. Let us further assume that the total millage or levy rate is $35.00 per $1,000 (3.50 percent) of taxable assessed value.

Next, let us assume that a property tax consultant like JMB Institutional Realty Corporation's newly formed tax appeal group is successful in reducing the assessed value of our West Coast office building from $16 million to $12 million. The annual tax savings will be $4,000,000 × .035 = $140,000.

Assume that the appropriate before-tax discount rate is 12 percent per annum and that the annual tax savings will last for ten years. The present value of $140,000 a year for the next ten years is

$$PV \text{ of tax savings} = \frac{\$140,000}{(1 + .12)^1} + \cdots + \frac{\$140,000}{(1 + .12)^{10}}$$
$$= \$791,031$$

Obviously, the higher the discount rate, the lower the present value. Time, too, is an element in these calculations. If we extend the series to 20 years (still with $140,000 of annual tax savings at the end of each year) at 12 percent per year, the present value of the annual tax savings would increase to $1,045,722. These examples could be multiplied. But the main point is clear: In instances where assessed values are out of line with the property's real value, filing a tax appeal can lead to significant tax savings for the existing property owner.

Now for a very subtle point. Suppose we were to turn this example around. That is, suppose that the true market value of the West Coast office building is $16 million, while its current assessed value is $12 million. In this case, the demand for the West Coast office building in all likelihood would increase and the price would go up by the present value of the anticipated tax savings. This means that the market value of the property would grow to

$$\$16,000,000 + \$791,031 = \$16,791,031$$

This is known as *tax capitalization*. Tax capitalization benefits the investor who currently owns the office building because any subsequent buyer would have to pay a higher price, $16,791,031, to acquire it.

HAZARD INSURANCE

The purpose of hazard insurance is to substitute certainty for uncertainty by shifting the risk of a disastrous event to an insurance company. Of course, a fee, termed an *insurance premium,* must be paid to the insurance company for accepting the risk. A contract (an insurance policy) between the two parties stipulates the details of the arrangement, including amount and time of coverage. The overall effect is to spread the cost of a disastrous event, which otherwise would fall on one person, over many persons exposed to the same hazard.

Manager's Insurance Responsibility

Normally, the property manager is responsible for arranging protection against all major insurable hazards. The manager's task, then, is to identify and evaluate the risk involved and to secure the best and most economical protection available in the insurance market. It follows that the manager should also keep accurate records regarding all insurance matters, and renew coverage well in advance of expirations.
Insurance coverage to be considered includes the following:

1. *Standard fire insurance.* Protects against all direct losses or damages to real property by fire, except losses caused by perils or forces specifically excluded in the policy.

2. *Extended coverage.* Broader protection, including risk compensation for losses due to perils excluded from a standard fire insurance policy, for example, explosion, windstorm, hail, riot, civil disturbance, aircraft, vehicles, and other miscellaneous causes. Cost is usually low.

3. *General liability.* Insures against liability imposed by law for injuries or damages caused to persons or properties of others.

4. *Workmen's compensation.* Employee protection against on-the-job injuries; required in most states.

5. *Inland marine insurance.* Protection against personal property losses, and more generally, damage to property that is mobile in nature.

6. *Casualty insurance.* Protects against losses due to theft, burglary, plate glass breakage, and the failure or breakdown of elevators, steam boilers, or machinery, as well as against other similar incidents. Policies may also be obtained to cover a variety of accident and health injuries.

7. *Rent insurance and consequential losses.* Compensates owner for consequential losses incident to damage or destruction of the property; also known as *business interruption insurance.*

Buying Insurance

Selecting a competent and cooperative agent is probably the first priority in buying insurance. An agent helps balance the costs against the choice of company and adequacy of coverage. Contracting with an insurance company that has a sound reputation and is financially capable is the next priority. Price considerations is third in priority. Assuming a capable agent and a strong company, let us look at price considerations.

Rates.   Insurance is based on the law of averages. Disastrous events are very property-specific, so which owners will suffer losses is impossible to predict. However, for a company insuring 10,000 to 20,000 similar properties, the incidence of loss can be statistically predicted. Knowing the expected total amount of losses and the total value of all the buildings, the company can calculate a premium rate per thousand dollars of value. In practice, the rate also covers administrative expenses and profits for the company.

Coinsurance.   From an owner's viewpoint, understanding the coinsurance requirement of an insurance contract is crucial. In figuring rates for various risks, the insurance company must take into account both the total premium revenues it will get and the risks and losses to be covered. From experience, insurers have found it necessary to use coinsurance. *Coinsurance* is a technique used to penalize policyholders who underinsure. Coinsurance or averaging clauses generally call for 80, 90, or 100 percent averaging; of these, 80 percent is the most popular.

An 80 percent clause does not mean that the insurance company will pay 80 percent of any loss, as many people think. Nor does it mean that with a total loss, they would be able to collect only 80 percent of the face amount of the policy. The typical 80 percent clause reads, in part: "This company shall not be liable for a greater proportion of any loss or damage to a property described herein than the sum hereby insured bears to the eighty percent (80%) of the actual cash value of said property at the time such loss shall happen, nor for more than the proportion that this policy bears to the total insurance thereon."

An example will show why coinsurance is needed. Most fire losses are partial. Thus, owner A, knowing that most losses are partial, might decide to carry only a nominal amount of insurance; for example, $20,000 worth on a building valued at $100,000. At a rate of $10.00 per thousand, the total premium would be $200. A second owner, B, not knowing that most losses are partial, insures for the entire $100,000 at a total premium of $1,000.

Without coinsurance, in the event of a $20,000 loss each would receive this amount as compensation, even though owner B paid five times as much for coverage. It could be argued that owner B had a greater limit of protection. But the chance of a total loss is not as great as that for a partial loss. Therefore, if the rate charged for the initial $20,000 of coverage were correct, it was excessive for the coverage beyond $20,000.

Let us reconsider the situations of owners A and B to see how insurance companies use the coinsurance requirement to correct for this imbalance. Figure 7–3 summarizes the discussion. Again the loss for each is $20,000.

Owner A carries only $20,000 of the required $80,000 coverage and becomes a coinsurer with the insurance company. The insurance company is responsible for 25 percent of any losses, ($20,000 ÷ $80,000 = 25%), while owner A is responsible for 75 percent of any losses (uncovered portion ÷ required coverage, or $60,000 ÷ $80,000). As shown in Figure 7–3, the insurance company therefore covers $5,000 of the loss and A absorbs the remaining $15,000.

Owner B, on the other hand, carries the required 80 percent insurance coverage and, therefore, receives compensation for 100 percent of its loss. Thus, if coinsurance is carried up to the required percentage, the policy can be considered as written without any coinsurance clause and will pay losses, dollar for dollar, up to its face amount. A loss of $80,000 would thus be completely covered. A loss in excess of the $80,000 coverage (80%) would fall on the owner, however.

Loss Adjustment

The insurance company should be notified immediately if a loss occurs. Also, the insured should act to protect the property from further damage, even to the extent of making temporary repairs. Full restoration should not be undertaken until a settlement with the insurance company has been reached. Estimates of cost to repair might also be obtained in order to reach an equitable settlement with the company.

FIGURE 7–3

Result of Underinsuring, with Coinsurance Requirement of 80 Percent

	OWNER A	OWNER B
SITUATION		
Actual cash value of building	$100,000	$100,000
Required coverage to meet coinsurance clause:		
80.00% of $100,000	$80,000	$80,000
Insurance coverage actually carried	$20,000	$80,000
Actual loss	$20,000	$20,000

CONSEQUENCES FOR OWNER A

Owner A required to carry $80,000 insurance and actually carried $20,000 of coverage. Insurance company therefore pays $20,000 / $80,000 of the $20,000 loss, or $5,000. Owner A is therefore responsible for balance, $15,000, of the actual loss.

CONSEQUENCES FOR OWNER B

Owner B required to carry $80,000 insurance and actually carried $80,000 of coverage. Insurance company therefore pays $80,000 / $80,000 of the $20,000 loss, or $20,000. Owner B is therefore covered for entire loss of $20,000.

CORPORATE REAL ESTATE ASSET MANAGEMENT

In most corporations the real estate manager is likely to be considered a specialist. The job of the manager is to ensure that real estate assets are managed to their full potential. This involves,

1. *Planning for additional capacity and making recommendations.* Plans for additional capacity are closely tied to the company's future plans for product development, production, and marketing.

2. *Screening for sites to consider.* The search for a new site may be the result of a need for additional capacity or a need to reduce operating expenses.

3. *Identifying surplus property or underutilized property.* This is done primarily for takeover prevention. Many takeover bids in the 1980s sought to force mature, cash-rich companies to pay out that cash to shareholders instead of plowing the money back into the business or using it to diversify. To effect these takeovers, the outside equity investors usually would borrow a major portion of the purchase price, using the firm's surplus or underutilized assets as collateral for the loan. Once the assets of the firm were taken over, the cash flows from operations were used to pay the principal and interest of the loan.

In some cases, the assets of the firm were sold to pay off the debt.

4. *Negotiating leases and purchase contracts.* Significant operating costs are associated with leasing or owning real estate. Michael Bell estimates that total occupancy costs for corporations can range between 5 and 8 percent of pretax gross sales, which can be upwards of 40 or 50 percent of net income.[a]

5. *Monitoring lease renewals, purchase options, tax assessments, and refinancing opportunities.* Companies are always looking for ways to cut expenses and improve performance.

6. *Redeploying nonprofitable assets.* Firms not only acquire businesses, they also sell businesses. Some corporations have restructured by selling businesses that are not profitable but have kept the real estate assets if the property might be more valuable in some other use. Corporate restructuring can also involve spinning off the firm's real estate assets into a limited partnership. Shareholders in a corporation pay tax twice—once at the corporate level and once at the personal level. In comparison, limited partnerships are taxed only at the personal level.

[a] Michael A. Bell, "The Importance of Sound Fixed-Asset Management," *Industrial Development* (January/February 1987), 151: 11–13.

SUMMARY

This chapter has provided a brief synopsis of routine property administrative issues, with an emphasis on merchandising space to secure suitable tenants at the best rents obtainable, on maintaining favorable tenant relations, collecting rents, purchasing supplies and authorizing wages, maintaining favorable employee relations, maintaining the property, and maintaining records and rendering reports. We also discussed the property tax process and hazard insurance considerations. It is important to realize that each assessing district, usually a county, has a board of review to consider protests from any owner that considers his or her property to be assessed at too high a value. This board considers all information available and makes a decision. Owners frequently hire appraisers to present evidence of value. If relief is denied, an owner may then petition the court for a judicial review.

KEY CONCEPTS

Assessed value   Amount of worth assigned to a property for property tax purposes; sometimes set by statute as a percentage of market value.

Business interruption insurance   Protection to a business owner from loss of income due to fire, flood, or other peril.

Coinsurance   Provision in a fire insurance policy to encourage adequate coverage; if a required percent of value is not insured against loss, the owner shares the risk of loss with the insurance company.

Effective rent   Rental income adjusted for concessions to tenants.

Tax base   Total assessed values of all properties in a tax district.

Tax capitalization   Present value of all future tax payments incurred or avoided.

Tax levy   Amount of property tax to be paid in a fiscal year, usually from 2 to 5 percent of value, depending on the jurisdiction.

QUESTIONS FOR REVIEW AND DISCUSSION

1. Discuss the several different functions of a property manager. Which function do you feel is the most difficult and why?

2. What is the difference between a property manager and an asset manager? How far should a property manager go in analyzing financial alternatives and recommending alternative decisions to an owner?

3. Is the property management process the same for all types of property? Discuss some similarities and differences.

4. What steps are involved in the property taxation process? What occurs during each phase?

5. Can assessed property values ever be appealed by property owners?

6. What different types of property insurance should be considered by an asset manager?

7. Explain coinsurance. Why is it used?

8. Identify and discuss briefly the three key issues in managing a property as a long-term investment.

9. What issues are important in buying insurance?

10. Is an owner's time well spent in seeking out and managing investment properties? Discuss.

1. The Plaza Landing Strip Center is a 50,000-square foot strip shopping center located in the southeastern United States. Management must decide between two strategies:

   Option 1: Lease the entire center to a national superstore grocery chain at $3.75 per square foot per year over the next 15 years.

   Option 2: Lease 25,000 square feet to a local anchor-tenant grocery store at $2.50 per square foot per year for 15 years and the remaining 25,000 square feet to specialty tenants at $12 per square foot per year for five years, followed by two successive five-year optional renewal periods.

   All leases are assumed to be triple-net (i.e., net of operating expenses, property taxes and insurance).

   a. Which option do you recommend? Assume that the required before-tax rate of return for option 1 is 10 percent. Further assume that the required before-tax rate of return under option 2 is 15 percent.

   b. Why is the required rate of return higher under option 2 than option 1? Briefly discuss.

   c. Why do you think specialty tenants are willing to pay higher rents than anchor tenants?

2. Calculate the annual effective rent for the following leases:

   a. A 10-year office lease, with free rent during the first year and a rental payment of $350,000 per year in years 2 through 10. The appropriate before-tax discount rate is 10 percent per annum. Total rentable area is 25,000 square feet.

   b. A fully indexed warehouse lease agreement that provides for rental increments in proportion to changes in the consumer price index. Rent payments begin at $275,000 per year and increase by 5 percent per year for five years. Total rentable area is 55,000 square feet. The appropriate discount rate is 8 percent per annum.

3. What is the total property tax levied against a property worth $150,000, assuming the assessor's office uses an assessed value of 60 percent of the market value and an exemption of $30,000 is granted to the property owner; the tax levy rate on this particular piece of property is 4 percent.

4. A building owner has a 90 percent coinsurance clause for fire insurance on a $600,000 building. If the building receives fire damage of $90,000 and the insurance policy is for $100,000, how much will the owner receive from the insurance company?

5. You own an office building worth $5 million. It is currently assessed at $6 million. The total millage or levy rate is $30.00 per $1,000 (3.00%) of taxable assessed value.

   a. Do you care whether the property is overassessed? Why or why not?

   b. You are successful in reducing the assessed value of the property to $5 million. The appropriate before-tax discount rate is 8 percent per annum and the annual tax savings will last for five years. Determine the present value of the annual tax savings.

CHAPTER 8

DISPOSITION OR ALIENATION DECISIONS

Chapter Outline

*The successful real estate deal is nothing more than a
series of crises tied together by a critical path.*

James A. Graaskamp

Our discussion in this chapter focuses primarily on the appropriate timing for disinvestment from one property and reinvestment in another. A shift in investment is indicated at such time as a higher rate of return might be earned by investing in and owning another property. Such analysis must take into account any difference in risk and any transaction costs that may be involved.

There follows a brief discussion of how to deal with distressed properties that are having difficulty attracting and keeping tenants or are otherwise failing to generate sufficient cash flow to pay the operating expenses and the debt service payment on the mortgage. Our aim here is to show, for a special set of assumptions, that an investor may want to hold on to a distressed property, at least temporarily while waiting for the market to rebound, before disinvesting.

A QUICK LOOK AT ORDINARY DISPOSITION DECISIONS

We are going to take a quick look at our Douglas Manor Apartments to illustrate how ordinary sell decisions are made. First we want to forecast the after-tax cash flows if we continue without change. Next, we calculate the after-tax cash flows if we divest. To decide whether to continue without change or divest, it is necessary to compute *incremental after-tax cash flows* by subtracting the after-tax cash flows of the divestment alternative from the after-tax cash flows of the continue-without-change alternative. These incremental after-tax cash flows can be called *relative cash flows,* and it is possible to compute the NPV of a series of relative cash flows. The recommended accept or reject criterion is to continue without change if the NPV of the incremental after-tax cash flows is equal to or greater than zero and to sell if the NPV is negative. This assumes, of course, that the investor can earn at least the required rate of return when reinvesting the after-tax proceeds in another investment.

Continue Without Change

The obvious place for the investor to begin is to make some assumptions about what would be likely to happen under a continue-without-change scenario. Thus, let us review the situation of Douglas Manor Apartments.

Having owned Douglas Manor for four years, the investor considers it time to evaluate his or her position. When Douglas Manor was acquired for $525,000, the expectation was that both NOI and value would increase by 5 percent per year; suppose, in fact, that the increases have only been 3 percent. Further, because of competition and a weak local economy, the investor expects the 3 percent growth rate to continue. Because income is off, selling prices are also down and are expected to remain that way over the next four years. Figures 8–1(a), 8–1(b), and 8–2 summarize the historical cash flows for Douglas Manor for years 1 through 4, and the projected flows for years 5 through 8.

The investor's net after-tax equity reversion of $610,956 at the end of year 4, as shown in Figure 8–2, is the appropriate base when making decisions about alternatives.

Cash flows for continuing without change for the next four years (years 5 through 8) are also summarized in Figures 8–1(a) and 8–1(b); net after-tax equity reversion at the end of year 8 is shown in Figure 8–2.

We are now ready to compute the incremental after-tax cash flows of continuing without change by subtracting the after-tax cash flows of the divestment alterna-

	HISTORICAL (YEARS 1–4)				PROJECTED (YEARS 5–8)			
	1	2	3	4	5	6	7	8
NOI, 3% Annual Growth	$64,000	$65,920	$67,898	$69,935	$72,033	$74,194	$76,419	$78,712
Less: Straight-line depreciation	16,399	16,399	16,399	16,399	16,399	16,399	16,399	16,399
Less: Interest paid	0	0	0	0	0	0	0	0
Taxable Income	$47,601	$49,521	$51,499	$53,535	$55,633	$57,794	$65,179	$67,626
Times: Investor's tax rate	0.36	0.36	0.36	0.36	0.36	0.36	0.36	0.36
Income Tax Payable	$17,136	$17,828	$18,540	$19,273	$20,028	$20,806	$23,464	$24,345

FIGURE 8–1(A)
Douglas Manor Apartments: Historical and Projected Cash Flows and Calculation of Annual Income Tax for Equity Owner in 36% Tax Bracket

	HISTORICAL (YEARS 1–4)				PROJECTED (YEARS 5–8)			
	1	2	3	4	5	6	7	8
NOI, 3% annual growth	$64,000	$65,920	$67,898	$69,935	$72,033	$74,194	$76,419	$78,712
Less: Debt service	0	0	0	0	0	0	0	0
Before-Tax Cash Flow	$64,000	$65,920	$67,898	$69,935	$72,033	$74,194	$76,419	$78,712
Less: Income tax payable	$17,126	$17,828	$18,540	$19,273	$20,028	$20,806	$23,464	$24,345
After-Tax Cash Flow	$46,864	$48,092	$49,358	$50,662	$52,005	$53,388	$52,955	$54,367

FIGURE 8–1(B)
Douglas Manor Apartments: Calculation of Annual After-Tax Cash Flow

		END OF YEAR 4		END OF YEAR 8	
Sales Price		$720,326		$810,733	
Less: Selling expenses		50,423		56,751	
Net Sales Price		$669,903		$753,982	
Less: Adjusted tax basis					
Basis beginning of year 1	$525,000		$525,000		
Less: Straight-line depreciation	65,596	495,404	131,192	393,808	
Capital Gain		$210,526		$360,174	
Times: Capital gains tax rate		0.28		0.28	
Taxes Due on Sale		$ 58,947		$100,849	
Net Sales Price		$669,903		$753,982	
Less: Mortgage balance		0		0	
Before-Tax Equity Reversion		$669,903		$753,982	
Less: Taxes due on sale		58,947		100,849	
After-Tax Equity Reversion		$610,956		$653,133	

FIGURE 8–2

Douglas Manor Apartments: After-Tax Equity Reversion

tive from the after-tax cash flows of the continue-without-change alternative. To illustrate, at the end of year 4, which is the current time period, the incremental after-tax cash flow is computed by subtracting the after-tax equity reversion, $610,956, from the after-tax cash flow from continuing without change, which by definition is zero. The result is a negative, after-tax incremental cash flow of $610,956. This $610,956 amount can be thought of as what the investor is foregoing today in return for a series of cash flows in the future.

At the end of year 5, which is the first year of continuing without change, the incremental after-tax cash flow is $52,005. Similarly, at the end of years 6, 7, and 8, the incremental after-tax cash flows are $53,388, $52,955, and $707,500, respectively. These incremental cash flows are the expected after-tax cash flows to be received if the investor sticks with the property. Note that the $707,500 cash flow at the end of year 8 is the sum of the after-tax cash flow from operation plus the expected after-tax equity reversion from sale.

These calculations are summarized below in tabular form:

END OF YEAR	(1) ATCF CONTINUE WITHOUT CHANGE	(2) ATER SELL	(3) = (1) − (2) DIFFERENTIAL CASH FLOW	(4) PV FACTOR @ 11%	(5) = (3) × (4) PV DIFFERENTIAL CASH FLOW
4	$0	$610,956	($610,956)	1.00000	($610,956)
5	52,005		52,005	0.90090	46,851
6	53,388		53,388	0.81162	43,331
7	52,955		52,955	0.73119	38,720
8	707,500		707,500	0.65873	466,051
NPV at End of Year 4 ÷ Beginning of Year 5					($16,003)
After-Tax IRR					10.17%

The net present value of the series of differential cash flows can be expressed as follows:

$$NPV = \frac{ATCF_1}{(1 + r)} + \frac{ATCF_2}{(1 + r)^2} + \cdots + \frac{ATCF_n}{(1 + r)^n} + \frac{ATER_n}{(1 + r)^n} - ATER_0$$

Here $ATCF_1, ATCF_2, \ldots, ATCF_n$ are the expected after-tax cash flows from continuing without change, $ATER_n$ is the expected after-tax equity reversion from the sale of the property in period n, and $ATER_0$ is the after-tax equity reversion from sale today, and r is the required rate of return. Implicit in these calculations is the assumption that the investor can earn at least r when reinvesting the after-tax proceeds from sale in another investment.

At an 11 percent required rate of return the NPV is $-\$16,003$. Thus the NPV rule tells us to sell the property. Now let us make sure that by reinvesting we will earn at least an 11 percent after-tax equity rate of return.

To Sell or Not to Sell

Obviously if you are going to persuade the owner of Douglas Manor Apartments to divest, you must be prepared to recommend an alternative use of the sales proceeds, which at the end of year 4, amount to $610,956 based on our earlier analysis.

Let us assume that the Swift Office Building, which the investor can purchase for $600,000, is identified as a potential alternative. The first year NOI from the Swift Office Building is projected at $85,200. Value and NOI are expected to grow by 4 percent per year. The land is valued at $108,000. This means the improvements of $492,000 would give a straight-line depreciation write-off of $12,615 per year over the 39-year life set by the IRS. See Figures 8–3 and 8–4 for cash flows.

FIGURE 8–3
Swift Office Building:
Cash Flow Projections
and Calculation of
Annual Income Tax
for Equity Owner in
36% Tax Bracket

	YEAR			
	1	2	3	4
NOI, 4% annual growth	$85,200	$88,608	$92,152	$95,838
Less: Straight-line depreciation	12,615	12,615	12,615	12,615
Interest paid	0	0	0	0
Taxable Income	$72,585	$75,993	$79,537	$83,223
Times: Investor's tax rate	0.36	0.36	0.36	0.36
Income Tax Payable	$26,131	$27,357	$28,633	$29,960

FIGURE 8–4
Swift Office Building:
Cash Flow Projections
and Calculation of
Annual After-Tax
Cash Flows

	YEAR			
	1	2	3	4
NOI, 4% annual growth	$85,200	$88,608	$92,152	$95,838
Less: Debt service	0	0	0	0
Before-Tax Cash Flow	$85,200	$88,608	$92,152	$95,838
Less: Income tax payable	26,131	27,357	28,633	29,960
After-tax cash flow	$59,069	$61,251	$63,519	$65,878

Sale of the Swift Office Building at the end of year 4 would result in a net after-tax equity reversion of $623,874 (see Figure 8–5). The result would be a four-year after-tax IRR of 11.20 percent, slightly above the investor's 11 percent required rate of return. NPV for the equity investment of $600,000 comes to $3,734. Thus, the Swift Office Building is a viable alternative for the investor.

However, in making the changeover, the investor would have an additional $10,956 to invest; this amount is the end-of-year 4 after-tax equity realized from selling Douglas Manor, $610,956, less the $600,000 cash payment for the Swift Office Building. The investor would also incur risk in the changeover in that he or she would be switching from a residential-type property, with which the investor is familiar, to a business-type property. In addition, considerable stress would be involved.

Making the Choice

The two alternatives facing the investor are summarized in Figure 8–6. Effectively the choices are as follows:

1. Continue to hold Douglas Manor, with an expected after-tax IRR of 10.17 percent and a NPV from the entire end-of-year 4 equity of −$16,003, which is clearly unacceptable provided you can earn 11 percent elsewhere.

2. Sell Douglas Manor and buy the Swift Office Building, which would provide a NPV of $3,734 and an after-tax IRR of 11.20 percent. The investor would have an excess of $10,956 to invest elsewhere or to use for other purposes. Note that the Swift Office Building in this case is representative of the many alternatives open to the investor.

Would there be other factors to consider? Possibly. But in financial terms, the sale and reinvest option looks like the most attractive alternative. The financial returns would clearly be greater, although some additional financial risk would be incurred by investing in a different type of property.

		END OF YEAR 4
Sales Price		$701,915
Less: Selling expenses		49,134
Net Sales Price		$652,781
Less: Adjusted tax basis		
Beginning of year 1 basis	$600,000	
Less: Straight-line depreciation	50,460	549,540
Capital Gain		$103,241
Times: Capital gains tax rate		0.28
Taxes Due on Sale		$28,907
Net Sales Price		$652,781
Less: Mortgage balance		0
Before-Tax Equity Reversion		$652,781
Less: Taxes due on sale		28,907
After-Tax Equity Reversion		$623,874

FIGURE 8–5
Swift Office Building: After-Tax Equity Reversion at End of Year 4

ALTERNATIVE	AFTER-TAX EQUITY INVESTMENT	NET PRESENT VALUE	AFTER-TAX IRR	CASH RELEASED FOR INVESTMENT ELSEWHERE
Continue without Change	$610,956	($16,003)	10.17%	None
Sell and Reinvest in Swift Office Building	$600,000	$3,743	11.20%	$10,956

FIGURE 8-6
Summary of Investment Alternatives

DEALING WITH DISTRESSED PROPERTIES

Now let us consider how to deal with *distressed properties*. Suppose you own outright a $10 million office building in Southern California. A recession hits and a large amount of space begins to sit empty. To make things more difficult, further suppose that Congress passes some new tax legislation—conceived in the spirit of protecting the industry from foolish management, but timed to catch even the best properties at a disadvantage.

Under these circumstances the value of your office building is likely to plummet. For the sake of this example, let us suppose that your office building is now worth only $7 million; you would be out $3 million if you were to sell today. And the latter value ignores transaction costs.

Not wanting to take a $3 million loss, you ask yourself: What if I were to hold on to the property for a while? Could I minimize my losses? You could potentially minimize losses. Could I expect to regain everything I lost and more? Perhaps. It all depends on when the Southern California real estate market rebounds and how high prices will rise.

To illustrate, assume that the Southern California real estate market is expected to rebound over the next four years, and that it will cost you between $250,000 and $1,250,000 a year in foregone revenue and carrying costs to hold the property during this period. A forecast of the risky before-tax cash outflows is shown below.

**Forecasted Opportunity Costs and Benefits of Holding
on to a Hypothetical Office Building
in Southern California**

YEAR	OPPORTUNITY COST	LOSS OF EQUITY WHEN SOLD
1	$1,250,000	
2	1,000,000	
3	750,000	
4	250,000	$0

To decide whether or not to continue to hold the property you would want to discount the cash outflows and choose the option that minimizes your losses. We should make several points here.

First, we know that if you were to quit the property today, without taking further risks you would lose roughly $3 million. We also know that property values are likely to recover over the next four years. In fact, we believe that by the end of year 4 property values will be at the same level they were before the recession and before Congress changed the tax laws. How do we know this? Because we expect the loss of equity upon sale at the end of year 4 to be exactly zero. However, to hold on to the property during the next four years is costly; the cost includes the carrying costs of holding vacant space.

Second, holding the property is a risky strategy. There is always the risk that the market will take longer to rebound than initially anticipated; for example, it may take as much as ten years. Land in Chicago, for example, sold for $11,000 an acre in 1836. By 1842 Chicago land prices had fallen to $100 an acre, and not until 1873, following a panic, a Civil War, and a great fire, did land values regain their 1836 values in nominal terms.[1] Obviously if it took ten years for the market to rebound, your opportunity costs of holding the property could escalate dramatically.

Third, to penalize the cash outflows associated with holding onto a property with a higher-than-average risk, they must have a higher present value. Thus, the expected future costs of holding on to the property should be evaluated using a lower-than-average discount rate. This risk adjustment for a cash outflow is the exact opposite of a normal risk adjustment for a cash inflow. Confused? Let us look at some numbers.

Assuming that you would normally require a 15 percent before-tax rate of return on the cash inflows from a property in financial distress, we can find the present value of the future holding costs as follows:

$$PV = \frac{CF_1}{(1 + r)} + \frac{CF_2}{(1 + r)^2} + \frac{CF_3}{(1 + r)^3} + \frac{CF_4}{(1 + r)^4}$$

$$= \frac{\$1,250,000}{(1 + .15)} + \frac{\$1,000,000}{(1 + .15)^2} + \frac{\$750,000}{(1 + .15)^3} + \frac{\$250,000}{(1 + .15)^4}$$

$$= \$2,479,176$$

Since the present value of the expected future holding costs is less than $3 million, we should hold on to the property.

However, if we truly want to penalize the cash outflows associated with holding onto a property with a higher-than-average risk, instead of discounting at a 15 percent before-tax rate of return, we should discount the cash outflows at, say, 4 percent. The difference of 11 percent represents the risk being absorbed by the investor. The result is

$$PV = \frac{CF_1}{(1 + r)} + \frac{CF_2}{(1 + r)^2} + \frac{CF_3}{(1 + r)^3} + \frac{CF_4}{(1 + r)^4}$$

$$= \frac{\$1,250,000}{(1 + .04)} + \frac{\$1,000,000}{(1 + .04)^2} + \frac{\$750,000}{(1 + .04)^3} + \frac{\$250,000}{(1 + .04)^4}$$

$$= \$3,006,928$$

[1] The effect of the decline in land values was to ruin most of those who bought land in Chicago prior to 1836. See Homer Hoyt, *One Hundred Years of Land Values in Chicago*. Chicago: University of Chicago Press, 1933.

Thus, there is a conflict: The present value of the expected future holding costs discounted at 4 percent is actually greater than $3 million. This suggests that we should sell the property today.

Fortunately, in our rather simple example this conflict is easily resolved. If the property were sold today, it might actually sell for only 75¢ on the dollar. The 25¢ discount is what would be needed to bring prices down to a level that would attract a potential buyer. Without a deeply discounted price, no bids are likely. On a $7 million office building in distress this could easily amount to an added loss of $1,750,000. Given this additional loss, we would conclude that the property is not worth selling quickly; instead, the best decision would be to continue to hold.

Lender Issues in Dealing with Distressed Properties

Consider for the moment actions of a typical bank or financial institution involved in working out real estate loan problems. When property values fall, the lender is likely to be left with little choice but to seek title to the property. This process is know as *foreclosure.* In a foreclosure, the lender petitions the proper court of jurisdiction for a foreclosure action. The courts then either set a time period within which the borrower must pay the debt or forever lose the right to redeem the property, or order a public sale of the mortgaged property (see Chapter 23). All in all, the foreclosure process can be rather lengthy and costly; with each passing day the bank must pay the ongoing operating costs that are due regardless of whether the property is vacant. Meanwhile, the property withers in the elements, and the market becomes increasingly aware of the white elephant sitting unsold.

To illustrate how the foreclosure process works, consider our office building in Southern California. Let us now assume that the property is mortgaged to the hilt. As before, we shall assume that vacancies rise and income falls. In turn, property values plummet. This is the pain phase of the investor/lender relationship; this is where mortgage delinquencies start and lenders begin to seek remedies. This phase is followed by a bail-out phase, where the lender must decide whether to bail out the project or foreclose on the borrower.

Either option—choosing to bail out the borrower or to foreclose—can be costly to the lender. For instance, suppose the bank has made a good-faith effort to reach a debt restructuring agreement with the owner of our office building but the attempt has been a failure. Alternatively, assume that it is bank policy not to reward failure to pay on time by agreeing to extend the due date of the loan or to recast the mortgage payment.

Equity investors are generally unwilling to contribute additional equity capital when the value of the property is less than the mortgage amount, because any subsequent increase in the equity value of the property will go directly to benefit the lender. Likewise, lenders are typically unwilling to bail out properties in distress because the borrower may forsake the usual objective of maximizing the overall market value of the property to pursue narrower self-interest instead. Frequently the borrower is concurrently experiencing other financial problems which may prevent him or her from properly overseeing management and/or providing the necessary compensation or incentives for management to do its job. The result is disinterested management, which further aggravates existing vacancies.

However, we should also note that no lender really wants to get the property back; owning property, especially distressed property, is bad news for the bank. First, the bank must recognize a loss on its books. If our $10 million office building has a $9 million mortgage balance, the bank will have to take a $2 million loss unless, in addition to the foreclosure, there is some other personal recourse against the borrower.[2] The calculations are as follows:

	BEFORE VALUE FALLS		AFTER FORECLOSURE
Market value of property	$10 million	Market value of property	$ 7 million
Less: Loan amount	$ 9 million	Less: Loan amount	$ 9 million
Equity Investment	$ 1 million	Loss to Lender	($2) million

$$\text{Loss to Equity Investor} = \text{Equity before} - \text{Equity after}$$
$$= \$1 \text{ million} - \$0 = \$1 \text{ million}$$

Before the decline in the value of the property, the investor has $1 million of equity in the property (the difference between the $10 million market value and the $9 million commercial mortgage). After values plummet and after foreclosure, the investor actually incurs a $1 million loss, and the potential loss to the lender is the difference between the $7 million market value and the $9 million loan amount. This $2 million loss means that the bank, in its statements, will have to lower its equity capital value by that amount. If a bank had many problem properties, the total losses could wipe out its total capital, thus forcing regulators to foreclose on the bank.

This example also assumes that the lender can dispose of the property. But the process of actually foreclosing on a property and selling it to another investor can bog down and keep the bank in an ownership role far beyond an economic point. To sell the property the lender will incur legal and administrative costs, and indirect costs. Someone in the lender's organization must manage the property while a buyer is being sought. Bank regulators will require that the lender hold additional capital to protect against subsequent loss on sale of the property.

Once the property has been foreclosed, the lender must make decisions similar to those faced by our equity investor. The primary exception is that the value of cash today to a bank is very high, which means that the bank may discount the cash outflows associated with holding the property at a higher-than-average risk even more than our equity investor. Thus, instead of discounting at a 4 percent before-tax rate, the bank may discount at 2 percent. The result is:

$$PV = \frac{CF_1}{(1+r)} + \frac{CF_2}{(1+r)^2} + \frac{CF_3}{(1+r)^3} + \frac{CF_4}{(1+r)^4}$$

$$= \frac{\$1,250,000}{(1+.02)} + \frac{\$1,000,000}{(1+.02)^2} + \frac{\$750,000}{(1+.02)^3} + \frac{\$250,000}{(1+.02)^4}$$

$$= \$3,124,362$$

[2] A mortgage note wherein the lender waives the right to a deficiency judgment for the difference between the mortgage amount and the property value is called a *nonrecourse loan*. Most commercial mortgage loans originated in the 1980s were nonrecourse loans.

Here again ignoring the fact that a fire-sale approach may be needed to sell the property immediately, the calculations suggest that, since the present value of the expected future holding costs is actually greater than $2 million, the lender should sell today rather than hold on to the property.

Early Warning Signals

Perhaps the best strategy for dealing with distressed properties is to forestall them by watching for early warning signals. The difficulties of most problem properties usually can be traced to one of the following factors—poor management, operating deficits, lack of capital improvements, or owners who need greater liquidity. Sometimes the problems are physical—deterioration of interiors and exteriors, problem tenants, neighborhood deterioration, functional obsolescence, adverse changes to frontage, increased traffic congestion, or worsened access in and out of the property.

Fixing these problems before they become major obstacles can save everyone a lot of grief. It helps the equity investor because he or she may be able to avoid foreclosure. Working hard to turn around a property may also allow the equity investor to borrow again another day.

SUMMARY

This chapter began with a discussion of the continue-without-change versus sell-and-reinvest decision for financially sound properties. To make this decision, one proceeds as follows:

1. Forecast the after-tax cash flows from continuing without change, including both the cash flows from operations and the equity reversion at a sale date some time in the not-too-distant future.

2. Calculate the after-tax equity reversion from divesting, assuming that the property were sold today.

3. Compute the incremental after-tax cash flows by subtracting the after-tax cash flows of the divestment alternative from the after-tax cash flows of the continue-without-change alternative.

4. Compute the NPV of this series of relative cash flows. The recommended accept or reject criterion is to continue without change if the NPV of the incremental after-tax cash flows is equal to or greater than zero and to sell if the NPV is negative.

Net present value can be expressed as follows:

$$NPV = \frac{ATCF_1}{(1 + r)} + \frac{ATCF_2}{(1 + r)^2} + \cdots + \frac{ATCF_n}{(1 + r)^n} + \frac{ATER_n}{(1 + r)^n} - ATER_0$$

Where $ATCF_1$, $ATCF_2$, . . . , $ATCF_n$, and $ATER_n$ are the expected after-tax cash flows from continuing without change, $ATER_0$ is the after-tax equity reversion from sale today, and r is the required rate of return.

This chapter also examined the continue-without-change versus sell-and-reinvest decision for distressed properties. Here the motivation underlying the disposition decision is completely different; rather than attempting to maximize wealth, owners of distressed properties often attempt to minimize losses. This means that the investor must first project the foregone revenue and carrying costs associated with holding on to the property. Next, he or she must determine the present value of these carrying costs. The calculation is as follows:

$$PV = \frac{CF_1}{(1 + r)} + \frac{CF_2}{(1 + r)^2} + \cdots + \frac{CF_n}{(1 + r)^n}$$

Here CF_1, CF_2, . . . ,CF_n are the expected opportunity costs of holding on to the property and r is the required rate of return. To penalize these cash outflows for higher-than-average risk, it follows that we must have a higher present value. Therefore, the expected future costs of holding on to the property should be evaluated with a lower-than-average discount rate, which is the exact opposite of a normal risk adjustment for a cash inflow.

Having done this, the investor will then want to compare the potential loss from sale today with the present value of the expected opportunity cost of holding on to the property. The decision rule is:

Hold If: PV of expected carrying costs ≤ Loss if sold today

or

Sell If: PV of expected carrying costs > Loss if sold today

These decision rules are designed to minimize the owner's losses. Faced with having to lower prices substantially in order to attract a potential buyer immediately, most owners are inclined to hold on to the property and hope that the real estate market will rebound.

Lenders are a different story. Owing to the high value they place on cash today, lenders are more likely to sell rather than to hold distressed properties. Lenders may also incur substantial administrative costs in dealing with distressed real estate. We should point out also that no lender really wants to foreclose on a problem property. If a bank has many properties, the total losses may wipe out its capital and force regulators to foreclose.

KEY CONCEPTS

Continue without change   Option that should be exercised if the present value of the after-tax cash flows from continuing to operate exceeds the present value of the after-tax proceeds from sale.

Sale and reinvest   Alternative that should be exercised if the present value of the after-tax proceeds from sale exceeds the present value of the after-tax cash flows from continuing to operate. Assumes that the investor can earn at least the required rate of return when reinvesting the after-tax proceeds in another investment.

Distressed properties   Properties that bring an insufficient return to the owner.

Incremental after-tax cash flows   Indicates the cost of selecting one alternative over another. In the continue without change decision, the incremental after-tax cash flows are computed by subtracting the after-tax cash flows of the disinvestment alternative from the after-tax cash flows of the continue-without-change alternative.

QUESTIONS FOR REVIEW AND DISCUSSION

1. In general terms, explain the process by which an owner decides whether to remain with a property or sell and reinvest the proceeds in another property.

2. How is the incremental after-tax cash flow calculated when deciding whether to divest a property?

3. What are the decision criteria used when considering the incremental after-tax cash flows on a project?

4. When evaluating risky, uncertain cash outflows, should a higher or lower discount rate be used? Why?

5. What is meant by foreclosure? Is it always the preferred option of the lender for a financially distressed property? Why or why not?

6. Would lenders use a lower or higher discount rate than private owners on risky future cash outflows?

7. What are some common early warning signals that a commercial property may be in financial distress?

PROBLEMS

1. A property has been held by an investor for six years, and the investor is now considering disposition. The investor expects the following cash flows.

    If:

    Continue to operate: The after-tax cash flow next year will be $72,000 and is expected to grow by 3 percent per year. The after-tax equity reversion is expected to be $780,000 if the property is sold at the end of two more years.

    Sell today: The net after-tax equity if sold today is $650,000.

    The investor requires an after-tax rate of return of 10 percent. The projection period is two years. Should the property be sold today? What is the after-tax NPV and IRR of the differential cash flows?

2. The owner of a financially distressed property in Texas can dispose of it at a $2 million loss today. If the period of recovery for the project is expected to be three years, with annual opportunity costs of $1,000,000, $800,000, and $600,000 respectively, should the property be sold? Assume that the original discount rate of 15 percent has been lowered to 5 percent due to the risky nature of the cash flows.

3. In problem 2, should the property be sold if the discount rate used is 8%?

4. Assume Ronald Smith bought Lincoln Towers for $640,000, of which $116,000 is attributable to the land. He is now at the end of year 2 and is considering several alternatives. He seeks you out, as a real estate consultant, and asks you to help analyze the following alternatives.

The property is 100 percent equity financed. Depreciation is 39-year straight-line cost recovery. The projection period is two years.

Assume Smith's EOY2 sales price would be $680,000 if sold at EOY2. NOI in the first year of the 2-year anticipated holding period is $72,000. NOI is expected to increase by $4,000 at the end of year 3. The disposition price is expected to increase by $40,000 per year. Selling expenses are 8 percent. The required rate of return is 10 percent.

Required:

(a) Compare the likely results from the two alternatives—continue to operate versus sale, and indicate which you recommend. Give reasons for your choice.

(b) What after-tax rate of return on equity will Ronald Smith receive if he does nothing?

PART TWO
APPRAISAL

CHAPTER 9

OVERVIEW OF THE APPRAISAL PROCESS

Chapter Outline

Nothing can have value without being an objective of utility. If it is useless, the labor contained in it is useless, cannot be reckoned as labor, and cannot therefore create value.

Karl Marx, *Das Kapital*

An *appraisal* is an estimate or opinion of the value of a property, or some interest therein, rendered by an impartial person skilled in the analysis and valuation of real estate; the value most often sought is market value, or the most probable selling price. An orderly, well-conceived set of procedures, termed the *appraisal process,* is used in making the estimate.

In this chapter we provide a brief overview of the real estate appraisal process. The discussion is limited to defining terms and providing a basic explanation of the process.

THE NEED FOR MARKET VALUE ESTIMATES

Situations in which a real estate decision must be made, an action taken, or a policy established usually turn on a market value estimate of real estate. Below are some examples:

Transfer of Ownership or Possession

Market value serves as a benchmark to both parties in buy–sell transactions. For example, assume that the market value or most likely selling price of a single-family residence is $100,000. A prudent buyer might well open negotiations at $80,000 and would not be willing to pay much in excess of $100,000. The owner certainly would not offer the property for sale at less than $100,000; most likely, the initial asking price would be $100,000 or perhaps even $120,000. Further, the owner would be very unlikely to accept less than $100,000 unless under great pressure to sell. Knowing market value makes the negotiations much more certain for both parties.

Market value is also important in renting property, because rent is usually a percentage of market value. Value estimates are also needed to establish a fair-value basis for tax-deferred exchanges and for minimum bids in property auctions.

Market value estimates are helpful in group negotiations, such as in settling an estate consisting of several parcels where several people are designated as heirs on a pro rata basis. In this kind of situation, it is often preferable to assign properties to individual heirs rather than to sell them and distribute the proceeds. Without objective value estimates, some of the heirs might feel that they were receiving a less-than-fair share of the estate, and considerable bitterness and litigation could result. This is also true for a business reorganization, a corporate merger, the issuance of new or additional stock by a corporation or trust, or a corporate bankruptcy.

Financing a Property Interest

The property is the real estate lender's security. Therefore, the lender wants assurance that the most probable selling price of the property is greater than the principal amount of the loan. As an example, suppose that a 90 percent loan were requested to finance the purchase of a single-family residence valued at $100,000, which sold at the owner's initial asking price of $120,000. A $108,000 loan might be implied, but this is $8,000 more than the $100,000 market value and $18,000 more than 90 percent of market value (90% × $100,000 = $90,000). If a $108,000 loan were made, the lender would have little or no cushion should a foreclosure become necessary within a few years; the lender's risk is much greater than is implied by the 90 percent loan-to-purchase-price ratio.

Public and private insurers of mortgage loans, such as the Federal Housing Administration (FHA) or Mortgage Guarantee Insurance Corporation (MGIC), want assurance that the security exceeds the insured principal by an established percentage. Extending this line of reasoning, a prospective purchaser of mortgage bonds wants assurance that adequate security is provided by the pledged property.

Taxing Property Interests

An error in estimating market value by an assessor directly affects the amount of property taxes levied against a property. In most areas, assessed value is some proportion of market value. Assume that assessed value is supposed to equal 60 percent of market value. Also assume that a residence with an actual market value of $100,000 is over-appraised at $130,000. The $30,000 difference translates into an overassessment of $18,000; at a 3 percent tax levy this means extra annual taxes of $540.

Market value estimates are important in state and federal tax situations as well. According to the IRS, the allocation between land and improvements is required to be in direct relation to the distribution made by the assessor. The allocation determines the annual depreciation, and the larger the allowable deduction, the less the taxes to be paid. An investor may take exception to the assessor's distribution and hire a real estate appraiser to make the determination. In addition, gift and inheritance taxes payable to federal and state governments depend directly on the market value of the property involved.

Compensation for Property Loss or Damage

Owners insure to protect against risk of property loss or damage caused by natural disasters such as fire, wind, flood, lightning, and earthquake. In some cases, this insurance is for the cost of replacement or reproduction of the property rather than for market value. But, if the loss is realized, the insurance settlement depends on the market value of the property.

Likewise, *eminent domain* actions—the right of a government to take private property for public uses or purposes, with payment of just compensation—constitute a continuing and major need for estimates of market value. If an entire property is condemned, the owner is entitled to just compensation equal to at least the market value of the property. If only part of the property is taken, the owner is usually entitled to compensation equal to the value of the part taken, plus the amount of any damages to the remainder. Often, the taking authority and the owner get separate market value estimates as a basis for determining just compensation. If a settlement cannot be negotiated, it is left up to the courts to decide.

Property Utilization

Finally, determining the best way to use a property requires a highest-and-best-use assessment. One way to determine the highest-and-best use of a property is to find that use which yields the greatest present value. This analysis is closely akin to market and feasibility analysis (discussed in Chapter 19) and should precede any decision concerning development or redevelopment of realty.

THE NATURE OF VALUE

Several attributes must be present for a parcel of real estate to have value. The first is *utility,* or the ability to satisfy human needs and desires by providing shelter, privacy, or income. Second, *effective demand* must be present for the services or amenities that the property produces. The third attribute is *relative scarcity;* that is, supply must be limited relative to demand. A fourth is *transferability,* meaning that rights of ownership or use can be conveyed from one person to another with relative ease. Finally, the property must be located in an environment of law and order so that investors will not suffer loss because of legal or political uncertainty.

Market Value

As mentioned, *market value* is the most basic value concept in real estate. An increasingly accepted definition of market value is *most probable selling price,* in cash. Two other widely used definitions are: (1) the amount in dollars, goods, or services for which a property may be exchanged, and (2) the present worth of future rights to the income or amenities generated by a property.

Whichever definition is used, market value is estimated by methods shown later in this chapter. In applying the methods the following assumptions apply.[1]

1. Real estate buyers and sellers act as rational persons, with reasonable but not perfect knowledge. This is realistic because almost all market participants gather information about conditions before they act.

2. Buyers and sellers act competitively and rationally in their own best interests to maximize their income or satisfactions.

3. Buyers and sellers act independently of each other—that is, without collusion, fraud, or misrepresentation. If this were not the case, some transaction prices might be severely distorted.

[1] See market value in *Real Estate Appraisal Terminology,* Rev. ed., compiled and edited by Byrl N. Boyce under the joint sponsorship of the American Institute of Real Estate Appraisers and the Society of Real Estate Appraisers. Cambridge, Mass: Ballinger, 1981.

4. Buyers and sellers are, typically, motivated to act without undue pressure. This means that properties placed on the market turn over or sell within a reasonable period. Thus, a forced sale or a sale occurring after the property has been exposed to the market for an extremely long time would not be considered typical.

5. Payment is made in cash in a manner consistent with the standards of the market; that is, the buyer uses financing terms generally available in the local market.

Market Value Versus Market Price

Market value does not necessarily equal market price. In fact, the market value for a property may be greater than, equal to, or less than its sale price in an actual market transaction. *Market price* is the amount negotiated between a buyer and a seller in a less-than-perfect market. Market price is an historical fact. Market value, on the other hand, is an estimated price made by an objective, experienced, knowledgeable appraiser. The estimate is made after looking at and studying a number of actual transactions and other market data.

Market Value Versus Cost

Market value may also be greater than, equal to, or less than the cost of a property. As used here, *cost* means the capital outlay, including overhead and financing expenses, for land, labor, materials, supervision, and profit necessary to bring a useful property into existence. It does not mean market price.

A rational developer or investor improves sites and constructs new buildings on them only if the expected market value equals or exceeds the cost of production. Developing a major property without adequate market analysis ignores the simple reality that cost does not necessarily mean value.

Value in Use Versus Value in Exchange

The worth of a property based on its utility to a specific user is its *value in use.* Utility for a specific user may mean certain types of amenities, income, or value the real estate contributes to an enterprise. Value in use depends on the unique judgments, standards, and demands of a particular user, and is independent of identifiable market information. Another term for value in use is *subjective value*—that is, value that is dependent on the nature and mental attitude of the person making the judgment. However, if one assumes that the viewpoint of the typical person is the same as subjective value, then the value-in-use estimate becomes consistent with most probable selling price, or market value.

Recognition of this special case leads us to *value in exchange,* which is the amount of money or purchasing power (in goods and services) for which the property might most probably be traded. When such exchanges take place, appraisers and others collect and analyze the values given in exchange to determine a value equivalent to most probable selling price. Effectively, these analysts make a neutral estimate of the value of the properties, termed *objective value.* Value in exchange then is roughly synonymous with objective value and with market value.

A rational owner retains a property as long as value in use exceeds value in exchange. With time, however, depreciation is used up as a tax shelter, community change may make a location obsolete, or the owner decides to retire. Thus, for a variety of reasons, value in use drops and eventually falls below value in exchange. At this point, disposition becomes advantageous and market activity results.

Figure 9-1, which shows the investment value of a small warehouse to the seller and a potential buyer, summarizes these points. From the seller's standpoint, the current value of the warehouse, $627,000, is based on its value in use. The buyer's investment value, on the other hand, is $663,500, which reflects a greater value in use.

Also shown in Figure 9-1 is the market value of the property. Obviously, the market value of the property needs to be greater than $627,000 in order for the owner to want to sell, and less than $663,500 in order for the potential buyer to want to buy.

The actual market value should fall somewhere between $627,000 and $663,500 depending on market conditions. For example, when the market is thin (i.e., few buyers and many sellers), the actual market value of the property is apt to be fairly close to $627,000. Conversely, when demand is high (i.e., many buyers and few sellers), the actual market value of the property is likely to be much closer to $663,500.

Other factors that may lead to higher market values include different expectations about the benefits the property will generate in the future, and different information levels about competing properties in the market.

THE APPRAISAL PROCESS

There are several elements or steps that make up what professional appraisers call the *framework* of the appraisal process. These steps, when taken in the order presented, allow a systematic analysis of the facts that bear upon and determine the market value of a specific parcel (see Figure 9–2).

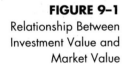

FIGURE 9–1
Relationship Between Investment Value and Market Value

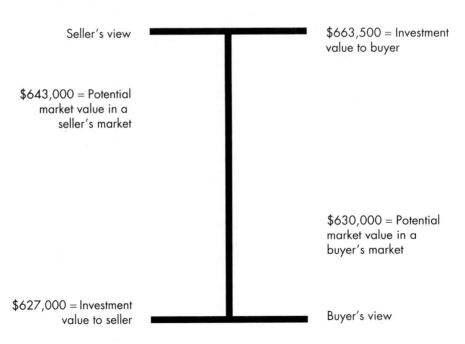

Seller's view

$643,000 = Potential market value in a seller's market

$627,000 = Investment value to seller

$663,500 = Investment value to buyer

$630,000 = Potential market value in a buyer's market

Buyer's view

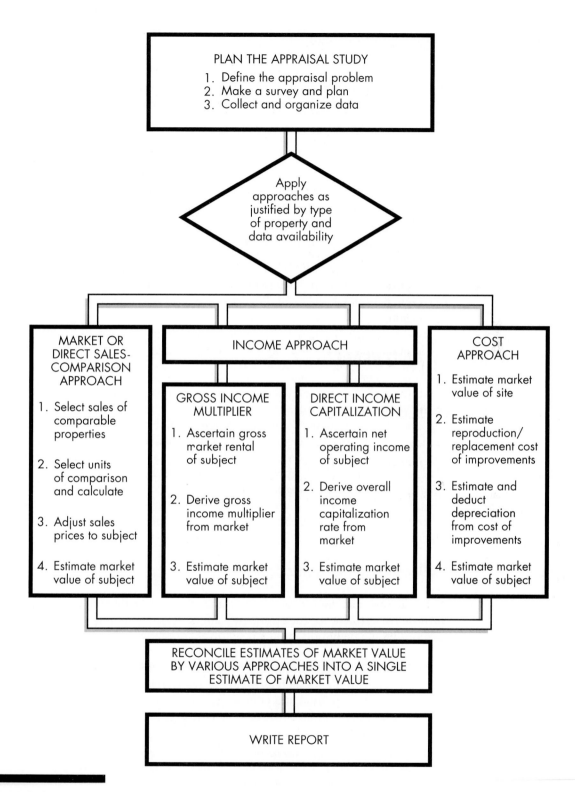

PLAN THE APPRAISAL STUDY
1. Define the appraisal problem
2. Make a survey and plan
3. Collect and organize data

Apply approaches as justified by type of property and data availability

MARKET OR DIRECT SALES-COMPARISON APPROACH

1. Select sales of comparable properties

2. Select units of comparison and calculate

3. Adjust sales prices to subject

4. Estimate market value of subject

INCOME APPROACH

GROSS INCOME MULTIPLIER

1. Ascertain gross market rental of subject

2. Derive gross income multiplier from market

3. Estimate market value of subject

DIRECT INCOME CAPITALIZATION

1. Ascertain net operating income of subject

2. Derive overall income capitalization rate from market

3. Estimate market value of subject

COST APPROACH

1. Estimate market value of site

2. Estimate reproduction/ replacement cost of improvements

3. Estimate and deduct depreciation from cost of improvements

4. Estimate market value of subject

RECONCILE ESTIMATES OF MARKET VALUE BY VARIOUS APPROACHES INTO A SINGLE ESTIMATE OF MARKET VALUE

WRITE REPORT

FIGURE 9–2
The Appraisal Process: Steps in Estimating Market Value

Defining the Problem

The *appraisal assignment* must be agreed upon jointly by the appraiser and by the owner or the owner's agent to ensure that the analysis and conclusions bear on the decision or action to be made. In defining the problem, agreement is needed on each of the following:

1. Specific identification of the property, preferably by both address and legal description.

2. Specific identification of the legal rights to be valued (see Chapter 26).

3. Specific purpose of the appraisal. For example, is the appraisal being done prior to putting the property up for sale? to obtain financing? for insurance purposes? for a condemnation procedure?

4. Specific date for which the value estimate is desired.

5. Specific value to be estimated; for example, market value, assessed value, condemnation damages, or other. Market value is the objective in most appraisal assignments.

MAKING A SURVEY AND PLAN

Next, the scope, character, and amount of work involved must be estimated. This determination constitutes the *appraisal plan.* This is quite simple and routine when valuing a one-family residence. However, when a major property or complex legal rights are involved, it is often necessary to check with data sources, such as brokers, lenders, title companies, and other appraisers. The highest and best use of the property must also be considered. The appraiser must also decide which of the alternative approaches to value—the market approach, the income approach, or the cost approach—should be utilized, the effort likely to be involved, and the fee. If not already agreed upon, the fee is usually cleared with the client before further work is undertaken.

Collecting and Organizing Data

National, regional, community, and neighborhood data are collected and analyzed to provide background for the appraisal plan. By way of example, the following considerations would be important in a residential appraisal:

1. *Physical and environmental data.* Here the emphasis is on topology and physical improvements such as rolling or flat terrain; natural beauty; drainage; quality of soil; condition and contour of roads; transportation and availability of essential public utilities; quality of housing; proximity to schools, stores, and recreational facilities.

2. *Demographic and social data.* Nature and characteristics of population, including lifestyle, care of homes, whether neighborhood is in a transition, and percentage of homeownership.

3. *Economic data.* Personal income per capita; income stability; homogeneity of professional or business activities; frequency of turnover; housing market price

levels and trends; assessment trends and tax levels; vacancies; and percentage of area development.

An on-site inspection of the subject property must then be made, followed by a written description of it. With knowledge of the subject property, the appraiser is in a much better position to collect data on comparable properties. Once collected, the data are sorted according to the direct sales comparison, cost, and income approaches. From this point on, the appraiser's attention is focused on one approach at a time.

PRINCIPLES OF APPRAISING

Over the years appraisers have developed the following *principles of valuation.*

1. *Supply and demand.* Market value is the result of supply and demand interaction.

2. *Change.* The forces of supply and demand are dynamic and change constantly, and therefore fluctuate in price and value. Thus, a market value estimate is valid only for a given date.

3. *Competition.* Prices are kept in line and market values established through continuous interaction of buyers, sellers, developers, and other market participants.

4. *Substitution.* A rational buyer will pay no more for a property than the cost of acquiring an equally desirable, alternative property.

5. *Variable proportions.* Real estate reaches its point of maximum productivity, or highest and best use, when the factors of production (usually considered to be land, labor, capital, and management) are in balance.

6. *Contribution or marginal productivity.* The value of any factor of production or component of a property depends on how much its presence adds to the overall value of the property.

7. *Highest and best use.* For market valuation purposes, real estate should be appraised at its highest and best use so that maximum value is recognized.

8. *Conformity.* A property reaches its maximum value when it is located in an environment of physical, economic, and social homogeneity or of compatible and harmonious land uses.

9. *Anticipation.* Market value equals the present worth of future income or amenities generated by a property, as viewed by typical buyers and sellers.

The first four principles involve the real estate market. The next three apply primarily to the property itself. The eighth principle concerns the neighborhood or area around the property. The ninth principle looks at the property's productivity from the viewpoint of a typical buyer or seller.

The principles of substitution, change, contribution, and highest and best use are generally considered the most important and, therefore, merit further explanation.

Principle of Substitution

According to the *principle of substitution,* a rational buyer will pay no more for a property than the cost of acquiring an equally desirable, alternative property. An equally desirable, alternative property means one of equal utility or productivity, with time costs or delays taken into account. The rational buyer is presumed to have the following three alternatives:

1. Buying an existing property with utility equal to the subject property. This alternative is the basis of the market or *direct sales-comparison approach* to estimating market value.

2. Buying a site and adding improvements to produce a property with utility equal to the subject property. This alternative is the basis of the *cost approach* to estimating market value.

3. Buying a property that produces an income stream of the same size and with the same risk as that produced by the subject property. This alternative is the basis of the *income approach* to estimating market value.

The latter approach cannot be utilized as one goes from income-producing to non-income-producing properties, such as single-family homes, churches, vacant lots, and timberland. With income-producing properties, annual rental income may be used as the basis of comparison for the income approach. Since annual rental data are not usually available for nonincome-producing properties, greater reliance must be placed on the direct sales-comparison and cost approaches.

Principle of Change

The *principle of change* reflects the dynamics of the forces of supply and demand that lead to price and value fluctuation. Because value changes constantly, a specific date must be attached to each estimate. Physical, social, political, and economic conditions are always in a state of transition—buildings suffer wear and tear, people move, laws change, and industries expand and contract. It is the appraiser's task to recognize these forces and to make a snapshot estimate of their cause-and-effect on the market value of the property.

Principle of Contribution or Marginal Productivity

The *principle of contribution* may be defined by saying that the value of any factor of production, or component of a property, depends on how much its presence adds to the overall value of the property. Alternatively, the value of the factor or component may be measured by how much its absence detracts from the overall value. Does the absence of a garage or a second bath reduce the value of a residence by some incremental amount? This principle serves as the basis for making adjustments among properties in the direct sales-comparison approach. It also provides the basis for estimating physical and functional depreciation in the cost approach.

Principle of Highest-and-Best Use

Finally the *principle of highest-and-best use* says that real estate should be appraised at its highest-and-best use for market-valuation purposes. There is a simple logic behind this principle; namely, a prudent owner will in self-interest put a property to the use that yields the greatest present value or return. To do otherwise would not be rational. And it is this value that is critical to any decision made about the property.

In applying this principle, it must be recognized that the value of an improved property may not be as great as that of the site, if the site were vacant and/or available for an alternative highest-and-best use. This would be the case, for example, if a private house were on a commercial site. In such a case the value of the site would exceed the value of the improved property, which would mean that the improvements were making no contribution to value and should be removed. On the other hand, if the value of the property were greater than that of the site, it would pay the owner to continue the use dictated by the improvements. A more detailed discussion of highest and best use is contained in Chapter 12.

ORGANIZING AND PERFORMING AN APPRAISAL OF A REGIONAL SHOPPING CENTER—AN EXAMPLE

Regional shopping centers are difficult to appraise. There are generally two major tenant types: anchor tenants and nonanchor tenants. Leading anchor tenants are often major department stores such as Macy's, Saks Fifth Avenue, Marshall Fields, and Bloomingdale's. Nonanchor tenants include smaller department and variety stores, ladies' and men's specialty shops, shoe stores, furniture and hardware stores, jewelry, greeting card, camera, and record stores, as well as restaurants and bookshops. The sheer number and diversity of tenants makes it difficult to estimate the scope, character, and amount of work involved in appraising a regional shopping center.

Defining the Trade Area.   The trade area served by the shopping center depends on the condition of roads, travel speed on roads, the ability to get into and out of the center, and the type of traffic using the roads. Normally, for a regional shopping center the primary trade area is limited to 30 minutes' travel time, but the center may draw from several suburban communities and the fringes of one or more large cities.[2] Some regional or super-regional shopping centers, like the newly developed Mall of America in Bloomington, Minnesota, can draw customers from all across the country. The size of the trade area will depend also on the number of stores in the center and the cumulative pull of the store mix. A good selection of merchandise in each store can create a greater customer draw than an otherwise comparable center offering a less desirable selection of merchandise.

Physical and Environmental Data.   A physical inspection of the property should be made to determine if major expenditures, like a new roof or storefront, or other capital investment must be made. The inspection should also reveal whether sufficient parking is available, whether traffic problems adversely affect the center, and whether there is any functional obsolescence. A tour of each store should be made to determine the product mix, selection of merchandise, and price ranges.

---

[2] A *primary trade area* is thought of as the geographic core from which a store or shopping center gets the most business. This is typically the area closest to the store and with the highest density of customers to population. A *secondary trade area* is that area adjoining the primary trade area and with the next highest ratio of customers to population. The *tertiary* (or *fringe*) *trade area* would be defined as the residual portions of the store's trade area.

Demographic and Social Data.   It is very necessary in appraising a regional shopping center to estimate total spending of the residents within the center's trade area.[3] After total spending for the trade area is estimated, one must determine how much purchasing power the site will attract. This entails dividing total spending among the competitive centers, based on the size, convenience, quality, attractiveness, and accessibility of each center. Collecting data on personal income per capita, income stability, and homogeneity of professional or business activity is also extremely important.

Forces of Supply and Demand.   A market survey of competing centers should be made. Each competing center should be scored in terms of store mix, price ranges for merchants, and volume of sales per square foot of retail area. A regional survey should also be made to determine changes in road patterns; general economic conditions, trends in wage rates and unemployment and new business entry into the area, and the effects of new governmental policy on the area. Consideration must also be given to estimating the entry of new households into the area. Change is a very important force in appraising shopping centers. In order for the center to be successful, the location must have a future and must be able to compete with potential future centers.

Income and Expense Data.   Property tax records should be inspected to determine current assessed values and whether assessed values are too high or too low. Estimates of future property tax rates should be made. Operating expenses should be examined to determine if there is a substantial understatement of current expenses. Rental rates and lease terms for every tenant should be reviewed. Percentage rent rates should also be given full consideration.[4]

Highest-and-Best-Use Analysis.   Identifying the highest and best use of the site is of utmost importance in the valuation of any property. If the value of the site exceeded the value of the total improved property, this would mean that the property should be made vacant by demolishing the shopping center (assuming that the return from the new improvements would more than offset the cost of demolishing the existing building and constructing a new one). Highest-and-best-use analysis should be done separately for the site as though vacant and for the property as improved.

Sales of Comparable Properties.   Identify similar, recently sold shopping centers for which pertinent data are available. Determine if these properties are comparable, according to terms of sale, time of sale, location, physical characteristics, economic characteristics, and use. Analyze the dissimilarities between the comparable properties and the subject property to determine the market value of the shopping center. Remember that an informed purchaser will pay no more for the shopping center than when he or she should have to pay for an existing property with equal utility. Lack of adequate market data may limit the usefulness of the sales-comparison approach in valuing a regional shopping center.

---

[3] Actually, total purchasing power in the trade area depends on the number of households in the trade area, the average income per household, and the average propensity for households to consume.

[4] Retail tenants typically pay a minimum fixed rental plus a percentage of rent over a sliding scale sales schedule. The percentage rent assures both tenant and owner of fairness. As more units of merchandise are sold, rents rise to reflect the increased popularity of the center.

Income Approach to Value. To complete the income approach, first estimate the net operating income of the property. Then determine an appropriate rate at which to discount the income stream. Value is determined as the present worth of the expected future stream of income.

Cost Approach to Value. The cost approach to value requires estimating the cost of the major site improvements and then adjusting for any loss in value of the property owing to diminished utility (e.g., accrued depreciation). Adding the land value to the net cost of the improvements enables one to arrive at the estimated market value of the shopping center under the cost approach. A rational investor will pay no more for the shopping center than the cost of acquiring a vacant site and constructing a building and other improvements to develop a property of equal utility.

Reconciliation. *Reconciliation* is the process of resolving differences in value and of researching a most probable sales price for the shopping center. Reconciliation involves weighing and comparing the indications of value according to the quality of the available data, the appropriateness of the approach for the type of property being analyzed, and the value being sought. Reconciliation is a thought and judgment process; it is not the simple averaging of the value indications. In some situations, appraisers attach a range, similar to the standard deviation, or to the market value estimate.

SUMMARY

The appraiser's role in most situations is to determine the amount, in cash, goods, or services, for which a property may be exchanged. An appraisal may also be requested when the financing of a property interest depends on a market value estimate of the property, or when owners take out insurance to protect against risk of property loss or damage, or when an investor takes exception with the taxes levied against the property, or simply to help the investor determine the best way to use a property.

The appraisal process is identical for all properties and entails:

1. *Defining the Problem.* Agreement is needed on the identification of the property and the legal rights to be valued, on the specific purpose of the appraisal, and the date for which the value estimate is desired.

2. *Making a survey and plan.* The appraiser must decide which of the several alternative approaches to value can be used and the effort likely to be involved, and the fee should be agreed upon. The three approaches to value are the sales-comparison approach, the income approach, and the cost approach. Reconciliation involves weighing and comparing the market value indications from the three approaches to value according to the quality of the available data and the appropriateness of the approach for the kind of property.

3. *Collecting and Organizing the Data.* National, regional, community, and neighborhood data must be collected and analyzed to provide a background for the specific approaches to value.

Underlying the appraisal process are several basic principles: (1) that a rational buyer will pay no more for the property than the cost of acquiring an equally desirable alternative property; (2) that the value of a property is the present value of the future benefits; (3) that real estate is a dynamic market, with social and economic forces constantly causing changes that affect the value of a property; (4) that the value of any component of a property depends on how much its presence adds to the overall value of the property; and (5) that the property is allocated to its highest-and-best use.

KEY CONCEPTS

Appraisal   An estimate of the value of a property, or of some interest therein.

Appraisal process   An orderly, well conceived set of procedures used in making an appraisal.

Market price   Amount actually negotiated between a buyer and a seller for a property; a historical fact.

Market value   The most probable selling price of a parcel of real estate; often equated to value in exchange. (More technical definitions are used by professional appraisers.)

Objective value   A "neutral" estimate of the value of properties based on market price information.

Subjective value   Dependence of worth on the nature and mental attitude of the person making the judgment.

Value in exchange   Price that a property would most probably bring if sold; synonymous with objective value or market value.

Value in use   Worth of a property based on its merits to a specific user; usually greater than market value.

QUESTIONS FOR REVIEW AND DISCUSSION

1. List and explain briefly three major reasons for appraisals.

2. Distinguish among the following:

    a. Market value

    b. Value in exchange

    c. Objective value

    d. Reproduction cost

    e. Market price

    f. Value in use

    g. Subjective value

    h. Replacement cost

3. List and explain at least three principles of market value appraising, including the principle of substitution.

4. What attributes are necessary for a parcel of real estate to have value?

5. When determining market value of a property, what assumptions are implicit in the valuation process?

6. What is meant by highest-and-best use? Describe a scenario whereby a current use is not the highest-and-best use?

7. Explain the purpose and process of reconciliation.

8. Generally speaking, when doing an appraisal to determine fair market value, should the current use or the highest-and-best use be valued?

9. What three techniques are commonly used to arrive at fair market value for appraisals?

PROBLEMS

1. A house sold six months ago for $70,000. Currently, a potential buyer wishes to build a small commercial building on the site. If this buyer is willing to pay $150,000 for the site and there are no other uses for the site other than its current use or a small commercial building, what is the highest and best use? If it cost $90,000 in administrative and legal fees to change the zoning on the site to allow for a commercial building, does the highest-and-best use for the site change?

2. A projected five-year income stream for an income-producing property is $75,000 during year 1, and grows at 3 percent per year thereafter. The cash throw-off from sale at the end of year 5 is expected to be $110,000. Using a 10 percent discount rate, what is the market value of the property using the income approach to value?

CHAPTER 10

INCOME-PROPERTY ANALYSIS AND APPRAISAL

Chapter Outline

There are few sorrows, however poignant,
in which a good income is of no avail.

Logan Pearsall Smith

In this chapter we extend the basic valuation concepts introduced in Chapter 3. Our attention here is directed to the estimation of market value for income-producing property. Income-producing real estate is generally owned as an investment. In turn, the value of any income property is a direct result of the quality, amount, and duration of the income it generates. That is, the higher the earning power of a property, the greater its value.

Valuing income properties involves estimating both market value and investment value. *Investment value* is the value to a specific investor and is akin to subjective value, or value in use. Market value, as discussed in Chapter 9, is the most probable selling price and is equivalent to objective value or value in exchange. Market value is based on impersonal, detached, market-oriented data and assumptions; investment value on the other hand depends on data and assumptions that are personal and subjective. Market and investment value may coincide if the data and assumptions of the specific investor are the same as those of the typical investor in the market.

Market value is clearly the focal point of almost any real estate decision. Whether buying, selling, investing, developing, lending, exchanging, renting, assessing, or acquiring property for public use, market value needs to be known for the decision and action to be sound.

HOW INCOME PROPERTIES ARE VALUED

We showed in Chapter 3 that the market value of an income-producing property is the present value of an expected cash flow stream. This is usually written as

$$MV_0 = \sum_{t=1}^{n} \frac{NOI_t}{(1 + r)^t} + \frac{MV_n}{(1 + r)^n}$$

where MV_0 is the current market value of the property, NOI_t is the property's net operating income at time t, MV_n is the expected sales price of the property at the end of n period, and n is some finite holding period. Here we ignore the effects of selling expenses on the net sales proceeds at disposition. The term Σ is a shorthand notation for the word *summation.* Therefore, the equation above could also be written as:

$$MV_0 = \frac{NOI_1}{(1 + r)^1} + \frac{NOI_2}{(1 + r)^2} + \cdots + \frac{NOI_n}{(1 + r)^n} + \frac{MV_n}{(1 + r)^n}$$

171

Notice that if this price formula holds, then investors n periods from now will also determine MV_n by looking at the property's net operating income and its expected sales proceeds over the m-period holding period from $t = n + 1$ to $t = n + m$. This means that we can express MV_n in terms of NOI_t and MV_{n+m}:

$$MV_n = \sum_{t=n+1}^{n+m} \frac{NOI_t}{(1 + r)^{t-n}} + \frac{MV_{n+m}}{(1 + r)^m}$$

The same is true for the value of the property when it is resold at time $n + m$:

$$MV_{n+m} = \sum_{t=n+m+1}^{n+m+k} \frac{NOI_t}{(1 + r)^{t-n-k}} + \frac{MV_{n+m+k}}{(1 + r)^k}$$

In this case we assume that the property will be held for k periods; that is, from time $n + m + 1$ to time $n + m + k$.

In principle, with an infinite horizon and an infinite chain of investors succeeding each other, the market value of the property is

$$MV_0 = \sum_{t=1}^{\infty} \frac{NOI_t}{(1 + r)^t}$$

where the sign ∞ is used to indicate infinity.

This discounted cash flow formula for the market value of real estate reduces to

$$MV_0 = \frac{NOI}{r - g} = \frac{NOI}{R_0}$$

assuming NOI is growing at a constant rate, g, and $g < r$. In valuation terminology, the above expression is known as the *direct income capitalization approach* and $R_0 = r - g$ is known as the *capitalization rate* or *going-in rate*. The idea of direct income capitalization is to convert a stream of expected future income payments into a lump sum, or capital, value. See Figure 10–1 for the steps involved.

RELATIONSHIP BETWEEN DISCOUNT RATES AND CAPITALIZATION RATES

It is extremely important to distinguish between discount rates and capitalization rates. As discussed in Chapter 3, discount rates represent the required rate of return, or yield, on real estate. For a retail shopping center, for example, pretax yields might range from 11 to 15 percent, depending on the risk involved. On a high-rise suburban office building pretax yields might range from 12 to 17 percent.

Capitalization rates, on the other hand, are net of value appreciation or depreciation. In times of rapid inflation, a very low capitalization rate is likely. Also, experience has shown that capitalization rates vary over time with the fluctuation in interest rates. To illustrate, consider the recent acquisition of South Hills Village Mall, one of Pittsburgh's oldest enclosed malls, by the New York-based O'Connor Group. The O'Connor Group purchased the 24-year-old mall on behalf of Shopping Center Associates, an investment group, and an unidentified investor.

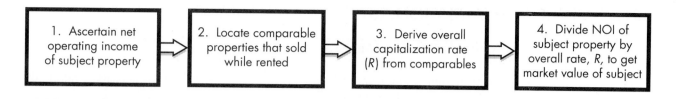

FIGURE 10–1
Steps in the Direct Capitalization Approach to Estimating Market Value

Suppose the O'Connor Group expects to earn an 11 percent pretax return on the investment. Further suppose that South Hills Village Mall is expected to appreciate by 3.5 percent per annum. This means

$$R_0 = r - g$$
$$= 11\% - 3.5\% = 7.5\%$$

The R_0 in this example is 7.5 percent. But the expected pretax rate of return on investment is 11 percent. The lower R_0 gives a higher value, reflecting favorable future income and/or capital gains expectations.

Notice that we could have just as easily dealt with the situation in which South Hills Village Mall was expected to depreciate by 3.5 percent per annum. In this case the overall capitalization rate is

$$R_0 = r - g$$
$$= 11\% - (-3.5\%) = 14.5\%$$

The effect of this assumption is to raise, rather than lower, the overall capitalization rate and to lower appraised value for a given NOI. The negative 3.5 percent premium in this case represents a *recapture premium*—that is, an amortization of the building component. This is as it should be; absent inflation, NOI must also provide for a return *of* the invested capital. Otherwise there would be no mechanism by which investors could recapture the building's future depreciation.

There is also the possibility that with a 25-year remaining economic life, South Hills Village Mall could depreciate in real terms by 1.5 percent per annum, while appreciating in nominal terms by 3.5 percent per annum. The net (of depreciation) recapture rate in this case is 2 percent and the overall capitalization rate applicable to the building is

$$R_0 = r - g$$
$$= 11\% - 2\% = 9\%$$

Appropriate capitalization rates are clearly influenced by the conditions under which the particular investment is being operated. Capitalization rates are also affected by prevailing interest rates, availability of funds, and risk.

DERIVING THE CAPITALIZATION RATE

Market-Extraction Method

Direct income capitalization is most meaningful when the capitalization rate is derived from the market. This is called the *market-extraction method.*

Assuming comparable income properties can be found, the only information required about each property is its net operating income and its sale price. Dividing the sale price into the net operating income yields

$$R_0 = r - g = \frac{NOI}{MV_0}$$

This is really only a reversal of the process of estimating MV_0.

With three comparable office buildings, the calculations might be as follows:

$$\text{For comparable 1} \quad R_0 = \frac{\$594,000}{\$6,000,000} = 0.0990, \text{ or } 9.9\%$$

$$\text{For comparable 2} \quad R_0 = \frac{\$748,000}{\$7,400,000} = 0.1011, \text{ or } 10.01\%$$

$$\text{For comparable 3} \quad R_0 = \frac{\$465,000}{\$4,680,000} = 0.0994, \text{ or } 9.94\%$$

On the basis of these three ratios, an overall capitalization rate of 10 percent would seem to be a reasonable reflection of what the market is actually doing.

Given an estimate of R_0, finding the indicated market value of an income-producing property is straightforward. The NOI of the subject property is divided by the market-derived overall capitalization rate, R_0.

The proper calculation is

$$MV_0 = \frac{NOI}{.1000} = \frac{\$780,000}{.1000} = \$7,800,000$$

assuming that NOI in a stabilized year of operation for the subject property is $780,000. With R_0 equal to 10 percent, we obtain an indicated market value of $7,800,000.

Band-of-Investment Method

Under the *band-of-investment method,* individual rates of interest applicable to properties that use both debt and equity financing are weighted to arrive at the market rate of capitalization. To illustrate: Assuming that first mortgage loans are made for up to 65 percent of property value at 8 percent interest for 20 years (monthly compounding), and that the equity balance requires a return of 12 percent—after provision for appreciation or depreciation—to be financially attractive to owners or investors, then the market rate would be as follows:

1. We know that the lender will require an 8 percent return on all funds advanced. We also know that the lender requires that the first mortgage loan be amortized

over 20 years, with monthly compounding. Thus, we must set aside an annuity each month to pay off the mortgage at the end of 20 years. The amount of the annuity at 8 percent interest for 20 years is

$$\text{Return of capital to lender} = \frac{i}{(1 + i)^n - 1}$$

$$= \frac{.08/12}{(1 + .08/12)^{240} - 1}$$

$$= .0017 \text{ per month}$$

$$= .0017 \times 12 = .0204 \text{ per annum}$$

This fraction is known as a *sinking fund factor*—that is, it is the amount that must be set aside each period to have $1 at the end of 20 years if we are paying an 8 percent rate. This fraction can also be computed using a financial calculator. Simply enter $1 for future value, 8% ÷ 12 for interest rate, 20 × 12 = 240 for the number of periods, and solve for the annuity payment. Then multiply by 12 to convert to an annual interest rate factor.

The total required payment to the lender is thus

$$\text{Mortgage constant} = \text{return on funds} + \text{return of capital to lender}$$
$$= .08 + .0204$$
$$= 10.04\%$$

2. We know that the equity investor requires a return of 12 percent after provision for appreciation or depreciation. Thus, the weighted average rate is

SPLIT INTEREST	PERCENT OF VALUE		SPLIT RATE	WEIGHTED RATE
First mortgage	65%	×	10.04%	= 6.53%
Equity	35%	×	12.00%	= 4.20%
Total	1.00			10.73%

If the net income of a property were $800,000 per annum, then the capitalized value of that income at 10.73 percent would be $800,000 divided by .1073, or $7,455,732. The income of $800,000 would be distributed as follows:

SPLIT INTEREST	VALUE		RATE OF EARNING		DOLLAR EARNINGS
First mortgage	$4,846,226	×	10.04%	=	$487,000
Equity	$2,609,506	×	12.00%	=	$313,000
Total	$7,455,732				$800,000

It is to be emphasized that the weighted average rate 10.73 percent in this example represents an *overall capitalization rate* for the property. It applies to any property that is 65 percent debt-financed that is priced to yield a total required payment to the lender of 10.04 percent and a cash-on-cash return to the equity investor of 12 percent. This 12 percent cash-on-cash return to the equity investor is known as the *equity dividend rate.*

Built-Up Method

Under the *built-up method,* the rate of capitalization would be a composite of the following: (1) pure interest, i.e., interest that can be secured on government bonds (adjusted for the tax savings associated with real estate); (2) rate for nonliquidity, i.e., rate necessary to compensate for relative inability to cash in the investment; (3) a recapture premium, i.e., a return of investment or an adjustment for appreciation; and (4) rate of risk. The risk rate varies with the type of investment.

To illustrate, the rate applicable to an equity property may be composed as follows:

Pure interest	6.50 percent
Nonliquidity	1.00 percent
Recapture premium	2.00 percent
Risk (of loss)	2.00 percent
Total	11.50 percent

The recapture premium in this case provides for a 2 percent return of investment, net of appreciation. This adjustment to the pure interest rate accounts for the fact that improvements have limited lives. It also supposedly accounts for the value of the land 10, 30, 50, or more years in the future, when its availability, free from present structural improvements, may be counted on, and it also accounts for any appreciation or depreciation in the value of the improvements.

Here is a simple example. We will make the following assumptions to demonstrate the application of the built-up method of capitalization.

Net operating income	$130,000
Anticipated economic life of structure	50 years
Pure interest rate	6.50%
Nonliquidity premium	2.00%
Recapture premium	2.00%
Risk premium	1.50%

The built-up rate is thus

$$R_0 = 6.50\% + 2.00\% + 2.00\% + 1.50\% = 12.00\%$$

which provides for an amortization rate of 2 percent per year (under the assumption that the property is expected to last fifty years).

The capitalized value of net income is

$$MV = \frac{NOI}{R_0}$$

$$= \frac{\$130,000}{.12}$$

$$= \$1,083,333$$

The higher the built-up rate of capitalization when applied to a given income, the lower the resultant value. To illustrate, suppose the built-up rate of capitalization were equal to 18 percent. With no change in net income, the capitalized value would be

$$
\begin{aligned}
MV &= \frac{NOI}{R_0} \\
&= \frac{\$130,000}{.18} \\
&= \$722,222
\end{aligned}
$$

To be conservative, therefore, many appraisers use a high built-up rate for capitalization of net income.

LIMITATIONS OF DIRECT CAPITALIZATION

The chief difficulty in the direct capitalization approach to value lies in the selection of a capitalization rate. In order to make the maximum use of the capitalization approach, the capitalization rate must accurately reflect the behavior of investors in the marketplace. This difficulty might explain why appraisers typically regard the capitalization rate as a ratio that is derived from the market. Recall that the ratio of net operating income to value is a direct measure of the capitalization rate on a specific property. Where such data are available and of sufficient quality, viewing the capitalization rate as a ratio provides the most compelling evidence of the equity yields necessary to attract potential investors. Where the data on net operating income or value are lacking, or are not clear, as frequently happens, the appraiser must select a capitalization rate by considering the equity yield rates and financing conditions available, plus the possibility of increased rentals and capital appreciation. In selecting a capitalization rate, certainty of the returns, the relative ease of liquidation of the investment, the relative burden of managing the investment,and the possibility of producing tax-sheltered cash flow must also be considered.

Also note that the income approach to value, as a rule, is limited to property that is used primarily for income or investment purposes. It does not provide an accurate valuation of owner-occupied homes because the benefits or amenities derived by owners are difficult to measure in terms of dollars, or even as hypothetical rental income. For apartment houses, commercial, or industrial properties, however, the income approach is applicable.

GROSS INCOME MULTIPLIER TECHNIQUE

The *gross income multiplier technique* is also used primarily for income-producing properties. A *gross income multiplier* (GIM) relates total annual income to market value. The basic steps in the GIM technique are: (1) ascertain the gross annual market income of the subject property, (2) derive a GIM from the market, and (3) apply the GIM to the subject property to estimate its market value. For small, one- to four-family residential properties, monthly rental is commonly used instead of gross annual market income.

Derivation of the market GIM is equivalent to extracting the market capitalization rate. That is, sales prices of comparable properties are divided by their respective gross annual incomes to get a range of GIMs. Sample calculations follow.

Suppose we collected a sample of three comparable brownstone rental dwelling units. The term *brownstone* is used as a generic word to denote small, urban, multiple dwellings (up to 10 units) that either are rented or sold as condominiums. These buildings may also be called *graystones* or *townhouses.* Dividing sales price by the gross annual market income gives a GIM. The calculations are:

$$GIM \text{ for a property} = \frac{\text{Sales price}}{\text{Gross annual income}}$$

$$GIM, \text{ comparable } 1 = \frac{\$610,000}{\$101,400} = 6.02$$

$$GIM, \text{ comparable } 2 = \frac{\$745,760}{\$124,500} = 5.99$$

$$GIM, \text{ comparable } 3 = \frac{\$680,000}{\$113,200} = 6.01$$

On the basis of these calculations, a market GIM of 6.00 seems reasonable for brownstone units in this particular neighborhood at this time.

Applying the market GIM to the gross annual income of the subject property, $108,000, gives an indicated market value of

$$\text{Indicated market value} = \text{Gross income} \times \text{Market-derived GIM}$$
$$= \$108,000 \times 6.00 = \$648,000$$

LIMITATIONS OF THE GIM TECHNIQUE

One of the major limitations of the gross income multiplier approach is that sales of some types of income properties occur infrequently; thus, the derivation of a market GIM must be based on limited information. In addition, rental data are not always available for deriving the multiplier. Another limitation is that gross rents are used instead of net operating income; if the building-to-land ratios differ, or if the buildings are different ages, the results may be distorted. Further, the GIM is subject to some distortion because adverse zoning, lack of maintenance, or heavy property taxes will negatively influence sale price with little effect on rental levels. Thus, unless the comparables are similar in all respects, a distorted GIM may be derived from the market. Finally, the technique is not useful for properties that are unique or that generate income in the form of amenities.

SUMMARY

The procedure whereby the market value of income-producing property is calculated by capitalizing the annual net income generated by the property at an overall capitalization rate is known as direct capitalization. The process can be summarized as follows:

$$MV_0 = \frac{NOI}{R_0}$$

where MV_0 is market value, NOI is annual net income, and R_0 is the capitalization rate necessary to attract investors.

The capitalization rate represents the required rate of return, or yield, on real estate, less the possibility of capital appreciation. Also considered by investors in selecting a capitalization rate are the certainty of the returns, the relative ease of liquidation of the investment, the relative burden of managing the investment, and the possibility of producing tax-sheltered cash flow. In order to make maximum use of the direct capitalization approach, the capitalization rate must accurately reflect the behavior of investors in the marketplace.

An alternative, income approach to value is the gross income multiplier (GIM) technique. The GIM approach to value relates total annual income to market value. The basic formula is

Indicated market value = Gross income × Market-derived GIM

The GIM multiplier is derived by looking at the sales prices of comparable properties, divided by their respective gross annual incomes.

KEY CONCEPTS

Band-of-investment method   A widely used approach to estimate an overall capitalization rate. It is based on the premise that debt and equity financing is typically involved in a real estate transaction.

Built-up method   A method of identifying the basic elements of the overall capitalization rate.

Direct income capitalization approach   Division of net operating income by an overall capitalization rate to arrive at market value.

Equity dividend rate   Income rate that reflects the relationship between equity income and equity capital.

Gross income multiplier (GIM)   A ratio derived from the market; sales price divided by annual gross income equals GIM.

Market-extraction method   Method used to estimate the overall capitalization rate by dividing the sale price of a comparable income property into the net operating income.

Overall capitalization rate   A ratio in property valuation; net operating income divided by sale price. Also known as the going-in rate.

Recapture premium   Provision for a return of investment, net of value appreciation.

Sinking fund factor   Amount that must be set aside each period to have $1 at some future point in time.

QUESTIONS FOR REVIEW AND DISCUSSION

1. What is the difference between investment value and market value? Are they ever the same?

2. Are capitalization rates the same as discount rates? If not, how do they differ?

3. What are some indirect factors that may affect the capitalization rate?

4. If a property is expected to decrease in value in the future, what will happen to the capitalization rate, all else being equal?

5. What three steps are involved in using the gross income multiplier approach to value?

6. What are some inherent weaknesses with the gross income multiplier approach?

7. Depreciation need not be considered in market value appraising because it is more than offset by inflation. Is this true? Discuss.

8. Is depreciation taken into account in the GIM technique of the income approach to value? If so, how? Explain.

9. How do market values adjust or change in response to changes in demand? How is changing value incorporated into estimates of value by appraisers?

10. Relate the following to the income approach to value:

    a. The three basic steps of the GIM technique

    b. Two appropriate applications of each

    c. Two limitations of each

PROBLEMS

1. An office building is expected to produce an initial income stream at the end of year 1 of $62,000 and to grow thereafter at 4 percent per year. If an investor expects a 10 percent rate of return, what is the value of the property with no appreciation or depreciation expected? What is the value of the property if the income stream is expected to decrease by 4 percent per year?

2. A 50,000-square foot warehouse will be depreciating at 5 percent per year. During the same period, the building will appreciate in nominal terms by 4.75 percent. If the initial income stream is $200,000 and the discount rate is 12 percent, what is the value of the property? If the building cost $20 per square foot to construct, how much is the land worth?

3. An office building situated on a 1-acre parcel of land has an expected gross income of $106,000 per year with a vacancy rate of 7.5 percent. What is the value of the property and improvements assuming a gross income multiplier of 6.5? If land in the area is worth $45,000 per acre, what is the value of the building?

4. You are a loan officer. An owner approaches your lending institution for a $1,000,000 mortgage loan. The parcel is vacant, with commercial zoning and an appraised market value of $500,000. The proposed improvements will cost $1,100,000, based on firm contractor estimates. No depreciation or diminished utility is expected because the structure would be well designed.

Your institution has an established policy of a 65 percent maximum loan-to-value ratio on commercial loans. The building is expected to have a 50-year economic life. The current interest rate is 12 percent. Expected potential gross income is $300,000 per annum. Vacancy losses are 5 percent. Operating expenses are $109,000 per annum. Local gross income multipliers for this type of property typically run about 5.2. Overall capitalization rates range from 11.1 to 11.3 percent in the area. Determine the following.

a. Indicated market value, using the GIM technique

b. Indicated market value, using the overall capitalization rate

c. Your estimate of market value, after reconciling the two approaches

d. Would the requested loan be within your institution's guidelines?

5. You are an appraiser for UWREC and are asked to appraise a 14,300-square-foot Class B office building in the central business district of Whereverville in 19xx. You are given the following information to use in valuing the property:

Potential gross income	$113,000
Vacancy and collection losses,	
5% of potential gross income	$16,500
Operating expenses	
Utilities	$18,200
Repairs	$5,600
Maintenance	$18,600
Property taxes	$19,000
Insurance	$5,100
Assumed growth rates per year	
Rental income	4%
Repairs and maintenance	6%
Property taxes	6%
Insurance	4.5%
Utilities	3%
Equity dividend rate	16%
Loan information	
Loan to value ratio	75%
Mortgage interest rate	10%
Loan amortization period	20 years

a. Determine the overall capitalization rate using the band-of-investment approach.

b. What elements go into calculating the equity dividend rate?

c. Compute the value of the office building using the direct capitalization method.

d. Determine the value of the office building using a before-tax discounted cash flow model. Assume that the expected selling price at the end of year 6 is 7.5 times the NOI. Selling expenses are expected to be 5 percent of the sales price.

CHAPTER 11

APPRAISING FOR SINGLE-FAMILY PROPERTIES

Chapter Outline

The true worth of anything is just as much as it will bring.
Unknown, *The Spectator*, 1908.

In appraising for single-family properties, the best approach is to identify similar, recently sold properties for which pertinent data are available, analyze the dissimilarities between the comparable properties and the subject property, and then estimate the market value of the subject property. For this *sales-comparison approach* to be useful, ample sales of equally comparable properties must be available.

The second-best approach is to rely on the cost approach to value, which works well for new or nearly new properties. The cost approach requires that you estimate the cost of the improvements—including any extras like a garage or carport, fireplace, and built-in appliances—deduct the loss in value caused by physical deterioration, functional obsolescence, and adverse economic influences, and then add the market value of the land.

Examples given in this chapter will show you how to apply the appraisal process to single-family residential properties. A time-tested, inside secret of successful residential appraisers is to choose your comparable properties wisely. A comparable property which matches the subject property in most respects will minimize the chance of errors when estimating the market value of the subject property. It is also important to note that the sales comparison approach can be applied in certain circumstances to nonresidential properties as well, provided, of course, ample sales of comparable properties are available.

DIRECT SALES-COMPARISON APPROACH

The direct sales-comparison approach to value, also termed the market approach, provides for the estimation of market value by referring to recent sales, or listing and offering prices, of comparable properties. The underlying assumption is that a potential owner will pay no more for the subject property than would probably have to be paid for another equally desirable property—that is, an existing property with utility equal to the subject property.

The direct sales-comparison approach involves four basic steps: (1) collect data on sales of comparable properties, (2) select units of comparison and do necessary calculations, (3) adjust sales prices to subject property, and (4) estimate market value of subject property (see Figure 11–1).

Collecting Data on Comparable Sales

The first step in the direct sales-comparison approach is to locate comparable properties, with the same highest and best use, which have sold recently. All comparable

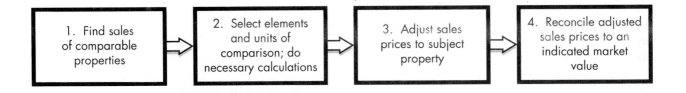

| 1. Find sales of comparable properties | ⟹ | 2. Select elements and units of comparison; do necessary calculations | ⟹ | 3. Adjust sales prices to subject property | ⟹ | 4. Reconcile adjusted sales prices to an indicated market value |

FIGURE 11–1
Steps in the Direct Sales-Comparison Approach to Market Value

properties should be reasonably similar to the subject with respect to size, design, type of construction, physical condition, and location. In an active residential real estate market, to qualify as a comparable property all properties should have sold within the last three months.

Selecting Units of Comparison

Between the comparable properties and the subject property there should be similarities in the number of rooms, bathrooms, bedrooms, size of lot, building age, style, and condition. Adjustments for any significant differences are to be made either in dollar terms or percentage terms. Adjustments in some circumstances can also be made in terms of dollars per square feet.

Adjustments

Adjustments are made from the comparables to the subject property. It would be improper to adjust from the subject to the comparable because the price of the subject is not known. Second, adjusting comparables to the subject provides a base market value for the subject—that is, each of the comparables is being compared with the subject rather than with each other. Generally speaking, the greater the likeness between a comparable and a subject property, the fewer the adjustments necessary and the more reliable the resulting value estimate. Listing and offering prices are sometimes used if a sufficient number of sales of comparable properties cannot be found.[1]

The ratio, sales price per square foot, is the one most frequently used in making adjustments from a comparable to a subject. Sales price per living unit, or per room, is also used in comparing single-family houses and condominiums.

Differences that require adjustment between comparables and a subject property fall into nine general categories: (1) the real property rights conveyed, (2) financing terms, (3) conditions of sale, (4) market conditions (i.e., time of sale), (5) location, (6) physical characteristics, (7) economic characteristics, (8) use, and (9) non-realty components of value.

Real Property Interests Conveyed. Transaction prices vary depending on the real property interest that is conveyed. Assume two comparable properties: Both properties border the Potomac River in Washington, D.C., and both properties were

---

[1] We advise extreme caution in using listing and offering prices if a sufficient number of sales of comparable properties cannot be found. Listing and offering prices often tend to overstate market values.

sold subject to a scenic easement which prevents the use of the property for construction of anything but low-rise structures thereby forever preserving the scenic beauty of a portion of the Potomac River. Further assume that the subject property borders the Potomac River but is sold free and clear of any scenic easements.

Now compare the subject property to the comparable properties. When residential real estate is sold subject to a scenic easement, the value reflects the rights in the property to build a larger house. Having said this, logically the subject property in our example should sell for more than the comparable properties, all else being equal. It is therefore extremely important to adjust for any differences in the real property interest that is being conveyed.

Financing Terms. Favorable financing terms typically result in a transaction price that is higher than a normal market transaction. For example, consider a buyer interested in acquiring a $100,000 single-family residence. The seller, eager to encourage the sale, offers to help finance the sale by lending $100,000 at a subsidized rate of 6 percent. The current market interest rate for this type of property is 10 percent.

The favorable financing terms in this case result in a savings of $278.02 per month on a 30-year mortgage.[2] The present value of these payment savings, discounted at the current market interest rate of 10 percent is

$$PV \text{ of payment savings} = \frac{\$278.02}{(1 + .10/12)^1} + \frac{\$278.02}{(1 + .10/12)^2} + \cdots + \frac{\$278.02}{(1 + .10/12)^{360}}$$

$$= \$31,681$$

Because the buyer cannot take advantage of the payment savings without purchasing the property, the present value of these payment savings should be added to the transaction price of the house:

$$\text{Transaction price} = MV_0 + \text{Present value of payment savings}$$
$$= \$100,000 + \$31,681$$
$$= \$131,681$$

For a $100,000 single-family residence, a buyer might pay as much as $131,681 in order to purchase the property at the subsidized finance rate.

[2] The monthly payment on a $100,000 mortgage with a 10 percent interest rate for 30 years is the payment that solves the following formula:

$$\$100,000 = \frac{\text{Payment}}{(1 + .10/12)^1} + \frac{\text{Payment}}{(1 + .10/12)^2} + \cdots + \frac{\text{Payment}}{(1 + .10/12)^{360}}$$

Solving for the monthly payment yields

$$\text{Payment} = \frac{\$100,000}{\frac{1}{(1 + .10/12)^1} + \frac{1}{(1 + .10/12)^2} + \cdots + \frac{1}{(1 + .10/12)^{360}}}$$

$$= \$877.57$$

Likewise, the monthly payment on a $100,000 mortgage with a 6 percent interest rate for 30 years is $599.55; thus, the monthly savings is $877.57 − $599.55 = $278.02. For a more in-depth discussion, see Chapter 20.

What if we were to use this transaction as a comparable? Clearly, the normal sale price of the property is

$$
\begin{aligned}
MV_0 &= \text{Transaction price} - \text{Present value of payment savings} \\
&= \$131,681 - \$31,681 \\
&= \$100,000
\end{aligned}
$$

Using $131,681 would overstate the property value under normal financing terms. Therefore, a negative adjustment is made to the comparable property for favorable financing terms.

Conditions of Sale. The price for a comparable property should reflect an arm's length, or neutral, value. Otherwise an adjustment to the price may be necessary. Differences in bargaining power between buyer and seller, undue pressure on either buyer or seller, or personal relationships within the transaction may all have caused the comparable price to be too high or too low. Price distortions can also result if an unusually high down payment is required or if one party knows more about market conditions than the other.

Market Conditions. If market conditions (e.g., amount of market activity, money availability, etc.) have changed between the time the comparable was sold and the date of the value estimate for the subject property an adjustment will be necessary. For example, higher interest rates may have slowed sales activity and lowered prices since the sale of the comparable.

Location. Locational adjustments become necessary if there are differences in either convenience or environment between the comparable and the subject property. A convenience adjustment is made if a comparable property has better or worse accessibility, or situs, than the subject property. Differences in housing quality, prevalence of deed restrictions, zoning, or neighborhood prestige all may lead to a location adjustment. Even differences in one-family houses in the same neighborhood, such as age, style, size, and condition, imply an adjustment for location.

Physical Characteristics. With single-family residential properties, differences in physical characteristics are the basis for adjustment between a comparable and a subject property. Thus, adjustments would be appropriate for differences in size, age, condition, number of rooms, number of baths, the presence or absence and size of a garage or carport, and the presence or absence of special features such as fireplaces, air conditioning, or a swimming pool.

Use. Differences in the use or the highest-and-best use of a comparable property versus a subject property can cause differences in transaction prices. For example, a piece of vacant land zoned for residential use, but which is purchased with the intention of converting the parcel to commercial use, may sell for a price that is above the market level for residential lots. Buyers may also pay more for an apartment complex purchased for conversion to condominiums.

Adjusting for differences in use or highest-and-best use is difficult. Sound advice, then, is to avoid using as a comparable, a property where there are differences in the use or the highest-and-best use.

Non-Realty Components of Value.   The non-realty components of value include furniture, fixtures, equipment, or other items that are not real property but are included in the sales price of either the comparable or the subject property. For example, in the appraisal of a single-family residence in which the seller offers the buyer a free Mercedes Benz, the value of the non-realty component must be recognized.

An Example of the Direct Sales-Comparison Approach

When using the direct sales-comparison approach, adjustments can be made either in dollar or percentage terms. Figure 11–2 shows the adjustments that might apply to a single-family residence. Note that adjustments for differences in market conditions, location, and physical characteristics are made in this example in percentage terms. In the following paragraphs we will explain the process of adjusting for comparables A and B; the reader is asked to rationalize the adjustments for C.

All sales are considered to be at arm's length and there are no special financing terms; thus, no adjustments are made for differences in financing terms or conditions of sale.[3] As for a time adjustment, values are assumed to be going up at a rate of 6 percent per year. Thus, the price of comparable A, which sold 6 months ago, is adjusted upward by 3 percent.[4] This yields a time-adjusted price for comparable A of $61.25 per square foot. The price of comparable B, which sold 5 months ago, is adjusted upward by 2.5 percent.

The subject is considered to have an average location both as to situs and environment. The convenience of comparable A is much better (which, in Figure 11–2, is indicated by above average ++); hence, a downward adjustment—in this case of 4 percent. Comparable B is slightly below average (which is indicated by below average −); hence, an upward adjustment of 2 percent is needed to adjust the price to the subject. Also, comparable A is judged to have a superior environment (above average +) relative to the subject; hence, the 2 percent downward adjustment.

Finally, adjustments are necessary for differences in physical characteristics. Comparable B is in slightly worse overall condition than the subject, and an upward adjustment of 1 percent results. Comparable A has more baths and more garage spaces than the subject, both of which require downward adjustments.

These adjustments lower the adjusted sale price of comparable A to $55.12 per square foot. Likewise, the adjusted sale price is $55.72 per square foot for comparable B and $55.56 per square foot for comparable C. Multiplying these square foot values by the area of the subject, 1,800 square feet, yields an indicated sales price range for the subject property of $99,216 to $100,296, or an average of $99,840.

Uses and Limitations

The direct sales-comparison method is well suited to making an objective estimate of a property's market value. It depends entirely on market information. Including sev-

---

[3] If adjustments for financing terms and conditions of sale were necessary, they would be made before the adjustments for market conditions, location, or physical characteristics.

[4] The adjustment for time of sale is

$$\text{Time of sale adjustment} = \frac{\text{No. months since sale of comparable}}{12} \times \text{Annual appreciation rate}$$

ITEM OF COMPARISON	SUBJECT PROPERTY	COMPARABLE A	COMPARABLE B	COMPARABLE C
		COMPARABLE SALES		
Sales price	—	$113,000	$95,000	$102,500
Unit size (square feet)	1,800	1,900	1,800	1,780
Lot size (square feet)	10,000	10,200	9,880	10,100
Sale price/square foot		$59.47	$52.78	$57.58
Real property interests conveyed	Maximum possible estate	Maximum possible estate	Maximum possible estate	Maximum possible estate
Adjusted price		$59.47	$52.78	$57.58
Financing		Conventional	Conventional	Conventional
Conditions of sale		Arm's length	Arm's length	Arm's length
Adjusted price		$59.47	$52.78	$57.58
Market conditions:				
Months since sale		6	5	1
% adjustment		3.00%	2.50%	0.50%
Adjusted price		$61.25	$54.10	$57.87
Location:				
Convenience (situs)	Average	Above average + +	Below average −	Above Average +
% adjustment		−4.00%	2.00%	−2.00%
Environment	Average	Above average +	Average	Average
% adjustment		−2.00%	0.00%	0.00%
Physical characteristics:				
Overall condition	Above average +	Above average +	Average	Average
% adjustment		0.00%	1.00%	0.00%
Number of baths	2.0	2.5	2.0	2.0
% adjustment		−2.00%	0.00%	0.00%
Garage spaces	2.0	3.0	2.0	3.0
% adjustment		−2.00%	0.00%	−2.00%
Final adjusted sales price/square foot		$55.12	$55.72	$55.56
Indicated MV of subject property		$99,216	$100,296	$100,008

FIGURE 11–2

Direct Sales-Comparison Adjustments for Single-Family Residence

eral comparables almost always ensures that the behavior of typical buyers and sellers is taken into account in the resulting value estimate. Also, the direct sales-comparison approach takes into account varying financing terms, inflation, and other market elements that influence the typical purchaser. Consequently, courts place greater emphasis and reliance on this method than on any other.

The method is most applicable when the market is active and actual sales data are plentiful and readily available. This means that the direct sales-comparison method is the one most appropriate for a widely bought and sold property type, such as vacant lots, one-family houses, and condominium units.

Lack of adequate market data is the method's major limitation. By default, the method is not applicable to the kind of property that is infrequently bought and sold or is unique—for example, a church. There are two other limitations: (1) sales of truly comparable properties must be selected, and (2) the value estimate is based on historical data. In the case of the latter limitation, there is an underlying assumption that past market trends continue on to the date of the value estimate.

The direct sales-comparison method also assumes that the property is in its highest-and-best use. What therefore might have originally been thought to be a comparable sale may not be so if the property were not allocated to its highest-and-best use.

COST APPROACH TO VALUE

The cost approach to value provides for the estimation of market value based on the cost of acquiring a vacant site and constructing a building and other improvements to develop a property. The cost approach to value is most often used when examining the feasibility of purchasing a vacant site and adding improvements versus purchasing an already improved property. To go from a vacant site to the subject property may involve adjustments in value caused by differences in utility and accrued depreciation. The underlying assumption is that a rational potential owner will not pay more for a property than the cost of producing, without undue delay, a substitute property with equal utility.

The Basic Steps

The cost approach to value involves the following basic steps: (1) estimate market value of subject site, (2) estimate reproduction cost of improvements to subject site, (3) estimate accrued depreciation and deduct from cost of improvements, and (4) add site value and depreciated costs of improvements together to get indicated market value of subject property (see Figure 11–3).

Land value is best established by the direct sales-comparison approach with similar sites.

Two ways to value the cost of new buildings are recognized. The first, *cost of replacement,* involves determining the cost of producing a building or other improvements with a utility equal to that of the subject property. Modern materials, design, and layout may be used, but the utility must be the same. *Cost of reproduction* involves determining how much it would cost to create an *exact* replica of the subject property.

After deciding whether to use replacement or reproduction cost, estimates of local construction costs per square foot or per cubic foot are obtained. The total "cost new" is then calculated by multiplying the area or volume of the improvements by the current local cost of construction.

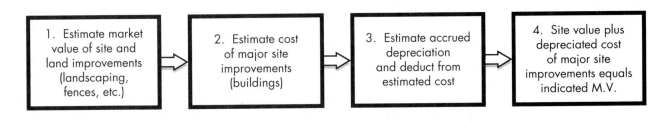

FIGURE 11–3
Basic Steps in Cost Approach to Value Method

Accrued depreciation is deducted from cost new to arrive at an indicated market value. Three types of depreciation are recognized (see Figure 11-4).

1. *Physical deterioration.* Loss in value brought about by wear-and-tear, acts of nature, or actions of the elements.

2. *Functional obsolescence.* Loss in value because of a property's inability to provide a service relative to a new property properly designed for the same use. The cause may be poor layout and design or inefficient building equipment—in short, improvements that are not up to current standards.

3. *External obsolescence.* Also termed economic, locational, or environmental obsolescence; loss in value of a site or property because of external or environmental factors that unfavorably affect the flow of income or benefits from the property, such as blight and declining demand.

An Example of the Cost Approach to Value Method

An example of the cost approach to value method seems appropriate here. To illustrate, consider the single-family residence in Figure 11-2. Assume that the cost to construct new improvements is $102,640 (see Figure 11-5). Further assume that the total loss in value from accrued depreciation is $23,240. The depreciated cost of the improvements to the site is therefore $79,400 (= cost to construct new improvements less accrued depreciation, or $102,640 − $23,240). Adding the market value of the site ($21,000) and the depreciated cost of the improvements together yields an indicated market value of $101,400.

Uses and Limitations

The cost approach to value has the greatest application in estimating the value of unique or special-purpose properties which have little or no market. Examples include churches, tank farms, and chemical plants. It is also well suited to new or nearly new properties where estimating depreciation is not difficult. The cost approach has

FIGURE 11–4
Types of Accrued
Depreciation

TYPE OF DEPRECIATION	EXPLANATION AND EXAMPLES
1. Physical deterioration	Parts of building completely used up, worn out, or deteriorated: peeling paint; leaky roof; heating, ventilating, air conditioning systems, appliances that will not work; storm damage. If deficiency involves foundation or structural mainframe, usually not curable.
2. Functional obsolescence	Aspects of building or property that work but are not up to current standards: outdated fixtures; lack of storage space; absence of a second bathroom; too few electrical outlets. If deficiency is due to architectural design, such as an inefficient floor plan, usually not curable.
3. External obsolescence	External or environmental factors that unfavorably affect the flow of benefits: neighborhood blight; noxious odors; unduly heavy traffic; nonconforming use nearby.

Land value (using direct sales comparison)		$ 14,000	
Plus: Landscaping, walks, drive, etc.		7,000	
Total site value		$ 21,000	$ 21,000
Cost to construct new improvement:			
Main structure: 1,800 square feet at $50/square foot		$ 90,000	
Garage area: 420 square feet at $12/square foot		5,040	
Miscellaneous (blinds, appliances, etc.)		7,600	
Total cost new		$102,640	
Less: Accrued depreciation			
Physical deterioration	$ 4,470		
Functional obsolescence	5,770		
External obsolescence	13,000		
Total depreciation	$23,240	− 23,240	
Depreciated value of improvements		$ 79,400	79,400
Indicated market value using cost approach			$101,400

FIGURE 11–5
Example of Cost Approach to Value

long been used in assessing for property tax purposes, which involves mass appraising and has usually demanded a standardized methodology. Property insurance adjustors rely on the cost approach because improvements often are only partially damaged or destroyed and must be either restored to their original design or completely torn down. Finally, the approach is very suitable in determining highest-and-best use of a vacant site.

One major limitation of the cost approach is that depreciation is very difficult to measure for older properties. Another is the great difficulty in allowing for differences in quality of improvements, e.g., design and style elements, kind and quality of materials, and quality of workmanship. Further, even getting an accurate estimate of cost new is difficult because costs may vary substantially from one builder to another. For these reasons, the cost approach is not as applicable as other approaches for older properties or properties that are frequently sold. Also, it is nearly impossible to find vacant lot sales to serve as comparables in determining site value in older, established neighborhoods.

RECONCILIATION

Each approach to value yields a distinct indication of market value. *Reconciliation* is the process of resolving differences in value and reaching a most-probable sales price for the property being analyzed. Reconciliation involves weighing and comparing the indications of value according to the quality of the available data and the appropriateness of the approach for the kind of property. Reconciliation is a thought and judgment process: It is not the simple averaging of the value indications. In some situations, appraisers produce a range of market value estimates, similar to a standard deviation in statistical analysis.

SUMMARY

The direct sales comparison approach to value is an extremely important tool available to residential real estate appraisers. The approach begins with obtaining prices of recent sales of properties similar to and competitive with the subject property. Adjustments to the prices of the comparable properties are then made to account for differences in real property interests conveyed, financing terms, conditions of sale, market conditions, location, physical characteristics, use, and nonreality components of value between the subject and comparable properties.

The validity of the direct sales comparison approach to value is limited primarily to very active residential real estate markets with frequent sales of comparable properties. Lack of truly comparable sales and the use of historical data may also limit the validity of the direct sales comparison approach.

The use of the cost approach to value serves primarily as a check of the direct sales comparison approach. The cost approach involves adding together the market value of the land and the reproduction cost of the improvements, each computed separately, and then deducting all accrued depreciation. Three types of accrued depreciation are recognized: physical deterioration, functional obsolescence, and economic obsolescence.

The chief difficulty of the cost approach to value lies in the realization that, at any given time, cost may or may not equal value depending on whether real estate markets are under- or overbuilt. Moreover, because of the difficulty involved in estimating accrued depreciation, the cost approach to value tends to be well suited only to new or nearly new properties.

KEY CONCEPTS

Cost approach to value   A method of valuing property based on site value plus current construction costs less accrued depreciation.

Direct sales-comparison approach   Method of valuing property based on recent sales prices of similar properties.

Reconciliation   Resolving differences in indications of value when estimating market value.

QUESTIONS FOR REVIEW AND DISCUSSION

1. What is the best approach to appraising single-family properties? What must be true about the data being used in order for this method to be effective?

2. What four steps are involved in the direct sales-comparison approach to value?

3. Is it correct to adjust value from the subject property to the comparable property or vice versa? Why?

4. What nine general categories are generally used when adjusting for differences between comparable properties and a subject property?

5. Explain how different financing terms can have an affect on the purchase price of a property.

6. If a comparable property has one less bedroom than a subject property, what adjustment would be made, and to which property would the adjustment be made?

7. What are the basic steps involved in the cost approach to value?

8. What are the three different types of depreciation?

9. When arriving at a final estimate of value for a subject property, is this estimate always a single number?

1. If a buyer of a comparable property receives seller financing of 4 percent, amortized over 20 years on the entire purchase price of $2,100,000, and the market rate for such a loan would have been 8 percent amortized over 20 years, how should the purchase price be adjusted to reflect the favorable financing terms?

2. Assume that a comparable property was sold six and a half months ago, and that similar properties have been depreciating by 5.2 percent per year. In addition, the comparable property contains two bedrooms and no garage, while the subject property has three bedrooms and a garage; analysis indicates that bedrooms add $700 of value per bedroom and garages add $400 of value. If the comparable property sold for $110,000, what is its adjusted sales price relative to the subject property?

3. Assume that a 32,000-square foot property has on it an old water tower that would cost $12,000 to demolish and remove from the site. The highest-and-best use for the property is a single-family house. If land for comparable property is worth $15 per square foot, what is the indicated value of the subject property using the cost approach to value?

4. You are appraising a vacant single-family residential lot in West Ridge, two blocks from Jefferson elementary school and three blocks from the Park Avenue neighborhood shopping center. Your client is contemplating buying the lot for personal use. The parcel is 80 by 120 feet, is located in the middle of the block, is level and on-grade with the street, and has an excellent view. The asking price is $40,000. Three sales of comparable lots, all on-grade, occurred in the last year.

   Comparable 1: 80 × 120 feet, and directly across the street, sold 2 months ago for $37,500, lacks a view
   Comparable 2: 70 × 120 feet, one block nearer school and shopping center, sold 3 months ago for $36,500, has excellent view
   Comparable 3: 80 × 120 feet, located one block nearer Jefferson school and neighborhood shopping center, sold 6 months ago for $40,000, very similar to the subject in all physical respects and has a comparable view

   Appropriate adjustments are as follows:

   For time: Values are increasing 1 percent per month
   For location: Being one block nearer school and shopping center adds 5 percent to land value. Being directly across street means exactly comparable to subject. Having high-quality view adds 5 percent to value relative to not having a view

   a. Set up a grid to adjust sales prices on a per square foot basis.

   b. Make necessary adjustments, and estimate the market value of the subject site.

   c. Is the proposed purchase at $40,000 a reasonable buy?

5. You are appraising a vacant downtown site, one and a half blocks from the main business area of Park City. The owner is contemplating a long-term lease to a local

parking lot operator. The subject parcel is 80 × 120 feet. It is located in the middle of the block, is level and on-grade with the street, and has a public rear alley. The offer is for $12,000 per year net. Three sales are available as comparables:

Comparable 1: 90 × 115 feet, directly across the street and sold 2 years ago for $82,000, level site with rear alley
Comparable 2: Corner parcel, 60 × 120 feet, one block south of subject, sold 2 months ago for $100,000, level with a rear alley
Comparable 3: 80 × 120 feet, located in the middle of the next block south, sold 6 months ago for $105,000, very similar to subject

Appropriate adjustments are as follows:

For time: Plus 10 percent per year
For location: Subject area is considered to be 10 percent better than that one block to the north and 10 percent less desirable than that one block to the south. Site across the street is comparable to the subject. A corner site is 20 percent superior to a midblock lot.

You are to analyze the property, with the following steps:

a. Diagram the locations of the vacant sites. Include some indication of relative desirability and values.

b. Set up a grid to adjust sales prices on a per square foot basis.

c. Estimate the market value of the subject site, and give recommendations for or against the proposed lease.

6. Subject property is a 75-year-old, single-family house in a residential neighborhood that is made up of homes similar in size, style, and age. The homes in the area appear to be well maintained and landscaped. The subject property is 1,150 square feet with a 1,050-square foot finished basement. It has an attached one-car garage, central air conditioning, and a fireplace. Subject property is in need of a new roof. Assume the subject property will be sold in October 19xx.

Three comparables are available:

Comparable 1: 67-year-old, 1,336-square foot single-family home located six blocks southwest of subject property. It does not have a finished basement or fireplace, but has an attached one-car garage and central air conditioning. The property was sold in June of the same year for $149,000.
Comparable 2: 65-year-old, 1,450-square foot single-family home located six blocks west of subject property. It has a partially finished basement (200 square feet), an attached one-car garage, fireplace, no central air conditioning, and a brand-new water heater and water softener. The property was sold in January of the same year for $134,000.
Comparable 3: 76-year-old, 1,823-square foot single-family home located two blocks southeast of the subject property. There is a 500-square foot finished basement, central air conditioning, attached one-car garage, and no fireplace. The property sold in June of the same year for $159,000.

The appropriate adjustments are as follows:

$2,000 per year for differences in age
9 percent per year for differences in the sales dates
$28 per square foot of finished basement

$800 for attached one-car garage

$8,200 for a fireplace

$1,500 for central air conditioning

$2,000 for a new water heater and softener

$4,000 for a new roof

a. Estimate the value of the subject property.

b. Discuss why the comparables selected are either good or bad for this appraisal of the subject property. How could they have been better? Worse?

c. What features of a home do you think most significantly affect its value and therefore must be accounted for in adjustments (e.g., number of bathrooms, swimming pool, etc.).

CHAPTER 12

ADVANCED APPRAISAL TOPICS

Chapter Outline

This chapter completes our discussion of appraisal. Here we will cover in depth the principle of highest-and-best use as it applies to appraisal theory. In any appraisal a determination first must be made as to whether the improvements constitute the highest-and-best use of the land. If they do, the appraiser proceeds, using either the income approach, direct sales-comparison approach, or cost approach to value. If the improvements do not constitute the highest-and-best use of the land, the appraiser must use caution in applying any of the three approaches to value, since the improvements would not be replaced or reproduced in their present use, type, or form.

The determination of the highest-and-best use of a given site at a given time requires careful study and expert analysis of the social, economic, and political forces that influence land utilization and income produced by the land over the estimated life of the proposed improvements.

Great care must be taken to employ land in such a manner that the present worth of future rights to income will be maximized. It is not unusual to find that the highest-and-best use of a property may be to leave it as a vacant site until such time as it ripens into a more productive use. This may be the case in cities that are undergoing rapid growth; in such a situation, future demand may warrant the construction of bigger and better improvements than those justified by the current market conditions.

Generally also, because of changes in the arts, in design, and in modes of community living, improvements erected many years ago rarely constitute the highest-and-best use of land. Where land is committed to a faulty or other-than-optimum use, it appears logical to charge the error in utilization against the value of the manmade improvements and not against the passive land that must be acted upon to yield an income. Most land, as is true of other scarce resources, is in competitive demand, and the prices bid for units or parcels of land reflect the varied use to which land can be put under alternative development. Because logically there can be but one optimum use of land at a given time under which the average net return over a period of years is highest, a choice must be made to determine which land use constitutes the highest-and-best use.

THE CONCEPT OF HIGHEST-AND-BEST USE

The concept of *highest-and-best use* can be illustrated with the help of Figure 12–1. In panel A, we have plotted the market value and construction cost (excluding land) of a hypothetical development project; in panel B we show the residual value of the land, which is simply the difference between market value and construction cost.

FIGURE 12–1
Market Value and
Construction Cost
of a Hypothetical
Development Project.
Residual Land Value
Is the Difference
Between Market Value
and Construction Cost.

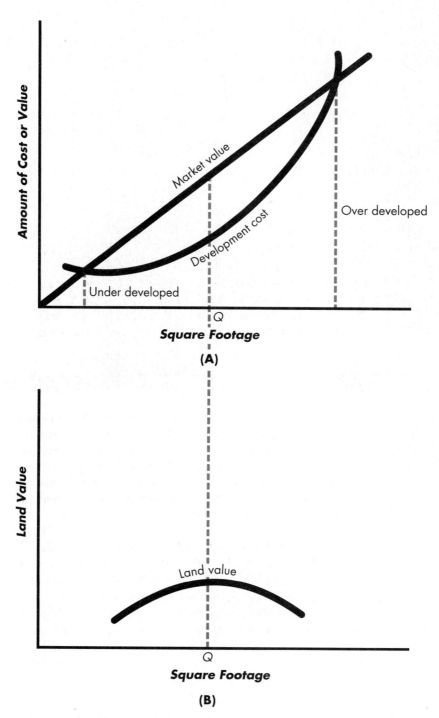

(A)

(B)

You can see that the residual value of the land varies with the gross building area. The greatest residual land value is attained at Q^*. Up to that point construction costs increase at a much slower rate than market value. Beyond Q^*, however, technological constraints will cause total construction costs to increase much more rapidly than market value.

This illustration would suggest that Q^* is the highest-and-best use or the optimum use of the site. After all, Q^* produces the highest residual value of the land. But wait, there is more!

Other Factors to Consider

Put yourself in the shoes of our hypothetical developer. What else might you like to know before concluding that point Q^* is the highest-and-best use? The answer: You need to know whether the intended use is *physically possible* and *legally permissible.*

In assessing physical possibility, the relevant questions are: Will the site support the use? What problems need correction? If there are problems that need correction, what is the cost to correct?

In terms of legal permissibility, the use must be evaluated for the following: Will the use comply with all regulations? Can it be brought into compliance? What is the risk and/or cost of noncompliance?

Therefore, regardless of whether or not point Q^* produces the highest residual land value, if the intended use is not physically possible or legally permissible, it cannot be the highest-and-best use of the land.

Testing for Highest-and-Best Use

Suppose a building site in a given community can be developed under existing and/or reasonably anticipated zoning restrictions for residential purposes only. Suppose, further, that preliminary studies and analysis of neighborhood characteristics and housing demand narrow the choice of possible and profitable site improvements to one of the following types of structure.

1. A single-story duplex building, with each rental unit containing two bedrooms, a dining-living room, a kitchen, and a tiled bath. Total improvements cost, $75,000.

2. A three-family apartment building, with each apartment containing two bedrooms, a dining-living room, a kitchen, and a tiled bath. Total improvements cost, $100,000.

Because the highest use of the building site is residential, as prescribed by the zoning laws, the determination still to be made is which of the two improvements described above constitutes the best use. Under the definition of highest-and-best use, it is necessary to determine the income-producing capacity of the land and, by the process of capitalization, find the income that yields the highest present value. Based on prevailing rentals of $600 a month for a four room and bath duplex and $500 per month for a four room and bath apartment unit, for similar residences in comparable neighborhoods, the procedure used to derive land income and land value is shown in Figure 12–2.

The conclusion can be drawn that the highest-and-best use of the building site under this study is a single-story duplex to be constructed at a cost of $75,000 and renting at $600 per month per dwelling unit. Under this highest-and-best use the land warrants a present value of $12,333. Under the next best type of improvement or utilization, both income attributable to and land value diminish.

The data in this example could also be processed using time-value-of-money techniques to ascertain the investment value of the alternative properties.

GROSS ANNUAL INCOME	SINGLE-STORY DUPLEX	TRIPLEX APARTMENT BUILDING
Duplex units: $600 per month × 2 units × 12 months	$14,400	
Triplex apartment: $500 per month × 3 units × 12 months		$18,000
Less: Vacancy and credit losses, and operating expenses, 35%	5,040	6,300
Annual net operating income	$ 9,360	$11,700
Less: Allowance for return on investment in the buildings, 9%, and recapture of the investment in buildings, 2%		
Duplex: 11% × $75,000	8,250	
Triplex: 11% × $100,000		11,000
Net income residual to land	$ 1,110	$ 700
Indicated market value of land capitalized at 9%		
Duplex: $1,110 ÷ .09	$12,333	
Triplex: $700 ÷ .09		$ 7,778

Because the market value of a given parcel of land is based on the income attributable to land under its highest-and-best use, it is important that care be taken to differentiate between (1) income derived from a specific use or agreed-upon rental, and (2) income that is economically warranted—that is, the residual income that remains when land has been put to its optimum use. The residual income is what remains after due economic shares have been allocated to labor (wages), coordination (entrepreneurial costs), and capital (interest and capital returns).

The income that is attributable to land under its highest-and-best use is referred to as *economic rent.* Economic rent is the income the land can or will produce if employed to its optimum capacity. Any other income agreed to or arbitrarily assigned to land is classified as *contract rent.* To the extent to which contract rent fails to equal economic rent, a proportional share of land value is transferred from the owner to the user or tenant.

A thorough understanding of the concept of highest-and-best use is of great importance in the effective and wise use of our land resources. Care must be taken when studying alternative long-term uses to select a use that is possible, legal, and economically warranted, yet will preserve the utility of the land and yield the highest possible present value.

Special Situations in Highest-and-Best-Use Analysis

In special situations, a decision tree approach to highest-and-best-use analysis can be used to determine the market value of the land. A *decision tree* is a graphic way of structuring complex problems that helps to direct the user to a solution.

Figure 12–3 illustrates a decision tree for a developer. The immediate problem is whether or not the developer will be able to get a zoning change. The land is currently zoned residential C, which permits single-family, detached residences, semi-detached residences containing not more than four dwelling units, and apartment houses. A zoning change from residential C to commercial A would permit office buildings, retail establishments, service shops, and restaurants. The developer foresees a 50 percent chance of a zoning change.

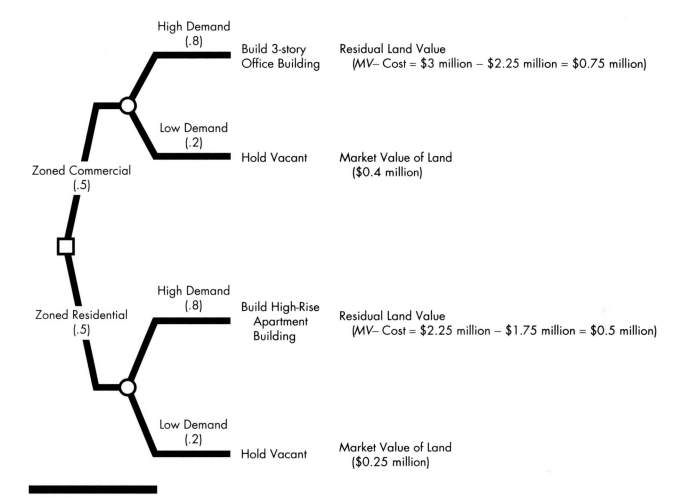

FIGURE 12–3
A Decision Tree for a Developer

The next problem is to determine what the developer should do if he or she is not successful in getting the land rezoned. We can solve that problem by deciding first what to do next year after construction is completed. To do this we start at the right side of the decision tree and work backwards. With an 80 percent chance of high demand for apartment units, we estimate that a high-rise apartment building would be worth $2.25 million, with the cost of improvements valued at $1.75 million and a residual land value of $0.5 million. If demand were low, we determine that the best option would be to hold the site vacant until such time as it ripened into a more productive use. Looking at comparable land sales for zoned residential use, we calculate that the market value of the vacant site is $0.25 million.

Now consider what the developer ought to do if the land were zoned commercial. Again, we start at the right side of the diagram and work backwards. If demand for office space were high, we estimate that a three-story office building would be worth $3 million, divided between construction costs of $2.25 million and a residual land value of $0.75 million. If demand were low, the best option would be to hold the site vacant. Evaluating the worth of the site if zoned commercial, we determine that the market value of the vacant land is $0.4 million.

The expected present value of the land is

$$\text{Present worth of land} = p \times \text{present worth if commercial} + (1 - p) \times \text{present worth if residential}$$

where p is the probability of the zoning change and $(1 - p)$ is the probability of not getting a zoning change.

We can compute the present worth of the land if zoned commercial as follows:

$$
\begin{aligned}
\text{present worth} &= \text{probability high demand} \times \text{present worth residual value high demand} \\
&\quad + \text{probability low demand} \times \text{present worth residual value low demand} \\
&= 0.8 \times \frac{\$0.75 \text{ million}}{(1 + .10)} + 0.2 \times \frac{\$0.40 \text{ million}}{(1 + .10)} \\
&= \$0.62 \text{ million}
\end{aligned}
$$

Similarly, to compute the present worth of the land if zoned residential, we calculate expected values and discount:

$$
\begin{aligned}
\text{present worth} &= \text{probability high demand} \times \text{present worth residual value high demand} \\
&\quad + \text{probability low demand} \times \text{present worth residual value low demand} \\
&= 0.8 \times \frac{\$0.50 \text{ million}}{(1 + .10)} + 0.2 \times \frac{\$0.25 \text{ million}}{(1 + .10)} \\
&= \$0.41 \text{ million}
\end{aligned}
$$

Thus the expected present worth of the land is $0.52 million:

$$
\begin{aligned}
\text{Present worth of land} &= p \times \text{present worth if commercial} + (1 - p) \times \text{present worth if residential} \\
&= 0.50 \times \$0.62 \text{ million} + 0.50 \times \$0.41 \text{ million} \\
&= \$0.52 \text{ million}
\end{aligned}
$$

We can complicate this example by introducing more options. For example, we could consider what the market value of the land would be if demand for office space were moderate, or if the developer were to do nothing until year 1 and then build. As we introduce more possibilities into this problem and as it becomes more complex, the decision tree becomes a more valuable tool for organizing the information necessary to calculate the value of the land.

VALUING LEASEHOLD INTERESTS

A *leasehold interest* is created when someone leases property and then subleases the premises to subtenants. There are several ways a leasehold interest can be created. Some investors lease improved real estate, modernize it, subdivide it, manage it, and sublet it. Others lease vacant land, erect a building thereon, and then rent the space in the building. In these lease situations, the tenant who initially leases the property or the vacant land possesses a leasehold.

Appraisal of a leasehold interest is straightforward. To illustrate the process, consider the case of a leasehold interest in vacant land. In this case a local investor leases a piece of vacant land, erects a free-standing grocery store, and then rents the building to a national food chain at a profit. The net income to the investor is calculated as follows:

Lease payment from national food chain	$515,625
Less: Operating expenses	103,125
Rental payment due landowner	82,500
Net income from leasehold	$330,000

This net income can be capitalized at an overall capitalization rate just like any other net income payment. For example, at a 10 percent capitalization rate the value of this leasehold interest is

$$MV_0 = \frac{NOI}{R_0}$$

$$= \frac{\$330,000}{0.10} = \$3,300,000$$

The capitalization rate in this case should be large enough to compensate the local investor for the opportunity cost of money, plus the additional risk associated with the investment. It should also include a return of capital as discussed in Chapter 10.

The size and quality of the national food chain has an important bearing on how much risk there is for the local investor. Before entering into a leasehold agreement, most investors try to assess the willingness as well as the ability of the national food chain to meet its financial obligations. Published sources such as Moody's and Standard and Poor's rating services can be used for this purpose.

Lease terms can also have an important effect on the riskiness of a leasehold interest. Most leases on commercial properties are lengthy and complex, and often contain renewal options. A *renewal option* gives the lessee the right to extend the lease term for a certain period, on specified terms, provided he or she is not in default. The lessee's option to renew is completely discretionary; landlords usually cannot enforce an automatic renewal clause against a tenant. This uncertainty surrounding the lease term makes valuing leases and leasehold interests problematical.

Finally, it is important to note that a leasehold interest is a unique asset, with risk characteristics shared by no other financial asset. This is particularly true if the leaseholder can make better use of the depreciation tax shelter generated by the structure than the landowner or the tenant.

It is also important to note that a leasehold interest can be extremely difficult to finance. Normally, a mortgage lender will not lend on a leasehold interest unless the landowner subordinates (i.e., takes an inferior position) his or her interest in the land to the mortgage on the leasehold. The reason is straightforward. Without having the landowner subordinate his or her interest in the land to the mortgage on the leaseholder, the mortgage lender is generally precluded from selling the property and using the sale proceeds to pay off the mortgage should the leaseholder default. After all, you can't sell what you don't own! Such a situation leaves the mortgage lender in the untenable situation of having to rely on the net income from the leasehold and wait for repayment, which is something most lenders are ill-equipped to do.

The person who conceivably stands to receive a windfall in this situation is the landowner. Why? Because he or she eventually will gain possession of the improvements when the ground lease terminates.

With so much to gain and everything to lose you can easily see why landowners are generally unwilling to subordinate their interest in the land to the mortgage on the leasehold. This creates a classic *Catch 22* predicament.

SUMMARY

The highest-and-best use of a given property is identified by taking the following steps:

1. Identify the uses that could apply to the property.
2. Determine if each use is physically possible and legally permissible.
3. Examine the quantity and quality of income from each use.
4. Choose the use that produces the highest residual land value.

In valuing a property, the appraiser should proceed with caution if the improvements do not constitute the highest-and-best use of the land. It is not unusual to find that the highest-and-best use may be to leave the site vacant until a later time. Likewise, improvements erected many years ago rarely constitute the highest-and-best use of land.

In special situations, a decision tree, which is a graphic way to structure complex problems, can be used to determine the market value of the land. To create a decision tree, you start at the right side of the decision tree and work backwards. At each decision point there is a payoff and a corresponding probability. Expected present values are then calculated by multiplying the present value of each possible payoff by its probability of occurrence and then summing these products.

When there are only two possible outcomes, the expected value of a piece of land is

$$\text{Present worth of land} = p \times \text{present worth if successful} + (1 - p) \times \text{present worth if failure}$$

where p is the probability of some event occurring and $(1 - p)$ is the probability that the event does not occur. If there are more than two possible outcomes, the decision tree becomes more complex.

Valuing leasehold interests can also be problematical. A leasehold interest is created when a person who leases property, in turn subleases the premises. A common example of a leasehold interest is when a developer leases vacant land, erects a building on it, and then rents the space in the building. A leasehold interest is valued by capitalizing the net income from the leasehold at a rate commensurate with the risks involved.

Financially feasible   An appraisal term applied to all uses that are profitable to investors; usually measured in terms of money, although consideration may be given to such things as amenities.

Highest-and-best use   The use of a parcel that produces the greatest present value; must be legal, possible, and probable.

Leasehold interest   Tenant's interest or position in a property under a lease.

Legally permissible   Usually the second area of inquiry in testing for highest-and-best use; the intended use must be legal and in compliance with all land use regulations, including private restrictions, zoning, building codes, historic district controls, and environmental regulations.

Physically possible   Usually the first area of inquiry in testing for highest-and-best use; test focuses on (1) whether the site supports the use, and (2) what problems, if any, need correction and what is the cost of curing the problems.

QUESTIONS FOR REVIEW AND DISCUSSION

1. What factors must be considered in arriving at the highest-and-best use of a property besides the residual land value? Briefly discuss.

2. Why is the income level generated by an income-producing property relevant in determining the highest-and-best use of a site? Explain.

3. Can the residual land value be calculated if probabilities are assigned for different uses? If so, how would this be done?

4. Explain the process used to value a leasehold interest.

5. How would the financing of a project for a developer with a leasehold interest negatively impact the owner of the land?

6. What factors can affect the riskiness of a leasehold interest?

7. Give an example of a situation where the highest-and-best use of a site is to keep it vacant. Give an example where the highest-and-best use is to leave it undeveloped.

PROBLEMS

1. Two potential uses are identified for a parcel. One use costs $240,000 to construct and provides an income of $50,000 per year; in order to proceed with this use, legal and consulting fees to receive a zoning variance will cost $22,000. Another use costs $310,000 and results in an income of $48,000 per year; due to physical constraints, however, $25,000 must be set aside to provide adequate stormwater drainage ponds for this use. If a capitalization rate of 12 percent is used in the first example, and a capitalization rate of 10 percent is used in the second, which use is the highest-and-best use?

2. An individual has a leasehold interest in an improved site that is leased out to a restaurant. Expenses associated with the leasehold interest in the land equal $45,000 per year. The rental payment on the leasehold is $67,500 per year and the restaurant subleases the land for a base rent of $200,000 per year plus 1 percent of annual net income. Assume the restaurant has a net income stream of $98,000 per year. What is the value of the leasehold interest at a capitalization rate of 11 percent?

3. Construct a decision tree to arrive at the net present value of a property with the following probabilities:

Residual land values are as follows for each scenario:

	HIGH DEMAND	LOW DEMAND
Office building	$345,000	$15,000
Industrial building	$ 70,000	$30,000
Residential building	$220,000	$45,000

Assume that the appropriate discount rate is 10 percent.

	PROBABILITY OF USE	PROBABILITY OF DEMAND		
		HIGH DEMAND	LOW DEMAND	TOTAL
Office	30%	30%	70%	100%
Industrial	60	60	40	100
Residential	10	60	40	100
	100%			

CHAPTER 13

PROPERTY DEVELOPMENT PROCESS

Chapter Outline

City building is just a privilege of citizenship.
Robert Thornton, Sr., former mayor of Dallas

An understanding of property development is important to an investor for at least two reasons. One reason is that buying vacant land and adding improvements is an alternative to buying an existing income property. Another is that after owning an improved property for several years, it may be necessary to modernize or redevelop it.

Whatever the situation, vacant or improved realty must produce a profit. That is, when a specific parcel of land is developed, each of the factors of production (labor, capital, and management) must earn a return sufficient to attract it to the project. Combining these factors in optimum proportions results in the property being developed to its highest-and-best use.

A parcel that does not promise an incremental profit is termed *submarginal.* Submarginal lands are areas such as deserts, jungles, arctic areas, marshes, and mountain tops. In some situations, however, a parcel may be submarginal in one use but promise a surplus in another. Thus, a parcel may have value as a site for a service station but not as a personal residence.

Competition to control and develop desirable properties is often very keen, making it necessary to acquire the site long before it is ripe for actual development. A *ripe property* is one that yields the maximum profit after all other factors of production have been satisfied. When the site has been acquired in advance, *carrying costs*—the expenses and outlays related to holding the site, for example, taxes—must be met during the ripening period. Thus, downtown sites are often devoted to interim uses, known as *taxpayers* (parking lots and one-story fast-food outlets are common), to meet carrying costs.

An economic anomaly that applies more to real estate development than almost any other activity is worth noting at this time. Real estate developments, such as apartment houses, shopping centers, office buildings, and hotels are often designed and built as one-of-a-kind projects. The total cost is also the average cost and the marginal cost; there are no second, third, or fourth projects over which the costs of mistakes may be spread. Therefore, a developer must be extremely careful when undertaking any project because the costs of any mistakes apply only to the project at hand.

HISTORY AND ECONOMICS OF PROPERTY DEVELOPMENT

Property development and redevelopment are market responses to the changing social and economic needs of a community. In a new and growing area, the need is simply for space—the extension of roads and utilities and the addition of structures to vacant sites. Later, the need is to adjust long-lived and functionally obsolete physical structures to the changing demands of a dynamic society.

Subdividing Versus Developing

Subdividing and developing are terms that are sometimes used interchangeably, but actually have very distinct meanings. *Subdividing* means the breaking up of vacant land into sites, to be used for one-family houses, office buildings, or warehouses. *Developing* is a broader concept, generally taken to mean taking a parcel of land and adding improvements to produce a completed, operational property. Adding improvements to subdivided land is also considered development. Development is a much more complex undertaking, requiring the coordination of many people and activities.

Changing Development Practices

During the boom period following World War I, land speculators often took advantage of the naivete of people desiring homes and of the lack of concern of community and governmental leaders. Planning, zoning, and subdivision regulations were not yet common. Subdivisions sprang up at random, especially in remote suburban areas, and were often miles away from utility services such as electricity, water, and waste disposal. Extravagant promotional and advertising campaigns were then set in motion. In turn, municipal authorities frequently jumped on the bandwagon and agreed to extend utilities, install paved roads, build schools, provide police and fire protection, and otherwise encourage the new development. Except in isolated cases, the expected rush to the suburbs did not occur and the cities found themselves heavily burdened with the long-term bonded debt floated to finance the ill-fated undertakings.

The Great Depression in the 1930s brought home to citizens everywhere the serious consequences of excessive development. States and federal agencies increasingly acted to prevent a recurrence of runaway subdivision and the attendant civic burden.

Following World War II, most cities initiated strict subdivision controls. Now, when subdivisions are proposed, assurances must be given, and often a performance bond posted, that all costs, from the grading and paving of streets to the installation of municipal services, can and will be borne by the subdivider. Necessary land for schools and other civic facilities must be immediately dedicated to public use. Often, proof that there is a demand for space must be provided before authority to subdivide is granted.

Developers are much more responsible now than in the past. The public expects greater livability in its communities and buys from the developers who offer the best values. Also, more land-use controls (community plans, zoning ordinances, subdivision regulations, building inspections) are in effect now than in the past. Consequently, the quality of development continues to improve.

Land-Use Succession—The Reason for Development

Land and space tend to go to the use that pays the owner the highest return (rent) or gives the owner the greatest value. Examples abound. Forest lands are cleared or marshes are drained to make way for farms. In turn, farmland is converted into residential neighborhoods, shopping centers, and industrial parks. Older houses are remodeled and converted to office use. Old factories, mills, breweries, and canneries are rehabilitated for shopping centers and other commercial uses. Houses and stores are removed to make way for bridges and freeways.

Almost every change increases the intensity of use, productivity, and value of the land involved and adds to the general welfare at the time it is made. In effect, each parcel, whether urban or rural, is continually seeking its highest-and-best use, unless prevented by institutional limitations (such as community plans and zoning ordinances) or lack of owner insight and initiative. Thus, each parcel is subject to continual development and redevelopment, a process termed *land-use succession.*

Land-use succession may better be visualized with the aid of a graph (see Figure 13–1). Effectively, each new or succeeding use must be so productive or profitable that it can absorb the old use. In the figure, use B might be a high-rise office building replacing an old, obsolete apartment building. The value of the site in office use is great enough to absorb the value of the site in residential use, plus the value of the depreciated building. If remodeling is involved, the new use must absorb the value of the property in its old use plus the construction costs involved.

Historically our cities have developed outward, or at the *extensive margin* where rents or values make it just barely financially feasible to convert land to urban areas and to add urban improvements. The energy crunch of the early 1970s, plus other factors, brought more growth upward, or at the *intensive margin* where rents or values make it just barely financially feasible to use urban land more intensely with the addition of more capital and labor.

During the 1980s some metropolitan areas—particularly those in the Northeast and Northcentral—decreased in size as people migrated from the northern states to states with better weather. A shift to a more service-oriented economy also brought dramatic changes to many metropolitan areas. Cities heavily dependent on traditional manufacturing declined, while cities that made the transition to the new service activities thrived.

Most cities in the United States during the 1980s also experienced the suburbanization of retailers and office firms as retailers moved to the suburbs to be close to their customers and clustered in malls to exploit shopping externalities, while many office firms moved to the suburbs as advances in communication technology (satellites, fiber-optics, and solid-state electronics) decreased the need to choose a central business district location.

FIGURE 13–1
Land-Use Succession
Results When a New
Use Is so Profitable That
It Can Absorb the Value
of the Property in its
Older Use

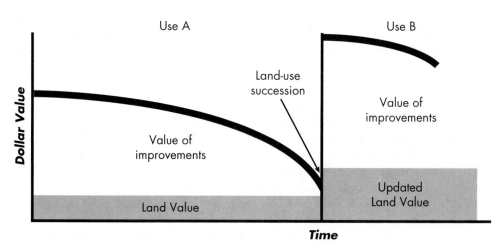

How can the development process be explained? What differentiates a successful real estate development from an unsuccessful development? Basically, there are three stages in a typical real estate development project: a preliminary planning stage, a final planning stage, and a project management stage wherein the improvements to the land are constructed and the completed project is rented or sold.

Preliminary Planning Stage

Initially, a developer must own or search for a property suitable for improvement. Once a property is located, its development possibilities must be checked out with the planning commission and other governmental agencies. A market analysis and highest-and-best use analysis are necessary to ascertain the probable use and the probable value of the land. If the situation looks right, a letter of intent or an option to purchase the land may be arranged with the owner.

Several other crucial activities should also be initiated during this stage. These include locating financial backing and submitting a preliminary development plan to the local planning commission and other agencies for tentative approval (see Figure 13–2). With tentative approval in hand, the final planning stage is entered. No definite time limit applies to the preliminary planning stage, but several months to several years is typical.

Final Planning Stage

In the final planning stage, any reservations or conditions attached to the preliminary plan must be removed or satisfied.

Covenants restricting the number and size of structures to be placed on the land, if desirable, must be written. Capital and operating budgets must be worked out to determine if the project is financially feasible. Based on the accounting data, if financial backing is not already in hand it must be arranged. Concurrently, a marketing and promotional program is drawn up.

By the end of the final planning stage, governmental approvals must be in hand and final budgets in place. If everything continues to appear feasible, the land is purchased (if not already owned). Local regulations usually stipulate one year as the maximum time allowed from preliminary plan approval to final plat approval. If the allowed time is exceeded, the developer is likely to have to begin all over again, which frequently involves having additional conditions attached to the project.

Project Management Stage

With all necessary approvals in hand, a developer can concentrate on marketing the project. Of course, other work is also going on. Utilities and streets must be installed or a performance bond put up to cover that portion of the development. If appropriate, deed restrictions must also be recorded. Finally, if improvements are to be added, arrangements must be made for architects, landscape architects, contractors, and others.

The construction stage and then the rental or sale of the properties may take several years to complete. If the project is subdivision, the developer may build

DEVELOPMENT STAGE	PHYSICAL	INSTITUTIONAL		ECONOMIC	
	PHYSICAL DESIGN AND DEVELOPMENT	GOVERNMENTAL	LEGAL	FINANCIAL	MARKETING AND PROMOTION
Preliminary Plans	Locate property if not already owned	Discuss possibilities with planning agency and others	Arrange for option to purchase land if not owned	Make estimate of cost and value of land	Market analysis
					Highest-and-best-use analysis
	Complete preliminary design	Tentative approvals		Locate financial backing	
				Feasibility analysis	
Final Plans	Details of final map of lots or subdivision	Work with planning and other agencies to get final approvals of proposed development	Develop restrictions to be placed on the land	Make up initial capital and operating budgets	Marketability study
			Purchase land, if not owned		Develop marketing and promotional program based on market analysis
		Approvals obtained		Verify backing	
				Make up final budgets	
Project Management	Install utilities and streets, build houses, etc., if part of operation	Record plat and controls	Transfer parcels as sold	Recheck profit picture	Initiate marketing program
				Pay bills, watch money come in	Rent space if ownership to be retained

FIGURE 13–2
The Property Development Process

model homes first. When homes are sold, clear title must be conveyed. If the project is a rental property, space must be leased or an equity owner must be found at this point to take control of the property. The disposition stage continues until all the parcels are sold or all space is rented.

Lenders take the risk that something can be built on schedule and on budget, and then sold, rented, or financed to pay back the borrowed money. In most development projects the uncertainties surrounding the project are due entirely to the fact that the decisions of the consumers of the services to be offered at the site are unknown. The developer is a speculator who produces a product in advance of orders. The development is planned in the expectation that there will be a demand for the space in the future.

In most instances, a developer needs external financing, either to help acquire the land or move forward on the improvements. One of three options is generally used: Bring in equity partners at the outset, arrange for debt financing, or combine equity with debt financing. Forming an equity partnership provides the much-needed seed money and often helps to spread the risk inherent in large real estate development projects. An equity partnership generally has more staying power than an individual, no matter what his or her financial capacity. Equity partners are exposed to only a share of the project's risk.

Sources of debt financing for development projects include banking institutions (commercial banks and thrifts), insurance companies, financial services companies, nondomestic banks, and, to some extent, Wall Street. These institutions typically will proceed with a development only if the pro forma return upon completion meets some minimum expectations. In the past, these expectations were fairly modest. For example, most retail developers believed in a 5–10 rule: modest 5 percent returns in the first few years of the project would be compensated for in the long run by rent growth and property appreciation. Together, they would yield returns in excess of 10 percent. This, of course, did not happen in the 1980s; instead of long-run rent growth and property appreciation, the real estate markets in most areas of the United States were over-stored, over-roomed, and over-built. Vacancies were excessive, rents were low, and prices fell precipitously.

Two types of loans are used to finance the development of income-producing properties and unimproved land: construction loans and land-development loans.

Construction Loans

A *construction loan* is made to finance the addition of improvements. It generally runs until the completion of the proposed improvements and, possibly, to the sale of the property.

A construction loan is distinctive in that the total amount of the loan is not fully paid out to the borrower at the outset of the project. Instead, funds are paid out in installments at agreed stages of construction. A lender's representative usually inspects and certifies satisfactory progress prior to each payout. Upon completion of the project, the construction loan is paid off by the borrower.

To obtain a construction loan the developer is usually required to get a permanent "take-out" commitment from a long-term lender. A *permanent take-out commitment* is an option-like agreement that gives the developer the right to borrow at a contractually specified interest rate within a set time period. The permanent take-out commitment is important because construction loans are usually granted only on the assurance that a long-term lender is obligated to make a "permanent" mortgage. In the absence of this assurance, construction lenders are unlikely to advance any funds.

The permanent take-out commitment creates a mechanism whereby a lender will provide funds so that the developer can repay the construction loan. Most permanent take-out commitments obtained prior to actual development include various contingencies. If the developer does not fulfill these contingencies, the permanent lender does not have to fund the loan. Common contingencies in a permanent take-out commitment include:

1. A completion date for the construction of the project.
2. Minimum leasing requirements.
3. Provisions for gap financing.

Gap financing is often needed if the permanent lender decides to advance only partial funding of the permanent mortgage. This can happen in cases where the developer faces cost overruns, or where the minimum leasing requirement is not being met. The "gap" in this case is the difference between the partial funding advanced by the permanent lender and the funds needed to repay the construction lender.

In a case where the borrower is unable or unwilling to repay, a construction lender may have to foreclose on the project. Construction lenders also face the risk that the developer will run into unforeseen problems, like strikes, unfavorable weather, structural or design problems, materials price increases, or the loss of a contractor or subcontractor. When project costs begin to exceed project value, the lender faces the possibility that the developer will abandon the project before completion rather than invest additional equity.

The following will illustrate how a construction loan works. TriStar Development Company has approached Community Bank for a construction loan to develop a strip shopping center on land they already own. They have already secured a $960,037 take-out commitment from a major life insurance company.

The interest rate on the construction loan is based on the prime rate plus 200 basis points. During the 5-month construction period, the prime rate is expected to be 8 percent per annum. Thus, the loan rate is expected to be 10 percent per annum, or 0.83 percent per month.

Closing costs and origination fees are $20,000. These costs are added to the cumulative loan balance at the closing of the construction loan. The timing of all other disbursements is shown in Figure 13–3.

FIGURE 13–3
Monthly Cash Draws on Construction Loan

MONTH	(1) NET CASH TO DEVELOPER FOR CONSTRUCTION COSTS	(2) CLOSING COSTS AND ORIGINATION FEES	(3) = (1) + (2) MONTHLY CASH DRAWS
Close	$ 0	$20,000	$ 20,000
1	$ 0		$ 0
2	$300,000		$300,000
3	$300,000		$300,000
4	$200,000		$200,000
5	$125,000		$125,000
Total	$925,000	$20,000	$945,000

The cumulative loan balance is shown in Figure 13–4. The interest computation is the monthly interest rate times the previous cumulative loan balance. For month 1, for example, the interest is 0.83 percent × $20,000 = $166. This amount is added to the previous cumulative loan balance, plus any monthly cash draw, to determine the cumulative loan balance at the end of the month.

You should now be able to work out the interest and cumulative loan balance computations for months 2 through 5. For month 2, the interest is 0.83 percent × $20,166 = $167 and the cumulative loan balance is $320,333 ($20,166 + $300,000 + $167), and so forth. The ending loan balance is $960,037, which will be repaid with funds advanced from the permanent lender. The *total interest costs* on this loan are $15,037 (the difference between the cumulative loan balance and the total monthly cash draws, or $960,037 − $945,000).

The *effective interest rate* on this construction loan is defined as the discount rate that makes the present value of the total net cash to the developer equal to the present value of the loan payoff. To find the effective interest rate for the construction loan to TriStar Development Company, we must solve for *IRR* in the following expression:

$$\frac{\$0}{(1 + IRR)} + \frac{\$300,000}{(1 + IRR)^2} + \frac{\$300,000}{(1 + IRR)^3} + \frac{\$200,000}{(1 + IRR)^4}$$

$$+ \frac{\$125,000}{(1 + IRR)^5} = \frac{\$960,037}{(1 + IRR)^5}$$

Solving for the *IRR* by trial and error yields 2.03 percent per month, or 24.38 percent per annum. To solve for *IRR* you can also treat this problem as series of cash inflows—the monthly cash draws—followed by a single lump-sum cash outflow—the loan payoff, net of the monthly cash draw in month 5.

To keep matters simple, we assumed that the construction loan rate in our example remained at 10 percent during the entire construction period. We could have made the problem slightly more realistic by assuming that the construction loan rate varied over the construction period. To recalculate the amount of interest for each month with a variable interest rate, one would first need to determine the value of the prime rate plus, in this case, 200 basis points. Then, as before, you would multi-

MONTH	(1) MONTHLY CASH DRAWS	(2) INTEREST[a]	(3) = (1) + (2) CUMULATIVE LOAN BALANCE
Close	$ 20,000	$ 0	$ 20,000
1	$ 0	$ 166	$ 20,166
2	$300,000	$ 167	$320,333
3	$300,000	$2,659	$622,992
4	$200,000	$5,171	$828,163
5	$125,000	$6,874	$960,037
Total	$945,000	$15,037	$960,037

FIGURE 13–4
Cumulative Loan Balance on Construction Loan

[a]Interest = monthly interest rate × previous cumulative loan balance.

ply the new monthly interest rate times the previous cumulative loan balance to determine the amount of interest for each month. The new cumulative loan balance is then derived as before.

We can also deal with cost overruns. Two cases should be considered. If the cost overrun is minor, in all likelihood it will be added to the cumulative loan balance and paid off with the construction loan. If it is major, however, the developer must be prepared to pay the overrun out of personal funds or take out a gap loan. We should also warn that a cost overrun can cause the permanent financing arrangement to be canceled, which would leave TriStar Development Company seeking another way to pay off the construction loan.

Land-Development Loans

Land-development loans are made for the purpose of acquiring, subdividing, and making improvements to raw, undeveloped land. In residential land development, the resulting improved land is sold off as individual sites to single-family builders or apartment developers. In business parks and industrial development, land developers prepare sites for sale to commercial developers. Land-developers must make decisions about optimal lot sizes, land use and traffic circulation plans, and amenities like lighting, subsurface improvements, and street improvements.

Repayment of a land-development loan ultimately depends on how many lots are sold and the price per lot. This makes land-development loans the riskiest of all real estate loans. As each lot is sold, the developer is given a release statement in which the lender waives all liens on the parcel sold. The release statement allows clear title to the lot to pass from the developer to the buyer of the parcel.

DEVELOPMENT POLICY ISSUES

Excessive development in the wake of falling demand, as occurred in commercial office space during the 1980s, can lead to overbuilding, rising vacancies, and falling rents. Excessive development can also cause physical problems, such as air pollution, traffic congestion, inadequate water supply, overburdened police and fire protection, deteriorated housing, and other public facility difficulties.

To curb the problems associated with excessive development some cities have adopted stringent land-use controls. These controls attempt to lessen street congestion, reduce fire hazards, promote health, and restrict population growth by regulating land-use through zoning and building ordinances. Stringent land-use regulations often result in certain structures or activities on the property being prohibited, and they make the land less desirable and less valuable. The prospective real estate developer should be knowledgeable about the ramifications of restrictive land-use controls.

Growth of our cities has also resulted in a problem known as *leap-frog development*. As central business districts grow and land values rise, it is not uncommon for speculators to buy land in the path of development and to hold it for appreciation. Problems arise when further development of the central business district is required. In such cases developers have shown a proclivity to leap-frog over the land held by speculators to buy less-expensive land further out, leaving a permanent ring around the business center that ultimately becomes slums and blighted areas.

Evidence of leap-frog development can be seen in almost every major city in the United States. Take, for example, the borough of Manhattan in New York City. New York City is the largest city in the United States and the nation's leading financial and cultural center. Each of its five boroughs—the Bronx, Manhattan, Queens, Brooklyn, and Richmond (Staten Island)—is a county. Evidence of leap-frog development patterns in Manhattan can be seen between the intensively developed financial district at the southern end and the central commercial district that starts at about 42nd Street, and includes Rockefeller Center between 48th and 51st Street and Fifth Avenue and the Avenue of the Americas. Leap-frog development patterns are also visible in Chicago, Detroit, and Los Angeles.

Another major factor in the planning for real estate development is the levying of development fees. With the development of real estate comes the need for expanded infrastructure in order to service the increased population; changes in traffic, schools, and municipal services are needed. Traditionally, this problem was handled by requiring the developer to dedicate land contiguous to the proposed site upon which the government could build the necessary facilities. Now, local communities often collect fees from developers, called *fees in lieu of dedication,* to be used to finance related facilities. Local communities may also collect *impact fees,* which are used to supplement the shortfall in other forms of financing for the city. Impact fees are normally paid as a condition of the issuance of a building permit. *Link-up fees* may require a developer to make improvements or contribute money to certain housing programs, the need for which has arisen by virtue of the new employment brought into the city by the development.

SUMMARY

Real estate development generally means combining land and improvements to produce a completed, operational property. Adding improvements to subdivided land is also considered development. A developer attempts to combine land with other factors of production (labor, capital, and management) in optimum proportions to develop the property to its highest-and-best use.

The reason for real estate development is land-use succession. Land and space tend to go to the use that pays the owner the highest return or gives the owner the greatest value. Almost every change in land use increases the intensity of use, productivity, and value of the land involved and adds to the general welfare at the time it is made. The highest-and-best use will be realized unless prevented by institutional limitations, such as community plans and zoning ordinances, or lack of owner insight and initiative.

KEY CONCEPTS

Carrying costs Expenses and outlays that have to be met until a property is ripe for development or redevelopment.

Construction loan   A short-term loan to cover the construction costs of a building or development project; differs from a permanent mortgage in that the loan proceeds are generally advanced in the form of installment payments as the work progresses.

Developing   Process of combining land and improvements to produce a completed, operational property.

Gap financing   Usually fills a temporary need until permanent financing is obtained; may also be used when permanent financing is difficult to obtain or is too expensive.

Impact fees   A municipal assessment against new development projects to compensate for the added costs of public services generated by the new construction.

Total interest costs   Difference between the cumulative construction loan balance and the total monthly cash draws.

Land-use succession   Continuing process of land development and redevelopment, as owners adjust properties to changing conditions.

Leap-frog development   Proclivity of developers to leap-frog over the land held by speculators to buy less expensive land further out, leaving a permanent ring around the business center that ultimately becomes slums and blighted areas.

Permanent take-out commitment   Commitment made in writing by the permanent lender to provide funds to the developer to repay a construction loan, provided certain contingencies are met.

Subdividing   The breaking up of a tract of land into smaller sites or plots; sites may be for homes, small offices, warehouses, etc.

Submarginal land   Lands (swamps, mountaintops, and deserts) not able to yield sufficient profit to financially justify their development.

QUESTIONS FOR REVIEW AND DISCUSSION

1. Define and explain the interrelationships among carrying costs, the investor, and a ripe property.

2. What are some examples of potential carrying costs for a parcel of land?

3. Give a brief historical overview of real estate development in the United States. Distinguish between subdividing and developing.

4. Explain briefly how the economics of land-use succession leads to property development. Give at least two examples of this process occurring.

5. State briefly the necessary relationship between costs and value in order for a property to be ripe for development.

6. What are some typical sources of debt financing?

7. What is the distinction between a construction loan and a permanent loan?

8. Under what conditions would a developer need to approach a lender for gap financing?

9. What is a land development loan? How is it usually paid off?

10. What is leap-frog development? Why does it occur?

11. What types of fees may be levied by cities prior to issuing a building permit to a developer? What effect do you think the decrease in development nationwide will have on the future viability of these fees?

12. Identify and discuss briefly the activities in each of the three stages of the property-development process.

13. Do zoning and other land-use controls affect profits realized by a developer? If so, how? Discuss.

14. Is the advance acquisition of land for development productive? Explain. Is it socially desirable?

15. Do we, as a society, need planning, zoning, subdivision regulations, and other land-use controls?

16. What major areas of your community are being developed from bare land now? What type of development is it: residential, commercial, or industrial? Is such development consistent with the economic and social outlook for your community?

PROBLEMS

1. Western State Bank agrees to make a construction loan to Acme Builders. The schedule of disbursements is given below. The interest rate will float at 3 percent above the prime rate. Interest is to be compounded monthly on the previous month's ending balance, and is to accrue. The prime rate is 7 percent, and it is assumed that it will remain so for the entire period.

MONTH	NET CASH TO DEVELOPER	CLOSING COSTS
0	$ 0	$50,000
1	$ 20,000	
2	$280,000	
3	$270,000	
4	$200,000	
5	$140,000	
6	$140,000	

a. What is the total loan amount?

b. What is the total interest costs on this loan?

c. What is the effective interest rate?

2. Assume in problem 1 that the prime rate jumps to 8 percent at the end of the third month and remains at that level for the remaining term of the construction loan.

   Required: (a) What is the total loan amount? (b) What is the interest carry? (c) What is the before-tax IRR to the lender?

3. The Property Shop has decided to develop a small medical building. The total project costs are $1,000,000 (including the cost of the land). The Property Shop will

be required to put up $200,000 in equity. The remainder is to be paid with a construction loan from Valley Bank. The loan rate is 8.5 percent for the entire 6-month construction period.

The Property Shop will need to borrow $25,000 at closing to pay for architect/engineering fees, legal fees, and other development costs. Closing costs and origination fees are $20,000. The timing of all other disbursements is shown below:

MONTH	NET CASH TO DEVELOPER	CLOSING COSTS
0	$ 25,000	$20,000
1	$100,000	
2	$150,000	
3	$150,000	
4	$100,000	
5	$100,000	
6	$139,000	

a. What is the total interest costs on this loan?

b. What is the effective interest rate on this construction loan?

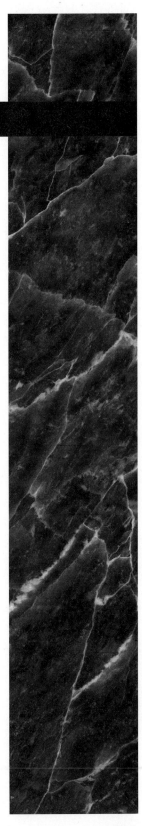

CHAPTER 14

ANALYSIS FOR PROPERTY DEVELOPMENT

Chapter Outline

City building is just a privilege of citizenship.
Robert Thornton, Sr., former mayor of Dallas

Analysis for property development requires the application of the combined skills of urban planners, architects, civil engineers, real estate consultants, and financiers, all cooperating on a project that must be sanctioned by various governmental agencies. Before proceeding with the acquisition of the land or expending any development costs, the entire project must be worked out on paper. Estimates must be made of investment, operating, and overhead costs. This should be followed by a market analysis, to determine the extent of present and reasonably anticipated demand for building sites in the area under development.

SITE SELECTION AND ANALYSIS

Judging whether a site is ready for change is probably the most basic decision of a subdivider or developer. Most other decisions in the development process flow from the site-selection decision. In many cases, the site-selection decision is made twice. It is made first upon acquisition, or even before, when committing resources to study the site and its potential for development. A second decision time comes when resources are committed to subdivide and/or develop the site. The second decision is of greater importance, in that an acquired site may be sold or held vacant or developed. It is also a much larger commitment.

Many elements are considered in site selection and analysis. These include:

1. Location or situs
2. Accessibility
3. Size and shape
4. Physical characteristics
5. Utilities and services
6. Applicable public regulations
7. Cost or value

These elements are considered here briefly as they apply to the major alternative uses: residential, commercial, and industrial.

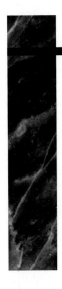

HANDICAP ACCESSIBILITY REQUIREMENTS

All public accommodations and commercial facilities are now required to comply with the 1991 Americans with Disabilities Act (ADA) and the American National Standards Institute (ANSI) accessibility standards for single-family and multifamily housing. Included in the ADA and ANSI regulations and accessibility standards are requirements for accessible new construction and alterations; removal of barriers in existing facilities; the provision of auxiliary aids for individuals with vision, speech, or hearing impairments; and requirements for nondiscriminatory policies and procedures.

The ADA also requires that all barriers at existing public accommodations and commercial facilities be removed to the maximum extent feasible. Severe fines can be imposed against the owner of the property if the regulations are not met.

Residential

Location is essentially the relation of a site to the other uses of land in the vicinity. A desirable residential location is largely determined by the location of the property relative to existing or future schools, churches, shopping centers, major roadways, and other urban facilities. Thus, adverse or conflicting land uses, such as air-polluting industrial plants, are best avoided when considering a residential site. Location and accessibility are closely related. Accessibility, you will remember, is the relative ease or convenience of getting to and from a particular parcel. Most trips from homes are to schools, shopping facilities, places of work, and homes of friends or relatives. Thus, close proximity to schools and shopping is important. Most wage earners are willing to commute up to an hour if the neighborhood and living environment are otherwise acceptable. Beyond close proximity, immediate access to freeways and mass transit is important to good accessibility.

Each site is unique in size, shape, and physical characteristics. The size and shape of a parcel must accommodate a reasonable layout for residential use. Similarly, the topography, soils, hydrology, trees and bushes, and other physical characteristics of a site must be suitable to residential development. The most desirable topography is gently rolling hills that allow adequate drainage and facilitate the creation of an interesting living environment. Fertile soils that support vegetation are also advantageous.

Relative availability of utilities such as water, sanitary sewers, and storm sewers, is critical to most residential development. These may be provided through private or public systems, with public systems being much preferred to assure continuity of service at a reasonable cost. The installation of utilities and streets is a major cost in development. On the other hand, electrical and telephone services are extended to most urban sites at the time of development without costs to the project. In many areas, gas is available on a no-cost basis also.

Cost is a final major consideration in selecting a site for development. If the cost or asking price is so high that little profit is likely, the site is unacceptable. On the other hand, if the market value of an owned site is higher than a developer considers justified, the site may be sold rather than developed.

Commercial

A distinct trade area is the prime consideration in locating a convenient commercial district. Population size and income levels must be examined in the market analysis and must justify the development. Then, the most accessible site to homes, one that cannot readily be cut off by competition, becomes important. Easy accessibility from several directions, without undue congestion and with easy entry onto the parcel itself, makes up a substantial part of this locational and accessibility need. High visibility to passing traffic is also a locational plus.

The size and shape of the site must be suited to the type of development proposed, with consideration given to easy and adequate parking for customers. Thus, while a 5- to 10-acre site may be adequate for a neighborhood shopping center, 80 to 100 acres or more are needed for a regional center. A large discount store might need 10 acres or more. Fast-food outlets and service stations increasingly need from 1 to 3 acres.

A level site, at or slightly above street level, is most desirable. Uneven terrain, or sites that are substantially above or below street level, discourage entry by potential customers and are to be avoided. All urban utilities and services are necessary for most commercial development. As is true for other types of development, proper zoning and other public approvals must be obtained before developing a commercial center or district. In addition, an environmental impact statement is required. And, finally, the cost or value of the site must be consistent with the proposed use to allow the developer an acceptable profit.

Industrial

Primary concerns in location and accessibility for industrial purposes are raw materials, labor, supplies and component parts, and the market for the finished product. Larger firms, such as metal and mineral processors, are tied to raw materials. Weight-gaining industries must locate near their markets. Most other manufacturers need only be sure of readily obtaining component parts, supplies, and services from suppliers. That makes proximity and access to a freeway or interstate highway highly important to them. Large plants may need railroad or water access, in addition. Immediate airport access is becoming increasingly important. An adequate labor pool with appropriate skills is necessary for any plant. But, except for the most specialized processes, labor may be readily obtained almost anywhere in the United States because of the high technical capability of our population.

An industrial park may occupy several hundred acres in a large metropolitan area. Of course, many parks and districts are much smaller. The size and shape of the parcel must accommodate a reasonable layout. That is, the parcel must not necessitate sites of odd and inefficient shape. The topography must be level for the most part, and the soil must have high load-bearing capability; sites with soft ground, such as marshes, are best avoided because they may not be able to support large buildings and heavy machines.

All utilities are required in an industrial area. In many cases, the utilities may have to be oversized to handle the many wastes resulting from the processes. Likewise, gas and electrical services may have to be oversized.

Highly restrictive local air and water pollution regulations discourage industrial location. In addition, some communities have a no-growth posture and are reluctant to accommodate the needs of prospective industries. An environmental impact statement is required when creating any industrial park or district. As with residential and commercial parcels, the cost or value of a site intended for industrial purposes must be in line with its profit potential.

IMPROVEMENT ANALYSIS

Improvement analysis is critical if the highest-and-best use of the site is to be realized. It is easy for a developer to overdevelop a property, for instance, by having heavier floor loads than those required in a regular office building, or higher ceilings, larger column spacing, and larger toilet rooms. Typically such amenities are required in the case of a new suburban office building if you wish to attract research and development tenants. In contrast, regular prospective office tenants are unlikely to pay much more than the going rate for these additional construction costs. It is also possible to underdevelop a property, for example, by not making the building flexible enough or developing only 40,000 square feet of office space when the site and market could support 240,000 square feet of office space.

Important factors to consider when analyzing building improvements include

1. Functional utility
2. Compatibility
3. Accommodation of specific activities
4. Ease and cost of maintenance
5. The building's form and ornamentation

Buildings come in all shapes and sizes. Newly constructed buildings often enjoy the broadest market appeal because of their architectural style and functional utility. Commercial tenants, for example, like the prestige of new buildings. Some commercial tenants, like IBM and Xerox, look at their buildings as *signature buildings,* and prefer structures that contain architectural features and physical amenities designed to display an impressive image.

Other physical characteristics to be considered when evaluating the improvements include the quantitative and qualitative construction details; an analysis of the mechanical systems, an analysis of the physical layout of the space, and special features, such as covered walkways, enclosed entry ways, location of the units within the structure, and atrium space. Poor traffic patterns inside the structure can contribute to functional obsolescence.

ANALYSIS FOR PROPERTY DEVELOPMENT

The analysis for developing a real estate investment is quite similar to that required when buying an investment. The main difference is that the costs incurred are for land plus improvements instead of for stocks or bonds. Also the details of construction management must be handled, and the delay for construction must be taken into account. A specific example seems appropriate at this point.

Black Oaks Case Data

To illustrate the analysis for property development, we now turn our attention to Black Oaks, a proposed 28-unit apartment building. The cost of land plus improvements are expected to be $1,001,000 (see Figure 14–1). Market and feasibility analysis, summarized in a pro forma annual operating schedule, indicate a first year NOI of $97,134 (see Figure 14–2).

Given this data, two separate and equally compelling analyses can be undertaken: a "front door" and "back door" approach to development feasibility.

Front Door Approach

The *front door approach* starts with the expected cost, or most likely purchase price, of the property, based on which required cash flows necessary to justify the investment are calculated. These cash flows are then compared with those that may be realized in the market.

To illustrate, let us consider Black Oaks. From Figure 14–1, expected development costs are estimated to be $1,001,000. Let us assume that Black Oaks has a 8 percent overall capitalization rate. Then

$$\text{Justified } NOI = R_0 \times \text{Development cost}$$

which follows from the fact that $MV_0 = NOI \div R_0$ (see Chapter 10). All that we have done is to substitute the expected development costs for MV_0 and solve for NOI.

To determine the justified potential gross income, note that

$$NOI = PGI \times (1 - v) - OE$$

where

PGI = potential gross income
v = vacancy rate, and
OE = operating expenses (including fixed and variable expenses)

Also note that we can write OE as

$$OE = \frac{OE}{PGI \times (1 - v)} PGI \times (1 - v)$$

$$= OER \times PGI \times (1 - v)$$

FIGURE 14–1
Black Oaks Apartments: Project Cost Summary

Land (including road improvements and installation of utilities)	$ 176,000
Improvements	
Building costs, including architectural fees	586,395
Financing and legal costs	96,080
Contingencies	40,000
Developer fees and profit	102,500
Total	$1,000,975
Rounded to	$1,001,000

Gross Scheduled Income		
1 BR units with 1½ baths: 20 at $450 per month		$ 9,000
2 BR units with 2½ baths: 4 at 600		2,400
3 BR units with 2½ baths: 4 at 695		2,780
Gross Monthly Income		$14,180
Gross Annual Income (gross monthly income × 12)		$170,160
Less: Vacancy and collection losses at 5%		8,508
Effective Gross Income		$161,652
Less: Total operating expenses		
Fixed		
Real estate taxes	$24,503	
Hazard insurance	1,702	
Licenses	200	
Variable		
Management at 5%	8,083	
Resident manager	6,000	
Custodian and gardener	8,000	
Workman's compensation and Social Security	1,555	
Advertising	1,020	
Utilities	1,455	
Elevator service	1,800	
Supplies	1,200	
Other (pool, etc.)	2,400	
Repair and maintenance	6,600	
Total	$64,518	64,518
Net Operating Income		$ 97,134

FIGURE 14–2
Black Oaks Apartments: Pro-Forma Annual Operating Statement

where

OER = operating expenses divided by effective gross income and, hence, can be considered a measure of the property's operating efficiency (see Chapter 3)

You can probably see where we are heading. By taking these three expressions, we can solve for the justified potential gross income needed to justify an 8 percent overall return on Black Oaks. With $v = .05$ and $OER = .40$, the calculation is

$$\text{Justified } PGI = \frac{R_0 \times \text{Development cost}}{(1 - v) \times (1 - OER)}$$

$$= \frac{.08 \times \$1,001,000}{(1 - .05) \times (1 - .40)}$$

$$= \$140,491$$

Justified potential gross income on a total development cost of $1,001,000 is, therefore, $140,491. Figure 14–2 shows that the expected potential gross income is $170,160. Thus, by the front door approach, Black Oaks appears feasible.

Back Door Approach

There are three versions of the back door approach. The basic approach starts with a scheduled gross income based on market rents; from this NOI is calculated. NOI provides the basis for determining the present worth of the building to the developer. A development project is feasible if its present worth exceeds the cost of development.

Basic Back Door Model.   To illustrate, consider the income and operating statement for Black Oaks apartment project shown in Figure 14–2. Applying an overall capitalization rate of 8 percent to the projected NOI of $97,134 gives a present worth of the apartment project to the developer of $1,214,175:

$$\frac{NOI}{R_0} = \frac{\$97,134}{.08} = \$1,214,175$$

This exceeds the $1,001,000 development cost, indicating that the project is feasible on a preliminary basis. Refined calculations involving discounted after-tax cash flows, as illustrated in Chapter 6, could be used to determine more specifically if the project is a desirable investment alternative. The back door approach to feasibility can also be extended to take into account the lender's perspective.

Back Door Model from the Lender's Perspective.   A second model is from the lender's perspective. Here is the set-up. Assume that Black Oaks is to be financed with both debt and equity. This is a fairly typical assumption. We will use a first-year return-on-cash equity investment of 5.25 percent. Further assume that local lenders require a minimum *debt-coverage ratio* of at least 1.20. This means there must be $1.20 of net operating income for every $1.00 of annual debt service.

Now for the analysis. We begin with the NOI of $97,134 for Black Oaks, which reflects current market rents. With a NOI of $97,134, a debt-coverage ratio of 1.20 means

$$\text{Debt-coverage ratio} = 1.20 = \frac{\text{Net operating income}}{\text{Annual debt service}}$$

or

$$1.20 = \frac{\$97,134}{\text{Annual debt service}}$$

or

$$\text{Annual debt service} = \frac{\$97,134}{1.20} = \$80,945$$

This implies a mortgage loan of no more than $911,261, assuming annual payments at 8 percent interest for 30 years. This amount is the present value of $80,945 per year discounted at 8 percent interest for 30 years. The formula is

$$PV = \frac{\text{Debt service}}{(1+i)^1} + \frac{\text{Debt service}}{(1+i)^2} + \cdots + \frac{\text{Debt service}}{(1+i)^{30}}$$

$$= \frac{\$80,945}{(1+.08)^1} + \frac{\$80,945}{(1+.08)^2} + \cdots + \frac{\$80,945}{(1+.08)^{30}}$$

$$= \$911,261$$

This loan amount is known as the *maximum supportable mortgage loan,* or, as it is sometimes called, the *justified mortgage loan amount.*

First year before-tax cash flow would be $16,189 ($97,134 − $80,945). Applying a return-on-cash equity investment of 5.25 percent to this annual before-tax cash flow yields a *justified equity investment* of $308,362. The calculations are as follows:

Net operating income	$ 97,134
Less: Annual debt service	80,945
Before-tax cash flow	$ 16,189
Divided by: Equity dividend rate	.0525
Justified equity investment	$308,362

The return-on-cash equity investment, or the *equity dividend rate* as it is commonly known, is a measure of the return on investment to the equity investor after all operating expenses and debt service payments. For Black Oaks, the equity dividend rate is

$$\text{Equity dividend rate} = \frac{\text{Before-tax cash flow}}{\text{Initial equity investment}}$$

$$= \frac{\$16,189}{\$308,362} = 5.25\%$$

In turn, the *present worth* of Black Oaks would be the justified mortgage loan amount plus the justified equity investment:

Present worth of project = Justified mortgage value + Justified equity value
$$= \$911,261 + \$308,362 = \$1,219,623$$

This amount is the maximum value of the property to the developer. Note that the present worth of the project to the developer should exceed total development costs if the project is to be financially feasible. This back door approach is summarized in Figure 14-3.

Back Door Model from the Developer's Perspective.   Now for a third back door model—this one taking into account the developer's perspective. First, we will calculate the maximum amount of money that the developer can spend on debt service payments without taking on an inordinate amount of default risk.

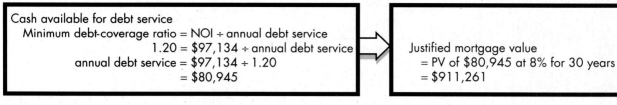

Cash Flow Amounts   Capital Amounts

Cash available for debt service
  Minimum debt-coverage ratio = NOI ÷ annual debt service
                    1.20 = $97,134 ÷ annual debt service   Justified mortgage value
       annual debt service = $97,134 ÷ 1.20   = PV of $80,945 at 8% for 30 years
                          = $80,945   = $911,261

                                                                        +

Before-tax cash flow = NOI – annual debt service   Justified equity value = $16,189
$97,134 – $80,945 = $16,189   capitalized at equity dividend rate

                                                             $16,189 ÷ .0525 = $308,362

                                                                        =

                                                             Total present worth to developer
                                                               = justified mortgage value +
                                                                 justified equity value

                                                             $911,261 + $308,362 = $1,219,623

FIGURE 14–3

Black Oaks Apartments: Back Door Analysis from the Lender's Perspective

Given Black Oaks' operating expenses of $64,518, a default ratio of 85 percent, which equals total annual operating expenses plus annual debt service divided by potential gross income, and first-year potential gross income of $170,160, based on current market rents, the maximum amount of money that a developer can spend on debt service payments can be calculated as follows:

$$\text{Default ratio} = \frac{\text{Operating expenses} + \text{Debt service payments}}{\text{Potential gross income}}$$

$$= \frac{\$64,518 + \text{Debt service payments}}{\$170,160} = .85$$

or

$$\text{Debt service payments} = .85 \times \$170,160 - \$64,518$$
$$= \$80,118$$

In turn, this implies a mortgage loan of no more than $901,951, assuming annual payments at 8 percent interest for 30 years, which is the present value of $80,118. The formula is

Maximum mortgage amount

$$= \frac{\text{Debt service}}{(1 + i)^1} + \frac{\text{Debt service}}{(1 + i)^2} + \cdots + \frac{\text{Debt service}}{(1 + i)^{30}}$$

$$= \frac{\$80,118}{(1 + .08)^1} + \frac{\$80,118}{(1 + .08)^2} + \cdots + \frac{\$80,118}{(1 + .08)^{30}}$$

$$= \$901,951$$

The cash available in the first year for pretax distribution and vacancy losses would be $25,524 ($170,160 − $64,518 − $80,118). So, with vacancy and collection losses of $8,508, first-year before-tax cash flow would be $17,016 ($25,524 − $8,508). This means a justified equity investment value of $324,114, assuming a 5.25 percent required equity dividend rate. The calculations are:

Potential gross income	$170,160
Less: Operating expense	64,518
Less: Annual debt service	80,118
Income available for risky cash flows	$ 25,524
Less: Vacancy and collection losses	8,508
Before-tax cash flow	$ 17,016
Divided by: Equity dividend rate	.0525
Justified equity investment	$324,114

The present worth of Black Oaks is $1,226,065 ($901,951 + $324,114), some $225,065 greater than the total development cost. Thus, with total investment value based on the developer's resources and criteria exceeding cost, the development of Black Oaks is feasible. These calculations are summarized in Figure 14-4.

RISK ANALYSIS

A final step in the analysis is to consider possible cost overruns and relevant financial ratios to assess the risk involved. The effect of cost overruns on property performance can easily be considered using a front door approach.

To illustrate, suppose you anticipate a 30 percent cost overrun for the Black Oaks Apartments project. This 30 percent cost overrun means that total development costs will be $1,301,300, up from $1,001,000. In turn, this means

$$\text{Justified potential gross income} = \frac{R_0 \times \text{Development cost}}{(1 - v) \times (1 - OER)}$$

$$= \frac{.08 \times \$1,301,300}{(1 - .05) \times (1 - .40)} = \$182,639$$

Thus, with a 30 percent cost overrun Black Oaks would no longer be feasible. Recall that potential gross income is only $170,160. And the *required* potential gross income on a total development cost of $1,301,300 is $182,639.

Cash Flow Amounts

Capital Amounts

Breakeven occupancy level
   Maximum default ratio = (Operating expense +
                          Debt service)/
                          Potential gross income
   85% = ($64,518 + Debt service)/$170,160
   Debt service = $170,160 × .85 - $64,518
   Debt service = $80,118

Justified mortgage value = PV of $80,118
   at 8% for 30 years
   = $901,951

+

Cash flow available for pretax
   distribution and vacancy losses = Potential gross income −
   Operating expense − Debt service
   = $170,160 − $64,518 − $80,118
   = $25,524

Before-tax cash flow = $25,524 − Vacancy losses
                     = $25,524 − $8,508
                     = $17,016

Justified equity value = $17,016
   capitalized at equity dividend rate

   $17,016 ÷ .0525 = $324,114

=

Total present worth to developer
   = justified mortgage value +
      justified equity value

   $901,951 + $324,114 = $1,226,065

FIGURE 14–4
Black Oaks Apartments: Back Door Analysis from the Developer's Perspective

The operating expense ratio for Black Oaks is

$$\text{Operating expense ratio} = \frac{\text{Operating expenses}}{\text{Potential gross income}} = \frac{\$64,518}{\$170,160} = 37.92\%$$

The operating expense ratio of 37.92 percent appears acceptable; a range of 38 to 40 percent is generally considered reasonable for new residential properties.

SUMMARY

Good development decisions require good cash flows. And good cash flows arise when a location has been wisely selected and when the right decisions have been made about the physical improvements to be added to the site.

Two methods are generally used to determine whether a development project is feasible: a front door approach and a back door approach. The front door approach to development feasibility starts with the expected cost of the property, from there the required cash flows necessary to justify the investment are calculated. The calculation is

$$\text{Justified potential gross income} = \frac{R_0 \times \text{Development cost}}{(1 - v) \times (1 - \text{Operating expense ratio})}$$

Projects where justified potential gross income is below expected potential gross income are considered feasible.

In contrast, the back door approach to development feasibility starts with the maximum gross income of the property and computes justified present worth of the project to the developer. In order to calculate justified present worth, we compute

$$\text{Justified } MV = \frac{NOI}{R_0}$$

Then if justified investment value is greater than development cost (including the market value of the land) the project is feasible.

KEY CONCEPTS

Back door approach Starts with the scheduled gross income, based on market rents, from which NOI is calculated. NOI provides the basis for determining justified investment value. Project is feasible if the justified investment value exceeds the cost of development.

Default ratio Identifies the level of occupancy at which a property's earnings exactly equal both operating expenses and required debt service.

Front door approach Starts with the expected cost, or most likely purchase price of the property, from which required cash flows necessary to justify the investment are calculated. These cash flows are then compared with those that may be realized in the market.

Justified equity investment Maximum amount the equity investor will be willing to commit to the project.

Maximum supportable mortgage loan Determined based either on minimum acceptable debt-coverage ratios or maximum acceptable loan-to-value ratios.

Total justified present worth to developer Maximum supportable mortgage loan plus justified cash equity investment.

QUESTIONS FOR REVIEW AND DISCUSSION

1. What are some important elements that should be considered in site selection and analysis?

2. What are some significant factors involved when analyzing commercial properties?

3. When was the Americans with Disabilities Act (ADA) passed? What are the main requirements of the ADA?

4. What is the front door approach to financial feasibility?

5. How does the back door approach to financial feasibility work?

6. How is the operating expense ratio calculated? What is a normal operating expense ratio for new residential developments?

7. What is the difference between using a discounted cash flow model versus a front door or back door model to analyze the financial feasibility of a project? Explain the shortcomings of each model.

PROBLEMS

1. A potential office building development costs $110 per square foot to construct, excluding land costs. The developer now holds an option to purchase the land for $20,000,000; the operating expense ratio is expected to be 40 percent, a stabilized occupancy level for the market is 90 percent, and the market capitalization rate is 8 percent. The building proposed by the developer contains 400,000 square feet of space and gross rents for the building are expected to be $26 per square foot. According to the front door approach to financial feasibility, should the developer move ahead with the project?

2. A potential new apartment complex is expected to earn an effective gross income of $650,000, while operating expenses are projected to be $235,000. Hard costs on the project are estimated to be $2,000,000, and soft costs will be 15 percent of hard costs. The land is expected to cost $1,800,000 and the market capitalization rate is 9 percent. Using the back door approach to financial feasibility, determine whether or not the project should be undertaken.

3. Assume that NOI for Black Oaks Apartments (see Figures 14–1 through 14–4) were not expected to increase at all over the four-year projection period and that the appropriate equity dividend rate is 12 percent. Would Black Oaks Apartments be viable as an investment?

4. Central Medical Building is a small two- to three-practice medical center planned for the remaining undeveloped lot just outside a major metropolitan area. The neighborhood is predominantly single-family dwellings with a limited number of low-rise and mid-rise apartment buildings. The plans call for a project totaling 4,500 square feet of rentable space with 12 parking spaces. The site is a small, triangular-shaped lot containing 4,215 square feet of land. The pro forma for the project is based on rents of $28 per square foot, plus a $25 per month per parking space fee to each tenant utilizing the on-site parking. Expenses for utilities and water, sewer, and trash pickup will be passed on to the tenants. A financial analysis of Central Medical Building suggests that the value equals or exceeds development cost (including land value). What aspects, if any, should be further investigated before the project is undertaken?

5. FBS Bank is considering financing a 90-unit multifamily development project for Hart Development Inc. The relevant facts are given below.

Site acquisition costs	$ 500,000
Construction costs	$4,450,000
Loan-to-value ratio	70%
Interest rate on a 25-year loan (monthly payments)	10%
Debt service coverage ratio	1.15
Equity dividend rate	16.5%
Default ratio	90%
Rent	$900 per unit
Operating expenses	$145 per unit
Vacancy rate	5%
Real estate taxes	$ 118,500
Replacement reserves	$ 86,400

a. Using the front door approach to financial feasibility, determine the rent required per unit. Is this project financially feasible?

b. Using the developer's back door approach to financial feasibility, can this project be justified?

c. Using the lender's back door approach to financial feasibility, determine whether this project is financially feasible.

d. What is the maximum investment that this project could support if the debt service coverage ratio were changed to 1.12?

e. What is the maximum investment that this project could support if the lender's interest rate were dropped to 8.5 percent?

CHAPTER 15

LAND DEVELOPMENT

Chapter Outline

The first man, who, having enclosed a piece of ground, bethought himself of saying, "This is mine," and found people willing to believe him, was the real founder of society.

Jean Jacques Rousseau

The speculative buying and selling of raw land can be extremely risky. Anyone who has bought raw land with the expectation of being able to resell the land at a future date at a profit has had to face this fact. Land development is an equally risky business. Acquiring raw land for subsequent development and resale is not a good investment for someone who is risk averse. Why? Because you can only make money in land development if you sell the land at a profit. Thus, if future demand should fail to materialize or land values fail to rise, rather than earning a return on any invested capital, you may actually lose money.

In this chapter we discuss the theories and practices of developing raw land as an investment.

THE LAND DEVELOPMENT PROCESS

The land development process involves three main steps:

1. First, you must determine which properties to buy and where. Land developers hope that extensive market analysis will assure that they are undertaking a profitable activity.

2. Second, you must decide whether (1) to do nothing to the land, hoping its value will increase sufficiently to provide a profit without the commensurate outlays for development costs, or (2) to subdivide the land into smaller parcels, perhaps adding streets and utilities, and then sell the developed parcels to builders and/or individuals. You might also consider placing some type of improvements on the sites.

3. Third, if you decide to develop, you have the problem of estimating the timing of the development. Unwarranted enthusiasm about future land values led developers in the early 1920s to lay out miles of streets and sidewalks for communities that went unused for thirty years.

Most of the profit in land development is made by subdividing the land into smaller parcels and adding street improvements and utilities. But this is also where all the risks are. Adding street improvements and utilities raises the investment costs. Higher investment costs, in turn, mean that land prices must increase all the more simply to reach a cost recovery point.

237

Financing arrangements for subdividing land can be complicated. A typical arrangement might call for a private investor to advance the funds in return for some percentage of profits and/or a piece of the equity. Because the land is vacant, it generates no income from operations during this period. Obviously, then, both the developer and the lender must look to the sale of the property for a return on their investment. The absence of any operating income also means that the developer must be responsible for carrying costs (e.g., real estate taxes, special assessments, and so on).

As with all other investments, timing in land development is critical. To realize substantial profits, you have to buy the land before its future becomes known to the market. This means that you might have to buy and hold the land for five, ten, or more years to realize a substantial profit. During this period, of course, a lot of changes could take place that would make the land much more valuable; but it is also true that changes in zoning, traffic patterns, population, surrounding land use, and political climate, could make the land much less valuable.

SITE ANALYSIS

By popular consensus, the three most important value characteristics of real estate are *location, location,* and *location.* This is why site analysis is so critical to land development.

Location has two distinct dimensions. One, termed *convenience* or *accessibility,* concerns the relative costs and the relative ease of getting to and from the site. The second, called *exposure* or *environment,* concerns what surrounds the parcel.

Convenience

A parcel of land can be put to only one of many possible uses at any given time. For example, a given site might be used for a residence, a professional office building, a gasoline service station, a dry cleaning store, or a tavern. What determines which use will win out in the competition among them? If all possible uses are feasible, convenience of location is usually the dominant consideration in the competition.

The importance of convenience can best be shown with an example. For most neighborhood convenience centers, driving times of 5 minutes may determine the retail trade area. The reason: When shopping for groceries, drugs, hardware, and liquors, consumers demand convenience. This means that neighborhood convenience centers must locate in proximity to homes and workplaces. Also, it means that neighborhood convenience centers must have easy entry and exit from the street.

Linked Activities.   Social and economic activities are interdependent. Families tend to be tied to nearby schools, stores, churches, work centers, and friends. Lawyers typically are in frequent contact with nearby court proceedings and records, clients, abstracting and title companies, and financial institutions. A drive-in restaurant attracts customers, needs deliveries of food and drink, and is the daily workplace of its employees. Each of these relationships is termed a *linkage,* or a relationship between two land-use activities that generates movement of people or goods between them.

A child going to school reflects a linkage. So does a parent going to the office or to the store for ice cream. A car getting gas at a service station constitutes a linkage, as does wheat going from the farm to a flour mill. The movement of cars from a factory in Detroit to a distributor in Denver is a linkage. All involve movement of people or goods.

A residence is considered to have an *outward orientation* in its linkages; each trip originates at the dwelling unit (see Figure 15-1). On the other hand, a shopping center, a factory, or an office complex has an *inward orientation;* most trips are initiated elsewhere and come to the activity (see Figure 15-2). Obviously, the better the linkages, the greater the productivity of the property.

Disutility of Travel. Moving people or goods between linked activities involves four types of costs. These costs are measured as disutilities, whether in dollars, time, or aggravation.

1. *Transportation Costs.* The out-of-pocket costs of movement are measured as fares on public transit or operating expenses for privately owned vehicles.

2. *Time Costs of Travel.* Time is required for a person or good to move from one site to another, from one economic activity to another. The speed of alternative transportation modes, traffic controls, congestion, and the efficiency of the street and road system all affect time costs of travel. The dollar cost of a trip can be calculated based on the time required for the trip and the value of the traveler's time. For goods, estimating the dollar cost of travel is much more difficult. It is a function of lost business when goods are not on hand, of spoilage because of delays in transit, or of lost personal or work time because of interrupted schedules.

3. *Terminal Costs.* Many types of linkage involve expenses at one or both ends. Terminal costs include dollars spent for loading docks, as well as for moving goods onto and from a truck or train. Parking an automobile during a downtown interview involves paying a parking fee, which is a terminal cost. Shopping centers absorb or internalize terminal costs to improve accessibility and reduce aggravation costs.

4. *Aggravation Costs.* Traveler irritation and annoyances caused by delay, congestion, bumping and shoving, and heat or cold are costs of travel that, on a personal level, enter into the costs of friction. Aggravation costs are very difficult to measure in dollar terms.

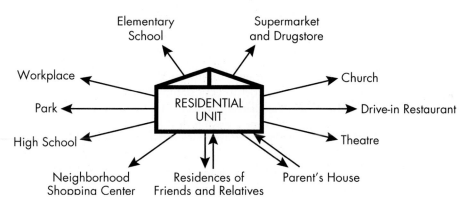

FIGURE 15-1
Linkages of a Residential Unit

FIGURE 15-2
Shopping Center
Linkages

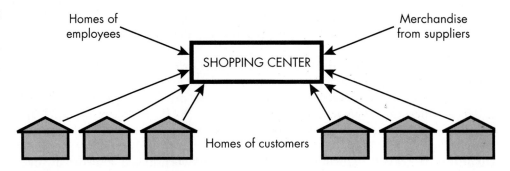

Since consumers attempt to minimize the costs and disutility of travel, the site with the lowest total disutility cost typically provides the greatest convenience or accessibility for a use.

Exposure

Exposure is the environment around a property as experienced by a user of the property. A good view, pleasant breezes, or nearness to centers of prestige and fashion provide a favorable exposure, or environment, and make the property more desirable and more valuable. On the other hand, a property subject to loud or untimely noises, to foul-smelling odors and smoke, to unduly high property taxes (without any corresponding public benefits or services), or a distressing view is said to have an unfavorable or negative exposure. Exposure affects the senses of people and is realized or experienced without moving from the site. Whether some "exposures," such as the social mix of a neighborhood, are considered favorable or unfavorable may depend on the user's perspective.

Favorable Exposure.   The primary benefits of exposure are aesthetic, satisfaction and prestige; for example, tree-lined residential streets or a Wall Street address for a financial house. High ground tends to possess these attributes to a greater extent than does a low-lying area. The reason why upper-income areas tend to dominate the hills in most urban areas is their more favorable exposure plus the ability of homeowners to outbid low-income families for these sites.

Social and business prestige are important determinants of location also. In the Washington, D.C. area, a Georgetown or Chevy Chase address carries high social acceptance. The same is true of the Gold Coast north of the Chicago Loop. Likewise, a Madison Avenue address in New York City is important for acceptance in the world of advertising. Every large metropolitan area has several premium areas. As might be expected, these are usually associated with desirable aesthetic qualities.

Unfavorable Exposure.   A social or economic activity prefers to avoid conditions that are distasteful, inharmonious, or objectionable. More than one slaughterhouse has been banned from a business district because it produced noxious odors. Slum areas are not inviting for high-income housing developments. Factories emitting excessive smoke cause residential areas downwind to become blighted. Polluted lakes and streams, trash dumps, open sewers, and sewage-disposal plants are all undesirable neighbors for most land-use activities. The result of unfavorable exposure is lower property values.

Properties suffer loss in value when other locations offer greater convenience or more favorable exposure; this is termed *locational obsolescence*. Factors that can lead to locational obsolescence include:

1. *Changes in Linked Activities.* The tendency of linked activities to relocate is an important determinant of locational obsolescence. For example, following World War II Sears initiated a policy of relocating to the edge of downtown areas or in new shopping centers. Montgomery Ward stayed downtown. For over three decades thereafter, Sears far outstripped Montgomery Ward in growth, although the two firms had started out approximately equal.

2. *Changes in Channels of Movement.* New modes of movement or new channels of movement mean new travel patterns. Thousands of motels, truck stops, and gasoline service stations were hurt by the construction of the interstate highway system. If higher energy costs cause a shift toward greater use of mass transit, central or downtown locations for restaurants and motels could increase in demand. On the other hand, drive-in restaurants would probably be seriously hurt by the shift.

3. *Changes in Nonlinked Establishments.* The development, removal, or relocation of unrelated activities may have widespread effects on spatial relationships. The development of a civic center may break up a retail shopping pattern. A large office building may touch off a whole series of moves by attorneys, engineers, realty brokers, and business services, leaving numerous vacancies in the process. Lower rents in older buildings tend to shift the makeup of tenants to businesses such as bill collectors, insurance adjusters, and printing agencies. A bookstore owner may find that his or her clientele has left, forcing either a move or a change in operational methods.

4. *Changes in the Nature of an Activity.* Changes in technology and in ways of conducting business affect the ability of a property to perform the desired functions for the use involved. For example, the use of electronic mail to send messages, documents, and data over computer lines has made some office firms less dependent on face-to-face contact and thus less likely to choose a central business district location.

Protecting Against Unfavorable Exposure

A user may gain some protection from unfavorable exposure by carefully considering the following factors when searching for a location.

1. Select a site or area that is subject to protective planning, zoning, or deed restrictions.

2. If possible, select a location with a physical buffer against possible blight. Freeways, a line of hills, or a river can provide such a buffer.

3. Promptly request enforcement of land-use controls when violations occur. If nearby land-use activities are unregulated and generate smog, dust, or unpleasant odors, initiate legal action to curtail or close them down as nuisance activities.

A SITE-EVALUATION CHECKLIST

A complete list of all the factors affecting site productivity is probably impossible; some are physical, some are legal, some are economic. The following categories account for those considered most important. Physical factors tend to be less important in site analysis if the property has already been developed and is in use, because they no longer determine the size and type of improvements. However, physical factors may be the primary determinant of the highest-and-best use for a vacant site. Off-site improvements necessary to make the site productive, such as road improvements and public utilities, are included as a part of site analysis.

The value or price of a site is generally on an as-is basis. And a lesser value should reflect a loss in productivity resulting from the absence of a service. If improvements and services have been added but not paid for, the value of the site is reduced by the amount of the unpaid costs or assessments.

Size and Shape

The size and shape of the site are of prime importance to productivity, particularly in urban areas. Lots that are small or are odd or irregularly shaped are difficult to develop and can accommodate only a limited number of uses. As a consequence, their value per unit of area is generally lower than that for parcels of standard size and shape.

For example, a lot that is triangular does not lend itself to the siting of a rectangular building. As a result, either land has to be wasted, or a triangular building, with higher construction costs and inefficient interior space arrangements, erected. Long, narrow lots are not desirable either; a lot 10 by 600 feet would not be practical as a site for a single-family residence even though it contained 6,000 square feet, a typical size lot in many communities.

Generally, land value per unit of area declines as the size of the parcel increases and the method of measuring areas changes. In rural areas, land values are lower, and size normally is stated in terms of acres rather than square feet.

Topography and Geology

Topography, the contours and slopes of the surface, and geology, the structure of the surface, determine the ability of a site to support buildings, suitability for cultivation, or other user purposes. The affects of topography and geology are interrelated. The contour of the land affects water flow and drainage; subsoil conditions also affect drainage; fertile soil eases landscaping problems. In developing a site, test borings help to foretell excavation and foundation needs. Rocks, gullies, quicksand, cliffs, or bog underlayment present special problems.

Topography must generally not be unduly rough for business, industrial, or agricultural uses. Rough terrain increases the costs of putting in roads and streets, installing utilities, and landscaping, in addition to increasing building costs. On the other hand, improved amenities—views and relative privacy—frequently result in builders of upper-income housing seeking out hilly terrain, even though the costs are greater.

Topography also has an important bearing on drainage and susceptibility to erosion, not only for the subject site but for adjoining land as well. The possibility of flooding is always an important factor. Stagnant or polluted waters can be a source of mosquitoes or disease and, therefore, a health hazard.

Soil and subsoil conditions bear directly on the income-producing ability of a site. Marshy conditions or subsurface rock usually mean greater difficulty and expense in development. Soil fertility tends to be of less importance in urban areas. In fringe areas not served by city sewer lines, soils must be relatively permeable in order to absorb septic tank effluent.

Roads and Public Utilities

Access to streets and roads is essential for each privately owned parcel of land in a community. Streets and roads facilitate movement between and among all sites, and thus serve them all. Without ready accessibility, transportation costs might become so great that most uses could not absorb them. Thus, a farm on a good road, or an industrial plant on a railroad or an interstate highway, tend to be prime property. In comparison, the value of a farm or plant that is inaccessible except by foot is almost certain to be extremely low. A completely inaccessible site has no value for all practical purposes.

Public utilities are also important to most sites. Telephone, gas, and electrical services are needed for rapid communication and for power. Sewers and water mains are necessary if septic tanks and wells cannot be accommodated. In many areas, storm-water sewers must be installed to prevent periodic flooding.

The value of a site is likely to be reduced where these services are not immediately available. That is, a site without water is worth less than a site with water.

Legal Limitations on Use

The highest-and-best use of a site may be limited by zoning, deed restrictions, easements, leases, liens, or other clouds on title. In the absence of legal limitations on use, highest-and-best use is determined by supply-and-demand.

If several legal limitations apply, the most limiting takes precedence. Thus, a site may be suitable, based on market demand, for a high-rise apartment building; zoned for a two-story apartment building; and limited by deed restriction to development as a single-family residence. The single-family use governs. If the deed restriction were removed, the zoning would control. Thus, restrictive zoning, an easement, or an awkward lease can reduce the productivity, and therefore the value, of a site just as surely as poor drainage, lack of access, or inconvenient size or shape. The cause is less tangible, but the effect on use and value is as real.

Lack of clear title or other title problems can also limit use and productivity. For example, three siblings may inherit a property as tenants-in-common. Unless all the siblings agree to the terms necessary for development, efforts by an investor to develop it further would be fruitless. Another example of an encumbrance that limits use and productivity is a power-line easement across a site. Assume that the easement limits construction to 32 feet in height. Even though demand justifies a seven-story building, which would be allowed by zoning, the use would be limited to a three-story building.

WHAT IS PLOTTAGE VALUE?

Sometimes, a value increment, called plottage value can be realized by bringing two or more smaller parcels of land under one ownership. *Plottage value* means that the value of the several parcels, when combined, is greater than the sum of the values of the individual parcels under separate ownership.

Plottage comes about because the larger, combined unit of land can be used more intensively or with lower costs than would be possible with the smaller parcels treated independently. Thus, combining two triangular business lots, for example, could produce a site able to accommodate a rectangular building. The benefit, as against two triangular-shaped buildings, would be lower construction costs and a more efficient arrangement of space. Another example of plottage value would be combining two single-family lots into a larger site on which a four-unit apartment building could be built—provided the latter use is allowed by the zoning ordinance.

However, note that, in some cases we may have the sum of the parts exceeding the value of the whole. This occurs when there is a possibility of excess supply. A neighborhood retail shopping center, for example, may have large widths. Large widths make it difficult to lease the property. By splitting up larger widths into smaller pieces, therefore, higher rents and greater occupancy rates can be realized.

LAND DEVELOPMENT FINANCING

Land-development loans work as follows. Disbursement of the funds occurs in stages, usually on a monthly basis, as determined by the need to pay for the land acquisition and development costs. Thus, the term of a land-development loan is as long as it takes to develop and sell the building sites. Interest is charged on the loan balance that is outstanding over any particular month. This interest is added to the beginning loan balance plus the monthly draw to determine the cumulative loan balance. Repayment of the loan is through the sale of the developed lots.

Here is an example: O&L Development Corporation is looking to borrow $636,000 in the form of a land-development loan. Okane Bank has expressed an interest. The project information is as follows:

Land acquisition costs	$350,000
Development costs	350,000
Total	$700,000
Market value of land after improvements	$945,000
Total number of parcels	90
Average lot price	$ 10,500

O&L Development Corporation must borrow $250,000 of the land cost at closing. The remaining land acquisition costs, $100,000, are to be paid directly by O&L Development Corporation as its equity contribution to the project. The interest rate is based on the prime rate plus 200 basis points. During the 10-month land-development loan period, the prime rate is expected to be 10 percent per annum. Thus, the loan rate is expected to be 12 percent per annum, or 1 percent per month.

Closing costs and origination fees are $36,000. The development costs of $350,000 will be borrowed in ten equal installments, beginning at the end of month 1. See Figure 15-3 for a summary of the monthly draws.

Note that in order to determine the amount needed each month to repay the loan, the initial draw at closing includes the $250,000 payment for the land plus the $36,000 for loan closing costs and origination fees. This is a typical practice. Most lenders add the loan origination fees and closing costs to the balance of the loan.

There will be a total of 90 parcels; sales are expected to begin in month 6 at a rate of 18 parcels a month. Each lot is to be sold for $10,500. As each site is sold, the land-development loan is repaid from the proceeds of the lot sales. The *release price* required by Okane Bank is the amount of principal and interest per parcel which will make the present value of the monthly draws equal to the present value of the repayments.

The calculations are set forth in Figure 15-4. Column 1 contains the monthly draws (see Figure 15-3). Each draw is discounted at a rate of 1 percent per month to determine its present value. The present value of the total monthly draws is $617,495 (see column 2).

Now compare the present value of the total monthly draws to the present value of the total repayments. The present value of the total repayments is set out in columns 3 and 4. The repayments are based on the release price per parcel times the number of lots sold in the period. The formula is

Repayments = Release price × Number of lots sold

The present value of each repayment is

Present value = Repayment × Present value factor
             = Release price × (Number of lots sold × Present value factor)

MONTH	(1) NET CASH TO DEVELOPER FOR LAND ACQUISITION AND LAND-DEVELOPMENT COSTS	(2) CLOSING COSTS AND ORIGINATION FEES	(3) = (1) + (2) MONTHLY CASH DRAWS
Close	$250,000	$36,000	$286,000
1	35,000		35,000
2	35,000		35,000
3	35,000		35,000
4	35,000		35,000
5	35,000		35,000
6	35,000		35,000
7	35,000		35,000
8	35,000		35,000
9	35,000		35,000
10	35,000		35,000
Total	$600,000	$36,000	$636,000

FIGURE 15-3
Monthly Cash Draws on Land-Development Loan

FIGURE 15–4
Calculation of Release
Price on a Land-
Development Loan

MONTH	(1) MONTHLY CASH DRAWS	(2) PV OF MONTHLY CASH DRAWS (@ 1% PER MONTH)	(3) REPAYMENTS (RELEASE PRICE × LOTS SOLD)	(4) PV OF REPAYMENTS (@ 1% PER MONTH)
Close	$286,000	$286,000		
1	35,000	34,653		
2	35,000	34,310		
3	35,000	33,971		
4	35,000	33,634		
5	35,000	33,301		
6	35,000	32,972	Release price × 18	Release price × 16.9568
7	35,000	32,645	Release price × 18	Release price × 16.7889
8	35,000	32,322	Release price × 18	Release price × 16.6227
9	35,000	32,002	Release price × 18	Release price × 16.4581
10	35,000	31,685	Release price × 18	Release price × 16.2952
Total		$617,495		Release price × 83.1217

Release price = $617,495 ÷ 83.1217
= $7,428.81

This present value is then totaled. The result is

Present Value of total repayments = Present value of repayments in month t
$+ \cdots$
+ Present value of repayments in
month $t + n$
= Release price × (number of lots sold in
month t × Present value factor) $+ \cdots$
+ Release price × (number of lots sold
in month $t + n$ × Present value factor)
= Release price × [(number of lots sold in
month t × Present value factor) $+ \cdots$
+ (number of lots sold in month $t + n$
× Present value factor)]

For the O&L land-development loan these unpleasant-looking formulas reduce to

Present Value of total repayments = Present value of repayments in month 6
$+ \cdots +$ Present value of repayments
in month 10
= Release price × (18 × 0.9420) $+ \cdots$
+ Release price × (18 × 0.9053)
= Release price × [(18 × 0.9420) $+ \cdots$
+ (18 × 0.9053)]
= Release price × 83.1217

We can now solve for the release price per parcel by setting the present value of the total repayments equal to the present value of the total monthly draws:

Present Value of total repayments = Present value of total monthly draws
Release price $\times$ 83.1217 = $617,495

or

Release price = $617,495 $\div$ 83.1217
= $7,428.81

This means that each time a parcel is sold O&L Development Corporation must pay $7,428.81 to Okane Bank from the proceeds of the lot sale.

The effective interest rate on this land development loan is defined as the rate of discount which makes the present value of the total net cash to the developer (see column 1 of Figure 15-3) equal to the present value of the total repayments (see Figure 15-4). This means that to find the effective interest rate for the land development loan to O&L Development Corporation, we must solve for IRR in the following expression:

$$\$250,000 + \frac{\$35,000}{(1 + IRR)} + \cdots + \frac{\$35,000}{(1 + IRR)^{10}}$$

$$= \frac{\$7,428.81 \times 18}{(1 + IRR)^{6}} + \cdots + \frac{\$7,428.81 \times 18}{(1 + IRR)^{10}}$$

Solving for IRR usually involves trial and error. In this case IRR is 2.23 percent per month, or 26.79 percent per annum.

Are you surprised at how high the effective interest rate is on this land development loan? You shouldn't be! The effective interest rate is much higher than the interest rate on the loan because of the $36,000 closing costs and origination fees. These fees can have an immense effect on the effective interest rate, especially if the loan is taken down slowly.

SUMMARY

The analyses required for moving raw land to finished development are complicated. To determine potential market demand, location and exposure must be considered. Changes in linked and nonlinked activities, disutility of travel, and nature of an activity must also be analyzed. The proximity to utilities, access roads, schools, police and fire protection, shopping, and employment are extremely important.

Legal limitations on the intended use for the site under consideration must also be examined. The highest-and-best use of a site may be limited by zoning, deed restrictions, easements, leases, liens, or other clouds on title.

Finally, the physical characteristics of the site must be examined. Size and shape are of prime importance to productivity. Topography and geology determine the suitability of a site for support of buildings, for cultivation, and for other purposes. In some cases a value increment, or plottage value, can be realized by bringing two or more smaller parcels of land together under one ownership.

KEY CONCEPTS

Accessibility   Relative ease or difficulty of getting to and from a property; a property that is easy to get to has good accessibility or convenience of location.

Convenience of location   Relative costs, in time and money, of getting to and from a property; lower costs means greater convenience or accessibility.

Disutility of travel   Costs of moving goods or people between linked land-use activities. Money, time, terminal, and aggravation costs.

Linkage   A relationship between two land-use activities that requires the movement of people or goods between them.

Locational obsolescence   Diminished utility of a site or property because of external factors of environment or location that unfavorably affect its ability to render services; results in a lower value.

Plottage value   Incremental value realized by combining two or more sites; the value of the larger parcel is greater than the combined values of the individual parcels.

QUESTIONS FOR REVIEW AND DISCUSSION

1. Why is land development risky? What are some possible techniques that can be used to minimize this risk?

2. At what stage is most of the profit in land development realized?

3. What are some possible reasons for the success of retail shopping centers located in the suburbs as compared to shopping centers located in central business districts?

4. Give examples of linkages that may be associated with a specific parcel of land directly off a major thoroughfare near several strip shopping centers.

5. What are some significant costs of friction that may be considered when thinking about traveling to a certain location?

6. Discuss some of the changes that can lead to locational obsolescence?

7. What are some legal limitations that should be considered when analyzing a site?

8. What issues other than legal limitations should be considered when undertaking a site analysis?

9. What is meant by plottage value? Describe a real world scenario in which this situation might occur.

PROBLEMS

1. A developer wishes to subdivide a parcel of land into two parcels. If the land is developed as a single parcel, its expected value is $850,000. To subdivide the land into two parcels, certain zoning changes and approvals will be necessary. The cost of obtaining these zoning changes and approvals is estimated to be $60,000. If the net operating income of each of the two lots is $45,000 per year

and the market capitalization rate is 10 percent, should the developer subdivide the land or not?

2. Assume in problem 1 that a new school goes up near the site and the value of the parcel as one piece increases to $1,200,000. Although the costs to subdivide remain the same, the net operating income of the two parcels increases to $70,000 each. Now what should the developer do?

3. Amida Development Company has approached First Bank for a land-development loan. Amida wishes to develop 60 acres of raw land, improving and subdividing it into 100 single-family residential lots. The average lot price is estimated to be $15,000.

The price of the land is $300,000. Amida Development Company has put down $60,000 to purchase the land. The remainder will be paid at closing.

The net cash to Amida Development Company is given below:

MONTH	NET CASH TO AMIDA DEVELOPMENT COMPANY FOR LAND-DEVELOPMENT COSTS
Close	$240,000
1	45,000
2	45,000
3	45,000
4	35,000
5	35,000
6	25,000
7	25,000
8	15,000
9	15,000
10	15,000
Total	$540,000

First Bank requires a 9 percent interest rate and a loan origination fee of $10,800. Parcel sales are expected to begin in month 7 at a rate of 20 parcels per month.

a. What is the release price per parcel?

b. What is the effective interest rate on this loan?

CHAPTER 16

ADVANCED PROPERTY DEVELOPMENT ISSUES

Chapter Outline

We shape our dwellings, and afterwards our dwellings shape us.
                                                        Winston Churchill

All developers struggle with the question of a *change-in-use*. Should a large, old house, for example, be converted into an office building? Should a gasoline service station be torn down to make way for an apartment building? A change-in-use involves the modification of an existing structure or its replacement by new improvements. The new use must be able to absorb the costs of conversion or replacement to be profitable and feasible.

Another type of transformation is a change in *intensity-of-use*. Adding another story to increase display and sales area is an intensity-of-use change, as is converting a large, old, single-family residence into several small apartment units. Although the type of use is not changed, the amount of economic or social activity on the site is modified. If the intensity is increased, the additional benefits must be great enough to justify the costs of the structural modifications.

A third type of adjustment is a change in *quality-of-use*. The nature of the benefits of using a property may be upgraded or downgraded. When creeping blight leads to the gradual deterioration in a residential neighborhood or a commercial area, the quality-of-use is downgraded. The rehabilitation of the Georgetown area in Washington, D.C., on the other hand, is an excellent example of upgrading the quality-of-use. Upgrading the quality-of-use depends on an explicit act by a manager or owner to take advantage of a favorable set of environmental conditions.

In this chapter we take up the issue of property redevelopment and modernization. But before doing so let us consider how to value intensity-of-use.

INTENSITY-OF-USE— THE CASE OF AN OFFICE BUILDING

Here is an interesting example of *intensity-of-use*. Consider a vacant site that is to be improved with an office building. The 10,000-square foot site—100 feet wide by 100 feet deep—was acquired for $600,000. Office space rents for $20 per square foot per year gross, which yields a net operating income of $12 per square foot. We shall assume that planning and zoning regulations allow 100 percent land coverage for office buildings, with no limit on height. We will also assume that the design of the building provides for 90 percent efficiency; that is, 90 percent of the building's area can be rented out. Finally, the ratio of annual net operating income to sales price for comparable properties approximates 10 percent. Building costs vary from $105 per square foot for the first story to $90 for the fourth and fifth stories, after which they increase by $5 per story. How many stories should the investor add to the land?

Figure 16–1 illustrates the calculations for valuing the intensity-of-use of the improvements. To begin, a one-story office building covering the entire 10,000 square foot site, with 90 percent efficiency, would provide 9,000 square feet of rentable area (see column 5). At $12 per square foot, an annual NOI of $108,000 would be realized.

Capitalized at 10 percent, the value realized would be $1,080,000 (column 10). However, the total cost for a one-story property would be $1,650,000, as shown in column 6; thus, the investor would suffer a loss of $570,000 (column 11). Adding a second story lowers the loss to $490,000, while yielding a positive marginal profit of $8.89 per square foot of rentable area added.

The marginal cost of a square foot drops as floors are added. Footings and other supports only have to be strengthened, and one roof serves all floors. Likewise, land costs fall from $600,000 ÷ 9,000 square feet = $66.67 per net rentable area with one-story, to $600,000 ÷ 18,000 square feet = $33.33 per net rentable area with two-stories, and so on. Offsetting these economies are the increasing costs of lifting materials to ever-higher levels, of installing elevators, and solving similar problems.

The marginal profit per square foot is maximized at $20 at four and five stories. Yet, it is only at the fifth floor that realized value equals costs incurred. It is clear that the building must be at least five stories. Even so, it pays the developer to add more stories because marginal profit is positive and total profit is still increasing. See Figure 16–2 for a graphic summary, floor by floor, of the interaction of total costs and total value for this example.

The marginal cost of $1,050,000 at the eighth story is just slightly exceeded by the $1,080,000 marginal value realized. At the ninth floor the point of diminishing returns has been reached and passed; the marginal cost of $1,100,000 is $20,000 greater than the marginal value. Or, we could say that at this point marginal cost equals marginal revenue, signaling that any additional space produced would result in ever-greater losses. Thus, the office building should be built to eight stories. At eight stories, profit is maximized at $240,000.

THE BUILDING-ENVELOPE CALCULATION

Now let us relax our assumption that planning and zoning regulations allow 100 percent land coverage for commercial uses. Instead, we shall assume that the land coverage requirements are as follows:

Front	20 feet
Rear	25 feet
Side	7.5 feet

This means that the structure must set back a minimum of 20 feet from the front, 25 feet from the rear, and 7.5 feet on either side. The area lost because of these *setback requirements* can be calculated as:

Front	(100 feet − 15 feet) × 20 feet	= 1,700 square feet
Rear	(100 feet − 15 feet) × 25 feet	= 2,125 square feet
Side	100 feet × 7.5 feet × 2	= 1,500 square feet
TOTAL	1,700 + 2,125 + 1,500	= 5,325 square feet

Note that in these calculations an adjustment is made to both the front and rear setback requirements to avoid double counting (see Figure 16–3).

	BUILDING				COSTS OF DEVELOPMENT					PROFIT ANALYSIS		
(1) NO. OF STORIES	(2) MARGINAL COST/ SQ. FT.	(3) MARGINAL COST PER STORY	(4) TOTAL ACCUMU-LATED COST	(5) NET RENTABLE AREA (SQ. FT.)	(6) TOTAL COST (LAND AND BUILDING)	(7) AVERAGE COST/ SQ. FT. OF RENTABLE AREA	(8) MARGINAL COST/ SQ. FT. OF RENTABLE AREA	(9) NET OP (ANNUAL)	(10) TOTAL VALUE (NOI ÷ .10)	(11) PROFIT (TOTAL VALUE MINUS TOTAL COST)	(12) AVERAGE PROFIT (LOSS)/ SQ. FT. OF RENTABLE AREA	(13) MARGINAL PROFIT (LOSS)/ SQ. FT. OF RENTABLE AREA
1	$105.00	$1,050,000	$1,050,000	9,000	$1,650,000	$183.33	$183.33	$108,000	$1,080,000	($570,000)	($63.33)	($63.33)
2	$100.00	1,000,000	2,050,000	18,000	2,650,000	147.22	90.00	216,000	2,160,000	(490,000)	(27.22)	8.89
3	95.00	950,000	3,000,000	27,000	3,600,000	133.33	85.50	324,000	3,240,000	(360,000)	(13.33)	14.44
4	90.00	900,000	3,900,000	36,000	4,500,000	125.00	81.00	432,000	4,320,000	(180,000)	(5.00)	20.00
5	90.00	900,000	4,800,000	45,000	5,400,000	120.00	81.00	540,000	5,400,000	0	0.00	20.00
6	95.00	950,000	5,750,000	54,000	6,350,000	117.59	85.50	648,000	6,480,000	130,000	2.41	14.44
7	100.00	1,000,000	6,750,000	63,000	7,350,000	116.67	90.00	756,000	7,560,000	210,000	3.33	8.89
8	105.00	1,050,000	7,800,000	72,000	8,400,000	116.67	94.50	864,000	8,640,000	240,000	3.33	3.33
9	110.00	1,100,000	8,900,000	81,000	9,500,000	117.28	99.00	972,000	9,720,000	220,000	2.72	(2.22)
10	115.00	1,150,000	10,050,000	90,000	10,650,000	118.33	103.50	1,080,000	10,800,000	150,000	1.67	(7.78)
11	120.00	1,200,000	11,250,000	99,000	11,850,000	119.70	108.00	1,188,000	11,880,000	30,000	0.30	(13.33)
12	125.00	1,250,000	12,500,000	108,000	13,100,000	121.30	112.50	1,296,000	12,960,000	(140,000)	(1.30)	(18.89)

FIGURE 16–1

Valuing Intensity-of-Use, Assuming No Setbacks and No Provision for Parking

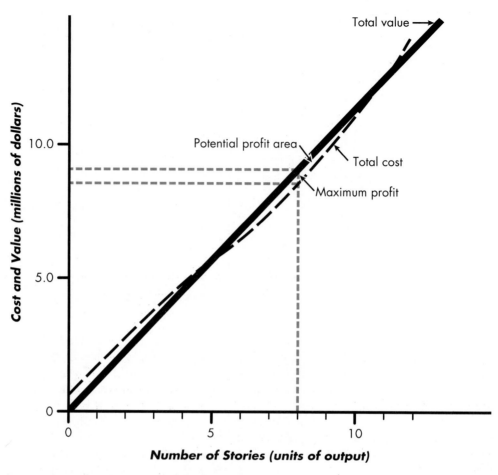

FIGURE 16–2
Total Value and Total
Cost Curves for Property
Improvement Analysis

Next, we calculate *total buildable area,* which is simply total lot area less area lost to setback requirements. The calculation is:

$$\text{Total buildable area} = \text{Total square feet} - \text{Area lost to setbacks}$$
$$= 10,000 - 5,325$$
$$= 4,675 \text{ square feet}$$

So, instead of having 10,000 square feet of buildable area as in our first example, we really have only 4,675 square feet of buildable area.[1]

But wait we are not done yet. We still need to account for parking. Industry standards for commercial structures typically require five parking spaces per 1,000

[1]Planning and zoning requirements may also impose limits on the amount of gross floor area. For example, assume that the gross floor area of the building cannot exceed two times the gross lot area. The maximum allowable floor area in this case would be:

$$\text{Allowable floor area} = \text{Lot area} \times \text{Floor area ratio}$$
$$= 10,000 \text{ square feet} \times 2$$
$$= 20,000 \text{ square feet}$$

Thus, a floor area ratio in this case means that an owner is permitted to construct a 20,000-square-foot office building

Rear

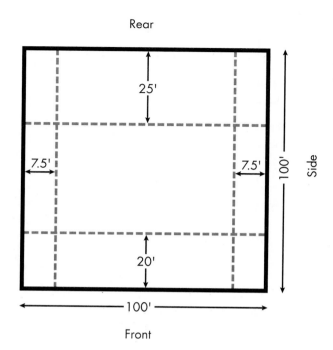

25'

7.5'   7.5'

100'
Side

20'

100'

Front

FIGURE 16–3
Area Lost Due to
Minimum Setback
Requirements

square feet of gross area. Keep in mind, too, that a parking space is roughly 300 square feet. Hence, developing five parking spaces would require 5 × 300 = 1500 square feet of buildable area. Likewise, developing ten parking spaces would require 3,000 square feet of buildable area, and so on.

Parking will obviously have a direct impact on the amount of building area. Consider our office building example, and assume for the moment that it should be built to one story. It will also be assumed that 4,675 square feet of total buildable area is available for parking or building. There are five parking stalls per 1,000 square feet of gross area, and each parking space is 300 square feet. Now our goal is to determine the maximum gross floor area of the building.

The astute reader will recognize that the total lot area covered by parking is simply gross building area times five parking stalls per 1,000 square feet of gross area times 300 square feet per stall. The gross area equals total lot area covered by the building, times the number of stories. Thus

Total buildable area = Lot area covered by building + Lot area covered by parking

Or,

Total buildable area = Lot area covered by building
+ Lot area covered by building

$$\times \text{Number of stories} \times \frac{5}{1,000 \text{ sq.ft.}} \times 300 \text{ sq.ft.}$$

Thus total buildable area is equal to:

Total buildable area = Lot area covered by building

$$\times \left[1 + \text{Number of stories} \times \frac{5}{1,000 \text{ sq.ft.}} \times 300 \text{ sq.ft.} \right]$$

We can now solve for lot area covered by building. Let total buildable area equal 4,675 square feet; and number of stories equal one. The calculations are:

$$\text{Lot area covered by building} = \frac{4,675 \text{ sq.ft.}}{\left[1 + 1 \times \dfrac{5}{1,000 \text{ sq.ft.}} \times 300 \text{ sq.ft.} \right]} = 1,870 \text{ sq.ft.}$$

For a two-story building, the lot area covered by building is

$$\text{Lot area covered by building} = \frac{4,675 \text{ sq.ft.}}{\left[1 + 2 \times \dfrac{5}{1,000 \text{ sq.ft.}} \times 300 \text{ sq.ft.} \right]} = 1,169 \text{ sq.ft.}$$

Likewise, for a three-story building, the lot area covered by building is

$$\text{Lot area covered by building} = \frac{4,675 \text{ sq.ft.}}{\left[1 + 3 \times \dfrac{5}{1,000 \text{ sq.ft.}} \times 300 \text{ sq.ft.} \right]} = 850 \text{ sq.ft.}$$

Figure 16–4 illustrates the relationship between number of stories and lot area covered by building. Also shown in Figure 16–4 is gross area.

Now let us determine the optimal number of stories. A one-story office building covering 1,870 square feet of lot area, with 90 percent efficiency, would provide 1,683 square feet of rentable area. At $12 per square foot, an annual NOI of $20,196 would be realized. Capitalized at 10 percent, the value realized would be $201,960. The total cost for a one-story property (including land and building) is $796,350, which yields the developer a loss of $594,390. Adding a second story decreases the developer's loss to $587,144. In fact, the developer loses money regardless of the number of stories built (see Figure 16–5).

Why? What has caused the project to become financially infeasible? The an-

FIGURE 16–4

Relationship Between Number of Stories and Lot Area Covered by Building

NUMBER OF STORIES	LOT AREA COVERED BY BUILDING	GROSS AREA
1	1,870	1,870
2	1,169	2,338
3	850	2,550
4	668	2,671
5	550	2,750
6	468	2,805
7	407	2,846
8	360	2,877

	BUILDING				COSTS OF DEVELOPMENT			PROFIT ANALYSIS		
(1)	(2)	(3)	(4)	(5)	(6)	(7)	(8)	(9)	(10)	(11)
NO. OF STORIES	MARGINAL COST/ SQ.FT.	MARGINAL COST PER STORY	TOTAL ACCUMU- LATED COST	NET RENTABLE AREA	TOTAL COST (LAND AND BUILDING)	AVERAGE COST/ SQ. FT. OF RENTABLE AREA	MARGINAL COST/ SQ. FT. OF RENTABLE AREA	NOI (ANNUAL)	TOTAL VALUE	PROFIT (LOSS)
1	105	$196,350	$196,350	1683	$796,350	$473.17	$473.17	$20,196	$201,960	−$594,390
2	100	43,244	239,594	2104	839,594	399.09	102.78	25,245	252,450	− 587,144
3	95	15,406	255,000	2295	855,000	372.55	80.56	27,540	275,400	− 579,600
4	90	5,464	260,464	2404	860,464	357.89	50.00	28,851	288,514	− 571,950
5	90	3,536	264,000	2475	864,000	349.09	50.00	29,700	297,000	− 567,000
6	95	4,813	268,813	2525	868,813	344.15	97.22	30,294	302,940	− 565,873
7	100	5,590	274,402	2561	874,402	341.42	152.78	30,733	307,330	− 567,072
8	105	6,098	280,500	2589	880,500	340.06	216.67	31,071	310,708	− 569,792

FIGURE 16–5
Valuing Intensity-of-Use Assuming Setback Requirements and Provision for Parking

swer, of course, is the cost of the land. Given the lot area lost to parking and minimum setback requirements, the land is now too costly. You can see this by looking at the average and marginal cost per square foot of rentable area.

One solution to the problem would be to renegotiate downward the price of the vacant lot. But note that even if you are successful in renegotiating the price of the land, development beyond one or two floors is highly unlikely. The reason is that the floor size becomes too small. With small floor plates, your building would appeal only to smaller tenants, which could make it very difficult to rent the space.

ANALYSIS FOR REDEVELOPMENT OR MODERNIZATION

Modernization or redevelopment is necessary to keep a property productive and in its highest-and-best use. The question becomes: "When is modernization appropriate, when is redevelopment needed?"

In simple terms, buildings are redeveloped or modernized to a former or improved condition when the marginal value created exceeds the marginal costs. The difference between modernization and redevelopment or renovation is renovation may include new construction or additions, but is usually performed without changing the basic plan or style of the structure.

Case: Douglas Manor Apartments

Let us return to the Douglas Manor Apartments example in Chapter 6. Suppose you are contemplating some modifications and modernization to the property. Total estimated cost of the modernization is $27,500. What you would like to know is, "Is this the best time to make these repairs?"

The only way to find the answer is to look at the net present value of the decision to modernize. To begin, let us suppose that the modernization will increase the annual NOI by $4,800, to $68,800, in year 1. The end-of-year 4 market value is expected to be $836,268. We shall continue to assume that you are in a 36 percent tax bracket.

From a tax depreciation standpoint, we know that the $27,500 modernization cost must be amortized over 27.5 years, meaning an additional $1,000 per year in straight-line cost recovery. Thus, total allowable depreciation would now be $17,399 per year. All other investment assumptions regarding Douglas Manor would hold as before, including a 5 percent growth rate.

Forecasted Cash Flows

Figures 16–6 and 16–7 show the revised annual NOI projections for Douglas Manor, including income taxes payable and the annual after-tax cash flow from operations. The format is almost identical to that in Figures 6–4 and 6–5. The after-tax cash flows from operations for years 1 to 4 are $50,296, $52,497, $54,809, and $57,236, respectively.

Figure 16–8 shows the calculation of the net after-tax equity reversion at the end of year 4, assuming modernization; the amount is $695,178. Again, the calculations closely parallel those in Chapter 6.

	YEAR			
	1	2	3	4
NOI	$68,800	$72,240	$75,852	$79,645
Less: Straight-line tax depreciation	17,399	17,399	17,399	17,399
Interest paid	0	0	0	0
Taxable Income	51,401	21,042	58,453	62,246
Times: Investor's tax rate	0.36	0.36	0.36	0.36
Income tax payable	$18,504	$19,743	$21,043	$22,409

FIGURE 16–6

Douglas Manor Apartments Modernized: Calculation of Annual Tax on Income for an Equity Owner in 36 Percent Tax Bracket

Marginal Net Present Value and Internal Rate of Return

Annual after-tax cash flows before and after modernization are shown in Figure 16–9. The increase in marginal revenues for years 1 through 3 is, respectively, $3,432, $3,585, and $3,747. Note that for year 4, the after-tax equity reversion (from disposition) is combined with after-tax cash flow from operations. The marginal equity investment for modernization is $27,500, and present value of the marginal after-tax cash flow for each of the four years is $3,432, $3,585, $3,747, and $49,928, respectively. The marginal cash flows are discounted at 12 percent.

Figure 16–9 shows that the accumulated present value of all marginal cash flows after taxes to the investment is $40,086 ($3,064 + $2,858 + $2,667 + $31,497). In turn, the NPV of the modernization is $12,586 ($40,086 − $27,500). Since net present value is positive, the modernization should be undertaken.

Alternatively, the analysis could be done by calculating the internal rate of return of the marginal cash flows. Based on a $27,500 initial investment, this calculates to 24.68 percent. Since this easily exceeds the 12 percent required rate of return, the program should be initiated.

An analysis for a major redevelopment of Douglas Manor, while more complex, would follow the same basic format. In summary, in order for the project to be financially feasible, the marginal revenues must justify the cost of modernization or redevelopment.

	YEAR			
	1	2	3	4
NOI	$68,800	$72,240	$75,852	$79,645
Less: Annual debt service	0	0	0	0
Before-tax cash flow	$68,800	$72,240	$75,852	$79,645
Less: Tax payable[a]	18,504	19,743	21,043	22,409
After-tax cash flow	$50,296	$52,497	$54,809	$57,236

[a] For tax payable, see Figure 6–4.

FIGURE 16–7

Douglas Manor Apartments Modernized: Calculation of After-Tax Cash Flows from Operations

FIGURE 16–8
Douglas Manor Apart-
ments Modernized:
Calculation of End-of-
Year 4 Taxes Due on
Sale and After-Tax
Equity Reversion

Sales Price, at end of year 4		$836,268
Less: Selling expenses @ 7%		58,539
Net Selling Price		$777,729
Less: Adjusted basis		
Purchase price	$552,500	
Less: Accumulated depreciation	69,596	482,904
Taxable Capital Gain		$294,825
Times: Capital gain tax rate		0.28
Taxes Due on Sale		$82,551

Sales Price, at end of year 4	$836,268
Less: Selling expenses @ 7%	58,539
Net Sales Price	$777,729
Less: Mortgage balance outstanding	0
Before-Tax Equity Reversion	$777,729
Less: Taxes due on sale	82,511
After-Tax Equity Reversion	$695,178

REDEVELOPMENT VERSUS RENOVATION

Suppose you must choose between the following two options:

Option 1: Spend $5 million to demolish the Rookery building, a 12-story office building located on LaSalle Street in Chicago's financial district, and $85 million to construct a new office building on the same site.

Option 2: Spend $90 million to renovate the Rookery building from top-to-bottom, including taking out and replacing the HVAC system, windows, elevators, life-safety systems, etc.

Which option should you choose? The answer is renovate. Here's why. By renovating the Rookery building, you would be able to depreciate the full $90 million in renovation expenditures. This means depreciation tax benefits of ($90 million ÷ 39) × .36 = $0.83 million per year, assuming a 36 percent marginal income tax rate.

In contrast, by choosing to demolish the Rookery building and construct a new building, you would be unable to depreciate the $5 million of demolition costs; instead, these expenditures would have to be capitalized into the value of the land and, consequently, cannot be depreciated. Your depreciation tax benefits, therefore, would be only ($85 million ÷ 39) × .36 = $0.78 million per year.

But wait we are not finished! The greater depreciation trades off higher tax savings now for a higher tax consequence at the time of sale. When the Rookery building is sold (say, at the end of five years), the additional taxes due on the sale are:

$$\text{Additional taxes due on sale} = \text{Capital gains tax rate} \times \text{Additional capital gains}$$
$$= \text{Capital gains tax rate} \times (\text{Accumulated depreciation if renovated} - \text{Accumulated depreciation if demolished})$$
$$= .28 \times (\$11.54\ million - \$10.90\ million)$$
$$= \$0.18\ million$$

	YEAR				
	0	1	2	3	4
After-Tax Cash Flows, after modernization	($27,500)	$50,296	$52,497	$54,809	$752,414
After-Tax Cash Flows, before modernization	0	46,864	48,912	51,062	702,851
Marginal Increase	($27,500)	$3,432	$3,585	$3,747	$49,563
Times: PV factor @12%	× 1.0000	× .8929	× .7972	× .7118	× .6355
PV of marginal increase	($27,500)	$3,064	$2,858	$2,667	$31,497
Accumulated present value of marginal after-tax cash flows	$40,086				
Net Present Value of modernization	$12,586				
After-Tax Internal Rate of Return to investor	24.68%				

FIGURE 16–9
Douglas Manor Apartments Modernized: Marginal Revenues, and the Internal Rate of Return to the Investor

We can now work out the net present value of the decision to renovate. The net present value is

$$NPV = PV \text{ of marginal tax depreciation benefits} - PV \text{ of additional capital gains tax}$$

$$= \left(\frac{\$0.05}{(1 + .06)} + \cdots + \frac{\$0.05}{(1 + .06)^5} \right) - \frac{\$0.22}{(1 + .06)^5}$$

$$= \$0.076 \text{ million}$$

The first term on the right hand side of the equation represents the present value of the additional savings resulting from the higher depreciation and the second term represents the additional capital gains taxes due on sale.

The net present value of renovating is $0.076 million. This obviously implies that renovating is more attractive. And that is exactly what happened to the Rookery building. In 1989, the Baldwin Development Company purchased the Rookery building and the land under it and announced a 100 percent gut renovation of the building. The total renovation costs were roughly $90 million.

What really swayed the Baldwin Development Company toward renovating the Rookery building was not the additional depreciation tax benefits. Rather, it was the 20 percent rehabilitation tax credit. The Baldwin Development Company knew beforehand that all qualified rehabilitation expenditures were eligible for a 20 percent rehabilitation tax credit. And they also knew that the Rookery building, which was built in 1888 and is on the National Register of Historic Places, would be eligible for this credit.

The effect of the rehabilitation tax credit is clearly to bias the redevelopment decision toward renovating and away from demolition. Obviously, in the case of the Rookery building, a 20 percent tax credit on all rehabilitation expenditures was too significant to be passed over by choosing to demolish the building and construct a new one.

INHERENT RISKS IN RENOVATING A PROPERTY

It is reasonable to ask whether renovations ever are financially feasible. In many cases, despite the tax credit renovations are not a good idea, especially when the renovation costs plus the initial cost of building are in excess of the cost of new construction, or when the renovated space is not as attractive to tenants as newly constructed space. Take, for example, the renovation of a dilapidated office building in a downtown location. The renovations may improve the building and make it into a prestige building. But a new construction would mean a prestige building. Hence, you still might not be able to attract tenants to the renovated property and you certainly might not be able to charge tenants higher rents. As a result you very likely would be unable to recoup your investment.

Nevertheless, some experts feel there is a niche for rehabilitation. The Kemper Investor Life Insurance and The Prime Group, for example, recently completed a $15 million renovation to the Plaza of the Americas in Dallas. The Plaza of the Americas consists of two 25-story office buildings, totaling 1 million square feet, plus a 100,000-square foot atrium. Another example of a recent renovation project is the 110-story, 4.5-million square foot Sears Tower in Chicago. The redevelopment of the Sears Tower included enlarging the building lobbies, modifying the elevator system, and the constructing a separate tourist entrance. As a result of the renovations, about 650,000 square feet of office leases at the Sears Tower were negotiated.

A lot of hotel owners also choose to renovate. One example is the Colony Square Hotel in Atlanta, which is the oldest hotel in Midtown, and is a few miles north of the downtown area on Peachtree Street. It is owned by Prudential Properties. Colony Square Hotel competes in the highly competitive market that serves the meetings and conventions industry, where expenditures on renovations are often viewed as essential.

The key to the renovation decision depends on finding properties that can compete successfully once the renovations are completed. Then, with a better product, you should be able to attract tenants to the property, tenants should be willing to pay higher rents, and you should be able to recoup the investment in a reasonable number of years (usually, 10 to 15 years). People who renovate, therefore, must have a very long-term outlook.

SUMMARY

Two important property development issues are addressed in this chapter: intensity-of-use and modernization or redevelopment decisions.

With respect to intensity-of-use, the theory suggests that improvements should be added to a vacant site (or to an existing property) to the point where the marginal dollar of cost produces a marginal dollar's worth of value. At that point the property is at its highest-and-best use.

The modernization or redevelopment decision can also be viewed as a sequence of steps. The first is to estimate the marginal benefits (i.e., the effect on the property's bottom line). The second is to compare the marginal benefits with the marginal costs: If the marginal benefits are greater than or equal to the marginal costs, then the correct decision is to undertake the project.

In this framework it is absolutely necessary that the developer be aware of underlying structural changes in demand or supply. Before doing any renovation, developers should also understand the factors that drive the local and regional economies and create the demand for real estate.

KEY CONCEPTS

Intensity-of-use   The relative amount of human and financial resources added to a site.

Marginal Internal Rate of Return   The rate of return that discounts the increase in marginal revenues to the exact amount of the additional costs of the investment.

Marginal Net Present Value   Present value of the increase in marginal revenues less all the additional costs of the investment.

Modernization   Process of taking corrective measures to bring a property into conformity with changes in style or additions to meet standards of current demands.

Renovation   To restore a property to its former condition; may include new construction or additions, but is usually performed without changing the exterior walls of the building.

Setback requirement   The amount of space required between the lot line and the building line.

QUESTIONS FOR REVIEW AND DISCUSSION

1. How can specific properties change over time?

2. In calculating the additional revenue that will be generated by a hotel expansion, what variable costs must be taken into account?

3. What is the principle of increasing and decreasing returns? How does it apply in the development of real estate?

4. At what point is redevelopment appropriate?

5. How can the feasibility of redevelopment be measured in financial terms?

6. At what point does the level of the marginal internal rate of return indicate that redevelopment is financially appropriate?

7. When considering redevelopment, what broad issues must be taken into account?

PROBLEMS

1. A large hotel is considering building an additional 75 rooms, which management feels would be occupied 30 percent of the time at $75 per night. The variable cost per occupied room is $25 per night, and construction costs are expected to be $80 per square foot (each new room is going to be 270 square feet). Property taxes and insurance total $6 per square foot, and the overall capitalization rate for hotel properties is 8 percent. Using this information, calculate whether or not the expansion is feasible.

2. The following marginal cash flows are expected from the renovation of a downtown office building: Initial construction costs will be $450,000; the after-tax cash flows for years 1–5 will increase by $62,000, and for years 6–9 will increase by $78,000; the after-tax cash flow for year 10, including reversion, will increase by $85,000. If the required rate of return on a similar type of property is 16 percent, should the improvements be undertaken?

3. Refer to Figure 16–1. If the marginal cost per square foot of rentable area started at $80 and increased $10 with each story added, what would be the optimal number of floors to be added to the site, if all other assumptions remained unchanged?

4. Analysis of a proposed rehabilitation is as follows.

	BEFORE	AFTER
Average rent per rentable square foot	$18	$20
Anticipated occupancy	90%	95%
Operating ratio	35%	30%
Net rentable square feet	70,000 sq. ft.	70,000 sq. ft.
Cost of the improvements		$500,000

Assume that the overall capitalization rate is 12 percent, both before and after the rehabilitation.

a. Should the rehabilitation project be undertaken?

b. Suppose building code violations were found, making the alternative either to improve or have the building condemned. Would the rehabilitation project be feasible in this case? Why?

5. Assume that you own a vacant lot that is 220 feet wide by 150 feet deep. The lot is zoned for apartment use with setback requirements of 30 feet for the front, 15 feet for the back, and 15 feet on each side. The building cannot occupy more than 50 percent of the lot area, and the floor area ratio is two to one.

a. With a lot area of 400 square feet per dwelling unit, what is the maximum allowable number of units for the site?

b. What is the total allowable floor area for the building?

c. If each floor is 15 feet high, how tall will the building be?

PART FOUR
SPATIAL ECONOMICS

CHAPTER 17

SPATIAL ECONOMICS AND URBAN AREA STRUCTURE

Chapter Outline

The test of a civilization is the power of drawing the most benefits out of its cities.
Ralph Waldo Emerson, Journals

Our attention, thus far, has been mainly on how to analyze a real estate investment. We have had little to say about spatial economics and urban area structure. In the following three chapters we examine the factors basic to the demand for all types of real estate.

URBAN AREA STRUCTURE

Urban areas change constantly. Usually they expand, although in some cases they do decline and contract. It is important, therefore, to understand why urban areas— like the New York-Northern New Jersey-Long Island metropolitan area or the San Francisco-Oakland-San Jose metropolitan area—exist and what causes urban areas to change.

Why Urban Areas Exist

Urban areas exist to exploit a variety of factors, including (1) savings in costs of social interaction, (2) internal economies of scale to firms, (3) external economies of scale to firms, (4) labor mobility or labor specialization, (5) greater consumer choice, and (6) fostering of innovation.

Savings in Costs of Social Interaction.   Most of us like social interaction, preferably on a face-to-face basis. Therefore, one factor in the development of urban areas is the need for social interaction. The closer together we live and the better the transportation technology, the lower the cost of this interaction.

Internal Economies of Scale.   A second factor in the development of urban areas is internal economies of scale. Using specialized labor and machinery to produce large numbers of units at reduced per unit costs is referred to as *internal economies of scale.* Henry Ford capitalized on the idea of internal economies of scale when he produced automobiles on an assembly line. Internal economies mean advantages to centralized production in factories, and lower prices for users and consumers. Internal economies favor the development of industrial cities.

External Economies of Scale.   To realize *external economies of scale,* firms have a tendency to locate in larger communities where adequate support services and supplies are readily available from others at a reasonable cost. There are many examples of external economies of scale. Corporate headquarters need to be close to financial intermediaries and advertising firms. Dressmakers cluster in Manhattan to facilitate comparison shopping and to locate close to common input suppliers. Small computer firms tend to cluster in the Silicon Valley in California and along Route 128 in Boston to locate close to the suppliers of electronic parts and near Stanford and MIT. Firms from different industries also tend to cluster in large cities to share common input suppliers.

Labor Specialization.   The larger the urban area, the greater is the feasibility of labor specialization. As individuals, we seek the work we do best or the work from which we derive the greatest satisfaction. At the same time, businesses want workers who are productive so that they can lower unit of output. An electrical engineer or machinist has far fewer opportunities for specialization in a small town than in a large metropolitan area. And, in the event of a layoff, the chances of a specialist finding a satisfactory job locally are much higher in a metropolitan area.

Greater Consumer Choice.   Economies of scale and labor specialization are limited by the size of the market. For example, unless the market can absorb one million cases of beer a day, it does little good to amass the facilities and people to produce one million cases. But, as communities grow larger, more and more firms find a market that is large enough for them to survive. Conversely, the greater the number of auto dealers, restaurants, law firms, schools, hardware stores, and shoe stores, the greater the choices available to citizens of a community.

Fostering Innovation.   An innovator or investor generally finds it easier to find needed equipment and services in a larger metropolitan area. This makes it easier to translate creative ideas into reality, although a determined innovator might succeed anywhere. The availability of supplies and services for an innovator is essentially an extension of the ideas of external economies of scale, labor specialization, and wider consumer choice. Fostering innovation may be a small factor relative to some of the earlier components of urbanizing forces, yet it does exert influence in the same direction.

Costs of Urbanization.   In fairness, there are also costs associated with urbanization. Urban life increases our exposure to contacts that are involuntary and often undesirable. Panhandlers, drug pushers, gamblers, and high-pressure sales people are all more likely to be encountered in metropolitan areas. We are also more tied to the "system" in urban areas. Thus, a strike of garbage handlers, of transportation workers, or of teachers is more likely in a city, and tends to have a greater debilitating effect on us than it would in a rural area. In a similar vein, we are committed to a greater support of things we may not use or believe in. For example, we pay taxes to support municipal parks, schools, and hospitals even though we may not use them. Air and water pollution, congestion, and the costs of commuting tend to be higher in urban areas. Hence, these items decrease the quality of life in cities and act toward decentralization or dispersal. Finally, anonymity is sometimes considered a cost of urbanization, although many people consider it a benefit.

Different Types of Urban Areas

Cities, broadly speaking, may be classified as primary and secondary urban centers. A *primary community* is one that has its own economic base—that is, its existence is not dependent on other communities within the state or metropolitan area. A *secondary community,* on the other hand, is a satellite whose size and strength depends on the primary community to which it owes its existence. The satellite communities are better known as bedroom towns and cities, where commuters (people who work where they would rather not live) reside. The economic strength of a satellite community depends entirely on the strength of its primary community.

Primary communities may be grouped into the following classes which, in a general sense, reflect their reason for existence:

Industrial cities	Detroit, Michigan; Pittsburgh, Pennsylvania
Commercial cities	Chicago, Illinois; San Francisco, California
Mining cities	Wheeling, West Virginia; Butte, Montana
Resort cities	Miami, Florida; Atlantic City, New Jersey; Scottsdale, Arizona
Political cities	Washington, D.C.; Tallahassee, Florida; Springfield, Illinois; Salem, Oregon
Educational cities	Chapel Hill, North Carolina; Ann Arbor, Michigan; Champaign-Urbana, Illinois; Corvallis, Oregon

Some communities have a diverse economic base and fall into two or more classifications. Thus, New York City is industrial and commercial, as well as being a tourist Mecca. Miami, Florida, which started as a resort city, is presently one of the most important commercial centers in the South, and has one of the largest international airports in the country. And Los Angeles, long known for movie making and citrus fruit, is important today as an international shipping center, second only to New York in shipping tonnage.

Where Do Urban Areas Locate?

Land is a resource that is necessary for almost all social and economic activities. But its characteristics vary from place to place. Topography and soil are both important for urban development, although soil fertility is generally not important, per se. Beyond these basic observations, what can we say about the location and growth patterns of cities?

Historically, defense was the primary consideration in the location of a city because invasion and conflict were common realities. Hence, Rome was founded on seven hills, Paris on an island, and London and Moscow in swamps. Walled cities were common in the Middle Ages.

As trade developed, settlements with the greatest comparative advantage for transportation and communication between producers and their markets prospered most. Under the *principle of comparative economic advantage* communities benefit most when they specialize in producing goods or services that cannot be provided as well by other communities.

The best locations for trade are the following:

1. On the shores of oceans or lakes yet convenient to the inland markets (e.g., San Francisco, Seattle, and Chicago).

2. At or near mouth of rivers (e.g., New York City, New Orleans, Philadelphia, and Portland, Oregon).

3. At the confluence of rivers or near other inland water transportation (e.g., Pittsburgh, St. Louis, Cincinnati, Omaha, and Syracuse).

4. At obstructions on a river requiring unloading and trans-shipment by another mode (e.g., St. Paul, Minnesota; and Albany, New York).

5. At river crossings (e.g., Rockford, Illinois; and Harrisburg, Pennsylvania).

6. At breaks in mountain chains or where mountain meets plain or at intersections of land trade routes (e.g., Denver, Salt Lake City, and Albuquerque).

7. At places where modes of transportation are serviced (e.g., Atlanta).

Note that water transportation was a major factor in the early development of the United States because large amounts of freight could be handled much more easily and at lower cost than by any other means at that time.

The emphasis on urban location and prosperity shifted to other factors with the Industrial Revolution. The most significant factors became the comparative advantage afforded by availability of raw materials, skilled labor, adequate power, and suitable climate. Nearness to market is important when product weight-gain or loss is involved. Following are some illustrative examples:

1. **Raw Materials.** The relative availability of coal and iron ore were important to the development of Pittsburgh; Birmingham, Alabama; and Gary, Indiana. Lumber mills were built near forests and at one time were prominent in the Midwest. Tacoma, Washington, and Eugene, Oregon, are leading mill towns. Today, however, faster second growth of timber is causing the lumber industry to move to the Southeast.

2. **Power.** Fall River, Massachusetts; Minneapolis; and Spokane all owe much of their early growth to the ready availability of low-cost water or hydroelectric power.

3. **Skilled Labor.** The auto industry has been concentrated largely in Ohio and Michigan because of the huge reservoir of skilled labor in those areas. Likewise, Seattle and Los Angeles have large reserves of skilled labor for airplane manufacture.

4. **Suitable Climate.** Tucson, Phoenix, San Diego, and Miami owe much of their growth to their pleasant climates. A general shift of economic activity to the Sun Belt is the current trend.

5. **Weight Gain or Loss.** A manufacturing process that involves a considerable weight gain is best located near the market for the product because the manufacturer avoids paying transportation costs on the gain in weight. Examples are soda pop and beer. Bulk, fragility, and perishability also increase the need to be near markets. With considerable weight loss, on the other hand, the manufacturer avoids unnecessary transportation costs by processing near the raw materials. Examples are copper mining and processing, and lumber manufacture. Some products, like grains, may be processed anywhere between producer and market, because little weight is gained or lost.

WHY DO URBAN AREAS GROW?

Many theories to explain the growth and location of activities in urban areas have been proposed. There are three that are particularly applicable. These are (1) the *concentric-circle theory,* (2) the *direction-of-least-resistance theory,* and (3) the *multiple-nuclei theory.*

The Concentric Circle Theory

Johann Heinrich von Thunen, an owner of a German estate, wrote *Der Isalierte Staat (The Isolated State)* in 1826, to explain the allocation of land to various activities. Von Thunen began by assuming a walled city or village in the middle of a level, productive, and isolated field or plain. So as not to influence or distort the analysis, climate, soils, topography, transportation, and other factors were all held constant. Automobiles and railroads were not yet known; goods were hauled by wagons, carried by hand, or in the case of livestock, driven. Any difference in the use of land could, therefore, be attributed entirely to differences in transportation costs or location (see Figure 17-1). For a technical explanation of von Thunen's theory see Raleigh Barlowe's *Land Resource Economics.*[1]

Von Thunen identified five zones, or *concentric circles*, outside the village or central city. Zone 1, immediately outside the walls of the city, would be used primarily for growing vegetables, and for tending milk cattle and egg-laying hens. These ac-

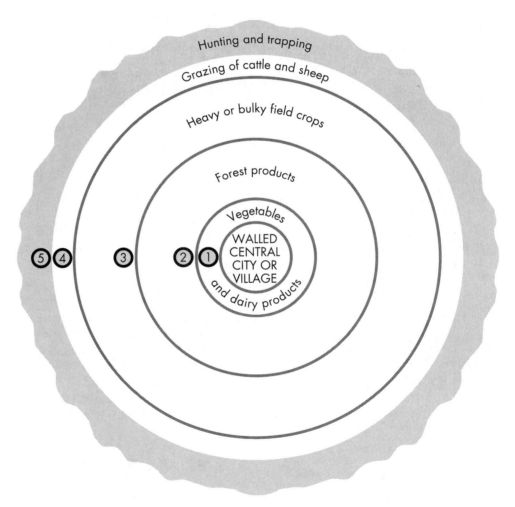

FIGURE 17-1
Concentric Circle Allocation of Space in an Isolated State

[1] Raleigh Barlowe, *Land Resource Economics,* 4th ed. Englewood Cliffs, N.J.: Prentice Hall, 1986, pp. 225–239.

tivities are intensive and involve many trips from the village, with the products often hand carried into the city. Forest products production turned out to be the best use for zone 2. Forest products are both bulky and heavy and were used for fuel and construction in von Thunen's day; hence, having them near the city saved considerable time and energy. Production of heavy or bulky field crops—potatoes, grain, hay—would be the main use of zone 3. Grazing of cattle and sheep was the appropriate use for zone 4, and the livestock could be driven as needed to zone 1 for slaughter or milking. The surrounding wilderness, zone 5, was appropriate for hunting and trapping.

Von Thunen's allocation of space was based on a product's net value after delivery in the city. Thus, both production and transportation costs were taken into account. Also, it was based entirely on the presumption of an open market; government control or intervention was not considered. The concern was only with rural land uses. And it was a steady state rather than a dynamic society.

Adjusting some of the assumptions in von Thunen's model results in a somewhat different pattern of activities. Assuming that a navigable stream flowing through the isolated state makes low-cost water transportation possible, results in an elongated settlement pattern, as shown in Figure 17–2a. While zone 1, vegetable and dairy products, remains relatively unchanged, zone 2, forestry, could be located at a greater distance from the center, if the activity were upstream. With improved land-transportation routes a star-shaped settlement pattern would result, as shown in Figure 17–2b. Relaxing or changing other von Thunen assumptions, such as soil fertility, topography, or number of city markets, would create other patterns.

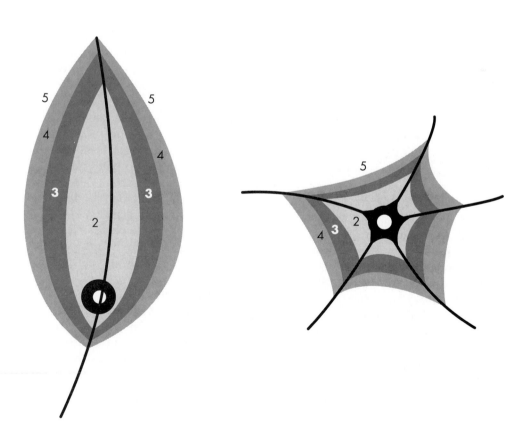

FIGURE 17–2
Settlement Patterns Resulting from Modified Von Thunen Assumptions

About one hundred years after von Thunen, in the 1920s, Ernest W. Burgess updated the concentric-circle theory to fit urban areas. According to Burgess, urban areas expand outward from a central business district of retail stores, office buildings, and factories. The next circle out is a zone of transition where low-income people live amid light manufacturing plants. Zone 3 houses workers for zones 1 and 2. High-income residences are in zone 4. Zone 5 consists of suburbs or semirural properties. At the time Burgess was writing, planning and zoning were relatively unknown, and automobiles and airplanes were just being introduced and their impact was not yet evident.

The Direction-of-Least-Resistance Theory

Richard M. Hurd, a mortgage banker, compiled information on the expansion and growth of more than 50 American cities. In 1903, Hurd wrote that cities grow in the direction of least resistance or greatest attraction.[2] The *direction-of-least-resistance* theory is really a modification of von Thunen's concentric-circle theory applied to modern urban areas, with some assumptions modified to take into account barriers to growth. Hurd stated his theory as follows:

> The point of contact differs according to the methods of transportation, whether by water, by turnpike, or by railroad. The forces of attractions and resistance include topography, the underlying material on which city builders work; external influences, projected into the city by trade routes; internal influences derived from located utilities, and finally the reactions and readjustments due to the continual harmonizing of conflicting elements. The influence of modern topography, all-powerful when cities start, is constantly modified by human labor, hills being cut down, waterfronts extended, and swamps, creeks and lowlands filled in, this, however, not taking place until the new building sites are worth more than the cost of filling and cutting. The measure of resistance to the city's growth is here changed from terms of land elevation or depression, and hence income cost, to terms of investment or capital cost. The most direct results of topography come from its control of transportation, the waterfronts locating exchange points for water commerce, and the water grade normally determining the location of the railroads entering the city.
>
> Growth in cities consists of movement away from the point of origin in all directions, except as topographically hindered, this movement being due both to aggregation at the edges and pressure from the center. Central growth takes place both from the heart of the city and from each sub-center of attraction, and axial growth pushes into outlying territory by means of railroads, turnpikes and street railroads. All cities are built up from these two influences, which vary in quantity, intensity and quality, the resulting districts overlapping, interpenetrating, neutralizing and harmonizing as the pressure of the city's growth brings them into contact with each other. The fact of vital interest is that, despite confusion from intermingling of utilities, the order of dependence of each definite district

[2] Richard M. Hurd, *Principles of City Land Values.* New York: The Record and the Guide, 1903, 1924, pp. 13–15.

on the other is always the same. Residences are early driven to the circumference, while business remains at the center, and as residences divide into various social grades, retail shops of corresponding grades follow them, and wholesale shops in turn follow the retailers, while institutions and various mixed utilities irregularly fill in the intermediate zone, and the banking and office section remains at the main business center. Complicating this broad outward movement of zones, axes of traffic project shops through residence areas, create business subcenters, where they intersect, and change circular cities into star-shaped cities. Central growth, due to proximity, and axial growth, due to accessibility, are summed up in the static power of established sections and the dynamic power of their chief lines of intercommunication.

Considerable research and writing have been done since Hurd made his statement. Yet no simpler, clearer, or more comprehensive statement about the dynamics of urban growth has since been made.

The Multiple-Nuclei Theory

In the 1930s, Homer Hoyt developed the sector theory, which is based on wedge-shaped neighborhoods surrounding a central business district. New, high-income residential areas were seen as developing along highways and near other fast transportation facilities. This theory is not too different from the route, or axial, theory suggested by a number or scholars. The latter theory says that an urban area tends to grow along its lines of transportation, because of the economic advantage of convenience that is made possible by the easy, low-cost movement. Both theories appear to be restatements of Hurd's direction-of-least-resistance theory.

Frederick Babcock, an appraiser who studied urban growth and change in the 1930s, focused on how urban change comes about. He characterized urban areas as *sliding, jumping,* and *bursting* in their growth.[3] One district expands by gradually encroaching upon or sliding into neighboring districts. Or, an expanding district will sometimes jump, or leap, over a barrier, such as another well-established district. Thus, an expanding business district may jump over a river, a civic center, or a university. Bursting occurs when a district expands by scattering to several new subdistricts. Thus, the pre-World War II central business districts of large metropolitan areas burst—and the suburban shopping center is the result. Similarly, manufacturing areas scattered from the central city to the suburbs, taking the form of industrial parks and districts.

Harris and Ullman advanced the idea of multiple nuclei, or clusters of development, in 1945.[4] Essentially, their theory is an extension of Babcock's with physical, economic, and social considerations taken into account. It also extends the idea that cities are a collection of areas devoted to various functional activities. Four reasons suggested by Harris and Ullman for the development of clusters, or nuclei, are:

1. Some activities require specialized facilities.

2. Like activities tend to group together because they mutually benefit from cohesion.

[3] Fredric Babock, *The Valuation of Real Estate.* New York: McGraw-Hill, 1932, p. 59.
[4] Chauncy D. Harris and Edward L. Ullman, "The Nature of Cities," in *Building the Future City, Annals of the American Academy of Political and Social Sciences* (November 1945, 7–17).

3. Unlike activities are sometimes adverse or detrimental to each other.

4. Some activities can afford the high rents of the most desirable sites, others cannot and must take less desirable sites.

The multiple-nuclei theory of land-use arrangements is based largely on the rent-paying ability of the various uses. The use able to pay the highest rent gets the most desirable site. The worth of a specific location depends on transportation and communication possibilities and the surrounding environment. Thus, business and industrial centers developed outside the central business district. Currently, these nuclei take the form of shopping centers, industrial parks, convention centers (often near major airports), and resort communities (functional areas) (see Figure 17-3).

RENT THEORY AND URBAN STRUCTURE

What land use pays the highest rent or gives the highest value to a site in an urban area? Rent theory says that the most accessible site is likely to be the most productive or most profitable. And, unless rivers or hills intervene, the most-central location in an urban area is the most accessible. What kinds of uses dominate our central business districts?

Early in this century, large department stores and other retail outlets occupied the prime sites in major cities. Office buildings, hotels, apartment buildings, and manufacturing plants were usually located nearby. Moving out from the central city, one-family homes became a dominant land use. Individual commercial and industrial districts sometimes developed along major arteries as wedges or sectors. Lot sizes increased as the edge of the city blended into the countryside. The hierarchy of land uses is diagrammed in Figure 17-4.

As the use of automobiles and trucks increased after World War II, industry moved to the suburbs. Residential neighborhoods followed, pulling commercial districts with them, and satellite villages were often engulfed by the rapid urban expansion. Industrial parks, shopping centers, recreation centers, and residential neighborhoods made up the new community fabric. The land-use structure became a pattern of more-or-less distinct, functional neighborhoods or districts superimposed upon a network of streets and highways. The typical value pattern that developed is shown in Figure 17-5. Thus, land-use patterns took on a structure that tended to minimize the costs of moving people and goods and that is best described by the multiple-nuclei concept.

Rivers, lakes, marshes, and hills all act as barriers to the normal expansion of urban areas. In accordance with Hurd's principle of the direction of least resistance, expansion takes place away from or around these barriers, or in the direction where the cost is less relative to the expected benefits. However, over time and with increasing growth, the time costs of travel around these barriers to the urban fringe steadily increase. At some point, it becomes feasible to incur the costs of bridging rivers and lakes, filling in marshes, and expanding into hilly areas. The Golden Gate Bridge of San Francisco, the Lake Pontchartrain Bridge near New Orleans, and the recent filling-in of the tidal marshes near Newark, New Jersey, for industrial development are examples of "delayed" development outward from an urban center.

Existing realty improvements tend to lag a community's social and economic needs. For example, several one-family houses or a church might have to be torn down to make way for a discount store. Likewise, the existing *urban infrastruc-*

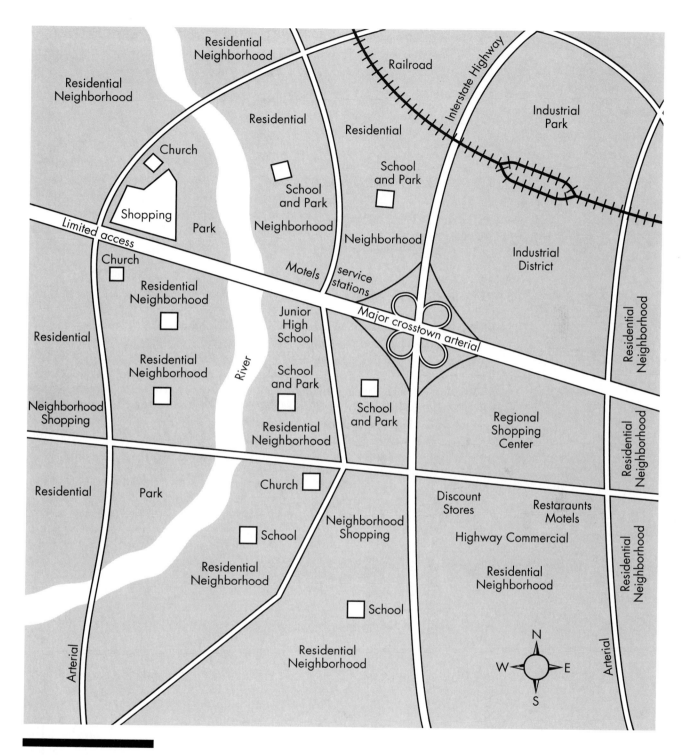

FIGURE 17–3

Multiple-Nuclei (Functional Activities) in a Modern Community

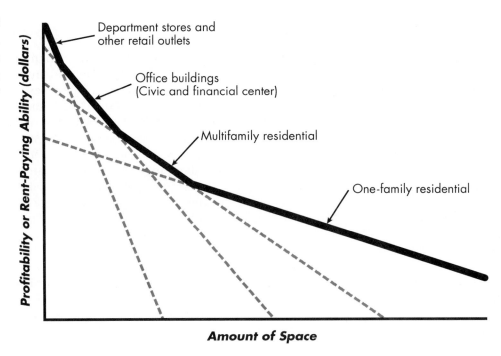

FIGURE 17–4
Hierarchy of Urban
Land Uses Based on
Rent-Paying Ability

ture—that is, the basic installations and facilities that serve the community—acts to retard urban adjustment. Schools; sewer and water systems; power and communications systems; and streets, freeways, and mass transit systems are all components of the urban infrastructure. Whether physical barriers or existing improvements, additional costs must be incurred for the area to be used more intensely. At some point, the potential benefits may justify the additional costs.

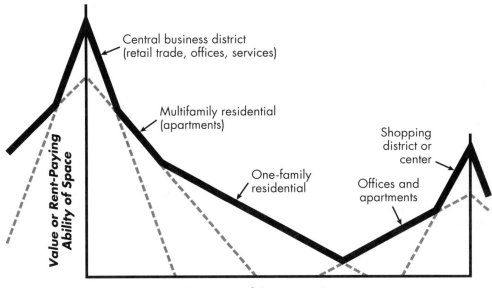

FIGURE 17–5
Schematic Diagram of
Various Land Uses
and Their Rent-Paying
Ability in a Large
Metropolitan Area

Basic Principles of Rent Theory

Let us now summarize our discussion by defining *rent theory* as an explanation of urban growth and change. First, land-use activities tend to locate at the point of greatest comparative advantage. Second, these land-use activities tend to compete based on their rent-paying ability. Over a period of time, the uses able to pay the highest rents, or prices, get the choicest locations, and a hierarchy of land uses develops. Department stores, office buildings, and apartment buildings get the choice, central urban sites. Moving out from the center, the hierarchy goes to one-family residences to field crops to grazing. Subcenters, for example, shopping centers and industrial parks, are interspersed into urban areas as businesspeople and others strive to minimize transportation costs relative to the benefits received from a particular location.

At any given time, an urban area may be expanding or contracting. Most of our experience is with expansion of the economic base and growth. Urban areas may grow outward or upward.

Outward expansion—the urbanization and development of new lands—is called growth at the *extensive margin*. The extensive margin is the point at which rents or values make it just barely feasible to convert land to urban uses and add improvements. The extensive margin is symbolized by land subdivision and development at the urban fringe. The building of large, sprawling regional and superregional shopping centers and the development of campus-style office buildings are also activities associated with the extensive margin.

Urban areas also expand upward, or at the *intensive margin*. The intensive margin is the point at which rents or values make it just barely feasible to use urban land more intensively by adding more capital and labor. Replacing old houses with a discount store is one example; converting an old factory or cannery into a shopping center and the development of shopping centers like the eight-story Water Tower Place in Chicago are others (see Figure 17–6).

Note that intensity-of-use and rent are related but do not always move in tandem. Rent is the payment for the use of realty. Generally, the higher the value of the site, the higher its rent-paying capacity and the greater its intensity-of-use. That is,

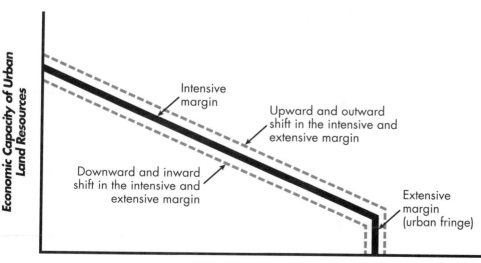

FIGURE 17–6
Intensive and Extensive Margins of Urban Land Uses

there must be some relationship between the value of a site and the amount of improvements added to the land. Intensity of use, rent, and value are all closely related to the highest and best uses of land.

Intensity-of-use is also the key to understanding why urban areas grow upward as well as outward. Neither urban nor rural land is productive in and of itself. Regardless of use—corn, wheat, office space, or residential units—all land requires the addition of labor, capital, and management. The factors of production must be combined so that each factor gets its greatest return. According to the *principle of proportionality* real estate reaches its maximum productivity, or highest-and-best use, when all the factors of production are in balance. The ability of a site to absorb human and capital resources is the *economic capacity of the land.* Additional investment is added until the marginal profit no longer is equal to or exceeds the marginal cost of investment.

Obviously, the more money spent on improvements, the more intensely the land is used; conversely, intense development requires that high values (economic capacity) be justified. Urban uses are generally much more intense than rural uses. And urban land values are generally higher than rural values. The highest-and-best use of a site is reached when no further value can be gained by the addition of resources; in fact, value can start to decrease. This is also known as the *principle of increasing and decreasing returns.* At the extensive margin, this point is reached when conversion of additional rural land to urban uses is just barely feasible economically. That is, a developer would earn no profit at all or only a minimally acceptable one after paying for the costs of subdividing and construction. At the intensive margin, this point is reached when the owner of a developed property who adds resources to rehabilitate or convert to another use realizes either no increase or only a small increment of value in excess of the costs incurred. In either case, if the returns were any lower the result would be a decision not to develop the land or rehabilitate the property.

EXAMPLE: THE TRADE-OFF BETWEEN LAND RENT AND DISTANCE TO THE CITY

To illustrate the trade-off between office rent per square foot and distance to the city center, let us consider the location decision for a hypothetical office firm. All office firms share two important characteristics: First, they gather, process, and distribute information, and they must be able to perform this service quickly. Second, office firms rely on face-to-face interaction with clients; it is important, therefore, for them to be conveniently located.

"Output" for our hypothetical office firm is meetings with clients, and employees must travel from the office to the city center to consult with the clients. The prices that the firm can charge for its services are determined by competition. Obviously, having high-priced employees spend time with clients in the central business district means that travel costs will increase substantially as the distance to the city center increases.

To see how this might affect the rent an office firm is willing to pay, imagine that our hypothetical office firm locates one block from the city center, and that travel costs are $12 per block (round-trip). With 2,400 consultations per week and a fee of $48 per consultation, the firm will earn $115,200 in gross revenues. From this, the firm must pay office rents and all travel costs, plus operating costs including a normal return on equity.

Travel costs per consultation are $12 (travel costs per block times the number of blocks to city center, or $12 × 1). Operating costs including a normal return on equity are taken to be $28,800. Thus, the maximum rent our firm can pay and still remain profitable is $57,600 (gross revenues minus all nonrent expenses, including operating costs plus a normal return on equity, and all travel costs, or $115,200 − $28,800 − $12 cost per consultation × 2,400 consultations per year).

As the firm moves away from the city center, the absolute maximum rent the firm can afford decreases because travel costs increase. To visualize this, suppose that our firm were located two blocks from the city center. You can see from Figure 17-7 that operating costs fall from $28,800 to $21,600 and travel costs increase from $12 to $24 per consultation. With no change in gross revenues, the maximum rent the firm can pay and still remain profitable is $36,000 (gross revenues of $115,200 minus all nonrent expenses, which include operating costs and a normal return on equity of $21,600, and travel costs of $24 per consultation times 2,400, or $57,600).

Now we are able to draw a bid-rent curve (see Figure 17-8). Panel A shows our office firm's total revenue, which is unaffected by location. It also shows total cost other than rent. As the firm moves away from the city center, the total cost curve increases. This increase is a direct result of the increased travel costs.

The difference between total revenue and total cost other than rent is the firm's pre-rent profit (see panel B of Figure 17-8). This is the firm's bid-rent curve, which shows the absolute maximum rent the firm is willing to pay for different locations.

With no other bidders, office firms with similar profiles would occupy all locations outward to the point where the bid-rent curve in panel B intersects the horizontal axis. However, this situation is clearly unrealistic. With other, different-use bidders, as in Figure 17-5, the uses able to pay the highest rents will get the choicest locations.

Bid-rent relationships help to explain why certain locations decline in value over time and why other locations experience a revival. A residential bid-rent function indicates how much households are willing to pay for housing at different locations in the city. Bid-rent functions are negatively sloped because travel costs increase with distance to the city center. With lower rents farther from the *city center,* land users and tenants tend to lease more space. Also, with lower land costs, suburban areas tend to expand horizontally rather than vertically.

SUMMARY

Most economic, social, and political forces are urbanizing in their effect; hence, the long-term trend toward larger and larger cities. Manufacturing, trade, education, and government are prime examples of activities that are more advantageously carried on with people concentrated in one place.

BLOCKS TO CITY CENTER	FIRM REVENUES	OPERATING COSTS	TRAVEL COSTS PER CONSULTATION[a]	TOTAL TRAVEL COSTS	TOTAL COSTS OTHER THAN RENT	PRE-RENT PROFIT
1	$115,200	$28,800	$12	$28,800	$ 57,600	$57,600
2	$115,200	$21,600	$24	$57,600	$ 79,200	$36,000
3	$115,200	$18,000	$36	$86,400	$104,400	$10,800

[a] Round-trip cost of $12 per block times number of blocks to city center.

FIGURE 17-7
Bid-Rent Function for Office Firm

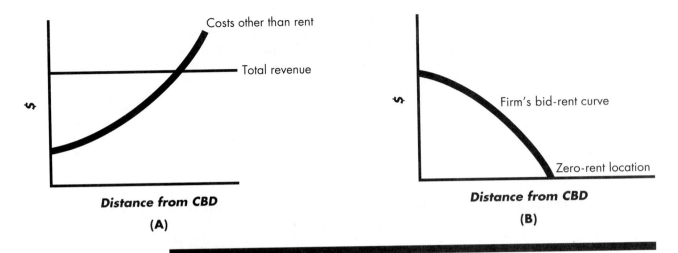

FIGURE 17-8
Bid-Rent Curve for a Hypothetical Office Firm

At the local level, urbanizing forces interact with the physical environment to create *functional areas,* which are the major building blocks of our urban areas. Residential neighborhoods, commercial districts, and industrial districts are the most obvious examples of functional areas. Streets and other components of the transportation system tie functional areas together by facilitating the movement of people and/or goods between them.

Several theories exist as to how cities were established and grew in response to the needs of people. First, there is the concentric-circle theory, which suggests that retail stores, office buildings, and factories tend to locate in the central business district. Immediately outside the central business district is a transition zone where low-income people live amid light manufacturing plants. Next is a zone housing workers for the two inner zones, then a zone for high-income residents, and lastly a zone consisting of suburbs or semirural-type properties.

Then there is the direction-of-least-resistance theory, which is actually an extension of the concentric-circle theory. The direction-of-least-resistance theory suggests that growth takes place in the direction of least resistance, both from the central heart of the city and from various subcenters. Resistance to urban growth is measured by the costs of investment or capital, infrastructure cost, and zoning constraints.

Third, there is the multiple-nuclei theory, where land use is based on the rent-paying ability of various activities. According to the latter theory, an urban area grows by scattering past, or sometimes leaping over, a barrier such as another well-established district, in its expansion. Clusters, or multiple nuclei, then develop owing to the fact that like activities tend to group together because they mutually benefit from cohesion, or because some activities require specialized facilities, or because some activities can better afford the high rents of the most desirable sites.

Rent theory suggests that over a period of time the uses that are able to pay the highest rents get the choicest location. In addition, rent theory posits a hierarchy of land uses. Starting at the central business district, department stores, office buildings, and apartment buildings will get the choice sites because they can afford the high rents of the most desirable sites. Moving out from the center, the hierarchy goes to one-family residences to field crops to grazing and forestry to submarginal lands.

The bid-rent curve shows the relationship between rent per square foot and distance to the city center. As the distance from the city center increases, landlords can expect to receive less rent per square foot. Note also that with lower rents tenants tend to lease more space. Thus, the amount of suburban office space per worker tends to be greater than downtown office space per worker. Also, because land costs are lower, suburban areas tend to expand horizontally rather than vertically.

KEY CONCEPTS

Bid-rent function   A schedule showing the rent a use or business activity can pay as an increasing amount of space is devoted to the use.

Concentric-circle theory   Von Thunen's proposal that land use is directly attributable to differences in transportation costs or location around a central city.

Direction-of-least-resistance theory   Hurd's theory of community growth that says cities grow in the direction of least resistance or greatest attraction. This theory is really an extension or modification of von Thunen's concentric-circle theory.

Extensive margin   The point at which rents or values make it financially feasible to add urban improvements and/or to convert farm land to urban uses; symbolized by land development at the urban fringe.

External economy of scale   Relocation of a firm in a community large enough to obtain support services and supplies from others at costs lower than it could obtain by providing the same services and supplies to itself.

Functional area   An area of specialized activity. Residential neighborhoods and commercial and industrial districts are the most obvious examples of functional areas.

Intensive margin   The point at which rents or values make it financially feasible to add more capital and labor so that urban land can be used more intensively; an example would be replacing old houses with a new discount store.

Internal economy of scale   Use of specialized labor and machinery within a firm to achieve greater output and reduced cost per unit. In turn, this usually means lower prices to users and consumers and a larger market share.

Multiple-nuclei theory   The Harris and Ullman proposal of clusters of development, which is an extension of the idea that cities are a collection of functional areas.

Principle of comparative economic advantage   Communities and regions specialize in activities that provide them with the greatest economic advantage relative to other communities or regions.

Principle of proportionality   When the factors of production are in balance with one another, real estate reaches its maximum productivity or highest-and-best use; also known as the principle of increasing and decreasing returns.

Urban infrastructure   Necessary facilities of an urban community, such as sewer, water, power, transportation, communications, and school systems.

1. Discuss six major forces behind urbanization. Give an example of each.

2. What is the difference between an external economy of scale and an internal economy of scale?

3. Explain briefly four benefits and three costs of urbanization.

4. Concentric-circle, direction-of-least-resistance, and multiple-nuclei are prominent theories of urban growth and development. Are the theories related in any way? Explain.

5. Do any of the theories in question 4 fit your community? Discuss.

6. Illustrate and explain briefly with bid-rent functions how space is allocated in a large hotel to maximize rent or value. Do the same for a department store.

7. What is the difference between intensive and extensive rent margins?

8. Explain the interrelationships, if any, among intensity-of-use, rent levels, value, and highest-and-best use for a specific site.

9. Is anonymity a cost or a benefit of urbanization? Explain.

10. Explain, in general terms, the interrelationships among site value, construction costs, and rent levels as they concern highest-and-best use of a specific site.

11. What is the main distinction between a primary community and a secondary community? Give an example of each type.

12. What are the different classes of primary communities?

13. List some of the factors that helped to determine the location of urban centers during different periods in history?

14. Which theory of urban growth best explains the development of strip centers along major roadways outside of the central business district?

15. According to rent theory, why are the most profitable land uses situated in the best locations? Are the best locations always in the central business district?

PROBLEMS

1. Assume a sales office locates at the center of a city. Travel costs are $25 per block each way, each sales call results in an average of $350 in revenue, and 3,500 sales calls are made each year to the city center. Operating costs are $35,000 per year. With this information, calculate how much the firm would be willing to pay in rent three blocks away? What about five blocks away?

2. In problem 1 above, if operating costs increase to $50,000 per year, but transportation costs decrease to $20 per block each way, how much would the firm be willing to pay in rent three blocks away? What about five blocks away?

3. Survey your community. Note where development and redevelopment is taking place. Are there any bypassed hills or marshes that look ripe for development? Can you identify where development and redevelopment is most likely to take place in the next five years?

CHAPTER 18

MORE ABOUT URBAN AREA STRUCTURE AND REAL ESTATE MARKETS

Chapter Outline

Divine nature made the country, human art built the cities.

Marcus Terentius Varro, a Roman polymath

In Chapter 17, we introduced the topic of urban growth theory and suggested that this theory could be restated as rent theory, which would reflect the many decisions by individual owners about the use of their property. Rent theory, or as it is sometimes called, value theory, is also the means by which local economic activity is related to real estate. The key to rent theory is the maximization of self-interest, expressed in monetary terms—that is, maximizing net profits, rents, and benefits.

In this chapter we look at the interaction of supply and demand in local real estate markets. The discussion begins with an examination of the types of real estate markets and their characteristics. We then look at the forces of supply and demand, and note that real estate prices, values, and sales activity, as well as construction and development activity, are directly influenced by per capita personal income at the local level. A direct relationship also exists between population trends and real estate values. Other things being equal, increasing population means increased demand for real estate services and, in turn, higher values. A declining population has the opposite effect. Institutional forces, including cultural, social, and religious beliefs and the governmental system, also affect land use. We conclude the chapter with a discussion of real estate market functions and market operations, and give a brief overview of local market indicators.

TYPES OF REAL ESTATE MARKETS

Typically real estate markets are classified according to the type of property traded. Each type of property may be further subdivided into smaller and more specialized market areas:

Residential: Urban; suburban; and rural.

Commercial: Office buildings; store properties; lofts; theaters; garages; and hotels and motels.

Agricultural: Timberland; pasture land; ranches; orchards; and open farmland (for produce, tobacco, cotton).

Special Purpose: Cemeteries; churches; clubs; golf courses; parks; and public properties (buildings, highways, streets).

Real estate markets may also be classified as to rights of ownership or use. Thus, we may speak of a rental market involving *transfer of space,* and an equity market involving *transfer of ownership.*

We might also recognize a buyer's market and a seller's market. A *buyer's market* occurs when the supply of goods and services greatly exceeds demand, thereby enabling purchasers to bargain for and get lower prices. In a buyer's market values fall. Conversely, a *seller's market* occurs when demand greatly exceeds supply, thereby enabling sellers to bargain for and get higher prices. Seller's markets result in rising values.

MARKET CHARACTERISTICS

Product characteristics such as fixed location, situs, heterogeneity, indestructibility, and durability cause the real estate market to differ from other kinds of markets in several ways.

Real Estate Markets Are Local

Fixity causes the market for real estate to be local in character; demand must come to the parcel. An oversupply of land or land improvements in a midwestern state is of no use in filling a market demand for like land or improvements in another region or metropolitan center. Therefore, real estate is extremely vulnerable to shifts in local demand. Further, a real estate broker in Los Angeles cannot well advise a business executive seeking a site in Atlanta.

Real Estate Is Not a Standardized Commodity

Real estate is heterogeneous. No two parcels of real estate are exactly alike; at the very least, each has a unique location. Even with two physically adjacent properties, situs and legal characteristics may cause a difference in relative value. One parcel may be zoned residential A, the other B, meaning that the allowed site uses are different. Or one parcel may be subject to deed restrictions that limit it to high-income residential use, and the other may be free of such limitations and thus open to any legal use.

The Market for Real Estate Is Diffused

Real estate markets are diffuse; wide fluctuations in value and in the number of transactions can occur from region to region as well as from state to state or community to community. The market for farmland in the United States, for instance, may be judged good, or active, when based on the number of sales and the increase in overall values. But this favorable average may be a composite derived from wheat, corn, tobacco, and cattle-raising regions, which might be more than offset by unfavorable activity in the cotton-growing region. Likewise, Phoenix, Arizona; Los Angeles, California; and Miami Beach, Florida, may record sharp gains in sales while activity in Tacoma, Washington, and Dallas, Texas, drops through the floor.

Poor Adjustment of Supply and Demand

Fixity prevents equalization of real estate supply and demand in an area, in a region, or nationally. On a local market level durability also causes maladjustments in supply and demand. Land itself is indestructible, and improvements, if properly maintained, may last a hundred years or more. Thus, if demand suddenly falls, the inability to adjust or withdraw supply causes real estate to become a drag on the market. An oversupply of space results in a buyer's market and lower values. Conversely, a sudden increase in demand creates a seller's market because additional space cannot be quickly built.

The Absence of Market Stabilizing Factors

Being heterogenous, real estate is nonfungible, that is, nonsubstitutable; in turn, this restricts the ability of sellers to ensure against a potential decrease in price before the real estate can be sold. It also discourages speculation, which leads to greater, not less, price volatility.

Normally, owners or speculators in fungible commodities like grains, energy, stock indexes, and livestock can ensure against a potential decrease in price by entering into a futures contract to deliver the commodity at some specified future time at a price now agreed upon but to be paid in the future at the time of delivery. If the seller is correct later and the price in the future is lower than the market's present prediction of the price, the seller can purchase the commodity, if not already owned, and deliver it to the buyer for the currently agreed-to higher price. This method of insulating against a potential price decline does not work well in the case of real estate. The nonfungibility of real estate means that sellers who currently do not own the real estate cannot simply settle at the time of delivery by purchasing some other property and delivering it to the buyer for the currently agreed-to higher price.

Transactions Are Private in Nature

Real estate transactions are very private. Buyers and sellers meet in confidence, often negotiate through brokers, and the bid and offering prices are rarely publicized. Also, not all deeds of record specify the actual dollar amounts paid. In these circumstances, personal contact with developers, builders, realtors, financial and legal specialists, property managers, and other real estate professionals often is necessary to obtain useful information.

FACTORS OF SUPPLY AND DEMAND

A real estate market is sensitive to local changes in demographic, economic, political, and social forces. Among the more important factors are the following.

1. Population: number, age/sex mix, and family composition
2. Employment and wage levels and stability of incomes
3. Personal savings, availability of mortgage funds, and interest rates
4. Sales prices, rent levels, and percentage of vacancies
5. Taxation rates and land-use controls, including rent controls
6. Availability and costs of land, labor, and building materials
7. Relative quality of existing structures and changes in construction technology

Population, employment, income, savings, and availability of credit combine to provide an effective demand. By itself, population without purchasing power represents raw or potential demand. *Effective demand,* therefore, is the desire for land or space armed with purchasing power.

Population

For most types of real estate population is a prerequisite of demand. An increase in the number of people means increased potential demand. And a decrease in population means declining demand. To go from potential demand to effective demand, the population must have wealth or income. For residential real estate, population is usually measured as the number of households rather than as the number of people.

Given population and purchasing power, demand then depends on the characteristics of the population. For example, an elderly population means fewer children per household and a demand for dwelling units with only one or two bedrooms. Alternatively, a community with many children under 18 years of age means strong demand for three- and four-bedroom dwelling units. More schools and playgrounds are also likely to be needed. A largely middle-aged population, most of whom work, is likely to translate into demand for two-and three-bedroom housing units of moderate-to-high value. With higher incomes, people generally want larger and more attractive places in which to live.

Wage Levels and Income Stability

The real estate market is sensitive to changes in wage levels, employment opportunities, and stability of income. Rental payments and housing costs are closely geared to ability to pay. In fact, there are definite rules-of-thumb accepted by mortgage lenders and federal housing agencies under which total housing costs should not exceed 25 to 35 percent of the wage earner's income. Homes are usually financed by mortgage loans, with payments made out of income on a monthly basis. But food, clothing, and transportation costs generally take priority over housing. Hence, income and the employment outlook must be positive for the demand for residential space to be strong.

Personal Savings, Credit Availability, and Interest Rates

Higher wages and salaries are significantly reflected in the increase in total disposable personal income, which rose from $722 billion in 1960 to $1,952.9 billion in 1980, and to $4,042.9 billion in 1990. During the same period, personal savings increased from $57.5 billion in 1980 to $153.8 billion, and to $175.6 billion in 1990. Personal savings plus investments by financial institutions provide the reservoir of mortgage funds. In turn, the size of the reservoir influences the availability of mortgage credit and interest rate levels.

The availability of mortgage credit and the level of interest rates act as a barometer of residential real estate market activity. A tightening of money, along with higher interest rates, immediately and negatively influences home construction and existing home sales. Easier availability and lower interest rates have the opposite effect. Since most homes are bought on credit, interest rates are an important part of a purchase transaction and often influence the transaction price. To many buyers, especially those who only make a small down payment, the most important consideration in buying a house is the size of the monthly payments for principal, interest, taxes and insurance. To those buyers the actual purchase price is just one of several financial factors.

Rent and Vacancy Levels

The rental market is highly competitive. If rents are set too high, tenants will economize on space and vacancies will result. For all practical purposes, housing supply cannot be withdrawn from the market. Competition to maintain full occupancy, therefore, forces prices into line. Vacancy rates that exceed 5 to 8 percent indicate either an oversupply of space or that the space is overpriced. In either case, construction is likely to be cut back until the market strengthens.

Taxation and Land-Use Controls

Taxation is sometimes used as a governmental tool to compel or deter real estate development or to direct the employment of land for particular uses. For example, vacant land is sometimes overassessed and taxed to stimulate its improvement. Likewise, owners of business properties and tenant-occupied properties often are assessed at a higher rate than owners of residential homes. Such tax policy is directly designed to encourage homeownership and the use of land.

Land-use controls also affect how real estate markets operate. Tighter controls and permit requirements drive real estate prices up, which tends to discourage sales and construction.

Costs of Land, Labor, and Building Materials

The availability and cost of land, and the price of labor and building materials affect the supply of real estate. Although the total amount of land is plentiful, land that is economically usable may be in short supply. Improvements in the form of roads, drainage, water, and other utilities must ordinarily be added to raw land before it can be subdivided and offered for sale. Such improvements are costly and often can be successfully made only with community sanction and on a relatively large scale. This scarcity of building sites causes upward pressure on the prices of existing properties and adversely affects market sales activity. On the other hand, speculative optimism can lead to an oversupply of improved land that results in a depressed market for months and even years.

Construction Technology and Building Quality

More buildings are torn down than fall down. This destruction of often physically sound structures is the result of changes in building methods and building obsolescence. Rapid advances in building design and methods of construction have sparked a demand for modern homes that offer more amenities of living. Improvements in heating, lighting, insulation, soundproofing, air conditioning, and interior design have brought about an active demand for home modernization and replacement that is likely to last for many years. Similar changes apply also to commercial and industrial buildings.

REAL ESTATE MARKET FUNCTIONS

The real estate market accomplishes its primary function, the exchange of space for money, by the way prices are set. Price is also the deciding factor for other real estate market functions:

1. Existing space is reallocated to alternative users based on their needs and relative ability to pay.
2. The quality and quantity of space is continually adjusted to meet changing conditions.
3. Land-use patterns are determined.
4. Price and value information is generated for the use of market participants in subsequent decisions.

In general, real estate market prices are an indication of real estate values. And the resulting pattern of land uses reflects the social and economic tastes and needs of the community.

Reallocation of Existing Space

In a free market, property sales occur only when they are mutually advantageous to both the buyer and the seller. The buyer would rather have the property than the money. The seller prefers the money. The real estate market, therefore, reallocates property ownership and redistributes space according to the preferences of financially capable property users.

Most sellers were once buyers, preferring property to the money. Over time, conditions may have changed to where the owner now prefers money to ownership. There are numerous reasons why owners opt to sell and buyers opt to purchase.

In addition to outright sales, the reallocation function also includes rentals and tax-deferred exchanges. Although we tend to focus on the sales transaction because it is most common, the concerns of a renter are essentially the same as those of a buyer, except that the control of the property is gained by leasing rather than by purchase.

Space Adjustment

Owners change how properties are used as they respond to market pressures and opportunities. Remodeling or renovation may be necessary to adjust to the changing need of the market. For example, if the value of a property converted to office use exceeds the value of the property in its current residential use plus the cost of conversion, a rational owner would convert the property to office space.

Likewise, if the demand for space exceeds the current supply, raw land must be subdivided and properties developed to increase the quantity of space. However, should demand decrease and property values decline, little or no space adjustment (remodeling or new construction) is likely. Space adjustment is discussed more fully on pages 290–294 in the section on real estate market operation.

Determination of Land Use

Land-use activities differ in profitability and in turn in their ability to pay for space. Because location greatly affects the ability to pay for space, various uses compete for the best sites. The expectation is that the highest-and-best use for each site will win the competition. At any time, there exists a definite pattern of land use that reflects the relative ability of users to pay for space.

Generate Information

Investors, lenders, managers, assessors, builders, developers, and brokers all want and use information about property sales for judgments and decisions that turn on value. An investor wishes to pay no more for a property than the amount for which a comparable property sold. On the other hand, an owner wishes to sell for no less. A lender does not want to lend more on a property than that for which it can be sold. Managers need value information to set rent levels, assessors to establish assessed values. Builders and developers make value judgments on structures to be built or projects to be undertaken. And brokers need value information to show clients that the transactions being proposed are sound. Price and value information are, therefore, important to the continuing operation and stability of the real estate market.

REAL ESTATE MARKET OPERATIONS

Supply and demand interact constantly in the real estate market causing both short-run and long-run adjustments.

The Dynamics of Supply and Demand

The real estate market acts much like any theoretical market in response to changes in supply and demand, although imperfections, such as lack of product standardization, long lead times for production of new supply, the use of leverage, and tax shelters, cause some deviations from the theory. Some of the guidelines to understanding the dynamics of the real estate market are as follows:

1. Units, or types, of real estate that are comparable in size and quality tend to sell at similar prices.
2. Prices tend to be stable if supply and demand are in balance.
3. If demand outruns existing supply, a seller's market is created and prices advance. Higher prices cut back on the number of units demanded and, at the same time, stimulate construction of new units. Several weeks, and often several months, are required for new supply to be produced after the need is recognized. New construction will continue until supply and demand are again in balance and prices have stabilized.

4. If supply exceeds demand, as in a declining community or region, a buyer's market exists and prices decline. Falling prices stimulate demand while discouraging new construction. Prices will continue to fall until supply and demand are again in balance.

5. The changing cost of credit has a significant impact, with lower interest rates stimulating demand.

Short-Run Adjustments

The demand for space is much more dynamic than the supply of space. If demand suddenly declines, excess supply cannot be removed from the market area. On the other hand, if demand suddenly surges, additional supply cannot be provided on short notice.

To illustrate, consider the housing market in a medium-sized community that is not tied to a large metropolitan area by commuters and is, therefore, independent of outside influences. For the purposes of this example, we assume that any one housing unit can be substituted for another of approximately equal quality. The short-run interaction among supply, demand, and price is shown in Figure 18–1.

In Figure 18–1, curve D_0 represents the original demand schedule for housing. Curve S represents the supply schedule. The vertical axis can represent either the rent, or sales price, of one housing unit. The horizontal axis indicates the number of housing units demanded or supplied.

The downward slope of the demand curve shows that more units will be demanded at a lower price than at a higher price. The upward slope of the supply curve says that more housing units will be supplied at a high price than at a lower price.

Supply and demand forces are in balance at the point where curves D_0 and S intersect. The price at this point is P_0, at which level X units of housing are demanded. A sudden increase in population or income would shift the demand schedule to the

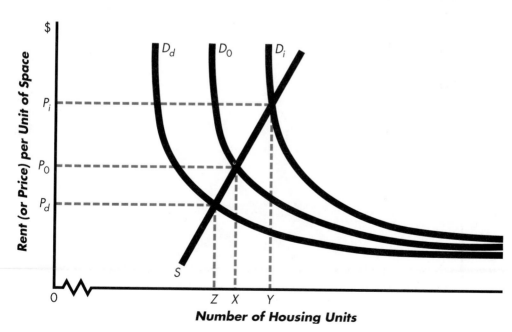

FIGURE 18–1
Short-Run Supply, Demand, and Price Relationship

right, curve D_i. Because new units cannot be quickly produced, the price rises sharply to P_i. At this price, Y units are demanded and supplied. Alternatively, a decline in demand, curve D_d, would cause the price to drop to P_d, with fewer units, Z, being demanded.

In the short run a sudden increase in demand cannot greatly increase the number of housing units supplied. Several weeks would be required, at a minimum, to increase supply, even though the price had increased to P_i. The additional amount of supply equals $Y - X$. This would come about, first, by vacancies being absorbed. Purchase and rental prices would then increase as demand pressed on supply. Some people would use their living space more intensely by doubling up—that is, by crowding more people into their dwellings. Their motives might be to earn more rent or to help friends and relatives forced out of other units by higher prices. Lower income people would be forced to double up because they could not afford the higher prices. Some families would find housing in the country or in the surrounding villages, and commute greater distances to work.

Long-Run Adjustments

The cost of building new housing units enters into the long-run determination of a new equilibrium. Assume that several new industries move into our medium-sized community over a period of years. The successive increases in demand are represented by curves D_1 and D_2 in Figure 18–2. A long-run cost curve is added in Figure 18–2 to recognize the cost of building an additional housing unit. The supply curves are short run because of the long lead time needed to build additional units.

In Figure 18–2, an increase in demand from curve D_0 to curve D_1, increases the short-run price above the marginal cost to produce an additional unit. This is represented by the intersection of curves S_0 and D_1. New housing units would be built (price exceeds cost) and eventually a new equilibrium is reached at a price of P_1 at the intersection of curves S_1 and D_1. Because the price at the intersection equals the cost of production, builders would not find it profitable to continue new construction beyond this point.

FIGURE 18–2
Long-Run Supply, Demand, Price, and Cost Relationship

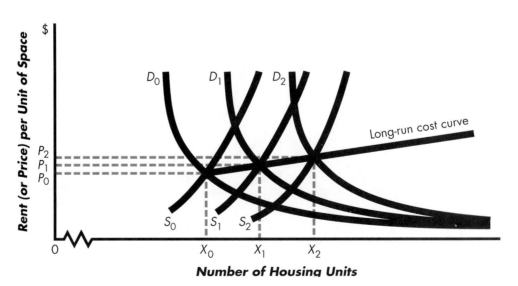

A second increase in demand, to curve D_2, would start the process again. With demand again exceeding supply, prices advance. Under conditions of steadily increasing demand, the costs of land, labor, and building materials all tend to increase because material suppliers and workers can bargain for higher prices and wages and almost always get the increase. Hence, the long-run cost curve slopes upward. Eventually, a new equilibrium is reached at the point where the long-run cost curve and curves D_2 and S_2 intersect. The new price level is P_2, where the number of housing units in the community has increased to X_2. The overall increase in housing units equals $X_2 - X_0$.

Little or no new construction would occur if demand decreased—that is, if the demand curve shifted to the left. The price would quickly drop below the cost curve, and no profit incentive would be present to justify construction of new housing units.

Are There Real Estate Cycles?

Some analysts and authors assert that population, income, and the economy interact to produce regular increases and declines, or cycles, in real estate sales and construction volume. Changes do occur in the level of these activities with the seasons and as a result of economic conditions. Seasonal fluctuations are regular, with higher levels of activity usually occurring in the summer. But, aside from seasonal variations, construction activity and real estate sales seems to fluctuate over periods of from three to seven or more years. Each period of expansion and interaction seems to be unique.

Real estate construction and sales activity seem more closely related to the cost and availability of financing than to any other factor. For example, shortages of credit in 1966, 1966–1970, 1973–1974, and 1979–1982 pushed interest rates up and resulted in sharp cutbacks in housing starts across the United States. Thus, an investor or developer might better look to current and likely monetary policy than to other economic data in deciding whether or not to take on a new project. The most recent recession in 1990–1991 was caused in large part by the tightening of underwriting standards on commercial real estate loans and the slow process of absorbing unemployed real estate resources into productive new endeavors.

Are Real Estate Markets Perfectly Competitive?

The conditions that are necessary for a market to be perfectly competitive are:

1. **Freedom.** Market operates without external (government) regulation or controls.

2. **Knowledge.** All participants have complete or perfect knowledge about competing goods, prices, and future expectations.

3. **Number of Participants.** Many buyers and sellers, none of whom are able to influence the market's operation.

4. **Commodity.** Product is homogeneous, identical, or fungible, and divisible into very small units for transactions.

5. **Mobility.** Product is readily transportable to satisfy excess demand conditions wherever and whenever they occur.

Markets range from perfectly competitive to imperfect. A *perfectly competitive market* is one in which all information concerning future risks and benefits for each commodity is available to all participants. Real estate markets are generally considered to be *imperfectly competitive* in that full information is usually not readily available to all participants. For one thing, information costs considerable money, time, and effort to collect and analyze. Therefore, less wealthy investors find it relatively more difficult than wealthy ones to acquire information. This means that market participants may be led to expect different returns and risks from real estate and may reach differing values for a given parcel of realty.

Several other factors act to keep real estate markets imperfect. Most properties are large, with a long economic life. A developed site cannot readily be broken up and sold in smaller units. Further, the fixed location of the physical property means that it cannot be used to satisfy supply and demand in other locations.

Are Real Estate Markets Efficient?

Perfect or not, how efficient are real estate markets? An *efficient market* is one in which changes in the outlook for a given property are quickly reflected in the property's probable selling price. Favorable information about a parcel causes an immediate increase in its value, and negative or unfavorable information pushes its value down. In an inefficient market, participants with greater knowledge or skill can use their knowledge to bargain more effectively.

Research has not provided a clear answer to the question, are real estate markets efficient? One thing does seem certain. Information is generally captured and disseminated rather slowly in real estate markets. But once information is known, the price of the real estate adjusts almost immediately to reflect the new information. To be a successful real estate investor one must understand the cause-and-effect market indicators of the real estate market.

LOCAL REAL ESTATE MARKET INDICATORS

Market information is extremely important to an investor who is considering developing or purchasing a property. Price levels and values are uncertain and risky; they do not rise and fall in regular cycles. However, uncertainty and risk may be reduced by monitoring and interpreting the key local market indicators for housing discussed here. These same indicators may be used to interpret change in other submarkets as well. We use the housing market as an example here because it is larger, more familiar, and has more transactions.

Supply and demand and real estate market theory must be understood to interpret local market indicators. As buyers or sellers, most of us are opportunists, with a desire to buy low and sell high. The indicators enable us to better follow this maximizing strategy. Market indicators help us identify buyer's markets and seller's markets, perhaps before they are widely recognized. But buyers must sometimes purchase in a seller's market, and sellers must sometimes sell in a buyer's market. The result is that prices advance or decline according to the forces of supply and demand.

Four categories of indicators are identified here. They are: (1) demand, (2) supply/demand interaction, (3) finance, and (4) construction or new supply (see Figure 18-3). Note that we do not include indicators of supply, even though 95 to 97 per-

MARKET INDICATORS	SOURCES OF INFORMATION
1. Demand	
a. Population	Population Center[a], Chamber of Commerce
b. Employment	Local U.S. Department of Labor office
c. Unemployment	Local U.S. Department of Labor office
d. Per capita personal income (wage levels)	Census data, local U.S. Department of Labor office
2. Supply/Demand Interaction	
a. Sales prices	Comparison of standard house with local sales prices
b. Rent levels	Comparison in market
c. Vacancy rate/utilization rate	Surveys, personal observation
d. Sales volume	Multiple listing service reports, want ads
3. Financial	
a. Relative availability of money	*Wall street Journal,* survey of local lenders
b. Cost of money (interest rates)	*Wall Street Journal,* survey of local lenders
c. Prime rate	*Wall Street Journal,* survey of local lenders
d. Foreclosure rates	Lenders, courthouse records
4. New Supply	
a. Subdivision activity	Plat records, court house
b. Building permits	Local housing office/Dodge reports[b]
c. Construction volume	Contractors, news reports
d. Construction costs	Contractors

FIGURE 18–3
Local Real Estate Market Indicators

[a] Many states provide population information, usually through a major university.
[b] The Dodge Reports provide construction activity and construction costs for the United States, states, metropolitan statistical areas, and counties. The data are published monthly, with annual summaries, through F. W. Dodge Division, McGraw-Hill Information Systems Company.

cent of the space that can have an influence on market activity in any year already exists at the beginning of the year. Demand is the dynamic force in real estate markets. Trends, rates of change, and direction of change in the four categories of indicators discussed below provide the most important information.

Demand Indicators

The four key demand indicators are (1) population, (2) employment, (3) unemployment, and (4) per capita personal income. Trends in these indicators tell a great deal about likely changes in effective demand.

Obviously, an increase in population means an increased desire for housing. And an increase in employment, along with high levels of employment, indicates economic growth and is likely to result in an inflow of additional workers and increased population. Per capita personal income tells how much purchasing power is available for housing. Declines in population and income obviously mean decreased effective demand.

Many states have Population Centers, usually at a major university, from which population data may be obtained. The U.S. Department of Labor provides employment, unemployment, and wage (income) information for most communities. Planning commissions and chambers of commerce often publish reports containing population and labor force information. And most newspapers periodically publish reviews and comments on the economic outlook for their area and region.

Supply/Demand Interaction

Price levels, vacancy rates, sales volume, and rent levels tell what is happening in regard to supply/demand interaction in local real estate. Information on these variables must generally be captured personally, since such data are not published on a regular basis.

Price-level information may be obtained by comparing prices for certain "standard" houses over time. That is, prototypical two-, three-, and four-bedroom houses might be priced on a comparative basis every few months. In like manner, rent levels for one-, two-, and three-bedroom apartments might be checked. The checking information may be retrieved by reading want ads for asking prices or rents on dwelling units offered for sale or rent. Also the summary of completed transactions published monthly by a multiple listing service could serve as a source of price information. Sales volume may also be estimated from this summary. A further indication of sales activity is the volume of deeds recorded by a county recorder. Again, trends and rates of change are vital information.

Vacancy rates tell what portion of the existing supply of space is not being utilized. Thus, the rate of property utilization in a community is the complement, or flip side, of the vacancy rate. Surveys by local apartment owners are sometimes made to determine vacancy rates. Checking with property managers and monitoring want ads may also indicate vacancy levels. New, unsold houses must also be counted as vacancies. An increasing vacancy rate foretells a weakening in prices or rents, while a declining rate suggests that rents and prices are likely to advance.

Financial Indicators

Key financial indicators provide information about the relative availability of money, the prime rate, local mortgage interest rate quotations, and the mortgage foreclosure rate.

The *prime rate* is the rate that major commercial banks charge large, well-established, financially sound companies for business loans. The rate tends to be uniform across the country and, in a sense, ties all financial markets together. An increase in the prime rate indicates a tightening in the money markets, while a decrease indicates easier money. Changes in the prime rate are widely quoted in the financial news. A change in the prime rate usually precedes a comparable shift in mortgage interest rates.

Mortgage foreclosure rates tell the number of borrowers who fail to live up to their mortgage contracts. Death and divorce, two major causes of foreclosure, tend to be relatively stable over time but the rate of unemployment fluctuates. Thus, a sudden increase in foreclosures is likely to have been preceded by layoffs and declining economic conditions. Foreclosures translate into a decline in demand, at least in the short run.

New Supply Indicators

Development and construction mean increases in the supply of real estate. Developers and builders generally add to supply only if they expect sales prices or market values to exceed costs. Starting construction of a new building means that an aspiring homeowner or investor has decided that value will exceed cost. In the short run, construction may continue as a builder strives to keep a crew going despite a discouraging market outlook. Key statistics in this area are subdivision activity, building permits, construction volume, and construction costs.

Subdivision requires several months to a year from approvals of the location and boundaries of individual properties to market availability of sites. Housing construction may take only two or three months, but it does not always follow immediately after the issuance of a building permit. These lags must be taken into account when interpreting development and construction indicators.

Building permits and the dollar amount of construction put-in-place tell of short-term increases in supply. These indicators must be related to effective demand. Subdivision activity indicates that the long-run outlook is promising. At the same time, ever-higher construction costs mean that less space is likely to be demanded and used.

Interrelatedness of Indicators

Real estate supply and demand forces exert pressures in many directions. Increasing births or incomes translate into greater demand. On the other hand, migration from one metropolitan area to better opportunities elsewhere decreases demand. Thus, the effect of supply and demand forces are interrelated. Likewise, market price and sales volume indicators may not all point in the same direction. The investor-analyst must read and interpret the signs provided by indicators on a continuing basis.

SUMMARY

Most of us, living as we do in the midst of local real estate markets, are intuitively aware of the forces of supply and demand. We know that demand may shift over time, and that the demand for space is much more dynamic than the supply. We also know that rents and prices are apt to increase if demand outruns existing supply, and rents and prices are prone to fall if supply exceeds demand.

No doubt you are also intuitively aware of the more important local demand indicators, like population, employment, unemployment, and per capita personal income. Trends in these indicators tell a great deal about likely changes in effective demand for real estate. Consider, for example, real estate prices in Southern California. We all know that California had been a growth state for many years. We also know that Southern California experienced vastly rising real estate rents and values during the 1970s and 1980s. Conversely, New Mexico can be considered a relatively slow-growth state. Compared to California, it had a fairly stable population during the 1970s and 1980s. In turn, construction and real estate activity were not as strong and values were not as high as in Southern California. However, at the same time New Mexico was not subject to the boom-and-bust real estate cycle that occurred in Southern California during the late 1980s and early 1990s.

Because real estate markets are essentially local in character, we must always pay attention to local supply indicators, like sales prices, rent levels, vacancy rates, and sales volume. Equally important are key financial indicators, like the relative availability of credit, the prime rate, and the mortgage foreclosure rate. An increase in the prime rate, which indicates a tightening in the money markets, can have an adverse effect on real estate markets. Likewise, an increase in mortgage foreclosure rates indicates a softening of the real estate market.

KEY CONCEPTS

Buyer's market   When supply greatly exceeds demand, purchasers are able to bargain for and get lower prices. The result is falling values.

Doubling up   Using living space more intensely; crowding more people into each dwelling unit.

Effective demand   Desire armed with purchasing power.

Efficient market   A market where changes in the outlook for a given commodity are quickly reflected in its probable selling price and value.

Perfect market   Where all the information relative to prices, risks, and benefits for each commodity is equally available to all participants. In addition the commodity must be easily divisible and readily transportable.

Potential demand   Raw desire for land or space; population.

Prime rate   The interest rate that major commercial banks charge large, well-established, financially sound companies on business loans.

Seller's market   When demand greatly exceeds supply, sellers are able to bargain for and get higher prices. The result is rising values.

QUESTIONS FOR REVIEW AND DISCUSSION

1. Name at least two submarkets for each of the following types of real estate:

   a. Residential

   b. Commercial

   c. Industrial

   d. Agricultural

   e. Special purpose

2. List and briefly describe at least four characteristics that make real estate markets unique.

3. List and briefly describe four demand and four supply forces of local real estate markets.

4. Describe briefly short-run and long-run adjustments in real estate markets. Illustrate with supply/demand diagrams.

5. Explain the need for market indicators.

6. Name and briefly discuss the nature of two market indicators in each of these four categories: (a) demand, (b) supply/demand interaction, (c) finance, and (d) new supply.

7. Identify and briefly describe three functions of real estate markets.

8. Would we need an urban real estate market if we did not have ownership rights in real property? Discuss.

9. Property owners sometimes oppose community growth even though values generally go up as a result. Is this rational? Explain.

10. What institutional forces may affect land-use decisions?

11. Why is it difficult for real estate markets to move toward equilibrium?

12. What demographic forces affect real estate markets? How?

13. How is potential demand different from effective demand?

14. Historically, what seems to be the most important factor in determining the level of real estate activity in the United States?

15. Discuss how a significant drop in interest rates can affect real estate markets both positively and negatively.

16. Explain how a long-term decrease in the unemployment rate can affect different classes of real estate.

17. Do you believe the real estate industry is cyclical in nature? Why or why not?

CHAPTER 19

REAL ESTATE MARKET AND FEASIBILITY ANALYSIS

Chapter Outline

*He reads much; he is a great observer, and he looks
quite through the deeds of men.*
William Shakespeare, *Julius Caesar*

A market study is a management tool for decision making and is used as well for planning and investment analysis. A *real estate market analysis* is a study to predict changes in the amount and types of real estate facilities needed in an area. The emphasis is usually on urban space needs—that is, residential, retail, office, and industrial space. The time horizon can vary from 1 or 2 years to 10 or more years. The larger the probable need and the greater the investment, the longer the study horizon is likely to be.

An investor needs market and feasibility information before purchasing any large property so as to assure that the outlook for the property is sound. This information also provides a basis for judging the amount to bid for the property. A developer would use a market study to judge whether or not a new shopping center is needed and where it should be located. At times, a market analysis, or what is sometimes called a *marketability* analysis, may be done to determine the competitive position of a proposed development at a particular location. Market studies are used to determine whether a property is being put to its highest-and-best use and merchandised to greatest advantage. New projects and redevelopments may also be analyzed to determine optimal siting in relation to schools and transportation, existing patterns of land use, public regulation, and neighborhood and social conditions. Luxury high-rise condominium units may be analyzed to determine the demographic and economic characteristics of the market for this type of housing.

A market study can help a lender decide whether to lend and how large a loan can be made to finance a development. What the lender really hopes for is to be able to forecast what the future market value of the property will be.

Sometimes a market study may reach out to study potential users of the property. For example, shoppers at a retail center may be questioned about their preferences and attitudes. A prospective investor seeking the right property, needs to know users' preferences as to location, site size and quality, and improvements. Finally, a market study can be helpful in obtaining necessary approvals from planning officials.

THE STUDY FRAMEWORK

Several distinct phases are involved in a market study. A decision regarding the type of real estate—office space, warehouses, or apartments—is presumed to have been made before deciding on the study. Also presumed is an awareness of the relation of the national and regional economy to the local economy.

1. **Market-area Delineation.** First, you must determine who are the likely consumers of the services to be offered at the subject property. This entails determining the potential *market,* or *trade area.* Market area is largely determined by the *range of influence,* or area of competition for the type of real estate under consideration. A housing study might cover a single community, for example. On the other hand, the range of influence for a regional shopping center might extend for 50 to 75 miles.

2. **Analysis of the Area's Economy.** Second, you must decide whether the market area is expanding or contracting. Analysis of an area's basic resources, employment, income, population, and economic trends provides a setting for detailed consideration of real estate needs. This is commonly called an analysis of the *economic base.*

3. **Estimation of Market Potential.** Third, you must consider the purchasing power of the market area. How much are consumers willing to spend for the type of real estate under consideration? Real estate supply factors that must be identified include an inventory of finished space, plus any current new construction, conversion, or demolition activity. Consumers may be loyal to a certain grocery chain, drug store, or dry cleaner. This loyalty may be based on the consumer's perception regarding price and quality of the merchandise being offered, or on perceived differences in the convenience associated with a specific retail establishment.

4. **Site Evaluation and Selection.** Site evaluation and selection is the fourth step in a market analysis. The site chosen can have a major impact on operating expenses. For example, to overcome a poor site, you may have to incur large advertising expenditures. Additionally, to the extent that consumers are not inclined to search for most types of merchandise, convenience of location may be the single most important ingredient for success.

5. **Projections and Conclusions.** Conclusions about the relative strength of market demand currently and into the future must be reached. The types of space needed at various prices or rent levels must be identified. Finally, a judgment on the share of the market that can be captured must be reached.

ESTIMATING POTENTIAL MARKET DEMAND FOR RETAIL USES—AN EXAMPLE

The market study area for retail properties is typically limited to a trade area or neighborhood. Here we follow a study for a supermarket. Groceries tend to be *convenience goods;* that is, people buy them close to home. They may shop on the way home from work or begin the shopping trip from home; in either case, they usually go to only one, two, or three of the nearest stores (i.e., stores within a five- to ten-minute drive). Knowing this, the analyst can establish a trade area based on several considerations:

1. **Neighborhood Boundaries.** Major streets and highways, freeways, railroad tracks, large parks, reservoirs, rivers, lakes, and steep hills may all serve as boundaries between neighborhoods.

2. **Social and Economic Groupings.** Neighborhoods tend to be made up of people of similar tastes and income levels. Observation of people's dress, cars, and housing gives a clue as to the extent of the similarity. Similar information can be obtained from census tract data.

3. **Travel Patterns.** Mode of travel affects where people buy food. Thus, street and traffic patterns for motor vehicles and public transit become important in delineating the trade area.

Let us now consider the potential purchasing power of the trade area. Estimates of potential purchasing power begin with a determination of the average household income in the retail trading area. Figure 19-1 shows the trade area for a hypothetical supermarket. Total purchasing power within the trade area is:

$$\text{Total purchasing power} = \text{Number of households} \times \text{Mean household income}$$
$$= 2000 \times \$40,000 = \$80,000,000$$

To find total potential sales, you simply multiply total purchasing power within the market area by the fraction of household income typically spent on groceries. In our example

$$\text{Total potential sales} = \text{Percent spent on groceries} \times \text{total purchasing power}$$
$$= .08 \times \$80,000,000 = \$6,400,000$$

But what about total potential sales at the site? Common sense tells us that it ought to depend on the opportunities supplied by the center, the competitive differential among sites, accessibility to the site, and the attraction held by the site for residents

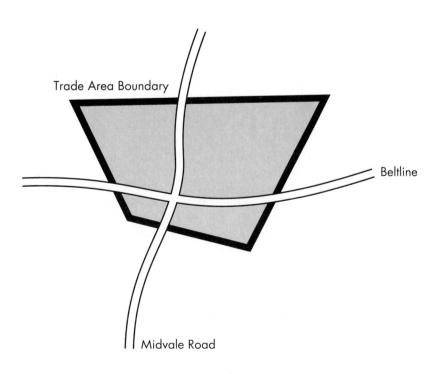

FIGURE 19-1
Market Area for a Neighborhood Supermarket.

within the market area. For our purposes let us suppose that the site is able to capture 80 percent of total potential sales. Then

$$\text{Total sales at site} = \text{Site capture rate} \times \text{Total potential sales}$$
$$= .80 \times \$6{,}400{,}000 = \$5{,}120{,}000$$

If this were a new, rather than an existing, center, we could use this information to determine the amount of space that should be built. To do this, you divide total estimated sales by average sales per square foot, which for supermarkets of this type is roughly \$275 per square foot. The result is

$$\text{Justifiable space} = \text{Total sales at site} \div \text{Sales per square foot}$$
$$= \$5{,}120{,}000 \div \$275 = 18{,}618 \text{ sq. ft.}$$

This calculation tells you that the trade area is capable of supporting a 18,618-square foot supermarket.

You may find when you perform these calculations that the amount of justifiable space at the site is too small compared with the competition. This could occur, for example, if the supermarkets in our trade area were larger, 35,000- to 50,000-square foot super stores, with high-volume grocery sections, beer/wine sections, a deli, and health and personal care sections. So be careful when you interpret the amount of justifiable space at the site.

ESTIMATING MARKET DEMAND FOR OFFICE USES—A MORE DIFFICULT EXAMPLE

Here is a tougher example. To estimate the market demand for office space, you first need to analyze the general rate of growth of business activity in the area in and around the city. A local economy that is expanding attracts additional workers and population. With increased economic activity and population, the office space needs of the area also increase.

To estimate the rate of growth of business activity in and around the city, we do economic-base analysis.

Economic-Base Analysis

In *economic-base analysis,* business activity is divided into two categories: base and service, or base and nonbase. *Base activity* produces goods or services that are exported "outside" (the area under analysis). Payment for the exported goods is in money, which, in turn, is used to buy other goods and services from the outside. The exchange enables the community or area to survive and to continue as an economic entity. Naturally enough, nonbase or *service activity* produces goods or services solely for local consumption. Base activity is also sometimes termed primary activity, in which case service activity is called secondary activity.

But how can base activity be identified? People who "know what the base is" believe they can easily identify base activity. In fact, the problem is not so simple. For example, should a department store, a bakery, a service station, or a university be classified as a base or a service activity? The answer depends to a large extent on the size of the community or area being studied.

Almost all economic activity in the United States is service activity—that is, less than 10 percent of the gross domestic product of most major urban areas in the United States is exported. If the study unit is a relatively small city of 50,000 people, the answer is more difficult. To the extent that the department store draws farmers as customers, or bakery goods are transported to neighboring communities, the department store and bakery are base activities. Likewise, a service station, located on a highway and catering to through traffic, is a base activity. Since a university draws students and funds from outside the city, it too contributes to the economic base of the city.

A *location quotient* (LQ) is commonly used to distinguish between the base and service portions of economic activity. A location quotient is the percentage of total local activity in an industry relative to the percentage of total national activity in the same industry:

$$LQ_i = (E_i / E_t) \div (US_i / US_t)$$

where

LQ_i = location quotient for industry i
E_i = local employment in industry i
E_t = total local employment
US_i = national employment for industry i, and
US_t = total national employment

Location quotients vary among regions due to differences in consumption and production. A location quotient of $LQ = 1$ for a particular industry means that, on average, the region has the same percentage of employment in that industry as the nation. Hence, the industry would in that region be service only. A location quotient of $LQ < 1$ implies that the area has less than its proportionate share of employment in a particular industry and had to import goods and services. A location quotient of $LQ > 1$ implies a greater than proportionate concentration of employment.

Using 1990 industry employment as the measure, the location quotient of Wisconsin dairy products is calculated as follows:

$$\frac{E_i}{E_t} \text{ for Wisconsin dairy products} = \frac{17,605}{1,948,856} \times 100 = 0.90\%$$

$$\frac{US_i}{US_t} \text{ for dairy products} = \frac{140,154}{93,476,000} \times 100 = 0.15\%$$

$$LQ \text{ for Wisconsin} = (E_i/E_t) \div (US_i/US_t)$$

$$= \frac{0.90\%}{0.15\%} = 6.00$$

An *LQ* of 6.00 implies that Wisconsin produces over six times its needs in dairy products. Obviously, dairy products are very important to the economic base of Wisconsin, which is known as the "land of dairy." Other *LQ*s are shown in Figure 19–2. Note the *LQ* of 1.88 for sausage products in Milwaukee County. At the other extreme, the very low *LQ* in mining says that Milwaukee County does not produce its proportional share of oil and gas. Finally, note that nonbase activities, such as retail trade, transportation, communications, public utilities, services, and public administration all have *LQ*s very near 1.

Economic-base analysis was originally designed as a tool to predict future population for a community. An analyst working only with employment data, might, for example, project total employment to the year 2000 based on trends and other information. This prediction can be accomplished by recognizing that total employment consists of

$$E_t = E_b + E_s$$

where

> E_t = total employment within a region or city
> E_b = total base employment within a region or city, and
> E_s = total service employment within a region or city

Suppose further that service employment, which is ancillary to base employment, can be expressed as a fraction of total employment:

$$E_s = kE_t \qquad 0 < k < 1$$

Here k is the ratio of service employment to total employment ($k = E_s/E_t$).

We can now figure out how total employment within a region or city is related to base employment. The relationship between total employment and base employment is

$$E_t = E_b \, (1/1 - k)$$

where $1/(1 - k)$ is the *employment multiplier.*

Now you have a formula for forecasting total employment based on your expectation of base employment. This is correct only if we know that the base employment multiplier in future periods will be the same as this year's.

Another way to express the relationship between total employment and base employment within a region or city is

$$\Delta E_t = \Delta E_b \, (1/1 - k)$$

where

> ΔE_t = change in total employment within a region or city, and
> ΔE_b = change in base employment within a region or city

Let us see how this formula can be used to estimate the change in total employment within Milwaukee county. Suppose base employment within Milwaukee County is expected to increase by 20 percent during the 1990–2000 period—that is, the number of jobs is expected to increase from 106,701 workers in 1990 to 128,041 workers in 2000, or a change of 21,340 jobs. With an employment multiplier of $1/(1 - 0.63) = 2.70$, the resulting change in total employment is 57,618 jobs.[1]

---

[1] Total service employment within Milwaukee County in 1990 includes retail trade, finance, insurance, real estate, and services, or 297,894 employees. The ratio of service employment to total employment is $297,894 \div 470,114 = 0.63$.

MAJOR INDUSTRY GROUP	UNITED STATES			STATE OF WISCONSIN			MILWAUKEE COUNTY		
	NUMBER EMPLOYED (000)	PERCENT DISTRI-BUTION	INDUSTRY LOCATIONAL QUOTIENT	NUMBER EMPLOYED	PERCENT DISTRI-BUTION	INDUSTRY LOCATIONAL QUOTIENT	NUMBER EMPLOYED	PERCENT DISTRI-BUTION	INDUSTRY LOCATIONAL QUOTIENT
Agriculture, forestry, & fisheries	531	0.57%	0.78	8,654	0.44%	0.78	850	0.18%	0.32
Mining	723	0.77%	0.13	1,944	0.10%	0.13	49	0.01%	0.01
Construction	5,239	5.60%	0.78	84,782	4.35%	0.78	15,300	3.25%	0.58
Manufacturing	19,173	20.51%	1.38	550,192	28.23%	1.38	106,701	22.70%	1.11
Lumber & Wood Products									
Primary metal industries									
Fabricated metal industries									
Machinery, except electrical									
Electrical machinery									
Motor vehicles & other trans.									
Food & kindred products									
Sausage products	78,799	0.08%	4.13	6,448	0.33%	4.13	685	0.15%	1.88
Dairy products	140,154	0.15%	6.00	17,605	0.90%	6.00			
Textile mill & fabricated									
Printing, publishing & allied									
Chemical & allied products									
Other nondurable goods									
Transport, communication & public utilities	5,592	5.98%	0.86	99,724	5.12%	0.86	23,144	4.92%	0.82
Wholesale trade	6,328	6.77%	0.89	118,056	6.06%	0.89	25,315	5.38%	0.80
Retail trade	19,815	21.20%	1.01	415,825	21.34%	1.01	86,958	18.50%	0.87
Finance, insurance & real estate	6,956	7.44%	0.89	129,017	6.62%	0.89	45,470	9.67%	1.30
Services	28,800	30.81%	0.89	536,208	27.51%	0.89	165,466	35.20%	1.14
Unclassified establishments	319	0.34%	0.67	4,454	0.23%	0.67	861	0.18%	0.54
Total	93,476	100.00%	—	1,948,856	100.00%	—	470,114	100.00%	—

SOURCE: Employment data from U.S. census; calculations by authors.

FIGURE 19–2

Location Quotients for the United States, the State of Wisconsin, and the Milwaukee County Area, 1990

This brings us now to the demand for office space. Estimating the demand for office space involves a two-part calculation. First, the projected change in total employment within Milwaukee County must be converted into a change in office employment. This is done by multiplying total employment by 24 percent, which is the ratio of office employment to total employment.

$$\text{Increase in office employment} = \text{Percent of office workers} \times \text{Increase in total employment}$$
$$= .24 \times 57,618 = 13,828$$

Next, we multiply the number of new office workers by office space per employee. Normally, this ratio is around 250 square feet per employee, but it varies by type of office occupation and city. Using 250 square feet per employee, we obtain

$$\text{Demand} = \text{Increase in office employment} \times \text{Office space per employee}$$
$$= 13,828 \times 250 = 3,457,000$$

Thus, a projected change of 13,828 office workers for the period 1990–2000 for a community such as Milwaukee County would mean an expected increase in the demand for office space of 3,457,000 square feet over the ten-year period, or 345,700 square feet per annum.

Limitations of Economic-Base Analysis.   Economic-base analysis is not without serious limitations. Without going through a detailed discussion, we should point out that recent research indicates that the employment multipliers for a region or city tend to be unstable in the short run, and that they vary from city to city. Small cities or regions normally are net "exporters"—that is, their "base" activity is high; consequently, the local multipliers are often between 1 and 2. As the size increases, there are greater opportunities to increase income by nonbase or service activity. This instability weakens the model as a reliable forecasting tool.

Shift-Share Analysis

Shift-share analysis breaks down employment growth (or decline) in a region over a given time period into three components: (1) a national growth effect, (2) an industry-mix effect, and (3) a competitive effect. Trends in each component are then analyzed to determine a top-down forecast of employment growth by industry sector.

To illustrate how shift-share analysis works, consider Figure 19–3. Panel A of Figure 19–3 shows the total employment by major industry sector (i.e., agriculture, manufacturing, and nonmanufacturing) for Milwaukee County and the United States in 1988 and 1990. Also shown is total employment for Milwaukee County and the United States over this same time period.

The overall rate of growth in the national economy during the 1988–1990 period is

$$\text{U.S. average growth rate} = \frac{93,476,000 - 87,882,000}{87,882,000} = 6.37\%$$

Thus, if Milwaukee County had grown as rapidly as the national economy over the 1988–1990 period, 50 new jobs would have been added in the agriculture sector

(A) DATA

SECTOR	MILWAUKEE COUNTY		UNITED STATES	
	1988	1990	1988	1990
Agriculture	788	850	462,000	531,000
Manufacturing	104,375	106,701	19,262,000	19,173,000
Nonmanufacturing	327,532	362,563	68,158,000	73,772,000
Total	432,695	470,114	87,882,000	93,476,000

(B) SHIFT-SHARE RESULTS

SECTOR	COMPONENTS		
		SHIFT	
	SHARE[a]	MIX[b]	COMPETITIVE[c]
Agriculture	50	68	−56
Manufacturing	6,649	−7,129	2,808
Service	20,864	6,125	8,057
Total	27,513	−936	10,809

[a] Share = Employment in local industry sector in base period × U.S. average growth rate.

[b] Mix = Employment in local industry sector in base period × (U.S. growth rate in industry sector − U.S. average growth rate).

[c] Competitive = Employment in local industry sector in base period × (Local growth rate in industry sector − U.S. growth rate in industry sector).

FIGURE 19–3
Shift-Share Analysis for Milwaukee County, Wisconsin

(agriculture sector employment in 1988 times U.S. growth rate, or 788 × 0.0637); 6,649 new jobs in the manufacturing sector (104,375 × 0.0637); and 20,864 new jobs in the nonmanufacturing sector (327,532 × 0.0637). These calculations are set out in the first column of Panel B in Figure 19–3.

The industry-mix effect for Milwaukee County indicates the extra (or reduced) growth because a particular industry is expected to grow more (or less) rapidly than the overall national average growth rate. Consider, for example, the agriculture sector in the United States. Between 1988 and 1990, it grew at a rate of

$$\text{U.S. growth rate in agriculture} = \frac{531,000 - 462,000}{462,000} = 14.94\%$$

or 8.57 percent faster than the overall U.S. economy (14.94 percent − 6.37 percent). Thus, a total of 68 new jobs would have been added in the agriculture sector in Milwaukee County if the local agriculture sector kept pace with industry-wide changes (agriculture sector employment in 1988 times excess rate of growth in the U.S. agriculture sector vis-à-vis the overall U.S. economy, or 788 × (0.1494 − 0.0637)). The industry-mix components for manufacturing and nonmanufacturing in Milwaukee County are −7,129 (104,375 × (−0.0046 − 0.0637)) and 6,125 (327,532 × (0.0824 − 0.0637)), respectively (see column (2) of Panel B in Figure 19–3). The industry-mix components can be used as an indicator of where to look for industry strengths and weaknesses.

The competitive-mix component for Milwaukee County is the difference between the actual change in employment and the employment change to be expected if the local industrial sector grew at the national rate. The actual change in employment in the agriculture sector in Milwaukee County is

$$\text{Milwaukee County growth rate in agriculture} = \frac{850 - 788}{788} = 7.87\%$$

or 7.07 percent slower than the U.S. growth rate in agriculture (7.87 percent − 14.94 percent). This indicates a less than favorable environment for agriculture in Milwaukee County. Because of this less than favorable environment for agriculture in Milwaukee County, total employment in the agriculture sector over the 1988–1990 period would have decreased by 56 jobs [agriculture sector employment in 1988 times excess growth rate in agriculture in Milwaukee County vis-à-vis the U.S. agriculture sectors, or 788 × (0.0787 − 0.1494)]. The competitive-mix components for manufacturing and nonmanufacturing in Milwaukee County are 2,808 [104,375 × (0.0223 + 0.0046)] and 8,057 [327,532 × (0.1070 − 0.0824)], respectively (see column (3) of Panel B in Figure 19–3). The positive competitive-mix components for manufacturing and nonmanufacturing indicate a favorable environment for both manufacturing and nonmanufacturing in Milwaukee County.

Another thing you should look at is whether both the industry mix and competitive components are positive or negative. If the two components are positive this symbolizes a robust national industry as well as a solid local market, whereas if both are negative this is indicative of a dwindling industry. You should also be on the alert for industries with negative industry mixes and positive competitive effects, especially if the overall effect is positive; this suggests that the local environment is compensating for a negative industry mix.

PROJECTING POPULATION FOR MILWAUKEE COUNTY—A THIRD EXAMPLE

The projected increase in total employment within Milwaukee County can easily be converted into a projected increase in total population by dividing the increase in total employment by the labor force participation rate for the projected period. The labor force participation rate which indicates the fraction of adult civilian population who are members of the labor force is about 42 percent, but it is rising slowly because of an increasing percentage of working women. Thus, a 1990–2000 projection of an increase of 57,618 workers for a community would mean an expected increase in population of about 137,186 people:

$$
\begin{aligned}
\text{Increase in population} &= \text{Increase in total employment} \\
&\quad \div \text{Labor force participation rate} \\
&= 57{,}618 \div .42 \\
&= 137{,}186
\end{aligned}
$$

The economic development implications of this forecast are as follows. Clearly, an increase of 137,186 people in the Milwaukee County area over the next ten years will mean more housing, an increase in retail shopping centers, and so on. Overall demand for residential dwelling units will increase by

$$\text{Increase in households} = \text{Increase population} \div \text{Household size}$$
$$= 137{,}186 \div 2.3 = 59{,}646$$

Of these estimated 59,646 new households in the Milwaukee County area over the next ten years, some will demand residential rental space and others will prefer to become homeowners. We can estimate the number of new homeowners and renters essentially as follows:

1. **New Homeowners.** To determine the number of new homeowners, multiply the number of new households in the Milwaukee County area by an aggregate homeownership rate. To illustrate, assume that 63 percent of all occupied dwelling units in Milwaukee County are owner-occupied (i.e., the aggregate homeownership rate is 63 percent). It follows then that the number of new homeowners will be $.63 \times 59{,}646 = 37{,}577$.

2. **Number of New Renters.** Estimate the number of new renters as a residual, or remainder, by subtracting the number of new homeowners from the number of new households in the Milwaukee County area. The result is $59{,}646 - 37{,}577 = 22{,}069$ new renter-occupied households.

Ultimately the type of housing desired and locational preferences will depend upon household characteristics such as age, family size, income, and lifestyle preferences.

FEASIBILITY ANALYSIS

A *feasibility analysis* is a study to determine the potential profitability of a specific real estate project. It extends economic base and market analysis to a specific real estate investment problem. Feasibility analysis takes into account market, physical, locational, legal, social, governmental, and financial factors. The project is considered financially feasible only if the value to be created exceeds the total costs to be incurred.

Everyone involved in an investment situation expects to benefit. The owner of the site or property wants the property to increase in value or to realize a profit on a sale. The user wants to get a property in a location that best serves his or her needs. The owner may become the user. The developer, brokers, architects, engineers, builders, lenders, and attorneys involved expect to receive reasonable fees or commissions. A feasibility analysis is made so that the initiator of the action minimizes risk while getting the greatest benefits possible.

Testing for Financial Feasibility

Feasibility analysis can be applied to three types of situations:

1. A site or property looking for a use.
2. A use looking for a site or a property with certain types of improvements.
3. An investor looking for the best profit opportunity available.

A Site Looking for a Use.   Feasibility analysis, in the case of a site looking for a use, begins with the selection of the three or four (or more) most likely uses for the property. The total cost involved in preparing the site for each of the uses is then determined. Costs include the cost of the site, or the market value if the investor already owns the site; site preparation costs such as soil tests, grading, and landscaping; fees for architects, engineers, and attorneys; brokerage commissions; financing charges; a developer's profit; and all other costs incidental to the development of the project.

The problem is to find a use able to realize enough value from the completed project to justify the costs. Some choices might be: An office building constructed at a total cost of $800,000. The present value of future rents must equal or exceed $800,000 for the project to be financially feasible. Or, the developer can buy an old, abandoned cannery for $1 million. Located near the waterfront, which is a major tourist attraction, it could be converted into a tourist shopping center at an additional cost of $2 million. The value in the new use must equal or exceed $3 million to justify the project. In a conversion or rehabilitation, the higher rents or benefits must be sufficient to justify the costs of modification.

A project would also be considered feasible if the owner expected to use the property and considered the costs reasonable and within his or her financial capacity.

A feasibility analysis for a site looking for a use ends with the selection of the highest-and-best use. Among financially feasible uses, the highest-and-best use typically is that use which produces the highest residual land value. Depending on the particular situation, the highest-and-best use also may be that use which produces the highest value consistent with the rate of return warranted by the market.

A Use Looking for a Site.   A user expects to realize benefits from a site, from its improvements, and from its location. A user values a property on the basis of its future returns. The cost of renting or owning must be less than the value of the benefits that will be realized for a property to be feasible.

Feasibility analysis in the case of a use looking for a site begins with a market analysis that shows an unsatisfied demand existing in a community. The demand might be for office space, for a retail trade area, or for three-bedroom apartments. Several alternative sites are selected for analysis. Based on the use under study, street patterns, traffic flow, lot size, location, zoning, actual or potential building size and shape, and neighborhood quality might be important considerations in selecting each of the sites. Based on the specific characteristics of each site, the future returns are estimated. From this, the amount that can be paid for the property is calculated. The site or property that best serves the use is selected.

Here is a simple example. After analysis, a merchant decides that the highest rent he or she can pay for a certain store is $24,000 per year. The owner wants $30,000. The property is not a feasible alternative for the merchant. Or, a developer estimates that apartment rentals justify a value of $17,000 per dwelling unit on a certain site. If the site costs $3,000 per dwelling unit and improvement costs are estimated at $13,000 per dwelling unit, the $17,000 value exceeds the total costs of $16,000. The project is feasible.

Investor Looking for a Profit Opportunity.   An investor may use market and feasibility analysis first to locate and then to choose from several profit opportunities. In the simplest situation, the investor may be trying to select the best of two or three investment opportunities available.

In a more complex situation the investor may try to combine a use and a site for profit. Thus, an investor may determine from market analysis that demand for a supermarket exists in a neighborhood. As a first step the investor might search out one or several suitable sites and take options on them. The investor then approaches supermarket chains to try to convince one of them to build a store on one of the sites under option. The effort ends when the store is built and put into operation.

SUMMARY

A real estate market analysis is a study to predict changes in the amount and types of real estate improvements needed in a community or area. Much judgment must be exercised in making and using a market study. Market studies are useful in determining when land at the urban fringe should be improved, as well as when the use of the improved site should change or increase in intensity. The study framework for an investment or development decision involves five steps:

1. Market-area delineation
2. Analysis of the area's economy
3. Estimation of market potential
4. Site evaluation and selection.
5. Projections and conclusions.

The range of influence, or area of competition, is the prime consideration in delineating the market area.

Economic-base analysis provides the umbrella for the market and feasibility analysis. Economic-base analysis involves determining the activities that drive the local economy, and projecting future changes. Factors of real estate supply and demand must be studied to relate the economic-base study to the use or site under study, both for a current and a long-run market outlook.

Feasibility analysis is the study of the profitability of a specific real estate project, taking account of market, physical, locational, legal, governmental, and financial factors. Feasibility tests differ depending on whether you have a site looking for a use, a use looking for a site, or an investor looking for the best profit opportunity available.

KEY CONCEPTS

Base activity An industry that produces goods or services for "export" outside the local area. The goods and services are paid for in money, which is returned to the local economy. Base activity is sometimes referred to as primary economic activity.

Feasibility analysis Study of the practicality (value exceeds cost) of a specific investment or development proposal. Extension of economic-base analysis and market analysis to a specific development or investment problem.

Location quotient (LQ) A ratio used to identify economic-base industries; equals the percent of total local activity in an industry divided by the percent of total national activity in the same industry.

Market analysis   Study to predict changes in the amount and types of real estate facilities needed in an area, with emphasis on urban space needs—residential, retail trade, office, and industrial.

Service activity   An industry that produces goods or services for local consumption or use; that is, not for export. Sometimes also referred to as secondary economic activity.

QUESTIONS FOR REVIEW AND DISCUSSION

1. Explain briefly the nature of a real estate market study and how it might be used by a developer, an investor or owner, and a prospective tenant.

2. List the phases of a market study in sequence, and briefly explain each phase.

3. What considerations enter into delineating a market area?

4. In economic-base analysis, what is a location quotient? Explain the use of an LQ in identifying the economic base of a community.

5. Identify and explain briefly the three types of situations for which feasibility analysis is suited.

6. Does a market study remove all the risk from a project for a developer or an investor? Discuss.

7. Is there a relationship among a market study, a feasibility study, and the highest-and-best use of a property? Explain.

8. What special factors would warrant consideration in making a market analysis for an office building? A shopping center? A supermarket? A warehouse?

9. What are some of the factors that influence trade-area boundaries for retail shopping centers?

10. How is a market-capture rate incorporated into the calculation of justifiable space for a given market area? Briefly discuss.

11. What are the limitations of economic-base analysis?

12. What is shift-share analysis? How are the different components calculated?

PROBLEMS

1. Using the data illustrated below:

	REGION A EMPLOYMENT	U.S. EMPLOYMENT
Printing/publishing	43,539	1,524,887
Apparel/accessory stores	18,805	1,156,594

   a. Calculate the location quotient for Region A in each of the two industries above. Assume that total employment in Region A for the same year was 1,796,474, while total employment in the United States was 87,881,632.

   b. Which industry is an export industry?

2. The following data are available for the printing/publishing industry employment levels:

CITY XYZ		U.S.	
T = 0	T = 1	T = 0	T = 1
31,703	43,539	1,286,520	1,524,887

Total employment in the United States grew from 72,971,338 in t = 0 to 87,881,632 in t = 1.

Required: (a) Using the above information, break down the growth rate of the printing industry in City XYZ into its three shift-share components. (b) Describe each component and what it represents.

3. A real estate company is considering construction of a shopping center to open in two years. Preliminary consultations with various retailers in the marketing area have been made. The retailers have expressed a willingness to lease space in the proposed shopping center. The land for the shopping center already belongs to the company, having been purchased eight years ago.

a. Outline the course of action you would follow in performing a feasibility analysis of the subject site. How does this differ from conducting a market analysis?

b. How would the structure of the feasibility analysis in this case differ if the real estate company began with a need for a site? Discuss.

c. What factors should be considered in selecting potential retailers? Discuss.

4. The following information is for Young City.

	1980	1990
Population	170,616	191,262
Households	68,996	80,047
Household size	2.47	2.39
Percent homeowners	0.63	0.61

a. Determine the average annual population growth rate for the years 1980 through 1990.

b. Use the average annual population growth rate to forecast population for the years 1990–2000.

c. Based on the economic development implications of your population forecast in b, forecast the number of new homeowners and renters for the years 1990–2000.

5. Your aunt died recently and willed you 31 acres of land on State Highway 33, which connects Sun City and Parkridge, two rapidly growing communities in the Sun Belt. The property has been in your aunt's family for over 110 years.

The 31 acres is actually made up of two parcels on opposite sides of Highway 33. The southern parcel contains 7 acres, has a cotton mill and an old, pole–type warehouse on it, and is bordered on the east by Avion Way, which comes off the highway and provides direct access to the airport. Avion Way is scheduled to be widened to four lanes, with a center boulevard, during the next year. Also, a railway line runs along the property's southern edge. It is doubtful that the improvements are consistent with today's highest-and-best use of the parcel. The larger parcel, which is vacant except for an old farmhouse where your aunt lived, fronts on Highway 33 for one-quarter mile, and is bordered on both the eastern and western sides by public streets.

Highway 33 carries considerable traffic. The parcels along it generally range in size from one-half to three acres, with mostly mixed, residential and highway commercial uses. Within five miles are many single family residences, apartment buildings, commercial and office buildings, medical buildings, two colleges and a state university, several churches, and a large county park. The metropolitan airport, recently expanded, is about three miles to the south, just beyond the East-West Interstate Highway.

The central business district of Sun City, population 210,000 and eight miles to the east, is undergoing a major face-lift as part of an urban renewal project. The Jackson County courthouse is in Sun City. Downtown Parkridge, population 80,000, is four miles to the west. Of the two cities, Parkridge is the faster growing. The cities are growing toward each other, for the most part. Most industrial expansion of consequence in the last two decades has been in unincorporated areas south of the interstate highway and the airport. Several high-technology firms have built plants there in recent years. Thus, the location of the parcels appears to preclude their being developed for industrial purposes.

Taxes on the parcels amount to about $30,000 per year, or $2,500 per month. The net income from operation of the mill has been sporadic; in fact, it is likely that the mill has been operating in the red since your aunt's death, 18 months ago. Having just entered the work force, your income is only about $1,600 per month, gross. Clearly, you must make some decisions.

All estate and probate problems have been resolved. Now, as the new owner, you are free to take whatever legal actions you deem necessary to preserve your position and to operate the properties at a profit. Major problems you now face are as follows.

a. Not being familiar with this real estate, you clearly need information and advice about it and how to operate it. How would you go about getting such information? Alternatives range from looking in the phone book and arranging an appointment with the broker with the biggest ad, to engaging a marketing and planning consultant, probably at a minimum cost of several thousand dollars.

b. The mill is operating at only partial capacity and probably at a loss. Might an adjustment in property taxes be sought? Assume that the assessed value and taxes are one-half on the land and one-half on the improvements. How might you find out about this?

c. Assume that property taxes are $16,000 on the smaller parcel and $14,000 on the larger. For the smaller parcel, the taxes on the land are $9,000 per year, which represents about 2 percent of its market value. What is a rough estimate of the market value of the land? What limitations attach to estimating value by this method?

d. What steps might you take to develop some personal idea of the highest-and-best use of the property?

e. Should the costs of demolishing the existing structures enter into your thinking and planning? What other alternatives are open to you regarding the improvements? Under what circumstances would you not demolish any structures?

f. Could and should the 7-acre parcel be developed independently of the larger parcel? What issues might be involved in making this decision?

g. In general, what effect are the following likely to have on the value of the land?
  (i) Sun City downtown renovation?
  (ii) Industrial expansion to the south?
  (iii) The recently expanded airport?
  (iv) The mixed, residential-commercial development along Highway 33?
  (v) The railway line along the edge of the smaller parcel?
  (vi) The scheduled widening of Avion Way?

h. In your investigations, you uncover a rumor that Highway 33 is to be rerouted along the interstate highway. What is the probable influence on the value of your parcels, if true?

i. What, in your opinion, is the feasibility of preserving the building on the smaller parcel and converting it into a:
  (i) Neighborhood shopping center?
  (ii) Recreational center?
  (iii) Retirement home?
  (iv) Public market?
  (v) Office complex?
  (vi) Research complex?

What additional information might you want before making a decision on any of these?

j. What, in your opinion, is the feasibility of developing the larger parcel into a:
  (i) Subdivision for one-family residences?
  (ii) Shopping center?
  (iii) Medical office center?
  (iv) Apartment complex?
  (v) Complex of four story office buildings?
  (vi) Race track?

What additional information might you want before making a decision on any of these?

k. Would any combination of the foregoing uses make sense? Why?

l. Given that you now have a clearer idea of what your alternatives are, what are your next steps?

PART FIVE
REAL ESTATE FINANCE

CHAPTER 20

MECHANICS OF FIXED-RATE MORTGAGE FINANCING

Chapter Outline

In a fixed-rate mortgage, a lender exchanges cash for a series of equal or uniform payments from the borrower. To determine the present value of the mortgage loan (which is the amount of money the lender is willing to advance to the borrower), these periodic debt service payments are discounted at a fixed interest rate. The general *present value formula* for a fixed-rate mortgage is

$$PV = \frac{DS}{(1 + i)} + \frac{DS}{(1 + i)^2} + \cdots + \frac{DS}{(1 + i)^n}$$

where DS is the periodic debt service payment received at the end of periods 1, 2, . . . , n; i is the interest rate; and n is the loan duration.

Alternatively, we could use the present value formula to find the periodic debt service payment that would pay off the loan over a specified duration and yield a desired rate of return to the lender.

$$PV = \frac{DS}{(1 + i)} + \frac{DS}{(1 + i)^2} + \cdots + \frac{DS}{(1 + i)^n}$$

implies that

$$DS = PV \left(\frac{1}{\dfrac{1}{(1 + i)} + \dfrac{1}{(1 + i)^2} + \cdots + \dfrac{1}{(1 + i)^n}} \right)$$

or

$$DS = PV \times \frac{1}{PVAIF_{i, n}}$$

where

$$PVAIF_{i, n} = \frac{1}{(1 + i)} + \frac{1}{(1 + i)^2} + \cdots + \frac{1}{(1 + i)_n}$$

The term $PVAIF_{i, N}$ is known as the *present value of an annuity factor*. The $PVAIF_{i, N}$ factor, used as a multiplier, converts a series of equal or level payments into a single,

320

lump-sum present value. Values of $PVAIF_{i,N}$ have been calculated for various values of i and N, and are shown in the time-value-of-money tables in the appendix.

A thorough understanding of these expressions is extremely important. Throughout this chapter we will use these expressions to answer questions like how to determine the outstanding loan balance on a fixed-rate mortgage at any given point in time, or how to determine the amount of interest paid on a fixed-rate mortgage. First though we shall look at some loan terminology and basic financial concepts.

LOAN TERMINOLOGY AND BASIC FINANCIAL CONCEPTS

Here are some very important loan terms and basic financial concepts.

1. **Loan-to-Value Ratio.** The amount of a property's market value that is borrowed is usually expressed as a percentage, called the *loan-to-value ratio* (*LTV*, sometimes *LVR*). An $800,000 loan on a $1 million commercial property illustrates the calculation of a LTV. The LTV ratio in this case is 80 percent.

$$\text{Market value loan} = \frac{\$800,000}{\$1,000,000} = 80\% = LTV$$

The higher the loan-to-value ratio, the higher the risk of default. A typical LTV on most loans is between 75 and 80 percent, but the LTV may go up to 90 or 95 percent if the borrower obtains mortgage insurance against some or all of the losses in the event of a default. The LTV required by a lender directly affects the amount of cash or down payment required by the borrower. If a lender is subject to a maximum LTV of 75 percent, a borrower with only $10,000 will not be able to bid for a property with a value in excess of

$$\frac{\text{Down payment}}{(1 - LTV)} = \frac{\$10,000}{(1 - .75)} = \$40,000 = \text{Maximum purchase price}$$

This is in contrast to a $100,000 property where a 90 percent LTV applies.

2. **Loan Principal.** The *principal of a loan* is the number of dollars actually borrowed, or the remaining balance of the loan. For income-producing properties, the amount an investor is able to borrow depends directly on the *debt-service coverage ratio* (*DCR*) required by the lender, which equals NOI divided by the annual debt service required for principal and interest:

$$\text{Debt-service coverage ratio} = \frac{\text{Annual NOI}}{\text{Annual debt service}}$$

No hard and fast rule for DCR is possible, but most lenders expect the DCR ratio to exceed 1.35 on most income-producing properties. A sound property, well located, and with a proven track record, may get approval with a slightly lower ratio.

3. **Interest Rate.** *Interest* is the rent or charge paid for the use of money. An *interest rate* is the amount paid to borrow money, calculated as a percentage of the amount borrowed. The higher the interest rate, the higher the interest charged. For example, at 6 percent, annual interest on a $800,000 fixed-rate mortgage equals $48,000 in year 1. At 9 percent, annual interest equals $72,000 in year 1.

   From a lender's point of view the interest rate charged to borrowers reflects several factors: (1) the lender's cost of money, (2) the interest rates being charged by other lenders, (3) the risks of the loan, based on the property's and the borrower's characteristics, and (4) the yields available on competitive investments such as Treasury bonds and consumer loans.

4. **Loan Duration.** *The duration of a loan* is the time given the borrower to repay the loan. A loan duration of from 20 to 30 years is typical for residential properties. The loan period for commercial loans is usually shorter, between 10 and 20 years.

5. **Loan Amortization.** *Amortization* means regular, periodic repayment of the principal. The repayment is usually made at the same time interest payments are made. The longer the amortization period, the smaller the periodic installments to repay the principal. If amortization is not required, interest must usually be paid periodically, with repayment of the entire loan principal on the last day of the contract. A loan may be partially amortizing, meaning that periodic payments are made to reduce the principal balance, but at some date the entire remaining balance must be repaid in a single, lump-sum payment.

6. **Debt Service.** The periodic payments for interest and (usually) principal reduction is termed *debt service.* If amortization is not called for (typically on construction loans), debt service consists of interest only. Debt service, in sum, reflects the principal amount, the interest rate, the duration, and the amortization schedule of a loan.

CALCULATING DEBT-SERVICE PAYMENTS

Let us now illustrate how to calculate the required annual debt service payment on a fixed-rate mortgage. Consider a $500,000 loan made at 12 percent for 25 years (compounded annually). The present value of this loan is

$$\$500,000 = \frac{DS}{(1 + .12)} + \frac{DS}{(1 + .12)^2} + \cdots + \frac{DS}{(1 + .12)^{25}}$$

which implies that

$$DS = \$500,000 \left(\frac{1}{\dfrac{1}{(1 + .12)} + \dfrac{1}{(1 + .12)^2} + \cdots + \dfrac{1}{(1 + .12)^{25}}} \right)$$

or

$$DS = \$500,000 \times \frac{1}{7.84314} = \$63,749.98$$

Is there an easier way to calculate the payment needed to amortize, or pay off, the loan over a specified time period? The answer is yes. To illustrate, suppose we wish to know the required annual debt service payment on a $1,000,000 loan made at 10 percent for 20 years (compounded annually). To compute the required annual debt service payment, we can multiply the $1,000,000 loan amount by an annual *principal recovery factor (PR factor)* at 10 percent for 20 years.

A principal recovery factor is a reciprocal of the PVAIF factor. The PR factor, sometimes known as the *mortgage constant (MC)*, converts a present lump-sum amount, the loan, into a series of future cash flows—that is, the debt-service payments. In fact, the PR factor equals 1 divided by the PVAIF factor,[1] and the calculation is

$$DS = \$1,000,000 \times 0.117460 = \$117,460$$

where the annual PR factor at 10 percent for 20 years is 0.117460 (see appendix). Alternatively, the debt service payment on this $1,000,000 fixed-rate mortgage can be computed just as easily using a financial calculator. The inputs for the financial keys would be PV = $1,000,000, i = 10 percent, and n = 20 years. Solving for PMT would yield an annual debt service payment of $117,460.

COMPOUNDING OR DISCOUNTING MORE THAN ONCE A YEAR

Note that the time-value-of-money elements must be modified when compounding or discounting takes place more than once a year. The necessary adjustments are as follows: (1) the interest rate must be divided by the number of periods per year to get the effective rate for the shorter period, and (2) the number of years must be multiplied by the number of periods per year to get the total number of periods. Thus, with monthly compounding, a 12 percent annual or nominal interest rate becomes a 1 percent per month effective interest rate.

$$\frac{12\%}{12 \text{ months}} = 1 \text{ Percent per month}$$

A 25-year loan becomes a 300-month loan (25 × 12). Finally, the monthly payments on a $500,000 fixed-rate mortgage at a 12 percent annual interest rate for 25 years become

$$\$500,000 = \frac{DS}{(1 + .01)} + \frac{DS}{(1 + .01)^2} + \cdots + \frac{DS}{(1 + .01)^{300}}$$

---

[1] The PR factor can also be thought of as the debt service payment on a $1 mortgage at an interest rate of i percent for n periods. Having just said that, the PR factor can easily be determined using a financial calculator. Simply enter $1 for PV, input the interest rate for i and the loan duration for n, and solve for the debt service payment (PMT).

which implies that

$$DS = \$500{,}000 \left(\frac{1}{\dfrac{1}{(1 + .01)} + \dfrac{1}{(1 + .01)^2} + \cdots + \dfrac{1}{(1 + .01)^{300}}} \right)$$

or

$$DS = \$500{,}000 \times \frac{1}{94.94655} = \$5{,}266.12$$

Most residential and commercial mortgages call for monthly payments.

Notice that the debt service payment is a function of the principal, interest rate, duration, and amortization schedule. The larger the principal amount, the greater the required debt service. Also notice that the higher the interest rate, the greater is the debt service. Increasing the interest rate on a $500,000 loan from 12 percent to 15 percent increases annual debt service payment from $63,749.98 to $77,349.70 (or 21 percent). However, going from 5 percent to 8 percent increases annual debt service payment from $35,476.23 to $46,839.39 (or 32 percent).

Duration has an inverse impact on debt service. The longer the duration, the smaller the debt service, although the relationship is not proportional. Thus, increasing the term of a $500,000 loan from 25 to 30 years only lowers debt service from $63,749.98 to $62,071.83.

OUTSTANDING LOAN BALANCE

Calculating the outstanding loan balance at any point in the life of the loan is not difficult: It is simply the present value of the remaining debt service payments. The formula is

$$\text{Loan outstanding, } EOY_t = \frac{DS}{(1 + i)} + \frac{DS}{(1 + i)^2} + \cdots + \frac{DS}{(1 + i)^{n-t}}$$

or

$$\text{Loan outstanding, } EOY_t = DS \times PVAIF_{i,\ n-t}$$

Note that this formula works with either annual or monthly compounding.

Our $500,000, 12 percent, 25-year loan with annual compounding can be used to illustrate the calculations. At the end of year 1, the loan balance is $496,250.02, calculated as follows:

$$\begin{aligned} \text{Loan outstanding, } EOY1 &= DS \times PVAIF_{12\%,\ 25-1} \\ &= \$63{,}749.98 \times 7.784316 \\ &= \$496{,}250.02 \end{aligned}$$

At the end of year 2, the loan balance is $492,050.03, calculated as follows:

$$\text{Loan outstanding, } EOY2 = DS \times PVAIF_{12\%,\ 25-2}$$
$$= \$63,749.98 \times 7.718434$$
$$= \$492,050.03$$

The procedure can be repeated for each year of the mortgage maturity. Notice that the balance owed during each year of the loan will drop off faster as the loan becomes older; that is, as the loan matures. Until that point very little is paid down on the outstanding loan balance (see Figure 20–1).

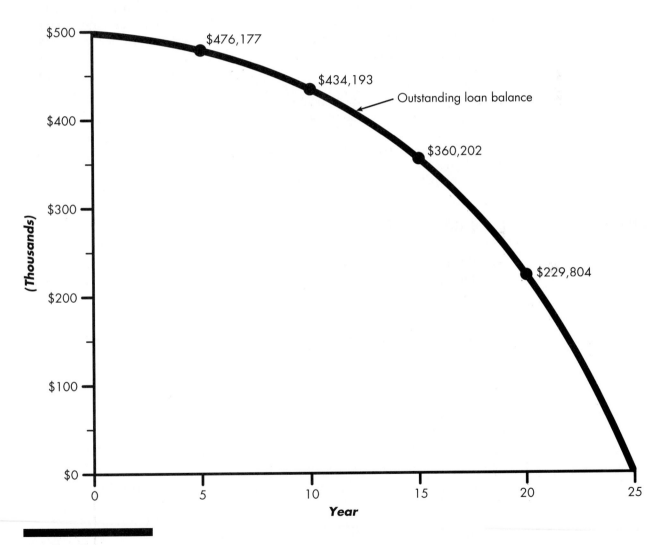

FIGURE 20–1
Outstanding Loan Balance on a $500,000, 12%, 25-Year, Amortizing Fixed-Rate Mortgage

INTEREST CALCULATIONS

Interest is usually calculated to the end of each payment period. In practice, debt service payments are customarily due on the first day of the following period. The payment therefore includes accumulated interest for the previous period plus any principal-reduction amount for the current period. Interest is deducted from each payment first, with the balance going to principal reduction. Interest is sometimes payable at the beginning of a payment period; when that is the case it is termed *interest due* or *interest due in advance*. Interest paid is of considerable value to a borrower because it is a tax-deductible expense for both home ownership and for real estate investments.

Interest calculations are shown here, first using annual payments, and then monthly payments. A $500,000, 12 percent, 25-year loan is used in our example.

Annual Payments. With annual payments, we earlier calculated debt service to be $63,749.98. We also know that debt service consists of interest and repayment of principal (amount borrowed). The amount of interest is simply the beginning of year principal times the annual rate:

$$\text{Interest in year 1} = \text{Loan balance, } BOY1 \times i$$
$$= \$500,000 \times .12$$
$$= \$60,000$$

The amount going to principal is

$$\text{Principal} = \text{Debt service} - \text{Interest}$$
$$= \$63,749.98 - \$60,000$$
$$= \$3,749.98$$

At the end of year 1, after the first payment, the loan amount outstanding is

$$\text{Loan outstanding, } EOY1 = \text{Loan Outstanding, } BOY1 - \text{Principal}$$
$$= \$500,000 - \$3,749.98$$
$$= \$496,250.02$$

Interest for year 2 would then equal $496,250.02 times 12 percent, or $59,550.

Note that debt service payments during the early part of the life go mostly to interest with a small portion to principal reduction. As the loan ages, the portion that goes to principal reduction increases while the portion to interest decreases (see Figure 20–2).

Total interest payable on a loan is easily calculated; it equals the total of all payments less the original principal. Thus, if our $500,000 loan were paid off on schedule over its full 25-year life, the total amount of interest paid would be $1,093,749.62, more than twice the initial amount borrowed.[2]

---

[2] Alternatively, the interest component of the debt service payment can be calculated as follows:

$$\text{Interest during time period } t = DS \times [1 - (1 + i)^{-(n-t-1)}]$$

To illustrate, let $DS = \$63,749.98$, $i = 12\%$, $n = 25$ years, and $t = 1$. Substituting these values into the above expression yields an annual interest expense in year 1 of $60,000.

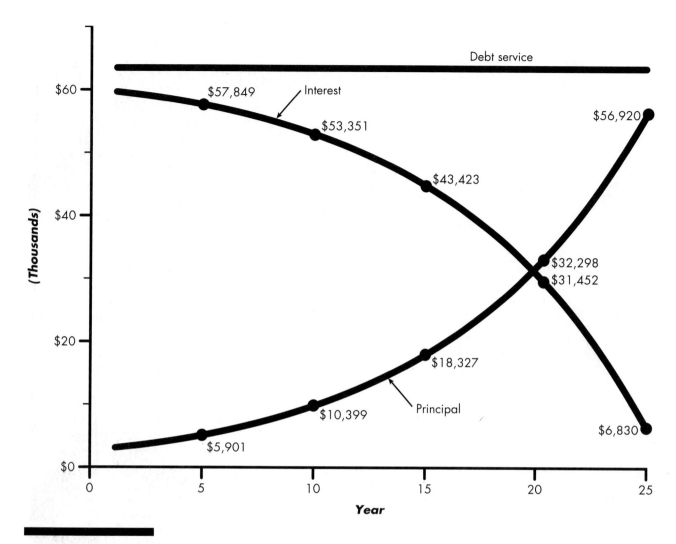

FIGURE 20–2

Allocation of Debt Service to Interest and Principal Reduction with a $500,000, 12%, 25-Year Amortizing Fixed-Rate Mortgage

Annual debt service	$63,749.98
Times: Number of payments	× 25
Total of all payments	$1,593,749.62
Less: Initial principal	500,000.00
Total interest payable over entire life of loan	$1,093,749.62

Monthly Payments. For monthly payments, the calculations are somewhat more involved. Let us return to our 12 percent, 25-year loan of $500,000, but now with monthly payments of $5,266.12, as calculated earlier, or $63,193.45 per year (12 × $5,266.12). Interest expense during month 1 can be calculated as follows.

$$\text{Interest in month 1} = \text{Loan balance, } BOM1 \times (i/12)$$
$$= \$500,000 \times .01 = \$5,000$$

Principal reduction in the first month is

$$\begin{aligned}
\text{Principal} &= \text{Debt service} - \text{Interest} \\
&= \$5,226.12 - \$5,000 \\
&= \$226.12
\end{aligned}$$

The loan amount outstanding at the end of month 1, or the beginning of month 2, is

$$\begin{aligned}
\text{Loan outstanding, } EOM1 &= \text{Loan outstanding, } BOM1 - \text{Principal} \\
&= \$500,000 - \$226.12 \\
&= \$499,773.88
\end{aligned}$$

Repeating these calculations, here is what you will find. In month 2, interest is $4,997.74 ($499,773.88 × .01) and principal reduction is 228.38 ($5,226.12 − $4,997.74), leaving a loan balance of $499,545.50 ($499,773.88 − $228.38). In month 3, interest is $4,995.46, principal is $230.66, and the loan balance at the end of the month is $499,314.84. And so on.

These calculations can become quite tedious if you are trying to amortize a 25-year loan with monthly mortgage payments. However, there is a shortcut. To understand how the shortcut works, let us take a look at what we know. We know that

$$\begin{aligned}
\text{Principal} &= \text{Loan outstanding, } BOM_t - \text{Loan Outstanding, } EOM_t \\
\text{Interest} &= \text{Debt service} - \text{Principal}
\end{aligned}$$

And we also know that the outstanding loan balance at any point in the life of the loan is simply the present value of the remaining debt service payments:

$$\text{Loan outstanding, } EOY_t = \frac{DS}{(1 + .01)} + \frac{DS}{(1 + .01)^2} + \cdots + \frac{DS}{(1 + .01)^{N-t}}$$

or

$$= DS \times PVAIF_{i,\,n-t}$$

So here is the shortcut. To compute the amount of interest expense in any given year, first determine the outstanding loan balance at the end of the year. Then calculate the amount of principal reduction by subtracting the outstanding loan balance at the end of the year from the loan balance at the beginning of the year. Having done that, you can compute the amount of interest expense by subtracting the principal reduction from total debt service during the year.

To illustrate, let us reconsider our $500,000, 12 percent, 25-year loan with monthly mortgage payments. The outstanding loan balance at the end of month 12, or at the end of year 1, is

$$\begin{aligned}
\text{Loan outstanding, } EOM12 &= \frac{\$5,266.12}{(1 + .01)} + \frac{\$5,266.12}{(1 + .01)^2} + \cdots + \frac{\$5,266.12}{(1 + .01)^{300-12}} \\
&= \$5,266.12 \times 94.30566 \\
&= \$496,624.92
\end{aligned}$$

The amount of principal reduction in year 1 is

$$\begin{aligned} \text{Principal} &= \text{Loan outstanding, } BOM1 - \text{Loan outstanding, } EOM12 \\ &= \$500,000 - \$496,624.92 \\ &= \$3,375.08 \end{aligned}$$

Total debt service during the year is $63,193.45. This means that the amount of interest is

$$\begin{aligned} \text{Interest} &= \text{Debt service} - \text{Principal} \\ &= \$63,193.45 - \$3,375.08 \\ &= \$59,818.37 \end{aligned}$$

Total interest payable over the life of the loan equals the total of all payments less the original principal:

Monthly debt service	$ 5,266.12
Times: Total number of payments	× 300
Total payments	$1,579,836.21
Less: Original principal	500,000.00
Total interest payable	$1,079,836.21

Note that yearly debt service is less with a monthly payment loan than with an annual payment loan, $63,193.45 versus $63,749.98. And also that less interest is payable overall, $1,079,836.21 versus $1,093,749.62. The amounts are less on a monthly payment loan because the principal repayment begins earlier with monthly payments. Thus, interest is paid on a slowly declining principal during the year.

An important principle is inherent in this information. Namely, the more frequent the compounding, other things being equal, the lower the yearly debt service and the less the interest paid in any given time.

LOAN AMORTIZATION SCHEDULE

A loan progress schedule to summarize the end-of-year principal balances and the interest paid during each year is necessary to determine tax-deductible interest in any given year. The calculations are easily done with a calculator, as an extension of the work done earlier. Our $500,000, 12 percent, 25-year, loan is used to illustrate the process (see Figure 20–3).

POINTS AND FEES

It is costly for lenders to originate mortgage loans. The property has to be appraised, the borrower has to be investigated, and the title to the property must be checked. To recover these costs, lenders usually charge the borrower an *origination* fee, or *discount points.*

FIGURE 20-3

Loan Amortization
Schedule for a
$500,000, 12%,
25-Year, Amortizing
Fixed-Rate Mortgage

YEAR	DEBT SERVICE	INTEREST[a]	PRINCIPAL[b]	LOAN OUTSTANDING[c]
0				$500,000.00
1	$63,749.98	$60,000.00	$3,749.98	$496,250.02
2	$63,749.98	$59,550.00	$4,199.98	$492,050.03
3	$63,749.98	$59,046.00	$4,703.98	$487,346.05
4	$63,749.98	$58,481.53	$5,268.46	$482,077.59
5	$63,749.98	$57,849.31	$5,900.67	$476,176.92
6	$63,749.98	$57,141.23	$6,608.75	$469,568.16
7	$63,749.98	$56,348.18	$7,401.81	$462,166.36
8	$63,749.98	$55,459.96	$8,290.02	$453,876.34
9	$63,749.98	$54,465.16	$9,284.82	$444,591.51
10	$63,749.98	$53,350.98	$10,399.00	$434,192.51
11	$63,749.98	$52,103.10	$11,646.88	$422,545.62
12	$63,749.98	$50,705.47	$13,044.51	$409,501.11
13	$63,749.98	$49,140.13	$14,609.85	$394,891.26
14	$63,749.98	$47,386.95	$16,363.03	$378,528.23
15	$63,749.98	$45,423.39	$18,326.60	$360,201.63
16	$63,749.98	$43,224.20	$20,525.79	$339,675.84
17	$63,749.98	$40,761.10	$22,988.88	$316,686.96
18	$63,749.98	$38,002.44	$25,747.55	$290,939.41
19	$63,749.98	$34,912.73	$28,837.26	$262,102.15
20	$63,749.98	$31,452.26	$32,297.73	$229,804.43
21	$63,749.98	$27,576.53	$36,173.45	$193,630.97
22	$63,749.98	$23,235.72	$40,514.27	$153,116.71
23	$63,749.98	$18,374.00	$45,375.98	$107,740.73
24	$63,749.98	$12,928.89	$50,821.10	$56,919.63
25	$63,749.98	$6,830.36	$56,919.63	($0.00)

[a] Interest = Loan outstanding, $BOY_t \times$ interest rate
[b] Principal = Debt service − Interest
[c] Loan outstanding, EOY_t = Loan outstanding, BOY_t − Principal

Origination fees and discount points are frequently used to increase the effective interest costs of the loan; as such, they provide negotiating flexibility in a market where interest rates fluctuate. That is, if the stated coupon rate on the mortgage loan is 10 percent, but the going market rate is 10.5 percent, the "real" mortgage rate can be raised to the market by charging points or loan fees. When interest rates are fluctuating, lenders prefer to adjust the origination fee rather than the stated rate to meet competition. Lenders also use origination fees and points to adjust for differences in risk between loans; thus, the higher the expected risk, the higher the origination fee.

When an origination fee is charged, debt service is nonetheless based on the face amount of the loan rather than on the net amount disbursed. Thus, debt service on a $50,000, 25-year loan at 10 percent would be computed on the $50,000 face amount. However, origination fees are deductions from the face amount of the loan. With a 2 percent origination fee of $1,000, the net amount disbursed would be $49,000 ($50,000 − $1,000 = $49,000).

Origination fees and points are often expressed in terms of percentages. For example, a loan origination fee of $1 million on a $10 million loan is discounted at 10 percent, or 10 points.

An Example—Discount Without Prepayment. The Urbandale Savings and Loan Association makes a $10 million, 12 percent loan for 25 years. Assume that the market interest rate is 13 percent. How many points must Urbandale Savings and Loan Association charge to raise the coupon rate to the market?

First, let us determine the yearly debt service payment. The debt service is based on the full face amount of the loan (which is $10 million in this case). At 12 percent annual compounding, the payment is

$$\text{Payment} = \text{Loan outstanding} \times PR \text{ factor @ 12\% for 25 years}$$
$$= \$10,000,000 \times 0.12749997 = \$1,274,99.70$$

Assuming no prepayment, Urbandale Savings and Loan Association stands to get $1,274,999.70 per year for the next 25 years. The market value of this loan equals the present value of $1,274,999.70 per year, discounted at 13 percent for 25 years, or $9,345,728.63:

$$PV = \frac{DS}{(1+i)} + \frac{DS}{(1+i)^2} + \cdots + \frac{DS}{(1+i)^n}$$
$$= DS \times PVAIF_{13\%,\,25}$$
$$= \$1,274,999.70 \times 7.3299850$$
$$= \$9,345,729 \text{ (rounded)}$$

The dollar discount is, therefore, $654,271 ($10,000,000 − $9,345,729). And the discount off the face value is 6.54 percent:

$$\text{Percentage discount} = \frac{\text{Dollar discount}}{\text{Loan outstanding}}$$
$$= \frac{\$654,271}{\$10,000,000}$$
$$= 6.54\%$$

An Example—Discount With Prepayment. Let us now change the situation slightly and assume prepayment at the end of year 15 of the loan. The prepayment equals the present value of the final 10 years of debt service at the 12 percent contract rate, or $7,204,032.66.

$$\text{Prepayment} = DS \times PVAIF_{12\%,\,10\text{ years}}$$
$$= \$1,274,999.70 \times 5.650223$$
$$= \$7,204,032.66$$

With prepayment at the end of year 15, Urbandale Savings and Loan Association would receive $1,274,999.70 per year for 15 years plus a one-time payment of $7,204,032.66 at the end of year 15 of the contract.

The present value of $1,274,999.70 per year for 15 years, discounted at the market rate, 13 percent, is $8,239,531 (rounded). The discounted value of the prepayment, $7,204,032.66, is $1,151,858 (rounded). Thus, the market value of the loan is $9,391,389 ($8,239,531 + $1,151,858).

In turn, the dollar discount is $608,611 ($10,000,000 − $9,391,389). This calculates to a discount off the face value of 6.09 percent ($608,611 ÷ $10,000,000).

The prepayment reduces the discount off the face value. The reason is that the payments from the end of year 15 to the end of year 25 are discounted at a lower rate, making their end of year 15 value larger. In turn, the market value of the loan is greater, meaning a smaller discount.

BORROWING COSTS AND MORTGAGE CHOICE

We end this chapter with a brief discussion of borrowing costs and the choice of mortgage loans. Lenders normally offer borrowers a wide variety of fixed-rate mortgages from which to choose. For instance, some lenders offer borrowers mortgage loans with high contract rates and low discount points, while other lenders offer loans with low contract rates and high discount points. The borrower's problem is to choose the mortgage contract that minimizes the effective cost of borrowing.

To illustrate how this should be done, consider the following problem. A borrower would like to finance a property with a $750,000 loan for 20 years at a 12 percent contract rate (compounded monthly). There are two alternatives. One is to take the loan at 12% but pay the lender a 4 percent origination fee. The other alternative is to take out a $750,000 fixed-rate mortgage for 20 years at a 13 percent interest rate with no discount points. Which loan is the better choice?

We can structure this problem by determining the IRR on the two loans. Let us consider the easier IRR calculation first. For the $750,000 fixed-rate mortgage at 13 percent with no discount points, the cash flows are

$$PV = DS \times PVAIF_{i, n}$$
$$\$750,000 = \$8,786.82 \times PVAIF_{1.08, 240}$$

The interest rate that equates the present value of the debt service payments to the present value of the mortgage loan is, by definition, known as the lender's IRR, or *effective cost of borrowing.*

Using trial-and-error procedures to solve for the effective cost of borrowing, yields an IRR of 1.08 percent, or 13 percent per annum. But this is as expected. In the absence of any discount points, the contract rate will always equal the effective cost of borrowing.

Now let us consider the $750,000 loan at 12 percent and 4 discount points. The cash flows are

$$PV = DS \times PVAIF_{i, N} + \text{Loan fees}$$
$$\$750,000 = \$8,258.15 \times PVAIF_{i, n} + \$30,000$$

Solving for IRR in this case is again done by a trial-and-error process. Assuming the loan is held to maturity, the result is

$$\$750,000 = \$8,258.15 \times PVAIF_{1.05, \, 240 \, \text{months}} + \$30,000$$

or $1.05 \times 12 = 12.65$ percent per annum. This yield is obviously lower than the 13 percent contract rate. Thus, the borrower would be better off choosing the $750,000 loan at 12 percent and paying the 4 discount points up front.

Note that we would get a much different answer if the borrower were to pay off the loan at the end of, say, five years. Why? Because we would be amortizing the $30,000 loan origination fee over a much shorter period. The IRR calculation is

$$PV = DS \times PVAIF_{i,60} + \text{Loan outstanding, } EOY5 \times PV1_{i,60} + \text{Loan fees}$$
$$= 8{,}258.15 \times PVAIF_{1.09,60} + \$688{,}082.47 \times PV1_{1.09,60} + 30{,}000$$

or $1.09 \times 12 = 13.13$ percent per annum. The reader should verify that nothing happens to the IRR on the $750,000 loan at 13 percent with no discount points, even though it, too, would presumably be prepaid at the end of 5 years.

SUMMARY

This chapter has dealt with the mechanics of determining debt service payments, interest expense, principal reduction, and loan balances on fixed-rate mortgages. Two essential relationships were introduced: (1) how to determine the present value of the mortgage (which is the amount of money the lender is willing to advance to the borrower); and (2) how to find the periodic debt service payment that will gradually pay off the loan over a specified duration and yield a desired rate of return to the lender.

The general present value formula for a fixed-rate mortgage is

$$PV = \frac{DS}{(1+i)} + \frac{DS}{(1+i)^2} + \cdots + \frac{DS}{(1+i)^n}$$

where DS is the periodic debt service payment received at the end of periods 1, 2, . . . , n; i is the interest rate, and n is the loan duration.

To determine the periodic debt service payment, one computes

$$DS = \text{Loan balance} \times \frac{1}{PVAIF_{i,n}}$$

or

$$DS = \text{Loan balance} \times PR \text{ factor}$$

where PR, which is equal to $1/PVAIF_{i,n}$, is known as the principal recovery factor, or mortgage constant. Values of $PVAIF_{i,n}$ and PR have been calculated for various values of i and n, and are shown in the time-value-of-money tables in the appendix.

KEY CONCEPTS

Amortization   Systematic repayment of a loan; the installments include both interest and partial debt reduction.

Debt service   Periodic installments of interest and partial repayment of a loan.

Duration of loan   The life, or contract period, of a loan; also known as the "term" of a loan.

Interest   The cost of money, or the price paid to borrow money.

Interest rate   Price, stated as a percent per year, paid to borrow money.

Loan discount   Amount subtracted from the face value of a loan when it is originated; may be expressed as a dollar amount or a percentage.

Loan-to-value ratio   The amount borrowed against a property divided by its market value, usually expressed as a percentage.

Principal of loan   The unamortized balance of a loan; amount owing.

Principal recovery factor (PR factor)   A time-value-of-money multiplier used to convert a current lump-sum payment into a series of equal future values.

QUESTIONS FOR REVIEW AND DISCUSSION

1. What is a loan-to-value ratio? Does a higher LTV provide more or less financial risk to a lender, all else being equal?

2. What is a debt-service coverage ratio?

3. What does amortization mean?

4. What adjustments need to be made when compounding or discounting takes place more than once a year?

5. Are most residential and commercial mortgages compounded monthly or annually?

6. How is the outstanding loan balance calculated?

7. How can lenders adjust the discount rate on the loan to increase the effective cost of borrowing on the loan?

8. When does the contract rate on a loan equal the effective cost of borrowing?

9. Explain how the duration of a loan can affect the effective cost of borrowing?

10. Distinguish between buying a loan at a 5-point discount off face value and discounting debt service for a loan at 5 percent.

11. The market rate is less than the contract rate of a loan. If the loan were sold by the lender, would it sell at a discount or premium?

12. As an annuity lengthens, what happens to the present value of the most distant payments? What does this mean for the present value of a series of payments as the maturity of the loan goes to infinity?

13. The amount, term, and interest rate for two loans are identical; however, one calls for monthly compounding, the other for annual. Will the annual debt service for the annual compounding loan be more than, equal to, or less than 12 times the monthly debt service? What is the source of the difference?

PROBLEMS

1. Construct a loan amortization table for a 10-year, $1,150,000 loan, amortized annually at 10 percent, with a 2 percent origination fee. What is the effective cost of borrowing? If no points are charged, what is the effective cost of borrowing?

2. A borrower has a choice between two $600,000 loans, both of which are amortized annually over ten years, but will be paid back after four years. The first loan is for 12 percent with no points or loan origination fees, and the second loan is at a coupon rate of 10 percent with a loan origination fee of $3,500. Which loan is more advantageous to the borrower?

3. What is the difference in the effective cost of borrowing between a $500,000 loan amortized annually at 12 percent over 10 years, with 4 points paid at the time of the loan origination, versus the same loan prepaid after 4 years?

4. Ann Cook obtains a 15 percent, $100,000 loan from the University Savings & Loan Association to be repaid over 25 years.

   a. What is the debt service with annual end-of-year payments?

   b. With monthly compounding and payments, what debt service is required?

   c. With annual compounding, how much interest would be paid in year 2 of the loan?

   d. With monthly compounding, how much interest would be paid in year 2 of the loan, assuming that all payments are made on schedule?

5. J. Alum takes out a $100,000 loan from the Student Credit Union at 12 percent with payments to made over 25 years.

   a. What is the annual debt service?

   b. If there is a monthly debt service, how much is it?

   c. What is the amount of interest paid in year 3, assuming a monthly debt service?

6. The market interest rate goes up to 15 percent at the end of year 2, and the Student Credit Union decides to sell the J. Alum loan. Assume annual payments.

   a. With no prepayment expected, what is the market value and what is the discount?

   b. With prepayment expected at the end of year 10, what is the market value and what is the discount?

7. Suppose, instead, that the market interest rate had dropped to 9 percent by the end of year 2 when the Student Credit Union decided to sell the J. Alum loan.

   a. What market value should a potential buyer place on the loan, assuming no prepayment is expected?

   b. What percent premium of face value does this represent? (Note: This is simply the converse of a percent discount.)

   c. Assuming prepayment at the end of year 10, what is the market value and what is the premium?

8. The Fifth National Bank of Clinton makes a 12 percent, 25-year, $40,000 mortgage loan with annual compounding to John L. Sullivan to finance a home he purchased. At the end of year 6, the bank needs the money and wishes to sell the loan in a 10 percent market.

   a. Assuming that all the payments have been made on schedule, what is the unamortized loan balance at the end of year 6?

   b. Assuming no prepayment, at what price is the loan likely to sell?

   c. Would the loan be selling for a discount or premium? What percent?

d. Assuming prepayment at the end of year 12 and sale of the loan at the end of year 6, at what price is the loan likely to sell?

e. Diamond Jim Brady buys the loan at the end of year 6 for $40,000. Assuming that it is not prepaid, what yield (IRR) should he realize?

f. If Diamond Jim Brady buys the loan at the end of year 6 for $40,000, assuming that it will be prepaid at the end of year 12, what yield (IRR) should he realize?

9. Jose LaGuadia takes out a $200,000 mortgage loan from the Bears Credit Union. The terms are 15 years, 9 percent, and annual payments. The credit union decides to sell the loan at the end of year 4 in a 12 percent market.

a. What is the loan balance at the end of year 4?

b. What amount will the credit union realize, assuming no prepayment is expected on the loan?

c. What is the dollar and percent discount for the loan in part b?

d. Assuming prepayment at the end of year 10 and sale of the loan at the end of year 4, at what price is the loan likely to sell?

e. Irena James buys the loan at the end of year 4 for $140,000. Assuming that it is not prepaid, what yield (IRR) should he realize?

f. If Irena James buys the loan at the end of year 4 for $140,000, assuming that it will be prepaid at the end of year 10, what yield (IRR) should be realized?

10. You are a loan officer for Acme Bank and are asked to calculate the bank's effective yield on a loan. The loan was for $1,000,000 at 9.5 percent, and 3 discount points were charged on the original loan amount. There is a 2 percent prepayment penalty on the outstanding mortgage balance when the loan is paid off in the sixth year. Assume the loan is fully amortized over 25 years, with annual payments. (Note: Prepayment penalty increases the amount paid to the lender in the sixth year.)

11. How many months does it take to amortize a loan with an outstanding loan balance of $135,895, monthly payments of $1,245, and an interest rate of 10 percent?

12. What is the outstanding loan balance at the end of year 15 on a 30-year, $750,000 loan at 8 percent with monthly amortization?

CHAPTER 21

DEBT AND EQUITY FINANCING OF REAL ESTATE

Chapter Outline

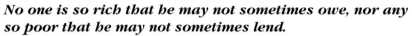

*No one is so rich that he may not sometimes owe, nor any
so poor that he may not sometimes lend.*

Rabelais

Most people must borrow to help finance the acquisition or development of real estate. In fact, the amount borrowed usually makes up much more than half, and sometimes more than 80 percent, of the property's value. The balance of the value, more or less 20 percent, is termed *equity.*

Debt financing is also used to magnify, or *leverage,* the rate of return on the equity investment. But, as the rate of return increases in tandem with the increase in the debt/equity ratio, so likewise does the risk of bankruptcy increase. In using debt to increase the rate of return on the equity investment, the investor must face the question, Is the increase in expected return exactly offset by an increase in risk?

In this chapter we discuss the general circumstances under which debt financing can be used to enhance the rate of return on the equity investment. We also discuss the various sources of equity and debt financing for commercial real estate.

EQUITY FINANCING

Individuals or groups of individuals provide the equity financing in most real estate projects.

Equity Financing by Individuals

At the time of purchase, a new owner usually obtains equity financing from personal funds, often from accumulated savings. This is especially true with the homebuyer, who does not want others sharing in his or her enjoyment of the dwelling. Also, the amount of money required to purchase a home is not usually large enough to require or justify group ownership. Finally, most lenders require individual ownership of a dwelling. Consequently, for homes and other low-value properties as well, the individual saves until he or she is able to put up the necessary equity for the desired purchase.

Equity Financing by Groups

An investor or speculator may not have the funds or the desire to carry the entire burden of equity ownership in a larger property. Thus, the investor or speculator will interest others, by a mutual contribution plan, in sharing in equity financing. Methods vary to suit the specific circumstances of each case. The following are the most usual.

General Partnerships. Many purchases are shared by just a few associates—generally not more than two or three. They may, and often do, speak of themselves as partners. They should also consider themselves joint venturers. Each contributes an agreed-upon share of the necessary equity financing—which may be used to purchase, and possibly for renovations or modernization work. Title to the property is usually taken in the name of all the partners, although sometimes one becomes the owner for the benefit of all. Their rights, obligations, and shares are agreed upon, ordinarily under a separate contract. Technically, they become joint tenants or tenants-in-common. The general partnership arrangement has the disadvantage that the death of any one of the owners may cause delay, taxation, and other inconveniences. Hence, it is normally used only when the term of ownership is expected to be short. It is not used when a large sum of money is involved, because the individuals may not wish to become personally liable for the full amount of any mortgage financing.

Limited Partnerships and Syndicates. A *syndicate* is a joint venture whereby two or more persons pool contributions which they use to purchase, hold, and dispose of real estate through the agency of a manager or other representative. Most real estate syndications are organized as limited partnerships with the syndicator acting as general partner and the investors being limited partners. The limited partners are passive investors who share in the profits. The general partner, on the other hand, organizes, operates, and is responsible for the entire partnership venture. Limited partnerships are frequently used to speculate in real estate. Corporate and trust arrangements are also used for syndicates. A syndication enables numerous persons each to take a small share in a project; if there is a loss, it is shared by the members. A syndicate is simple to create and easy to terminate. The members are not generally interested in long-term ownership, but are seeking a quick turnover with profit. Often they go on to other, similar endeavors.

Corporations. A real estate corporation may be organized with the property in question as the principal asset. The organizer of the corporation can then issue stock to raise the funds necessary for the purchase. This method is simple and inexpensive. Death of any stockholder creates no problem, because the corporation is a separate entity. Mortgage obligations are executed in the name of the corporation, so that no stockholder becomes personally liable; yet each shares in any profit in accordance with her or his stock holdings. A major disadvantage with Corporations, however, is that profits are subject to double taxation. They are taxed once when earned by the corporation and then taxed again when distributed to shareholders as dividend income.

Condominiums. A condominium arrangement may be used to own and finance a multi-unit residential or commercial complex. Each condominium unit must be financed by its individual owner, however. In turn, default by one condominium owner does not obligate other owners to pick up the payments to protect themselves. The unit in default simply goes through foreclosure proceedings the same as any other mortgaged property. Some builders and developers of multi-unit structures deem it wise to consider the feasibility of alternative permanent financing in case the condominium units do not attract purchasers as anticipated. Such standby financing prevents a costly delay when the form of ownership is changed to meet shifting housing demands or investment market conditions.

Cooperatives.   Tenant, or cooperative, ownership is a type of multiple ownership with profits and losses shared by the respective owners. It has come into general use to describe apartment buildings taken over by a group of individual tenants, to be owned, occupied, and operated by them for their mutual benefit and profit. Briefly, it is ownership by an occupying group: a highly restricted community under one roof. It differs from single-home ownership in the sense that the tenant-owner does not have the same responsibilities toward his or her home as the owner of a single-family home. Cooperative ownership is, customarily, corporate ownership, with each tenant-owner a stockholder and holding his or her apartment under a proprietary lease.

A cooperative housing project generally is a multifamily structure, commonly known as a garden apartment, or is an elevator-type building. The building as a rule, is managed for the cooperative owners by a managing agent who is compensated on a salary or commission basis. Members of the cooperative venture occupy individual apartment units and can use or sell the premises subject only to restrictions imposed by the cooperative to protect the quality of the investment and the general amenities of the property. In addition to the initial equity interest, each owner-occupant pays a monthly charge (rent) as a proportionate share to cover mortgage amortization, interest, taxes, hazard insurance, operating costs, use of common utilities, and managerial expenses.

Real Estate Investment Trusts (REITs).   REITs are much like corporations. The typical equity REIT will purchase a building or buildings, finance part of the building or buildings with debt, and issue shares in the corporation or trust to raise the rest of the cash. These shares are usually traded in small dollar units, ranging from $10 to $20 and up, and can change hands quickly, like any other stock.

What differentiates REITs from regular or C corporations is that REITs are not taxed at the corporate level. To avoid paying the corporate tax, all REITs must meet a number of qualifications established by the IRS:

1. There is the "five and fewer rule." Shares must be held by at least 100 persons, and the five biggest investors may not together own more than half the shares. The exception to this rule is investments made by pension funds. Pension fund investments in REITs are ascribed to the beneficiaries of the fund and not to the individual fund. This allows a large pension fund with many beneficiaries to own as much as 100 percent of the REIT.

2. At least 75 percent of the assets must consist of real estate, mortgage notes, cash, cash items, or government securities.

3. At least 75 percent of gross income must come from rents, mortgage investment income, and gain on the sale of real estate.

4. Less than 30 percent of gross income may be derived from the sale or disposition of stock or securities held for less than six months and real property held for less than four years. This restriction prevents REITs from speculating in real estate by actively selling properties.

5. One or more trustee must manage the REIT.

6. At least 95 percent of annual taxable income must be distributed to shareholders.

Investors in REITs receive dividend distributions each year reflecting the performance of the underlying assets. A number of REITs pay out much more than 95 percent of taxable income in a calendar year. They are able to do so because of depreciation and other tax shelter items, which create bookkeeping losses to avoid or defer paying taxes on income.

Many REITs attempt to maintain a stable dividend over time and raise the dividend only when reasonably confident that the higher dividend can be maintained. All things being equal, investors may consider dividend stability a positive utility and be willing to pay a premium for it.

REIT investors also receive the benefit of skilled real estate advice. Some REITs have internal managers, while others use external advisors. The role of the external advisor is to control the day-to-day operations of the REIT and provide investment counsel. REIT advisors are frequently subsidiaries of large commercial banks, life insurance companies, real estate mortgage banking firms, and financial conglomerates. REIT advisors are often paid an advisory fee that is tied to the profitability of the REIT's portfolio. Some advisors are also paid an acquisition or disposition fee.

A major drawback of the REIT form of ownership is that tax losses cannot be passed through to investors. For REITs that are reasonably sure they will incur a tax loss, this restriction reduces the tax benefits accruing to REIT shareholders, which, in turn, reduces the value of REIT status.

There are three general types of REITs: equity REITs, mortgage REITs, and hybrids. *Equity REITs* take equity positions in new or existing real estate projects. *Mortgage REITs* primarily buy and sell real estate mortgages. Major sources of income for mortgage REITs are mortgage interest, origination fees, and profits earned from the buying and selling of long-term mortgages. *Hybrid REITs* are a combination of equity and mortgage REITs; they earn profits from rental income and capital gains, as well as mortgage interest and placement fees.

A rush of new REITs has taken place over the past few years. To some extent this surge in REIT offerings reflects the desire for increased liquidity. It also reflects the fact that REIT prices have picked up greatly relative to the late 1980s. Many institutional property owners are eyeing REITs as means of divesting themselves of commercial property. IBM's pension fund, for example, recently sold several shopping centers to a REIT in exchange for $48 million in cash and $13 million worth of shares in the trust. Taubman, a large shopping center developer, recently set up a REIT in order to slim down its real estate holdings. Some of the larger REITs include New Plan, Weingarten, Washington, Santa Anita, and Bershire.

Annualized equity REIT dividend yields relative to 10-year U.S. Treasury yields during the 1985–1992 period are shown in Figure 21–1. You can see that equity REIT dividend yields are relatively high, ranging from 7 to 11 percent per year. You can also see that the yield spread between REITs and Treasury securities varies considerably, from a low of −200 basis points, which is minus 2 percentage points (1 percentage point is equivalent to 100 basis points), to a high of 275 basis points, or 2.75 percentage points.

Figure 21–2 focuses on equity REIT returns relative to returns on real estate investments made by private-sector institutions, and shows that REIT returns and the Frank Russell Company/National Council of Real Estate Investment Fiduciaries (FRC/NCREIF) return series are quite diverse. We noted earlier (in Chapter 4) that the FRC/NCREIF property index reflects the performance of institutional-grade properties held in a fiduciary setting. One reason for the discrepancy between equity REIT re-

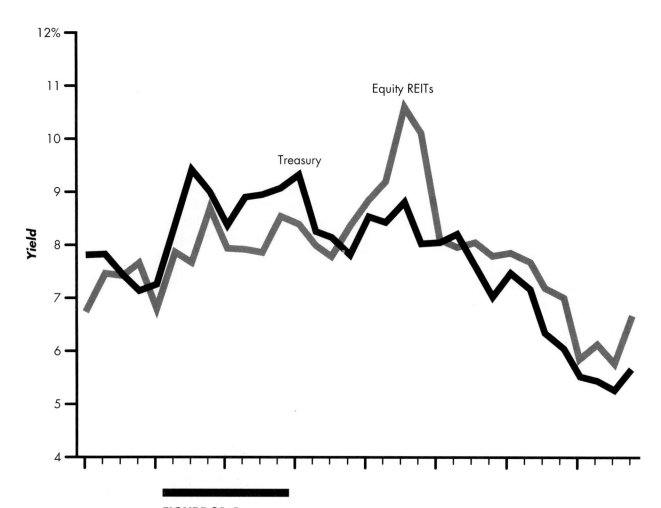

FIGURE 21-1

Equity REIT Returns Versus 10-year U.S. Treasury Yields

Source: The Complete Guide to the Real Estate Investment Trust Industry, National Association of Real Estate Investment Trusts, 1994; and *Federal Reserve Bulletin,* Federal Reserve Board, various issues.

turns and the FRC/NCREIF return series is that REIT investors tend to value external factors, such as company management and its ability to identify and create investment opportunities through active management of the real estate. The FRC/NCREIF property index includes a premium for liquidity whereas the equity REIT index does not.

DEBT FINANCING

As an investor, you need to choose the type of debt that makes sense for your project. Many commercial mortgages, which are used to finance retail properties, office buildings, and industrial/warehouse properties, are either nonamortizing or partially amortizing and mature with an outstanding principal balance, or balloon payment. Some mortgages are interest-only, with a balloon payment; others are zero-coupon mortgages. Interest rates on commercial mortgages may be fixed or adjustable.

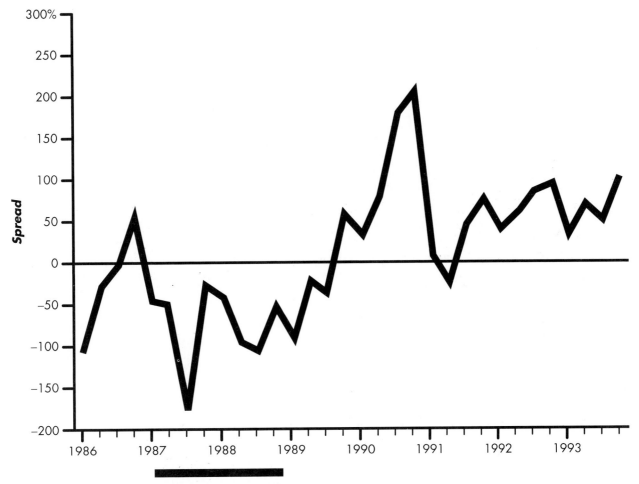

FIGURE 21-1 *(continued)*

Payment Structure

Commercial mortgages use one of four basic payment terms.

> fully amortizing
> partially amortizing, with a balloon payment
> interest-only
> zero coupon

Fully Amortizing. *A fully amortizing mortgage* is considered the least risky. A fully amortizing mortgage provides for the gradual repayment of the debt by means of systematic payments of both principal and interest over a set period so that there is a zero balance at the end of the period. The outstanding mortgage balance, as we saw in Chapter 20, is reduced, or amortized, over the life of the loan. For this reason, fully amortizing mortgages are also known as *self-liquidating mortgages.*

Recall from Chapter 20 that the monthly payment on a fully amortized $2 million commercial mortgage at 12 percent interest for 25 years can be calculated as follows:

$$\$2,000,000 = \frac{DS}{(1 + .01)} + \frac{DS}{(1 + .01)^2} + \cdots + \frac{DS}{(1 + .01)^{300}}$$

which implies that

$$DS = \$2,000,000 \left(\frac{1}{\dfrac{1}{(1 + .01)} + \dfrac{1}{(1 + .01)^2} + \cdots + \dfrac{1}{(1 + .01)^{300}}} \right)$$

or

$$DS = \$2,000,000 \times \frac{1}{94.94655} = \$21,064.48$$

At the beginning of the loan period, the monthly payment will go primarily to payment of interest and only a small amount will go toward the principal. As the principal amount is reduced, the interest is calculated on an increasingly lower amount, and the monthly payment of interest decreases while the balance credited toward principal increases. At loan maturity, the outstanding loan balance will be completely amortized.

Amortization periods for commercial mortgage loans typically are between 10 and 25 years. Some commercial mortgage loans may carry even shorter terms, but as the amortization period becomes shorter, the debt service obligation becomes higher. For example, on a fully amortized $2 million commercial mortgage at 12 percent interest for 10 years, the monthly payment is:

$$DS = \$2,000,000 \times \frac{1}{69.70052} = \$28,694.19$$

Going from a 25-year amortization period to a 10-year amortization period increases the monthly loan payment from $21,064.48 to $28,694.19, or a 36 percent increase.

Partially Amortizing. A *partially amortizing mortgage,* or *balloon mortgage,* is considered more risky than fully amortizing debt. A balloon mortgage is often used in commercial and industrial real estate loans with very stable and secure tenants. The amortized payments are based on a payment schedule that is longer than the actual term of the loan. For example, a 25-year, $6 million, partially amortizing commercial mortgage loan at 12 percent (monthly compounding), with a balloon payment at the end of 5 years carries with it a monthly payment of:

$$\$6,000,000 = \frac{DS}{(1 + .01)} + \frac{DS}{(1 + .01)^2} + \cdots + \frac{DS}{(1 + .01)^{300}}$$

which implies that

$$DS = \$6,000,000 \left(\frac{1}{\dfrac{1}{(1 + .01)} + \dfrac{1}{(1 + .01)^2} + \cdots + \dfrac{1}{(1 + .01)^{300}}} \right)$$

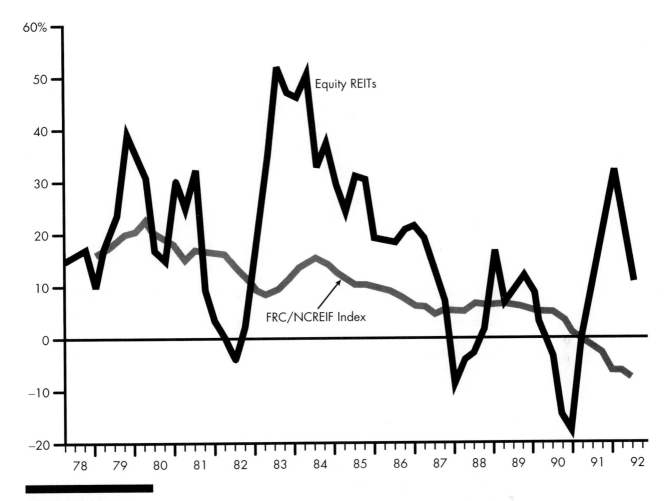

FIGURE 21–2

Equity REIT Index Versus FRC/NCREIF Property Index

Source: The Complete Guide to the Real Estate Investment Trust Industry, National Association of Real Estate Investment Trusts, 1994; and *The NCREIF Real Estate Performance Report,* National Council of Real Estate Investment Fiduciaries and Frank Russell Company, various issues.

or

$$DS = \$6,000,000 \times \frac{1}{94.94655} = \$63,193.45$$

At the end of year 5, or at the end of 60 months, a balloon payment of \$5,739,192 must be made:

$$\text{Loan outstanding, } EOM60 = DS \times PVAIF_{1\%, \, 300-60}$$
$$= \$63,193.45 \times 90.81942$$
$$= \$5,739,192$$

Typically, the borrower will expect to refinance the balloon payment at the end of the loan agreement into a new mortgage, thus introducing refinancing risk. Various factors, like an increase in interest rates, a decline in property values, a weakening of the borrower's financial status, a relatively large number of vacancies, tight credit conditions, and weak real estate market conditions, may impair the borrower's ability to refinance.

Interest-Only.   An interest-only mortgage is considerably more risky than a fully or partially amortizing mortgage. On an interest-only mortgage, there is no gradual buildup of equity by the owner, which means that the mortgage lender's risk remains constant throughout the life of the loan rather than diminishing over time. Also, there are the added risks associated with the need to refinance the outstanding loan balance at maturity.

To illustrate, the monthly payment on a $12 million interest-only commercial mortgage loan at 10 percent for 10 years is:

$$\text{Interest-only payment} = \text{Loan outstanding} \times \text{Interest rate}$$
$$= \$12{,}000{,}000 \times (.10/12) = \$100{,}000$$

At the end of 10 years, the outstanding loan balance is $12 million. Whether the borrower can pay back the outstanding loan balance at maturity will depend on the property and on market conditions. For instance, there is the risk that the property, having aged, may not be as attractive to prospective lenders as other buildings. There is also the risk that the market may be in a downturn at the time of maturity, or that interest rates may be prohibitively high.

Zero Coupon.   *Zero-coupon debt* is the riskiest type of financing. Where fully amortizing debt has equity buildup, zero-coupon mortgages have equity erosion over time because interest accrues over the term of the loan and becomes principal. Zero-coupon debt also has substantial refinancing risk.

These points can be illustrated by a simple example. Suppose financing for an office building includes a note that accrues interest but neither interest nor principal is repaid until the property is sold. The note is for $10 million at 8 percent for 20 years, compounded annually. The original issue price is:

$$\text{Issue price} = PV \text{ of loan amount}$$
$$= \frac{\text{Loan amount}}{(1 + i)^n}$$
$$= \frac{\$10{,}000{,}000}{(1 + .08)^{20}} = \$2{,}145{,}482$$

The *issue price* of $2,145,482 is the amount of cash the borrower receives at origination.

As the loan ages, the interest income that accrues each year is added to the principal of the loan. Interest in year 1, for example, is calculated as follows:

$$\text{Interest, } EOY1 = \text{Loan outstanding, } BOY1 \times \text{Interest rate}$$
$$= \$2{,}145{,}482 \times .08 = \$171{,}639$$

The outstanding loan balance at the end of year 1 is then:

$$\text{Loan outstanding, } EOY1 = \text{Loan outstanding, } BOY1 + \text{Interest}$$
$$= \$2{,}145{,}482 + \$171{,}639 = \$2{,}317{,}121$$

Repeating these calculations, the outstanding loan balance at the end of year 2 is $2,502,491 ($2,317,121 + .08 × $2,317,122 = $2,502,491). The outstanding loan balance at the end of year 3 is $2,702,690 ($2,502,491 + .08 × $2,502,491 = $2,702,690). And so on, until the borrower owes $10 million at the end of year 20.

A major drawback of the zero-coupon mortgage is that the holder of the mortgage is taxed on the interest income that accrues each year even though payment will not be received until maturity. Colloquially, this is termed *taxing of phantom income*. The taxing of phantom income results in a negative cash flow for the holder of the mortgage.

From the borrower's viewpoint, he or she is able to deduct the accrued interest expense each year. In our $10 million zero-coupon mortgage, for example, the borrower is able to deduct $171,369 of interest in year 1, $185,370 in year 2, $200,199 in year 3, and so on. Because no cash payments are made, the ability to deduct the accrued interest each year results in a tax-sheltered cash flow for the borrower. Suppose, for example, that the borrower is in a 36 percent marginal tax bracket. An interest expense of $171,369 in year 1 will result in a tax savings of $171,369 × 0.36 = $61,693. The tax savings in year 2 is $185,370 × 0.36 = $66,733, and the tax savings in year 3 is $200,199 × 0.36 = $72,072.

Fixed Versus Floating Rate

It is not uncommon for commercial mortgages to allow the interest rate to increase or decrease directly with the fluctuations in the prime rate (i.e., the rate that banks charge their most-favored customers) or the London Interbank Offer Rate (LIBOR). *Floating-rate* commercial mortgages are viewed as inherently more risky (in terms of default) than fixed-rate mortgages. The potential inability to meet an increase in debt service payments in the future increases the risk that the borrower may default. The presence of a floating rate also lessens somewhat the reliance of the credit analysis on the debt-coverage ratio.

As an illustration of a floating rate note, consider the following example. The borrower purchases a $6 million office building today with a $5 million floating-rate, interest-only, commercial mortgage at an initial rate of 7 percent for 20 years, compounded monthly. Adjustments to the interest rate are made monthly. No restrictions are placed on the maximum amount of the interest rate change.

The initial monthly payment on the floating-rate note is easily determined as follows:

$$\text{Payment} = \text{Loan outstanding, } BOM1 \times \text{Interest rate}$$
$$= \$5,000,000 \times (.07/12) = \$29,167$$

Next, suppose that at the end of the first month, the interest rate is now 7.5 percent. The new payment is:

$$\text{Payment} = \text{Loan outstanding, } BOM2 \times \text{Interest rate}$$
$$= \$5,000,000 \times (.075/12) = \$31,250$$

Notice that as a result of the increase in the interest rate from 7 to 7.5 percent, the monthly payment increased by $2,083, from $29,167 to $31,250. With no commensurate increase in operating revenues, the higher monthly payment increases the risk that the borrower may eventually default.

Other Important Terms in Commercial Mortgages

Commercial mortgages often contain either a lock-out provision or a yield mainte- nance agreement. A *lock-out provision* prohibits repayment of the mortgage prior to maturity. That means that the borrower is prohibited from repaying the mortgage in order to replace it with another lower-rate mortgage.

A *yield-maintenance agreement* is designed to discourage prepayment and to compensate lenders for reinvestment costs during periods of falling interest rates. The amount of the yield-maintenance premium depends on how much interest rates fall between the mortgage-origination date and the prepayment date, and the length of the remaining yield-maintenance period. The more interest rates fall during the pe- riod and the longer the remaining yield-maintenance period, the higher the charge made upon prepayment.

To illustrate, consider a $1 million commercial mortgage at 8.5 percent in- terest for 25 years, monthly compounding. The mortgage provides for yield-main- tenance premiums to be paid to the lender for any unscheduled principal pay- ment during the first six years. Let us further suppose that the mortgage is prepaid at the end of month 60; thus, there is one year remaining in the yield-maintenance period.

Assume that the yield on Treasury securities on the mortgage origination date was 7 percent. Further assume that at prepayment the Treasury yield is 5 percent. This represents a lost interest spread of 2 percent per annum, or 2% ÷ 12 = 0.17% per month, which is multiplied by the monthly balance in the yield-maintenance pe- riod to determine the dollar amount of the lost interest spread.

Here are the calculations. With one year remaining in the yield-maintenance pe- riod, the premium is:

Yield maintenance premium

$$= PV \text{ of lost interest income}$$

$$= \frac{\text{Loan balance, } EOM61 \times \text{Lost spread}}{(1 + r)} + \cdots$$

$$+ \frac{\text{Loan balance, } EOM72 \times \text{Lost spread}}{(1 + r)^{12}}$$

$$= \frac{\$926{,}390 \times .0017}{(1 + .0042)} + \frac{\$924{,}900 \times .0017}{(1 + .0042)^2} + \frac{\$923{,}399 \times .0017}{(1 + .0042)^3}$$

$$+ \frac{\$921{,}887 \times .0017}{(1 + .0042)^4} + \frac{\$920{,}365 \times .0017}{(1 + .0042)^5} + \frac{\$918{,}832 \times .0017}{(1 + .0042)^6}$$

$$+ \frac{\$917{,}288 \times .0017}{(1 + .0042)^7} + \frac{\$915{,}733 \times .0017}{(1 + .0042)^8} + \frac{\$914{,}168 \times .0017}{(1 + .0042)^9}$$

$$+ \frac{\$912{,}591 \times .0017}{(1 + .0042)^{10}} + \frac{\$911{,}003 \times .0017}{(1 + .0042)^{11}} + \frac{\$909{,}403 \times .0017}{(1 + .0042)^{12}}$$

$$= \$17{,}294$$

The values $926,390, $924,900, . . . , $909,403 represent the outstanding loan balance at the end of month 61 through the end of month 72, respectively (or months 1 through 12 of the remaining yield-maintenance period). The present value of the lost interest income is discounted at 0.42 percent per month (5% ÷ 12 = .42%), which is the lender's reinvestment rate at the prepayment date.

The critical point, of course, is that because of the yield maintenance premium, the present worth of the payment savings associated with taking out a new loan must be in excess of $17,294 before any rational investor would refinance, holding all else constant.

Some examples will clarify this point. First, let us assume that the investor can refinance the outstanding loan balance at the end of month 60 at 8.25 percent for 20 years, compounded monthly. We shall also assume the new mortgage loan can be prepaid at any time without a yield-maintenance premium. This simplifying assumption makes the calculations just a little bit easier. Later we will relax this assumption.

The monthly payment on the old mortgage is $8,052.27. The monthly payment on a new loan of $927,870 at 8.25 percent interest for 20 years is $7,906.06. Hence, the monthly payment savings is $146.21.

The present worth of these monthly payment savings, discounted at the investor's required rate of return of 15 percent for the next twenty years (the anticipated holding period), is:

$$PV \text{ of benefits} = PV \text{ of monthly payment savings}$$
$$= \$146.21 \times 75.9414632 = \$11,103$$

Clearly, the smart thing to do in this case is not to refinance. Why? Because the present worth of the payment savings is less than the yield-maintenance charge.

Now let us assume that the investor can refinance at 7 percent for 20 years, compounded monthly, all else being the same. In this case, the monthly payment savings is $858.50, based on a monthly payment on the new mortgage of $7,193.77. The present worth of these payment savings discounted at 15 percent for the next twenty years is $65,197. In comparison, the yield-maintenance premium is $17,294. Hence, the net present value of refinancing is $65,197 − $17,294 = $48,103.

The smart thing to do in this case is to refinance. Why? Because you are better off by $48,103 in present value dollars after paying the yield-maintenance charge. In fact, you could pay up to $48,103 in financing costs (i.e., discount points, loan origination fees, etc.) to take out the new loan and still be better off.

Next, suppose that the new mortgage, just like the old mortgage loan, provides for a yield-maintenance premium to be paid to the lender for any unscheduled principal payment during the first six years. How does this change the decision to refinance? Or does it? Actually, with an anticipated holding period of 20 years, none of the calculations is affected. Why? Because the yield-maintenance premium on the new loan never comes into play. It would affect the decision to refinance only if the investor's anticipated holding period were less than 6 years.

To illustrate, assume that the investor's anticipated holding period, instead of 20 years, is 5 years. Continuing with the above example, we shall assume that the investor can refinance at 7 percent with a 20-year amortization period, compounded monthly. The monthly payment savings is $858.50 over the next five years. At the end of month 120, which is the end of month 60 of the investor's anticipated holding period, the outstanding loan balance on the old mortgage would be $817,706, whereas the outstanding loan balance on the new mortgage is \$800,349, a difference of \$17,357.

To determine the yield-maintenance premium on the new mortgage when the loan is prepaid, assume that the Treasury yield for the new mortgage at origination was 5 percent. Further assume that when the new mortgage is prepaid the Treasury yield is 4 percent. With one year remaining in the yield-maintenance period on the new loan, the yield-maintenance premium on the new mortgage loan is:

Yield maintenance premium
$$= PV \text{ of lost interest income}$$

$$= \frac{\text{Loan balance, } EOM61 \times \text{Lost spread}}{(1 + r)} + \cdots$$

$$+ \frac{\text{Loan balance, } EOM72 \times \text{Lost spread}}{(1 + r)^{12}}$$

$$= \frac{\$797,824 \times .0008}{(1 + .0033)} + \frac{\$795,284 \times .0008}{(1 + .0033)^2} + \frac{\$792,730 \times .0008}{(1 + .0033)^3}$$

$$+ \frac{\$790,160 \times .0008}{(1 + .0033)^4} + \frac{\$787,576 \times .0008}{(1 + .0033)^5} + \frac{\$784,976 \times .0008}{(1 + .0033)^6}$$

$$+ \frac{\$782,362 \times .0008}{(1 + .0033)^7} + \frac{\$779,732 \times .0008}{(1 + .0033)^8} + \frac{\$777,086 \times .0008}{(1 + .0033)^9}$$

$$+ \frac{\$774,425 \times .0008}{(1 + .0033)^{10}} + \frac{\$771,749 \times .0008}{(1 + .0033)^{11}} + \frac{\$769,057 \times .0008}{(1 + .0033)^{12}}$$

$$= \$7,363$$

The values \$797,824, \$795,284, ..., \$769,057 are the monthly loan balances outstanding at the end of month 61 through the end of month 72 on the new mortgage loan. The lost interest spread is 5% − 4% = 1% per annum, or 1% ÷ 12 = 0.08% per month. The lender's reinvestment rate is 4% ÷ 12 = 0.33% per month.

Now we can calculate the net present value of refinancing, assuming a required rate of return of 15 percent. The calculation is:

$$NPV \text{ of refinancing} = PV \text{ of benefits} - \text{Yield maintenance premium on old loan}$$
$$= \$858.50 \times 42.0345918 + \$17,357 \times .4745676$$
$$- \$7,363 \times .4745676 - \$17,294$$
$$= \$23,536$$

Here, \$858.50 × 42.0345918 = \$36,087 is the present worth of the monthly payment savings and \$17,357 × .4745676 = \$8,237 is the present worth of payment savings when the loan balance is prepaid at the end of the investor's anticipated five-year holding period. The term \$7,363 × .4745676 = \$3,494 is the present value of the yield-maintenance charge on the new loan. Note that this term is a cash outflow (i.e., an expense to be paid by the investor when the new mortgage loan is prepaid). Lastly, the term \$17,294 is the yield-maintenance premium payable on the old loan.

Despite the shorter anticipated holding period and the existence of a yield-maintenance penalty on the new loan, the refinance decision is still a go. Why? Because the net present value, albeit smaller, is still a positive number. Here the investor can pay up to $23,536 in financing costs to take out the new loan and still be better off.

Before leaving this example, we should point out that the greater the remaining yield-maintenance period, the greater the yield-maintenance premium. This is an extremely important observation, because it says that the prepayment protection on commercial mortgages with yield-maintenance agreements will decline over time. That is, as the end of the yield-maintenance period approaches, the less its impact on the borrower's decision to refinance.

Sources of Debt Financing

The words *commercial mortgage* conjure up images of million dollar loans from insurance companies or REITs and sometimes even pension funds to fund superregional shopping centers and large office buildings in places like New York City, Chicago, and Los Angeles. Commercial mortgages are also used to fund community and large neighborhood shopping centers, and one-tenant and multitenant commercial realty in downtown districts of secondary and tertiary cities and towns like Madison, Wisconsin, or West Palm Beach, Florida.

Financing for commercial properties is rarely obtained prior to an investor obtaining a commitment from a tenant with a national credit rating and/or several local tenants agreeing to a long-term lease. Sources of debt financing for commercial real estate include:

Savings and loan associations
Commercial banks
Mutual savings banks
Mortgage companies
Real Estate Investment Trusts
Life insurance companies
Pension funds

Savings and Loan Associations. *Savings and loan associations (S&Ls)* specialize in home mortgages. By historical standards, in dollar terms these associations have traditionally accounted for more than one-third of all mortgage loans outstanding, and nearly one-half of all home mortgage loans. In recent years, the share of home mortgage loans held by S&Ls has decreased substantially.

Here is a little bit of history. S&Ls have been active mortgage lenders for over 100 years. Yet regulation of their activities on a national scale did not begin until 1932 when Congress created the Federal Home Loan Bank (FHLB) system. All federally chartered S&Ls are currently regulated by the Office of Thrift Supervision (which took over for the FHLB system when the Federal Savings and Loan Insurance Corporation—a part of the FHLB system—went bankrupt in 1989). Also, almost all savings and loan associations, if qualified, belong to the Savings Association Insurance Fund (SAIF), which was created by Congress in 1989. SAIF insures public deposits with member institutions for up to $100,000 per account. Both the Office of Thrift Supervision and the SAIF are under the Federal Deposit Insurance Corporation (FDIC).

S&Ls may make conventional home mortgage loans for up to 80 percent, and sometimes 95 percent, of either the purchase price or appraised market value, whichever is less, of any home offered as security. The loans must be amortized on a monthly basis and have a maximum life of 40 years. Almost all loans with high loan-to-value ratios are made on an insured or guaranteed basis.

First mortgage loans may also be made on commercial properties, churches, and other improved properties up to a maximum loan-to-value ratio of 75 percent. S&Ls may also make loans for property improvement, alteration, repair, and equipment. Finally, mobile homes may be financed by S&Ls.

During the 1980s S&Ls were involved in the nation's worst banking scandal in history. Brought on by a surge in interest rates in the early 1980s, a rash of bad real estate loans in the mid-1980s, and fraud, approximately 1,000 S&Ls failed during the 1980s. Estimates of the costs to bail out the industry—which is ongoing—are between $150 and $200 billion in present value terms. To put this in perspective, the federal government currently spends about $230 billion on public education. The Vietnam War cost roughly $172 billion in today's dollars. In comparison, the federal government spends about $2 billion a year for research on cancer and heart disease.

Commercial Banks.   Commercial banks are required by law to maintain relatively greater liquidity of their assets than are other financial institutions, because they are more subject to unanticipated withdrawals of funds by the very nature of their operation. Thus, although some 14,000 commercial banks control approximately one-half of Americans' savings, their role in mortgage lending continues to be a secondary activity. Even so, commercial banks currently are, by far, the largest mortgage lenders. Making short-term commercial loans to local business firms is their primary lending activity. Short-term loans enable the banks to meet their liquidity requirements and, at the same time, maximize their profits.

Commercial banks may make uninsured conventional loans on homes for up to 80 percent of the lesser of the purchase price or appraised market value. The loans may be made, if fully amortized, for up to 30 years. Insured conventional loans may be made for up to 95 percent loan-to-value ratio. Commercial banks may also make construction loans for up to 24 months.

Commercial banks generally increase their mortgage lending activity when demand for local business loans is slow. They decrease mortgage lending activity when business loan demand is strong. That is, they tend to make real estate loans only when funds exceed local business needs. Recent improvements in the secondary mortgage market have lessened the pressure on commercial banks to avoid mortgage lending activity. With an active secondary mortgage market, a bank may sell off mortgages at almost any time to increase cash on hand. Thus, mortgage loans have become increasingly more liquid.

Mutual Savings Banks.   Mutual savings banks traditionally accounted for approximately one-eighth of all savings in the United States, about three-fourths of which is invested in mortgage loans. Thus, mutual savings banks have historically accounted for approximately 10 percent of all mortgage loans outstanding.

All mutual savings banks in the United States are state chartered. Most of them are located in the middle Atlantic states and in New England, with nearly seven-eighths in the states of New York, Massachusetts, Connecticut, Pennsylvania, and New Jersey. From the viewpoint of mortgage borrowers, the difference between savings and loan associations and mutual savings banks is slight.

In almost all states, mutual savings banks may make insured conventional loans up to 80 percent, and sometimes up to 95 percent, of a property's value with a duration of up to 30 years. Conventional, uninsured loans may generally be made for up to 80 percent of value, also with an amortization period of up to 30 years. In a few states, uninsured conventional loans may be made for up to 90 percent of value.

Mortgage Companies. Mortgage bankers and mortgage brokers hold little long-term mortgage debt. Instead, they service secondary lenders—life insurance companies, pension funds, and government agencies—that buy mortgages as long-term investments as opposed to other types of securities, such as government and corporate bonds. *Mortgage bankers* charge a fee to originate and service loans for these secondary lenders. *Mortgage brokers* originate loans, for a fee, but do not service them. The secondary lenders must then arrange to have them serviced elsewhere, often through mortgage bankers. Mortgage bankers sometimes originate loans first and look for a buyer later if the loan presents a profit opportunity.

Eastern and Midwestern banks and savings and loan associations sometimes become secondary lenders when they accumulate surplus funds that cannot otherwise be placed profitably; they use the surplus funds to buy loans, secured by properties in other regions, through mortgage bankers and brokers.

Mortgage bankers generally charge three-eighths of 1 percent of the outstanding loan balance per year as a servicing fee. Thus, an outstanding loan balance of $100,000 yields $375 per year to a mortgage banker. Since the $375 must cover the cost of accounting, filing, making monthly statements, correspondence, and office overhead, it means that the mortgage banker must service a large volume of loans to have a profitable operation.

Real Estate Investment Trusts (REITs). Mortgage REITs specialize in financing apartment buildings, large office buildings, shopping centers, health care facilities, and hotels. Mortgage REITs lend money and receive income in the form of interest, which by statute must be passed through to investors in order to avoid double taxation.

One of the more notable mortgage REITs is Rockefeller Center Properties, Inc., formed to permit public investment in a portion of Rockefellar Center. The net proceeds from the Rockefellar Center Properties common stock offering were used by the company to make a mortgage loan to two partnerships, which together own most of the land and buildings known as Rockefellar Center in New York City. Rockefellar Center Properties has the option to convert its mortgage to a partial equity interest in the property. Rockefellar Center includes 12 buildings, with approximately 6.2 million square feet of rentable office, retail, storage, and studio space (including the NBC TV studios). Other mortgage REITs include Countrywide Mortgage Investments, Inc., Lomas & Nettleton Mortgage Investors, Mellon Participating Mortgage Trust, and Pension Properties Trust. The magnitude of funds invested by mortgage REITs currently is approximately $25 billion.

Life Insurance Companies. Life insurance companies concentrate their mortgage lending efforts in multifamily and commercial properties. Larger loans and higher interest rates on loans for these properties make lending on them more profitable. Also, a share of the equity returns, including participation in the income generated by the property, is frequently arranged. Mortgage lending is particularly advantageous to life insurance companies because of the long-term nature of their insurance policy obligations. Actuaries are able to forecast the dollar requirements of their policy obligations and match them up with mortgages of appropriate terms.

Larger insurance companies—like Prudential with over $110 billion of assets—make mortgages on a national scale. Some loans are made through branch offices, but many are made through mortgage bankers and brokers. Extremely large loans are usually arranged from the home office. Life insurance companies have considerable flexibility in their mortgage lending, but they generally limit loans to two-thirds of appraised value, with amortization periods of up to 30 years. The magnitude of the funds invested in equity real estate by insurance companies currently runs from 3 to 5 percent of total real estate assets. Life insurance companies hold mortgages for about 6.5 percent, which amounts to about $250 billion, or 17 percent of their total assets of $1.5 trillion.

Pension Funds. Public and private pension funds have two main assets: The amount of assets that the firm or public entity has already put aside in the pension fund, and the value of the regular contributions to the fund that the firm or public entity plans to make in the future for its current employees. These assets are generally invested by the pension fund in high-yielding investments. Proceeds from these investments are then used to pay for employee retirement benefits.

Most pension funds hold from less than 1 percent of their assets up to 5 percent of their assets in real estate and real estate loans. For example, private pension funds hold less than one-half of 1 percent of their total assets in mortgages. State and local retirement funds hold about 3 percent of their total assets in mortgages, primarily residential mortgages. In addition, both private and public pension funds hold between 4 and 5 percent of their assets in securities backed by mortgages.

Do not be misled by these numbers, however. When we say that pension funds invest only a small percent of their assets in real estate, that is true. But together private, uninsured pension and state and local retirement funds have about $2 trillion of assets. That means they hold somewhere between $20 and $100 billion of real estate and real estate loans. We should also point out that most of these investments are backed by investment-grade real estate of large magnitude ($5 to $10 million). So if you are seeking to finance a 4-million square-foot superregional shopping center like the Mall of America in Bloomington, Minnesota, which is near Minneapolis, you might try a large pension fund. (Actual financing for the Mall of America, which opened in August 1992, was provided by TIAA/CREF, a large pension fund.)

LAND-CONTRACT FINANCING

Buyers sometimes lack an adequate down payment to qualify for a loan from an established financial institution. Or they want to preserve an existing loan on the property being bought. Or the property for which the loan is being sought will not qualify for a mortgage loan, because it is vacant or located in a run-down area. In all these situations, a land contract may serve as a suitable financing alternative.

A *land contract* is a written agreement between a seller (vendor) and a buyer (vendee) for the sale of real property over an extended time, and with title remaining in the seller until the terms of the arrangement are met. The buyer usually takes possession when the contract is made. Payments are credited toward the purchase price in a manner parallel to that by which a mortgage loan is amortized. A land contract is also known as a *contract for deed*, an *installment land contract*, or a *real estate contract*.

Example. Assume that a 20-unit apartment building is being sold on a land contract for $1 million. The seller has an existing mortgage of $700,000 at an interest rate of 8 percent; the seller's equity in the property is, therefore, $300,000.

The buyer puts $50,000 down, and agrees to make payments sufficient to cover the interest and to reduce the principal balance due the seller from $950,000 to $800,000 by the end of five years. The buyer may refinance at any time, but must refinance before the end of the sixth year. The interest rate on the unpaid land contract balance is 10 percent.

From a buyer's viewpoint, a land contract is similar to a partially amortizing loan in that payments go for interest and principal reduction. However, the seller retains legal title and continues to pay debt service on the existing mortgage loan against the property. Thus, both parties may be in highly leveraged positions. The transaction now looks like this:

	VALUE ALLOCATION	INTEREST
Contract sale price	$1,000,000	
Less: Buyer's down payment	− 50,000	
Amount of contract balance @ 10%	$ 950,000	$95,000
Less: Seller's mortgage loan @ 8%	− 700,000	−56,000
Owner-seller's equity	$ 250,000	$39,000

Amortization aside, the seller receives $95,000 in interest in the first year (10% × $950,000), while paying $56,000 interest on the original loan (8% × $700,000). The difference is $39,000. At the same time, the owner-seller's equity amounts to only $250,000. This produces a rate of return to the owner-seller of 15.6 percent ($39,000 ÷ $250,000). Thus, the buyer gets a 95-percent, loan-to-value ratio loan, and the seller both disposes of the property and stands to earn over 15 percent on the $250,000 loan to the buyer.

Using Land-Contract Financing

A land contract is at one time extremely useful and extremely risky. It serves as a sales, financing, and tax-avoidance instrument. The buyer makes only a nominal, or "thin," down payment, which certainly helps in making the sale. At the same time, a plus for a seller is that the transaction may be set up quickly, with no delay in arranging financing that would allow a hot prospect to cool off. The buyer gets a high loan-to-value ratio loan that calls for regular payments (usually monthly), over a number of years, at a competitive rate of interest. By receiving the sales price over several years, the seller pays taxes at a lower rate than if the full sales price had been received all in one year. Further, the buyer agrees to pay the annual taxes and insurance premiums on the property and to maintain the property in a reasonable condition, which means the seller has few carrying costs for the investment. At the same time, some definite risks or concerns are involved.

Seller Considerations. Traditionally, land contracts have been written to protect the seller. As mentioned, the buyer may be making only a thin down payment, may have a weak credit rating, and the property may be marginal. In these situations, the seller wants to be able to recover the property with a minimum of time and expense in the case of buyer default.

Another concern for the seller is the need to coordinate any required balloon payment or any prepayment privileges in the land contract with comparable privileges in the original mortgage against the property. Failure to do so might mean that the buyer has the right to prepay the land contract even though the seller could not, or would prefer not to, prepay the mortgage. In such a situation, the seller is liable to a heavy prepayment penalty to the mortgagee or a breach of contract suit from the buyer for failure to perform.

Despite these considerations, however, a land contract makes possible the sale and financing of a property, which would be very difficult to arrange in other ways, while fully protecting the seller.

Buyer Considerations. A land contract gives a buyer time to build up equity in the property, to the point where more traditional financing becomes possible. At the same time, several cautions should be exercised by a buyer in using a land contract.

First, evidence of clear and marketable title should be required at the time the land contract is drawn up. Failure to assure clear title might mean that the buyer could make payments for several years only to find that the seller cannot deliver marketable title.

Second, the transaction should be handled by a disinterested third person until the satisfaction of the terms. Failure to have a deed signed by the seller immediately delivered to a disinterested third person might result in delay and added cost to the buyer should the seller die or become incapacitated later on. Also, it is usually advisable to have the periodic land contracts payments paid to a disinterested third person to ensure that debt service payments for the original mortgage are being made on schedule.

Third, the land contract, or notice of the land contract, should be recorded immediately, particularly if the buyer does not take actual possession, as would be the case with a vacant lot. Without recording or possession by the buyer, the seller could conceivably sell the lot several times and leave town. The several buyers would be left with a serious and expensive litigation problem in addition to being out a large amount of cash.

Last, the seller should not be permitted to put the buyer's equity up as collateral for another loan. A simple clause in the contract to this effect, along with recording, would accomplish this restraint. To illustrate the problem, let us return to our earlier land contract example.

Assume that it is five years later and the balance of the land contract has been paid down to $800,000. Meanwhile, the value of the property has increased to $1,300,000. The buyer's equity should, therefore, be $500,000. But suppose that the seller had refinanced the property with a $1,100,000 mortgage six months ago and then left the area for whereabouts unknown. The buyer's equity has been reduced to $200,000 ($1,300,000 − $1,100,000). Of course, the buyer also has a legal claim for $300,000 against the seller, assuming the seller can be found!

Defaulting on a Land Contract

Several options are open to the seller if a buyer defaults, including forfeiture, a sale of the property to the buyer for cash, a foreclosure suit, or a suit for damages.

The seller may declare that the buyer has forfeited the rights to the property and retain as damages any amounts paid or improvements made by the buyer. Second, the seller may compel the buyer to purchase the property for cash. This option would probably be exercised if the unpaid balance of the land contract exceeded the value of the property and if the buyer were financially able. Third, the seller could file a foreclosure suit and seek to have the property sold. Finally, the seller could file suit for damages against the buyer if none of the foregoing options seemed satisfactory.

FINANCIAL LEVERAGE

In science, leverage means the physical use of a lever to gain a mechanical advantage in applying a force to an object. The longer the distance from the force to the pivot point, relative to the distance from the pivot point to the object, the greater the magnification of the force being applied.

The concept of leverage carries over to economics and finance. An investor can control a high-value property with a small equity investment by borrowing a major percentage of the value. In turn, the investor's gains or losses are magnified, which leads to positive and negative financial leverage. *Positive financial leverage* occurs when borrowing magnifies or increases the rate of return earned on the equity portion of the investment. For this to happen, the property or investment must earn a higher rate of return than the interest charged for the borrowed money. If the property earns at the same rate as the cost of the borrowed money, no gain or loss is realized from leverage. If the property earns at a lower rate, *negative financial leverage* results. A more familiar term for financial leverage is *trading on the equity*, meaning exploiting or taking the best possible advantage of an equity position in an investment.

A gain or loss from financial leverage may be realized in two distinct ways, as illustrated by the following examples.

Gain from Leverage Through Value Increases

Assume that an investor owns a $1,000,000 property with an $800,000 nonamortizing mortgage loan against it. The investor's equity in the property is $200,000. Next assume that the value of the property were to increase to $1,200,000. Since all of the $1,200,000 increase in value accrues entirely to the owner-investor, the value of the equity position doubles from $200,000 to $400,000. Thus, there has been a 100 percent increase in equity resulting from a 20 percent increase in the property's value, or an increase of 5:1 for every 1 percent increase in the value of the property. The debt, $800,000, remains unchanged.

INTEREST IN PROPERTY	INITIAL EQUITY POSITION	POSITION AFTER INCREASE IN PROPERTY VALUE
Market value	$1,000,000	$1,200,000
Debt (fixed)	− 800,000	− 800,000
Owner's equity	$ 200,000	$ 400,000

Gain from Leverage Through Cash Flow

A second example shows the gain from leverage resulting from differences in cash flows. The facts are simplified to make the principle of positive financial leverage stand out. Assume that a commercial lot worth $1,000,000 is under a long-term net lease for $100,000 per year; that is, the tenant pays all the operating costs. Without debt financing, the rate of return to the owner is 10 percent ($100,000 ÷ $1,000,000 = 10%). But, suppose the owner obtains a long-term loan against the property of $900,000 at 9 percent interest with no amortization required. That is, only the interest payments of $81,000 need to be paid each year ($900,000 × 9% = $81,000). The difference in income of $19,000 ($100,000 − $81,000 = $19,000) goes entirely to the equity position, which is now $100,000 ($1,000,000 − $900,000 = $100,000). The rate of return has been leveraged up to 19 percent.

Total annual net income from lease	$100,000
Less: Interest on fixed debt ($900,000 × 9%)	− 81,000
Net cash flow to equity	$ 19,000
Dividedly: Equity position ($1,000,000 − $900,000)	$100,000
Rate of return	19%

The advantages of financial leverage are not received without cost. The borrower incurs an increased risk of loss of income or of the property if reality does not live up to expectations. Thus, in the first example, a 10 percent decrease in the value of the property would reduce the equity position by 50 percent. In the second example, a decrease in net income of $10,000, or 10 percent, would reduce the rate of return to 9 percent, a decline of slightly more than 50 percent. Under worse circumstances, the equity position could become a liability. Use of leverage always increases the risk of loss to the equity position.

In using leverage it is important to distinguish between expected and unexpected events. Large gains may be realized from using leverage, when favorable events develop. Less gain, or even losses, might result from rates of growth that are slower than those foreseen when the investment was made. Thus, investors who used leverage with expectations of earning large gains through value increases during the rapid period of growth in Houston, Texas, that was based both on the oil boom and NASA's flight schedule, undoubtedly were met with large losses when the Houston real estate market collapsed in the 1980s as a result of the OPEC Crisis and the loss of the space shuttle. In a parallel sense, the sudden discovery of gold in Colorado would probably give Denver investors profits over-and-above anything they might have expected from using leverage.

MEASURING THE IMPACT OF FINANCIAL LEVERAGE ON THE INTERNAL RATE OF RETURN

To illustrate the potential impact of financial leverage on an investor's IRR, consider an investor who has $2 million in cash available for investment. Imagine the following very simple world. The investor is considering a proposal to invest $2 million in a 25,000-square-foot office building. The project proposal is summarized in Figures

	YEAR				
	1	2	3	4	5
Net Operating Income	$372,000	$366,600	$361,038	$355,309	$349,408
Less: Straight-line tax depreciation	41,026	41,026	41,026	41,026	41,026
Less: Interest paid	0	0	0	0	0
Taxable Income	330,974	325,574	320,012	314,283	308,382
Times: Investor's tax rate	0.36	0.36	0.36	0.36	0.36
Income Tax Payable	$119,151	$117,207	$115,204	$113,142	$111,018

21–3 and 21–4. The revenue figures assume a fixed market rent of $24 per square foot per annum and a vacancy rate of 8 percent for years 1 through 5. The operating costs of $7.20 per square foot include all fixed and variable expenses, and are forecasted to increase by 3 percent per year. The depreciable basis of the property is $1.6 million. Depreciation is computed using the straight-line method with a 39-year useful life. The investor is in a 36 percent marginal tax bracket; the capital gains tax rate is 28 percent.

Information about the expected resale value of the property is contained in Figure 21–5. At the end of year 5 the resale value is forecasted to be $2,550,000. Selling expenses of 6 percent are typical. The after-tax equity reversion is the net sales proceeds minus the mortgage balance outstanding and less the taxes due on sale.

In the absence of any financial leverage, the net present value of the property, discounted at 12 percent, is:

$$NPV = \frac{ATCF_1}{(1 + r_a)} + \frac{ATCF_2}{(1 + r_a)^2} + \cdots + \frac{ATCF_5}{(1 + r_a)^5} + \frac{ATER}{(1 + r_a)^5} - MV = 0$$

$$= \frac{\$252,849}{(1 + .12)} + \frac{\$249,393}{(1 + .12)^2} + \frac{\$245,834}{(1 + .12)^3} + \frac{\$242,167}{(1 + .12)^4} + \frac{\$238,390}{(1 + .12)^5}$$

$$+ \frac{\$2,228,404}{(1 + .12)^5} - \$2,000,000 = \$153,179$$

The IRR on this $2 million investment is 14.06 percent.

Now let us assume that the investor uses $1.5 million of borrowed funds to finance the purchase. The mortgage loan will be repaid in equal monthly installments

FIGURE 21–4
After-Tax Cash Flows
from Operations:
Unleveraged

	YEAR				
	1	2	3	4	5
Net Operating Income	$372,000	$366,600	$361,038	$355,309	$349,408
Less: Annual debt service	0	0	0	0	0
Before-Tax Cash Flow	$372,000	$366,600	$361,038	$355,309	$349,408
Less: Tax payable[a]	119,151	117,207	115,204	113,142	111,018
After-Tax Cash Flow	$252,849	$249,393	$245,834	$242,167	$238,390

[a] See Figure 21-3.

Sales Price, end of year 4		$2,550,000
Less: Selling expenses @ 6%		153,000
Net Sales Price		$2,397,000
Less: Adjusted basis		
Purchase price	$2,000,000	
Less: Accumulated depreciation	205,128	$1,794,872
Taxable Capital Gain		$ 602,128
Times: Capital gains tax rate		0.28
Taxes Due on Sale		$ 168,596

Sales Price, end of year 4	$2,550,000
Less: Selling expenses @ 6%	153,000
Net Sales Price	$2,397,000
Less: Mortgage balance outstanding	0
Before-Tax Equity Reversion	$2,397,000
Less: Taxes due on sale	168,596
After-Tax Equity Reversion	$2,228,404

over 25 years, with an interest rate of 9 percent. The monthly debt service payments are $12,587.95. Annual debt service is simply 12 times this amount, or approximately $151,055.

As a consequence of the decision to borrow $1.5 million, the investor's equity position is reduced to $500,000. Likewise, the after-tax cash flows to the investor are reduced to $150,150 in year 1 and to $133,092 in year 5 (see Figures 21–6 and 21–7). The impact on the investor's after-tax equity reversion is shown in Figure 21–8.

Repeating the same net present value calculations we find that

$$NPV = \frac{ATCF_1}{(1 + r_a)} + \frac{ATCF_2}{(1 + r_a)^2} + \cdots + \frac{ATCF_5}{(1 + r_a)^5} + \frac{ATER}{(1 + r_a)^5}$$

$$- (MV - \text{Loan balance}) = 0$$

$$= \frac{\$150,150}{(1 + .20)} + \frac{\$146,129}{(1 + .20)^2} + \frac{\$141,951}{(1 + .20)^3} + \frac{\$137,608}{(1 + .20)^4} + \frac{\$133,092}{(1 + .20)^5}$$

$$+ \frac{\$829,317}{(1 + .20)^5} - (\$2,000,000 - \$1,500,000) = \$261,884$$

	YEAR				
	1	2	3	4	5
Net Operating Income	$372,000	$366,600	$361,038	$355,309	$349,408
Less: Straight-line tax depreciation	41,026	41,026	41,026	41,026	41,026
Interest paid	134,321	132,751	131,034	129,156	127,102
Taxable Income	196,653	192,823	188,978	185,127	181,280
Times: Investor's tax rate	0.36	0.36	0.36	0.36	0.36
Income Tax Payable	$70,795	$69,416	$68,032	$66,646	$65,261

	YEAR				
	1	2	3	4	5
Net Operating Income	$372,000	$366,600	$361,038	$355,309	$349,408
Less: Annual debt service	151,055	151,055	151,055	151,055	151,055
Before-Tax Cash Flow	$220,945	$215,545	$209,983	$204,254	$198,353
Less: Tax payable[a]	70,795	69,416	68,032	66,646	65,261
After-Tax Cash Flow	$150,150	$146,129	$141,951	$137,608	$133,092

[a] See Figure 21–6.

FIGURE 21–7
After-Tax Cash Flows from Operations: $1.5 Million Mortgage

Here we discount the investor's after-tax cash flows and after-tax equity reversion at a 20 percent rate to reflect the increase in risk associated with using leverage. We have also adjusted the cost of the investment. Instead of using an investment of $2 million, we use the equity investment of $500,000, which is the purchase price of the property less the $1.5 million in borrowed funds.

The IRR for this project is now 35.42 percent on an investment of $500,000, or 21.36 percentage points higher. This increase comes about because of the favorable after-tax spread between the return on the property—which is 14.06 percent assuming 100 percent equity funding—and the cost of borrowing—which is 6.48 percent on an after-tax basis [9% × (1 − 0.36) = 5.76%].

Again we should stress that the increased after-tax IRR is not received without cost. The greater the amount of leverage, the greater the risk that the equity investor may have to invest additional funds or default on the mortgage note.

So, while we cannot tell you whether using leverage is good or bad, we can tell you to avoid borrowing for investments that earn less than the cost of the debt. In such circumstances, the leverage is negative and your return on equity will decrease. Try, for example, borrowing money at an after-tax rate of 10 percent and invest it at 8 percent after-tax. You obviously would wind up losing 2 percent on every dollar

Sales Price, end of year 4		$2,550,000
Less: selling expenses @ 6%		153,000
Net Sales Price		$2,397,000
Less: Adjusted basis		
Purchase price	$2,000,000	
Less: Accumulated depreciation	205,128	$1,794,872
Taxable Capital Gain		$ 602,128
Times: Investor's tax rate		0.28
Taxes Due on Sale		$ 168,596
Sales Price, end of year 4		$2,550,000
Less: selling expenses @ 6%		153,000
Net Sales Price		$2,397,000
Less: Mortgage balance outstanding		1,399,087
Before-Tax Equity Reversion		$ 997,913
Less: Taxes due on sale		168,596
After-Tax Equity Reversion		$ 829,317

FIGURE 21–8
Taxes Due on Sale at End of Year 5 and After-Tax Equity Reversion: $1.5 Million Mortgage

borrowed. At a 5:1 leverage ratio (i.e., $5 of debt for every $1 of equity), your rate of return would fall by 10 percent ($5 \times 2\% = 10\%$). It is also conceivable that a small negative spread between the rate of return on the property and the cost of borrowing could actually result in a negative IRR.

SUMMARY

The methods of raising equity capital vary to suit the specific circumstances of investment. The most usual methods of raising equity capital include general partnerships, limited partnerships and syndicates, corporations, condominiums, cooperatives, and real estate investment trusts.

You may also find that it is advantageous to borrow money in order to finance the acquisition. By borrowing money, investors are able to magnify, or leverage, the rate of return on equity so long as the rate of return exceeds the cost of borrowing. When this happens, the gain from leverage is said to be favorable (or positive). If the investment earns less than the cost of the debt, the gain from leverage is unfavorable (or negative).

The use of leverage to acquire an investment is accompanied by added uncertainty and the risk of not being able to meet the debt service payments, and the greater the amount of leverage, the greater the amount of risk. Thus, before borrowing you must ask yourself, will the expected increase in return on equity outweigh the possible increase in risk from the use of borrowed funds?

KEY CONCEPTS

Balloon mortgage   A loan whose last payment is much larger than preceding payments.

Equity   The market, or disposition, value of a property, less any debt against it; an owner's interest in a property.

Leverage (financial)   Use of borrowed money to finance a property; the impact may be positive or negative. Also known as trading on the equity.

Land contract   A method of buying and financing a property whereby the purchaser gets occupancy but the seller retains title. Also called a contract for deed.

Lock-out provision   Prohibits repayment of the mortgage prior to maturity.

Yield-maintenance premium   Designed to discourage prepayment and to compensate lenders for reinvestment costs during periods of falling interest rates.

Zero-coupon debt   A mortgage agreement where the interest accrues over the term of the loan and becomes principal. Zero-coupon debt has substantial refinancing risk.

QUESTIONS FOR REVIEW AND DISCUSSION

1. What are some of the different forms of equity financing? What are the advantages and disadvantages of each method?

2. How is a REIT different from a regular corporation?

3. What qualifications must be met in order for a REIT to remain exempt from corporate income taxes?

4. What are the different payment structures associated with debt financing? How does each method work?

5. What is a lock-out provision? Why would a lender want a lock-out provision in a loan agreement?

6. What is a yield-maintenance agreement?

7. Discuss the different sources of debt financing.

8. What is a mortgage REIT?

9. How does leveraging work? What makes leveraging risky?

PROBLEMS

1. A developer wishes to prepay with one year of a 6-year yield-maintenance agreement still in place. The existing mortgage is a 30-year, $650,000 mortgage, which is being amortized monthly at 12 percent. The current mortgage rate is 10 percent, with a 25-year maturity and no discount points. Since loan origination, the Treasury benchmark rate has dropped from 8 to 5 percent.

   a. What is the amount of the yield-maintenance premium?

   b. What is the net present value of refinancing? Assume that the required rate of return is 15 percent.

2. What is the net savings to a developer who refinances a 30-year, $700,000 mortgage, amortized monthly at 11 percent during the 60th month at a new rate of 9 percent for the remaining term (25 years). Assume that there is no yield-maintenance penalty, but that a new, loan origination fee of 2 percent is charged. The opportunity cost of funds equals 10 percent.

3. As a real estate investor, you are considering refinancing a small office building that was purchased three years ago for $500,000. The original mortgage had a 25-year term, 12 percent interest rate, 1 discount point, a prepayment penalty of 3 percent of the outstanding loan balance, required monthly payments, and a loan-to-value ratio of 85 percent. The building has been depreciated using the straight-line recovery method.

   The building is expected to generate a net operating income of $35,000 this coming year, and NOI is expected to increase at 4 percent per year. The current market value of the building is $600,000. You can refinance with an adjustable-rate mortgage with 1 discount point, 5 percent prepayment penalty, and an 85 percent loan-to-value ratio. The contract rate is 8.5 percent, and is indexed to the prime rate plus 300 basis points. The loan has a floor of 5.5 percent and a cap of 15.5 percent. Payments are made monthly and adjustments are made annually, with a maximum periodic adjustment of 250 basis points.

   You plan on selling the building in five years for an estimated $750,000, with 5 percent selling expenses. During this time period, the prime rate is expected to increase by 150 basis points annually. You are in a 28 percent marginal income tax bracket and have an after-tax required rate of return of 14 percent. Your capital gains tax rate is 28 percent. Should you refinance? Refinancing costs are $5,000.

4. B. Smith buys a vacant lot, agreeing to pay $24,000, with $4,000 initial down payment. Shortly after, rezoning is requested and obtained, increasing the lot's value to $36,000.

   a. What percentage increase in property value and in equity has taken place?

   b. Is this positive leverage?

5. An investor plans to develop a new sports bar on Maple Boulevard. The sports bar will offer some unique amenities, along with excellent food. The plans include a baseball dugout, second-floor sky boxes that can be rented out for private parties, fenced-in basketball area, two indoor sand volleyball courts, electronic games, and two satellite dishes with 15 TVs and an electronic scoreboard. The volleyball courts will be the backbone of the operations and should keep a steady stream of customers coming through the doors. The area is targeted for employment and population growth.

   A pro forma operating statement for year 1 is given below.

Revenues	
Bar sales	$ 891,000
Food sales	$ 420,750
Other income	$ 54,100
Total	$1,365,850
Less: Cost of goods sold	$ 489,700
Gross profit	$ 876,150
Less: Operating expenses	$ 763,907
Net operating income	$ 166,343

The project is expected to cost $1,020,000 (including land costs). The improvements represent 80 percent of cost, and depreciation will be based on the current tax law. Net operating income is expected to increase at the rate of 2 percent per year for the next five years. The expected selling price at the end of year 5 is 16 times the NOI. Selling expenses are expected to be 5 percent of the sales price. The holding period is 5 years. The investor's marginal income tax rate is 28 percent; and the capital gains tax rate is 28 percent.

   a. Compute the before- and after-tax IRR assuming 100 percent equity.

   b. An 80 percent loan can be obtained at an 8.5 percent interest rate for 15 years with monthly compounding. Calculate the expected before- and after-tax IRR on equity.

   c. Is there positive financial leverage with the proposed 80 percent loan?

6. A $200,000 loan is arranged at 10 percent interest, compounded annually, and with 30-year amortization, but with a balloon payment due at the end of year 12.

   a. How much is the debt service?

   b. What would be the amount of the end of year 12 balloon payment?

CHAPTER 22

FINANCING HOMEOWNERSHIP

Chapter Outline

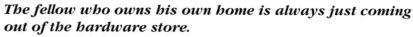

The fellow who owns his own home is always just coming out of the hardware store.

Kim Hubbard, in *Bartlett's Unfamiliar Quotations*

Homeownership has long been part of the Great American Dream. In 1900, 47 percent of all dwelling units were owner-occupied; by 1950, 55 percent were. Currently, about two-thirds of all residential units are owner-occupied.

The choices of the types of housing has also increased. Condominiums, cooperatives, and mobile homes are now widely accepted as alternatives to detached single-family residences. Changing life styles, as well as higher costs, account for this acceptance.

The purpose of this chapter is to outline the key decisions relative to owning a home. The two basic decisions are: (1) How much can I afford to pay for housing? and (2) Should I rent or buy? Tax treatment of homeownership and alternative methods of financing are also discussed.

DETERMINING HOUSING AFFORDABILITY

The primary considerations of a lender in making a mortgage loan are the applicant's ability to pay and motivation to own. And, for most people, obtaining a loan is a necessary prerequisite to homeownership. Since we assume motivation, let us look at how a lender is likely to evaluate an applicant's ability to carry a loan. Using Federal Home Loan Mortgage Corporation (FHLMC) guidelines, we can then extend the analysis to determine how much housing one can afford.

Annual Stabilized Income

The ability to carry a loan depends on recognized earning capability, which, under the FHLMC guidelines, is called *annual stabilized income.* Annual stabilized income begins with a person's yearly wages or salary. To this is added income from overtime, commissions, bonuses, dividends, interest, alimony, welfare, and the net rent from any income property owned. Payments for alimony and/or child support are deducted from annual stabilized income. Two years' experience on these additions and deductions is required for the figures to be fully accepted. As a case example, let us assume the B's want to buy a house.

One of the prospective buyers, has an annual salary of $24,000; the other earns $18,000 a year. They have little additional income from investments. However, they project that their earnings will have increased to $48,000 by the time they are ready to purchase.

Proportion for Housing. The FHLMC guidelines allow 25 percent of annual stabilized income for housing expenses. *Housing expenses* include loan interest, repayment of principal, hazard insurance premiums, and property taxes. Collectively, these expenses are frequently referred to as *PITI* (Principal, Interest, Taxes, Insurance) or PIIT. Payments for mortgage insurance, homeowner association dues, and ground rental payments are also included, if they are payable. Utility charges are not included.

Alternatively, the guidelines allow up to 33 percent of annual stabilized income for housing expenses plus other required periodic payments. The other payments would include outlays for such items as utilities, installment debt, alimony, and child support. An additional 10 percent may be added to these limits, if justified by a large down payment, a substantial net worth, or a demonstrated ability and willingness to devote a larger portion of income for housing expense. Thus, outside maximums of 28 percent and 36 percent of income may be devoted to housing. So, what does this all mean?

The 25 Percent Rule

The buyers ask the loan officer at the Urbandale Savings and Loan Association about current lending terms. The officer tells them that fixed-rate mortgage loans, for 80 percent of value, are now being made at 12 percent, with amortization calculated on a 30-year life. The loan officer also informs them that property taxes and mortgage insurance typically run about 3 percent of market value in Urbandale.

Under the *25 percent rule*, the amount that would be available for housing is $12,000 per year ($48,000 × 25 percent). This amount must cover PITI.

$$\text{Amount available} = \text{Debt service} + \text{Property taxes and insurance}$$
$$\$12,000 = 80\% \times \text{Purchase price} \times PR_{12\%,30} + 3\% \times \text{Purchase price}$$

Where $PR_{12\%,30}$ refers to the principal recovery factor at 12 percent for 30 years (see Chapter 20). For this example, we are using annual time-value-of-money factors; in practice, monthly factors are usually used.

Inserting the principal recovery factor, we are in a position to solve for what purchase price the buyers can afford.

$$\$12,000 = 0.80 \times \text{Purchase price} \times 0.124144 + 0.03 \times \text{Purchase price}$$
$$= 0.099315 \times \text{Purchase price} + 0.03 \times \text{Purchase price}$$
$$= 0.129315 \times \text{Purchase price}$$

$$\text{Purchase price} = \frac{\$12,000}{0.129315} = \$92,797$$

Thus, it appears that the buyers can afford to pay up to $92,800 (rounded) for a home. Do the figures check out? The loan would be for 80 percent of $92,800, or $74,200. Debt service payments plus property taxes and insurance total to $12,000:

Annual debt service on loan	($74,200 × 0.124144)	$ 9,216
Taxes and insurance at 3%	($92,800 × 0.03)	$ 2,784
Total required for PITI		$12,000

For a loan of $92,800, a cash down payment of $18,560, or 20 percent of the purchase price, would be required. Given the above calculations, the buyers now have an indication of how much they can afford for housing. But there is a second way to determine the amount.

The 33 Percent Rule

Under the *33 percent rule,* utilities and installment debt are taken into account. Thus, 33 percent of annual stabilized income must cover PITI, plus utility costs and installment debt. The relationship is as follows:

$$\text{Amount available} = \text{Debt service} + \text{Property taxes and insurance} + \text{Utilities plus installment debt}$$

The buyers estimate that installment debt on a car will be $2,544 per year. Also, they determine that they can expect to pay about $95 per month, or $1,140 per year, for utilities should they buy a house. The amount available under the 33 percent rule is thus $15,840 per year ($48,000 × 33%). Inserting the known information into the equation gives:

$$\$15,840 = 0.80 \times \text{Purchase price} \times 0.124144 + 0.03 \times \text{Purchase price} + (\$2,544 + \$1,140)$$
$$= 0.099315 \times \text{Purchase price} + 0.03 \times \text{Purchase price} + \$3,684$$

We are now in the position to solve for the purchase price:

$$\$12,156 = 0.129315 \times \text{Purchase price}$$
$$\text{Purchase price} = \frac{12,156}{0.129315} = \$94,003$$

With a purchase price of $94,000, the loan amount would be $75,200 and the required down payment would be $18,800. Annual debt service would be $9,335.60. Based on the 3 percent estimated by the bank, property taxes and hazard insurance would be $2,820. These amounts, plus $3,684 for installment payments, total to $15,839.60—just short of the $15,840 available each year.

After looking at available housing in the $85,000 to $95,000 range, the buyers decide to investigate whether they should rent or buy. Before taking up the rent or buy decision, we need a look at some of the federal tax aspects of owning a personal residence.

FEDERAL TAX LAWS AND HOMEOWNERSHIP

The owner-occupant of a personal residence does not get all the advantages of an owner-investor in other types of real estate. For one thing, annual depreciation may not be taken on a personal residence. Also, a personal residence is not like-kind property in a tax-deferred exchange for business or investment.

On the other hand, interest on a mortgage loan and real property taxes can both be used as direct offsets against ordinary income to reduce taxes payable. Thus, a homeowner in the 28 percent tax bracket, with property tax payments of $1,500 and interest payments of $3,000 in a given year, pays $1,260 less in income tax as a result ($4,500 × 28 percent). Renters get no such tax deduction. Interest and tax deductions, therefore, constitute a substantial advantage to homeownership as against renting.

Limitation on Interest Deduction

The allowable deduction for interest on loans secured by a person's primary or secondary residence is limited to the amount of interest on up to $1 million of debt, provided that the loan is used for the acquisition of the house. Mortgages obtained after purchase are subject to tighter restrictions. The rule is as follows: A taxpayer can deduct unlimited interest on post-acquisition borrowing, provided the debt is used to finance additions or alterations to the residence. Interest on up to $100,000 of other mortgage debt (home equity loans) can also be deducted, except for interest on debt that exceeds the property's current market value.

To illustrate, consider a taxpayer who acquires a $2.5 million residence by taking out a $2 million mortgage at 12 percent interest for 30 years, compounded monthly. Scheduled monthly payments are:

$$\text{Debt service} = \text{Loan outstanding} \times \text{Principal recovery factor}$$
$$= \$2,000,000 \times 0.010286 = \$20,572$$

The outstanding loan balance at the end of month 12, or end of year 1, is:

$$\text{Loan outstanding, } EOM12 = \frac{\$20,572}{(1+.01)} + \frac{\$20,572}{(1+.01)^2} + \cdots$$
$$+ \frac{\$20,572}{(1+.01)^{300-12}}$$
$$= \$20,572 \times 96.86554 = \$1,992,742$$

The amount of principal reduction in year 1 is:

$$\text{Principal} = \text{Loan Outstanding, } BOM1 - \text{Loan Outstanding, } EOM12$$
$$= \$2,000,000 - \$1,992,742 = \$7,258$$

Total debt service during the year is $246,867. This means that the amount of interest is:

$$\text{Interest} = \text{Debt service} - \text{Principal}$$
$$= \$246,867 - \$7,258 = \$239,609$$

In comparison, interest in year 1 on $1 million, at 12 percent for 30 years, compounded monthly, is $119,805. This means that in year 1 the allowable interest deduction is only $119,805, rather than $239,609. Note that this upper limit on the amount of interest that is fully deductible affects relatively few households.

Here is another example. A homeowner purchases a $500,000 residence by taking out a $300,000 first mortgage. The taxpayer's equity in the property is $200,000.

Suppose that the taxpayer then takes out a new, $150,000 second mortgage for purposes other than additions and alterations. From a tax standpoint here is what we know. A homeowner can never deduct interest on other mortgage debt in excess of the principal of the original mortgage plus $100,000. In this case this means that the taxpayer is allowed to deduct interest on only $100,000 of the new $150,000 second mortgage. The interest on the remaining $50,000 is nondeductible for tax purposes.

You may ask what if the borrower purchased the $500,000 property with, say, a $425,000 mortgage. In this case the home's current market value is the binding constraint. Assuming the taxpayer were still able to obtain a new, $150,000 second mortgage for purposes other than additions and alterations—which is a big assumption since the taxpayer's equity in the property is only $75,000—interest on only $75,000 could be deducted for tax purposes. The reason: No interest can be deducted on debt that exceeds the property's current market value.

Here is still another example. Consider a household that has refinanced. The original mortgage was for $200,000, and the refinanced mortgage was for $250,000. Suppose the taxpayer takes out a new, $100,000 second mortgage for purposes other than additions and alterations. The current market value of the property is $350,000. The amount of interest on the second mortgage that would be fully deductible is limited to $100,000 − ($250,000 − $200,000) = $50,000.

Loan Fees and Points

The tax treatment of loan fees and points depends on whether the fees are paid on acquisition debt or for refinancing. Loan fees and points on acquisition debt are treated as interest if paid separately to the lender and not subtracted from the loan. Points paid for refinancing must be amortized over the life of the loan.

Relief on Rollover

Congress has enacted special relief provisions, called a *rollover,* to minimize the tax impact on sale and repurchase of a personal residence. Under this rollover legislation, a capital gain from the sale of a personal residence is rolled over—that is, the tax is postponed—if a replacement residence is bought or built at a cost equal to or greater than the adjusted sale price of the old residence. The replacement residence must be purchased or built within the 48-month period beginning 24 months before and ending 24 months after the date of sale of the old residence (see Figure 22–1). The *date of sale* is when title passes; in an installment sale, the date of sale is when the buyer moves into possession and has assumed all the benefits and burdens of ownership, even though delivery of the deed is delayed to a later time.

The *adjusted sale price* equals the full price or contract price, less selling expense and less fixing-up expense. Selling expenses are primarily brokerage fees, prepayment penalties, and legal fees. Fixing-up expenses are noncapital outlays made to assist in the sale of the residence, such as painting, minor repairs, landscaping, and so on.

Example. Together two homeowners had purchased a Denver residence for $60,000 in 1986. In November 1994, the homeowners' employer transferred them to Chicago. The old residence was promptly sold for $94,000, with title transferred in January 1995. Selling expenses of $8,000 were incurred in the sale. The homeowners realized a gain of $26,000:

Sales price	$94,000
Less: Selling expenses	−8,000
Adjusted sales price	$86,000
Less: Purchase price (tax basis)	60,000
Long-term capital gain	$26,000

If the couple buy a home for $76,000 in Chicago, they would be taxed on a capital gain of $10,000 ($86,000 − $76,000), and their basis would remain at $60,000. Purchase of a new residence for $86,000 would mean no tax, and the basis would continue at $60,000. Purchase of a replacement residence for $100,000 would again mean no tax, but the basis would be increased to $74,000 ($100,000 less $26,000 unrecognized gain, or $60,000 plus $14,000 additional input).

All the cash proceeds from the sale need not be reinvested in the replacement residence. That is, a loan may be used to finance part of the purchase price of the new dwelling. But the new residence must be occupied within the period stipulated. And the replacement residence will not be considered a new residence if it is sold before the disposition of the old residence. Finally, a condominium or a cooperative unit qualifies as a replacement residence for a detached single-family house.

Relief on Sale by Elderly

Elderly citizens, 55 and over, are entitled to a once-in-a-lifetime capital gain exclusion of $125,000 on the sale of a personal residence. The property must have been used as the principal residence for three of the five years immediately preceding the sale. This exclusion recognizes that the value in a residence may be a basic source of retirement income of senior citizens. Also, elderly citizens often need and want less living space because of smaller family size and reduced income. Thus, this option may be taken even though the move is to a smaller dwelling unit, to a retirement home, or to the home of a son or daughter.

A married couple is treated as one taxpayer under this exclusion. Both spouses are treated as satisfying the requirements, if either is 55 at the time of the sale and meets the three- of five-year holding provision. The one-time exemption means that if the exemption is used to avoid taxes on a gain of $80,000 on one sale, the taxpayer may not later claim a second exemption of up to $45,000.

Example.　A couple, ages 56 and 57, sell their principal residence for $260,000. Their adjusted tax basis in the home is $100,000. Their fixing-up and selling expenses

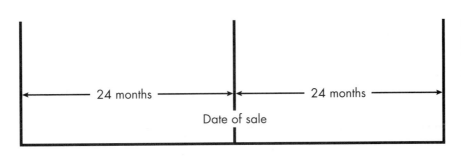

FIGURE 22–1
Tax-Exempt Rollover Period for Sale of Personal Residence

amount to $20,000, making the adjusted sales price $240,000. The taxable gain is $15,000, computed as follows.

Sales price	$260,000
Less: Fixing-up expenses	−20,000
Adjusted sales price	$240,000
Less: Adjusted tax basis	−100,000
Long-term capital gain	$140,000
Less: One-time exclusion	−125,000
Taxable gain	$ 15,000

The couple would pay capital gains taxes on the $15,000 at a 15 percent or 28 percent rate, depending on the amount of income they earned in the year of the sale.

Conversion to Income Property

The owner of a personal residence, upon moving, may convert it to an income property rather than sell it. The owner can then realize rental income, tax shelter, and capital appreciation and at the same time, avoid any selling expenses. But the property cannot be represented as an income property, and depreciation taken, while it stands vacant and up for sale. The intent must be to convert to an income property, as evidenced by the owner's affirmative actions. The property need not actually be rented; however, rental is prima facie proof that it has reached the status of income property.

RENT OR BUY?

Renting is sometimes a better choice than owning, and an economic comparison between renting and buying is worthwhile for anyone facing that decision. Then, based on one's own value system, a choice can be made with full knowledge of the implications.

Pros and Cons of Owning

Owning is usually perceived to offer intangibles that renting does not, such as greater status, financial security, stability, ego satisfaction, privacy, and personal freedom. Ownership is also perceived as being more desirable for a family with children. The explicit financial benefits of owning include value appreciation, the taxes on which can often be deferred or avoided, and deduction of interest and property taxes on income tax returns.

But the opportunity costs of owning must also be considered. The foregone return on the equity invested in a home, including closing costs at purchase, is often overlooked. This opportunity cost equals the rate of return that might be earned if the money were invested elsewhere.

A second, less tangible opportunity cost involves the activities foregone by the owner because of the need to repair and maintain the residence. Instead of repainting the house or repairing a faucet, the owner could be taking a nap, watching television, traveling, or water skiing.

Risk is a factor also. Major repairs, such as dry rot or termites, or a cracked foundation, or a roof leaking can add to the costs of owning. Taking out a mortgage loan involves financial risk. Some risks, however, such as liability for injuries on the premises, can be covered by insurance.

Transfer costs, financing costs, and administrative or maintenance costs must also be taken into account. Transfer costs include the outlays for attorney's fees, title searches, surveys, recording the deed and mortgage, loan processing, and appraisals. Transfer costs can run as high as 10 percent of value, although 6 to 8 percent is more typical. Interest on borrowed money and mortgage insurance premiums are the main financial costs of owning. Administrative or maintenance costs include annual property taxes, hazard insurance premiums, and the cost of repairs or replacements necessary to keep the property livable. Over a long period, the average annual outlays for painting, yardwork, equipment maintenance, and roof repair can be about 2 percent of value. Property taxes and homeowners' insurance typically amount to 2 to 3 percent in urban areas, and may sometimes be higher.

Pros and Cons of Renting

Mobility is a major advantage of renting. Thus adjusting to changing family size, income levels, or job locations can be easier. In some cases, for example, for adult households rental units may provide greater convenience and more amenities for living, and reduce the amount of time required to maintain the property. If the roof springs a leak or other problems come up, the risk and responsibility for correcting it is with the landlord. Further, the money not used to buy a home may be invested elsewhere to enhance further the renter's income and wealth. Also, in a renter's market during an economic downturn, renting can be a major bargain. Finally, when a renter wants to move, it can generally be done on short notice, with perhaps the loss of a deposit. A renter need not worry about selling a property when interest rates are extremely high or times are economically difficult.

Renting, however, is not always a clear choice. Renters get no direct tax benefits.

A renter also foregoes an opportunity cost by not realizing value appreciation of a home; on the other hand, the risk of value depreciation is avoided. Finally, renters are typically required to deposit a month's rent as security or for cleaning costs. However, if the unit is properly maintained, these are eventually recovered.

Rent Capitalization

A rent or buy decision should obviously be based on more than a simple comparison of monthly rent versus monthly PITI payments on a mortgage loan. But there is a way to do a "quick and dirty" analysis to help in deciding whether renting is feasible. Consider the following:

Let us return to the B's search for alternatives. They have now located a very nice condominium that is being offered for rent at $800 per month. "Is it a good deal?"

By comparing the rental unit to several other comparable condominiums up for sale, it is determined that the market value of the rental unit is about $100,000. From this the B's conclude that from an investment standpoint it would cost them in excess of $1,000 per month to purchase a comparable condominium. Here are the calculations in summary:

Condominium Market Value	$100,000
Times: Loan-to-value ratio	.75
Mortgage amount	$ 75,000
Times: Annual principal recovery factor @ 12% for 30 years	.12414
Annual debt service	$ 9,311

Equity funds also are expected to earn a 12 percent equity dividend rate. This implies a minimum annual cash flow to the B's of $3,000:

Condominium Market Value	$100,000
Times: One minus loan-to-value ratio	× .25
Equity amount	$ 25,000
Times: Equity dividend rate of 12%	.1200
Annual cash flow to equity investors	$ 3,000

The opportunity cost of buying a comparable condominium unit therefore is $12,311 (annual debt services plus annual cash flow to equity investors, or $9,311 + $3,000), or $1,026 per month.

Note that by adding property taxes, insurance, and maintenance to the $1,026 per month opportunity cost of owning would additionally raise the cost of owning. Thus, it would appear in this case that renting is clearly the better choice, at least in the short-run.

Net After-Tax Costs

Comparison of after-tax costs and benefits provides a much more accurate way to decide which alternative offers the greatest economic advantage. The analysis involves quantifying costs and benefits. The assumptions and calculations for a five-year projection are shown in Figures 22–2 and 22–3. Figure 22–4 extends the analysis in Figure 22–3 to ten years.

The rent or buy decision illustrated in Figures 22–3 and 22–4 involves a dwelling offered for rent at 1 percent of its $100,000 market value. If the dwelling is purchased, a 20 percent down payment would be required, with the balance financed by a 30-year, 12 percent loan. Closing costs are estimated to be 2 percent of the purchase price. The rental and market value, and other expenses are considered to increase by 5 percent per year. The owner's combined state and federal tax rate is 28 percent. Finally, if purchased, the owner is assumed to avoid any capital gains tax upon disposition by rolling ownership over within 24 months.

Transaction costs are prorated on a straight-line basis over the years of ownership. Thus, if the dwelling were owned for only one year, transaction costs of $9,000 (2 percent on purchase and 7 percent on sale) would be spread over the one year. If owned for two years, the average closing cost would drop to $1,000 ($2,000 ÷ 2). If sold at the end of year 2, selling expenses of $7,350 ($105,000 × 7%) would be spread over two years at an average of $3,675. By similar calculations, average closing and selling costs for a three-year holding period would be $667 and $2,573, respectively.

Rent payments are the major costs for a tenant, amounting to $12,000 in year 1. A major benefit to the renter is the interest earned on money not used for a down pay-

PROPERTY AND OWNER		FINANCING							
MARKET VALUE	BUYING COSTS (% OF MARKET VALUE)	SELLING COSTS (% OF MARKET VALUE)	ANNUAL CHANGE IN MARKET VALUE, RENT, AND EXPENSES	OWNER'S TAX BRACKET	DOWN PAYMENT (% OF MARKET VALUE)	LOAN TERM (YEARS)	INTEREST RATE (NOMINAL)	LOAN TO VALUE RATIO	OPPOR-TUNITY COST OF CAPITAL
$100,000	2.00%	7.00%	5.00%	28%	20%	30	12.00%	80.00%	10%

RENTAL DATA			RENTER'S INSURANCE		ANNUAL EXPENSES (% OF MARKET VALUE)		
INITIAL MONTHLY RENTAL	REQUIRED SECURITY DEPOSIT	GROSS RENT MULTIPLIER	(% OF MARKET VALUE)	RENTER'S CAPITAL INVESTED	PROPERTY TAXES	HAZARD INSURANCE	MAINTENANCE
$1,000	$1,500	100	0.20%	$20,500	2.00%	0.50%	1.00%

	YEAR 1	YEAR 2	YEAR 3	YEAR 4	YEAR 5
Beginning-of-year market value	$100,000	$105,000	$110,250	$115,763	$121,551
Monthly rental	$ 1,000	$ 1,050	$ 1,103	$ 1,158	$ 1,216
Gross rent multiplier	100	100	100	100	100

[a] Homeowner is assumed to avoid capital gains tax by buying another unit of equal or greater value within 24 months.

FIGURE 22-2

Assumptions for a One- to Five-Year Projection of the Net After-Tax Costs of Owning Versus Renting

ment or closing costs. Thus, $22,000, less $1,500 required for a deposit, is available for investment at 10 percent, earning $2,050 in year 1. This $2,050 is subject to tax at 28 percent, leaving a net benefit of $1,476. The invested funds in year 2 are presumed to be $21,976, (20,500 + $1,476).

Results of the analysis show that renting costs about $5,000 less in year 1, $10,724 versus $15,841 (see Figure 22–4). In year 2, the difference narrows to $688. And from year 3 on, renting is more costly, approaching $4,000 by the end of year 10.

The example makes it quite clear that renting is almost certain to cost less when occupancy is less than two years. Three years appears to be the breakeven period; this is consistent with conventional wisdom. But caution is advised; a slight change in assumptions quickly changes the result. A property appreciation rate of 2 percent results in renting always having the lower net cost. And a 10 percent per year property value increase makes ownership break even with renting at the end of year 1.

HOW HOUSES ARE FINANCED

There are a number of ways to finance houses. One of the most common methods is to take out a conventional loan.

Conventional Loan. A *conventional loan* is one *not* backed by government—that is, it is *not* insured by the Federal Housing Administration (FHA) nor guaranteed by

	RENT	OWN	RENT	OWN	RENT	OWN	RENT	OWN	RENT	OWN
Costs										
Average buying expenses		$ 2,000		$ 1,000		$ 667		$ 500		$ 400
Interest on loan		9,584		9,548		9,506		9,459		9,407
Property taxes, annual		2,000		2,100		2,205		2,315		2,431
Hazard insurance		500		525		551		579		608
Renter's insurance	$ 200		$ 210		$ 221		$ 232		$ 243	
Annual maintenance		1,000		1,050		1,103		1,158		1,216
Equity opportunity cost		2,000		2,529		3,087		3,675		4,295
Annual rent (12 × month)	12,000		12,600		13,230		13,892		14,586	
Average selling expenses		7,000		3,675		2,573		2,026		1,702
Total cost per year	$12,200	$24,084	$12,810	$20,427	$13,451	$19,691	$14,123	$19,712	$14,829	$20,058
Benefits										
Renter's return on money not invested in equity at rate of 10% minus taxes at 28%	$ 1,476		$ 1,582		$ 1,696		$ 1,818		$ 1,949	
Income tax savings										
For interest paid		$ 2,684		$ 2,673		$ 2,662		$ 2,649		$ 2,634
For property taxes paid		$ 560		$ 588		$ 617		$ 648		$ 681
Equity build-up-app'n		$ 5,000		$ 5,250		$ 5,513		$ 5,788		$ 6,078
Total benefits per year	$ 1,476	$ 8,244	$ 1,582	$ 8,511	$ 1,696	$ 8,792	$ 1,818	$ 9,085	$ 1,949	$ 9,392
Net cost per year	$10,724	$15,841	$11,228	$11,915	$11,754	$10,899	$12,305	$10,627	$12,880	$10,666
Net advantage to buying		($ 5,117)		($ 688)		$ 855		$ 1,678		$ 2,214

FIGURE 22–3

Net Costs of Owning Versus Renting for One to Five Years of Occupancy

the Veterans Administration (VA). The term *conventional loan* developed historically. When FHA loans were first introduced in the 1930s, borrowers were given the choice of an FHA-insured or a conventional loan. Conventional loans, which are contracts between private parties, are much less subject to government regulation than are FHA or VA loans. Further, conventional loans are traditionally made at lower loan-to-value ratios than FHA or VA loans because the lenders have less protection in default and foreclosure. Private mortgage insurance is an option with conventional loans, however.

FHA-Insured Loan. The Federal Housing Administration insures lenders against loss in return for fees or premiums paid by borrowers on what are popularly referred to as *FHA mortgages.* The FHA, an agency of the U.S. Government, does not, itself, lend money; it insures loans, for the entire principal, made by approved lenders under regulated conditions and terms.

VA-Guaranteed Loan. A mortgage loan that is partially guaranteed against loss by the Veterans Administration is termed a *VA* or *GI* mortgage. The VA sets no maximum amount for the loan, although there is a maximum guarantee. Also, unlike the FHA, if no financial institution will make a loan to an eligible veteran, the VA will make the loan itself. The guaranteed loan must initially be made to a qualified veteran or the dependent of a qualified veteran, usually a surviving spouse, and requires a *certificate of*

	NET COST TO		
YEAR	RENT	OWN	NET ADVANTAGE TO OWNING
1	($10,724)	($15,841)	($5,117)
2	(11,228)	(11,915)	(688)
3	(11,754)	(10,899)	855
4	(12,305)	(10,627)	1,678
5	(12,880)	(10,666)	2,214
6	(13,481)	(10,873)	2,608
7	(14,113)	(11,188)	2,926
8	(14,774)	(11,580)	3,194
9	(15,465)	(12,035)	3,430
10	(16,187)	(12,543)	3,645

FIGURE 22–4 Growth Rate: 5.00 Percent. Net After-Tax Cost of Owning Versus Renting for One to Ten Years of Occupancy

eligibility from the VA. The lending institution makes the loan from its own funds and gets the guarantee from the VA. The loan may later be taken over by a nonveteran. A number of states sponsor loans to former service personnel, which are commonly referred to as *state VA* or *state GI* loans.

Privately Insured Loan.   A conventional loan, on which the lender is partially protected against loss by a private mortgage insurance company in return for a fee or premium, is termed a *privately insured loan*. The insurance companies, therefore, compete directly with the FHA and VA. Almost all states allow lenders to make loans up to 95 percent of value with private mortgage insurance.

Private mortgage insurance, for single-family residences began with the Mortgage Guarantee Insurance Company of Milwaukee, Wisconsin, in 1957. Spectacular growth followed because of lower costs and shorter turnaround times on applications for loan insurance as compared with the FHA and VA. Acceptance of private mortgage insurance for secondary mortgage market purposes began in the early 1970s. Private mortgage insurance is now used for loans on apartment and office buildings, stores, warehouses, and leaseholds, although the rates for these types of properties are higher than for single-family homes.

Private mortgage insurance covers only the top 20 to 25 percent of a loan, which is the portion most exposed to risk and loss. Thus, a lender can make a 90 to 95 percent loan with private mortgage insurance with the same risk as an uninsured loan for 70 to 75 percent of value. With only a 5 to 10 percent down payment required, many more people can qualify for loans. Later in the life of the mortgage, with the loan-to-value ratio lowered to 70 to 75 percent, the insurance may be discontinued by the borrower. The FHA, in contrast, insures the loan for its entire life. The cost of private mortgage insurance is, therefore, much less than for FHA insurance.

Purchase-Money Mortgage Loan.   A *purchase-money mortgage* is a mortgage given by a buyer to a seller that secures all, or a portion, of the purchase price of a property. Thus, the seller is financing, or partially financing, the transaction. The loan becomes active at the exact time that title is passed, giving the seller's claim priority over any lien that might develop against the property due to the purchaser's actions. The legal presumption is that since the property was pledged at the time title passed, no other party could have developed a prior claim. The words *purchase-money mort-*

gage are commonly included in the deed to give notice of its existence. Some states do not recognize a deficiency judgment on a purchase-money mortgage, on the presumption that the seller-lender may recover the original property and thus be no worse off after a foreclosure than if the sale had not occurred and no mortgage had been made.

Second or Junior Mortgage Loan.   A mortgage with priority as a lien over all other mortgages against a property is a *first mortgage*. A mortgage subsequent in priority to a first mortgage is a *second mortgage*. And a mortgage with two mortgages of higher priority is a third mortgage. Mortgages have been stacked six and seven deep as to priority. The collective name for mortgages lower in priority than the first mortgage is *junior mortgages*. It follows that the lower the priority of a mortgage, the greater the risk of loss to the lender involved.

Home Equity Line of Credit.   Home equity lines of credit have become increasingly popular since their introduction in the early 1980s. They are a form of junior mortgages. Home equity loans are used by many homeowners to obtain money for nonhousing purposes, like purchasing a car. Interest on home equity loans is usually fully deductible (subject to some constraints, see discussion of junior loans), while interest on consumer loans (e.g., automobile loans, credit cards, etc.) is not deductible. Thus, if a taxpayer had a $10,000 home equity line of credit at 8 percent interest for three years, compounded annually, the interest in year 1 would be $800. With a marginal tax rate of 28 percent, the total tax savings would be $224 ($800 × 0.28 = $224), assuming, of course, that the taxpayer itemizes. In contrast, if the taxpayer had a $10,000 automobile loan, none of the interest would be tax deductible. This would amount to a loss in tax savings of $224. In this case it is clear that the home equity line of credit is cheaper on an after-tax basis.

HOUSING AFFORDABILITY AND LOAN REPAYMENT PLANS

At one time, real estate was financed with straight-term loans that called for periodic payments of interest at a fixed rate and a lump-sum repayment of the principal. Real estate loans are now made with a wide variety of repayment plans, each of which is designed to solve a particular problem. Needless to say, choosing between the alternative plans is a major decision for a borrower.

Fixed-Rate Mortgage

A *fixed-rate mortgage* is a loan in which the interest rate is fixed for the entire term of the loan. The typical home mortgage borrower prefers a fixed-rate mortgage. Why? Because a fixed-rate mortgage clearly offers the best protection against a general, persistent rise in prices. To illustrate a simple example, suppose you were a lender. If you were to lend $100,000 for one year at 3 percent and if in a year all prices were to double, you would suffer a loss in real purchasing power. You would get back $103,000, but at the new prices it would buy only as much as $51,500 would have at the old prices. If you were the borrower, however, you would have borrowed $100,000 and paid back $51,500 in real terms. In this example the nominal rate is

3 percent and the *realized real rate*—the nominal rate less inflation—is a negative 48.5 percent per year.

Of course, no lender would charge a 3 percent nominal interest rate if all prices were expected to double in a year. In reality, to protect against a rise in prices, the lender charges the borrower a much higher interest rate. And herein lies the problem for the fixed-rate mortgage borrower. The higher the interest rate, the greater the debt service. The greater the debt service, the more difficult it is for families with limited cash for a down payment or limited cash income to be able to borrow the amount they need to purchase a house.

Consider the following example. Suppose a family wishes to purchase a $112,500 house. Property taxes and hazard insurance, estimated at 3 percent of the purchase price, are $3,375. Under the 25 percent rule, the income the family has available for housing is $11,500. With a $22,500 down payment, they can just qualify for a 30-year, $90,000 loan at 8 percent interest, with monthly payments of $660.39. The calculations are:

Annual debt service ($660.39 × 12)	$ 7,924.66
Taxes and insurance at 3% ($112,500 × 0.03)	3,375.00
Total required for PITI	$11,299.66

Increasing the interest rate on the $90,000 loan from 8 to 11 percent increases the monthly debt service from $660.39 to $857.09. Total payments required for PITI would be $13,660.09 ($857.09 × 12 = $10,285.09, plus taxes and insurance of $3,375). But this means that the family can no longer qualify for the $90,000 loan and is unable to purchase the $112,500 house unless they can make a bigger down payment.

To buy the house, the family would need to increase the down payment by $18,902.30. With $11,500 of income available for housing and property taxes and hazard insurance at $3,375, they can afford a monthly debt service payment of $677.08 [($11,500 − $3,375) ÷ 12.] The maximum loan amount at 11 percent for 30 years is

$$\text{Loan outstanding} = \frac{DS}{(1 + i)} + \frac{DS}{(1 + i)^2} + \cdots + \frac{DS}{(1 + i)^n}$$

$$= \frac{\$677.08}{(1 + 0.917)} + \frac{\$677.08}{(1 + 0.917)^2} + \cdots + \frac{\$677.08}{(1 + 0.917)^{360}}$$

$$= \$677.08 \times 105.006346$$

$$= \$71,097.70$$

With a $71,097.70 maximum loan amount, the down payment must be $41,402.30, or 37 percent of the purchase price.

If the family cannot afford a larger down payment, another solution would be to look for a cheaper house. At 11 percent for 30 years the purchase price of the home that is affordable with $11,500 available for housing is:

Amount available = Debt service + Property taxes and insurance

$11,500 = 80% × Purchase price × $PR_{11\%,\ 30}$ + 3% × Purchase price

$$= 0.80 \times \text{Purchase price} \times 0.115025 + 0.03$$
$$\times \text{Purchase price}$$
$$= 0.092020 \times \text{Purchase price} + 0.03$$
$$\times \text{Purchase price}$$
$$= 0.122020 \times \text{Purchase price}$$
$$\text{Purchase price} = \$94{,}250 \text{ (rounded)}$$

As you will recall, *PR* is the principal recovery factor. In this instance, it is 11 percent for 30 years.

A third possibility is to opt for an adjustable-rate mortgage with lower current payments. However, if interest rates rise in the future, the monthly payment on this type of mortgage will also increase.

Adjustable-Rate Mortgage

An adjustable-rate mortgage, or ARM, is a loan on which the interest rate can increase or decrease, depending on the fluctuations of a designated index. Allowing the interest rate to fluctuate shifts the risk of increasing interest rates to the borrower, but a decrease in interest rates benefits the borrower.

There are various types of ARMs. Some ARMs are amortizing loans, with level debt-service payments. Thus, if the interest rate increases, the life of the loan is extended; if interest rates decrease, the term is shortened. Most ARMs, however, will fix the term of the loan and vary the debt service.

Often ARM loans have a maximum interest-rate adjustment per year (called an *interest rate cap*) and a maximum payment adjustment per year (called a *debt-service cap*). ARMs that include a debt-service cap are susceptible to negative amortization in which the loan balance may actually increase over the term of the loan rather than decrease. Interest rate fluctuations on ARMs may also be subject to a maximum *life-of-loan cap* which establishes a ceiling that the rate on the loan can never exceed.

ARMs allow lenders to continue making loans without fear of being locked into below-market rates. Hence, ARM lending helps maintain a more even flow of funds into real estate. At times, they have been the dominant lending arrangement. More often than not, however, borrowers must be enticed into taking out an ARM. This enticement usually comes in the form of a reduced initial interest rate, a so-called *teaser rate*.

Monthly payments on an ARM are calculated as follows: Consider a one-year, $100,000 ARM at an initial interest rate of 5 percent, with a 30-year amortization period. The initial monthly payments would be:

$$DS = \text{Loan outstanding} \times PR \text{ factor}$$
$$= \$100{,}000 \times 0.005956 = \$536.82$$

Note that these payments will remain fixed until the loan anniversary. The outstanding loan balance at the end of month 12, is:

$$\text{Loan outstanding, } EOM12 = \frac{DS}{(1 + i)} + \frac{DS}{(1 + i)^2} + \cdots + \frac{DS}{(1 + i)^{n-12}}$$

$$= \frac{\$536.82}{(1 + 0.00417)} + \frac{\$536.82}{(1 + 0.00417)^2}$$

$$+ \cdots + \frac{\$536.82}{(1 + 0.00417)^{348}}$$
$$= \$98,524.63$$

At the loan anniversary there are several possibilities. The lender can change the amount of the payment depending on the direction of interest rates, can keep the payment constant and reduce or extend the maturity date, or do a combination of the two. Our analysis will assume that the lender simply changes the periodic payment amount.

In this particular case, suppose at the end of the first year, the interest rate had increased to 9 percent. The new principal recovery factor at 9 percent interest for the remaining mortgage term (29 years) is 0.0081016. And the new monthly payment is:

$DS =$ Loan outstanding, $EOM12 \times PR$ factor
$\qquad = \$98,524.63 \times 0.0081016 = \$798.20$

At the end of year 2, the outstanding loan balance is \$97,783.31.

We can now determine the monthly payments for year 3 as follows: If at the end of the second year, the interest rate were 11 percent, the new principal recovery factor for the remaining mortgage term (28 years) would be 0.0096148. This means that the new monthly payment would be \$940.17 (\$97,783.31 × 0.0096148). Payments in subsequent years are determine in a similar fashion.

The message of all this is quite simple. A one-year ARM with a 30-year amortization period can be thought of as a 30-year, fixed-rate mortgage that is refinanced yearly at prevailing interest rates. Because the loan is refinanced every year, lenders do not have to take into account the expected inflation rate risk when pricing the loan. In turn, this means the borrower's initial monthly payment will be lower. And with a lower initial monthly payment, the borrower is normally able to qualify for a larger loan.

With an annual interest rate cap, a life-of-loan cap, or both, the monthly ARM payment calculations become more involved. To illustrate, let us reconsider our one-year, \$100,000 ARM at 5 percent with the 30-year life. Assume that each annual rate adjustment can be no greater than 2 percent and that the rate can be raised no more than 5 percent over the life of the loan. This means that at the end of year 1, instead of the rate increasing to 9 percent, the maximum rate that can be charged is 7 percent. (The maximum rate over the life of the loan is 10 percent.) Thus, payments in year 2 would be:

$DS =$ Loan outstanding, $EOM12 \times PR$ factor$_{7\%, 29}$
$\qquad = \$98,524.63 \times 0.0067213 = \$662.21$

What happens to the 2 percent interest rate differential between the 9 percent prevailing rate and the 7 percent ARM coupon rate? The answer is, it represents lost interest income to the lender. However before jumping to the conclusion that an ARM with an annual or life-of-loan interest rate cap is a bargain from the borrower's point of view, we should point out that these types of ARMs have slightly higher rates than ARMs without rate caps. Thus, lenders making ARM loans with annual or life-of-loan rate caps earn a higher initial rate that compensates for any lost future interest income should the rate caps become binding.

Some ARMs allow you to hold the payment constant and increase the outstanding loan balance each month. Under this option, the outstanding loan balance is increased to cover the accrued interest each month. To illustrate, suppose you were to take out a one-year, $100,000 ARM at an initial interest rate of 5 percent and a 30-year life, with no interest rate caps. The monthly payments in year 1 are $536.82 and the outstanding loan balance at the end of month 12 is $98,524.63. Assume that the maximum payment adjustment is 7.5 percent.

The interest rate at the end of year 1 is 9 percent. Thus, in year 2 the monthly payment should be $798.20 per month, which is an increase of $261.38 or 48.7 percent ($261.38 ÷ $536.82). However, the actual payment increase can be no more than 7.5 percent, or $40.26 per month, making the new monthly payment in year 2 $577.08. But this payment is not sufficient to cover the accrued interest each month. The total accrued interest for year 2 is 8,949.37.[1] The annual debt service is $577.08 times 12, or $6,924.96; the principal reduction is $6,924.96 less 8,949.37 equals a negative $2,024.41. Therefore, the outstanding loan balance at the end of month 24 is:

$$\text{Loan outstanding, } EOM24 = \text{Loan outstanding, } EOM12 - \text{Principal reduction}$$
$$= \$98,524.63 - (\$2,204.41)$$
$$= \$100,549.04$$

Notice that as a result of the payment cap, the outstanding loan balance at the end of month 24 increased by $2,024.41, going from $98,524.63 to $100,549.04. This increase in the outstanding loan balance is called *negative amortization*.

Note that most ARMs that allow negative amortization will also have a provision in the loan agreement that periodically—say, every 5 years—any negative amortization amounts must be absorbed by higher payments. Such a provision may result in a payment increase that exceeds the stipulated maximum payment adjustment.

Wraparound Mortgage

A *wraparound mortgage* is created when a second mortgage, made with a new lender, takes over the debt service payments on the first loan. The face amount of the wraparound loan is equal to the total of the first loan, plus the amount of money advanced by the second lender; hence, the *wrapping*. The amount of money actually advanced by the second lender is equal to the amount of the new loan less the remaining unamortized balance of the existing first loan. The borrower's debt service is based on the larger second loan. Thus, the wraparound mortgage envelops the existing mortgage even though it is subordinate to the existing loan.

A wraparound mortgage can be extremely advantageous, both from the borrower's and the lender's point of view, provided the existing loan has an interest rate that is well below current market rates. This enables the lender to charge an interest rate on the wraparound mortgage that is higher than the rate on the existing loan but, typically, is less than the going rate for new loans.

[1]The accrued interest in month 13 is $98,524.63 × (.09/12) = $738.93, and the outstanding loan balance at the end of month 13 is $98,524.63 + $738.93 − $577.08 = $98,686.48. For month 14, then, the accrued intrest is $98,686.48 × (.09/12) = $740.15 and the outstanding loan balance at the end of month 14 is $98,686.48 − $740.15 2 $577.08 = $98,849.55. Repeating these calculations for months 15–24 and summing the accrued interest for each month, you will find that the total accrued interest in year 2 is $8,949.37.

Here is a simple example. A seller has a fixed-rate mortgage at 7 percent interest, with monthly payments of $665.30. The unpaid principal on the mortgage is $94,131.59 and the remaining term to maturity is 25 years. Prevailing market interest rates are 11 percent.

Now let us suppose you are a buyer interested in the seller's house. The asking price is $125,000. You have $20,000 available in cash. Thus, you need to borrow $105,000 to complete the purchase. Unfortunately, you cannot qualify for a $105,000 loan at prevailing interest rates because the monthly PITI payments are too high.

Rather than looking for a more affordable house, you ask the seller whether he or she would be willing to make a wraparound mortgage for $105,000 at 9 percent for 25 years. The total wrap payment would be $881.16, which you can easily afford.

In making a $105,000 wraparound mortgage, the seller advances $10,868.41 ($105,000 − $94,131.59) of the purchase price. On this $10,868.41 investment, the seller nets $215.86 ($881.16 − $665.30) per month for the next 25 years after paying the debt service on the first mortgage. The IRR on the seller's investment is:

$$\frac{\$215.86}{(1+i)} + \frac{\$215.86}{(1+i)^2} + \cdots + \frac{215.86}{(1+i)^{300}} = \$10,868.41$$

Solving for IRR using trial-and-error yields 23.77 percent per annum, which is much higher than market rates.

A wraparound mortgage can be a win-win situation for both the buyer and seller. The buyer gets his or her needed financing. The seller receives a return that is much higher than market rates. The drawback is finding a loan that does not have to be paid off when the property is sold. It also is vital to find a loan that has an interest rate well below current market rates.

Graduated-Payment Mortgage

A *graduated-payment mortgage (GPM)* loan provides for low debt service payments initially, with regular increases for several years until a level is reached where the payments will amortize the loan over its remaining term. Debt service increases typically range from 2½ to 7½ percent per year. The interest rate may be fixed or variable. Sometimes, payments in the early years will not cover all the interest due on the loan; in this case, the shortfall is added to the principal.

GPM loans are best suited to situations where the borrower expects that increases in income will be at about the same rate as the scheduled increases in debt service. Thus, a GPM is sometimes called a young-people's loan, because it seems to best suit the needs of those who are just forming households and have increasing incomes. If the interest rate is adjustable, this becomes a *graduated-payment adjustable mortgage (GPAM)* loan.

Growing-Equity Mortgage

A *growing-equity mortgage (GEM)* requires variable payments tied to a borrower's ability to pay. However, in a GEM loan the increase is not tied to a fixed schedule as it is in the GPM arrangement. Instead, payments are adjusted annually to reflect 75 percent of the rate of change in a national index of per capita disposable personal income. A GEM loan is most likely to be made to a borrower who expects her or his income to rise significantly and, therefore, may be able to pay off the loan well ahead of its maturity date. Increases in debt service above the original payment schedule are used entirely to repay principal; hence, the borrower's equity builds up more quickly than with a standard loan.

The lender benefits from a GEM loan. There is higher cash flow and greater liquidity. Also lenders find the rapid amortization and shorter terms attractive. This normally translates into a slightly lower interest rate for the borrower. Why? Because a GEM loan that pays off in 15 years or less is usually less costly to originate than a fixed-rate mortgage that pays off in 30 years. There is also less risk of default on GEM loans compared to fixed-rate mortgages, which means lower interest rates.

Reverse-Annuity Mortgage

Reverse annuity mortgages (RAMs) are specifically designed for the growing number of elderly homeowners with a significant portion of their assets tied up in the equity of their home and little, if any, cash assets. RAM loans allow these homeowners to annuitize their equity in the home without having to sell the residence.

Here is how a RAM loan works. Upon signing the loan agreement, the owner-borrower receives periodic (monthly) payments over the term of the loan, which enable the owner-borrower to meet living expenses. The loan is repayable, with interest, upon a specific event, such as the sale of the property or the death of the owner, or at a specific date.

The cash flows with a RAM loan are, therefore, the opposite of those under a traditional mortgage arrangement, hence the name. Consider the case of homeowners who have the following net worth:

Cash	$ 10,000
Other assets	$ 5,000
Real estate	$250,000
Total assets	$265,000
Debt	$ 2,000
Total Net Worth	$263,000

The homeowners have $10,000 in cash, and $5,000 in other investments. The remainder of their assets, $250,000, represents equity in their principal residence. On the liability side, the homeowners have a small amount of consumer debt. Their total net worth is estimated to be $263,000. The homeowners' primary source of income is Social Security. To supplement that, they have been considering a $125,000 RAM loan at 8 percent for 10 years. The monthly annuity needed to accumulate a balance of $125,000 at the end of 10 years at 8 percent interest is:

$$DS \times (1 + i)^{120} + DS \times (1 + i)^{119} + \cdots + DS = \$125,000$$

We can solve for *DS* as follows:

$$DS = \$125,000 \ \frac{1}{(1 + i)^{120} + (1 + i)^{119} + \cdots + 1}$$

$$= \$125,000 \, \frac{i}{(1 + i)^{120} - 1}$$

$$= \$125,000 \times SFF_{0.67\%, \, 120}$$
$$= \$125,000 \times 0.0054661$$
$$= \$683.26$$

The SFF factor used in these expressions is known as a *sinking fund factor*. It is the annuity that would build up to $1 in cash by the end of 10 years, assuming an interest rate of 8 percent with monthly compounding.

To compute the SFF factor at 8 percent for 10 years on your financial calculator, the keystrokes are as follows: First, since you need to accumulate $1 in cash by the end of 10 years, let future value equal $1. Second, let the interest rate be 0.667 percent ($8\% \div 12$), and let the number of periods equal 120 (10×12). Solve for the amount of the annuity. The SFF factor at 8 percent for 10 years with monthly payments is 0.0054661. This is then multiplied by $125,000 to yield a monthly annuity payment of $683.26 for 120 months, or $8,199.14 per year for 10 years.

At the end of 10 years, or upon the sale of the property or death of the owners, the loan must be repaid with interest. If the property were sold after five years, for example, the homeowners would owe the lender:

$$\text{Loan outstanding, } EOM60 = DS \times (1 + i)^{60} + DS \times (1 + i)^{59} + \cdots + DS$$

$$= \$683.26 \times [(1 + i)^{60} + (1 + i)^{59} + \cdots + 1]$$

$$= \$683.26 \, \frac{(1 + i)^{120} - 1}{i}$$

$$= \$683.26 \, \frac{1}{SFF_{0.67\%, \, 60}}$$

$$= \$683.26 \, \frac{1}{.0136097} = \$50,203.91$$

The risk in a RAM loan is that the owner-borrower will outlive the loan. Then what happens? Technically, the owner-borrower has no choice. He or she will either have to come up with the cash to pay off the loan, or sell the property and repay the loan out of the sales proceeds. Politically, however, it is not that simple; no lender wants to evict elderly households. That is why most existing RAM programs will allow the owner-borrower to remain in the house even after the loan is due.

Another problem for lenders is that RAMs create "phantom income." Despite the fact that the lender does not receive payment on a RAM loan until the house is sold, or upon death of the owner and sale of the property, the lender must recognize the accrued interest income each year. Thus, the lender has a positive tax liability each year without any cash to pay it.

How risky a RAM is depends on the loan value relative to the property value. If property values were to fall, the sales proceeds might not be sufficient to pay off the loan.

Shared-Appreciation Mortgage

A loan in which any value increase in the property is split proportionately between the borrower and lender is termed a *shared-appreciation mortgage (SAM)*. In return for the right to share in appreciation, a SAM loan carries a below-market interest rate, which results in lower monthly debt service payments for the borrower. It is expected that the lender's share of the value increase will raise the effective yield on the loan above the market rate.

The borrower makes a lump-sum settlement if the property is sold or the loan prepaid before the specified maturity date. If the loan runs its full term, the lender typically guarantees to refinance the entire property at the appreciated value.

A SAM loan involves risk for both the lender and borrower. For the lender, the higher rate of return may not be realized. For the borrower, refinancing at the appreciated value may require a larger loan at an uncertain future market interest rate. Thus, the borrower may no longer be able to afford the property.

Blended Mortgage

When refinancing a property or when assuming a loan in a sale, lenders and borrowers sometimes compromise on the interest rate. Thus, the new rate is somewhere between the low rate on the original, older loan and the current market rate. In effect, there is a blending of the two rates; hence, the new loan is often termed a *blended mortgage*. It should be recognized that such a compromise is really not an alternative mortgage instrument. The compromise is an extremely practical way of solving a knotty problem for all parties involved, however.

Buydown Mortgage

Sometimes the difficulties in qualifying for a fixed-rate loan can be solved by taking out a *buydown mortgage.* In a buydown mortgage, a third party, typically the developer or seller, pays a fee to the lender to buy down the payments and interest rate for the borrower for a specified time period. Developers buy down the payments and interest rate purely as a marketing device. During periods of high interest rates, a buydown mortgage can make the property affordable to buyers who almost, but not quite, qualify for a fixed-rate mortgage at prevailing market rates.

The amount of the buydown fee that is paid by the developer or seller to the lender at loan origination is determined as follows: Consider a 30-year, $80,000 fixed-rate mortgage at a current interest rate of 13 percent. The monthly payment on this loan is $884.96. Assume that the prospective borrower can almost, but not quite, qualify for this mortgage. Let us further assume that the developer offers to buy down the borrower's monthly payment to $643.70 for years 1 through 3. In years 4 through 30, the borrower's monthly payment will increase to $884.96.

The buydown fee paid to the lender at the time of loan origination is the present value of the payment differential discounted at 13 percent (which is the required yield to the lender):

Buydown fee = *PV* of payment differential

$$= \frac{\$241.23}{(1 + .0108)} + \frac{\$241.23}{(1 + .0108)^2} + \cdots + \frac{\$241.23}{(1 + .0108)^{36}}$$

$$= \$7,159.50$$

The buydown fee in this example costs the developer $7,159.50, which is absorbed as a marketing cost, or is built into the price of the home. To the extent that the developer is successful in building part or all of the $7,159.50 into the price of the home, most if not all of the direct cost benefits to the borrower are negated. Still, having a buydown mortgage can be a good selling point because buydown mortgages have low initial payments, thus allowing many more borrowers to qualify for a loan. Of course, low initial payments can be a curse as well as a blessing. After the buydown period expires, borrowers may be subject to payment shock when their monthly payment increases and their income may not.

SUMMARY

Many of the factors considered in any real estate investment are also those one looks for in buying a house. The list includes location, location, and location; accessibility to schools, stores, churches, work, and friends; and sound structural characteristics.

In financing homeownership, buyers typically hope to qualify for a mortgage that will enable them to buy the home they want in the shortest possible time, with the least bother, and on the best-available terms. Ordinarily most people begin by seeking a standard, fixed-rate mortgage, because such a mortgage clearly offers the best protection against inflation. However, fixed-rate mortgages tend to have high interest rates and high initial monthly payments, which makes it difficult for borrowers to qualify.

There are many alternatives to the fixed-rate mortgage. They include adjustable-rate mortgages, where the interest rate paid by the borrower increases or decreases in response to fluctuations in an underlying index; graduated-payment mortgages, which provide for low, initial debt service payments, which are then increased over several years until a level is reached where the payments amortize the loan over its remaining term; buydown mortgages, where a third party, typically the developer or seller, pays a fee to the lender to buy down the payments and interest rate for the borrower for a specified time period; and a variety of alternative mortgage instruments.

Here are some things to remember about these loans. Lower initial payments usually come at a cost. Normally, the cost is the risk that payments could go above those for a fixed-rate mortgage. Sometimes, however, the cost may be hidden in a higher purchase price, as is the case in a buydown mortgage.

So when selecting a mortgage, consider your choices carefully. First, determine whether the mortgage will make the purchase possible. Then assess the risks of higher charges in the future.

KEY CONCEPTS

Adjustable rate mortgage   Loan arrangement in which the interest rate rises or falls in line with a prespecified index.

Adjusted sales price   Full sales contract price, less selling expense and fixing-up expense.

Annual stabilized income   Income from salary or wages, plus two years' experience of income from bonuses, commissions, etc.

Conventional loan   Real estate loan that is not FHA-insured or VA-guaranteed.

Date of sale   Date on which title passes. Used for purposes of determining capital gain or rollover.

FHA mortgage   Lender is insured against loss on a mortgage loan by the Federal Housing Administration.

Fixed-rate mortgage   A loan on which one interest rate applies over the entire life.

Housing expenses   Payments for housing; includes debt service, hazard insurance, and property taxes.

Junior mortgage   Generic name for any mortgage lower in priority than a first mortgage.

PITI   Principal, interest, property taxes, insurance; components of housing expense.

Purchase-money mortgage   Mortgage that pledges a property as collateral for a loan to finance its purchase.

Rent capitalization   Conversion of rent demanded (or payable) into the market value of a dwelling unit.

Rollover   Buying or building a replacement residence, at a cost equal to or greater than the adjusted sale price of the previous residence, within 24 months to postpone any capital gains tax payable.

Second mortgage   A mortgage immediately behind another mortgage in priority of claim.

33 percent rule   An FHLMC guideline that allows up to 33 percent of annual stabilized income for housing expenses and other required periodic payments, such as outlays for utilities, installment debt, alimony, and child support.

25 percent rule   An FHLMC guideline that allows 25 percent of annual stabilized income for housing expenses.

VA mortgage   A mortgage loan on which the lender is guaranteed against loss by the Veteran's Administration; also called a GI loan.

Wraparound mortgage   A mortgage that envelops an existing mortgage on a property although it is subordinate to the existing loan.

QUESTIONS FOR REVIEW AND DISCUSSION

1. Explain briefly how annual stabilized income relates to the affordability of housing.

2. What is the 33 percent rule? How is it applied?

3. Identify and explain two tax benefits that an owner gets which are not generally available to a renter.

4. Are there any direct tax benefits that a tenant gets which are not available to an owner? Are there any indirect benefits?

5. Explain the rollover of a personal residence in detail. What is the time frame for allowing the rollover of capital gains into the purchase of another residence?

6. Does an owner realize any intangible benefits not available to a renter? If so, what are they?

7. What extra costs does an owner have that a tenant does not have?

8. Currently what percentage of residential units are owner-occupied?

9. Other than debt service, what are some expenses associated with home owner-ship?

10. Are depreciation allowances allowed on personal residences?

11. What payments made by homeowners are tax deductible?

12. What is the maximum allowable tax deduction for interest payments?

13. What kind of capital gains exclusion is allowed for homeowners 55 and over?

14. Discuss the advantages and disadvantages of owning a home.

15. What are the different kinds of mortgages available to a homebuyer? How do they differ?

16. How does a reverse-annuity mortgage work? Who would be most likely to use this method as a financing tool?

PROBLEMS

1. Assume a couple is interested in purchasing a home and has an annual stabilized income of $70,000. Taxes and insurance are expected to be 5 percent of the market value of the home. Current loan terms for a fixed-rate mortgage on an owner-occupied house are: 80 percent loan-to-value ratio, 30 years, 8 percent, annual amortization. Using the 25 percent rule, what is the maximum purchase price of a home these buyers can afford?

2. A property was purchased for $55,000 in 1983. In 1989, the owner sold the home for $78,000. Selling expenses were 6 percent of the sales price. If a new home were purchased by the same individual within two years for $95,000, what would be the taxable capital gain? What would be the new adjusted basis?

3. A $90,000 RAM is issued to an elderly couple at 8 percent, with a monthly amortization period of ten years. How much will the couple receive each month? What is the balance owed on the mortgage at the end of year 5?

4. A buyer has an annual stabilized income of $50,000 and can afford only a 10 percent down payment to buy a house. Local lenders are making 90 percent loans at 12 percent, compounded monthly, with amortization over 25 years. Hazard insurance and property taxes in the community generally run about 2 percent of a house's market value. Using the 25 percent rule, how much housing can the buyer reasonably afford?

5. Assume that the buyer in problem 4 has monthly installment payments of $300. Using the 33 percent guideline, how much housing can the buyer afford?

6. The Nutleys ask you how much housing they can afford. You determine that they have a gross income of $36,000. You know that local lenders are making 90 percent, 30-year loans at 9 percent, compounded monthly. Also, property taxes and hazard insurance come to 2.4 percent per year in your experience. The Nutleys tell you they have long-term installment obligations of $240 per month.

a. How much housing can they afford under the 25 percent rule?

b. How much under the 33 percent rule?

c. Check your answers by comparing the monthly payments on your answers in a and b with the amounts the Nutleys can afford.

7. A couple, both 55, sell their house, realizing a $75,000 long-term capital gain. They decide to avoid taxes on the gain by taking advantage of the $125,000 exemption allowed senior citizens. They then buy a smaller house for $80,000, the value of which increases sharply. Six years later they sell the house for $125,000, net, after selling expenses. They take their situation to a certified public accountant, asking that the $45,000 gain be offset by the $50,000 of the senior citizen exemption they did not use earlier. What is the result?

8. Local lenders are making loans at 9 percent, compounded monthly. The buyers figure that they can afford $700 per month for housing. They have located a condominium, valued at $75,000, which can be rented for $700. On the basis of rent capitalization, would you advise them to rent or to consider buying? What would the result be if the market interest rate were 12 percent? 15 percent?

9. An employee is being transferred to Cambridge, Mass., for a two-year assignment. The employee has located a house for $100,000. A similar house is available at a rental of $1,000 per month, which is the amount the employee can afford for housing. Housing values in the community are expected to increase 11 percent per year for the next few years. All other information is the same as shown in Figure 22–2. You are asked, as a housing consultant, whether to buy or rent. On the basis of a two-year, net after tax, buy or rent comparison, what do you advise?

10. A 24-year loan is initiated for $50,000 at 9 percent with annual debt service. Assume it is an adjustable-rate mortgage, with interest rates subject to change at the end of every third year. At the end of year 3, the market interest rate is 12 percent.

a. What is the loan balance and debt service at the beginning of year 4?

b. Suppose that the ARM has a life-of-loan interest rate cap of 11 percent. Shortly after initiation, the index interest rate increases to 13 percent and remains there. What is the loan balance at the end of year 3? What is the annual debt service in year 4?

11. You have decided to purchase a home. The cost of the house is $150,000 and you have four financing options available to you (assume 30-year mortgages with monthly payments and full amortization for all four options).

Mortgage A: 9 percent fixed-rate mortgage, with no discount points or prepayment penalty. The loan-to-value ratio is 80 percent.
Mortgage B: 8.5 percent, fixed-rate mortgage, with 2 discount points and no prepayment penalty. The loan-to-value ratio is also 80 percent.
Mortgage C: Adjustable-rate mortgage, with 1 discount point and no prepayment penalty. The current contract rate is 5.5 percent. The rate is indexed to the prime rate plus 250 basis points. The loan has a floor of 4.5 percent and a cap of 15.5 percent. Adjustments are made annually, with a maximum periodic adjustment of 200 basis points. The loan-to-value ratio is 80 percent.
Mortgage D: Adjustable-rate mortgage, with no discount points and a 2 percent prepayment penalty. The contract rate is 6 percent and is indexed to the prime

rate plus 300 basis points. The loan has a floor of 5.5 percent and a cap of 14 percent. Adjustments are made annually, with a maximum periodic adjustment of 150 basis points. The loan-to-value ratio is 80 percent.

a. Which of the two fixed-rate mortgages will have the lower effective cost to you if you live in the house for 20 years?

b. Which of the two adjustable-rate mortgages will have the lower effective cost to you if you live in the house for five years? Assume that the prime rate increases by 175 basis points each year.

c. Which of the four mortgages will have the lowest effective cost to you if you live in the house for five years? Assume that the prime rate increases by 150 basis points each year.

CHAPTER 23

MORTGAGE UNDERWRITING

The house was more covered with mortgages than paint.

George Ade, American humorist and playwright

Lenders are continually faced with a wide variety of loan requests. The owner of a shopping center, for example, may want to expand the business and increase profits by completely renovating the property. Or the shopping center owner may want to attract new customers by including another full-line department store. An investor looking for profit opportunities may want to buy a piece of land next to a big motel on the outskirts of town and put up a small 20-room motel with a mama-papa management team. A trial attorney just out of law school may want to buy a condominium close to work. In each case, the lender will be asked to invest in the project by advancing a sum of money. And in each case the lender must decide whether the borrower has the ability and the desire to meet the down payment and the monthly or annual debt service payments.

If the lender is rational, he or she will evaluate both the borrower and the property, weighing the risk of default against potential profits. Only if the borrower can reasonably be expected to meet regular monthly or annual payments without difficulty will the loan be considered. Nor does the lender evaluate only the borrower's ability to meet the debt service payments. As long as there is any probability of default, the lender will also be concerned as to whether the property will provide enough value so that the lender can expect to recover his or her investment.

From the lender's point of view, deciding whether the borrower qualifies for a mortgage is termed *mortgage underwriting*. For lender and borrower alike the mortgage underwriting process begins with a loan application and interview.

APPLYING FOR A LOAN

Exactly what is involved in obtaining a real estate loan? Lenders, for the most part, want to make loans on high-quality properties to creditworthy borrowers. On the other hand, borrowers want the lowest possible interest rates and, therefore, shop lenders and terms. A borrower may also negotiate to avoid interest rate adjustments and penalties for early repayment. The application process is where lenders and borrowers come together.

A brief overview of the mechanics of the loan application process seems appropriate before getting into legalities and negotiations. Initial information requirements are well illustrated by the Federal Home Loan Mortgage Corporation/Federal National Mortgage Association (FHLMC/FNMA) loan application form shown in Figure 23-1. The entire application procedure involves several basic steps:

1. The prospective borrower shops to obtain information on the financial terms and repayment schedule required by different lenders.

Uniform Residential Loan Application

FIGURE 23-1
FHLMC/FNMA Loan
Application

This application is designed to be completed by the applicant(s) with the lender's assistance. Applicants should complete this form as "Borrower" or "Co Borrower", as applicable. Co-Borrower information must also be provided (and the appropriate box checked) when ☐ the income or assets of a person other than the "Borrower" (including the Borrower's spouse) will be used as a basis for loan qualification or ☐ the income or assets of the Borrower's spouse will not be used as a basis for loan qualification, but his or her liabilities must be considered because the Borrower resides in a community property state, the security property is located in a community property state, or the Borrower is relying on other property located in a community property state as a basis for repayment of the loan.

I. TYPE OF MORTGAGE AND TERMS OF LOAN

Mortgage Applied for:	☐ VA ☐ Conventional ☐ Other:		Agency Case Number	Lender Case No.
	☐ FHA ☐ FmHA			

Amount	Interest Rate	No. of Months	Amortization Type	☐ Fixed Rate ☐ GPM	☐ Other (explain): ____ ☐ ARM (type): ____
$	%				

II. PROPERTY INFORMATION AND PURPOSE OF LOAN

Subject Property Address (street, city, state, & ZIP)	No. of Units

Legal Description of Subject Property (attach description if necessary)	Year Built

Purpose of Loan	☐ Purchase ☐ Construction ☐ Other (explain):	Property will be: ☐ Primary Residence ☐ Secondary Residence ☐ Investment
	☐ Refinance ☐ Construction-Permanent	

Complete this line if construction or construction-permanent loan.

Year Lot Acquired	Original Cost	Amount Existing Liens	(a) Present Value of Lot	(b) Cost of Improvements	Total (a + b)
	$	$	$	$	$

Complete this line if this is a refinance loan.

Year Acquired	Original Cost	Amount Existing Liens	Purpose of Refinance	Describe Improvements ☐ made ☐ to be made
	$	$		Cost: $

Title will be held in what Name(s)	Manner in which Title will be held	Estate will be held in: ☐ Fee Simple ☐ Leasehold (show expiration date)

Source of Down Payment, Settlement Charges and/or Subordinate Financing (explain)

III. BORROWER INFORMATION

Borrower	Co Borrower

Borrower's Name (include Jr. or Sr. if applicable)	Co-Borrower's Name (include Jr. or Sr. if applicable)

Social Security Number	Home Phone (incl. area code)	Age	Yrs. School	Social Security Number	Home Phone (incl. area code)	Age	Yrs. School

☐ Married ☐ Unmarried (include single, divorced, widowed) ☐ Separated	Dependents (not listed by Co-Borrower) no. / ages	☐ Married ☐ Unmarried (include single, divorced, widowed) ☐ Separated	Dependents (not listed by Borrower) no. / ages

Present Address (street, city, state, ZIP) ☐ Own ☐ Rent ____ No. Yrs.	Present Address (street, city, state, ZIP) ☐ Own ☐ Rent ____ No. Yrs.

If residing at present address for less than two years, complete the following:

Former Address (street, city, state, ZIP) ☐ Own ☐ Rent ____ No. Yrs.	Former Address (street, city, state, ZIP) ☐ Own ☐ Rent ____ No. Yrs.

Former Address (street, city, state, ZIP) ☐ Own ☐ Rent ____ No. Yrs.	Former Address (street, city, state, ZIP) ☐ Own ☐ Rent ____ No. Yrs.

IV. EMPLOYMENT INFORMATION

Borrower	Co Borrower

Name & Address of Employer ☐ Self Employed	Yrs. on this job	Name & Address of Employer ☐ Self Employed	Yrs. on this job
	Yrs. employed in this line of work/profession		Yrs. employed in this line of work/profession

Position/Title/Type of Business	Business Phone (incl. area code)	Position/Title/Type of Business	Business Phone (incl. area code)

If employed in current position for less than two years or if currently employed in more than one position, complete the following:

Name & Address of Employer ☐ Self Employed	Dates (from - to)	Name & Address of Employer ☐ Self Employed	Dates (from - to)
	Monthly Income $		Monthly Income $

Position/Title/Type of Business	Business Phone (incl. area code)	Position/Title/Type of Business	Business Phone (incl. area code)

Name & Address of Employer ☐ Self Employed	Dates (from - to)	Name & Address of Employer ☐ Self Employed	Dates (from - to)
	Monthly Income $		Monthly Income $

Position/Title/Type of Business	Business Phone (incl. area code)	Position/Title/Type of Business	Business Phone (incl. area code)

Freddie Mac Form 65   10/92   Page 1 of 4   Fannie Mae Form 1003   10/92

FIGURE 23-1
(continued)

V. MONTHLY INCOME AND COMBINED HOUSING EXPENSE INFORMATION

Gross Monthly Income	Borrower	Co-Borrower	Total	Combined Monthly Housing Expense	Present	Proposed
Base Empl. Income *	$	$	$	Rent	$	
Overtime				First Mortgage (P&I)		$
Bonuses				Other Financing (P&I)		
Commissions				Hazard Insurance		
Dividends/Interest				Real Estate Taxes		
Net Rental Income				Mortgage Insurance		
Other (before completing, see the notice in "describe other income" below)				Homeowner Assn. Dues		
				Other:		
Total	$	$	$	**Total**	$	$

* Self Employed Borrower(s) may be required to provide additional documentation such as tax returns and financial statements.

Describe Other Income   *Notice:* Alimony, child support, or separate maintenance income need not be revealed if the Borrower (B) or Co-Borrower (C) does not choose to have it considered for repaying this loan.

B/C		Monthly Amount
		$

VI. ASSETS AND LIABILITIES

This Statement and any applicable supporting schedules may be completed jointly by both married and unmarried Co-Borrowers if their assets and liabilities are sufficiently joined so that the Statement can be meaningfully and fairly presented on a combined basis; otherwise separate Statements and Schedules are required. If the Co-Borrower section was completed about a spouse, this Statement and supporting schedules must be completed about that spouse also.   Completed ☐ Jointly ☐ Not Jointly

ASSETS Description	Cash or Market Value	Liabilities and Pledged Assets. List the creditor's name, address and account number for all outstanding debts, including automobile loans, revolving charge accounts, real estate loans, alimony, child support, stock pledges, etc. Use continuation sheet, if necessary. Indicate by (*) those liabilities which will be satisfied upon sale of real estate owned or upon refinancing of the subject property.		
		LIABILITIES	Monthly Payt. & Mos. Left to Pay	Unpaid Balance
Cash deposit toward purchase held by:	$	Name and address of Company	$ Payt./Mos.	$
List checking and savings accounts below				
Name and address of Bank, S&L, or Credit Union				
		Acct. no.		
		Name and address of Company	$ Payt./Mos.	$
Acct. no.	$			
Name and address of Bank, S&L, or Credit Union				
		Acct. no.		
		Name and address of Company	$ Payt./Mos.	$
Acct. no.	$			
Name and address of Bank, S&L, or Credit Union				
		Acct. no.		
		Name and address of Company	$ Payt./Mos.	$
Acct. no.	$			
Name and address of Bank, S&L, or Credit Union				
		Acct. no.		
		Name and address of Company	$ Payt./Mos.	$
Acct. no.	$			
Stocks & Bonds (Company name/number & description)	$			
		Acct. no.		
		Name and address of Company	$ Payt./Mos.	$
Life insurance net cash value	$			
Face amount: $				
Subtotal Liquid Assets	$			
Real estate owned (enter market value from schedule of real estate owned)	$	Acct. no.		
Vested interest in retirement fund	$	Name and address of Company	$ Payt./Mos.	$
Net worth of business(es) owned (attach financial statement)	$			
Automobiles owned (make and year)	$			
		Acct. no.		
		Alimony/Child Support/Separate Maintenance Payments Owed to:	$	
Other Assets (itemize)	$	Job Related Expense (child care, union dues, etc.)	$	
		Total Monthly Payments	$	
Total Assets a.	$		**Total Liabilities b.**	$

Freddie Mac Form 65   10/92   Page 2 of 4   Fannie Mae Form 1003   10/92

2. The prospective borrower completes and submits a loan application form to the lender of choice.

3. The lender provides a good-faith estimate of closing costs to borrower.

4. The lender obtains a credit report on applicant.

5. If a residential loan is requested, the lender verifies the applicant's employment data. If the borrower is self-employed, or is an investor, the lender is likely to ask to see the borrower's income tax returns for at least the two immediately prior years.

6. The lender verifies that equity funds are available to meet down payment and closing cost requirements.

7. The lender obtains an appraisal of the subject property to assure that its market value represents adequate security for the requested loan; that is, that an acceptable loan-to-value ratio is present.

8. Approval for loan insurance or guarantee is obtained from the Federal Housing Administration (FHA), a private mortgage insurance company, or the Veterans Administration (VA).

9. The lender's loan committee reviews all information and makes a go or no go decision. If go, the loan is made; if no go, the applicant is notified, and the file is closed.

10. The lender obtains evidence that the title to the property is free from significant defects. This is usually done through a title report which shows the current state of the title along with recorded objections to clear title.

Borrowers pay all the costs involved in obtaining a mortgage. The costs can include a credit report, an appraisal, a title report, attorney's fee, and recording fees. Additional information and documentation are required for FHA, VA, or private mortgage insurance.

LOAN DOCUMENTS

Two separate legal instruments are executed to document a loan on real estate. The first is either a mortgage or a *trust deed* in which title to the property is transferred to a third party as security for an obligation owed by the borrower. The second is a promissory note; in some states, a personal bond is used instead. A *promissory note* is a written commitment to repay a debt, and it serves as evidence of the debt. A *personal bond* is an interest-bearing certificate containing a promise to pay a certain sum on a specified date, and thus is similar to a promissory note. Usually only the mortgage or trust deed is recorded. Figure 23–2 summarizes the purposes and legal requirements for loan documentation.

Even though mortgages and trust deeds are both commonly referred to as mortgages, they are distinct instruments, with very different consequences if default occurs. In fact, a mortgage or a trust deed only become meaningful if default occurs.

Both a mortgage and a trust deed pledge real property as security for a debt or other obligation. The property remains pledged until the debt is cleared or satisfied. The borrower in the contract is called the *mortgagor;* the lender is the *mortgagee.*

FIGURE 23–2

Legal Instruments
Required for Loan
Documentation

DOCUMENT	PURPOSE OR EFFECT	LEGAL REQUIREMENTS
Mortgage	Creates and pledges a property interest for the protection of the mortgagee-lender	1. In writing 2. Adequately identify property 3. Identify borrower and lender (and trustee)
Trust deed	Creates a property interest to be held by the trustee for the lender-beneficiary	4. Proper wording of pledge 5. Signature of mortgagor-borrower 6. Voluntary delivery and acceptance
Promissory note or personal bond	Creates a personal obligation of borrower to repay debt according to agreed terms or schedule	1. A written instrument 2. A borrower (obligee) with contractual capacity 3. A lender (obligor) with contractual capacity 4. A promise or covenant by borrower to pay a specific sum 5. Terms of payment 6. A default clause, including reference to the mortgage or trust deed 7. Proper execution 8. Voluntary delivery and acceptance

The mortgage and promissory note used as illustrations later in this chapter were developed jointly by the Federal National Mortgage Association (FNMA) and the Federal Home Loan Mortgage Corporation (FHLMC). These instruments are as uniform as possible from state to state.

Mortgages. A mortgage pledges property as security (collateral) for a debt. The arrangement gives the lender the legal right to foreclose—that is, have the property sold to satisfy the debt if it is not repaid on schedule. At the same time, the borrower gets the right to occupy and use the property as long as payments are made. The accompanying promissory note, which is a separate agreement, evidences the debt. The technical name for this is *hypothecation,* meaning the borrower retains the right of occupancy and use of the property while it serves as collateral for a loan. A mortgage is a two-party transaction, as shown in Figure 23–3.

Trust Deeds. A trust deed is often used in place of a mortgage, for reasons of time and convenience to the lender should default occur. A trust deed, instead of being merely a claim or lien on the property, actually conveys title to the pledged property to a third party (trustee) to be held as security for the debt owed the lender, who is also the beneficiary of the arrangement. A separate promissory note is still used to evidence the debt.

Note that a trust deed creates a three-party arrangement, as shown in Figure 23–4. The owner-borrower-trustor receives money and, at the same time, (1) conveys title to the trustee and (2) gives a promissory note to the lender-beneficiary. The

FIGURE 23–3
The Two-Party Mortgage Transaction

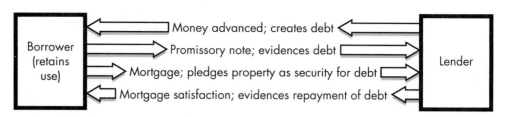

trustee holds title to the property as security for the lender in case of default by the borrower.

If default occurs, the trustee usually has automatic power of sale. *Power of sale* means the right to sell without court proceedings, which considerably shortens the time required by the lender to get satisfaction. Thus, after three or four payments are missed, the lender may request sale, with satisfaction often realized in from 6 to 12 months.

Promissory Notes. A promissory note or bond evidences debt, makes it the personal obligation of the borrower, and gives life to a mortgage or trust deed. The note also contains the financial terms surrounding the debt. If the debt is unenforceable for any reason, the mortgage or trust deed is also unenforceable (see Figure 23–5).

The note, which is a personal obligation of the borrower, expands the lender's rights in case of default. If only a mortgage or trust deed were used, the borrower might abandon the property, move elsewhere, and have no further personal obligation or liability regarding the loan. The note is enforceable wherever the borrower might take up residence.

In the note shown, the amount and date appear in the heading, followed by numbered, specific clauses.

1. **Mortgagee and terms.** The mortgagee is identified, along with the interest rate, maturity date, monthly debt service amount, and place of payment. Payments are to be made on the first day of each month at the Urbandale Savings and Loan.

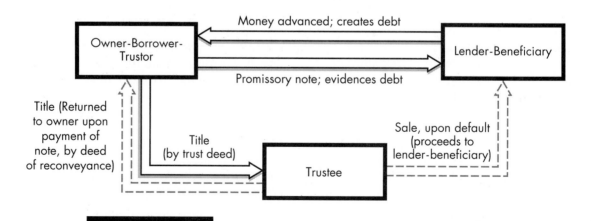

FIGURE 23–4
The Three-Party Trust Deed Arrangement

NOTE

(Multifamily)

US $ 500,000 ....

Urbandale

...., Texas

City

January 15 ...., 19 89

1. FOR VALUE RECEIVED, the undersigned promise to pay ....Urbandale Savings and Loan Association
...., or order, the principal sum of Five Hundred Thousand
...and no/100 ($500,000.00)................................. Dollars, with interest on the un-
paid principal balance from the date of this Note, until paid, at the rate of ...10.... percent per annum. The
principal and interest shall be payable at Urbandale Savings and Loan Association, 300 North
Main, Urbandale
...Four Thousand Five Hundred Forty Three and fifty......... in consecutive monthly installments of
....) on the ...1st............. day of each month beginning ...March 1st.........., 1989
(herein "amortization commencement date"), until the entire indebtedness evidenced hereby is fully paid,
except that any remaining indebtedness, if not sooner paid, shall be due and payable on the ..1st........
day of ...February.................., 2006.......

2. If the amortization commencement date is more than .30.... calendar days from the date of this Note, the undersigned shall pay the holder hereof interest only on the outstanding principal balance of this Note at the rate
of .10.... percent per annum in ...one......... installments beginning .15 January.........
19..89.. and on ..no other.. thereafter until the
amortization commencement date, at which time any remaining interest payable pursuant to this paragraph (and
not paid as a part of the first monthly installment of principal and interest) shall be paid.

3. If any installment under this Note is not paid when due, the unpaid principal balance of this Note shall bear
interest during the period of delinquency at a rate of ..10..... percent per annum, or, if such increased rate of
interest may not be collected from the undersigned under applicable law, then at the maximum increased rate
of interest, if any, which may be collected from the undersigned under applicable law; and, at the option of
the holder hereof, the entire principal amount outstanding hereunder and accrued interest thereon shall at once
become due and payable. Failure to exercise such option shall not constitute a waiver of the right to exercise
such option if the undersigned is in default hereunder. In the event of any default in the payment of this Note,
and if the same is referred to an attorney at law for collection or suit is brought hereon, the undersigned shall
pay the holder hereof, in either case, all expenses and costs of collection, including, but not limited to, attorney's
fees.

4. The undersigned shall pay to the holder hereof on demand a late charge of ...2...... percent of any installment
not received by the holder hereof within ...15...... calendar days after the day the installment is due.

5. The undersigned shall have the right to prepay the principal amount outstanding hereunder in whole or
in part at any time after the amortization commencement date, provided that the holder hereof may require that
any partial prepayments shall be made on the date monthly installments are due and shall be in the amount of that
part of one or more monthly installments which would be applicable to principal and further provided that
the undersigned has given the holder hereof written notice of the amount intended to be prepaid at least
five (5)............ days prior to such prepayment. The undersigned shall pay the holder hereof together with
any prepayments (including prepayments occurring as a result of the acceleration by the holder hereof of the
principal amount of this Note, but excluding prepayments occurring because of the application by the holder hereof
of insurance or condemnation awards or proceeds pursuant to a Deed of Trust securing this Note) a percentage
of the amount prepaid in excess of any amount upon which a charge is not permitted by applicable law as
follows: ..4...... percent of the sums prepaid in the first year from the amortization commencement date, the
percentage payable declining by the number one (1) each year thereafter until the percentage payable is ...0.....
percent, which percentage shall be payable for the remaining term of the Note. Prepayments shall be applied
against the outstanding principal balance of this Note and shall not extend or postpone the due date of any
subsequent monthly installments or change the amount of such installments, unless the holder hereof shall
otherwise agree in writing.

6. From time to time, without affecting the obligation of the undersigned or the successors or assigns of the
undersigned to pay the outstanding principal balance of this Note and observe the covenants of the undersigned contained herein, without affecting the guaranty of any person, corporation, partnership or other
entity for payment of the outstanding principal balance of this Note, without giving notice to or obtaining the
consent of the undersigned, the successors or assigns of the undersigned or guarantors, and without liability
on the part of the holder hereof, the holder hereof may, at the option of the holder hereof, extend the time for
payment of said outstanding principal balance or any part thereof, reduce the payments thereon, release anyone
liable on any of said outstanding principal balance, accept a renewal of this Note, modify the terms and time
of payment of said outstanding principal balance or join in any extension or subordination agreement, and
agree in writing with the undersigned to modify the rate of interest or period of amortization of this Note or
change the amount of the monthly installments payable hereunder.

7. Presentment, notice of dishonor, and protest are hereby waived by all makers, sureties, guarantors and
endorsers hereof. This Note shall be the joint and several obligation of all makers, sureties, guarantors and
endorsers, and shall be binding upon them and their heirs, personal representatives, successors and assigns.

8. The indebtedness evidenced by this Note is secured by a Deed of Trust, dated of even date herewith, and
reference is made thereto for rights as to acceleration of the indebtedness evidenced by this Note.

Douglas Manor
2001 Century Drive
Urbandale, Texas 00000
(property address)

/s/Gerald I. Investor

/s/Nancy O. Investor

TEXAS—FHLMC—3/71—Over Four Families

FIGURE 23–5

A Promissory Note

2. **Adjustment of payment date.** Interest only is to be paid for first partial month so principal payments may be scheduled on the first of the month.

3. **Default and acceleration.** The noteholder has the right to accelerate or call for immediate payment of the entire outstanding principal plus accrued interest, if the contract is breached, e.g., by late payments. Acceleration is the first step in foreclosure.

4. **Late charge.** If payment is over 15 days late, a penalty is specified.

5. **Prepayment provisions.** Borrower may prepay, but only under stated conditions. The prepayment penalty, as negotiated when the loan was taken out, is included as part of the agreement.

6. **Negotiability.** The security and negotiability of the note is protected by stating that any modification to the terms shall not affect the obligation of the borrower to abide by the terms and to repay the principal of the note.

7. **Joint and several.** Makers, endorsers, and others waive the right to protest or to deny the note as their obligation, individually or jointly.

8. **Reference to security instrument.** This promissory note is secured by either a mortgage or a trust deed.

THE DEBT-FINANCING PROCESS

The debt-financing process breaks down into three basic stages: (1) initiation, (2) interim or servicing, and (3) termination. These phases apply, regardless of the type of loan involved (see Figure 23–6).

Loan Initiation

A lender must make several basic decisions in making the loan. The applicant must be judged to have an acceptable credit rating and adequate income as evidence of being financially responsible. Also, the relative size of the loan must be determined. A residential loan is not likely to be initiated in excess of 90 to 95 percent of the market value of the pledged property. Assuming that all the lender's criteria are met, the loan application is approved. The borrower signs the mortgage and note and meets other settlement requirements, and the loan contract is made.

FIGURE 23–6
Decisions or Actions Required in the Debt-Financing Process

INITIATION PHASE	INTERIM OR SERVICING PHASE	TERMINATION PHASE
Loan processing	Debt service payments	Mutual agreement
Application	made on schedule	Pay on schedule
Borrower analysis	Possible change of	Default and
Property analysis	ownership with	Voluntary sale, or
Financial analysis	Assumption of loan, or	Deed in lieu of foreclo-
Letter of commitment	Taking subject to	sure, or
Loan closing		Foreclosure and sale

Interim or Servicing Phase

As long as all terms of the contract are met, the agreement is continued without interruption. The borrower must make scheduled payments of principal and interest to the lender and meet other obligations as set forth in the trust deed.

A borrower may, unless prohibited by an *alienation* or *due-on-sale* clause, sell the pledged property without paying off the loan. (A due-on-sale clause means exactly what it says. If the property is sold, the loan must be paid off with the proceeds of the sale.) The life of the loan is thereby continued even though ownership of the property has changed. The new buyer, in these circumstances, may take title "subject to" the loan or may take title and "assume and promise to pay" the loan. The distinction between the two alternatives is substantial. Most new loan agreements include "due-on-sale" clauses to prohibit the sale of the pledged property and continuation of the loan without prior consent from the lender.

Taking Subject to a Loan.   *Taking title subject to a loan* means that the buyer does not take over legal responsibility for the repayment of the debt. Thus, if unable to meet required debt service payments, the buyer may simply walk away from the property without further obligation to the lender.

Even so, it is usually in the buyer's interest to continue debt service payments as long as the buyer has an equity interest in the property. Not only would the buyer risk the loss of the property in this case, but could also lose his or her equity.

Assuming and Promising to Pay a Loan.   Agreement by a grantee (usually a buyer) to accept responsibility for repayment of an existing loan against a property is termed *assumption.* The buyer agrees to pay debt service and to pay any deficiency should a default occur. Unless released, the seller continues to be liable to the lender for payment of the loan as well. The release of a seller-borrower in an assumption is termed *novation,* which means that a new contractual obligation has been substituted for an old one by mutual agreement of all parties concerned.

Loan Termination

Termination by Satisfying the Contract.   Upon meeting all the requirements of a mortgage loan contract, a borrower is released from the obligation and is entitled to a receipt acknowledging payment, variously known as a *mortgage satisfaction,* a release, or a discharge. Recording a release ends the lien or claim against the pledged property. Under trust deed financing, the trustee provides a deed of release to clear the record.

Termination by Mutual Agreement.   A borrower may refinance or recast a loan prior to complete repayment, provided the lender or the contract so permits. *Refinancing* means obtaining a new and larger loan, usually at new terms. *Recasting* means keeping the same size loan but changing the interest rate and/or the amortization period, usually to reduce required debt service. Finally, the loan may be prepaid, as when a property is sold and the buyer obtains new financing.

What happens if a lender refuses to give the release? Almost all mortgages and trust deeds contain a defeasance clause to protect the borrower upon complete repayment of the loan. A *defeasance clause* states that if the loan and interest are paid in full, the rights and interests of the lender in the property cease. Thus, without a debt, the mortgage or trust deed is not enforceable.

Finally, even when a loan is in default, the parties may work out ways to avoid foreclosure. If the value exceeds the loan balance, the owner-borrower may voluntarily sell the property rather than go into foreclosure. Or, the parties may "voluntarily" agree to a *deed in lieu of foreclosure* instead. Such a compromise is often reached when the owner's equity in the property is less than the expected costs of foreclosure and yet the property has enough value so that the lender will not get seriously hurt. Effectively, the lender agrees to take the property in satisfaction of the debt if the borrower signs it over promptly. Both save time and money. Of course, the lender must then manage and dispose of the property.

Termination by Foreclosure.   Termination by *foreclosure* is a legal procedure whereby property used as security for a debt is sold to satisfy the debt in the event of default. The importance of the foreclosure suit, and the time required for satisfaction, depend on the state in which the property is located. Mortgage law in some states is based on the principles of title theory, while in other states it is based on lien theory. Some legal scholars say that there are also intermediate theory states, which use a blend of the other two. For brevity and clarity, the lien and title theories are emphasized here.

In early times, when real estate was used as security for a mortgage loan, the borrower deeded the property outright to the lender, who became its legal owner. The borrower usually retained possession, but upon default, the lender immediately took possession. Today, in title theory states, a limited form of legal title is still conveyed to the lender when a property is mortgaged. On default, the lender has the right of possession, which is not usually exercised for residences. For commercial and investment properties, the right is usually exercised through the collection of rents by the lender or the lender's representative. Even so, foreclosure proceedings must be initiated and completed by the mortgagee to clear the title.

In lien theory states, title remains with the borrower, who remains in possession, even after default. The mortgagee must initiate and complete foreclosure proceedings to get satisfaction from the pledged property. In intermediate states, title remains with the borrower until default, at which point it passes to the lender.

Over the years the distinction between title theory and lien theory states has blurred. The main difference is that rents from and possession of income properties are more readily realized by a lender in title theory states. In both classes of states, foreclosure means eventually selling the pledged property and paying off the debt with the proceeds.

Lenders recognize that borrowers miss payments occasionally and that most borrowers live up to their obligations if given an opportunity. In extended default, however, a lender must eventually file a foreclosure suit. The suit demands immediate payment of the debt and invokes the acceleration clause found in nearly every mortgage. The *acceleration* clause gives the lender the right to declare all remaining debt service payments of the loan due and payable immediately. Without an acceleration clause, a lender would have to sue for each payment as it became due. If the remaining debt service is not paid, the mortgage says that the property may be disposed of at a judicial or foreclosure sale to raise money to pay the debt. Figure 23–7 summarizes the mortgage foreclosure process.

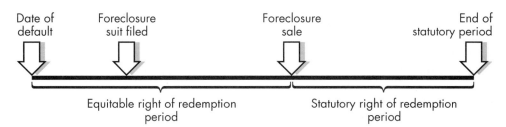

Date of default   Foreclosure suit filed   Foreclosure sale   End of statutory period

Equitable right of redemption period

Statutory right of redemption period

FIGURE 23–7
The Mortgage Foreclosure Process

A borrower may recover the property under an *equitable right of redemption* up until the foreclosure sale; this right is also called the *equity of redemption.* In exercising the equitable right of redemption, the borrower must make up all back payments and pay any costs of foreclosure incurred by the lender. The equitable right of redemption cannot be waived or cut off except by a foreclosure sale.

Some states give the borrower a statutory right of redemption after the foreclosure sale. A *statutory right of redemption* allows a borrower to recover foreclosed property for a limited time after the judicial sale by payment of the sales price plus foreclosure costs plus any other costs or losses incurred by the lender. For example, a foreclosed borrower might arrange another loan to redeem a property that is rapidly increasing in value. Or, a foreclosed borrower who suddenly comes into a large inheritance might then have the means to recover a favorite property.

Any surplus in a judicial sale goes to the borrower. In some states, if the price is less than the debt plus interest plus foreclosure costs, a lender may obtain a deficiency judgment against the borrower. A *deficiency judgment* is a judicial decree in favor of a lender for that portion of the mortgage debt and foreclosure costs that remains unsatisfied from the proceeds of the judicial sale. The judgment attaches to real and personal property of the mortgagor.

Trust Deed Foreclosure. Upon default, the trustee has authority, under the power of sale, in almost every state to promptly sell the pledged property. Many of the time-consuming requirements of mortgage foreclosure are therefore avoided. Further, the borrower is usually not entitled to any redemption rights after the trustee's sale. At the same time, a deficiency judgment is usually not recognized when the power of sale is exercised.

PROVISIONS OF MORTGAGES AND TRUST DEEDS

Mortgages and trust deeds, as mentioned, are very similar except in foreclosure. Each clearly establishes the realty that is to secure the debt. Each refers to a promissory note as evidence of the debt. Each identifies the borrower and the lender. Each contains an accurate legal description of the pledged property. Each must be signed by all parties with an interest in the realty, although the lender may sign neither.

The following are generally considered the most important borrower obligations and, hence, are consistently provided for in a mortgage or trust deed:

1. Make debt service payments in accordance with the note.
2. Pay all real estate taxes as they are levied.

3. Provide adequate hazard insurance to protect the lender against loss if the property is damaged or destroyed by fire, wind, or other peril.

4. Maintain the property in good repair at all times.

5. Obtain authorization from the lender before substantially altering the property.

In addition, the following are usually, but not always, provided for in a mortgage or trust deed:

1. Reserve right of lender or noteholder to inspect and protect the property.

2. Stipulate that debt service payments apply to taxes first, insurance second, interest third, and principal reduction fourth.

3. Stipulate that proceeds from insurance or condemnation go to the lender first, with any excess going to the borrower.

4. Reserve right of lender to approve transfer of ownership of secured property and assumption of the loan, including renegotiation of the interest rate (alienation or due-on-sale clause).

A prospective borrower needs to know and understand the specific clauses of the pledging document. The FNMA/FHLMC uniform instrument, discussed here, contains all these provisions, and more, within its 26 clauses or covenants. Much lender experience went into the development of this pledging document, so that it would have wide acceptability. Thus, rarely are provisions of a mortgage or trust deed negotiable to a borrower. Violation of any of the provisions constitutes default and sets the stage for possible foreclosure.

Each clause is discussed here only briefly as to purpose or content. The clauses are taken up in the same order as they appear in Figure 23–8. The reader may wish to closely study the specific wording of each convenant.

Uniform Covenants

1. *Payment of Principal and Interest.* Borrower agrees to make payments of debt service promptly and otherwise payments as agreed—as for example, for a late charge.

2. *Funds for Taxes and Insurance.* Borrower agrees to make monthly deposits with the lender for property taxes, hazard insurance, mortgage insurance (if any), water and sewer charges (if any), and rents or ground rents (if any). Lender is to make these annual payments when due.

3. *Application of Payments.* Noteholder is awarded some discretion in applying payments to taxes, insurance, interest, and rents. (For one- to four-family residences, payments apply first to insurance and taxes as necessary, second to interest on the principal, and third to reduction of the principal.)

4. *Charges, Liens.* Borrower agrees to pay any charges or liens against the property promptly. Also, the borrower agrees not to allow inferior or lower-priority liens to develop.

5. *Hazard Insurance.* Borrower is required to keep the property insured against fire and other hazards up to the amount of the loan balance, and against rent

losses, with the insurance proceeds payable to the noteholder and any excess paid the borrower.

6. *Property Preservation and Maintenance.* Borrower agrees to maintain the property in good repair and not permit its waste or deterioration. Borrower further agrees that fixtures, buildings, equipment, and other improvements shall not be removed or demolished without prior written consent from the noteholder.

7. *Use of Property.* Borrower agrees not to change the use of the property unless otherwise agreed to or required by law. Even a change in zoning is subject to review by the noteholder.

8. *Protection of Lender's Security.* Lender may protect the secured property by any actions necessary if the borrower fails to do so.

9. *Inspection.* Noteholder has reasonable entry to the property for inspections to assure its maintenance, safety, and proper operation.

10. *Books and Records.* Lender is permitted reasonable access to the borrower's books and other financial records concerning the property.

11. *Condemnation.* Proceeds from condemnation shall first go to pay lender expenses and the debt, with any excess going to the owner.

12. *Borrower Not Released.* Lender does not release the lien or forgive any of the borrower's repayment obligation by extending time for payment or by failure to press for payment. That is, the lender loses no rights by being courteous and considerate in dealing with the borrower or debtor.

13. *Forbearance by Lender not a Waiver.* Noteholder forbearance—postponing action to a later time—does not waive or preclude exercise of a right or remedy. Thus, for example, in default, payment may be demanded immediately or at a later time, without damage to the noteholder.

14. *Estoppel Certificate.* Borrower agrees to provide lender an estoppel certificate on demand. An estoppel certificate is a written statement that, when signed and given to another person, legally "stops" or prevents the signer from saying subsequently that the facts are different from those set forth. Such a certificate is usually used to verify the loan balance upon sale and assignment of the mortgage.

15. *UCC Security Agreement.* Borrower agrees to provide statements and to pay recording charges necessary to bring the mortgage into compliance with the Uniform Commercial Code.

16. *Leases of the Property.* Borrower promises to provide lender with copies of leases and side agreements with tenants, on request.

17. *Remedies Cumulative.* Lender remedies are distinct and cumulative and may therefore be exercised concurrently, independently, or successively.

18. *Acceleration Upon Borrower Insolvency.* Lender may require immediate repayment of the debt upon the borrower's insolvency, as evidenced by filing for bankruptcy.

19. *Transfer of Borrower's Interests: Assumption.* On sale or transfer of ownership, lender may require immediate repayment or renegotiate and extend the loan, e.g., at a higher interest rate. This is often called the due-on-sale or alienation clause.

FIGURE 23–8
FNMA/FHLMC Uniform
Instrument

Uniform Covenants. Borrower and Lender covenant and agree as follows:

1. PAYMENT OF PRINCIPAL AND INTEREST. Borrower shall promptly pay when due the principal of and interest on the indebtedness evidenced by the Note, any prepayment and late charges provided in the Note and all other sums secured by this Instrument.

2. FUNDS FOR TAXES, INSURANCE AND OTHER CHARGES. Subject to applicable law or to a written waiver by Lender, Borrower shall pay to Lender on the day monthly installments of principal or interest are payable under the Note (or on another day designated in writing by Lender), until the Note is paid in full, a sum (herein "Funds") equal to one-twelfth of (a) the yearly water and sewer rates and taxes and assessments which may be levied on the Property, (b) the yearly ground rents, if any, (c) the yearly premium installments for fire and other hazard insurance, rent loss insurance and such other insurance covering the Property as Lender may require pursuant to paragraph 5 hereof, (d) the yearly premium installments for mortgage insurance, if any, and (e) if this Instrument is on a leasehold, the yearly fixed rents, if any, under the ground lease, all as reasonably estimated initially and from time to time by Lender on the basis of assessments and bills and reasonable estimates thereof. Any waiver by Lender of a requirement that Borrower pay such Funds may be revoked by Lender, in Lender's sole discretion, at any time upon notice in writing to Borrower. Lender may require Borrower to pay to Lender, in advance, such other Funds for other taxes, charges, premiums, assessments and impositions in connection with Borrower or the Property which Lender shall reasonably deem necessary to protect Lender's interests (herein "Other Impositions"). Unless otherwise provided by applicable law, Lender may require Funds for Other Impositions to be paid by Borrower in a lump sum or in periodic installments, at Lender's option.

The Funds shall be held in an institution(s) the deposits or accounts of which are insured or guaranteed by a Federal or state agency (including Lender if Lender is such an institution). Lender shall apply the Funds to pay said rates, rents, taxes, assessments, insurance premiums and Other Impositions so long as Borrower is not in breach of any covenant or agreement of Borrower in this Instrument. Lender shall make no charge for so holding and applying the Funds, analyzing said account or for verifying and compiling said assessments and bills, unless Lender pays Borrower interest, earnings or profits on the Funds and applicable law permits Lender to make such a charge. Borrower and Lender may agree in writing at the time of execution of this Instrument that interest on the Funds shall be paid to Borrower, and unless such agreement is made or applicable law requires interest, earnings or profits to be paid, Lender shall not be required to pay Borrower any interest, earnings or profits on the Funds. Lender shall give to Borrower, without charge, an annual accounting of the Funds in Lender's normal format showing credits and debits to the Funds and the purpose for which each debit to the Funds was made. The Funds are pledged as additional security for the sums secured by this Instrument.

If the amount of the Funds held by Lender at the time of the annual accounting thereof shall exceed the amount deemed necessary by Lender to provide for the payment of water and sewer rates, taxes, assessments, insurance premiums, rents and Other Impositions, as they fall due, such excess shall be credited to Borrower on the next monthly installment or installments of Funds due. If at any time the amount of the Funds held by Lender shall be less than the amount deemed necessary by Lender to pay water and sewer rates, taxes, assessments, insurance premiums, rents and Other Impositions, as they fall due, Borrower shall pay to Lender any amount necessary to make up the deficiency within thirty days after notice from Lender to Borrower requesting payment thereof.

Upon Borrower's breach of any covenant or agreement of Borrower in this Instrument, Lender may apply, in any amount and in any order as Lender shall determine in Lender's sole discretion, any Funds held by Lender at the time of application (i) to pay rates, rents, taxes, assessments, insurance premiums and Other Impositions which are now or will hereafter become due, or (ii) as a credit against sums secured by this Instrument. Upon payment in full of all sums secured by this Instrument, Lender shall promptly refund to Borrower any Funds held by Lender.

3. APPLICATION OF PAYMENTS. Unless applicable law provides otherwise, all payments received by Lender from Borrower under the Note or this Instrument shall be applied by Lender in the following order of priority: (i) amounts payable to Lender by Borrower under paragraph 2 hereof; (ii) interest payable on the Note; (iii) principal of the Note; (iv) interest payable on advances made pursuant to paragraph 8 hereof; (v) principal of advances made pursuant to paragraph 8 hereof; (vi) interest payable on any Future Advance, provided that if more than one Future Advance is outstanding, Lender may apply payments received among the amounts of interest payable on the Future Advances in such order as Lender, in Lender's sole discretion, may determine; (vii) principal of any Future Advance, provided that if more than one Future Advance is outstanding, Lender may apply payments received among the principal balances of the Future Advances in such order as Lender, in Lender's sole discretion, may determine; and (viii) any other sums secured by this Instrument in such order as Lender, at Lender's option, may determine; provided, however, that Lender may, at Lender's option, apply any sums payable pursuant to paragraph 8 hereof prior to interest on and principal of the Note, but such application shall not otherwise affect the order of priority of application specified in this paragraph 3.

4. CHARGES; LIENS. Borrower shall pay all water and sewer rates, rents, taxes, assessments, premiums, and Other Impositions attributable to the Property at Lender's option in the manner provided under paragraph 2 hereof or, if not paid in such manner, by Borrower making payment, when due, directly to the payee thereof, or in such other manner as Lender may designate in writing. Borrower shall promptly furnish to Lender all notices of amounts due under this paragraph 4, and in the event Borrower shall make payment directly, Borrower shall promptly furnish to Lender receipts evidencing such payments. Borrower shall promptly discharge any lien which has, or may have, priority over or equality with, the lien of this Instrument, and Borrower shall pay, when due, the claims of all persons supplying labor or materials to or in connection with the Property. Without Lender's prior written permission, Borrower shall not allow any lien inferior to this Instrument to be perfected against the Property.

5. HAZARD INSURANCE. Borrower shall keep the improvements now existing or hereafter erected on the Property insured by carriers at all times satisfactory to Lender against loss by fire, hazards included within the term "extended coverage", rent loss and such other hazards, casualties, liabilities and contingencies as Lender (and, if this Instrument is on a leasehold, the ground lease) shall require and in such amounts and for such periods as Lender shall require. All premiums on insurance policies shall be paid, at Lender's option, in the manner provided under paragraph 2 hereof, or by Borrower making payment, when due, directly to the carrier, or in such other manner as Lender may designate in writing.

All insurance policies and renewals thereof shall be in a form acceptable to Lender and shall include a standard mortgage clause in favor of and in form acceptable to Lender. Lender shall have the right to hold the policies, and Borrower shall promptly furnish to Lender all renewal notices and all receipts of paid premiums. At least thirty days prior to the expiration date of a policy, Borrower shall deliver to Lender a renewal policy in form satisfactory to Lender. If this Instrument is on a leasehold, Borrower shall furnish Lender a duplicate of all policies, renewal notices, renewal policies and receipts of paid premiums if, by virtue of the ground lease, the originals thereof may not be supplied by Borrower to Lender.

In the event of loss, Borrower shall give immediate written notice to the insurance carrier and to Lender. Borrower hereby authorizes and empowers Lender as attorney-in-fact for Borrower to make proof of loss, to adjust and compromise any claim under insurance policies, to appear in and prosecute any action arising from such insurance policies, to collect and receive insurance proceeds, and to deduct therefrom Lender's expenses incurred in the collection of such proceeds; provided however, that nothing contained in this paragraph 5 shall require Lender to incur any expense or take any action hereunder. Borrower further authorizes Lender, at Lender's option, (a) to hold the balance of such proceeds to be used to reimburse Borrower for the cost of reconstruction or repair of the Property or (b) to apply the balance of such proceeds to the payment of the sums secured by this Instrument, whether or not then due, in the order of application set forth in paragraph 3 hereof (subject, however, to the rights of the lessor under the ground lease if this Instrument is on a leasehold).

If the insurance proceeds are held by Lender to reimburse Borrower for the cost of restoration and repair of the Property, the Property shall be restored to the equivalent of its original condition or such other condition as Lender may approve in writing. Lender may, at Lender's option, condition disbursement of said proceeds on Lender's approval of such plans and specifications of an architect satisfactory to Lender, contractor's cost estimates, architect's certificates, waivers of liens, sworn statements of mechanics and materialmen and such other evidence of costs, percentage completion of construction, application of payments, and satisfaction of liens as Lender may reasonably require. If the insurance proceeds are applied to the payment of the sums secured by this Instrument, any such application of proceeds to principal shall not extend or postpone the due dates of the monthly installments referred to in paragraphs 1 and 2 hereof or change the amounts of such installments. If the Property is sold pursuant to paragraph 27 hereof or if Lender acquires title to the Property, Lender shall have all of the right, title and interest of Borrower in and to any insurance policies and unearned premiums thereon and in and to the proceeds resulting from any damage to the Property prior to such sale or acquisition.

6. PRESERVATION AND MAINTENANCE OF PROPERTY; LEASEHOLDS. Borrower (a) shall not commit waste or permit impairment or deterioration of the Property, (b) shall not abandon the Property, (c) shall restore or repair promptly and in a good and workmanlike manner all

Uniform Covenants—Multifamily—1/77—**FNMA/FHLMC Uniform Instrument** *(page 3 of 8 pages)*

or any part of the Property to the equivalent of its original condition, or such other condition as Lender may approve in writing, in the event of any damage, injury or loss thereto, whether or not insurance proceeds are available to cover in whole or in part the costs of such restoration or repair, (d) shall keep the Property, including improvements, fixtures, equipment, machinery and appliances thereon in good repair and shall replace fixtures, equipment, machinery and appliances on the Property when necessary to keep such items in good repair, (e) shall comply with all laws, ordinances, regulations and requirements of any governmental body applicable to the Property, (f) shall provide for professional management of the Property by a residential rental property manager satisfactory to Lender pursuant to a contract approved by Lender in writing, unless such requirement shall be waived by Lender in writing, (g) shall generally operate and maintain the Property in a manner to ensure maximum rentals, and (h) shall give notice in writing to Lender of and, unless otherwise directed in writing by Lender, appear in and defend any action or proceeding purporting to affect the Property, the security of this Instrument or the rights or powers of Lender. Neither Borrower nor any tenant or other person shall remove, demolish or alter any improvement now existing or hereafter erected on the Property or any fixture, equipment, machinery or appliance in or on the Property except when incident to the replacement of fixtures, equipment, machinery and appliances with items of like kind.

If this Instrument is on a leasehold, Borrower (i) shall comply with the provisions of the ground lease, (ii) shall give immediate written notice to Lender of any default by lessor under the ground lease or of any notice received by Borrower from such lessor of any default under the ground lease by Borrower, (iii) shall exercise any option to renew or extend the ground lease and give written confirmation thereof to Lender within thirty days after such option becomes exercisable, (iv) shall give immediate written notice to Lender of the commencement of any remedial proceedings under the ground lease by any party thereto and, if required by Lender, shall permit Lender as Borrower's attorney-in-fact to control and act for Borrower in any such remedial proceedings and (v) shall within thirty days after request by Lender obtain from the lessor under the ground lease and deliver to Lender the lessor's estoppel certificate required thereunder, if any. Borrower hereby expressly transfers and assigns to Lender the benefit of all covenants contained in the ground lease, whether or not such covenants run with the land, but Lender shall have no liability with respect to such covenants nor any other covenants contained in the ground lease.

Borrower shall not surrender the leasehold estate and interests herein conveyed nor terminate or cancel the ground lease creating said estate and interests, and Borrower shall not, without the express written consent of Lender, alter or amend said ground lease. Borrower covenants and agrees that there shall not be a merger of the ground lease, or of the leasehold estate created thereby, with the fee estate covered by the ground lease by reason of said leasehold estate or said fee estate, or any part of either, coming into common ownership, unless Lender shall consent in writing to such merger; if Borrower shall acquire such fee estate, then this Instrument shall simultaneously and without further action be spread so as to become a lien on such fee estate.

7. USE OF PROPERTY. Unless required by applicable law or unless Lender has otherwise agreed in writing, Borrower shall not allow changes in the use for which all or any part of the Property was intended at the time this Instrument was executed. Borrower shall not initiate or acquiesce in a change in the zoning classification of the Property without Lender's prior written consent.

8. PROTECTION OF LENDER'S SECURITY. If Borrower fails to perform the covenants and agreements contained in this Instrument, or if any action or proceeding is commenced which affects the Property or title thereto or the interest of Lender therein, including, but not limited to, eminent domain, insolvency, code enforcement, or arrangements or proceedings involving a bankrupt or decedent, then Lender at Lender's option may make such appearances, disburse such sums and take such action as Lender deems necessary, in its sole discretion, to protect Lender's interest, including, but not limited to, (i) disbursement of attorney's fees, (ii) entry upon the Property to make repairs, (iii) procurement of satisfactory insurance as provided in paragraph 5 hereof, and (iv) if this Instrument is on a leasehold, exercise of any option to renew or extend the ground lease on behalf of Borrower and the curing of any default of Borrower in the terms and conditions of the ground lease.

Any amounts disbursed by Lender pursuant to this paragraph 8, with interest thereon, shall become additional indebtedness of Borrower secured by this Instrument. Unless Borrower and Lender agree to other terms of payment, such amounts shall be immediately due and payable and shall bear interest from the date of disbursement at the rate stated in the Note unless collection from Borrower of interest at such rate would be contrary to applicable law, in which event such amounts shall bear interest at the highest rate which may be collected from Borrower under applicable law. Borrower hereby covenants and agrees that Lender shall be subrogated to the lien of any mortgage or other lien discharged, in whole or in part, by the indebtedness secured hereby. Nothing contained in this paragraph 8 shall require Lender to incur any expense or take any action hereunder.

9. INSPECTION. Lender may make or cause to be made reasonable entries upon and inspections of the Property.

10. BOOKS AND RECORDS. Borrower shall keep and maintain at all times at Borrower's address stated below, or such other place as Lender may approve in writing, complete and accurate books of accounts and records adequate to reflect correctly the results of the operation of the Property and copies of all written contracts, leases and other instruments which affect the Property. Such books, records, contracts, leases and other instruments shall be subject to examination and inspection at any reasonable time by Lender. Upon Lender's request, Borrower shall furnish to Lender, within one hundred and twenty days after the end of each fiscal year of Borrower, a balance sheet, a statement of income and expenses of the Property and a statement of changes in financial position, each in reasonable detail and certified by Borrower and, if Lender shall require, by an independent certified public accountant. Borrower shall furnish, together with the foregoing financial statements and at any other time upon Lender's request, a rent schedule for the Property, certified by Borrower, showing the name of each tenant, and for each tenant, the space occupied, the lease expiration date, the rent payable and the rent paid.

11. CONDEMNATION. Borrower shall promptly notify Lender of any action or proceeding relating to any condemnation or other taking, whether direct or indirect, of the Property, or part thereof, and Borrower shall appear in and prosecute any such action or proceeding unless otherwise directed by Lender in writing. Borrower authorizes Lender, at Lender's option, as attorney-in-fact for Borrower, to commence, appear in and prosecute, in Lender's or Borrower's name, any action or proceeding relating to any condemnation or other taking of the Property, whether direct or indirect, and to settle or compromise any claim in connection with such condemnation or other taking. The proceeds of any award, payment or claim for damages, direct or consequential, in connection with any condemnation or other taking, whether direct or indirect, of the Property, or part thereof, or for conveyances in lieu of condemnation, are hereby assigned to and shall be paid to Lender subject, if this Instrument is on a leasehold, to the rights of lessor under the ground lease.

Borrower authorizes Lender to apply such awards, payments, proceeds or damages, after the deduction of Lender's expenses incurred in the collection of such amounts, at Lender's option, to restoration or repair of the Property or to payment of the sums secured by this Instrument, whether or not then due, in the order of application set forth in paragraph 3 hereof, with the balance, if any, to Borrower. Unless Borrower and Lender otherwise agree in writing, any application of proceeds to principal shall not extend or postpone the due date of the monthly installments referred to in paragraphs 1 and 2 hereof or change the amount of such installments. Borrower agrees to execute such further evidence of assignment of any awards, proceeds, damages or claims arising in connection with such condemnation or taking as Lender may require.

12. BORROWER AND LIEN NOT RELEASED. From time to time, Lender may, at Lender's option, without giving notice to or obtaining the consent of Borrower, Borrower's successors or assigns or of any junior lienholder or guarantors, without liability on Lender's part and notwithstanding Borrower's breach of any covenant or agreement of Borrower in this Instrument, extend the time for payment of said indebtedness or any part thereof, reduce the payments thereon, release anyone liable on any of said indebtedness, accept a renewal note or notes therefor, modify the terms and time of payment of said indebtedness, release from the lien of this Instrument any part of the Property, take or release other or additional security, reconvey any part of the Property, consent to any map or plan of the Property, consent to the granting of any easement, join in any extension or subordination agreement, and agree in writing with Borrower to modify the rate of interest or period of amortization of the Note or change the amount of the monthly installments payable thereunder. Any actions taken by Lender pursuant to the terms of this paragraph 12 shall not affect the obligation of Borrower or Borrower's successors or assigns to pay the sums secured by this Instrument and to observe the covenants of Borrower contained herein, shall not affect the guaranty of any person, corporation, partnership or other entity for payment of the indebtedness secured hereby, and shall not affect the lien or priority of lien hereof on the Property. Borrower shall pay Lender a reasonable service charge, together with such title insurance premiums and attorney's fees as may be incurred at Lender's option, for any such action if taken at Borrower's request.

13. FORBEARANCE BY LENDER NOT A WAIVER. Any forbearance by Lender in exercising any right or remedy hereunder, or otherwise afforded by applicable law, shall not be a waiver of or preclude the exercise of any right or remedy. The acceptance by Lender of payment of any sum secured by this Instrument after the due date of such payment shall not be a waiver of Lender's right to either require prompt payment when due of all other sums so secured or to declare a default for failure to make prompt payment. The procurement of insurance or the payment of taxes or other liens or charges by Lender shall not be a waiver of Lender's right to accelerate the maturity of the indebtedness secured by this Instrument, nor shall Lender's receipt of any awards, proceeds or damages under paragraphs 5 and 11 hereof operate to cure or waive Borrower's default in payment of sums secured by this Instrument.

(page 4 of 8 pages)

FIGURE 23–8
(continued)

FIGURE 23–8
(continued)

14. ESTOPPEL CERTIFICATE. Borrower shall within ten days of a written request from Lender furnish Lender with a written statement, duly acknowledged, setting forth the sums secured by this Instrument and any right of set-off, counterclaim or other defense which exists against such sums and the obligations of this Instrument.

15. UNIFORM COMMERCIAL CODE SECURITY AGREEMENT. This Instrument is intended to be a security agreement pursuant to the Uniform Commercial Code for any of the items specified above as part of the Property which, under applicable law, may be subject to a security interest pursuant to the Uniform Commercial Code, and Borrower hereby grants Lender a security interest in said items. Borrower agrees that Lender may file this Instrument, or a reproduction thereof, in the real estate records or other appropriate index, as a financing statement for any of the items specified above as part of the Property. Any reproduction of this Instrument or of any other security agreement or financing statement shall be sufficient as a financing statement. In addition, Borrower agrees to execute and deliver to Lender, upon Lender's request, any financing statements, as well as extensions, renewals and amendments thereof, and reproductions of this Instrument in such form as Lender may require to perfect a security interest with respect to said items. Borrower shall pay all costs of filing such financing statements and any extensions, renewals, amendments and releases thereof, and shall pay all reasonable costs and expenses of any record searches for financing statements Lender may reasonably require. Without the prior written consent of Lender, Borrower shall not create or suffer to be created pursuant to the Uniform Commercial Code any other security interest in said items, including replacements and additions thereto. Upon Borrower's breach of any covenant or agreement of Borrower contained in this Instrument, including the covenants to pay when due all sums secured by this Instrument, Lender shall have the remedies of a secured party under the Uniform Commercial Code and, at Lender's option, may also invoke the remedies provided in paragraph 27 of this Instrument as to such items. In exercising any of said remedies, Lender may proceed against the items of real property and any items of personal property specified above as part of the Property separately or together and in any order whatsoever, without in any way affecting the availability of Lender's remedies under the Uniform Commercial Code or of the remedies provided in paragraph 27 of this Instrument.

16. LEASES OF THE PROPERTY. As used in this paragraph 16, the word "lease" shall mean "sublease" if this Instrument is on a leasehold. Borrower shall comply with and observe Borrower's obligations as landlord under all leases of the Property or any part thereof. Borrower will not lease any portion of the Property for non-residential use except with the prior written approval of Lender. Borrower, at Lender's request, shall furnish Lender with executed copies of all leases now existing or hereafter made of all or any part of the Property, and all leases now or hereafter entered into will be in form and substance subject to the approval of Lender. All leases of the Property shall specifically provide that such leases are subordinate to this Instrument; that the tenant attorns to Lender, such attornment to be effective upon Lender's acquisition of title to the Property; that the tenant agrees to execute such further evidences of attornment as Lender may from time to time request; that the attornment of the tenant shall not be terminated by foreclosure; and that Lender may, at Lender's option, accept or reject such attornments. Borrower shall not, without Lender's written consent, execute, modify, surrender or terminate, either orally or in writing, any lease now existing or hereafter made of all or any part of the Property providing for a term of three years or more, permit an assignment or sublease of such a lease without Lender's written consent, or request or consent to the subordination of any lease of all or any part of the Property to any lien subordinate to this Instrument. If Borrower becomes aware that any tenant proposes to do, or is doing, any act or thing which may give rise to any right of set-off against rent, Borrower shall (i) take such steps as shall be reasonably calculated to prevent the accrual of any right to a set-off against rent, (ii) notify Lender thereof and of the amount of said set-offs, and (iii) within ten days after such accrual, reimburse the tenant who shall have acquired such right to set-off or take such other steps as shall effectively discharge such set-off and as shall assure that rents thereafter due shall continue to be payable without set-off or deduction.

Upon Lender's request, Borrower shall assign to Lender, by written instrument satisfactory to Lender, all leases now existing or hereafter made of all or any part of the Property and all security deposits made by tenants in connection with such leases of the Property. Upon assignment by Borrower to Lender of any leases of the Property, Lender shall have all of the rights and powers possessed by Borrower prior to such assignment and Lender shall have the right to modify, extend or terminate such existing leases and to execute new leases, in Lender's sole discretion.

17. REMEDIES CUMULATIVE. Each remedy provided in this Instrument is distinct and cumulative to all other rights or remedies under this Instrument or afforded by law or equity, and may be exercised concurrently, independently, or successively, in any order whatsoever.

18. ACCELERATION IN CASE OF BORROWER'S INSOLVENCY. If Borrower shall voluntarily file a petition under the Federal Bankruptcy Act, as such Act may from time to time be amended, or under any similar or successor Federal statute relating to bankruptcy, insolvency, arrangements or reorganizations, or under any state bankruptcy or insolvency act, or file an answer in an involuntary proceeding admitting insolvency or inability to pay debts, or if Borrower shall fail to obtain a vacation or stay of involuntary proceedings brought for the reorganization, dissolution or liquidation of Borrower, or if Borrower shall be adjudged a bankrupt, or if a trustee or receiver shall be appointed for Borrower or Borrower's property, or if the Property shall become subject to the jurisdiction of a Federal bankruptcy court or similar state court, or if Borrower shall make an assignment for the benefit of Borrower's creditors, or if there is an attachment, execution or other judicial seizure of any portion of Borrower's assets and such seizure is not discharged within ten days, then Lender may, at Lender's option, declare all of the sums secured by this Instrument to be immediately due and payable without prior notice to Borrower, and Lender may invoke any remedies permitted by paragraph 27 of this Instrument. Any attorney's fees and other expenses incurred by Lender in connection with Borrower's bankruptcy or any of the other aforesaid events shall be additional indebtedness of Borrower secured by this Instrument pursuant to paragraph 8 hereof.

19. TRANSFERS OF THE PROPERTY OR BENEFICIAL INTERESTS IN BORROWER; ASSUMPTION. On sale or transfer of (i) all or any part of the Property, or any interest therein, or (ii) beneficial interests in Borrower (if Borrower is not a natural person or persons but is a corporation, partnership, trust or other legal entity), Lender may, at Lender's option, declare all of the sums secured by this Instrument to be immediately due and payable, and Lender may invoke any remedies permitted by paragraph 27 of this Instrument. This option shall not apply in case of

    (a) transfers by devise or descent or by operation of law upon the death of a joint tenant or a partner;

    (b) sales or transfers when the transferee's creditworthiness and management ability are satisfactory to Lender and the transferee has executed, prior to the sale or transfer, a written assumption agreement containing such terms as Lender may require, including, if required by Lender, an increase in the rate of interest payable under the Note;

    (c) the grant of a leasehold interest in a part of the Property of three years or less (or such longer lease term as Lender may permit by prior written approval) not containing an option to purchase (except any interest in the ground lease, if this Instrument is on a leasehold);

    (d) sales or transfers of beneficial interests in Borrower provided that such sales or transfers, together with any prior sales or transfers of beneficial interests in Borrower, but excluding sales or transfers under subparagraphs (a) and (b) above, do not result in more than 49% of the beneficial interests in Borrower having been sold or transferred since commencement of amortization of the Note; and

    (e) sales or transfers of fixtures or any personal property pursuant to the first paragraph of paragraph 6 hereof.

20. NOTICE. Except for any notice required under applicable law to be given in another manner, (a) any notice to Borrower provided for in this Instrument or in the Note shall be given by mailing such notice by certified mail addressed to Borrower at Borrower's address stated below or at such other address as Borrower may designate by notice to Lender as provided herein, and (b) any notice to Lender shall be given by certified mail, return receipt requested, to Lender's address stated herein or to such other address as Lender may designate by notice to Borrower as provided herein. Any notice provided for in this Instrument or in the Note shall be deemed to have been given to Borrower or Lender when given in the manner designated herein.

21. SUCCESSORS AND ASSIGNS BOUND; JOINT AND SEVERAL LIABILITY; AGENTS; CAPTIONS. The covenants and agreements herein contained shall bind, and the rights hereunder shall inure to, the respective successors and assigns of Lender and Borrower, subject to the provisions of paragraph 19 hereof. All covenants and agreements of Borrower shall be joint and several. In exercising any rights hereunder or taking any actions provided for herein, Lender may act through its employees, agents or independent contractors as authorized by Lender. The captions and headings of the paragraphs of this Instrument are for convenience only and are not to be used to interpret or define the provisions hereof.

22. UNIFORM MULTIFAMILY INSTRUMENT; GOVERNING LAW; SEVERABILITY. This form of multifamily instrument combines uniform covenants for national use and non-uniform covenants with limited variations by jurisdiction to constitute a uniform security instrument covering real property and related fixtures and personal property. This Instrument shall be governed by the law of the jurisdiction in which the Property is located. In the event that any provision of this Instrument or the Note conflicts with applicable law, such conflict shall not affect other provisions of this Instrument or the Note which can be given effect without the conflicting provisions, and to this end the provisions of this

(page 5 of 8 pages)

FIGURE 23–8
(continued)

Instrument and the Note are declared to be severable. In the event that any applicable law limiting the amount of interest or other charges permitted to be collected from Borrower is interpreted so that any charge provided for in this Instrument or in the Note, whether considered separately or together with other charges levied in connection with this Instrument and the Note, violates such law, and Borrower is entitled to the benefit of such law, such charge is hereby reduced to the extent necessary to eliminate such violation. The amounts, if any, previously paid to Lender in excess of the amounts payable to Lender pursuant to such charges as reduced shall be applied by Lender to reduce the principal of the indebtedness evidenced by the Note. For the purpose of determining whether any applicable law limiting the amount of interest or other charges permitted to be collected from Borrower has been violated, all indebtedness which is secured by this Instrument or evidenced by the Note and which constitutes interest, as well as all other charges levied in connection with such indebtedness which constitute interest, shall be deemed to be allocated and spread over the stated term of the Note. Unless otherwise required by applicable law, such allocation and spreading shall be effected in such a manner that the rate of interest computed thereby is uniform throughout the stated term of the Note.

23. WAIVER OF STATUTE OF LIMITATIONS. Borrower hereby waives the right to assert any statute of limitations as a bar to the enforcement of the lien of this Instrument or to any action brought to enforce the Note or any other obligation secured by this Instrument.

24. WAIVER OF MARSHALLING. Notwithstanding the existence of any other security interests in the Property held by Lender or by any other party, Lender shall have the right to determine the order in which any or all of the Property shall be subjected to the remedies provided herein. Lender shall have the right to determine the order in which any or all portions of the indebtedness secured hereby are satisfied from the proceeds realized upon the exercise of the remedies provided herein. Borrower, any party who consents to this Instrument and any party who now or hereafter acquires a security interest in the Property and who has actual or constructive notice hereof hereby waives any and all right to require the marshalling of assets in connection with the exercise of any of the remedies permitted by applicable law or provided herein.

25. CONSTRUCTION LOAN PROVISIONS. Borrower agrees to comply with the covenants and conditions of the Construction Loan Agreement, if any, which is hereby incorporated by reference in and made a part of this Instrument. All advances made by Lender pursuant to the Construction Loan Agreement shall be indebtedness of Borrower secured by this Instrument, and such advances may be obligatory as provided in the Construction Loan Agreement. All sums disbursed by Lender prior to completion of the improvements to protect the security of this Instrument up to the principal amount of the Note shall be treated as disbursements pursuant to the Construction Loan Agreement. All such sums shall bear interest from the date of disbursement at the rate stated in the Note, unless collection from Borrower of interest at such rate would be contrary to applicable law in which event such amounts shall bear interest at the highest rate which may be collected from Borrower under applicable law and shall be payable upon notice from Lender to Borrower requesting payment therefor.

From time to time as Lender deems necessary to protect Lender's interests, Borrower shall, upon request of Lender, execute and deliver to Lender, in such form as Lender shall direct, assignments of any and all rights or claims which relate to the construction of the Property and which Borrower may have against any party supplying or who has supplied labor, materials or services in connection with construction of the Property. In case of breach by Borrower of the covenants and conditions of the Construction Loan Agreement, Lender, at Lender's option, with or without entry upon the Property, (i) may invoke any of the rights or remedies provided in the Construction Loan Agreement, (ii) may accelerate the sums secured by this Instrument and invoke those remedies provided in paragraph 27 hereof, or (iii) may do both. If, after the commencement of amortization of the Note, the Note and this Instrument are sold by Lender, from and after such sale the Construction Loan Agreement shall cease to be a part of this Instrument and Borrower shall not assert any right of set-off, counterclaim or other claim or defense arising out of or in connection with the Construction Loan Agreement against the obligations of the Note and this Instrument.

26. ASSIGNMENT OF RENTS; APPOINTMENT OF RECEIVER; LENDER IN POSSESSION. As part of the consideration for the indebtedness evidenced by the Note, Borrower hereby absolutely and unconditionally assigns and transfers to Lender all the rents and revenues of the Property, including those now due, past due, or to become due by virtue of any lease or other agreement for the occupancy or use of all or any part of the Property, regardless of to whom the rents and revenues of the Property are payable. Borrower hereby authorizes Lender or Lender's agents to collect the aforesaid rents and revenues and hereby directs each tenant of the Property to pay such rents to Lender or Lender's agents; provided, however, that prior to written notice given by Lender to Borrower of the breach by Borrower of any covenant or agreement of Borrower in this Instrument, Borrower shall collect and receive all rents and revenues of the Property as trustee for the benefit of Lender and Borrower, to apply the rents and revenues so collected to the sums secured by this Instrument in the order provided in paragraph 3 hereof with the balance, so long as no such breach has occurred, to the account of Borrower, it being intended by Borrower and Lender that this assignment of rents constitutes an absolute assignment and not an assignment for additional security only. Upon delivery of written notice by Lender to Borrower of the breach by Borrower of any covenant or agreement of Borrower in this Instrument, and without the necessity of Lender entering upon and taking and maintaining full control of the Property in person, by agent or by a court-appointed receiver, Lender shall immediately be entitled to possession of all rents and revenues of the Property as specified in this paragraph 26 as the same become due and payable, including but not limited to rents then due and unpaid, and all such rents shall immediately upon delivery of such notice be held by Borrower as trustee for the benefit of Lender only; provided, however, that the written notice by Lender to Borrower of the breach by Borrower shall contain a statement that Lender exercises its rights to such rents. Borrower agrees that commencing upon delivery of such written notice of Borrower's breach by Lender to Borrower, each tenant of the Property shall make such rents payable to and pay such rents to Lender or Lender's agents on Lender's written demand to each tenant therefor, delivered to each tenant personally, by mail or by delivering such demand to each rental unit, without any liability on the part of said tenant to inquire further as to the existence of a default by Borrower.

Borrower hereby covenants that Borrower has not executed any prior assignment of said rents, that Borrower has not performed, and will not perform, any acts or has not executed, and will not execute, any instrument which would prevent Lender from exercising its rights under this paragraph 26, and that at the time of execution of this Instrument there has been no anticipation or prepayment of any of the rents of the Property for more than two months prior to the due dates of such rents. Borrower covenants that Borrower will not hereafter collect or accept payment of any rents of the Property more than two months prior to the due dates of such rents. Borrower further covenants that Borrower will execute and deliver to Lender such further assignments of rents and revenues of the Property as Lender may from time to time request.

Upon Borrower's breach of any covenant or agreement of Borrower in this Instrument, Lender may in person, by agent or by a court-appointed receiver, regardless of the adequacy of Lender's security, enter upon and take and maintain full control of the Property in order to perform all acts necessary and appropriate for the operation and maintenance thereof including, but not limited to, the execution, cancellation or modification of leases, the collection of all rents and revenues of the Property, the making of repairs to the Property and the execution or termination of contracts providing for the management or maintenance of the Property, all on such terms as are deemed best to protect the security of this Instrument. In the event Lender elects to seek the appointment of a receiver for the Property upon Borrower's breach of any covenant or agreement of Borrower in this Instrument, Borrower hereby expressly consents to the appointment of such receiver. Lender or the receiver shall be entitled to receive a reasonable fee for so managing the Property.

All rents and revenues collected subsequent to delivery of written notice by Lender to Borrower of the breach by Borrower of any covenant or agreement of Borrower in this Instrument shall be applied first to the costs, if any, of taking control of and managing the Property and collecting the rents, including, but not limited to, attorney's fees, receiver's fees, premiums on receiver's bonds, costs of repairs to the Property, premiums on insurance policies, taxes, assessments and other charges on the Property, and the costs of discharging any obligation or liability of Borrower as lessor or landlord of the Property and then to the sums secured by this Instrument. Lender or the receiver shall have access to the books and records used in the operation and maintenance of the Property and shall be liable to account only for those rents actually received. Lender shall not be liable to Borrower, anyone claiming under or through Borrower or anyone having an interest in the Property by reason of anything done or left undone by Lender under this paragraph 26.

If the rents of the Property are not sufficient to meet the costs, if any, of taking control of and managing the Property and collecting the rents, any funds expended by Lender for such purposes shall become indebtedness of Borrower to Lender secured by this Instrument pursuant to paragraph 8 hereof. Unless Lender and Borrower agree in writing to other terms of payment, such amounts shall be payable upon notice from Lender to Borrower requesting payment thereof and shall bear interest from the date of disbursement at the rate stated in the Note unless payment of interest at such rate would be contrary to applicable law, in which event such amounts shall bear interest at the highest rate which may be collected from Borrower under applicable law.

Any entering upon and taking and maintaining of control of the Property by Lender or the receiver and any application of rents as provided herein shall not cure or waive any default hereunder or invalidate any other right or remedy of Lender under applicable law or provided herein. This assignment of rents of the Property shall terminate at such time as this Instrument ceases to secure indebtedness held by Lender.

Uniform Covenants—Multifamily—1/77—FNMA/FHLMC Uniform Instrument   *(page 6 of 8 pages)*

20. *Notice.* Certified mail must be used by the lender or borrower to give notice of changes of name or address, default and foreclosure, sale of the property, or damage or destruction to the property to the other.

21. *Successors and Assigns Bound.* People taking over the legal positions of the lender and/or borrower at a later time are equally bound by the contract provisions, jointly and severally.

22. *Governing Law and Severability.* Conflicts between the uniform instrument and local law are to be resolved according to the law of the jurisdiction in which the property is located. And any such conflict shall not invalidate the remaining provisions of the instrument. This provision, dividing the instrument into distinct, independent obligations or agreements, any one of which may be removed without affecting the others, is termed the *severability clause.*

23. *Waiver of Statute of Limitations.* Borrower waives any statute of limitations rights to provisions in the mortgage.

24. *Waiver to Marshalling of Assets.* Right to the marshalling of assets (arranging in a certain order) in connection with default remedies in the contract is waived by the borrower, giving the lender greater freedom in pursuing remedies under the instrument.

25. *Construction Loan Provisions.* A construction loan may be made and tied into the instrument.

26. *Assignment of Rents.* Upon breach of a condition, and with proper notice, rents are to be paid to a receiver, to better protect the lender's interests. A receiver is an officer of the court appointed to take possession and control of the property of concern in a suit.

Nonuniform Covenants

State statutes are specific and often vary substantially. Thus, the FNMA/FHLMC instruments provide for state-specific covenants to comply with such statutes. For the instrument in Figure 23-5, these nonuniform covenants are as follows:

27. *Acceleration: Remedies.* Lender may declare all sums secured by the mortgage to be due and payable immediately. Lender shall also be allowed to collect all costs of remedies, such as attorney's fees, abstracts, title reports, and other expenses.

28. *Release.* Lender will terminate this instrument upon payment of all sums due (desistance clause).

29. *Attorneys' Fees.* Attorneys' fees shall include fees awarded by an appellate court.

30. *Future Advances.* Lender, at borrower's request, may advance additional money, which also will be secured by this mortgage (open-end provision).

LENDER RISKS

Real estate can almost always be financed if one is willing to pay the price by way of interest rates and other terms of borrowing. A sophisticated investor makes it a point to know the procedures of borrowing and to borrow at the most opportune time and on the most advantageous terms. Advantageous borrowing begins by understanding money market conditions. For example, the inverse relationship between money supply and interest rates is an economic fact of life. The time required for a change in monetary conditions to be reflected in a changed level of residential construction is uncertain and depends on several complex factors. Nevertheless, the basic relationship continues; when plenty of money is available, interest rates drop, and vice versa.

A further consideration for the potential borrower is approaching the right institutions for the kind of loan desired. Savings and loan associations and mutual savings banks lend much more readily on one-family houses than do life insurance companies or commercial banks. Commercial banks and life insurance companies, however, are more likely to make loans on farms and commercial properties. And, of course, individual lenders must be approached for purchase-money mortgages and land contracts for undeveloped land.

A third major consideration is lender risk, of which a potential borrower must be aware. Lenders continually balance opportunities for profits against risk, or the probability of loss of profit and principal. Lenders operate on the principle that as risk increases, profits should also increase. Mortgage lenders have three major sources of risk: (1) the borrower, (2) the property, and (3) their overall portfolio.

Borrower Risk

A lender's risk analysis in making a loan begins with the borrower. The categories of concern are: (1) credit rating, (2) assets, or net worth, (3) earning capacity or income, and (4) motivation. A lender is likely to have accept-reject guidelines for each category.

A credit rating may be obtained simply by ordering a credit report on the prospective borrower. The borrower's credit experience and reputation must show an acceptably stable performance, including job and income patterns and family life. Both the credit report and the borrower's application provide information on assets owned, or net worth, including savings and checking account balances.

The borrower's monthly or annual income must show a capability of making the principal, interest, taxes, and insurance payments for the desired loan. For a homeowner loan, the usual rule is that PITI must not exceed one-fourth, or 25 percent, of the borrower's gross monthly income. For investment property the lender looks more to the property as security for the loan.

The borrower's motivation is the final and perhaps the most important of the four categories. Motivation means that the borrower has sufficient incentive and desire to meet the requirements of the loan. A young family wishing to own their own home is usually considered highly motivated. Motivation may be judged in several ways. A strong credit report, a steady accumulation of assets, and rising income all indicate strong motivation.

Property Risk

In analyzing property risk, three categories of concern must be addressed: (1) on-site characteristics, (2) location, and (3) marketability. For owner-occupied dwellings borrower risks are generally more important than are property risks, because the borrower is the primary source of money to meet the loan payments. But for investment properties, where the value may be many, many times the borrower's income, the property must be looked to more strongly for security.

The size, shape, and topography of a site are the first considerations in judging on-site characteristics. These characteristics must be complementary to the improvements and the use. Next, the size, condition, functional capability, mechanical equipment, and appearance of any improvements are taken into account.

Location means relative ease of accessibility, as discussed in Chapter 15. Location also concerns neighborhood features and government factors. A good deal of emphasis is also placed on special amenities that may raise values.

Marketability risk pertains largely to market value and the economic makeup of the community. A growing community with diversified industries provides greater marketability, for example, than does a community with one industry that is declining. Also, stable employment and economic patterns are preferable to cyclical patterns.

Portfolio Risk

Owning and managing a large number of investments involves many risks; collectively they are called *portfolio risks*. For a mortgage lender, these risks may be categorized as: (1) administrative, (2) investment, and (3) mix and turnover, or diversification, perils.

Administrative risk is inherent in making and servicing loans that might lead to losses. The chance of error in the property file and in keeping records of payments is ever present. Another administrative risk would be overlooking some item during required periodic inspections to ensure upkeep and maintenance.

Investment risk is the chance that an adequate rate of return will not be realized on loans. A loan may go sour for two reasons. First, the borrower might not be able to keep up with increasing costs of operation, in which event abandonment or foreclosure could result. Second, if the property's value declines faster than the loan is amortized, in a foreclosure the unamortized principal plus foreclosure expenses might exceed the disposition value of the property.

Portfolio diversification is advantageous if the risks tend to offset each other or are unlikely to occur at the same time. If all the properties in the portfolio are not influenced in the same way at the same time, some risk is avoided. Diversifying a real estate portfolio means that not all loans are made in the same community, nor all borrowers employed in the same industry, nor do they have the same occupation.

LENDER PROCEDURES AND COMMITMENTS

Making an application is the first step in obtaining a loan. Information required by lenders includes: (1) the amount of the loan desired, (2) identification of the property to be pledged as security, and (3) annual income, kind of employment, and other financial information on the applicant. If the property and the applicant are acceptable, a loan commitment is made.

A *loan commitment* is a written pledge, promise, or letter of agreement to lend or advance money under specified terms and conditions. The commitment states the amount, the interest rate, and the life of the loan, along with any other terms demanded by the lender. In most cases, the applicant has the right to seek for other lenders if the amount and terms of the commitment are unacceptable. At the same time, the lender usually includes a termination date on the commitment, after which the offer to make the loan is withdrawn.

The four commonly used loan commitments are: (1) firm, (2) conditional, (3) takeout, and (4) standby. The first two commitments, firm and conditional, are the most applicable to consumer loans on residential properties. Takeout and standby commitments are important to builder-lender transactions, as well as to transactions between lending agencies themselves.

A *firm commitment* is a definite offer to make a loan at stated terms and conditions. For all practical purposes, the borrower-applicant need only accept the offer and prepare for the loan closing. Nearly all commitments to homebuyers and small investors are firm commitments.

A *conditional commitment* is an agreement to make a loan subject to certain limitations or provisions. The provision may be completion of construction or development of a property. The Federal Housing Administration commonly issues conditional commitments that depend on a builder finding an acceptable buyer-borrower for a speculative house. The builder accepts the risk of finding an acceptable buyer, but because the property is already approved, the conditional commitment facilitates the sale of the house.

A *takeout commitment* is an agreement by one lender to make a permanent loan to "take" another lender out of a temporary loan. Takeouts are common in construction loans. A takeout commitment is also a firm agreement to buy a loan for an originating lender at a definite price. A takeout commitment is commonly used between financial institutions and government agencies. For example, a takeout commitment may be given by a governmental agency, such as the Government National Mortgage Association, to a local lender, such as a bank. The government agency agrees to buy and take over a mortgage loan from a local lender as soon as the loan is closed and all contingencies surrounding the loan are satisfied. The local lender is usually considered contractually bound to sell the loan at the stipulated price. The price to be paid for the loan is included in the written commitment. Takeout commitments usually involve properties under construction or development.

A *standby commitment* is the promise to buy a loan from a second lender, without the initial lender being obligated to sell the loan. That is, a standby commitment gives the owner of a loan the option to sell or not to sell the loan at the stipulated price. A standby commitment is usually issued by a large institutional lender, such as a life insurance company, to a local bank or mortgage banker.

FEDERAL LAWS AFFECTING LENDING

The following brief summary is offered only to alert the reader to the many applicable regulations and their general content.

Equal Credit Opportunity Act

The Equal Credit Opportunity Act (ECOA), enacted in 1974, forbids discrimination by mortgage lenders because of race, color, religion, national origin, age, sex, or marital status, or because all or part of an applicant's income is from a public assistance program. ECOA is implemented by the Federal Reserve System as Regulation B. Persons desiring credit must be informed of their rights under the act prior to completing an application. The reason for denial of credit must be given, upon request.

Truth-in-Lending Act

The Truth-in-Lending (TIL) Act requires full disclosure of loan costs. TIL is, in truth, Title I of the Consumer Credit Protection Act and is implemented by the Federal Reserve System as Regulation Z. Under the act, a lender is required to provide advance disclosure of finance charges and loan terms, such as the interest rate, origination fees, due date of payments, prepayment fees, and late payment fees, so that borrowers may shop for the least-cost or most-advantageous credit terms. Note that the act does not regulate the cost of credit or set maximum allowable interest rates.

Coverage.   To begin with, the Truth-in-Lending Act applies only to lenders who "regularly extend or arrange credit." Further, Regulation Z applies to loans for personal, household, or family residences if four or more payments are involved. A lease in which the lessee's obligation is less than $25,000 is also covered if the duration is greater than four months. A private party taking back a purchase-money mortgage on the sale of a residence is exempt. Also, credit transactions on investment property are exempt.

Finance Charges and the Annual Percentage Rate.   Finance charges include all the costs associated with a loan that are directly or indirectly payable by a borrower and are required by a lender as a precondition to making the loan. Examples are interest, origination fees, finder's fees, and service or carrying charges. Real estate purchase costs, such as title insurance, recording fees, appraisal fees, and legal fees that would be incurred whether or not the loan were taken out are not included. These costs must be itemized and disclosed, however.

Disclosure of finance charges must be made in terms of an *annual percentage rate, APR*. Regulation Z specifies how the APR is to be calculated. The disclosure must be to within one-eighth of one percent, based on the amount actually disbursed. Because the APR reduces the cost of the loan to a single number, it facilitates comparison shopping.

Here is an example. Consider a 30-year, $90,000 mortgage at 10 percent with 3 discount points, or $2,700. The monthly payments are $789.81.

$$DS = \text{Loan outstanding} \times \text{PR factor}$$
$$= \$90,000 \times 0.008776 = \$789.81$$

The effective yield on the loan assuming no prepayments is 10.37 percent per annum ($0.864\% \times 12$):

$$\text{Loan outstanding} = DS \times PVAIF_{i,\,n} + \text{Loan costs}$$
$$\$90,000 = \$789.81 \times PVAIF_{0.864,\,360} + \$2,700$$

Rounding to the nearest one-eighth of one percent, the APR is 10⅜ percent or 10.375 percent per annum.

Recission.   Regulation Z provides a limited right to rescind certain mortgage transactions like the taking of a second mortgage. This right to rescission is intended to protect homeowners from unscrupulous sellers of home improvements, appliances, or furniture. The right to rescission does not apply to a mortgage or trust deed.

Usury Laws.   Most states have *usury laws* that set a maximum level of interest that may be charged on various types of loans. Note, however, that these laws do not pertain to residential mortgage loans.

SUMMARY

The mortgage underwriting process involves several steps. The first step is to collect information on both the property and the borrower.

The next step is to qualify the property and the borrower. The categories of concern are the on-site characteristics, location and marketability of the property, and the credit rating, assets and liabilities, income, and motivation of the borrower.

Having qualified the property and the borrower, most lenders will issue a firm commitment to residential homebuyers. A firm commitment obligates the lender to make a loan to the borrower at stated terms and conditions. The commitment usually includes a termination date, after which the offer to make the loan is withdrawn.

Two separate legal instruments are executed to document a loan on real estate: the first is a mortgage or trust deed and the second is a promissory note. The mortgage or trust deed pledges the property as security for the debt. The promissory note is a written commitment to repay the debt.

Generally, all mortgages contain many clauses such as provisions for the use of the property, forbearance by the lender, acceleration of the debt upon borrower insolvency, transfer of the borrower's interests, and assignment of rents. Also, the mortgage obligates the borrower to maintain the property in good repair and not permit its waste or deterioration.

There are no guarantees in mortgage underwriting. After doing their best to evaluate both the borrower and the property, and weighing the risks of default against potential profits, lenders still must accept some risks. Should the borrower lose his or her job and stop making payments on the mortgage or should the property depreciate in value, the lender may be forced to foreclose and take a loss on the property. If the local economy turns down, the lender may be forced to take back properties that a few years ago had been completely leased but are now sitting empty.

One way to compare different loan terms on a mortgage is to calculate the annual percentage rate. Because the APR states the cost of the loan as a single number, it facilitates comparison shopping. The APR is calculated by taking into account all the costs associated with a loan that are directly or indirectly payable by a borrower and required by a lender as a precondition to making the loan. The formula is:

$$\text{Loan outstanding} = DS \times PVAIF_{i, n} + \text{Loan costs}$$

Examples of costs associated with the loan are interest, origination fees, finder's fees, and service or carrying charges. Real estate purchase costs, such as title insurance, recording fees, appraisal fees, and legal fees, which would be incurred whether the loan were taken out or not, are not included in the finance charges.

KEY CONCEPTS

Acceleration clause   Provision that allows a lender to require immediate repayment of the entire loan if the borrower defaults.

Alienation or due-on-sale clause   Provision in a mortgage loan giving the lender the right to require immediate repayment if the property is sold or otherwise conveyed.

Assumption (of a loan)   Agreement by a buyer to accept responsibility for repayment of an existing loan against a property.

Borrower risk   A type of lender risk that comes about if the borrower is not able to meet loan payments.

Deed in lieu of foreclosure   When an owner-borrower who is in default voluntarily conveys title to the lender to avoid the costs of foreclosure.

Defeasance clause   Provision that defeats or voids any mortgage claim if the secured debt is fully repaid on time.

Deficiency judgment   A judicial decree in favor of a lender for the unsatisfied portion of the mortgage debt and foreclosure costs.

Equitable right of redemption   The right of a borrower to recover a mortgaged property by paying the amounts due on a delinquent loan prior to the foreclosure sale.

Foreclosure   A legal process to force the sale of a pledged property to satisfy an unpaid debt.

Mortgage satisfaction   Receipt or certificate from a lender stating that the loan has been repaid in full.

Novation   Replacing an old contract with a new one.

Portfolio risk   Chance that a lender will not realize an expected rate of return on an entire portfolio of loans.

Power of sale   Right of a lender to hold a foreclosure sale without going to court.

Promissory note   A written statement evidencing a debt and containing a commitment to repay the debt.

Severability clause   Provision that the invalidation of one clause in a contract will not invalidate the other clauses.

Statutory right of redemption   Borrower's right to recover a property after a foreclosure sale by paying all accumulated charges on the defaulted loan.

Taking subject to a loan   A buyer taking title to a property subject to an existing loan, but without obligation to repay the loan.

Usury   When a rate of interest that is higher than that permitted by law is charged on a loan.

QUESTIONS FOR REVIEW AND DISCUSSION

1. Explain the debt-financing process.

    a. What are the main legal documents involved?

    b. Who are the main parties involved?

    c. What is the legal process of foreclosure upon default?

2. How does the debt-financing process differ when a trust deed is used to secure the debt?

3. What purpose is served by the promissory note in debt financing?

4. State at least four major provisions of the security instrument that is common to both mortgages and trust deeds.

5. What are the purposes or functions of the following?

   a. Defeasance clause

   b. Assignment of rents

   c. Acceleration of the debt

   d. Taking subject to a loan

   e. Deed in lieu of foreclosure

6. Distinguish between an equitable right of redemption and a statutory right of redemption.

7. Distinguish between a deficiency judgment and a defeasance clause.

8. Does the lender or the borrower have the greater power in debt-financing negotiations? Discuss.

9. What risks must be considered by a lender prior to making a loan?

10. What is a loan commitment? What are the four commonly used loan commitments?

11. What are the main provisions of the Truth-in-Lending Act?

12. How can a comparison of the cost to the borrower be made between differently structured loans?

PROBLEMS

1. What is the APR on a 10-year, $250,000 loan, amortized annually at 10 percent, with 5 points, assuming no prepayment?

2. What is the APR on a 30-year, $400,000 loan, amortized monthly at 8 percent, with 3 points, assuming no prepayment? What is the APR on this loan, assuming no points?

3. If finance charges are $4,000 on a $750,000 loan amortized monthly at 8 percent for 10 years, what is the APR on the loan?

CHAPTER 24

MORTGAGE SECURITIZATION

Chapter Outline

*Finance is the art of passing currency from hand to hand
until it finally disappears.*
Robert W. Sarnoff

Most residential single-family mortgage loans originated in the United States are converted into securities that are sold to investors in a secondary mortgage market. The process of converting mortgages into securities and selling the securities to investors in a secondary market is known as *securitization* or *collateralization.* Lenders who sell their mortgages in these markets do so in anticipation of a profit. Often the lender earns a servicing fee as well, for collecting payments on the underlying mortgages, keeping the books, and following up on delinquent loans.

Mortgage securitization has brought new sources of capital into the mortgage market, improved the efficiency of the mortgage market by standardizing underwriting guidelines, enhanced the marketability and liquidity of residential mortgages by creating mortgage securities that trade the way bonds are traded, and eliminated the mismatch of mortgage funds and the demand for mortgages between fast- and slow-growing areas.

In this chapter we will see that the superior returns, high-credit quality, and significant liquidity available from investments in residential mortgage securities are tempered by the risk of prepayment. You will also find that the terms, concepts, and facts presented in Chapters 20–23 are essential for analyzing and evaluating mortgage securities.

SECONDARY LENDERS

To understand the workings of the secondary mortgage market, you must appreciate the difference between primary and secondary lenders. *Primary lenders* originate loans or supply loans directly to borrowers. Savings and loan associations, mutual savings banks, commercial banks, mortgage bankers, and life insurance companies make up the bulk of primary lenders.

Secondary lenders buy loans from or originate them through someone else. Federally supported agencies, pension funds, and some life insurance companies are the major secondary lenders.

If left to themselves, primary lenders would soon run out of money to lend in periods of tight money. The federal government has worked to develop secondary mortgage institutions, such as the Federal Home Loan Bank Systems, the Federal Home Loan Mortgage Corporation (FHLMC), the Federal National Mortgage Association (FNMA), and the Government National Mortgage Association (GNMA) to add liquidity to mortgage markets (see Figure 24-1). These agencies either advance money to primary lenders or buy mortgages from them. In both cases funds are released that primary lenders can use to make more mortgages.

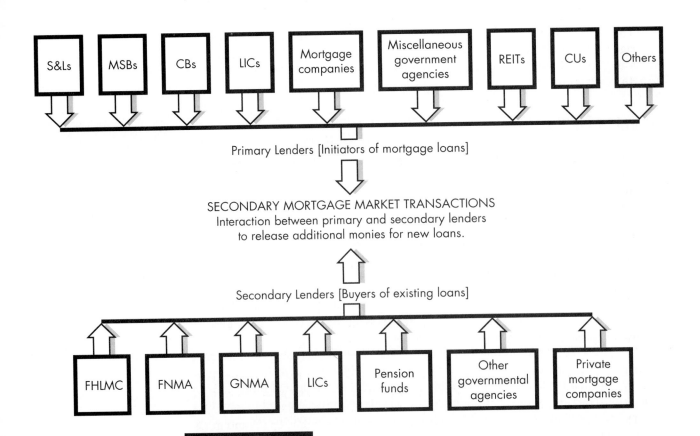

FIGURE 24–1

The Secondary Mortgage Market

The main secondary lenders are agencies of the federal government, and life insurance companies. Commercial banks and savings and loan associations sometimes act as secondary lenders if the profit opportunities elsewhere exceed those locally. Increasingly pension funds are also investing in mortgages. The combined activities of all these lenders means that mortgage underwriting is no longer bound by a strictly local market; the secondary mortgage market links the entire U.S. capital and mortgage markets.

Primary lenders may also participate in the secondary market. For example, a New York mutual savings bank with excess funds may buy mortgages from a savings and loan in Colorado where funds are scarce. Or a life insurance company may buy loans from mortgage bankers in several states. FHA-insured and VA-guaranteed loans facilitate the buying and selling of mortgages in the secondary market because of their standardized terms. Privately insured conventional loans with uniform FNMA/FHLMC instruments also give lenders protection and standardized terms. The result of all this buying and selling activity among lenders is higher liquidity for mortgages and a broadening of the mortgage market. In addition, because commercial banks and life insurance companies are active in mortgage markets, mortgages must be directly competitive with other investments—stocks and bonds—to compete for funds. This competition means that mortgages and home construction are increasingly tied to the supply and demand for money over the entire economy.

There are also a number of organizations that offer protection to holders of mortgage loans, thus additionally facilitating the purchase and sale of loans in the secondary mortgage market. These organizations include private insurance corporations, the FHA, the VA, and the Farmers Home Administration (FmHA).

Federal Home Loan Bank System

The Federal Home Loan Bank (FHLB) system was created by Congress during the financial crisis of the 1930s. The purpose was to establish a source of central credit for the nation's home financing institutions. This initial purpose has expanded into five functions:

1. To link mortgage lenders to the nation's capital markets.
2. To serve as a source of secondary credit for member institutions during periods of heavy withdrawal demand.
3. To smooth out seasonal differences between savings flows and loan changes.
4. To facilitate the flow of funds from capital-surplus areas to capital-deficit areas.
5. To generally stabilize residential construction and financing.

The FHLB advances funds to members in need, consistent with the foregoing functions. The system does not operate as a secondary mortgage market facility per se. FHLB advances are a relatively cheap source of funds.

The Federal Home Loan Bank system is made up of 12 regional banks and member institutions. Membership is open to savings and loan associations, mutual savings banks, commercial banks, and life insurance companies.

Federal Home Loan Mortgage Corporation

The Federal Home Loan Mortgage Corporation (FHLMC) was initially created by Congress in 1970. The nickname for FHLMC is Freddie Mac. Freddie Mac functions as a secondary mortgage market facility; it buys and sells conventional, FHA-insured, and VA-guaranteed mortgages. The FHLMC is currently a privately-owned corporation.

In recent years, the FHLMC has promoted the development of *mortgage-backed securities,* called *collateralized mortgage obligations* (CMOs). Mortgage-backed securities generally "pass through" principal and interest, as it is received, to holders of the securities on a prorata basis. The CMO provides a unique repayment structure that appeals to a wide variety of investors. CMOs are divided into three classes: short, intermediate, and long-term. All holders receive semiannual payment of interest at the certificate rate. Holders of first-class, short-term certificates receive all the payments of principal from the collateralized loans until they are fully repaid. Next, holders of intermediate certificates receive all the payments of principal. And, of course, long-term holders are repaid their principal last. This unique repayment schedule reduces the uncertainty of holders as to the length of their investment. Pension funds have found the intermediate and long-term certificates particularly attractive.

The declared goal of the FHLMC is to make mortgages as liquid and attractive as other securities; in the past, mortgages have been considered a relatively illiquid investment. *Liquidity* refers to the ease and speed with which an investment can be converted into cash and to the cash-to-value ratio realized. The easier the conversion into cash and the higher the cash-to-value ratio, the more liquid the investment.

The FHLMC seeks to accomplish its goal in several ways:

1. By development, in conjunction with the Federal National Mortgage Association, of uniform mortgage instruments with standardized terms to facilitate the ready buying and selling of conventional mortgages in secondary mortgage markets.

2. By the purchase and sale of conventional mortgage loans on a whole and a participation basis. Participation means that two or more investors or lenders share in the ownership of the loan.

3. By the purchase and sale of FHA-insured and VA-guaranteed loans on a continuing basis.

Federal National Mortgage Association

The Federal National Mortgage Association (FNMA), which is nicknamed Fannie Mae, was created by Congress in 1938. Fannie Mae is a government-sponsored corporation, but its stock is privately owned. This unique combination of interests makes FNMA a private corporation with a public purpose.

The basic purpose of FNMA is to provide a secondary market for residential loans. FNMA buys, services, and sells loans to fulfill this purpose. It deals in conventional, FHA-insured, and VA-guaranteed loans, and buys mortgages when loanable funds are in short supply and sells them when funds are plentiful. FNMA and FHLMC jointly developed uniform instruments for conventional mortgage loans to facilitate their use in the secondary mortgage market.

Government National Mortgage Association

The Government National Mortgage Association (GNMA), referred to as Ginnie Mae, was created by Congress in 1968. Ginnie Mae is entirely owned by the federal government, and its financial activities are supported by borrowings from the federal government. In fact, Ginnie Mae is an agency of the Department of Housing and Urban Development and has its operating policies set by the HUD secretary. GNMA has three main functions: (1) to provide special assistance for disadvantaged residential borrowers, (2) to raise additional funds for residential lending, and (3) mortgage portfolio management and liquidation.

The special-assistance function involves providing funds for low-cost housing and for residential mortgages in underdeveloped, capital-scarce areas. The fundraising function is to stabilize mortgage lending and home construction activities. The primary vehicle used to accomplish these two functions is the issuance of government-guaranteed securities.

GNMA guarantees mortgage-backed securities secured by government-insured (FHA) or government-guaranteed (VA) loans. The loans underlying the guarantee are pooled, a covering security is issued, and repayments from the pool are used to pay off the security. Two basic types of securities are issued: pass-throughs and bonds. The *pass-through* provides monthly payments of principal and interest to the security holder. The bond provides semiannual payments of principal and interest. Debt service from the pool of mortgages is used to make payments on the securities. The funds raised from sale of the security are used to purchase additional mortgages.

As a result of these programs, GNMA carries a very large portfolio of mortgages, which requires continuing management. GNMA's mission is to buy, service, and sell mortgages in an orderly manner that will have a minimum adverse effect on the residential mortgage market and result in minimum loss to the federal government.

Private Mortgage Corporations

Some private mortgage insurance corporations organize subsidiary mortgage corporations to invest reserves in mortgages. Prepayments and monthly debt service on the mortgages are used to pay claims on insured mortgages on which lenders lost money. These companies constitute a private, secondary mortgage lender or investor. The largest of these firms is the MGIC Mortgage Corporation, called Maggy Mae.

MORTGAGE-BACKED SECURITIES

There are several kinds of mortgage-backed securities. Following are definitions of the various kinds of mortgage-backed securities.

1. **Pass-through securities.** Pass-through securities are formed when individual mortgage loans are pooled and undivided interests (i.e., prorata interests) in the pool are sold. The cash flow from the underlying mortgages is passed through to the holder of the securities in the form of monthly payments. These monthly payments include scheduled payments and partial and full prepayments. A partial prepayment occurs when an individual mortgage borrower makes a monthly payment that is greater than the amount actually due. The excess payment is used to reduce the outstanding loan balance. Full prepayments occur when the borrower repays the remaining principal before the final, scheduled payment month.

   There are four types of mortgage pass-through securities:

   GNMA pass-throughs
   FHLMC participation certificates
   FNMA mortgage-backed securities
   private pass-throughs

   GNMA pass-through securities are made up of pools of FHA-insured or VA-guaranteed mortgage loans and sold in denominations of $25,000. Each pool must be made up of mortgages that carry the same interest rate and maturity. The minimum, single-family pool size is $1 million for level-payment mortgages. The timely payment of principal and interest on these securities is guaranteed by GNMA, and is known as a *credit enhancement.* The guarantee obligates GNMA to step in and make scheduled payments to the investor should the loan servicer fail to perform. GNMA pass-through securities are very popular. Since the individual mortgage loans are insured by the FHA or guaranteed by the VA, the risk of a default loss is slight. GNMA also securitizes graduated-payment, growing-equity, buydown, and manufactured-home loans.

   FHLMC participation certificates are made up of conventional mortgages. FHLMC participation certificates, or PCs, were first introduced in 1971. Minimum pool size is $100 million. The larger pool size means that prepayments are often more predictable than those of GNMAs. Payments are made monthly. Every conventional mortgage with a loan-to-value ratio greater than 80 percent must be insured against default by a private mortgage insurance company. No loan amount in excess of the conforming loan limit (which changes each year based on a Congressionally mandated formula) can be sold to FHLMC and placed in a PC. The 1993 conforming loan limit is $203,150. Higher loan limits apply in Alaska, Hawaii, Guam and the Virgin Islands; and for multiunit houses. The loans may be new originations or seasoned mortgages that were originated more than one year ago. FHLMC PCs trade in a liquid market, but they are not as liquid as GNMAs. FHLMC guarantees only the timely payment of interest and the ultimate payment of principal on all mortgages that make up the pool. FHLMC also sells FHA/VA PCs made up of pools of fixed-rate, level-payment, and fully amortizing, first-lien home mortgages insured by the FHA or guaranteed by the VA.

FNMA mortgage-backed securities are similar to FHLMC PCs. They are made up of conventional, conforming, single-family home mortgages. Minimum pool size is $1 million. FNMA guarantees the timely payment of interest and principal. FNMA also guarantees principal payments resulting from foreclosures and prepayments. FNMA also sells FHA/VA mortgage-backed securities made up of pools of FHA or VA loans no more than one-year old.

Private pass-throughs are made up of high-balance conventional mortgages that exceed the Congressionally established limits on loan size for secondary-market loan purchases by FHLMC and FNMA. The first private pass-through security was issued by the Bank of America in 1977. These so-called jumbo, conventional loans lack uniform underwriting guidelines as compared to conforming loans. Private pass-throughs are usually sold to pension funds, S&Ls, commercial banks, insurance companies, and other investors.

There are two basic types of private pass-through securities: fixed-rate and adjustable-rate pass-throughs. Fixed-rate pass-throughs are similar to FNMA mortgage-backed securities. Adjustable-rate pass-throughs are made up of conventional, adjustable-rate mortgages. The pass-through rate on an adjustable-rate mortgage-backed security may vary periodically during the life of the security. Private pass-through securities must register with the Securities Exchange Commission (SEC).

2. *Mortgage-Backed Bonds.* A mortgage-backed bond is a general debt obligation of the issuer that is collateralized by a pool of mortgages. The bond is structured so that the cash flow from the mortgages securing it will provide for the full and timely repayment of the bond. Bond interest payments are made semiannually. A mortgage-backed bond normally has a fixed note rate with a specific maturity. Mortgage-backed bonds are also ordinarily *overcollateralized.* Overcollateralization requires that more mortgages secure the bond than the bond is worth. This ensures against issuer defaults on scheduled interest and/or principal payments.

3. *Collateralized Mortgage Obligations (CMOs).* A CMO is a mortgage-backed bond with multiple classes of bonds instead of one. Each class has a stated maturity. These include short, intermediate, and long-term classes, or so-called *tranches.* Short-term certificates receive all payments of principal from the collateralized loans until they are fully repaid. Next, holders of intermediate certificates receive all payments of principal. And so on. The maturities and average lives of each tranche can be structured to meet market demands.

4. *Stripped Mortgage-Backed Securities.* There are two types of stripped mortgage-backed securities: interest-only (IO) and principal-only (PO) securities. In these securities the interest and principal payments are separated. The IO holder receives all interest payments; the PO holder receives all principal payments, including principal prepayments.

Cash Flows on Mortgage-Backed Securities

Mortgage-backed securities do not perform like bonds or other traditional fixed-income investments. Bond holders receive interest payments semiannually, with principal paid at maturity. Mortgage-backed security holders receive monthly payments. The monthly payments are comprised of interest plus scheduled, as well as unscheduled, principal payments on the underlying mortgages, less a servicing fee.

Analysis of the cash flows of mortgage-backed securities would be straightforward were it not for the unscheduled principal payments, or prepayments, on the underlying mortgages. Because these prepayments are highly uncertain, mortgage-backed securities have, for most of their history, traded at considerably higher yields than comparable Treasury securities.

Here is why prepayments on mortgage-backed securities are so important. Mortgage-backed securities in the secondary market often trade at a *premium*—that is, at a price above face value. For example, a $100 million mortgage-backed security that sells for $102 million is selling at a premium of $2 million.

Mortgage-backed securities sell at a premium when the market interest rate is less than the contract rate, or original interest rate, on the underlying mortgages. When mortgages are pooled the rate for the mortgage-backed security is usually the same or close to the rate on the underlying mortgages. However, over time, market rates may change.

When market rates are low, borrowers tend to refinance existing high-rate mortgages. Wouldn't you? If you had taken out a 30-year, $100,000, 12 percent mortgage loan five years ago and the current market rate is 8 percent, it would make sense to refinance. The monthly payments would fall from $1,028.61 to $753.78, assuming a loan that would cover the remaining principal balance of $97,663.22 at 8 percent for 25 years. The present value of the $274.83 monthly savings, discounted at 8 percent for 25 years, is $35,608.22. If financing costs on the new loan were 3 percent, or $2,929.90, the net present value of refinancing is $35,608.22 − $2,929.90 = $32,678.32.

Now let us look at what happens to mortgage-backed security holders when borrowers pay off their mortgage balances. The mortgage-backed security holders would receive the remaining face value, or par amount, of the underlying mortgages. They paid a premium for the mortgage-backed security, however. Thus, in this situation the mortgage-backed security holders would be hurt by an increase in prepayments.

There is another side to this picture, however. Mortgage-backed securities sometimes sell at a discount—that is, investors pay less than the face value. This happens when market interest rates are above the contract rate on the underlying mortgages, and the discount gives the investor a higher rate of return.

A discount on a mortgage-backed security gives holders a capital gain should borrowers pay off their mortgage balances. Consider a $100 million mortgage-backed security that sold for $97 million. If all borrowers were to pay off their mortgage balances, the security holders would receive $100 million. Since they paid $97 million for the mortgage-backed security, they would earn an unexpected profit of $3 million.

Historically mortgages are prepaid in from 8 to 12 years. However, prepayment rates are subject to a great deal of variability; they come about because a borrower

1. Sells to a buyer who obtains new financing and thus the existing loan is paid off

2. Refinances at a lower interest rate

3. Decides to pay off all or a portion of the mortgage balance

4. Defaults, which is followed by foreclosure

Sales and refinancings are less likely when interest rates are high or are going up. Defaults are less likely as property values rise and loan-to-value ratios fall.

The prepayment rate also varies widely among states and regions. California is known as a relatively fast prepayment state. The mid-West is typically thought of as a slow prepayment region. Some of the reasons for this difference in prepayment rates have to do with the strength and diversity of the local economy, the strength of local demand, and state and local regulations regarding such things as interest rates, mortgage terms, and foreclosure laws.

Seasoning also affects prepayment rates. Seasoning refers to the age of the mortgages in the pool. Typically the relationship between prepayment rates and seasoning is positive; in early years the prepayments go up at an increasing rate, then the rate of increase slows down. Finally, after a number of years, the rate tends to level off, or burn out, because beyond a certain age families tend to remain in their existing homes.

Refinancing as a reason for prepayment is closely related to the fluctuations in the market interest rate. Twice in the past decade borrowers have taken advantage of low interest rates by refinancing. The first refinancing boom was in 1986–1987 and the second in 1992.

Forecasting Prepayments

The prepayment rate is expressed as the percentage of mortgages in a pool that prepay in a period (see Figure 24–2).

For a typical mortgage-backed security, the prepayment rate starts out at about 0.2 percent annually in the first month; it increases by 0.2 percent each month for 30 months, and then levels off at 6 percent annually. Thus, on a 30-year, fixed-rate mortgage pool, 6 percent of the mortgages remaining should prepay every year after the thirtieth month.[1]

The higher the mortgage interest rate, the higher the prepayment rate. Initially, the increase is relatively small. However, as the spread between the mortgage interest rate and the current market rate reaches levels where many borrowers find it worthwhile to refinance, prepayment rates will increase significantly.

Likewise, mortgages with rates below the current rate tend to prepay more slowly. The prepayment rate slows down as the spread between the mortgage interest rate and the current market rate gets more negative. But the prepayment rate

[1] This prepayment model is known as the Public Securities Association (PSA) prepayment model. The PSA consists of major dealers in the market for mortgage securities.

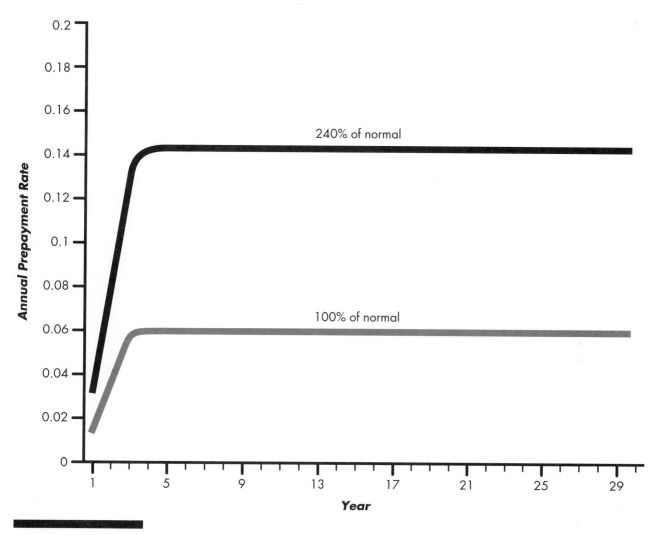

FIGURE 24–2

Typical Prepayment Pattern on a Pool of 30-Year, Standard, Fixed-Rate Mortgages

never slows to zero, because housing turnover and other factors cause some prepayments even for mortgage loans with below-market interest rates.

A simple example shows how to calculate the cash flows on a mortgage-backed security.

Figure 24–3 shows the expected annual interest and principal (both scheduled amortization and unscheduled prepayments) payments on a $100 million, 30-year, 10% mortgage-backed security. Normally, one would forecast the expected cash flows on a mortgage-backed security assuming monthly amortization, since payments are made monthly. We have assumed annual amortization in this example to simplify the calculations.

We also need to make a number of assumptions about the expected prepayment rates. First, we need to specify how quickly the mortgage pool is likely to pay off. Usually this is expressed as a multiple of the "normal" prepayment experience. For example, 0 percent of normal means no prepayments, 100 percent of normal

YEAR	BEGINNING BALANCE	INTEREST	SCHEDULED AMORTIZATION	PREPAYMENTS	DEBT SERVICE	CASH FLOWS
1	$100,000,000	$10,000,000	$607,925	$1,292,097	$10,607,925	$11,900,022
2	$98,099,978	$9,809,998	$660,024	$3,605,278	$10,470,022	$14,075,300
3	$93,834,676	$9,383,468	$699,163	$5,355,292	$10,082,631	$15,437,923
4	$87,780,221	$8,778,022	$724,858	$5,223,322	$9,502,880	$14,726,201
5	$81,832,041	$8,183,204	$749,503	$4,864,952	$8,932,707	$13,797,659
6	$76,217,586	$7,621,759	$774,986	$4,526,556	$8,396,745	$12,923,301
7	$70,916,044	$7,091,604	$801,335	$4,206,883	$7,892,940	$12,099,822
8	$65,907,826	$6,590,783	$828,581	$3,904,755	$7,419,363	$11,324,118
9	$61,174,491	$6,117,449	$856,753	$3,619,064	$6,974,202	$10,593,266
10	$56,698,674	$5,669,867	$885,882	$3,348,767	$6,555,750	$9,904,517
11	$52,464,024	$5,246,402	$916,002	$3,092,881	$6,162,405	$9,255,286
12	$48,455,141	$4,845,514	$947,146	$2,850,480	$5,792,660	$8,643,140
13	$44,657,515	$4,465,751	$979,349	$2,620,690	$5,445,101	$8,065,791
14	$41,057,475	$4,105,748	$1,012,647	$2,402,690	$5,118,395	$7,521,084
15	$37,642,139	$3,764,214	$1,047,077	$2,195,704	$4,811,291	$7,006,995
16	$34,399,358	$3,439,936	$1,082,678	$1,999,001	$4,522,614	$6,521,614
17	$31,317,679	$3,131,768	$1,119,489	$1,811,891	$4,251,257	$6,063,148
18	$28,386,299	$2,838,630	$1,157,551	$1,633,725	$3,996,181	$5,629,906
19	$25,595,023	$2,559,502	$1,196,908	$1,463,887	$3,756,410	$5,220,297
20	$22,934,228	$2,293,423	$1,237,603	$1,301,797	$3,531,026	$4,832,823
21	$20,394,827	$2,039,483	$1,279,682	$1,146,909	$3,319,164	$4,466,073
22	$17,968,237	$1,796,824	$1,323,191	$998,703	$3,120,014	$4,118,717
23	$15,646,344	$1,564,634	$1,368,179	$856,690	$2,932,814	$3,789,503
24	$13,421,475	$1,342,147	$1,414,697	$720,407	$2,756,845	$3,477,251
25	$11,286,371	$1,128,637	$1,462,797	$589,414	$2,591,434	$3,180,848
26	$9,234,159	$923,416	$1,512,532	$463,298	$2,435,948	$2,899,246
27	$7,258,330	$725,833	$1,563,958	$341,662	$2,289,791	$2,631,453
28	$5,352,709	$535,271	$1,617,133	$224,135	$2,152,404	$2,376,538
29	$3,511,442	$351,144	$1,672,115	$110,360	$2,023,259	$2,133,619
30	$1,728,967	$172,897	$1,728,967	$0	$1,901,864	$1,901,864

FIGURE 24–3

Expected Annual Interest and Principal Payments on a $100 Million, 10 Percent, 30-Year Mortgage-Backed Security

refers to the normal prepayment experience, and 200 percent of normal means that a pool is experiencing prepayment at twice the normal rate. In our example we assume 100 percent of normal.

Second, because we have assumed annual rather than monthly amortization, we also need to specify an annual prepayment rate. In practice, this problem is a moot issue since amortization is usually done monthly. In terms of Figure 24–3, here is what we have done about the expected prepayment rates. In year 1, the prepayment rate is taken to be 1.30 percent, which assumes a pool that prepays at a 0.2 percent annual rate in the first month and increases by 0.2 percent per month in months 2 through 12

The prepayment rate in year 2 is taken to be 3.7 percent which assumes a pool that prepays at a 2.6 percent annual rate in month 13 and increases by 0.2 percent per month in months 14 through 24. In year 3, the prepayment rate is 5.75 percent, which is the average annual rate assuming a pool that prepays at 5 percent in month 25 and increases by 0.2 percent per month until it levels off at 6 percent annually. In years 4 through 30 the prepayment rate is 6 percent.

Now for the cash flow calculations. Calculating the expected prepayments each year is easy.

$$\text{Prepayments} = (\text{Loan outstanding}, BOY_t - \text{Scheduled amortization}) \times \text{Prepayment rate}$$

The hard part is to work out the annual debt service payment. Why? Because the debt service payment depends on the outstanding loan balance after accounting for prepayments. That makes sense; if some loans were paid off in the first year, you would not expect to receive the same debt service payment in year 2. Hence, the debt service payment in year 2 is based on the outstanding loan balance after all prepayments.

Let us try to put some numbers into the equation. At the beginning of year 1, the outstanding loan balance is, by definition, $100 million. At 10 percent interest for 30 years, the debt service payment is:

$$DS = \text{Loan outstanding}, BOY1 \times PR_{10\%, 30}$$
$$= \$100,000,000 \times 0.106007925 = \$10,607,925$$

The interest in year 1 is $10 million ($100 million $\times$ 10%). This means that the scheduled amortization is $10,607,925 minus $10,000,000, or $607,925. Remember that principal reduction can be backed into by subtracting the amount of interest paid from the annual debt service payment.

We can now calculate the expected prepayment in year 1:

$$\text{Prepayments} = (\text{Loan outstanding}, BOY1 - \text{Scheduled amortization}) \times \text{Prepayment rate}$$
$$= (\$100,000,000 - \$607,925) \times 0.0130 = \$1,292,097$$

The total cash flow on our $100 million, 30-year, 10 percent, mortgage-backed security in year 1 is therefore:

$$\text{Cash flow} = \text{Debt service} + \text{Prepayments}$$
$$= \$10,607,925 + \$1,292,097 = \$11,900,022$$

This is shown in column 7 of Figure 24–3.

Now for the hard part. A total of $1,900,022 ($607,925 + $1,292,097) in principal, including both scheduled and unscheduled, was paid off in year 1. This leaves an outstanding loan balance at the end of year 1, or the beginning of year 2, of:

$$\text{Loan outstanding}, EOY1 = \text{Loan outstanding}, BOY1 - \text{Scheduled amortization} - \text{Prepayment}$$
$$= \$100,000,000 - \$607,925 - \$1,292,097 = \$98,099,978$$

At 10 percent interest for 29 years, the debt service payment in year 2 is:

$$DS = \text{Loan outstanding}, BOY2 \times PR_{10\%, 29}$$
$$= \$98,099,978 \times 0.106728075 = \$10,470,022$$

It should be noted that this is 98.7 percent of $10,607,925, which makes sense since the pool survival rate at the end of year 1 is 98.7 percent. In this context, the *pool survival rate* measures the percentage of the outstanding mortgages in a pool at the beginning of the period that remain outstanding at the end of the period. In our example the survival rate for year 1 is 1.000 minus 0.013, or 98.7 percent.

Repeating the interest, scheduled amortization, prepayment, and cash flow calculations for year 2 using an annual prepayment rate of 3.7 percent, we find that

$$\text{Interest} = \$98,099,978 \times .10 = \$9,809,998$$
$$\text{Scheduled amortization} = \$10,470,022 - \$9,809,998 = \$660,024$$
$$\text{Prepayment} = (\$98,099,978 - \$660,024) \times 3.7\% = \$3,605,278$$
$$\text{Cash flow} = \$10,470,022 + \$3,605,278 = \$14,075,300$$

In this case the outstanding loan balance at the end of year 2, or beginning of year 3, is:

$$\text{Loan outstanding, } EOY2 = \text{Loan outstanding, } BOY2 - \text{Scheduled amortization}$$
$$- \text{Prepayment}$$
$$= \$98,099,978 - \$660,024 - \$3,605,278$$
$$= \$93,834,676$$

At 10 percent interest for 28 years, the debt service payment in year 3 is:

$$DS = \text{Loan outstanding, } BOY3 \times PR_{10\%, \, 28}$$
$$= \$93,834,676 \times 0.107451013 = \$10,082,631$$

As a check, note that the pool survival rate at the end of year 2 is 95.0 percent ($0.987 \times [1.000 - .037]$), which is the pool survival rate at the beginning of the period, times the percentage of the outstanding mortgages at the beginning of the period that remain outstanding in year 2. This implies that the debt service payment in year 3 should be 95.0 percent of $10,607,925, or $10,082,631.

The remaining calculations for years 3 through 30 are shown in Figure 24–3. Two important points should be made. First, remember that in year 3 the annual prepayment rate is 5.75 percent and in years 4–30 the annual prepayment rate is 6 percent. Second, you can check the debt service calculations by computing the pool survival rate. The pool survival rate at the end of each period is the pool survival rate at the beginning of the period times the percentage of the outstanding mortgages at the beginning of the period that remain outstanding during the period. To illustrate, the pool survival rate at the end of year 3 is 0.950 times ($1.000 - .057$), or 89.6 percent. At the end of year 4, the pool survival rate is 0.896 times ($1.000 - 0.060$), or 84.2 percent. And so forth.

Value of a Mortgage-Backed Security

If you have digested what we have said so far, you can appreciate why mortgage-backed securities are hard to value. Fortunately for us, once we have calculated expected cash flows from a mortgage pool, valuing the security is an easy matter. The value of a mortgage-backed security is the present value of the expected cash flows, discounted at the investor's required rate of return.

Let us reconsider our example in Figure 24–3. The cash flows in years 1 through 30 are summarized in Figure 24–4. The investor's required rate of return in this example is assumed to be 9 percent. Discounting the cash flows in years 1 through 30 at 9 percent yields the market value of this mortgage-backed security to the investor; it is $106,510,953.

Several points should be made about this market value:

1. We have already made the point that higher-coupon mortgages have higher prepayment rates. This means that over time, if the market interest rate falls, prepayments will increase, thereby reducing the average life of the security. The decline in the market interest rate means that each debt service payment is discounted by a smaller factor, thus raising the present value of the security. However, a faster prepayment rate means that the market value of the mortgage-backed security will not increase by as much as other fixed-income securi-

YEAR	CASH FLOWS	PV FACTOR	PRESENT VALUE
1	$11,900,022	0.917431193	$10,917,451
2	$14,075,300	0.841679993	$11,846,899
3	$15,437,923	0.77218348	$11,920,909
4	$14,726,201	0.708425211	$10,432,412
5	$13,797,659	0.649931386	$8,967,532
6	$12,923,301	0.596267327	$7,705,742
7	$12,099,822	0.547034245	$6,619,017
8	$11,324,118	0.50186628	$5,683,193
9	$10,593,266	0.46042778	$4,877,434
10	$9,904,517	0.422410807	$4,183,775
11	$9,255,286	0.38753285	$3,586,727
12	$8,643,140	0.355534725	$3,072,936
13	$8,065,791	0.326178647	$2,630,889
14	$7,521,084	0.299246465	$2,250,658
15	$7,006,995	0.274538041	$1,923,687
16	$6,521,614	0.251869763	$1,642,597
17	$6,063,148	0.231073177	$1,401,031
18	$5,629,906	0.21199374	$1,193,505
19	$5,220,297	0.19448967	$1,015,294
20	$4,832,823	0.17843089	$862,325
21	$4,466,073	0.163698064	$731,088
22	$4,118,717	0.15018171	$618,556
23	$3,789,503	0.137781385	$522,123
24	$3,477,251	0.126404941	$439,542
25	$3,180,848	0.115967836	$368,876
26	$2,899,246	0.10639251	$308,458
27	$2,631,453	0.097607807	$256,850
28	$2,376,538	0.089548447	$212,815
29	$2,133,619	0.082154538	$175,286
30	$1,901,864	0.075371136	$143,346
		Market Value	$106,510,953

FIGURE 24–4
Present Value of Cash Flows on a $100 Million, 10 Percent, 30-Year, Mortgage-Backed Security Discounted at 9 Percent

ties because of the potential loss of value as borrowers prepay at par, rather than market value.

2. Conversely, if the market interest rate increases, prepayments slow down and the average life of the security increases. A higher market interest rate means that each future debt service payment will be discounted at a higher factor, thus lowering the present value. Compounding this fall in market value is a slower prepayment rate. In periods of rising market interest rates, therefore, prices of mortgage-backed securities tend to fall faster than prices of other fixed-income securities.

Figure 24–5 summarizes these observations. The dashed line in Figure 24–5 shows the market value of a $100 million, 30-year, 10 percent, mortgage-backed security as the market interest rate increases from 7 to 13 percent. The market values assume that the prepayment rate increases as the spread between the coupon rate and the current market rate grows wider. The solid line in Figure 24–5 shows the market value of the same security assuming a constant prepayment speed.

Notice that this price difference between the dashed line and the solid line widens as the market interest rate falls. This difference reflects the value of the borrower's prepayment option. Thus, at a 7 percent yield, rational investors expect to pay a much lower price for a fast prepayment mortgage pool than they are willing to pay for a mortgage pool with a constant prepayment rate. The faster prepayments decrease realized yields on mortgage-backed securities, which, in turn, lead to lower prices.

COLLATERALIZED MORTGAGE OBLIGATIONS

The concept behind collateralized mortgage obligations (CMOs) is as follows: Take a pool of mortgages and divide the cash flows from the pool into classes, with each class having a stated maturity. Prioritize the cash flows so that the short-term classes are paid off first. Then price the cash flows according to the required yields of in-

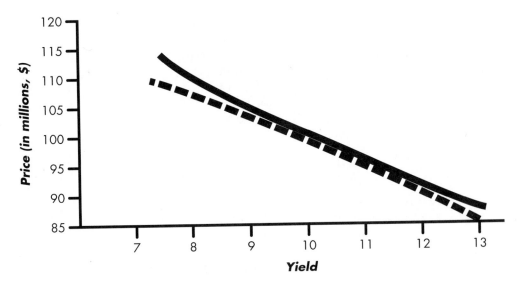

FIGURE 24–5

Market Value of a $100 Million, 10 percent Mortgage-Backed Security Under Various Interest Rate Scenarios

vestors seeking short-term securities and those seeking longer-term securities. If done correctly, the value of the part will exceed the value of the whole.

Slicing the cash flows into parts and then selling the individual parts to different investors is akin to the way chicken is packaged and sold in the supermarket. In most supermarkets, the whole chicken is cut up into various parts—legs, thighs, and breasts. The packages of like parts are then sold to people who prefer those parts. And the parts are priced so that the sum of the individual parts is greater than the value of the whole chicken.

Here is an example. Suppose you were to take the $100 million, 10 percent, 30-year mortgage-backed security shown in Figure 24-3 and create a CMO with the following classes:

	CLASS 1	CLASS 2	RESIDUAL
Coupon	9.75%	10.50%	—
Principal amount	$50 million	$45 million	$5 million

Normally CMO bonds pay interest semiannually; however for this example we will assume annual payments. Class 1 bonds have a coupon rate of 9.75 percent. They receive annual interest payments and also receive scheduled and nonscheduled principal payments for 11 years. Class 2 bonds have a coupon rate of 10.50 percent. Initially they receive interest payments only. Starting with year 11, after Class 1 investors have been paid off, they receive not only the annual interest payments but also scheduled and nonscheduled principal payments.

Note that the residual class does not have a specified coupon rate. The residual class is a contingency fund which receives whatever cash flows are left over after payments have been made to Class 1 bondholders, including any reinvestment income. A danger exists in most CMOs that the passthrough income on the underlying mortgages will be less than the amount promised to the CMO holders. Thus, in our example the residual class ensures that Class 2 holders will receive a 10.50 percent coupon payment for as long as the bonds are outstanding.

Figures 24-6, 24-7, and 24-8 show the cash flows to Class 1 and 2 bond holders, and the residual cash flows, respectively. These cash flows are calculated as fol-

YEAR	BEGINNING BALANCE	INTEREST	SCHEDULED AMORTIZATION	PREPAYMENTS	CASH FLOW
1	$50,000,000	$4,875,000	$607,925	$1,292,097	$6,775,022
2	$48,099,978	$4,689,748	$660,024	$3,605,278	$8,955,050
3	$43,834,676	$4,273,881	$699,163	$5,355,292	$10,328,336
4	$37,780,221	$3,683,572	$724,858	$5,223,322	$9,631,751
5	$31,832,041	$3,103,624	$749,503	$4,864,952	$8,718,079
6	$26,217,586	$2,556,215	$774,986	$4,526,556	$7,857,757
7	$20,916,044	$2,039,314	$801,335	$4,206,883	$7,047,532
8	$15,907,826	$1,551,013	$828,581	$3,904,755	$6,284,349
9	$11,174,491	$1,089,513	$856,753	$3,619,064	$5,565,330
10	$6,698,674	$653,121	$885,882	$3,348,767	$4,887,770
11	$2,464,024	$240,242	$916,002	$1,548,022	$2,704,266

FIGURE 24–6
Expected Annual Cash Flows on a $50 Million, 9.75%, Class 1, CMO Certificate

FIGURE 24–7

Expected Annual Cash Flows on a $45 Million, 10.50%, Class 2, CMO Certificate

YEAR	BEGINNING BALANCE	INTEREST	SCHEDULED AMORTIZATION	PREPAYMENTS	CASH FLOW
1	$45,000,000	$4,725,000	$0	$0	$4,725,000
2	$45,000,000	$4,725,000	$0	$0	$4,725,000
3	$45,000,000	$4,725,000	$0	$0	$4,725,000
4	$45,000,000	$4,725,000	$0	$0	$4,725,000
5	$45,000,000	$4,725,000	$0	$0	$4,725,000
6	$45,000,000	$4,725,000	$0	$0	$4,725,000
7	$45,000,000	$4,725,000	$0	$0	$4,725,000
8	$45,000,000	$4,725,000	$0	$0	$4,725,000
9	$45,000,000	$4,725,000	$0	$0	$4,725,000
10	$45,000,000	$4,725,000	$0	$0	$4,725,000
11	$45,000,000	$4,725,000	$0	$1,544,859	$6,269,859
12	$43,455,141	$4,562,790	$947,146	$2,850,480	$8,360,416
13	$39,657,515	$4,164,039	$979,349	$2,620,690	$7,764,078
14	$36,057,475	$3,786,035	$1,012,647	$2,402,690	$7,201,372
15	$32,642,139	$3,427,425	$1,047,077	$2,195,704	$6,670,205
16	$29,399,358	$3,086,933	$1,082,678	$1,999,001	$6,168,611
17	$26,317,679	$2,763,356	$1,119,489	$1,811,891	$5,694,737
18	$23,386,299	$2,455,561	$1,157,551	$1,633,725	$5,246,838
19	$20,595,023	$2,162,477	$1,196,908	$1,463,887	$4,823,272
20	$17,934,228	$1,883,094	$1,237,603	$1,301,797	$4,422,494
21	$15,394,827	$1,616,457	$1,279,682	$1,146,909	$4,043,047
22	$12,968,237	$1,361,665	$1,323,191	$998,703	$3,683,558
23	$10,646,344	$1,117,866	$1,368,179	$856,690	$3,342,735
24	$8,421,475	$884,255	$1,414,697	$720,407	$3,019,359
25	$6,286,371	$660,069	$1,462,797	$589,414	$2,712,280
26	$4,234,159	$444,587	$1,512,532	$463,298	$2,420,416
27	$2,258,330	$237,125	$1,563,958	$341,662	$2,142,745
28	$352,709	$37,034	$352,709	$0	$389,744

lows. From Figure 24–3, we know that the total cash flow on the underlying mortgages in year 1 is $11,900,022, of which $10,000,000 is interest and $1,900,022 is principal. Class 1 holders are promised $4,875,000 ($50,000,000 × .0975) of interest in year 1. Class 2 holders are promised $4,725,000 ($45,000,000 × .1050) of interest in year 1. The remaining interest income of $400,000 goes to the residual class ($10,000,000 − $4,875,000 − $4,725,000).

The Class 1 bonds will receive all the scheduled and nonscheduled principal payments in year 1, and will continue to receive these payments in years 2 through 11, at which time the Class 1 bonds are paid off. The total cash flow to the Class 1 bonds in year 1 is $6,775,022 ($4,875,000 + $607,925 + $1,292,097).

At the beginning of year 2, Class 1 has an outstanding loan balance of $48,099,978, which is the outstanding loan balance at the beginning of year 1, $50,000,000, less the scheduled and unscheduled principal payments of $1,900,022. In year 2 interest promised to Class 1 holders is $4,689,748 ($48,099,978 × .0975); Class 2 holders get $4,725,000 ($45,000,000 × .1050). Total interest payments for the two classes are $9,414,748, which leaves a residual interest income of $395,250.

YEAR	BEGINNING BALANCE	INTEREST	SCHEDULED AMORTIZATION	PREPAYMENTS	CASH FLOW
1	$5,000,000	$400,000	$0	$0	$400,000
2	$5,000,000	$395,250	$0	$0	$395,250
3	$5,000,000	$384,587	$0	$0	$384,587
4	$5,000,000	$369,451	$0	$0	$369,451
5	$5,000,000	$354,580	$0	$0	$354,580
6	$5,000,000	$340,544	$0	$0	$340,544
7	$5,000,000	$327,290	$0	$0	$327,290
8	$5,000,000	$314,770	$0	$0	$314,770
9	$5,000,000	$302,936	$0	$0	$302,936
10	$5,000,000	$291,747	$0	$0	$291,747
11	$5,000,000	$281,160	$0	$0	$281,160
12	$5,000,000	$282,724	$0	$0	$282,724
13	$5,000,000	$301,712	$0	$0	$301,712
14	$5,000,000	$319,713	$0	$0	$319,713
15	$5,000,000	$336,789	$0	$0	$336,789
16	$5,000,000	$353,003	$0	$0	$353,003
17	$5,000,000	$368,412	$0	$0	$368,412
18	$5,000,000	$383,069	$0	$0	$383,069
19	$5,000,000	$397,025	$0	$0	$397,025
20	$5,000,000	$410,329	$0	$0	$410,329
21	$5,000,000	$423,026	$0	$0	$423,026
22	$5,000,000	$435,159	$0	$0	$435,159
23	$5,000,000	$446,768	$0	$0	$446,768
24	$5,000,000	$457,893	$0	$0	$457,893
25	$5,000,000	$468,568	$0	$0	$468,568
26	$5,000,000	$478,829	$0	$0	$478,829
27	$5,000,000	$488,708	$0	$0	$488,708
28	$5,000,000	$498,236	$1,264,423	$224,135	$1,986,794
29	$3,511,442	$351,144	$1,672,115	$110,360	$2,133,619
30	$1,728,967	$172,897	$1,728,967	$0	$1,901,864

FIGURE 24-8
Expected Annual Cash Flows on a $5 Million, Residual Class CMO Certificate

The remaining calculations are shown in Figures 24-6, 24-7, and 24-8. In year 11, a portion of the principal prepayment shifts to Class 2 as the Class 1 bonds are paid off. In year 28, a portion of the scheduled amortization and all of the principal prepayments shift to the residual class.

Now let us show you the market values of these bonds. The value of the Class 1 bond is equal to the cash payments discounted at the investor's required rate of return:

$$MV = \frac{\$6,775,022}{(1 + .08)} + \frac{\$8,955,050}{(1 + .08)^2} + \cdots + \frac{\$2,704,266}{(1 + .08)^{11}}$$

$$= \$53,829,622$$

where 8 percent is the Class 1 investor's required rate of return.

At 8.75 percent, the value of the Class 2 bond is $51,914,277 and the value of the residual class is $4,209,679 (discount the cash flows in column 5 of Figures 24-7 and 24–8 at 8.75 percent to arrive at these numbers). Collectively, the value of the CMO is \$108,953,578 (\$53,829,622 + \$51,914,277 + \$4,209,679), which exceeds the value of the underlying mortgage pool as determined above.

SECURITIZATION OF COMMERCIAL MORTGAGES

The securitization of commercial mortgages is clearly in its embryonic stage. To date, less than 5 percent of all commercial mortgage debt outstanding has been securitized, and most of the activity has been tied to the efforts of the Resolution Trust Corporation (RTC), an instrumentality of the U.S. government that was set up in 1989, to dispose of the assets of failed S&Ls formerly insured by the Federal Savings and Loan Insurance Corporation.

The process for securitizing commercial mortgages is as follows. Start with a pool of commercial mortgages backed by income-producing properties, such as office buildings, retail shopping centers, industrial/warehouse properties, and hotels. Issue a CMO with two classes against the pool of mortgages—a class A bond and a class B bond. Take part of the sales proceeds and establish a reserve fund that will be used to provide protection against default. The size of the reserve fund depends on the pool's credit risk, the desired rating level, and whether other credit enhancements are available. Alternatively, the CMO can be overcollateralized by placing the mortgages in a pool whose value exceeds that of the certificates in the pool.

Also, prioritize the cash flows so that all principal payments, including principal payments received upon foreclosure, go to pay off class A bondholders first. Once class A bondholders are paid off, then class B bondholders will be paid off, assuming that defaults have not eroded their certificate principal balance.

Do something similar with respect to interest payments as well. Allocate accrued interest on the principal balance during the preceding month at the related passthrough rate. Make the distribution of interest to class B holders subordinate to distribution of interest to the class A holders. No distribution of interest will then be permitted to class B until the interest payable to class A has been paid.

The resulting CMO is called a *senior-subordinate structure.* The senior securities are the class A certificates. The subordinate securities are the class B certificates. Generally, the senior-subordinate structure prevents the subordinate securities, or so-called *junior* certificates, from receiving interest or principal payments until the senior certificate holders have been fully paid. This reduces principal exposure and risk as to timely payment of interest and principal for senior certificate holders. In turn, these risks are absorbed by the junior certificate holders.

Obviously, the main drawback in securitizing commercial mortgages is finding buyers for the junior securities, called the *B pieces.* B pieces may be rated or unrated by the rating agencies. Unrated securities are generally considered to be well below investment grade, with considerable uncertainty as to timely payment of interest. Protection factors are narrow. And risk can be substantial with unfavorable economic conditions. Normally, B pieces are deemed to be unacceptable investments for S&Ls, commercial banks, life insurance companies, and pension fund investors. Thus, the market for such securities is quite limited.

There is also the problem of trying to securitize nothing but commercial loans on foreclosed properties or loans with high debt-to-income ratios, or loans with no down payments, poor payment records, and loans that are delinquent. The riskier the underlying assets, the larger the reserve fund needed against potential losses.

SUMMARY

Residential mortgage securitization plays a vital role in channeling funds into the housing market. Roughly 40 to 50 percent of all single-family, conventional, home mortgage debt outstanding is securitized. And more than 85 percent of all FHA and VA mortgage debt is securitized.

Several types of mortgage securities exist: mortgage passthrough securities, mortgage-backed bonds, collateralized mortgage obligations, and stripped mortgage-backed securities. Here is a brief summary of each type.

Mortgage passthrough securities include GNMA passthroughs, FHLMC participation certificates, FNMA mortgage-backed securities, and private passthroughs.

Mortgage-backed bonds are a general debt obligation of the issuer and are collateralized by a pool of mortgages. The bonds are structured so that the mortgages securing them will generate enough cash flow to provide for the full and timely repayment of the bonds.

CMOs are mortgage-backed bonds with multiple classes of bonds instead of one. Each class has a stated maturity. These include short, intermediate, and long-term classes. The idea behind a *CMO* is simple—the holders of short-term certificates receive all payments and prepayments of principal from the collateralized loans until they are fully repaid. Next, holders of intermediate certificates receive all payments and prepayments of principal. And so on. CMOs can be structured to meet market demand.

There are two types of stripped mortgage-backed securities: interest-only (IO) and principal-only (PO) securities. In these securities the interest and principal payments are separated. The IO holder receives all interest payments while the PO holder receives all principal payments, including principal prepayments.

Pricing of mortgage-backed securities is complicated by the fact that very few mortgages are held to maturity. Historically, mortgages are prepaid in from 8 to 12 years; however, prepayment rates vary widely. Prepayments come about when a borrower refinances at a lower interest rate, sells the house, pays off the mortgage for any reason, or loses the property through foreclosure. Prepayments are less likely as interest rates rise, and they slow down as the pool ages. Prepayments can also vary widely among states and regions.

Valuing a mortgage-backed security or a mortgage-backed bond requires two steps. In the first step you need to forecast the expected cash flows on the underlying mortgages. In a CMO, you will also need to prioritize the cash flows for the different classes. The second step is to discount the cash flows at the investor's required rate of return. The market value of the security is equal to the discounted present value of the expected cash flows.

Securitization of commercial mortgages is in its infancy. Part of the reason is that issuers have been trying to securitize problem loans. Generally, securitizing such commercial mortgage loans requires a reserve fund and significant overcollateralization, plus a subordinate class of certificates to raise the rating on the senior class.

KEY CONCEPTS

Collateralized mortgage obligation (CMO) A mortgage paythrough bond.

Fannie Mae Federal National Mortgage Association (FNMA); a government-sponsored secondary lender.

Freddie Mac Federal Home Loan Mortgage Corporation (FHLMC); an active participant in secondary mortgage markets.

Ginnie Mae Government National Mortgage Association (GNMA); a government-sponsored corporation created to provide special assistance mortgage money for disadvantaged residential borrowers.

Mortgage-backed bond Similar to corporate bonds, except that the issuer pledges a pool of mortgages as security for the bonds.

Mortgage-backed security Represents an undivided ownership interest in a pool of mortgages with interest and principal being passed through to investors as received from borrowers; the pool may consist of one or many mortgages.

Secondary mortgage market The selling and buying of existing mortgage loans.

QUESTIONS FOR REVIEW AND DISCUSSION

1. What is the secondary mortgage market?

2. What are some of the benefits of mortgage securitization?

3. What is a primary lender? What financial institutions are most likely to be primary lenders?

4. What is a secondary lender? What institutions make up the bulk of secondary lenders?

5. Discuss the different types of mortgage-backed securities. Which type of mortgage-backed security is broken up into different maturity schedules?

6. What aspect of mortgage-backed securities creates risk or uncertainty as to expected returns to an investor?

7. How is the value of a mortgage-backed security calculated?

8. With a CMO, which class, or tranche, faces the most risk? Why?

9. Distinguish between securitization of residential mortgages and commercial mortgages? Include in your discussion the potential drawbacks in securitizing commercial mortgages.

10. Explain why, when market interest rates on mortgages are 8 percent, the price of a 10 percent mortgage-backed security may fall.

PROBLEMS

1. Ace Savings and Loan Association is issuing a $5 million mortgage-backed security with an 8 percent contract rate and 30-year term. Assume that the mortgages in the pool will prepay at the rate of 10 percent per year. Also assume annual compounding.

a. What would be the price that Ace Savings and Loan Association could obtain if market interest rates were 9 percent?

b. What if interest rates were 7 percent?

c. If interest rates were 9 percent and prepayments were to slow down to 6 percent, what price could Ace Savings and Loan Association obtain?

d. If interest rates were 7 percent and prepayments were to increase to 20 percent, what would the value be of this mortgage-backed security?

2. A 10 percent, 30-year, $2,500,000 mortgage-backed security is expected to have a constant prepayment rate of 12 percent per year. Assume annual compounding.

a. What is the expected yield if the price is $2,550,000?

b. If the expected yield is 10 percent, what should the price be?

3. Assume you are going to issue a $1,000,000 collateralized mortgage obligation. The collateral will consist of ten $100,000 fixed-rate mortgages with 9 percent contract rates and 30-year loan terms. The CMO will contain three classes of securities, with the third being a residual class:

	CMO TRANCHES		
	CLASS 1	CLASS 2	RESIDUAL
Price	$570,000	$430,000	$30,000
Coupon	9.75%	9.5%	

The underlying mortgages are paid annually, and the payments made to the investors in each of the classes are made annually. The expected prepayment rate is 10 percent.

a. If class 1 security holders demand a 10 percent required return, what is the value of the class 1 security?

b. Determine the value of the class 2 security. Assume class 2 security holders demand a 9.75 percent return.

c. If the residual holders demand a 12 percent rate of return, what is the value of the residual tranche?

d. How much will you, as issuer, receive as proceeds from the CMO issue?

4. Look up the price of a 8 percent, 30-year, GNMA security in a recent issue of the *Wall Street Journal.*

a. How much higher (or lower) is the GNMA equivalent yield than the yield on a Treasury bond with a similar maturity?

b. Would you expect the GNMA yield to be more or less than the Treasury yield?

PART SIX
LAW AND BROKERAGE

CHAPTER 25

PROPERTY DESCRIPTIONS AND PUBLIC RECORDS

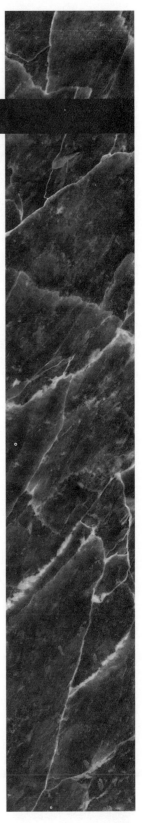

Chapter Outline

But that land—it is one thing that will still be there when I come back—land is always there.

Pearl S. Buck, *A House Divided*

An accurate, clear, and complete system of description is necessary in order to package real estate as a commodity because real estate involves both ownership and value. Physical descriptions establish boundaries, calculate area, and note location relative to other properties. Legal descriptions identify the rights owned and trace the transfer of ownership from one person to another.

WHAT IS REAL PROPERTY?

Real property is a legal concept; it is used to mean *ownership of rights* in real estate. They are rights to control, to use, to exclude, to dispose of, or to otherwise capture the benefits of real estate. The term real property is what makes physical real estate a flexible commodity; real property can be split up in many, many ways, as we shall see in the next chapter. The term real property is often used interchangeably with the terms land, real estate and realty; yet each is a distinct concept. A dictionary definition of *land* is that it is the solid part of the earth not covered by water. *Realty* and *real estate* are essentially identical concepts that include land, land improvements, and the natural assets of land such as oil, water, and minerals. For the rest of our discussion we shall use the four terms interchangeably.

To understand modern property descriptions, we must go back to land in its most basic definition, and to when there were few people relative to the amount of land. As the population increased and crowded more closely on the land, a system of physical property descriptions gradually came into use.

Current legal descriptions of most real property begin with physical boundaries. Initially, only surface descriptions were of concern. The surface description was considered to extend in the shape of an inverted pyramid from the center of the earth to the limits of the sky, as portrayed in Figure 25–1. Thus, the surface description was adequate, whether the land were used for farming or for an apartment building.

Later, real estate came to include both the land and *permanent improvements* to the land. These improvements might be above or below the surface of the earth or something that affects the utility of a given parcel, such as fertilizer added to enrich the soil.

Today, even more complicated descriptions are necessary because real property is more than three-dimensional space, though we might begin with a physical description. Property rights have come to be described as air rights, surface rights, and subsurface rights. More difficult to describe are water and mineral rights. And, today, a "right to light" (sunshine) appears to be evolving.

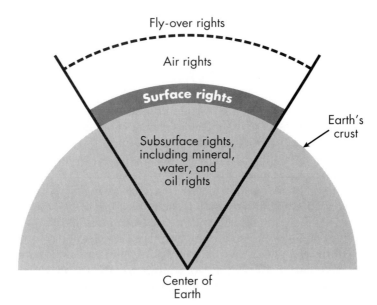

Fly-over rights

Air rights

Surface rights

Subsurface rights,
including mineral,
water, and
oil rights

Earth's
crust

Center of
Earth

FIGURE 25–1
Real Estate Extends from
the Center of the Earth
to the Tops of the
Highest Manmade
Improvements, Above
Which Common Fly-
Over Rights Exist

Thus, real property, as the object of ownership, may be described in many ways. Before going farther in our effort to describe real property, we need to distinguish between real and personal property.

Real Versus Personal Property

We begin with a basic relationship: Personalty is to personal property as realty is to real property. That is, if realty is the object of ownership for real property, then personalty is the object of ownership for personal property. *Personalty* means physical objects that are movable and not attached to the land, such as cars, typewriters, and furniture. And *personal property* refers to ownership rights and privileges in these movable things. In addition to being easily moved, personal property is sometimes consumed or destroyed, and is usually considered as something temporary or transient. Real property, on the other hand, refers to something that is fixed and permanent. A legal distinction is that a deed is used to transfer ownership of real property, whereas a bill of sale is used to transfer ownership of personal property. But the actual distinction is sometimes more subtle, and in specific situations, a line must be drawn between the two. How then do we determine whether an object is personal or real property? We begin by defining real estate more fully and then move on to a discussion of fixtures.

Land and Land Improvements

Real estate includes permanent improvements to a site, as well as the land itself. Houses, stores, factories, office buildings, schools, outbuildings, fences, and landscaping are clearly permanent improvements. By law and tradition, conveying ownership of a parcel of land also conveys ownership of any improvements thereon. In a similar sense, trees, natural vegetation, and assorted perennial plants, which do not require annual cultivation, are considered real estate. The term for them is *fructus naturales* (fruit of nature). On the other hand, annual cultivated crops (e.g., corn, potatoes, and cotton) are considered personal property even though they are attached to the earth. They are called *fructus industriales* (fruit of industry), or *emblements.*

Fixtures

A "movable" item may be considered to be personal property, or *chattel,* or it may be real property, or a *fixture.* Track lighting in a building, for example, is usually considered to be part of the real estate and is termed a fixture. That is, it is movable personal property annexed, affixed, or installed so as to be considered part of the real estate. But, when such items are not part of a building they are considered personal property. In a plumber's shop a bathroom sink is personal property, a chattel; it becomes real property, a fixture, when installed in a house.

The determination is particularly important at the time of sale and conveyance, of mortgaging, of lease termination, and of assessment for property tax purposes. A sales contract and deed convey ownership of land and fixtures, but not of chattels. A fixture is part of the security for a mortgage loan; a chattel is not. A tenant installation, if a fixture, may not be removed at the end of a lease. Fixtures that have become part of the realty so as to lose their character as chattels also become real estate for property tax purposes.

Several tests are used to determine if an article is a fixture. Meeting or passing the tests makes the item at issue a fixture and, therefore, real property.

1. *Manner of Attachment.* Generally, if the article is annexed to the land or building, and to remove it would leave the building or land incomplete, it is a fixture. Thus, installed electrical wiring, water pipes, a furnace, and wood siding are fixtures.

2. *Manner of Adaption.* An article specially constructed or fitted to a particular structure, or designed and installed to carry out the purposes of the property, is usually considered a fixture. In other words, the article is essential to the ordinary and convenient use of the property. Thus drapes cut and sewn for particular windows, screens and storm windows fitted to a house, and a front door key are almost certainly fixtures.

3. *Intent, Relationship,* or *Agreement of Parties.* The reasonably presumable intent of the person placing the article is probably most important in making the determination of an item as a fixture. Kratovil and Werner say that tests 1 and 2 are important, but "once the intention is determined, it must govern."[1] The test is based on the nature of the article, the manner of adaption, the manner of annexation, and all pertinent circumstances. Thus an owner's statements to neighbors may show whether or not an article was intended to become a fixture. An agreement between parties before an item is annexed would make intent clear and avoid later differences and a possible legal suit.

The relation between parties is often such that a presumable intention is inferred by the courts. For example, an owner may be presumed to be permanently annexing the article. And a tenant is ordinarily bound to leave articles fastened to the building. Even so, if a property is leased for business, it is a general rule that *trade fixtures,* such as

---

[1] Robert Kratovil and Raymond J. Werner, *Real Estate Law,* 9th ed. Englewood Cliffs, N.J.: Prentice Hall, 1988.

shelves, counters, and showcases, do not become real fixtures. But such equipment must be removed before the lease expires. And a renewal that fails to state that the equipment is to remain the tenant's property may deprive the tenant of ownership.

LEGAL DESCRIPTIONS OF REAL PROPERTY

For most legal purposes, real estate must be identifiable with reference only to documents. Courts consider a description adequate if a competent surveyor can exactly locate the parcel from it. In other words, a *legal description* is a specific and unique identification of a property that is recognized and acceptable in a court of law.

A street address is the simplest form of property description, but a street address is not specific enough for most legal documents or for court purposes. Other methods of legally describing real estate are therefore needed.

The three accepted methods of legally describing real estate, which we will describe later in the chapter, are (1) *metes and bounds,* (2) government, or rectangular, survey, and (3) recorded *plat.* A fourth method, the state plane-coordinate system, is gradually being accepted as a supplement to the foregoing three methods.

Any one of these methods provides a description suitable for use in a sales contract, mortgage, deed, or court of law. Description by recorded plat is used mostly in urban areas. Metes and bounds descriptions are used in urban areas to describe parcels that have been split off and developed individually—that is, the parcels were not part of a larger recorded plat. The rectangular, or governmental, survey system is used mainly in rural areas for large acreages; it is too crude for smaller, urban parcels. Except for condominium descriptions, these methods describe only the land; they do not describe improvements to a parcel.

A brief description of the elements of surveying is appropriate before taking up the methods themselves.

Elements of Surveying

Several considerations are common to all systems of describing real estate. To begin, any land description should contain (1) a definite point of beginning (POB), (2) definite corners, or turning points, (3) specific directions and distances for borders or boundaries, (4) closure, or a return to the point of beginning, and (5) the area enclosed in accepted units of measurement.

A point of beginning is where a real estate description begins. Ideally, a point of beginning ties into a larger system of property descriptions so that the resulting legal description relates the subject parcel to other parcels and to the rest of the world. In addition, a basic knowledge of units of measurement for angles or bearings, distances, and areas is needed in order to freely understand fully legal descriptions.

Angle Measurement. An angle measurement is a direction from an imaginary north-south line passing through a corner or turning point on a property. An angle measurement is measured east or west of the imaginary line and cannot exceed 90 degrees. For example, assume a circular compass properly oriented and set exactly over the corner point of a property, as in Figure 25–2. A line running just slightly north of due east might have a bearing of "north, 89 degrees east." A 3-degree more southerly line would have a bearing "south 88 degrees east." A minute, in angle measurement, equals one-sixtieth of a degree.

FIGURE 25–2
Illustration of Angle
Measurements

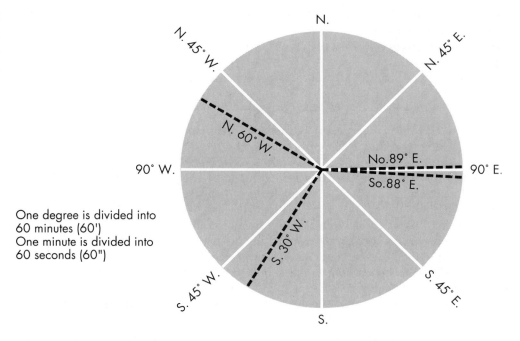

One degree is divided into
60 minutes (60')
One minute is divided into
60 seconds (60")

Distance Measurement. Distance measurements in surveying have traditionally been in miles, rods, feet, and inches. A mile equals 5,280 feet, or 320 rods. A rod, which equals 16½ feet, was a convenient unit of measurement in centuries past; it is not used much now because steel tapes and other new methods of measurement are faster and more accurate.

Area Measurement. Areas are most commonly measured in square feet, acres, and square miles, or sections. An *acre* is a measure of land that contains 43,560 square feet. A square mile—that is, a section—covers 640 acres. A table for conversion from English to metric measurements and vice versa is given in the appendix.

Elevation Measurement. A final element of surveying is elevation. Elevations are usually measured from mean sea level in New York Harbor, which is the basic elevation datum or point of reference for the United States. Elevations are important in establishing limits on heights of buildings and other structures and in setting grades for streets and highways. Condominium developments also depend on accurate elevation data.

Permanent reference points, called *benchmarks,* have been created and are located throughout the country to aid surveyors in work involving elevations. That is, a surveyor may take an elevation from a local benchmark and need not measure from a basic benchmark that is miles from the parcel under survey. Benchmark locations may be obtained from the United States Geological Survey, if needed.

Metes and Bounds Descriptions

Metes and bounds means measures and boundaries; the edges of a property are, of course, its limits and boundaries. Metes and bounds descriptions are widely used in the eastern United States. They are also used in other parts of the country to describe irregular or unplatted tracts in conjunction with the rectangular survey system. A metes and bounds description can be highly accurate when it is developed and written by a competent surveyor using precision equipment; it can also be quite complex. A metes and bounds description for parcel Z, shown in Figure 25–3, might be as follows:

All that tract or parcel of land situated in the Town of East Hampton, County of Suffolk and State of New York, bounded and described as follows: BEGINNING at the junction of the westerly line of land of James McKinney and the southerly side of Further Land, and running thence along the land of said James McKinney, south 18 degrees 17 minutes 30 seconds east 430 and 5/100 feet; thence along the land of said James McKinney north 71 degrees 42 minutes 30 seconds east, 383 and 52/100 feet to land of Rachel Van Houten; thence along the land of said Rachel Van Houten south 21 degrees 36 minutes 30 seconds east 895 and 82/100 feet to a point; thence still along the land of Rachel Van Houten south 21 degrees 16 minutes 20 seconds east 699 and 31/100 feet to the proposed Atlantic Avenue Highway, thence along said Atlantic Avenue south 72 degrees 42 minutes 40 seconds west 1387 and 50/100 feet; thence

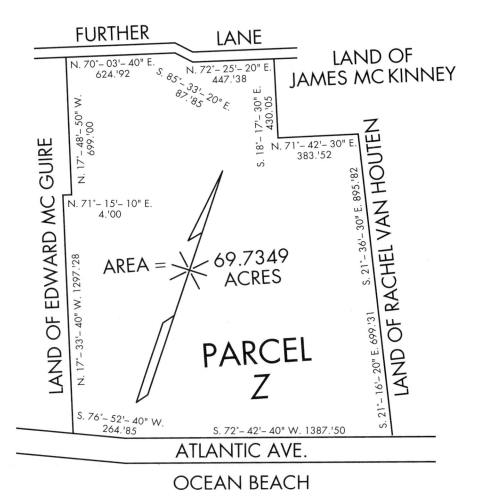

FIGURE 25–3
Parcel Z Based on Metes and Bounds Description

continuing along said Atlantic Avenue south 76 degrees 52 minutes 40 seconds west 264 and 85/100 feet to land of Edward J. McGuire; thence along the lands of said Edward J. McGuire north 17 degrees 33 minutes 40 seconds west 1297 and 28/100 feet, thence north 71 degrees 15 minutes 10 seconds east 4 feet; thence continuing along the land of said Edward J. McGuire north 17 degrees 48 minutes 50 seconds west 699 feet to Further Lane Highway; thence along said Further Lane Highway north 70 degrees 3 minutes 40 seconds east 624 and 92/100 feet, thence continuing along said Further Lane Highway south 85 degrees 33 minutes 20 seconds east 87 and 85/100 feet; thence continuing along said Further Lane Highway north 72 degrees 25 minutes 20 seconds east 447 and 38/100 feet to the point or place of beginning.

Containing by actual measurement as per survey dated April 10, 1971, of Nathan F. Tiffany 69.7349 acres. Atlantic Beach, New Jersey.

A simple variation of the metes and bounds system of identifying real estate is based on monuments. A *monument* is an identifiable landmark that serves as a corner of a property. A monument description, which does not require exact measurements or directions, is acceptable whenever land is not too valuable and the expense of a detailed, accurate survey would be out of proportion to the value. Monument descriptions are not widely used today, although at one time they were prevalent.

Monuments may be tangible or intangible. If they are tangible, they are either natural or artificial. Rivers, lakes, streams, trees, creeks, springs, and the like are natural monuments. Fences, walls, houses, canals, streets, stakes, and posts are artificial monuments. The center line of a street is an example of an intangible monument. Since all monuments are susceptible to destruction, removal, or shifting, they should be used only when necessary, and then every available identifying fact should be stated; for example, not merely "a tree," but "an old oak tree." Thus, even after the tree has become a stump, it may still be identified as oak and distinct from other trees.

Government or Rectangular Survey Descriptions

The *government, or rectangular, survey system* was approved by the United States Congress in 1785 to establish a standardized system of property descriptions. It is relatively simple in operation, at least for rural lands, is easily the most general survey system, and is used in 30 states. The New England states, the Atlantic Coast states, Southeastern Ohio, and Texas are not covered.

The General Framework.   This system is based on surveying lines that run north and south, called *principal meridians,* and east and west, called *base lines.* A map showing the location of the several principal meridians and their base lines in the United States is in Figure 25–4.

Guide meridians were established by the surveyors to minimize errors in measurement caused by the curvature of the earth. Guide meridians run parallel to the principal meridian at 24-mile intervals and converge as one goes north. In a comparable manner, *standard parallels* run east and west at 24-mile intervals, north and south of the base lines. Thus, surveyors created areas called *checks* or *quadrangles,* 24 miles on each side.

FIGURE 25–4

Principal Meridians and Their Base Lines Within the United States

These checks are further subdivided into 16 areas, each measuring 6 miles by 6 miles (36 square miles) called *townships.* The townships are again subdivided into *sections,* each a mile square and containing 640 acres. In turn, the sections are further split up into halves, quarters, or smaller parcels as needed to describe individual land holdings.

To identify the exact location of a given 36-square-mile township, the east-west rows of townships, parallel to the base line, are numbered as *tiers* 1, 2, 3, and so forth, north or south, of a given base line. The north-south columns of townships, parallel to the meridians, are called *ranges* and are numbered 1, 2, 3, and so forth, east or west of a principal meridian. The general system is illustrated in Figure 25–5.

Sections in a township are identified by number and are related to adjoining sections, as indicated in Figure 25–6.

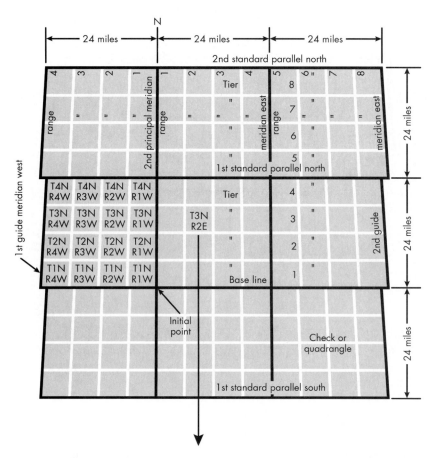

FIGURE 25–5

Designation of Townships by Tiers and Ranges

In describing a section, as in Figure 25–6, it is customary to state first the number of the section, then tier and range: "Section 12, Tier 3 North, Range 2 East of the principal named meridian." It may be abbreviated: "Sect. 12, T.3 N., R. 2 E., . . . County, State of . . ."

Specific Description.   The description of a specific parcel is relatively simple. For example, the parcel designated as Parcel X in Figure 25–7 is "northeast one-fourth of the northwest one-fourth of Section 12," and so on. Parcel Y's description is "west one-half of the southwest one-fourth of Section 12," and so on.

The acreage of each parcel can be determined quickly by working backward in the legal description from the section area of 640 acres. For example, areas of parcels X and Y are calculated as follows:

Parcel X:	NE 1/4 of NW 1/4 of Section 12
	1/4 × 1/4 × 640 acres = 40 acres
Parcel Y:	W 1/2 of SW 1/4 of Section 12
	1/2 × 1/4 × 640 acres = 80 acres

Occasionally, a section is incomplete because it extends into the ocean, a lake, or a river. If parcels in the section are irregular in shape, a standard legal description based

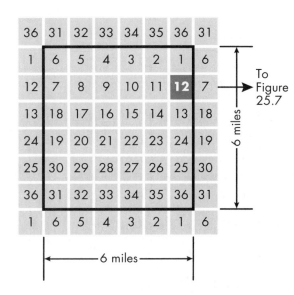

on the government survey system is not suitable for them. These incomplete lots are called *government lots* or *irregular lots.* In these situations, a metes and bounds description is made up for the irregular parcel and tied back to a point of beginning based on the rectangular survey system.

Recorded Plat Descriptions

The government survey system is extremely cumbersome for describing the small parcels commonly found in urban areas. The descriptions become much too involved. A more efficient and widely accepted way of describing property is by *recorded plat,* as a subdivision or a condominium. A *plat* is a drawing or map that is entered into the public record, and shows actual or proposed property lines, building setback lines, and so on.

Subdivision Plat.   Subdividing requires a very accurate initial survey map of a tract of land. The land is then divided into streets, lots, and blocks. Often restrictions that would maintain specific standards for the subdivision are either included on the subdivision map or are filed with it. The map and subdivision restrictions are all entered into the public record as a plat. The map assigns numbers to the various blocks and lots for convenience of identification, and the map usually bears a subdivision title, the owner's and surveyor's names, the date of survey, and the date of approval by community or county officials. Figure 25–8 is a simplified illustration of a small tract that the owner subdivided into lots.

   The subdivision plat map exactly describes the size and location of each lot by the metes and bounds property description system. Once the subdivision plat map has been recorded, only the plat name need be referred to insofar as lots and blocks in the subdivision are concerned. Lot 8, Block 3 in Green Acres Subdivision, Rustic County, Wisconsin, would therefore constitute a complete and adequate legal description. Reference to the plat map would show the exact location, shape, size and dimensions of the lot and would give considerable additional information about it.

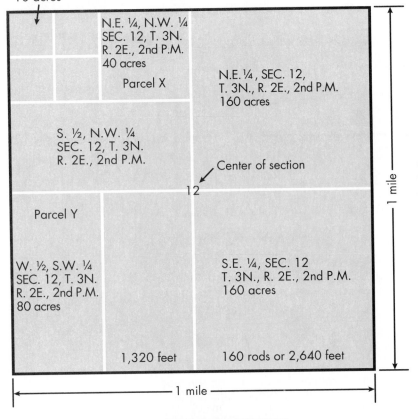

N.W. ¼, N.W. ¼, N.W. ¼
SEC. 12, T. 3N.
R. 2E., 2nd P.M.
10 acres

N.E. ¼, N.W. ¼
SEC. 12, T. 3N.
R. 2E., 2nd P.M.
40 acres

Parcel X

N.E. ¼, SEC. 12,
T. 3N., R. 2E., 2nd P.M.
160 acres

S. ½, N.W. ¼
SEC. 12, T. 3N.
R. 2E., 2nd P.M.

Center of section

12

Parcel Y

W. ½, S.W. ¼
SEC. 12, T. 3N.
R. 2E., 2nd P.M.
80 acres

S.E. ¼, SEC. 12
T. 3N., R. 2E., 2nd P.M.
160 acres

1,320 feet

160 rods or 2,640 feet

1 mile

1 mile

One rod = 16Ω feet
One mile = 320 rods or 5,280 feet
A square mile or section = 640 acres
One acre = 43,560 square feet

FIGURE 25–7
Measurements and Subdivisions of a Section

Condominium Plat. Condominium ownership is created by a special condominium law that permits individual interests and estates to be established within a total and larger property estate. The individual estates are technically established by use of vertical and horizontal planes (surfaces) that are usually identified vertically, such as the walls (not room partitions) of the unit, and horizontally, such as the floors and ceilings of the unit. It is here that elevation above sea level becomes critical.

The exact location of the building or buildings on the site and the exact location of the units within the buildings are described in the plat and in the architectural plans. Each is also described in legal language in a master deed. After all the individual unit estates have been described in the total property estate, all of what remains, such as the land and the structural parts of the buildings, becomes a common estate to be owned jointly by the owners of the individual unit estates. Thus, each condominium owner owns his or her individual unit estate and an undivided interest in the common estate.

Recording of the master deed extends the condominium laws of the state in which the condominium is located to the individual units of ownership. The master deed also establishes an association to look after the use and maintenance of the com-

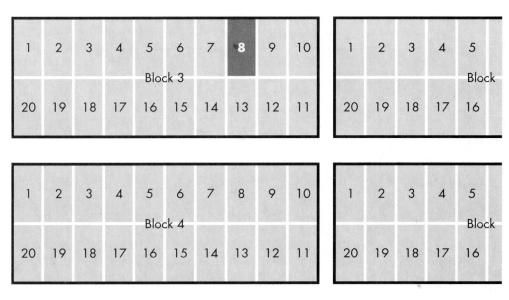

FIGURE 25-8
Green Acres Sub-
division, Rustic County,
Wisconsin

mon estate. The association is governed by a board of directors elected from among the owners of the individual units. Membership, with its attendant rights and responsibilities, applies to each unit.

After recording, condominium units may be legally identified by reference to the plat or master deed. The complex three-dimensional descriptions need not be repeated in deeds, mortgages, or contracts.

The State Plane-Coordinate System

The state plane-coordinate system is intended to supplement other methods of describing real estate. The system provides a definite and very accurate means of identifying parcels, even if landmarks, monuments, and other points of origin are destroyed, moved, or otherwise obliterated.

The coordinate system is based on a system of coordinate grids for each state, with the state flattened mathematically into a level plane. Points in each grid are identified by longitude and latitude, much as a ship's navigator might do at sea; thus, the need for physical landmarks is avoided. Because of the complexity of the state plane-coordinate system, property owners and lawyers are likely to continue to rely on traditional methods of describing realty. The system simply provides a certain means of locating critical points of beginning from which other methods of describing parcels may take off.

Description by Rights

Ownership may sometimes involve only air rights or riparian rights. Air rights are described in a similar manner to condominium rights. For example, rights of development over railroad tracks and cemeteries have been sold off in many larger cities. A legal description of air rights in a deed might convey all development rights 280 feet above mean sea level and up. To be useful, the description must also provide for the location and placement of footings and pillars placed among the railroad tracks, grave sites, and other surface uses to support any structure built in the air space.

PROPERTY DESCRIPTIONS AND PUBLIC RECORDS   **453**

Riparian rights are the right of use and enjoyment of the waters of a stream or lake by the owner of land bordering the body of water. Riparian rights are usually not subject to physical survey per se. If they are, the survey is only incidental to more complex legal considerations involving interaction with other property owners, relocation of streams, and the rights to shut off or restrict the flow of water. These rights should be clearly set forth in any legal document.

A seller must use care to convey only what is owned. Generally, this can best be accomplished by using the identical description under which the property was acquired.

PUBLIC RECORDS

Anyone who has an interest in realty must give notice to the world to protect that interest. Notice may be actual or constructive. Possession of realty is legally considered *actual notice* to the world of an interest in the property. Entering a legal instrument that evidences an interest in real estate into the public records is considered *constructive notice.* In turn, the public record serves as a source of information to anyone about to enter into a transaction concerning the real estate, such as lenders, potential tenants, or interested buyers.

Public records are maintained by local governments in all states in accordance with recording acts, and they provide a central repository or storehouse for certain kinds of information. Recording acts provide for the registration of every legal instrument creating, transferring, mortgaging, assigning, or otherwise affecting title to realty. Public records thus are designed to protect against fraud and to reinforce the Statute of Frauds. The records are maintained by city, town, and county officials under titles like clerk, recorder, treasurer, or tax collector. Public records include many documents affecting title to real and personal property, taxes, special assessments, ordinances, and building and zoning codes. See Figure 25-9 for an overview of the public records system.

Historically, possession of realty served as actual notice of an interest in realty and was adequate for almost all purposes. Modern society is complex, however, and a more efficient and effective system of notice became necessary. For example, owner A might sell property to B, conveying title with a deed. But, if B does not take possession, A might also sell to C, who upon moving into occupancy acquires a claim of title superior to that of B. Or A might obtain cash under a mortgage from D, after the sale to B, and subsequently leave the area. Either situation involves fraud and many legal problems. Recording deeds and mortgages gives constructive notice of the interest to all parties and is recognized as notice equal to actual possession. As a general rule, recording acts give legal priority to interests according to the sequence in which they are recorded. "First in time is first in line."

Real Property Title Records

Recording of a deed is highly recommended to give constructive notice to all persons of the grantee's interest in the property. Both the obligation and the benefit of recording go to the new owner. Recording is doubly important when vacant land is involved or when the new owner does not take immediate possession. Failure to record or to occupy gives a seller an opportunity to sell a second time to another buyer. If the sec-

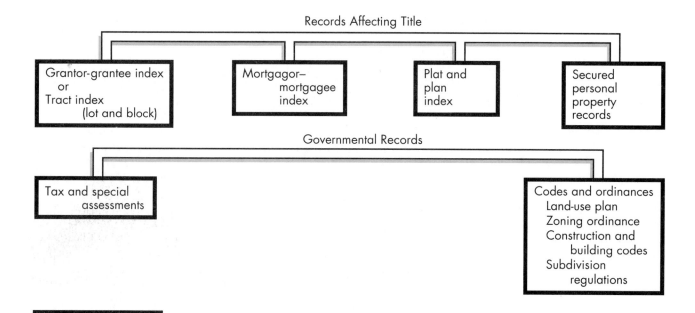

FIGURE 25–9
Public Records of Real Property

ond buyer records or occupies first, a claim of ownership superior to the first buyer's is realized. The first buyer's only recourse, for all practical purposes, would be against the fraudulent grantor. Two systems are used to maintain title records: the first is a grantor-grantee index; the second is a tract, or lot and block, index.

Grantor-Grantee Index. A *grantor* is the party conveying property ownership by way of a deed; a *grantee* is the party receiving title or ownership. A *grantor-grantee index* lists deeds according to the last name of the previous owner (grantor) and of the new owner (grantee). Thus, a title search can be initiated and a *chain of title* can be run if the name of either is known. In running a chain of title, the grantor is regarded as a grantee in a previous transaction. When located in the grantee index, the previous grantor's name then becomes immediately available.

Tract Index. A *tract index,* or a *lot and block index,* lists deeds and other documents affecting specific properties according to their legal descriptions rather than by grantor-grantee. In urban areas, the name of the subdivision in which the property is located will often serve as the key to entering the index. Alternatively, maps of the area will include a distinct number for each block. Transactions involving individual lots on the block can then be ascertained by looking in the index itself.

Entry into a tract index is more difficult in rural areas where the classification system is more involved because the property has a distinct legal description. The general system of the tract index in rural areas is based on identifying properties by township and by section. A chain of title can be run more easily with a tract index because all transactions involving a specific property are recorded on the same page. A tract index, however, is considered more difficult and more expensive to maintain than is a grantor-grantee index.

Mortgagor-Mortgagee Records

In nearly every state, mortgages are accepted for recording in, and constructive notice is given by, a *mortgagor-mortgagee index.* A mortgagor is the party receiving money in exchange for a claim against property; a mortgagee advances the money. A mortgagor-mortgagee index functions in a manner very similar to a grantor-grantee index; that is, the transaction may be entered into the index with either the name of the borrower-mortgagor or the lender-mortgagee. When a mortgage lien has been satisfied, this also is entered in the index. In some states mortgages are filed and recorded in the same grantor-grantee index that is used for deeds.

Plat and Plan Records

Maps, restrictions, architectural plans, and other pertinent information on subdivision and condominium plats are maintained as a part of the public record. The plats are a particularly excellent source of information on easements and restrictions on a specific plat. Parcel and building dimensions and building layout can also be readily determined from this source.

Secured Personal Property Records

The *Uniform Commercial Code* is a set of laws governing the sale, financing, and use as security of personal property. The code provides that items of personal property may be purchased on a conditional sales contract, which is also termed a security agreement. Legally, purchase by conditional sales contract means that title does not pass until full payment is made. In the meantime, a short version of the security agreement, termed a financing statement, is entered into the public record to give constructive notice of a collateral lien on the property. For owners of real estate, this notice is of considerable importance for items like water heaters, boilers, appliances, draperies, and other equipment which are frequently classed as fixtures. The items do not become fixtures, or part of the real estate, until the security agreement is satisfied. That is, important components of a property may not actually be a part of the realty. Notice of the financing statement is usually entered in the mortgagor-mortgagee index.

SUMMARY

Land surveys and property descriptions are needed for positive identification of parcels of real estate whenever title is transferred. Legal descriptions also provide boundary and size data, and provide a basis for subsequent division of the parcel into smaller units.

Urban properties are most often described by lot and block in a tract subdivision. Rural properties are generally described by reference to the government or rectangular survey. Sometimes, where land value is low and exact area is not critical, a monument description is used.

The government survey is based on a national system of base lines and meridians. Quadrangles, 24 miles on a side, are measured off the base lines and meridians. Townships, 6 miles on a side, are also measured and numbered east and west of the meridian and north and south of the base line. Each township contains 36 sections of 640 acres each.

A condominium project is made part of the public record in much the same way as a subdivision development. Subsequently, condominium units can be briefly described by reference to the recorded information.

KEY CONCEPTS

Acre   A unit of land 43,560 square feet in area.

Actual notice   Knowledge of an interest in real property imputed to all the world because claimant was or is in actual possession of the property.

Base line   An imaginary east-west line, north and south of which are rows of townships; used in the government rectangular-survey system.

Benchmark   A fixed point of known elevation used by land surveyors; e.g., to establish the floors and ceilings of condominium units.

Constructive notice   Knowledge presumed of everyone, by law, as a result of properly entering documents and/or other information into the public record.

Fixture   Item of personal property attached to a land or building in such a manner as to be legally considered part of the real estate.

Grantor/grantee   A grantor is the party named in a deed as conveying property ownership; a grantee is the party receiving title or ownership.

Grantor-grantee index   A public record filing system used to locate ownership documents, primarily deeds.

Guide meridian   North-south survey lines used to correct for earth's curvature.

Legal description   An identification of a specific parcel of real property that is unique to the parcel.

Metes and bounds   Describing real property using "measures" of distance and "boundaries" as markers or survey lines.

Monument   A point used as a marker in describing real estate; e.g., an iron pipe, a large boulder, or a tree.

Personal property   Any property that is not realty; usually movable objects. Also refers to ownership of movable objects such as books, bikes, or bread. Sometimes referred to as personalty.

Plat   A drawing or map that shows boundaries, shapes and sizes, and locations of individual parcels of real estate; used for example for subdivisions.

Principal meridian   A north-south survey line used as a reference in the government or rectangular survey system.

Range   A column of townships, east or west of a principal meridian, in the government or rectangular survey system.

Real estate   Land, including oil, water, and minerals, and improvements to the land; often equated with real property and realty.

Real property   Ownership right of use, control, and disposition of real estate.

Realty   See also Real estate; Real property.

Rectangular survey system   Government grid arrangement for legally describing land that uses principal meridians and base lines as references.

Riparian rights   The right of use and enjoyment of the waters of a stream or lake by the owner of land bordering the body of water.

Section   A square unit of land in the rectangular survey system measuring one mile on each side; 640 acres.

Standard parallel   East-west survey lines at 24-mile intervals north or south of standard parallels in the rectangular survey system.

Tier   A row of townships, north or south of a base line, in the rectangular survey system.

Township   Land units in the rectangular survey system, 6-miles square (36 sections), defined by the intersections of tier and range lines.

Tract index   Public record filing system, listing documents affecting each parcel of land.

Uniform Commercial Code   A set of laws governing the sale, financing, and use as security of personal property.

QUESTIONS FOR REVIEW AND DISCUSSION

1. What is a fixture? When is the identification of a fixture important? Not important? When are the following fixtures: key, storm windows, hot-water heater?

2. Explain the following methods of describing realty in detail.

   a. Metes and bounds

   b. The government survey system

   c. The recorded plat

3. Are there occasions when the above three methods or systems are not adequate to describe realty? Explain.

4. What effect would the adoption of the metric system have on legal descriptions of real estate, if any? Discuss.

5. The rectangular survey system is obsolete for describing real estate and should be replaced. Discuss.

6. Explain briefly the nature and use of the following public record indexes:

   a. Grantor-grantee

   b. Tract

   c. Mortgagor-mortgagee

   d. Secured personal property

7. From a grantee's viewpoint why should a deed be recorded? From a lender's? A lessee's?

You are asked by an investor to help identify and otherwise describe some properties.

1. Begin by making a square approximately 2 inches or 5 centimeters on each side on a sheet of paper, to represent Section 31, T.2N, R.5W, which is where the parcels are located. Sketch the parcels of land within the section:

   a. N.E.1/4

   b. S.E.1/4 of the S.E.1/4

   c. W.1/2 of the N.W.1/4 of the S.W.1/4

   d. S.W.1/4 of the N.W.1/4 of the N.W.1/4

   e. W.1/2 of the N.E.1/4 of the N.E.1/4 of the N.W.1/4

2. How many acres are there in each parcel of problem 1?

3. How many miles are there from the eastern edge of Sect. 31, T.2N, R.5W to the western edge of Sect. 36, T.2N, R.3W?

4. How far is it from the northern edge of Sect. 31, T.2N., R.5W. to the northern border of Sect. 6, T.1N, R.5W?

5. A buyer receives a deed to property. The buyer moves into the property but does not record the deed. To what extent are the buyer's rights in the property protected?

6. An investor obtains a mortgage loan for $500,000. The mortgagee fails to record the mortgage. To what extent is the mortgage valid?

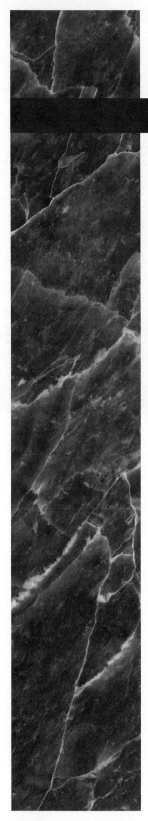

CHAPTER 26

REAL PROPERTY RIGHTS AND INTERESTS

Chapter Outline

Property has its duties as well as its rights.

Thomas Drummond, Letter to the Tipperary Magistrates, 1838

Property rights are the true commodity in the real estate market, even though attention is usually focused on the physical realty. The main ownership rights are *control, possession, use and enjoyment, exclusion,* and *disposition.* Control means the right to build or remove buildings, to grant easements, to impose covenants or conditions, to lease, to agree to a lien, or to act in any other way that allows an encumbrance to be placed against the property. Occupying the property as a home or using it as a place of business are ways of enjoying ownership. Keeping others off the property for privacy is exclusion. And the rights of disposition include selling or refusing to sell, giving the property to others by gift or will, and even abandonment.

Ownership of real estate is commonly considered a bundle of rights (see Figure 26-1). Law and order provided by a government serves to preserve, protect, and enforce the rights. When any of the rights are given up—for example, if an easement is granted or a mortgage lien is placed against the property—the value of the bundle is reduced. The purpose of this chapter is to explain the bundle of rights, the forms of ownership of the bundle, and the ways in which the bundle may be reduced.

Knowledge of property rights is extremely important because the decisions and actions an owner may take are implied in the rights owned. Lack of complete or clear

RIGHT OR BENEFIT	STICK IN BUNDLE
Control	Mortgage
	Lease
	Impose covenants or conditions
	Grant easements
	Grant license
	Build or remove structures
Use and enjoyment	Occupy as residence
	Use as place of business
	Farm
	Mine/drill for oil, etc.
	Place of recreation
Exclusion	Maintain privacy
	Nontrespass
Disposition	Sell or refuse to sell
	Gift
	Will
	Abandon

FIGURE 26-1
Ownership of Real Property is a Bundle of Rights

ownership translates directly into risk of loss of ownership because of poor title. *Title* is another way of saying ownership of real property. Having high-quality title of the right type reduces investor risks, enhances value, and increases owner flexibility in administering the property.

FREEHOLD OWNERSHIP INTERESTS

An ownership interest in real property is termed an *estate*. Basically estates are classified according to the time of enjoyment; there are two major classes: (1) freehold, and (2) nonfreehold. The term *freehold* has its origins in the English feudal system; it is land held by a free man. A freehold estate continues for an indeterminate period of time and is considered real property. Title to most freehold estates is held for the lifetime of the owner, unless sold or otherwise disposed of, and then passed on to an heir. Title may be held for the lifetime of some other designated person whose life expectancy is uncertain. The time of possession may be now or in the future. The most common freehold estates are fee simple, qualified fees, life estates, and remainders, which we will discuss in the following pages.

A *nonfreehold estate,* also termed a *leasehold estate* or less than freehold estate, endures for a determinate time only—that is, for a period measured in years, months, weeks, or days. Leasehold estates are personal rather than real property.

Transactions involving real property interests are subject in every state to a set of laws, called the *Statute of Frauds.* These laws require, among other things, that any contract creating or transferring an interest in land or realty be in writing to be enforceable at law. The laws also state that oral testimony to alter or vary the terms of such written agreements is not admissible as evidence in court.

Estates in real estate may also be classified according to:

1. Quantity or completeness of the interest
2. Time when interest is active and benefits are realized
3. Number and relationship of the concerned parties

In our discussion of interests, the terms tenancy and estate are often used interchangeably even though technically they do not mean the same thing. A *tenancy* is the manner of owning an estate, or interest in land; for example, a possessory right or interest. Stating ownership by tenancy gives more specific information about the interest held, as will be seen shortly. See Figure 26–2 for an overview of how estates and tenancies fit together. Leasehold estates will be discussed in Chapter 27.

Completeness of Ownership

Fee Simple.   *Fee, fee simple,* and *fee simple absolute* all mean the same thing; namely, complete or absolute ownership of realty subject only to certain limitations imposed by the government. Fee simple is the most complete bundle of rights that anyone can acquire in the United States.

The fee simple owner of real property may use it or dispose of it in any legal way, including passing it on by will. Further, a fee owner may divide up the title in any of several ways; this is termed *fee splitting.* Splitting up the fee is usually in terms

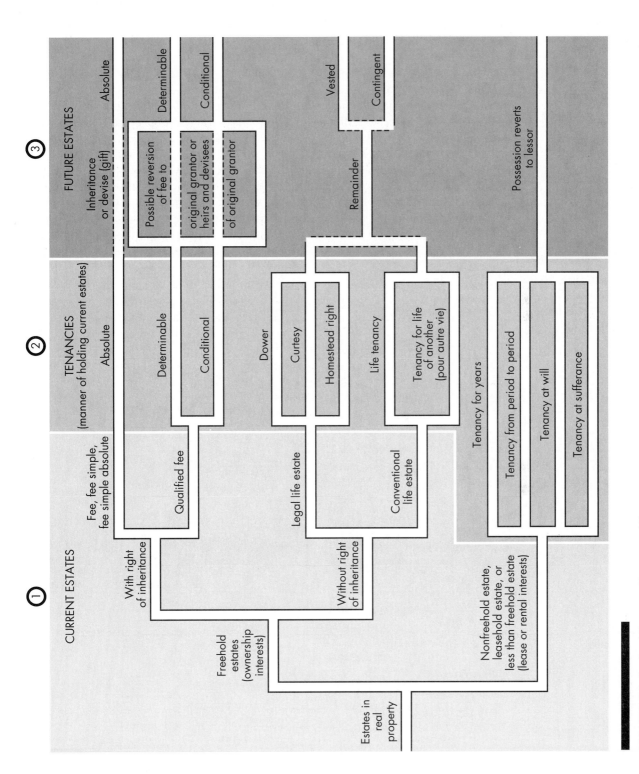

FIGURE 26-2 Real Property Estates and Tenancies

CURRENT ESTATES ①

TENANCIES ②
(manner of holding current estates)

FUTURE ESTATES ③

Estates in real property

Freehold estates (ownership interests)

Nonfreehold estate, leasehold estate, or less than freehold estate (lease or rental interests)

With right of inheritance

Without right of inheritance

Fee, fee simple, fee simple absolute

Qualified fee

Legal life estate

Conventional life estate

Absolute

Determinable

Conditional

Dower

Curtesy

Homestead right

Life tenancy

Tenancy for life of another (pour autre vie)

Tenancy for years

Tenancy from period to period

Tenancy at will

Tenancy at sufferance

Inheritance or devise (gift)

Possible reversion of fee to

original grantor or heirs and devisees

of original grantor

Remainder

Possession reverts to lessor

Absolute

Determinable

Conditional

Vested

Contingent

463

of completeness, time, or number of owners. For example, three rights in a single parcel could be assigned to three different persons—the air rights to one, surface rights to the second, and subsurface rights to the third. Or title might be split between a present owner and a future owner. See Figure 26-3 for the many ways in which a fee interest may be split.

Most realty is held in fee simple, and the term *ownership* ordinarily means such a position. However, concurrent ownership (two or more owners) is often involved. All other estates are less than fee simple and, in fact, are some portion of it. All the lesser parts, if gathered together again, would make the fee simple estate complete or whole again.

Qualified Fee.   A qualified fee estate is a fee estate with a limitation imposed by the person creating the estate. Breaching the limitation may result in title being taken away from one owner and being placed in another. For example, Brown deeds land to a church "so long as" it is used for religious or educational purposes. If the land

FIGURE 26–3
Alternative Ways in Which a Fee Interest May Be Split

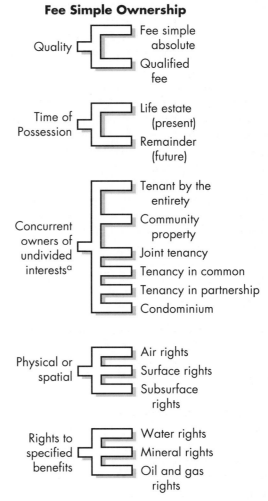

Fee Simple Ownership

Quality
- Fee simple absolute
- Qualified fee

Time of Possession
- Life estate (present)
- Remainder (future)

Concurrent owners of undivided interests[a]
- Tenant by the entirety
- Community property
- Joint tenancy
- Tenancy in common
- Tenancy in partnership
- Condominium

Physical or spatial
- Air rights
- Surface rights
- Subsurface rights

Rights to specified benefits
- Water rights
- Mineral rights
- Oil and gas rights

[a]Ownership of corporation is personal property even though the business entity owns real property. Also, leases and cooperatives constitute personal property.

were used otherwise—for a tavern or gambling house—the condition is violated. Title to land would then automatically revert to the grantor, or his or her heirs. In this case, the church's interest in the land is a qualified fee provided a certain prescribed use continues. Had Brown conveyed the land to the church "on the condition that" it is used for religious or educational purposes, then it would be up to Brown, or his or her heirs, to physically retake possession of the property within a reasonable period of time after the breach.

Time When Active

An ownership interest limited to the life of a natural person is a *life estate,* and the owner of a life estate is a *life tenant.* Life estates split a fee simple according to time. The interest may be measured by the life tenant's own life or by that of another person, termed *pour autre vie.* A life estate may be created by will, by deed, or by operation of the law. The future possession of the ownership interest, which becomes effective at the end of a life estate, is known as a *remainder.* The person designated to receive the remainder interest is a *remainderman.*

A life tenant has certain rights and duties. A life tenant may sell, lease, encumber, or otherwise dispose of the interest. At the same time, the remainderman's interest must be kept in mind. Hence, while the tenant is entitled to the income and use of the land, he or she is also obliged to keep the property in fair repair and to pay the usual, normal carrying charges, including taxes. The life tenant must also pay the interest on any mortgage. Any buildings erected on the land become the property of the remainderman. Because the rights cease at death, a life tenant is said to hold title without right of inheritance. Also, if the life tenant obtains a mortgage, the lien automatically expires at the end of the life estate.

Conventional Life Estates. A life estate created by will or deed is termed a *conventional life estate.* For example, a man wills land to his wife for as long as she lives and, then, upon her death, to his daughter. Upon his death, his wife becomes a life tenant and owns a life estate—the right to full use of the property for life. The daughter has a remainder position, which is the right to receive and use the property after the wife's death. Upon the wife's death, the fee is reunited in the daughter, who then becomes the owner of a fee simple interest.

Legal Life Estates. Life estates may also be created by law, which are termed *legal life estates.* Dower, curtesy, and homestead rights are legal life estates. Dower and curtesy were developed under English common law and are almost extinct now. In states where they are recognized, the division of property in a divorce terminates them.

An estate for life, given by law to a wife, in all property owned by a husband at any time during marriage is termed *dower.* Where dower still exists, the requirements are (1) a valid marriage, (2) ownership of real property by husband, and (3) his death. The interest attaches as soon as the property is acquired or the marriage takes place and cannot be cut off without the wife's consent. For this reason, she needs to sign the deed when she and her husband convey property by mutual consent. Upon his death she usually gets a one-third life estate in all the real property owned by her husband. Dower was intended to give a wife a means of support after the husband's death. While the husband lives, the wife's rights are *inchoate* or inactive.

Curtesy is the interest, given by law to a husband, in real property owned by his wife. Requirements are (1) a valid marriage and birth of a child, (2) sole ownership of the property by the wife at her death, (3) her death, and (4) no disposition of the property by her will. This interest does not attach until the wife's death, and she may defeat it by deed in her lifetime or by her will, in either case without her husband's consent. If the curtesy right is created, it usually entitles the husband to all the net income as long as he lives.

A protection of residence that precludes its attachment or forced sale for non-payment of debt, except for mortgage and tax liens, is a *homestead right*. This protection is statutory in origin; hence its details vary from state to state. It usually has two purposes: (1) to exempt the home from general debts, and (2) to provide a widow (sometimes a widower) with a home for life. In most states, the value and area of the exempt homestead are limited. Usually, the dwelling must be occupied as the family home, and a written declaration of homestead must be filed. It is then free from general claims for debts, except those that are a lien on the property, such as taxes and mortgages. Homesteads in a few states are exempt from taxes up to a certain assessed value, which is termed a homestead exemption. Homestead protection or rights should not be confused with this homestead exemption.

Number and Relationship of Owners

Real property may be owned by one or more persons. One person holding ownership gives sole title and is termed a *tenancy in severalty*. Two or more people holding title together are termed *concurrent owners*. In the latter circumstance, the owners frequently use or manage the real property as a single unit without regard to the number of owners; that is, each holds an undivided interest.

Tenancy by the Entirety. A husband and wife, owning property as one person, is a *tenancy by the entirety*. The legal fiction of a husband and wife being one originated in English common law. As tenants by the entirety, neither can convey the property or force a partition during the marriage. If either dies, the entire property is owned by the survivor. A divorce converts the arrangement into a tenancy in common, unless the property is disposed of or awarded to one party. A tenancy by the entirety is very useful in the purchase of home by a husband and wife, since it makes certain that the survivor will continue to own the residence regardless of whether a will is drawn. Tenancy by the entirety is not recognized in community property states.

Community Property. Community property, which is of Spanish origin and applies only to property held by a married couple, is a recognized form of ownership in eight states—Washington, Idaho, Nevada, California, Arizona, New Mexico, Texas, and Louisiana. Thus, while community property is not designated as a tenancy, it has the same effect.

The community property system recognizes two kinds of property, community and separate, rather than personal and real. *Community property* means that any property acquired by a husband and wife during their marriage, individually or jointly, is held equally by each of them. The death of either gives full title to the survivor.

Separate property is property owned by either the husband or the wife before their marriage, or received by either after their marriage through gift or inheritance, which is specifically excluded from classification as community property. Separate

property is free of any claim or interest by the other spouse. Each spouse, therefore, has full ownership and control of separate property and may sell, will, or give the property away or place a mortgage against it. Income or profit from separate property is also separate property. All property not classed as separate property is community property. Dower and curtesy are not recognized in community property states.

The rules are not uniform in the states that recognize community property. In most, the wife or husband is automatically entitled to one-half of the real and personal property, or income, of the spouse. A divorce or mutual agreement dissolves the community ownership and divides the property between the two parties.

Our laws are continually being challenged and modified. For example, "Do unmarried cohabitants, or *par vivants,* develop community property rights?" In one case, Lee Marvin, the actor, lived with Michelle Triola for several years, although he did not marry her. She did not work outside the domicile during this time, and she legally changed her last name to Marvin. Subsequently, they parted. She sued for one-half of his income during the period they lived together. The court ruled that Lee Marvin must only pay $104,000 "for rehabilitation purposes," in that no contract was reached. Even this award was overturned on appeal. Other cases indicate that where couples live together, share assets, and jointly invest, a property settlement is appropriate.

Joint Tenancy.   Ownership of an undivided interest by two or more owners, not related by marriage and with right of survivorship, is *joint tenancy. Right of survivorship* means that if one owner dies, his or her interest passes to the remaining owners. The death of one of the owners is often referred to as the "grand incident" of this form of ownership. The right of survivorship has caused joint tenancy to sometimes be referred to as a "poor man's will". In fact, a will is not replaced because only one property is affected.

Joint tenancy is not favored by the courts between people not related by marriage. Many states have abolished joint tenancy, except that the right of survivorship may still be created if specified in the deed. For a joint tenancy to stand up in a court contest, it must be proved that the joint owners have the four unities required of a joint tenancy: (1) equal interests, (2) title acquired by a single deed, (3) title acquired at the same time, and (4) the same undivided possession of the entire property. A breach of any one of these unities in a conveyance means that a tenancy in common rather than a joint tenancy was created. Needless to say, owners in a joint tenancy share equally in the income and expenses of ownership.

Tenancy in Common.   Ownership by two or more parties, **without** the right of survivorship, is called a *tenancy in common.* Thus, with the death of one of the owners, title to the deceased's share passes to his or her heirs or devisees. That is, the surviving owner or owners do not become owners of the interest of the one who died. Further, if the deceased had two or more heirs they are presumed to receive and hold the real property as tenants in common.

Tenants in common may have equal or unequal shares. They share in the income and are obligated to contribute to expenses according to their prorata share of ownership. They may all join to sell the property. Or, one may sell his or her interest, in which case the purchaser becomes a tenant in common with the others. If one owner wishes the property to be sold and the others do not, an action for *partition* may be brought, in which event the property is sold at an auction and each owner is paid his or her proportional share of the proceeds.

Tenancy in Partnership.   A partnership is an organizational arrangement whereby two or more people join their expertise and resources to conduct business for profit. Under the Uniform Partnership Act, articles of partnership are required to be drawn up and filed with a public official to form a partnership. The partnership operates as a business entity, with its own name. However, it is not a corporation or trust.

Two kinds of partnership interests are legally recognized: general and limited. The *general partner* (or partners) operates and manages the business and may be held liable for all losses and obligations of the entity not met by the other partners. A *limited partner* is exempt by law from liability in excess of his or her contribution. A limited partner, also termed a silent partner, may not participate in operations and management under penalty of losing the exempt or limited liability status. A limited partnership must have at least one general partner who conducts business for the entity.

The Uniform Partnership Act provides that realty acquired in the name of a partnership, general or limited, is owned by the partners as a *tenancy in partnership*. Tenancy in partnership carries with it the right of survivorship, which is necessary for the entity to continue uninterrupted business operations. The estate of the deceased partner is entitled to an accounting and a prorata share of the profits and net worth as of the time of death.

Condominium Ownership

Condominium ownership is holding a fractional interest in a larger property, part of which is separate and unique to each owner (the condominium unit) and part of which is held in general by all the owners (the common elements). Condominium ownership is similar to holding tenancy in common, except that a portion of the fractional share is held as a separate or divided interest. The larger property is, of course, the entire condominium development. An owner of a fractional share holds it in fee simple and may dispose of it without obligation to the other owner or owners.

Condominium co-ownership is most often used for multifamily residential properties. Each owner possesses an exclusive right to use, occupy, mortgage, and dispose of his or her particular dwelling, plus an undivided interest in the areas and fixtures that serve all owners in common. Each deed is subject to identical covenants and restrictions governing the repair and maintenance of the building. Owning an individual residential condominium offers tax advantages identical to those enjoyed by owners of detached, single-family properties.

Condominium ownership dates back to ancient Rome. Legislation introducing condominium ownership into the United States was initially passed in the early 1960s. As a rule, the legislation requires the separate assessment and taxation of each space unit and its common interests. The legislation, therefore, stops the assessor from treating any part of the common elements of the property as a separate parcel for taxation purposes. As a rule, too, statutes bar the placement of mechanic's or other liens on the common elements of a property held jointly by two or more owners.

The condominium arrangement requires the formation of a central administrative body to act on behalf of all the owners for operation of the larger property as an integral whole. Thus, all co-owners must share the expenses of operation and maintenance, which are levied as monthly assessments to each according to his or her prorata share. Owners, too, are bound to observe recorded rules and regulations governing use and occupancy of both the individually owned premises and those held in common. An owner cannot ordinarily be ousted or dispossessed (as can a defaulting tenant) for infraction of bylaws or regulations, but is subject to such court actions as necessary to compel compliance.

Condominium ownership is not limited to residential units. Business and industrial properties may also be subdivided into condominium units. Indeed, parking areas have been subdivided into condo parking spaces, and yacht clubs have been broken into condo boat slips. Also, increasingly recreational housing is being split into time-share condominiums; thus, a unit may have 50 different owners, each with the right of full use for one week per year.

Nonfreehold or Leasehold Interests

Owners frequently give possession and use rights in real estate to other parties in exchange for rent by way of a contract termed a *lease.* A nonfreehold or leasehold estate, limited to right of occupancy and use only, is thereby created. The party to whom the property is rented is a *lessee* or *tenant.* The owner in a lease arrangement is termed a *lessor* or *landlord.* And the owner's position is termed a *leased fee.* Leasing is discussed much more completely in the next chapter.

OWNING REAL ESTATE BY BUSINESS ORGANIZATIONS

A discussion of forms of ownership would not be complete without taking up corporations and trusts in their several forms. A corporation can own real estate as an estate in severalty. This means that the owners of a corporation, i.e, the shareholders, control and get the benefits of the real estate. However, they also are penalized by double taxation when the real estate is owned by the corporation.

Figure 26-4 provides a comparison of the several forms of real estate ownership for investment purposes. Emphasis is on the extent of exposure to liability, to tax implications, to duration of the arrangement, to the ease of transferability of the interest, and to the form of management. The term *full flow through* means that the income is not taxed at the initial level—that is, in its ownership form.

Corporation

A corporation is a legal entity whose rights to do business are essentially the same as those of an individual. The entity is owned by stockholders, who can be many in number, and has continuous existence regardless of any changes in ownership. A corporation limits the liability of owners to the amount invested in the organization. A corporation ceases to exist only if dissolved according to proper legal process.

The major disadvantages of the corporate form for real estate ownership and investment purposes are that (1) the costs of organizing and maintaining the corporation are relatively high, (2) the profits are subject to double taxation—taxable to the corporation and taxable to the shareholder upon distribution, and (3) corporations are subject to more governmental regulation, at all levels, than are most other forms of business organization.

A Subchapter S corporation, a hybrid of the partnership and corporate forms of organization, is frequently used to hold real estate. A Subchapter S corporation may

OWNERSHIP FORM	LIABILITY EXPOSURE	TAX STATUS	LIFE DURATION	TRANSFER-ABILITY	MANAGEMENT FORM
Individual (as condo or coop)	Unlimited	Full flow through, one level	Death terminates	Transferable	Personal
General partnership	Unlimited	Full flow through, one level	Terminated by death or withdrawal	Nontransferable	By mutual agreement, with equal say by each usually
Limited partnership	Limited for limited partners	Full flow through, one level	As agreed in organizational contract	Restricted transferability	Decisions by general partners; no say by limited partners
Corporation	Limited	No flow through, two levels	Perpetual	Easily transferable	Shareholder control, with board of directors
S-corporation	Limited	Full flow through, one level	Perpetual, if guidelines met	Easily transferable[a]	Shareholder control[a]
REIT	Limited	Substantial flow through, one level	Perpetual	Easily transferable[b]	Decisions by trustees

[a] Maximum number of stockholders is 35.
[b] Minimum number of shareholder-beneficiaries is 100.

FIGURE 26–4
Comparison of Ownership Forms for Real Estate Investment Purposes

have up to 35 shareholders, all of one class, who enjoy limited liability. Unlike a limited partnership, these shareholders may participate in centralized management decisions without jeopardizing their limited liability status. Further, shares are more easily transferred than are limited partner interests. At the same time, profits are exempt from corporate income taxes if distributed to shareholders immediately at the end of each accounting period. Operating losses may also be passed through to shareholders, with certain restrictions, to be used as tax deductions. Finally, a Subchapter S corporation may have perpetual life, provided that certain guidelines are not violated.

Trust

A trust is a fiduciary arrangement whereby property is turned over to an individual or an institution, termed a *trustee,* to be held and administered for the profit and/or advantage of some person or organization, termed the beneficiary. The person setting up a trust is termed a *trustor* or *creator.* The trustee acts for the trust, which may hold property in its own name, just as an individual or a corporation does. The trustee is obligated to act solely for the benefit of the beneficiary. Two kinds of trust are mainly used in owning realty: a real estate investment trust and an express private trust.

Real estate investment trusts (REITs) are much like corporations. People buy shares (of beneficial interest) and, thereby, join together to the real estate with limited liability. At the same time, double taxation of profits may be avoided by meeting the requirements of the trust laws—that is, paying out earnings in the year earned.

An *express private trust* usually involves only a small number of beneficiaries, often a spouse and children. An express private trust may be created during one's lifetime (a living or *inter vivos* trust) or upon one's death (*testamentary trust*). The main advantages of a private trust are savings in estate taxes and extended protection for the beneficiary, who may not be familiar with business affairs.

Cooperative

Ownership of shares in a cooperative venture entitling the owner to occupy and use a specific space or unit, usually an apartment, under a proprietary lease is *cooperative ownership*. The cooperative form of mutual ownership differs from a condominium in that the ownership of the entire property (land and improvements) is acquired by a corporation or trust. As a rule, the property is financed for up to 80 percent of its value with a mortgage loan; the balance is obtained from the sale of equity shares. Each buyer acquires a proprietary lease that is subordinate to financing taken on by the corporation.

A *proprietary lease* is an agreement, with the attributes of ownership, under which a tenant-shareholder in a cooperative occupies space designated according to the shares owned. The lease terms stipulate the payment of rent to the corporation to cover prorata shares of the amounts necessary to meet mortgage debt, maintenance expenditures, property taxes, and building-related expenditures, such as hazard insurance and replacement reserves. Because of the priority of the financing, a default in payments by the corporation due to a default in payments by some proprietary tenants, affects occupancy and title of all cooperative participants.

Syndicates and Joint Ventures

Two other forms of organization often mentioned in regard to owning real estate are syndicates or joint ventures; neither is a distinct legal entity in and of itself. A coming together of two or more persons or firms for a single project is commonly termed a *joint venture*. A *syndicate* is the coming together of individuals, and sometimes of individuals and organizations, to conduct business and to make investments on a continuing basis. Either may take the form of a partnership, corporation, or trust. Personal and financial abilities are pooled because the members believe that as a group they will be able to accomplish ends that each could not undertake and complete by acting separately. The term syndicate is used because it connotes an organization that has limited goals, usually of an investment nature.

ENCUMBRANCES TO OWNERSHIP

As stated earlier, the value of fee ownership is decreased as each right is given up or as each encumbrance is placed against it. An *encumbrance* is a claim against clear title of, or a limitation on use of, a property. An encumbrance is a result of a defect in the line of ownership or of some action, or nonaction, of the owner. An encumbrance is often referred to as a *cloud on title*.

Investor-owners need to know the causes and implications of encumbrances because losses due to lack of knowledge can amount to thousands of dollars. An encumbrance of a slightly less serious nature may result in title being unmarketable, meaning that a buyer is not obligated to accept a clouded title to a property. Most encumbrances are created voluntarily, but some are created involuntarily by action of law, such as when an owner ignores someone's rights. In addition to defects of title, encumbrances may take the form of liens, deed restrictions, leases, easements, and encroachments.

Figure 26-5 summarizes the many encumbrances that may accrue against property, as well as the limitations to ownership imposed by public bodies. Public limitations are discussed at length in Chapter 28. A written lease extending beyond the closing date in a sales transaction is an encumbrance. Other leases are not usually considered an encumbrance unless time of occupancy and use is of the essence to the buyer. Leases are discussed at length in the next chapter.

Liens

A *lien* is a claim to have a debt or other obligation satisfied out of property belonging to another. Common examples are mortgage liens, mechanic's liens, property tax liens, and judgment liens. A lien generally signifies a debtor–creditor relationship between the property owner and the lienholder. The creditor, if not otherwise satisfied, may initiate an action at law to have the debtor's property sold to satisfy the claim. In most cases, a lien results from a contract voluntarily entered into by an owner, but not always. Paying property taxes, for example, is certainly not done voluntarily, except by a great stretch of the imagination.

Note that a lien does not transfer title to the lienholder. And, where more than one lien is filed against a property, the one recorded first has highest priority of claim.

FIGURE 26-5
Limitations and
Encumbrances to Fee
Ownership

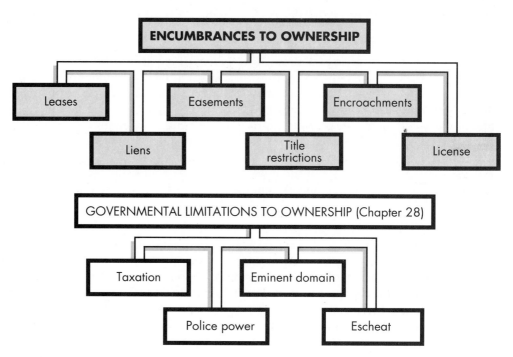

The general rule is, "First in time is first in line." However, property tax liens imposed by law take priority over all other liens.

A mortgage lien is created when property is pledged as security for a loan; it is specific to the property pledged.

Anyone performing work or furnishing materials toward the improvement of realty expects to be paid. In the event of nonpayment, the worker or material supplier has a specific, statutory claim for payment against the property, termed a *mechanic's lien*. The rationale is that the labor and materials enhance the property's value, and it would be a great injustice to let an owner avoid payment of a claim so closely connected to the property's value.

A tax lien is a claim against property due to nonpayment of income, inheritance, or property taxes by an owner. A tax lien results from an implied contract in which the property owner owes tax payments to the government in return for protection, services, and other benefits received. The property tax lien is the most common and is property-specific.

A judgment lien is a court declaration of an individual's indebtedness to another, including the amount. A judgment lien means that a claim in the amount of the court declaration is placed against all property owned by the debtor. Thus, a judgment lien is a general, or nonspecific, lien.

Easements

An *easement* is a right or privilege to use the land of another for certain purposes, such as party driveways, ingress and egress, or drainage. An easement is a nonpossessory real property right, meaning that the holder of the easement does not have the right to occupy the property subject to the easement.

Easements are usually created by deed or by contract. For example, a rancher may sell off a section of land near a river, but include in the sales contract and deed an easement to obtain and move water across the alienated land. Easements, except

THE HIGH COST OF IGNORING LIENS

In 1973 a law student in Sacramento, California, went to small claims court to recover a $50 cleaning deposit, plus $200 in damages from a building owner. The owner refused to pay. In 1976 the owner's property, a 95-unit apartment complex valued at $1.5 million was sold at auction to satisfy the claim. Only the student showed up at the auction, and in satisfaction of the default judgment, now put at $449, the student received a certificate of sale for the property. A one-year-and-one-day statutory period allowed for redemption of publicly auctioned property passed without the certificate being redeemed, so the student became legal owner of the property.

In 1985 a court debt of $554 resulted in a prime piece of Florida Keys real estate, valued at $301,675, being auctioned off for $1.00. The only and winning bid at the auction was made by none other than the instigator of the auction, appropriately named Richard Fast.

those for utilities and services, may be regarded as encumbrances to clear title in a sales transaction if detrimental to the use of the land. An investor should distinguish between the several types of easements and the implications of each.

Easement Appurtenant.   An access right of way across an adjacent property, a joint driveway, or the right to use a party wall are examples of an *appurtenant easement*. A party wall is an exterior building wall that straddles the property line and is used jointly by the adjacent property owners. Title is held to the part of the wall on one's own property, and an easement is held in the remainder. A written party-wall agreement is best used to create and control the use of this easement. An easement appurtenant is considered part of the land and is said to "run with the land." Appurtenant means belonging to, or going with, another thing.

An easement appurtenant results in a slight gain or loss in real property rights (and values). The parcel benefitted is known as the dominant estate. The parcel subject to the easement is known as the servient estate. The dominant parcel, of course, benefits and gains value, whereas the servient parcel becomes less desirable. Naturally enough, an easement resulting in a property's becoming a servient estate is regarded as an encumbrance to clear or marketable title.

An easement appurtenant requires at least two parcels of realty owned by different parties. The parcels are usually but not necessarily adjacent. Although the parcels need not be adjacent, the dominant parcel must be at the beginning or end of the easement. For example, a road or right-of-way could cross several servient parcels to serve a dominant parcel (see Figure 26–6).

Easement in Gross.   An *easement in gross* is a personal right to use the property of another. Neither adjacent nor nearby property need be owned to possess the right.

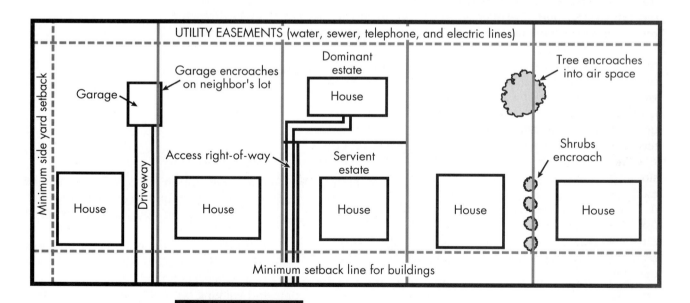

FIGURE 26–6
Typical Encumbrances

Examples of easements in gross are rights-of-way for pipelines, power lines, sewer lines, or roads used by public service companies.

Easement by Prescription. An *easement by prescription* is created by open, unauthorized, continuous use of a servient parcel for the prescriptive period. A prescriptive period is from 10 to 20 years in most states. The use must also have been without the approval of the owner of the encumbered parcel and notorious to the point that the owner could learn of it.

Termination. Easements may be terminated by any one of several ways.

1. Consolidation or merger, as when the dominant and servient parcels are brought under one ownership.
2. Agreement, as when the owner of the dominant parcel releases the right of easement to the servient owner, possibly for a price.
3. Completion of purpose, as when the easement is no longer needed. A right-of-way easement of necessity ends if alternate access to the landlocked parcel is gained by its owner.
4. Abandonment or lack of use.

Title Restrictions

A *title restriction* is a covenant (promise) or condition entered into the public record to limit the nature or intensity of use of land. For example, a property may be limited by a title restriction to one-family residential use or to having no residence smaller than 1,500 square feet. Or the requirement may be "not to keep goats, chickens, or pigs on the premises." Setback and side yard standards may be imposed by title restriction (see Figure 26–6) as well as by a zoning ordinance.

Title restrictions were traditionally entered into the public record on a deed at the time of conveyance of title to another and were originally known as deed restrictions. The restrictions now are commonly entered into the public record by subdividers and developers. In effect, rights are exchanged on all parcels to promote or enhance the value of the entire development. The purpose is to protect neighborhood quality and to preserve and enhance property values. Thus, the more appropriate term is title restrictions.

Restrictions are usually enforced by means of court injunction. In a subdivision or condominium development, the homeowners' association typically sees to enforcement.

Title restrictions that do not contain their own time limit (effective for 30 years from this date, for example) are terminated by the law of the state in which the property is located. A deed restriction may be, but need not be, an encumbrance to marketable title; it depends on the effect of the restriction on the use and value of the parcel.

Encroachments

An *encroachment* occurs when a building or other improvement, such as a fence or driveway, illegally intrudes on or into the property of another owner. Intrusion of a garage overhang or tree limbs are examples. The owner of the property intruded upon can require removal, and failure to do so may weaken his or her title. On the other side, a new owner of the encroaching property may be stuck with the unexpected expense of moving a building or cutting back a stately tree (see Figure 26–6).

An abstract of title or title insurance policy is not likely to evidence an encroachment unless it existed and was picked up in a previous transaction. That is, a physical inspection of a property, and sometimes a survey as well, is needed to ascertain that an encroachment exists. An encroachment is a title encumbrance and must be cleared up for marketable title to be conveyed to a buyer.

Licenses

A *license* is the privilege to use or enter the premises, granted by someone in legal possession of realty. The right to attend a ball game after purchase of a ticket or to hunt or fish on a farmer's land are examples. As a general rule, a license may be canceled at the will of an owner and is not usually considered an encumbrance to clear title.

SUMMARY

Real property rights and interests include rights of control, possession, use and enjoyment, exclusion, and disposition. Private limitations or encumbrances to ownership can be created voluntarily or involuntarily. Voluntary limitations include liens, easements, deed restrictions, and leases. Involuntary limitations come about by operation of law, as for example, the creation of a lien against property for failure to pay taxes or as a result of bankruptcy.

Fee simple is the most complete form of property ownership. Joint tenancy is ownership by two or more persons, with the right of survivorship at the death of any one owner. Tenancy-in-common interests in real estate may be passed on by will to designated heirs or beneficiaries of the deceased owner. Tenancy by the entirety is ownership by a husband and wife, which cannot be broken without their mutual consent.

Dower is the interest of a wife in her husband's property owned at his death. Curtesy is the legal interest of a husband in property owned by his wife on the date of her death. In community property states husband and wife share equally in the ownership of real estate acquired during the marriage. Forms of business or group ownership of real estate include condominiums, cooperatives, partnerships, corporations, syndicates, joint ventures, and trusts.

KEY CONCEPTS

Community property   Property acquired by a husband and wife during their marriage, with each owning a one-half interest.

Condominium   Individual ownership of a unit of space in developed real estate, plus an undivided ownership of common areas.

Cooperative   Ownership of real property by a corporation or trust, with shareholders occupying specific units of space under proprietary leases.

Deed restriction   A limitation on the nature or intensity of use of real property entered in the public record; title restriction is now the preferred term.

Easement   Right to use the land of another for certain purposes, such as ingress and egress, or drainage.

Encroachment   Unauthorized intrusion of a building or other improvement onto the land or into the airspace of an adjoining property.

Encumbrance   Any impediment to clear title, such as a lien, lease, or easement.

Estate   Extent and quality of one's interest in land or other property.

Fee, fee simple, fee simple absolute   Terms used interchangeably for the most complete bundle of rights one can own in land or real property.

Homestead   Occupancy of a residence as a home; a right often protected by state laws known as homestead exemptions.

Joint tenancy   Undivided co-ownership of property that features the right of survivorship.

Lease   An agreement giving the rights of possession and use of real estate to another person in exchange for rent.

License   Freedom to act; for example, to enter onto a property with the permission of the party in legal possession of the property.

Lien   A right or claim, secured by the property of another, to have a debt or other obligation satisfied.

Life estate   Ownership of the right to use real estate during the lifetime of a specified person.

Separate property   Property owned by a spouse that is excluded from community property status; property owned prior to marriage or received through gift or inheritance after marriage.

Statute of Frauds   Law requiring that certain contracts must be written to be legally enforceable; includes any agreement creating or transferring an interest in real property.

Tenancy   The manner in which something, such as an interest in land or real estate, is owned.

Tenancy by the Entirety   Form of joint ownership of property by a husband and wife, with right of survivorship. Neither spouse can dispose of the interest without the consent of the other.

Tenancy in Common   Ownership of property by two or more persons, without right of survivorship; shares need not be equal.

Tenancy in Partnership   Ownership of real estate acquired in the name of a partnership; carries with it the right of survivorship, which enables the partnership to continue uninterrupted business operations. Property may not be disposed of without consent of all partners.

Tenancy in Severalty   Sole ownership of property by one person.

Title   Ownership of property; sometimes involves necessary documentation to evidence legal ownership.

QUESTIONS FOR REVIEW AND DISCUSSION

1. Define and distinguish among the following:

   a. A freehold estate and a leasehold estate

   b. A conventional life estate and a legal life estate

   c. Estate and tenancy

2. Define and distinguish among the following:

   a. Tenancy in severalty

   b. Tenancy by the entirety

   c. Joint tenancy

   d. Tenancy in common

   e. Community property

3. List and explain briefly the four tenancies of leasehold estates.

4. Is government necessary for the existence of private property? Discuss.

5. Are there interests in real estate that do not involve ownership or possession? Discuss.

6. Does condominium ownership make sense in a rural setting? If so, are there some other forms of ownership that make more sense to accomplish the same purpose? Discuss.

7. Are the laws concerning ownership of real estate changing? In what ways? Give examples.

8. Distinguish between easement appurtenant and easement in gross. What is the usual purpose of each?

9. Identify and explain briefly two encumbrances, not due to defect in title, in addition to liens, easements, and deed restrictions.

10. Giving tax liens priority, by law, is unfair to other lienholders. Discuss.

11. It has been proposed that a statute of limitations is needed to remove encumbrances as clouds on title; thus, liens, easements, and deed restrictions would become ineffective after some stipulated period, say 15 years. Discuss. What are the implications?

12. When is a deed restriction not an encumbrance? Discuss.

PROBLEMS

1. Able, owner of 160 acres of land along a river sells half to Baker. An easement of access to the river for recreational purposes for Baker's benefit is written into the deed, although no right to use the frontage on the river is included. Baker later sells off five 10-acre parcels to other persons. Are these subsequent purchasers entitled to use the access easement across Able's land to the river? Discuss.

2. A, B, and C own land as joint tenants. C conveys his third to D and dies shortly after. A and B object, claiming that the conveyance is not valid without their

approval. A and B further claim that the conveyance, if legal, makes D a joint tenant also. The case is taken to court. What is the result?

3. Smith is looking for a home. One property is interesting, but upon investigation Smith determines the following. What effect does each have on value or on Smith's probable offering price?

   a. Garage encroaches on neighbor's lot

   b. Easement appurtenant to cross neighbor's lot to next street

   c. Utility easement for 9 feet along rear lot line

   d. Occupant's written lease for another six months

   e. Ownership by two brothers as tenants in common

CHAPTER 27

LEASING AND LEASE ANALYSIS

Chapter Outline

An owner may exchange possession and use rights in real estate to another person for rent by way of a lease. A *leasehold estate,* meaning right of occupancy only, is thereby created. The owner's interest in a rented property is termed a *leased fee.* The person to whom the property is rented is a lessee or tenant.

One of the important advantages of leasing space is that no capital investment is required of the tenant. Each of us is likely to be either a landlord or a tenant at some point during our lifetime. Students become tenants when signing a lease for a dorm room, an apartment, or a house. As an owner or a tenant we must understand leasing in order to make intelligent decisions when negotiating a rental agreement. Therefore, this chapter covers the basic terminology of leasing, the kinds of and typical covenants or clauses of leases, and the ways of terminating leases. Emphasis is on residential property, although key points regarding commercial or industrial property are included. Brief attention is also given to the relative negotiating positions of the parties and to some of the broader issues involved in negotiation, mainly to tenant unions.

CREATING A VALID LEASE

A lease can be an oral agreement under which the property is rented for a short term or a lengthy document containing many special provisions and covenants. Most state fraud statutes require that a lease for more than one year be in writing; it follows that a lease for less than one year may be oral. Written or oral, a leasehold interest is legally personal property.

A lease can be an encumbrance to clear title. And leases for three years or more are recordable in most states. However, recording may not be a crucial issue since possession gives actual notice of a tenant's claim in a property. Some leases are not recorded because the parties wish to avoid revealing rents, terms, and other contents of the agreement.

Essential Elements of a Lease

No particular wording or form of agreement is required by statute to create a valid lease. It is sufficient in law, if the intention is expressed to transfer from one to another possession of certain real property for a determinate length of time. Substance, not form, is what counts.

A long-term lease must contain the essential elements of a valid contract to be enforceable. These are: (1) that the parties be legally competent, (2) that the objective be legal, (3) that there be a mutual agreement or meeting of the minds, and (4) that consideration be given. Additional elements necessary to make the contract a lease include: (1) a named lessor and lessee, (2) adequate description of premises, (3) an agreement to let and take, or conveyance of the premises from the lessor to the lessee, (4) starting time and length of the arrangement, (5) agreed rental, and, (6) that it be in writing with signatures.

Basic Terminology

The party selling the right of occupancy and use in a lease is the *lessor* or *landlord*. The party buying is the *lessee* or *tenant*.

Four distinct tenancies are possible in leasing property: (1) tenancy for years, (2) tenancy from period to period, or periodic tenancy, (3) tenancy at will, and (4) tenancy at sufferance. The rights of the lessee become weaker as the lessee goes from a tenancy for years to a tenancy at sufferance. The emphasis here is on tenancy for years and periodic tenancy. Tenancy, again, means the manner or conditions under which a property is held.

Tenancy for Years.   A leasing agreement for a specific or definite period of time is a *tenancy for years*. Such an agreement is usually for more than one year and is usually written. The time may actually be for one month, six months, one year, or more than one year. A written lease for nine months creates a leasehold estate, or tenancy for years, just as a lease for 99 years does. In both cases, the time of occupancy and use is definite. The tenant is required to vacate the property and return possession to the landlord at the end of a tenancy for years without notice being required of the landlord. A tenant continuing in possession beyond the end of the lease is a *holdover*. In a holdover situation, the landlord may evict the tenant or elect to hold the tenant for a further period of one year. By mutual agreement of the parties, the lease agreement may be converted from a tenancy for years to a tenancy from period to period.

Tenancy from Period to Period.   A tenancy of uncertain duration—for example, month to month or year to year—is termed a *tenancy from period to period* or a *periodic tenancy*. The tenancy is usually from month to month for apartments in urban areas, and continues until the landlord or tenant gives notice of termination. The rental period usually determines the length of notice required. That is, a week's notice is required to end a week-to-week tenancy. Only a month's notice is likely to be required to terminate a year-to-year tenancy, however. A lessee holding over from a tenancy for years, where rental payments are made monthly, is likely to create a month-to-month tenancy.

Other Tenancies.   A lessee allowed to hold over with the consent of, but subject to eviction at the will of, the lessor creates a *tenancy at will*. Note that the option to hold over is exclusive to the landlord. Holding over without any justification other than the implied consent of the lessor creates a *tenancy at sufferance,* which is the weakest possible estate in realty. The tenant must vacate the premises in such a situation at the will of the landlord.

Broadly speaking, leases are classified as either short term or long term. This division is rather arbitrary and has no particular legal significance. Generally, however, commercial or industrial leases extending over ten or more years may appropriately be referred to as long-term leases. Typically these leases are lengthy documents containing many special provisions and landlord-tenant covenants. At the same time, three years would be considered a long-term lease for residential use. And a ground lease, defined later in this section, would be considered long term only if it exceeded 21 years.

The most usual lease classification system is by rental payment method. Ground leases and sale-and-leaseback arrangements are also classifications of leases. Note that these classifications may overlap and therefore are not mutually exclusive. For example, a sale-and-leaseback arrangement might actually be a ground lease calling for a net rental.

Classification by Rental Payment Agreement

Beginning with the most common, rental payment agreements may be classified as follows:

Percentage Lease.   An agreement whereby rent is a specified proportion of sales or income generated through tenant use of a property is called a *percentage lease*. A floor, or minimum rent, may be included to assure the owner of some basic income from the property.

The percentage of gross sales lease has gained steadily in popularity for commercial properties. Generally, such a lease provides for a minimum rental ranging from 40 to 80 percent of amounts considered fair in relation to property value. Percentage rentals may range from as low as two percent of gross sales for department stores or supermarkets to as high as 75 percent for parking lot operations.

Insofar as the landlord's income is directly related to the success of the tenant's operations, the lease generally includes clauses to ensure continuous and effective store operation. Agreement on methods of accounting and on a periodic audit is also generally included. The landlord, in turn, is expected to promise to maintain the property in prime operating condition and to exclude competitors from other nearby owned properties.

Index Lease.   Index leases came into vogue during the recent years of high inflation. An *index lease* provides either for rental adjustment in direct proportion to increases in taxes, insurance, and operating costs, or provides for rental increments in proportion to changes in cost-of-living or wholesale price indexes. Index leases are more likely to be used where property values are going up but no easy measure of the value increase is available. Examples are warehouses, factories, and office buildings.

Net Lease.   A rental agreement requiring the tenant to pay all maintenance costs, insurance premiums, and property taxes is a *net lease*. Net leases generally run for ten years or more. A net lease assures an owner of a certain rate of return from an investment while shifting the burden of meeting increasing operating costs and taxes to the tenant. Net leases are deemed suitable for large office, commercial, and industrial properties. They are preferred by investment trusts and insurance companies that acquire real estate under purchase-and-leaseback agreements.

Gross Lease. An arrangement calling for a fixed rental to be paid periodically throughout its entire life is a flat lease; it may also be called a straight or fixed-rental lease. This arrangement, which at one time enjoyed wide use and popularity, has come into gradual disuse for long-term leases because of inflation. When the amount of rents is fixed for a long period, a declining dollar value deprives the landlord (owner) of a competitive return in proportion to the value of the property. A flat lease requiring the lessor to pay all property carrying charges, such as taxes, insurance, and maintenance is called a *gross lease.*

Graduated Lease. A *graduated lease* that calls for periodic increases in the rental is intended to give the tenant lower operating expenses during the early, formative years of a business enterprise. In turn, the landlord shares in business growth through successively higher rental payments. This lease arrangement, which is also called a *step-up* lease, may result in excessive rents when growth fails to occur, thus causing business failure. Conceivably, step-down rentals might be used for an older property.

Reappraisal Lease. A *reappraisal lease* calls for a property's value and rental amount to be reestablished at agreed intervals, usually three to five years. Reappraisal leases are rarely used today because reappraisals are expensive and time consuming. Also, they often involve lengthy litigation due to conflicting value estimates between landlords and tenants.

Ground Lease

A *ground lease* provides use and occupancy of a vacant site in return for rental payments. The agreement usually contains a provision that a building is to be erected by the tenant. Frequently, the agreement contains a further provision that the building becomes the property of the landlord at the end of the lease term. The lease may also provide that at the expiration of the term, the landlord will pay the tenant all or part of the cost or appraised value of the building. The term of the lease, including renewal privileges, must therefore be long enough to allow the tenant to amortize the cost of the building during occupancy.

Ground rent is often a certain percentage of the value of the land. The tenant pays all taxes and other charges, the landlord's rent being net. No set rules govern ground leases. Each bargain is specifically negotiated. The provisions mentioned here merely suggest what might be agreed upon.

Sale and Leaseback

The transfer of title of a property for consideration (sale) with the simultaneous renting back to the seller (leaseback) on specified terms is a *sale-and-leaseback arrangement.* From the buyer's viewpoint, the arrangement is a purchase and leaseback. Businesses with large investments in real estate find it profitable to sell their holdings, thereby freeing up capital for expansion or operating use. The properties thus sold are leased back under custom-designed long-term agreements. Institutional investors, mainly major insurance companies, have found that real estate occupied on a long-term basis by reliable tenants with high credit ratings is an excellent and secure investment.

In arranging a sale and leaseback, the parties exchange instruments. The seller, generally a corporation, deeds the realty to the buyer, and the buyer in turn leases the property to the seller under previously agreed-upon terms.

The leases extend for 20 to 30 years, with options to renew for like periods. The rent is usually net to the new owner, the seller–lessee being required to pay all operating expenses, including taxes, maintenance, and insurance. Thus the risk of a lower than expected rate of return to the buyer–lessor is reduced. The seller-lessee, in turn, obtains 100 percent financing and also enjoys significant income tax advantages, since the rent becomes a tax-deductible cost of business. Such deductions are considerably larger than an owner's deductions would be for interest on mortgage debt, real estate taxes, and depreciation.

TYPICAL LEASE CLAUSES

A number of clauses appear in most leases, for the benefit of the landlord or the tenant. Figure 27–1 illustrates a typical apartment lease.

Landlord Rights and Obligations

Quiet enjoyment, meaning the right of possession and use without undue interference from others, is the primary covenant made by a landlord. There is an implied covenant of fitness for use. For example, if a landlord leases space in an apartment or office building, there is an implied covenant that the portions of the building used by all tenants are fit for the use for which they are intended. Many states have recently passed landlord–tenant laws requiring that the premises be kept in good repair. Failure to maintain may give the tenants the right to withhold rental payments or to apply the payments toward repair and maintenance.

The covenant of possession is that the tenant can hold possession against everyone, including the landlord. The lease usually allows the landlord to show the property to a prospective tenant or purchaser for a short period before expiration, with reasonable notice. Also the lease usually gives the landlord the right to enter and make necessary repairs to comply with governmental requirements. Thus, the landlord gives the tenant possession, subject only to the conditions in the lease.

Tenant Rights and Obligations

Certain rights and obligations go to the tenant in making a lease. Some rights, as follows, are automatic unless otherwise agreed to in the lease: (1) use of the premises in any legal manner, (2) security deposit not required, (3) able to sublet, (4) able to assign, (5) able to mortgage, and (6) redemption.

Use of Premises.   Unless restricted by agreement or zoning, a tenant may use the premises in any legal manner. Other occupants of other parts of the property may not be interfered with, however. The purpose for which the premises are to be used is often stated in the lease as, for example, "private dwelling," "boardinghouse," "retail drugstore," and so on. The lease may contain a clause that the premises cannot be used for any purpose that is extra hazardous, objectionable, detrimental to the local neighborhood, or similarly undesirable. Also, the tenant may vacate or give up use of the property, termed *abandonment,* before the lease expires; however, the tenant continues to be liable for rental payments.

FORM No. 818 ©1994 NC
STEVENS-NESS LAW PUBLISHING CO., PORTLAND, OR 97204

RENTAL AGREEMENT (Dwelling Unit – Residence Oregon)

THIS AGREEMENT, entered into in duplicate this _____10th_____ day of _____September_____, 19 _94_, by and between ___Evans Real Estate Management Co._____, lessor, and___Otto and Mary Mobile_____, lessee;

WITNESSETH: That for and in consideration of the payment of the rents and the performance of the terms of lessee's covenants herein contained, lessor does hereby demise and let unto the lessee and lessee hires from lessor for use as a residence those certain premises described as ___Unit II, Douglas Manor_____

located at ___2001 Century Drive, Urbandale, Anystate_____

☒ on a month to month tenancy beginning _____September 16_____, 19 _94_ (Indicate
☐ for a term of _____ commencing _____, 19_____, and ending _____, 19_____ which)

at a rental of $___520.00___ per month, payable monthly in advance on the _____1st_____ day of each and every month. Rents are payable at the following address: ___Evans Management Co., 41 East Third, Urbandale, Anystate 00000_____

It is agreed that if rent is unpaid after 5:00 p.m. 4 days following due date, the lessee shall pay a one-time late charge of $_____. The charge shall apply to each late payment of rent. Any dishonored check shall be treated as unpaid rent and be subject to the same late charge, plus a $_____ special handling fee and must be made good by cash money order or certified check within 24 hours of notification.

It is further mutually agreed between the parties as follows:

1. The premises shall be occupied by no more than _____ occupants.

2. Lessee shall not violate any city or county ordinance or state or federal law in or about the premises.

3. Lessee shall not sub-let the demised premises, or any part thereof, or assign this lease without the lessor's written consent.

4. If lessee fails to pay rent or other charges promptly when due, or to comply with any other term or condition hereof, lessor at lessor's option, and after proper written notice, may terminate this tenancy.

5. Lessee shall maintain the premises in a clean and sanitary condition at all times, and upon the termination of the tenancy shall surrender same to lessor in as good condition as when received, ordinary wear and tear and damage by the elements excepted; a fee is herewith paid, no part of which is refundable, for cleaning up and restoring the premises in the amount of $_____.

6. To permit lessor at any and all reasonable times, upon 24 hours' notice to lessee, to enter and go upon the premises for the purpose of examining their condition, or to make such repairs and alterations as lessor shall deem necessary or to show the leased premises to prospective purchasers, mortgagees, tenants, workers or contractors, provided always that in case of emergency lessor may enter the premises without notice.

7. There shall be working locks on all outside doors; lessor shall provide lessee with keys for same.

8. Lessee ☐, Lessor ☐ shall properly cultivate, care for and adequately water the lawn, shrubbery and grounds.

9. Lessor shall supply electric wiring, plumbing facilities which produce hot and cold running, safe drinking water and adequate heating facilities.

10. Lessee shall pay for all natural gas, electricity, and telephone service. All other services will be paid for by Lessor and Lessee as follows:

	Lessee	Lessor		Lessee	Lessor
Water	☒	☐	Garbage Service	☐	☒
Sewer	☐	☒	Cable TV	☒	☐

11. Lessor shall provide lessee with a working smoke detector, including working batteries, at the time tenancy commences. Lessee shall test any detector so provided at least once every six months, replace batteries as needed, notify lessor in writing of any operating deficiencies, and shall not remove or tamper with any properly functioning detector or remove working batteries from the same.

12. Lessee agrees to assume all liability for, and to hold lessor harmless from, all damages and all costs and fees in the defense thereof, caused by the negligence or willful act of lessee or lessee's invitees or guests, in or upon any part of the demised premises, and to be responsible for any damage or breakage to lessee's equipment, fixtures or appliances therein or thereon, not caused by lessor's misconduct or willful neglect.

13. Nothing herein shall be construed as waiving any of the rights provided by law of either party hereto.

14. In the event any suit or action is brought to collect rents or to enforce any provision of this agreement or to repossess the premises, reasonable attorney fees may be awarded by the trial court to the prevailing party in such suit or action, together with costs and necessary disbursements. On appeal, if any, similar reasonable attorney fees, costs and disbursements may be awarded by the appellate court to the party prevailing on such appeal.

15. The lessor, after 24 hours' written notice specifying the causes, may immediately terminate this agreement and take possession in the manner provided in ORS 105.105 to 105.165, if (a) Lessee, someone in lessee's control or lessee's pet seriously threatens immediately to inflict personal injury, or inflicts any substantial personal injury, upon the lessor or other tenants; (b) Lessee, someone in lessee's control, or lessee's pet inflicts any substantial personal injury upon a neighbor living in the immediate vicinity of the premises or upon a person other than lessee on the premises with permission of lessor or another lessee; (c) Lessee or someone in lessee's control intentionally inflicts any substantial damage to the premises; (d) Lessee has vacated the premises, the person in possession is holding contrary to a written rental agreement that prohibits subleasing the premises to another or allowing another person to occupy the premises without the written permission of lessor, and lessor has not knowingly accepted rent from the person in possession; or (e) Lessee or someone in lessee's control commits any act which is outrageous in the extreme.

16. Lessee shall not allow any undriveable vehicle to remain on the premises for more than 24 hours. No car repairs are to be made on the premises, including minor maintenance such as an oil change.

17. Upon termination of this Rental Agreement or the surrender or abandonment of the premises, and it reasonably appearing to lessor that lessee has left property upon the premises with no intention of asserting further claim to such property or the premises, or if lessee has been continuously absent for 7 days after termination of the tenancy by an unexecuted court order, or if lessor elects to remove such property pursuant to ORS 90.425(1) lessor may give lessee not less than 15 days' written notice by first class mail endorsed "Please Forward", to lessee's last known address and to any alternate address of lessee known to lessor, that the property is considered abandoned and unless the property is removed from the premises or place of safekeeping by a date specified in the notice, the property will be sold or otherwise disposed of and the proceeds of sale, if any, applied as provided by law.

18. The owner (or ___Evans Real Estate Mgt. Co.___
agent for service) is
Address ___41 East Third_____
___Urbandale, Anystate_____ Phone ___123-4567___
The manager is ___H. "Handy" Overseer_____
Address ___41 East Third_____
___Urbandale, Anystate_____ Phone ___123-8910___

19. A notice of nonpayment of rent or 24-hour termination is deemed served on the day it is both mailed by first class mail to lessee at the premises and also attached securely to the main entrance of that portion of the premises of which lessee has possession and/or has leased hereby.

20. Any holding over by lessee after the expiration of this agreement or any extension thereof, shall be as a tenancy at sufferance.

21. If this is a month-to-month tenancy only, then, except as otherwise provided by statute, this agreement may be terminated by either party giving the other at any time not less than 30 days' notice in writing prior to the date designated in the tenancy termination notice, whereupon the tenancy shall terminate on the date designated.

22. Lessor acknowledges the receipt of $___400.00___ as a security deposit, of which lessor may claim all or part thereof reasonably necessary to remedy lessee's defaults in the performance of this agreement (including nonpayment of past-due rent) and to repair damage to the premises caused by lessee, not including ordinary wear and tear. To claim all or part of this deposit, lessor shall give lessee, within thirty (30) days after termination of the tenancy and delivery of possession of the premises to lessor, a written accounting which states specifically the basis or bases of the claim, and the portion not so claimed shall be returned to lessee within thirty days. Lessor may recover damages in excess of the security deposit to which lessor may be entitled. Lessor also acknowledges receipt of the sum of $___N.A.___ to insure the return of _____ keys to the dwelling unit. This sum shall be refunded upon the return of all such keys.

23. Pets are allowed ☒, not allowed ☐ (indicate which). If allowed, "pets" consist of ___One cat_____
Lessee will be held responsible for all damage caused by pets and pay an additional non-refundable fee of $___100.00___ prior to bringing a pet onto the leased premises.

24. Failure by the lessor at any time to require performance by the lessee of any provision hereof shall in no way affect lessor's right hereunder to enforce the same, nor shall any waiver by the lessor of any breach of any provision hereof be held to be a waiver of any succeeding breach of any provision, or as a waiver of the provision itself.

25. The following personal property is included and to be left upon the premises when tenancy is terminated: ___range, refrigerator, electric, globes, carpeting, drapes, fire alarm_____

26. Additional provisions: ___Door to kitchen cabinet to be repaired___
_____

Lessee
Further
Agrees {
1. That lessee has personally inspected the premises and finds them satisfactory at the time of execution of this agreement;
2. That lessee has read this agreement and all the stipulations contained in the lease agreement.
3. That no promises have been made to lessee except as contained in this agreement and lease, except the following: ___None___

IN WITNESS WHEREOF, the parties hereto have executed this agreement in duplicate the day and year first above written and lessee acknowledges receipt of a copy of this agreement.

/s/ Handy Overseer _____ /s/ Otto Mobile _____
                                                    Lessor   /s/ Mary Mobile _____ Lessee
for Evans Real Estate Management Co.

The words lessee and lessor shall include the plural as well as the singular.   S-N landlord and tenant notices include Form Nos. 829, 960, 971, 972 and 973.

FIGURE 27–1

Typical Apartment Lease

Security Deposits. A landlord may properly require a security deposit to insure performance of the lease terms. This deposit may be cash, negotiable securities, or a bond executed by a surety company. A transfer of the property to another owner by the lessor does not, of itself, include the security deposit. That is, the lessor's covenant to return the deposit to the lessee is personal.

Right to Sublet.   A re-renting of a portion of the tenant's rights held under a lease is a *subletting* or *subleasing.* The original tenant becomes a *sublessor;* the party who occupies the space is a *sublessee.* A landlord may include a clause against subletting to maintain control of occupancy.

Assignment of Lease.   A tenant may also assign rights held under a lease, unless otherwise agreed. An *assignment* is a transfer of all of a tenant's rights in a lease. Although a landlord might have included a clause against assignment, given a stable alternate tenant, the landlord may waive the clause and agree to a proposed assignment. A lease, once assigned, is generally considered freely assignable. In such event, the usual rule is that the original tenant-lessee can be held liable for rents under a lease even though it has been assigned and reassigned.

Mortgaging the Leasehold.   A leasehold may be mortgaged unless the lease says otherwise. Unless otherwise agreed, the mortgage lien would not have any greater claim on the property than that held by the tenant under the lease.

Right of Redemption.   A lessee has a *right of redemption* in some states. That is, if dispossessed when more than five years of the lease are unexpired, the tenant has a right to pay all arrears and again obtain possession of the property. In a negotiated lease the tenant usually waives this right of redemption.

Jointly Negotiated Covenants

The following clauses are not standard to most leases.

Lease-Purchase Option.   A provision giving the tenant the right to purchase the premises at a certain price during the lease is called a *lease option,* or a *lease-purchase option.* Frequently, if the option is exercised within the first year, the rental for the first year applies to the purchase price. A lease option is used when an owner wants to sell to a tenant who is undecided about purchasing or who does not have an adequate down payment. A lease option has priority over any other prospective purchaser's right to purchase.

Right of Renewal.   A right of one or more renewals may be included in a lease, with rents adjusted from the initial lease payments. Renewal certainty gives the tenant a more stable basis for planning operations and the owner more stability of income.

Subordination.   Date of occupancy or recording establishes the priority of a tenant's claim to occupancy. Other liens and claims of record when the lease is made are superior to the rights of the tenant. A mortgage made after the lease, would, therefore be subordinate to the lease.

But a lease may contain a clause stating that it will be subordinate to, or have lower priority than, later mortgages, up to a certain amount. This *subordination clause* permits the landlord to increase the existing mortgages up to the agreed amount. On the other hand, the lease may be for a vacant site on which the tenant proposes to build substantial improvements. In this situation, the lessee may negotiate a clause with the owner-landlord that subordinates the fee ownership position to the proposed mortgage, up to an agreed amount.

In any event, an owner, a tenant, and a tentative lender should be aware of the significance of a subordinated position. There is a case on record in which a bank loaned $82,000 on a piece of property and ignored the rights of the people in possession. The mortgage was afterward foreclosed. It was then found that the property was occupied by tenants under a 10-year lease, with the option of a further 13-year renewal at an annual rent of $6,000, an amount entirely inadequate to service a loan of $82,000.

Liability after Reentry.   A lease may include a provision that if a tenant is dispossessed by a legal action known as a summary proceeding or abandons the property, the landlord must sublease the premises as an agent of the tenant. If the landlord re-lets the premises, the tenant must be credited with any money collected from the sublessee.

Improvements and Repairs.   A lease usually provides that no alterations to the building may be made without prior consent of the landlord. If improvements are made they become the property of the landlord, unless otherwise agreed. It is proper in some cases to provide that some or all improvements may be removed at, or prior to, the expiration of the lease. Thus, trade fixtures and machinery installed by the tenant are usually considered personal property and are removable when the tenant vacates.

The general rule is that neither party to a lease is required to make repairs, but the tenant is required to surrender the premises at the expiration of the lease in as good a condition as they were at the beginning, reasonable wear-and-tear and damage by the elements excepted. In a multitenant property, there is no legal requirement that the landlord make ordinary repairs for the upkeep of the property except that the building must be kept tenantable. Failure to do so may allow the tenants to move out on the grounds of having been constructively evicted.

Liens.   The tenant may make repairs, alterations, or improvements to the premises with the consent of the landlord. If then the tenant neglects to pay for the work performed, mechanics and materialmen may enforce their liens against the landlord's property. At the same time, the tenant may be held personally liable.

The landlord may demand further protection from liens by requiring that the tenant deposit cash or file a bond as a guarantee that the cost of repairs, alterations, or improvements will be paid. This requirement is very important in leases that require the tenant to undertake such work.

Damage Claims.   Agreement is desirable in a lease as to which party (landlord or tenant) is liable for claims developing from ownership, occupation, or use of the property. These claims may be made by persons injured on the property, or they may be made by persons damaged away from the property as, for example, when a fire spreads from the property. With liability clarified, the party bearing the risk may obtain protection through insurance.

A landlord or tenant is not responsible for an accident unless it was caused by the negligence of one of them. And, neither is liable for an injury caused by a negligent condition, unless either actually knew or should have known of the condition.

Damage and/or Destruction of Premises. Unless otherwise agreed, a lessee of a site must continue to pay rent even if the building thereon or other improvements are destroyed by fire, flood, wind, or other acts of God. This rule does not apply to a lease of an apartment, office, or some other portion of a building, since such an arrangement is not a lease of land.

In the event that partial destruction makes a building untenantable or unusable, the landlord must make repairs in a "reasonable" time. And if the premises are damaged and made unsuitable for occupancy before the tenant takes possession, the tenant may end the lease without liability to the landlord. A damage clause in a lease would, of course, enable the parties to clearly define their relationship and to protect themselves accordingly.

Compliance with Governmental Regulations. A clause concerning responsibility for compliance with governmental regulations may be included in a lease.

TERMINATION OF LEASES

A lease may be terminated by expiration of the term, mutual agreement of the parties (surrender), dispossession and/or eviction, eminent domain when the leased property is taken for public purposes, mortgage foreclosure, and/or upon bankruptcy of the tenant.

Term Expiration

Written leases end on the last day of their term, without notice. Tenancies from period to period and tenancies at will continue, or are self-renewing, until notice of termination is given.

Mutual Agreement

A tenant and landlord may end a lease by a mutual arrangement of surrender and acceptance, which may be by an expressed or implied agreement as well as by an oral or written agreement. With a recorded lease, the parties are advised to write out, sign, and record any agreement to surrender.

Dispossess and/or Eviction

A breach of conditions, followed by dispossession proceedings, may terminate a lease. The conditions may be divided into two classes, those for which the landlord dispossesses the tenant by summary proceedings and those for which summary proceedings may not be brought. Summary dispossession proceedings may be used to terminate a lease for the following reasons:

1. Nonpayment of rent.
2. Holding over at the end of the term.
3. Unlawful use of the premises.
4. Nonpayment of taxes, assignments, or other charges when, under the terms of the lease, the tenant undertook to pay them.

A landlord has the right to recover possession from a tenant through a summary proceeding known as dispossession or eviction. An eviction may be either actual or constructive. An *actual eviction* occurs if the tenant is ousted from the premises in whole or in part, by an act of the landlord. *Constructive eviction* occurs when the physical condition of the leased premises has changed, owing to some act or failure to act of the landlord, so that the tenant is unable to occupy the premises for the purposes intended. No claim of constructive eviction will be allowed unless the tenant actually removes from the premises while the condition exists. If the tenant removes and can prove a valid case, the lease is terminated. The tenant may also be able to recover damages for the landlord's breach of contract.

Eminent Domain

When leased property is taken for public purposes under the right of *eminent domain,* leases on it terminate. The tenant is given an opportunity to prove the value of the unexpired term of the lease in the proceeding under which the property is taken and may receive an award for it.

Mortgage Foreclosure

The foreclosure of a mortgage or other lien terminates a leasehold estate, provided that the lease is subordinate to the lien being foreclosed. The lessee must be made a party in the foreclosure suit for this to occur. Also, a lease may provide for termination upon bankruptcy of the tenant, especially when the tenant is unable to provide adequate assurances to the lessor that he or she has the financial wherewithal to be able to perform under the lease in the future.

TENANT UNIONS

Tenants and landlords need each other. Landlords have space to sell. Tenants need places to live or to do business. Both benefit when the right tenant gets the right space. The tenant gets greater satisfaction or does more business. The landlord gets higher rent and, in turn, greater property value.

At the same time, the interests of the tenants and landlords are in direct conflict, in a sense comparable to that of mortgagor and mortgagee. The negotiation between them goes on continually in one form or another. An important development in this negotiation/competition—tenant unions—is outside the traditional landlord-tenant relationship as discussed earlier. Even so, a brief look at the nature and implications of tenant unions seems warranted.

Tenant unions came into being because of abusive practices by some landlords. In apartment house operation particularly the landlord is generally more knowledgeable and financially stronger than any individual tenant. The situation is similar to that of a large employer with many employees. Organizing into unions increases the bargaining power of the tenants.

Tenant unions usually seek to (1) negotiate better leases and conditions for tenants, and (2) establish a grievance procedure for dissatisfied tenants. Tenant unions have also been instrumental in getting landlord-tenant statutes passed in many states; these statutes put tenants on a more even footing with owners.

Tenant unions have successfully called rent strikes to withhold rent payments to enforce their demands. The reasons for a rent strike might involve lack of security against criminal acts on the premises, wrongful eviction of tenants, or serious hazards that create building code violations.

Courts have held that if rents are paid into escrow in such strikes, retaliatory evictions are illegal. A *retaliatory eviction* is the removal of a tenant from a property as punishment for the tenant's asserting his or her rights. Thus, landlords may not retaliate against tenants for joining tenant unions, for reporting violations of building codes or other local regulations, or for legally withholding rents. The movement toward tenant unions seems healthy for responsible landlords and for society as a whole, as well as for tenants.

SUMMARY

A lease gives a tenant the right to occupy and use certain premises in return for periodic rental payments to the landlord. Leases or rental arrangements for up to one year may be made orally. In most states, leases for more than one year must be written.

An interest (possession) in real estate held under a lease is a tenancy. A tenancy may be definite—for a specific time—or indefinite—for an uncertain time. The most common indefinite tenancies are the periodic, at will, and by sufferance.

Leases are often classified according to the methods used to determine the amount of periodic rent payments. Using this kind of classification system, the most popular leases are the percentage-of-gross-sales lease, the index lease, and the net lease. The ground lease and the sale-and-leaseback agreement are special-purpose rental contracts.

In leasing premises, the landlord promises possession, quiet enjoyment, and fitness for uses. The tenant may use the premises in any legal manner that is not precluded by the lease and that does not interfere with other occupants of the building. The tenant may assign or mortgage rights held under a lease, or sublet the premises unless specifically prohibited by the lease. Joint negotiation between the landlord and tenant usually determines the security to be furnished, the additional charges to be paid by the tenant, and the rights of each party in case of fire or other destruction of the premises. Leases may be terminated by expiration, surrender and acceptance, breach of conditions, actual or constructive eviction, eminent domain, property destruction, tenant bankruptcy, or mortgage foreclosure.

KEY CONCEPTS

Abandonment   When tenant vacates or gives up possession before a lease expires; tenant may continue to be liable for rental payments.

Assignment   Transfer of all of a lessee's rights to another party.

Eviction, actual   Tenant removed from premises through direct action of a landlord.

Eviction, constructive   Tenant removed from premises through indirect action of a landlord; for example, when physical conditions make continued occupancy hazardous or unsuitable for purposes intended and landlord fails or refuses to correct situation.

Gross lease   Where tenant pays a fixed rent and the landlord pays all property expenses.

Ground lease   Contract giving right of use of land.

Index lease   Agreement providing for rental adjustment based on changes in an agreed-upon index, such as the consumer price index.

Lease option   Provision giving a tenant the right to purchase an occupied property at a specified price and within a stipulated time; also called a lease-purchase option.

Leased fee   Owner's interest or position in a leased property.

Leasehold estate   Tenant's interest or position in a property under lease.

Lessee/tenant   One who occupies a property in exchange for rental payments.

Lessor/landlord   One who gives up the right of occupancy and use of property in exchange for rent.

Net lease   Rental payments to an owner where the tenant agrees to pay the costs of hazard insurance, property taxes, and maintenance.

Percentage lease   Rental payments by tenant are calculated as a proportion of sales or other income generated by the property.

Quiet enjoyment   Right of possession and use of a property without undue disturbance or interference by others.

Retaliatory eviction   Removal of a tenant from a property as punishment for the tenant asserting his or her rights; generally illegal.

Sale and leaseback   Transfer of property ownership (sale) with the simultaneous renting back of the premises to the seller (leaseback).

Sublessee   A tenant who rents from a prior lessee.

Sublessor   A lessee who re-rents to another lessee.

Sublet   Transfer of only a portion of a tenant's rights to another party.

Subordination clause   A clause in a lien, lease, or other document establishing relative priority of claim on the property.

Tenancy for years   Renting a property for a specified time, usually under a written lease agreement.

Tenancy from period to period   Renting a property for a period of uncertain duration; also known a periodic tenancy.

QUESTIONS FOR REVIEW AND DISCUSSION

1. Explain clearly the distinction between tenancy for years and tenancy from year to year.

2. What are the advantages and disadvantages of a written tenancy for years relative to a periodic tenancy from the viewpoint of the tenant.

3. Explain these rental payment plan arrangements:

    a. Percentage

    b. Flat

    c. Net

d. Graduated

e. Index

f. Reappraisal

4. Explain the following concepts of clauses as they relate to leasing:

　a. Use of premises

　b. Right to sublet

　c. Right to assign

　d. Right to mortgage

　e. Lease option

　f. Subordination

5. List and explain at least four ways for ending a lease.

6. A property is under lease on a long-term, step-up lease. The neighborhood deteriorates and the property's value declines. Who benefits, if anyone? Explain.

7. Compare the advantages of leasing with the advantages of buying a business property. Is there a time when either is clearly more appropriate?

8. Is there a landlord-tenant code in your state? If so, what are its main provisions? If not, where are the major laws pertaining to landlord and tenant rights found?

PROBLEMS

1. N occupied a cabin on H's farm, without any provision for rent or duration. Both recognized that either could terminate the arrangement at any time. N died. H cleaned up the cabin, locked the door, and placed N's belongings on the porch. W, N's executor now claims the right to occupy the cabin as a continuation of the lease arrangement. Does W have this right? Explain.

2. J rented a luxury apartment in Tudor Towers for $1,000 per month on a 2-year lease on December 10. Shortly after, he received a job offer he could not refuse in another city. He re-rented the apartment to E for $1,200 per month for the remainder of the lease. Nothing is said in the original lease about assignment or subleasing of rights. Now the owner of Tudor Towers objects to the re-renting and threatens to sue J. What are J's rights in this situation?

3. A and B rent a building from W to establish a restaurant and tavern on a 1-year lease. They add a storage room in the rear and arrange for the installation of a bar, kitchen equipment, booths, and miscellaneous other items, all of which are attached to the building. The business is unusually successful, and A and B decide to move to larger quarters at the end of the year. Upon moving, they start to remove the improvements. W objects and threatens to sue, saying that all improvements become the property of the landlord unless otherwise agreed. Since no such other agreement was reached, what is the result?

4. E was instrumental in organizing a tenant union. As a result of the union, many tenants, including E, paid their rent into an escrow account until certain improvements were made to the property. When E's lease ended, the landlord refused to renew. E feels that she is being punished for her actions. What rights does she have? Can she be evicted under these circumstances?

CHAPTER 28

GOVERNMENTAL LIMITATIONS TO OWNERSHIP

Chapter Outline

Society in every state is a blessing, but government, even in its best state is but a necessary evil; in its worst state, an intolerable one.

Thomas Paine, *Common Sense,* 1776

The system of property ownership in the United States is a mix of the feudal and *allodial* systems of ownership brought from Europe. Under the English feudal system, a king or sovereign owned all the land, with subjects obtaining use of the land in return for services and allegiance. Under the allodial system initiated in France in 1789 following the Revolution, only private ownership was recognized; no rights were reserved by a sovereign authority. Combining the two systems in the United States gives private ownership rights to the individual, with the state reserving the rights of police power, eminent domain, taxation, and escheat. The reservation of these four rights remains the same, regardless of how the fee estate is split up.

Escheat is the reversion, or automatic conveyance, of realty to the state upon an owner's death, when no will, heirs, or other legal claimants to title can be found. In fact, escheat is seldom exercised because someone almost always has a title claim. Also, for all practical purposes, escheat is not a restriction on ownership; it simply serves to keep property productive and "in the system." Real estate is too valuable to society to go unused.

The right of government to regulate (police power), to condemn (eminent domain), and to tax make up a substantial portion of the "rules of the game" for real estate; hence, an understanding of this chapter is crucial for investors and practitioners. Government reserves these powers in order to look after public health, welfare, and safety; to facilitate growth and to meet communities' changing social and economic needs; and to financially maintain themselves. We look at these three governmental reservations of powers to see how they constrain a rational investor in developing and using land. Overall, we believe these restrictions yield positive results for society.

POLICE POWER

The right of *police power* allows government, through due process of law, to protect public health, welfare, safety, and morals. Villages, cities, and counties all have rights of police power based on state enabling acts that grant express authority to carry out needed regulatory activities. The enabling legislation provides the basis for planning, zoning ordinances, subdivision regulations, building and housing codes, rent controls, and other land use regulations. Generally, compensation need not be paid for lowered property values resulting from the use of police power. Let us look briefly at how this power to regulate came into being.

Nuisance Laws

A *nuisance* is the interference with a neighbor's use and quiet enjoyment of land, other than by trespass or direct physical invasion. In English common law, if Able cuts a tree on Baker's land, it is trespass, and Baker can bring a civil action at law, sue, and get compensation or redress. But if Able remains on his own land and operates a pig farm, a chemical plant, a blasting operation, or a naughty house, no trespass has occurred, even though the stench, chemical fumes, falling dirt and debris, and offense to public morals substantially interfere with Baker's use of his land. Even though there was no trespass, common law came to recognize that these conditions constituted a moral wrong, a private nuisance for which the originator could be held liable. In modern times, particles of energy, light, dust, or gas from a neighboring property; storage of explosives or radioactive materials; noise from an airport; acid rain; street litter; and even failure to drain mosquito-breeding waters are considered a nuisance or *trespass*.

In economics, such nuisances are called externalities, indirect costs, or spillover effects. Thus, an *externality* is when my behavior indirectly affects others, positively or negatively, without their concurrence or agreement. Externalities result in the market not allocating resources efficiently, thus keeping the economy from realizing its full potential.

Private efforts to control externalities are made mainly through deed or title restrictions. But, title restrictions have two major drawbacks. First, they are limited in geographic area; a developer cannot, for example, control land uses outside a subdivision. Second, an overt effort by the developer or owners within the subdivision is required for enforcement.

Thus, where negative externalities exist, the only truly socially satisfactory solution is a collective one—government regulation through planning, zoning, etc. Other possibilities do exist; for example, a tax or penalty can be imposed on the person creating the nuisance in order to force him or her to cease or to control the activity. But, our concern is with the various uses of police power.

Planning

A *master plan* is a comprehensive scheme that sets forth the ways and means by which a community can adjust its physical makeup to social and economic changes. It involves a systematic process that includes data collection, classification, and analysis. Almost every community—city, county, village, or metropolitan area—has a master plan. Planning itself is not a solution to externalities, but it does provide an underlying rationale for the many other forms of regulation.

Growth in population, commerce, manufacturing, and other activities necessitates development and improvement of a community's infrastructure: roads, sewers, water systems, schools, hospitals, and other public facilities. Depreciation and evolving technology also make infrastructure changes necessary. One major purpose of planning is to create and maintain a high-quality environment with stable property values; a second is to avoid wasteful mistakes in developing the infrastructure that result from poor coordination, duplication, and overbuilding.

A master plan really consists of several coordinated plans for land use, transportation, schools, and other public facilities. It must, at the very least, be based on studies of (1) population, (2) the economic base, (3) land use, and (4) transportation of the area or community. In turn, the master plan provides the underlying rationale for a community's zoning ordinances, subdivision regulations, and construction and building codes, our most often employed land use controls. *Land-use controls,* which are used to regulate and guide use of realty, are achieved through governmental regulation or by private parties through deed restrictions.

Experience shows that for a master plan to effectively meet a community's needs, it must be:

1. In scale with the population and economic outlook of the community.
2. In scale with the current and future financial resources of the community.
3. Balanced and attractive in design relative to the environment to be created and maintained.
4. In keeping with community sentiments on an attractive environment.
5. Flexible and easily updated to accommodate changing conditions and projections.

Zoning

Zoning is community regulation of land use, population density, and building size and appearance, and it is easily the most significant legal technique used to regulate

DISCONTINUANCE OF A NUISANCE THROUGH ZONING
HADACHECK V. LOS ANGELES
(U. S. SUPREME COURT REPORTS); 239 U.S. 394 (1915)

Hadacheck v. Los Angeles is a landmark case that tied together nuisance law and a justification for zoning.

In 1902 the Hadacheck Co. bought eight acres of land that contained valuable deposits of clay suitable for making bricks. Subsequently, kilns, buildings and machinery for the manufacture of brick were assembled on the site and the manufacture of brick was begun. The operation generated considerable smoke and dust, which interfered with the residential properties that developed in the surrounding area.

The entire area was later annexed to Los Angeles, and a three-square-mile district around the plant was given a zoning classification that made it "unlawful for any person to establish or operate a brickyard or brick kiln, or any establishment, factory or place for the manufacture

or burning of brick. . . ." Extensive litigation followed, with the case being taken to the California Supreme Court, and eventually to the U.S. Supreme Court. The residential neighbors gave extensive evidence of the interference with their rights due to the brick manufacturing operations.

The final judgment closed down the brick-making operation, with no damages being payable, although the court recognized "that the value of investments made in the business prior to any legislative action will be greatly diminished." The court also refused to recognize Hadacheck's claim of a preemptive right to carry on its business because it had been "in that locality for a long period." The company was not enjoined from removing the clay for manufacture into bricks at another location.

externalities. It involves dividing the community into districts in order to regulate land use by type (residential, commercial, and so forth); by intensity (one-family, multifamily, and so forth), and by height, bulk, and appearance. A zoning ordinance must undergo public review before being enacted into law.

Increasingly, land uses are organized by performance class rather than by district; using performance standards to define classes is called *performance zoning*. Performance zoning establishes districts that allow or accept uses, regardless of type, if they meet certain standards relative to density, appearance, traffic generation, and pollution origination. Thus, uses that do not adversely affect each other and may, in fact, complement each other, may be placed in the same class or district.

Zoning Ordinances.   In addition to written regulations a zoning ordinance usually includes a zoning map. The following are typical standards covered by the ordinance.

1. The community is divided into districts, with the land use in each specified as residential, commercial, industrial, or agricultural.

2. Standards limiting the height and bulk of buildings are set for each district.

3. Standards regulating the proportion of a lot that can be built on, including detailed front-, side-, and backyard set-back requirements, are set for each district.

4. By regulating the foregoing factors, limits are set on population density in the various districts. This procedure is called *density zoning*.

A properly drawn zoning ordinance does not concern itself with the following kinds of standards:

1. Specifying building materials and construction methods. (These are governed by construction or building codes.)

2. Setting minimum construction costs. (A public ordinance cannot legally set such a standard, but such standards may be set by private deed restrictions.)

3. Regulation of street design and installation of utilities, or reservation of land for park or school sites. (This is governed primarily by subdivision regulations, along with street or public works departments, the park department, and the school board.)

Height, Bulk, and Area Regulations.   Building height and bulk restrictions prevent the taking over of air, ventilation, and sunlight by one parcel at the unreasonable expense of another parcel. The restrictions also limit fire risks, population density, and street congestion. Building heights are generally limited to a certain number of stories (e.g., 1½, 2, 2½, 10, etc.)

Floor-area ratio (FAR) zoning is a form of performance zoning that is widely used to make possible greater design flexibility in a district while limiting population and development density. FAR is the relationship of building coverage to site area. For example, a FAR of 2.0 means that an owner is permitted to construct a two-story building over the entire lot, a four-story building over one-half of the lot, or an eight-story building over one-fourth of the lot. Any combination of fraction-of-lot coverage times the number of stories, therefore, may not exceed the allowed FAR of 2.0 (see Figure 28–1).

To ensure that adequate sunlight be available on a continuing basis, right-to-light zoning might modify FAR zoning, as shown in Figure 28–2.

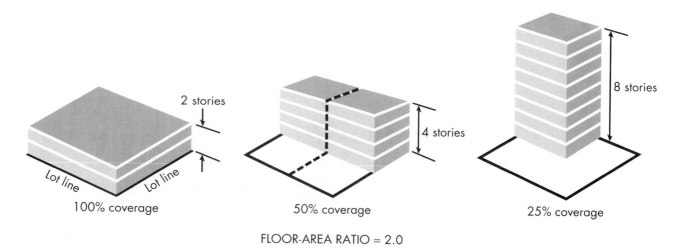

FIGURE 28-1
Floor-Area Ratio Zoning—an Example of Performance Zoning

Multiple-Use Zoning.   Allowing several compatible but different uses in a district is called multiple-use zoning. Thus, offices and small stores may be allowed in the same district as apartments or condominiums, an arrangement that may work to the benefit of all concerned. In fact, these uses may be combined into one project, termed a *planned-unit development (PUD),* as a result of a transfer of development rights. In a planned-unit development improvements are added to realty at the same overall density as in conventional development, but the improvements are clustered, resulting in more open common areas. For example, assume a 10-acre parcel is zoned for four dwelling units per acre. A developer is limited to 40 one-family houses by conventional zoning. With PUD, the developer might construct four closely clustered, ten-unit buildings, leaving the balance of the acreage for open space. PUD may be used in residential, commercial, or industrial development. PUD zoning is also termed *cluster zoning,* and is a form of density zoning.

   Transferable development rights means that one parcel may be developed more intensely if another parcel is developed less intensely. Development rights may be sold by one owner to another, thereby adding flexibility and variety to an area without increasing its overall density. In the planned-unit example, if some commercial development rights were also acquired, stores could be included in the project. However, some other project would go without stores because those rights had been acquired by the PUD. This, of course, would be an extension of the multiple-use zoning concept.

Zoning Challenges and/or Negotiations.   An owner, or potential owner, may petition for changes in, or relief from, a zoning ordinance by a direct challenge or in either of the following ways:

   A *zoning variance* is a deviation from a zoning ordinance granted because strict enforcement would result in undue hardship on a property owner. With a zoning variance the usual rules are simply set aside. An example would be a case where a lot is so steep that front-yard setback requirements cannot be met with reasonable expense. A variance must not violate the intent or spirit of the ordinance.

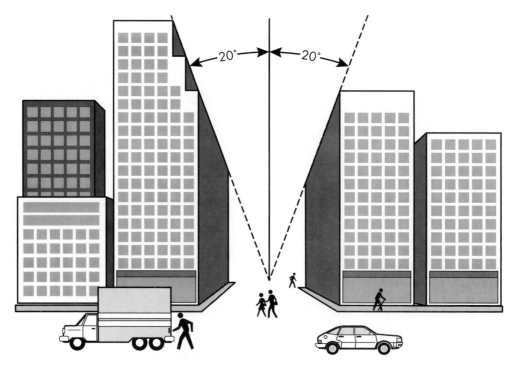

FIGURE 28-2
Right-to-Light
Performance Zoning

A technique known as contract zoning is sometimes used to fine-tune a zoning ordinance. *Contract zoning* refers to a situation where an owner, by title restriction or side agreement, limits a property's use in return for a new zoning classification. For example, a parcel is rezoned as commercial; at the same time the owner records a title restriction limiting use to one-story professional offices. Contract zoning is not a recognized legal concept.

An owner may try to circumvent the zoning board appeals process by going through the courts and challenging the zoning ordinance itself. The legal requirements of a valid ordinance are as follows:

1. Use districts must be provided for by enabling legislation and applicable regulations must be uniform for each classification and kind of building. A reasonable rationale for classifying districts differently must exist.

2. An entire jurisdiction (such as a city) and not just small, isolated areas must be zoned.

3. Parcels must not be zoned for uses they cannot physically accommodate.

A challenge on any of these points would argue that the ordinance is not based on a well-conceived land use or master plan. Also, a challenge might be based on the idea that an ordinance is arbitrary, unreasonable, destructive, or confiscatory in application.

Finally, zoning may not be used to discriminate against minorities or low-income people, which discrimination is termed *exclusionary zoning.* For example, a high-income residential district, by setting unreasonably large, minimum lot sizes or floor-area requirements, or high construction quality standards makes it improbable that low- and moderately-low income groups can afford to settle in the district.

Nonconforming Uses.   Existing uses or structures that are inconsistent with the applicable zoning are termed *nonconforming uses,* and they may be legal or illegal. If they existed prior to the original adoption of the ordinance, they are legal nonconforming uses, and are allowed to continue subject to several provisions. To require their removal would inflict severe and unreasonable financial hardship on owners. Generally, the provisions regulating a nonconforming use prohibit the following:

1. Enlargement.

2. Rebuilding or reconstruction after a specified percentage of damage or destruction, usually 50 percent.

3. Changing to another nonconforming use.

4. Resumption after a stated period of discontinuance, usually one year.

New uses and structures must conform to current zoning. To introduce a use or to build a structure inconsistent with the ordinance is to create an illegal nonconforming use, which would be subject to immediate removal without compensation.

A parcel or small area may not be rezoned for a use or structure that is inconsistent with the overall plan or ordinance; this is called *spot zoning* and is illegal. An owner who is adversely affected by a proposed rezoning of a nearby parcel may successfully challenge it in court if it can be proved that the proposed use is unclear, discriminatory, unreasonable, not for the protection of the public health, safety and general welfare, or not applied to all property in a similar manner.

Zoning and Value.   On a community-wide basis zoning does not create value in real estate. Market demand for a use is the basis of value, whether it involves an office building, a shopping center, or an apartment building. At the same time, a well-conceived master plan, together with appropriate zoning, must prevail in order for all the land in the community to realize its greatest value. If demand for a use is not present, commercial, industrial, or multifamily zoning will not enhance a property's value, except perhaps in the mind of the owner.

Zoning does channel values, however. Thus, obtaining a rezoning to commercial, for example, where market demand exists will enhance the value of the parcel. But, rezoning all the land in the community to commercial would not increase the total value of all the commercially zoned parcels. In fact, inappropriate zoning may distort or alter the use to which a parcel can be put, limiting it to less than its highest-and-best use and its greatest value potential.

Occasionally, a master plan or zoning ordinance will reclassify a property from a high-value use, such as commercial or industrial, to a low-value use, such as single-family residential. This is called *down zoning.* An owner must be constantly aware of the possibility of down zoning. If demand for the high-value use exists, down zoning could mean a substantial loss to the owner. On the other hand, such a rezoning may simply be a recognition of reality.

Zoning is intended to stabilize values; it does not prevent value declines. Zoning cannot prevent aging and obsolescence of structures, factors that are likely to lower values.

Subdivision Regulations

Locally adopted laws governing the conversion of raw land into building sites are called subdivision regulations. The regulations work primarily through plat approval procedures. That is, a subdivider or developer is not permitted to split up land until the planning commission has approved a plat of the proposed project, based on its compliance with standards and requirements set forth in the regulations.

In almost all states, a comprehensive plan, a major street plan, or an official map must have been adopted to provide a legal basis for the implementation of subdivision regulations and to serve as evidence that the regulations are not arbitrary or discriminatory. Such plans coordinate the layout of a particular subdivision with others in the area, and also provide for rights-of-way for major thoroughfares, easements for utility lines, and school and park locations.

The elements controlled by most subdivision regulations are as follows:

1. Rights-of-way for streets, alleys, cul-de-sacs, highways, and walkways. The right-of-way covers location, alignment, width, grade, surfacing material, and possible dedication to the community.

2. Lots and blocks. Regulations cover minimum dimensions and setback lines of buildings.

3. Utilities. Easements are provided for sewer, water, and power lines; assurance of pure water and ability to dispose of wastes without health problems is given.

4. Areas are reserved for schools, parks, open space, and other public uses.

Increasingly development charges are incorporated into subdivision ordinances. A *development charge* is a fee that is imposed on the subdivider or developer by the community to pay for the proportional costs of waste-disposal facilities, roads, water storage tanks, and the like, necessitated by the new subdivision. The intent is to have the owners of the newly developed parcels pay for the marginal costs of new facilities rather than place the burden on the citizenry in general.

Environmental impact studies are required for large development projects. An *environmental impact study* is an investigation and analysis to determine the long-run physical effects of a proposed land use on its surroundings and the long-run economic and social effects on other people. The purpose of an environmental impact study is to bring together in one report the likely costs and benefits of a project before it is approved for development. For example, an environmental impact study for a proposed shopping center would document the expected effects on auto traffic, air quality, the waste-disposal system, energy demand, employment, and vegetation. If these public sector costs are too substantial, the proposal might require modification to obtain approval.

Building Codes

Building codes take up where subdivision regulations leave off; that is, they apply mainly to improvements to the land. The objective is public safety and protection against negative externalities. The object is to prevent a hazard that might result in a loss of life or that might spill over onto neighboring parcels. Thus, the focus is on such concerns as fireproof construction, means of emergency exit, windows, load and stress, size and location of rooms, adequacy of ventilation, sanitation facilities, electrical wiring and equipment, mechanical equipment, and lighting at exits. Several separate codes, such as an electrical, plumbing, and fire code, may make up the building codes.

Codes are particularly stringent for buildings likely to be occupied by large numbers of people, such as apartment buildings, schools, churches, hospitals, and office buildings. Special provisions also usually apply to potentially hazardous structures such as amusement parks, canopies, roof signs, grandstands, grain elevators, or cleaning plants.

Enforcement begins with the requirement that a building permit be obtained for new construction or alterations. Both the zoning ordinance and the building codes must be complied with. Also, blueprints must pass examination before a building permit is issued. Construction is inspected as it progresses. When there is full compliance with all codes, a *certificate of occupancy,* which is an official notice that all code inspections were passed and that the structure is fit for use, is granted.

Rent Controls

A *rent control* is a governmental limitation on the amount of rent that may be charged for apartments or other space units. Rent controls are often sought by tenant unions on the argument that housing is required by everyone and tends to be unique in that supply cannot be expanded quickly in response to increased demand. Thus, tenants have little choice but to pay increased rents when demand outruns supply.

What are the implications of rent control? Assuming inflation, the immediate effect is to squeeze profits from a landlord, which leads to neglect of property maintenance. Property values drop both because rent increases are limited and property maintenance is neglected. Lower property values cause property taxes to local government to drop, resulting in tighter budgets and reduced services. Owners seek relief by trying to convert to condominiums or to demolish and rebuild in a use that is not subject to controls. If their efforts are unsuccessful and all profits are squeezed out of ownership, properties are abandoned and severe blight and slums result. But the problems are broader. Investors restrict the development of new housing projects to communities without controls. And lenders avoid making loans on properties in rent control areas. The result is more blight and urban deterioration. In the end, even the people intended to receive the benefits of rent controls lose out.

Rent controls are intended to benefit those with low incomes, although those who actually benefit do not necessarily have low incomes. Further, both liberal and conservative economists agree that the costs to society as a whole appear to outweigh the benefits. The effect is to transfer wealth from landlords to tenants. But providing relief for low-income people should fall on the whole of society rather than on property owners.

Frederick Hayek, a conservative, Nobel Prize winning economist, had this to say about rent controls. "If this account seems to boil down to a catalogue of inequities to be laid at the door of rent control, that is no mere coincidence, but inevitable. . . . I doubt very much whether theoretical research into the same problem carried out by someone of a different political-economic persuasion than myself could lead to a different conclusion."[1] And he was right. Gunnar Myrdal, a liberal economist, who also

---

[1] A.F. Hayek, "The Repercussion of Rent Restrictions," in *Rent Control, A Popular Paradox, Evidence on the Economic Effect of Rent Control.* Vancouver, B.C.: The Fraser Institute, 1975, p. 80.

won a Nobel Prize, had this view. "Rent control has in certain Western countries constituted, maybe, the worst example of poor planning by governments lacking courage and vision."[2]

Miscellaneous Controls

As a rule, fire and sanitation departments are empowered to make periodic inspections and to order compliance with directives to ensure safe and sanitary use and occupancy of buildings. Proper enforcement of fire control and sanitation ordinances may go a long way toward retarding housing blight and eventual elimination of unsightly and unsafe city slums. In almost all states, there are health regulations for wells, septic tanks, and other waste-disposal installations.

EMINENT DOMAIN

Eminent domain is the right of a governmental or quasi-governmental agency to take private property for public uses or purposes. Eminent domain literally means "highest authority or dominion." The right is based on the premise that an owner should sometimes be required to give up property, for just compensation, so that the common good or welfare may be advanced. As a last resort land for streets, parks, schools, and other public buildings, and for public or social purposes, is acquired through eminent domain. However, most organizations try to acquire desired properties by negotiation before exercising their right of eminent domain.

The taking is without the consent of the owner and requires payment of reasonable or just compensation. This is sometimes called condemnation, or the right of expropriation. Semipublic organizations, such as railroads, public utility companies and universities, may exercise eminent domain for limited purposes.

Need for Eminent Domain

The right of eminent domain is needed because our society and economy changes continually. For example, in the 1930s nearly half the population lived in rural areas and sociologists predicted that the U.S. population would mature and stabilize at 150 million by 1950. Automobiles were still a relatively new mode of transportation. Air travel was only for the wealthy, and most intercity passenger and freight transportation was provided by the railroads. Now, in the 1990s, the resident U.S. population exceeds 249 million people, about three-fourths of whom live in urban areas. Almost everyone drives an automobile, and air travel is much more common than travel by rail. Trucks haul a large share of intercity freight.

With the growth in population and shift from rural to urban areas, the power of eminent domain is needed to acquire property for highway construction, public building sites, flood control projects, and airport expansion. The power of eminent domain also has been legally exercised to acquire land in urban renewal areas for later resale to and redevelopment by profit-seeking individuals and corporations. Thus, the emphasis on public purposes is not limited to public need and use.

[2] As quoted by Sven Oydefelt in "The Rise and Fall of Swedish Rent Control," in *Rent Control, A Popular Paradox, Evidence on the Economic Effect of Rent Control.* Vancouver, B.C.: The Fraser Institute, 1975, p. 169.

Just Compensation

Just compensation is payment for property taken and is almost universally defined as the fair market value of the property. Many states pay severance damages to owners if only part of a property is taken but the value of the remainder is lowered as a result of the taking. That is, fair market value is paid for the portion of the property taken, and additional payment is made for any reduction in value to the remainder. An example is the taking of a portion of the property—such as the front 20 feet—leaving fee simple rights in the remaining land as the residual. In this case, compensation would be paid for the portion of the property that was confiscated plus for any damage occurred to the residual by the taking. Air rights or subsurface rights of a property also could be taken, leaving the surface rights as the residual.

Compensation is not usually paid for certain damages suffered by an owner. Examples are: (1) loss of business profits or goodwill; (2) moving costs (although the federal government and some states do pay these in some situations, independent of the court's decision); (3) additional costs of securing replacement housing or facilities; and (4) adverse effects of having as a new neighbor such improvements as an airport or a sewage treatment plant.

TAXATION AND SPECIAL ASSESSMENTS

Governments cannot function without the power to levy and collect taxes. The U.S. Supreme Court has noted, "The power to tax is the one great power upon which the whole national fabric is based. It is as necessary to the existence and prosperity of the nation as the air he breathes is to the natural man. It is not only the power to destroy but also the power to keep alive."[3]

Local governments rely heavily on property tax revenues to finance themselves. The taxes are levied on an *ad valorem basis,* which means that the tax is levied on each property according to its value, usually market value. Thus, each parcel must be periodically appraised and an assessed value placed on it. *Assessed value* means the amount in dollars assigned to a parcel by the tax administrator. Assessed value may be equal to or be a proportion of market value, and it varies directly with market value.

Annual property taxes typically run about 2 to 4 percent of market value, which is a lot of money to most owners. Thus, concerns of fairness in levying the tax and of efficiency in how the money is used become important. If used wisely, taxes may benefit an owner in that they help to provide police and fire protection, schools, parks, and a road system, all of which can enhance the value of a property.

From the community's viewpoint, the property tax is an efficient way to raise a large amount of revenue quickly and at relatively low cost. There are several reasons for this efficiency: (1) Most property in a community is subject to the tax, which makes for a large tax base. (2) Parcels are fixed in location; thus, values can be established and the taxes levied and collected without undue effort. If they are not paid, liens can be recorded and enforced. (3) The federal government is precluded from taxing real property by the Constitution. (4) Because property values tend to keep up with inflation, tax revenues also tend to rise with inflation. The main limitation to using the property tax is that property maintenance and new construction are inhibited because the tax is levied according to value.

---

[3] *Nichol v. Ames,* 173 U.S. 508 (1899).

Uniformity in Assessment

Equity, or fair tax treatment, is a major concern of owners, who feel that properties of comparable value should pay comparable taxes. If all property is assessed at the same proportion of market value this does occur. Thus, a store with a market value of $500,000 that is assessed at $300,000 is receiving the same treatment as a residence with a market value of $200,000 that is assessed at $120,000. Each is assessed at 60 percent of its market price. The store will pay 2.5 times more in property taxes, regardless of the rate at which taxes are levied, because its value is that much greater.

Tax Exemptions

Tax-exempt properties are a second equity issue of concern to owners. Property owned by government and nonprofit institutions, such as churches, hospitals, and private schools, are usually not required to pay property taxes. But they require services like fire and police protection regardless of their tax status. An indirect burden also exists. Streets and sewer, water, and power lines must sometimes be extended greater distances to serve publically owned properties, thereby constituting an extra cost to private owners. In recognition of the extra burden placed on local facilities, payments in lieu of taxes are often made in situations like this.

A tax exemption may benefit a private owner. In some states, such as Florida for example, homeowners are given a homestead exemption from assessed value by statute. An exemption of $25,000 is typical, with it being doubled for owners who are 65 and over. Assuming a 3 percent tax rate, each $10,000 of exemption means $300 less per year in taxes.

Special Assessments

Special assessments are charges upon real property to pay all or part of the cost of a local improvement that benefits the property. Assessments are not annual charges, as taxes are, and they are not apportioned according to the value of the property affected. For example, all lots fronting on a certain street are benefited by the paving of the street and are equally assessed for it, even though corner lots may have a greater value than inside lots. The value of a building is not considered in apportioning a special assessment because it is assumed that the land receives all the benefit. Sometimes special assessments are spread over a large area, with the properties nearest the improvement being assessed a greater proportion of the charge than more remote properties, the rate decreasing with the distance from the improvement.

Only where local improvements are beneficial—that is, where they increase the value of the affected properties—will courts sanction the levying of special assessments. In a court case, homeowners in Miami Beach, Florida, challenged the right of the municipality to levy assessments for the widening of Indian Creek Drive. The homeowners contended that widening the drive from 25 to 40 feet was initiated to relieve congested traffic on another street. They also contended that, as a result of the widening, Indian Creek Drive had turned into a noisy, heavily traveled thoroughfare used by the public generally, and that the effect was to lessen the value and desirability of their homes. The state supreme court in a 4-to-3 decision held for the homeowners, arguing that homeowners cannot be required to pay for the widening of a street when it results in increased traffic and decreases the desirability of their homes.

Special assessments become liens when they are definitely known and fixed. They may be divided into installments payable over a period of five to ten years or more, with interest charged on the deferred installments.

SUMMARY

Government limitations to ownership are intended to rationalize the process of urban development so that a more desirable community results. Urban land is too great a resource to allow its development and use to be left to chance.

The aims of land-use planning are to stimulate citizen participation in solving community problems, to coordinate civic developments, and to stabilize property values by promoting orderly growth. Economic base and population data, and land-use information must be collected and analyzed before preparing a master plan for a city. The master plan is intended to guide future growth, retard neighborhood blight, and to promote balanced, efficient land-use arrangements.

Zoning is a means of implementing the land-use plan. Zoning is used to regulate land use, to control the height and bulk of buildings, and to limit the density of development.

Eminent domain is the right of public or semipublic bodies to take property for public purposes without the consent of the owner. Just compensation, usually the fair market value of the property, must be paid to the owner for the property taken. The right of eminent domain is needed to aid in the redevelopment of our cities and to change and expand transportation and information transmission networks to serve the needs of the society.

KEY CONCEPTS

Ad valorem   According to value; typically real property is taxed in proportion to its market value.

Assessed value   Worth assigned a property for purposes of taxation; usually varies directly with market value.

Certificate of occupancy   An official statement that all required inspections were made and passed and that a structure is fit for use.

Contract zoning   Title restriction or side agreement that limits a property's use in return for a new zoning classification.

Density zoning   Limits on population density in various districts established or implemented through a zoning ordinance.

Development charge   Fee imposed to pay the proportional costs of new community infrastructure, such as waste-disposal facilities, roads, water storage tanks, etc. necessitated by the property being developed.

Down zoning   Rezoning from a high-intensity to a low-intensity use; likely to lower the value of a parcel.

Eminent domain   Right of a government to take private property for public uses or purposes; payment of just compensation is required.

Environmental impact study   Report concerning the long-run physical, economic, and social effects of a proposed development project.

Escheat   Conveyance of realty to the state after an owner's death, when no will, heirs, or other legal claimants to title can be found.

Exclusionary zoning   Zoning intended to discriminate against some group; e.g., an extra-large lot size would discriminate against low-income families.

Externality   When acts of an individual or a firm indirectly affect others without their consent; effects may be positive or negative.

Floor-area ratio (FAR) zoning   Regulation of building area to site area relationship; a form of density zoning.

Just compensation   Required payment for property taken; almost universally defined as the market value of the property.

Land-use control   Public or private legal restriction on how a parcel of land may be used.

Master plan   A document to guide a community's future physical growth as it adjusts to social and economic change; also called a comprehensive plan.

Nonconforming use   An existing land use or structure that is inconsistent with current zoning.

Nuisance   Interference without consent with a neighbor's use and quiet enjoyment of land other than by trespass or direct physical invasion.

Performance zoning   Zoning for a land use, the intensity or nature of which is defined in terms of standards to be met; e.g., FAR zoning.

Rent control   Governmental limitation on the amount that an owner-landlord may charge.

Special assessment   A charge upon private property to pay all or part of the cost of a local improvement that may benefit the property.

Transferable development right   Allowing the sale of the right to develop, so that one parcel may be developed more intensely if another parcel is developed less intensely; allows greater flexibility and variety in zoning and development of an area without increasing its overall density.

Zoning   Parcel-specific, public regulation of the use of land.

Zoning variance   A deviation from a zoning law granted to alleviate hardship.

QUESTIONS FOR REVIEW AND DISCUSSION

1. Briefly identify and explain the nature of the three main governmental limitations to private ownership of real estate.
2. Explain the need for land-use controls. Name and briefly explain four controls. Does an owner have any rights relative to these controls? Explain.
3. What are purposes of urban planning? Do you agree with them? Discuss.
4. Does zoning create value? Might zoning destroy value? Discuss.
5. Explain the need for eminent domain. What are an owner's rights relative to eminent domain?

6. Explain the need for taxation. Does an owner have any rights relative to taxation? Explain.

7. What is a special assessment? Is it related to land value in any way?

8. Is the real property tax system efficient? Is it equitable and fair? Discuss.

9. A ceiling on property taxes, as a percentage of market value, is frequently proposed. What would be the effects of such a ceiling? Would a 2 percent ceiling affect your community? A 1 percent ceiling?

10. What are the trends in the use of police power? Eminent domain? Taxation? Discuss.

PROBLEMS

1. B owns a 12,000-square foot lot zoned "residential 6,000," meaning that one dwelling unit may be built for each 6,000 square feet of area. Sales of similar lots show that lots sell for $8,000 per dwelling unit. B applies for a rezoning to "residential 2,000."

   a. If B gets the rezoning, how much will the lot increase in value, assuming that the sales price per dwelling unit remains the same?

   b. What factors might make this value increment larger or smaller?

2. The Investors own a 12,000-square foot lot next to B's. Their lot is also rezoned to "residential 2,000." However, it has a deed restriction limiting its development to a one-family residence. What impact on value is likely as a result of the zoning change?

3. W has owned a condominium unit on the twelfth floor of Lakeview Towers for 12 years. A developer is building a 20-story building across the street, which the zoning allows, thereby spoiling the view. W sues to have construction stopped, claiming a scenic easement based on the continuous use of the view for more than ten years, the time required to acquire an easement by prescription according to state law. What is the result? Discuss.

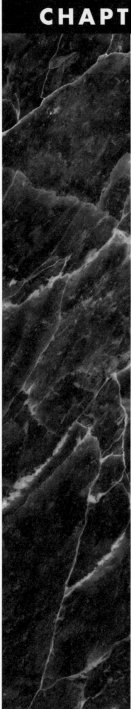

CHAPTER 29

THE INVESTOR-BROKER RELATIONSHIP

Chapter Outline

Let us begin anew—remembering on both sides that civility is not a sign of weakness, and sincerity is always subject to proof. Let us never negotiate out of fear. But let us never fear to negotiate.
John F. Kennedy, 35th President of the United States

A real estate broker is anyone who, for a fee or commission, is engaged to negotiate the sale, purchase, lease, or exchange of realty or to arrange financing of realty. Brokerage specialization has now reached the stage where individuals—and entire organizations—specialize either in the buying or selling of commercial or residential properties or in the leasing of commercial or residential properties. Other organizations, however, continue to provide a wide variety of functions and services, including appraising, brokerage, counseling, construction and development, financing, and insurance.

In looking at the investor-broker relationship, our concern is primarily with the legal and service relationship between an investor and a broker as it occurs in a buy-sell transaction. In the transaction, the broker is a negotiator and takes neither title nor possession of the realty. At the same time, the actions and success of the broker are of vital importance to the investor.

THE LAW OF AGENCY

Agency is the relationship created when one person is given the right to act on behalf of, or under the control of, another. In financial matters like the buying, selling, or leasing of property, the agency is considered a *fiduciary relationship*, in that trust and faith between the parties are expected and necessary.

The law of agency concerns the legal rights, duties, and liabilities of the principal, agent, and third parties based on contracts and/or relationships between them. It involves aspects of the law of contract and the law of torts. A *tort* is a wrongful or damaging act committed against another, for which a civil action may be brought. Causing personal injury to another, damaging another's property, fraud, and misrepresentation are examples of torts.

A person acting for or representing another, with the latter's authority, is an *agent*. Thus, a real estate broker is an agent in selling property for an owner under a listing agreement. The person for whom an agent acts is a *principal*. An owner, therefore, becomes a principal when he or she signs a listing agreement with a broker.

Agency in real estate traditionally involves three parties: a principal, an agent, and a third party. A potential buyer, such as an investor negotiating to purchase a property, is a *third party* in the typical real estate sales transaction (see Figure 29-1). The broker usually does not represent the buyer. The salespeople employed by the

FIGURE 29–1
Traditional Real Estate
Agency Relationship

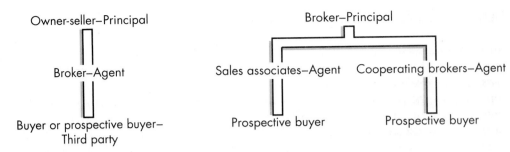

broker may perform activities such as negotiating contracts for sale, but must perform them in the name of the broker; that is, salespeople are agents of the broker.

A principal known or identified to a third party is a *disclosed principal.* A partially disclosed principal is one not known or identified to the third party, although the agent acknowledges that a principal is involved. Finally, an *undisclosed principal* is one who is secretly represented by an agent who appears to be acting in self-interest.

Duties, Liabilities, and Rights of a Principal

A principal's main duties to an agent are to compensate in accordance with the contract of employment. Thus, with the typical listing agreement, the owner must pay a commission to the broker when a "ready, willing, and able" buyer has been found. An owner also has a duty to give the broker-agent complete and accurate information when listing a property to be sold, leased, or exchanged.

A principal is liable on all agreements or contracts made by an agent within the authority given the agent. *Unauthorized agreements* are those outside or beyond the authority given the agent. A principal is also liable for unauthorized agreements if they are subsequently affirmed or ratified with full knowledge of the pertinent facts. Most listing agreements clearly spell out the authority given a broker, and that authority does not usually include signing or accepting an offer to purchase the subject property.

In the matter of torts, there is an important distinction between a salesperson who is engaged by a broker as an employee and a salesperson who operates as an independent contractor. Both employees and independent contractors are personally liable for their own acts, but they are not liable for torts committed by their principals. And a principal may become jointly liable for a tort committed by an employee within the scope of the employment agreement or under the direction of the principal.

Note, however, that a principal is not generally liable for acts of an independent contractor. An *independent contractor* is a person who retains personal control over work details while performing a service or task for an employer. A broker engaged to sell a property for an owner is almost certainly an independent contractor. A salesperson, working for a broker, may or may not be an independent contractor; the work relationship would be the primary determinant as to whether the salesperson were an independent contractor. The greater the control exercised by the broker, the less the likelihood that the salesperson is an independent contractor.

A disclosed principal may enforce any contract made with a third party by an authorized agent for the principal's benefit. A real estate broker ordinarily does not enter contracts for a principal, but such action is possible.

Duties, Liabilities, and Rights of an Agent

An agent's duties to a principal are: (1) to use reasonable care, (2) to obey reasonable instructions, (3) to give accountability, (4) to be loyal, and (5) to give notice. Using *reasonable care* means that the agent must be diligent and must act in good faith in representing the principal. And the agent is expected to follow or obey all *reasonable instructions* of a principal, assuming that the instructions pertain to the purpose of the principal-agent relationship. Following instructions includes keeping within the authority given by the principal. Instructions creating a tort or criminal situation would not be reasonable. An agent also has a legal duty of *accountability*—that is, to account for all money or property to the principal, including keeping adequate records concerning such money or property. In addition, it is illegal for a broker to commingle or mix personal funds and funds of a principal.

Loyalty means that the agent must not benefit from the relationship, except through compensation from the principal and unless otherwise agreed. Faithful performance is another term for loyalty. A broker, therefore, may not represent both parties in a buy-sell transaction without the knowledge and consent of both. Representing two principals is called *dual* or *divided agency*. Contracts involving agent disloyalty are voidable at the option of the principal, in that the broker cannot get the highest possible price for the seller and at the same time get the lowest possible price for the buyer. It follows that a broker cannot collect a commission for arranging a voided contract. If a broker acts for both buyer and seller, with the full knowledge of both, the dual agency rule does not apply. In this situation the broker is termed a *middleman.*

Giving notice to a principal means that any information given the agent must be communicated immediately to the principal. Any knowledge given the agent legally binds the principal. Therefore, it follows that the agent is bound to keep the principal informed of any important facts concerning the object of the agency arrangement.

An agent is not personally liable for contracts entered into for the benefit of the principal. However, an agent exceeding his or her authority does incur personal liability, unless such act is affirmed or ratified by the principal. A broker is authorized only to negotiate for the principal—that is, a broker is usually engaged only to find a buyer and not to make a sales contract. Therefore, a broker usually does not operate in a situation where the authority of the agency agreement might be exceeded. However, if a principal lacks legal competence to make a valid agency contract (because of insanity or being underage), the agent incurs personal liability for any resulting contract.

An agent has a right to enforce a contract of a principal against a third party in which an interest is held. Thus, a broker may enforce a sales contract between an owner and a buyer because of an anticipated commission. Finally, a broker derives authority from an owner through the listing agreement; to enforce the collection of a commission, a broker must have the agreement in writing. The salespersons also operate under the law of agency, with the broker as the principal.

LISTING AGREEMENTS

A *listing agreement* is a written contract of employment of a broker by a principal to buy, sell, or lease real estate. A listing agreement creates the traditional principal-agent relationship discussed above. After successfully completing a buy-sell or leasing transaction, the broker must show that a listing agreement was made with the owner to enforce his or her right to the commission. Most listing agreements provide that a broker may engage salespersons to help conduct the negotiations.

A broker may also contract with a buyer; in that case the broker becomes an agent of the buyer. A broker may not represent both buyer and seller without the knowledge and consent of both parties.

The listing agreement is the foundation of the broker's business. Out of it arise the broker's relation of trust and confidence with his or her principal and the broker's rights for compensation. It is highly important, therefore, that any person engaging in the real estate business fully understand the rights and obligations underlying the different kinds of listing contracts.

Strictly speaking, the typical listing is not a contract. At most, it may be classified as a unilateral contract that becomes an actual or bilateral contract upon performance by the broker. However, a listing agreement that contains promises by a broker to make a diligent effort and promises by an owner to pay some minimum monetary consideration and a commission becomes a bilateral contract even without performance. Lacking consideration, a unilateral contract is revocable until performance by either party at any time, even though a definite time is stipulated in the listing agreement.

There are five listing agreements in general use: (1) open, (2) exclusive agency, (3) exclusive right to sell, (4) multiple, and (5) net. Open and net listing agreements may be reached orally in some states. However, to enforce a claim for the collection of a commission, better brokers prefer written listings. In fact, most brokers refuse to handle or promote a property without a written listing.

Open Listing

An *open listing* occurs when an owner-principal offers several brokers an equal chance to sell realty. The broker who actually arranges the sale receives compensation. The owner must remain neutral in the competition between the brokers to avoid obligation for a commission to more than one broker. With this type of listing the owner may reserve the right to personally sell the realty without becoming liable for a commission, and usually does so.

The sale of the property terminates the open listing. Usually, the owner need not notify the agents since, under the law effective in almost all states, the sale cancels all outstanding listings. This safeguards the owner against paying more than one commission.

Exclusive-Agency Listing

In an *exclusive-agency listing* only one broker is engaged to sell realty for a commission, with a right retained by the owner to personally sell or rent the property without being obligated to pay a commission to the broker. An exclusive-agency listing contains the words "exclusive agency." The purpose of the exclusive-agency listing is to give the broker holding the listing an opportunity to apply "best efforts" without interference or competition from other brokers. In nearly every state, an exclusive-agency listing binds the owner to pay a commission to the broker named in the listing agreement in the event of a sale by that broker or any other broker.

An exclusive-agency listing does not entitle the broker to compensation when the property is sold by the owner to a prospect not procured by the broker. This listing is also revocable, unless a consideration was made. Further, the listing may be terminated if the broker has not performed, in which case the owner's liability is limited to the value of any services actually performed by the broker.

Exclusive Right-to-Sell Listing

An *exclusive right-to-sell listing* is the engagement of one broker to sell realty, with a commission due to the broker regardless of who sells the property, owner included. That is, the owner gives up the rights to personally sell the realty and avoid paying a commission. An exclusive right-to-sell listing contains the words "exclusive right." This listing is similar in all respects to the exclusive agency, except that a commission is due to the broker named in the contract if the property is sold within the time limit specified in the contract—regardless of who sells the property. An owner may reserve the right to sell to certain parties, who are or have been negotiating with the owner for the property, by including their names as exceptions in the contract. Figure 29–2 shows an exclusive right-to-sell listing contract that may also serve as a multiple-listing agreement.

Multiple Listing

Brokers commonly form into groups, termed *multiple-listing services,* in which each member agrees to share any listings in his or her office with others in the group. Members of the group use a multiple-listing service (MLS) agreement that is actually a special version of the exclusive right-to-sell listing agreement; it provides that any member of the MLS group who sells the realty will share in the commission as a cooperating broker. An MLS listing arrangement is advantageous to an owner in that the property gets wider exposure, which tends to mean a higher price and a shorter selling time. Sales commissions are shared between the listing and selling broker, with a small percentage going to the MLS organization. In a typical MLS sale, the commission is shared as follows:

1. From 5 to 10 percent of the gross commission goes to the multiple-listing service to cover operating expenses and general overhead.
2. From 50 to 60 percent of the remainder goes to the selling broker.
3. The balance goes to the listing broker.

For example, assume a $1,000 commission, with 5 percent going to the MLS organization, and a 50-50 distribution of the remainder. The proceeds would be distributed as follows: $50 (5% × $1,000) to the listing bureau; $475 (50% × $950) to the broker effecting the sale; and $475 (50% × $950) to the broker who initiated the listing.

Net Listing

A *net listing* is an agreement whereby an owner engages a broker to sell realty at a fixed, or minimum, price, with any excess to be considered as the broker's commission. A net listing is, therefore, a contract to obtain a minimum price for the owner. In some states, the broker cannot lawfully obtain a compensation greater than the usual and customary rate of compensation without the specific knowledge and con-

No. 678 © Rev. OE
Stevens-Ness L.P.Co.
Portland, OR 97204

REAL ESTATE BROKER'S   **EMPLOYMENT CONTRACT**
(involving lease and lessee's interest only; Use Form 676)

APARTMENT, HOTEL,
ROOMING HOUSE,
MOTEL

Name of property __Douglas Manor__

Location __2001 Century Drive, Urbandale, Anystate, 00000__ _____Tel._____ Legal Description __Lots 16 & 17__

__Edgewood South Subdivision__

(If said property is incorrectly described, owner hereby expressly authorizes broker subsequently to write in hereon or attach hereto, the correct legal description thereof.)

City __Urbandale__, County __Rustic__, State and Zip __Anystate 00000__; for better description see owner's title deed on record, now made a part hereof.

No. of apts. __16__, No. of rms. __72__; No. of __4__ rm. apts __8__; No. of __5__ rm. apts. __8__; No. of ___ rm. apts. ___. Does structure need remodeling or renovating? Yes ☐; No ☒.

Selling price, free of encumbrances: $ __680,000__; Terms: __Cash__

Is personal property included in this listing? Yes ☐; No ☐; if so, is signed inventory attached? Yes ☐; No ☐; to be attached? Yes ☐; No ☐.

To __Ivan M. Evans__ Broker, City __Urbandale__ State __Anystate__ __September 1st__, 19 __94__

FOR VALUE RECEIVED, you hereby are employed to sell or exchange the property described hereon at the selling price and on the terms noted. You hereby are authorized to accept a deposit on the purchase price. You may, if desired, secure the cooperation of any other broker, or group of brokers, in procuring a sale of said property. In the event that you, or any other brokers cooperating with you, shall find a buyer ready and willing to enter into a deal for said price and terms, or such other terms and price as I may accept, or that during your employment you supply me with the name of or place me in contact with a buyer to or through whom at any time within 90 days after the termination of said employment I may sell

__6% on 1st $100,000; 4% on excess of 100,000 (see below)__

or convey said property, I hereby agree to pay you in cash for your services a commission equal in amount to ____ % of the above stated selling price. I agree to convey said real estate to the purchaser by a good and sufficient deed, to assign the outstanding lease(s), if any, to transfer and deliver said personal property, if any, by good and sufficient bill of sale and to furnish title insurance in an amount equal to the selling price insuring marketable title to said real estate and good right to convey. I hereby warrant that the information shown hereon is true, that I am the owner of said property, that my title thereto is a good and marketable title, that the same is free of encumbrances except as shown hereafter under "Financial Details" and except taxes levied on said property for the current tax year which are to be pro rated between the seller and buyer. In case of an exchange, I have no objection to your representing and accepting compensation from the other party to the exchange as well as myself. I hereby authorize you and your customers to enter any part of said property at any reasonable time to show same. Also, I authorize you, at any time, to fill in and complete all or any part of the "Information Data" below, except financial details. The following items are to be left upon the premises as part of the property purchased. All irrigation, plumbing, ventilation, cooling and heating fixtures and equipment (including stoker and oil tanks but excluding fire place fixtures and equipment), water heaters, attached electric light and bathroom fixtures, light bulbs and fluorescent lamps, venetian blinds, wall-to-wall carpeting, awnings, window and door screens, storm doors and windows, attached floor coverings, attached

__stove and refrigerator to be regarded as fixtures also.__

television antenna, all plants, shrubs and trees and all fixtures except: _____

The following personal property is also included as a __none__

part of the property to be offered for sale for said price _____

_____ (or see signed inventory, if any, attached). This agreement expires at midnight on __December 31__, 19 __94__, but I further allow you a reasonable time thereafter to close any deal on which earnest money is then deposited. In case of suit or action on this contract, it is agreed between us that the trial and appellate courts may allow the prevailing party therein such sum as may be adjudged that party's reasonable attorney's fees. It is further agreed that my signature affixed to the renewal clause below shall have the effect of renewing and extending your employment to a new date to be fixed by me on the same terms and all with the same effect as if the said new date had been fixed above as the expiration date of your employment. Forfeited earnest money, if any, after deduction of any title insurance and escrow cancellation charges, will be disbursed in the following manner:

_____ (delete if inapplicable).

*THIS LISTING IS AN EXCLUSIVE LISTING and you hereby are granted the absolute, sole and exclusive right to sell or exchange the said described property. In the event of any sale, by me or any other person, or of exchange or conveyance of said property, or any part thereof, during the term of your exclusive employment, or in case I withdraw the authority hereby given prior to said expiration date, I agree to pay you the said commission just the same as if a sale had actually been consummated by you.

I HEREBY CERTIFY THAT I HAVE READ AND RECEIVED A CARBON COPY OF THIS CONTRACT.

Accepted: __September 1st__, 19 __94__

__Ivan M. Evans, Realtor__ Broker   __/s/ Wendy Wells__ Owner

Owner's Address __Unit 77, Condominium Towers,__ City __Urbandale__ State __Anystate__ Zip __00000__ Phone __345-2020__

FOR VALUE RECEIVED, the above broker's employment hereby is renewed and extended to and including _____, 19 ____.

Accepted: _____, 19 ____ Owner

_____ Broker   _____ Owner

-------- FOLD ON DOTTED LINE FOR INSERTION IN RING BINDER --------

FINANCIAL DETAILS

Selling price (free of encumbrances)

$ __680,000__ Terms: __cash__

__Mortgage not assumable__

Payments include: Prin. __X__ Int. __X__ Taxes __X__ Ins. __X__
(Check items to be included in payments)

Interest on deferred payments __none__ %

Fire ins. $ _____ Ann'l prem. $ _____

Taxes last fiscal year $ _____

ENCUMBRANCES   **PAYABLE**

1st mtg. $ __481,647__ Int. __9__ % __mo__

2nd mtg. $ _____ Int. ____ %

Contr. bal. $ _____ Int. ____ %

Delinquent taxes $ __none__

Municipal liens $ __none__

OPERATION

Gross annual income $ __106,667__

Gross annual outgo $ __34,000__

Net annual income $ __72,667__

CHATTELS

What included in this sale (check items involved)

Outstanding lease _____, Furniture _____

Fixtures __X__ _____, Equipment _____

Goodwill _____, Assumed Name _____

For details as to chattels included in sale:

See above _____ See signed inventory _____

Are chattels fully paid for _____ Are chattels mtg'd _____

Possession may be had __at closing__

8412

APARTMENT ☒   **HOTEL** ☐   **ROOMING HOUSE** ☐   **MOTEL** ☐ _____ ☐

(REAL ESTATE INVOLVED - WITH OR WITHOUT OUTSTANDING LEASE)   **INFORMATIVE DATA** Office Listing No. _____

Name of property __Douglas Manor__

Location __2001 Century Drive, Urbandale, Anystate 00000__

Name of owner __Wendy Wells__ Tel. __345-2020__

Owner has: Abstract _____ Title Insurance _____ Cert. of Title _____ Contract _____ Deed _____

Type of construction: _____

LEASE	HOW MANY	UTILITIES - METERS	DISTANCES
Is lease outstanding? Yes ___ No ___	Total No. of units __16__ Furn. __Un-F.__	Water Gen. __1__ Pvt. __16__	City center __2 1/2 mis__
Name of lessor _____	1 bedrm. apt. _____	Elect. Gen. __1__ Pvt. __16__	Shopping center __1 mi__
Name of lessee _____	2 bedrm. apt. __8__	Gas Gen. __1__ Pvt. __16__	Bus stop __in front__
Date of lease _____, 19 ___	__3 bdrm. apt. 8__		Grade school __6 blks__
Expiration date _____, 19 ___	Rooms _____	Phone Pub. __1__ Pvt. ___ Pay __X__	High School __8 blks__
Monthly rent $ _____		Sewer __yes__	__university 1 mi__
Are rents paid to date? Yes ___ No ___		Pvt. __16__ Pub. ___	__waterfront-6 blk__
Any option to renew? Yes ___ No ___	Baths __16__	Heating __forced air__	
If so, for how long _____	Showers __24__	Type __gas__	
If so, for what rent $ _____	Toilets __24__	Refrigerators __yes__	
Rent paid in advance? Yes ___ No ___	Elevator __yes__	How Many __16__	
If so, how much $ _____	Type __Otis-auto__	Ranges __various__	
Is lease otherwise secured? _____	Garage __Under-adequate for 28 cars__	How Many __yes__	**EMPLOYEES**
If so, how secured _____		Type __16__	Operating help _____
		Garb. Dis. __various__	Maids _____
Can lessee assign without lessor's		Laundry Fac __coin op__	Janitors _____
consent? Yes ___ No ___		__4 washers__	Other _____
	Smoke Alarm ___ All Units ___	__2 dryers__	

Remarks __commission 6% on 1st 100,000; 4% in excess of $100,000, payable only on closing__

Listed by __H. Ardent__

Signs permitted __yes__

Will consider exchange for __much larger property__   Inspected by _____

BROKER'S COPY

*TO MAKE NON-EXCLUSIVE—Strike complete paragraph following asterisk (*) in Employment Contract and have owner initial deletion.

FIGURE 29–2
Real Estate Broker's Employment Contract

sent of the owner. Given the imperfect nature of real estate markets and the difficulty in estimating the most-probable sales price, a net listing may give rise to a charge of fraud against the broker, although the possibility of this is less with an experienced investor-owner than with a typical homeowner.

As mentioned, a listing contract must generally be in writing in order for a broker to enforce the right to collect a commission. Several additional critical issues also must be resolved to create a fully satisfactory listing agreement.

Asking Price

In self-interest, an owner wants the highest possible sales price and therefore prefers a high asking price. A broker ordinarily prefers to list a property at a price low enough to make a quick sale likely. A broker, however, as an agent in a fiduciary relationship, has the duty of keeping the principal informed of all material facts affecting the agency relationship. This duty includes providing knowledge of the market value of the property. In fact, the broker, as a real estate practitioner, has an obligation to document that any suggested listing price is not too low. Information from sales of comparable properties is one generally accepted way of documenting value. An owner is generally advised to list at a price above indicated market value. This takes account of possible inflation in values and retains room for bargaining. A property that sells too quickly may very well have been listed at too low a price.

Reservation of Right to Sell

In an open listing, any broker selling the property is entitled to a commission; of course, the owner may personally sell the property and pay no commission. In an exclusive right-to-sell agreement, the listing broker is entitled to a commission if the property is sold by anyone, including the owner. An owner may retain a right to sell without a commission being required, however; the owner simply writes the names of the parties with whom negotiations have been or are being conducted into the contract as exceptions, along with a reservation of the right to sell to one of them without liability for a commission.

Broker Compensation

To an owner, the crucial number is the net sales price realized after payment of a sales commission. The most usual arrangement is for a broker to get some percentage of the selling price for a commission. And commission rates are largely set by local area custom. However, brokers are prohibited from collusion in setting commission rates by the Sherman Act and the Clayton Antitrust Act, which prohibit monopolies and agreements in restraint of trade. The anticollusion law means that brokers may charge what the traffic will bear; and owners are free to negotiate with the broker on the amount of commission to be paid. Brokers may not, in turn, cite local custom as a reason for not cutting a commission.

The amount of commission, or the method of determining the commission, is best included in the listing agreement. It follows that flat and percentage commissions are possible, individually or in combination. Also, a net listing may be used.

Flat Commission.   Some costs, such as advertising, office expenses, broker's time, and overhead, are almost certain to be incurred in selling any property. Thus, some flat amount, say, $1,000, might be justified, regardless of whether a small lot or a large house is being sold. When a flat commission is paid, an owner may quickly determine the net amount to be realized from a sale. For example:

Sales price	$100,000
Less: Broker's flat commission	1,000
Seller's net	$ 99,000

Percentage Commission.   Brokers typically get 5 to 7 percent of the sales price as commission. Thus, a sale for $100,000 with a 6 percent commission would net a seller $94,000.

Sales price	$100,000
Less: Brokerage commission	6,000
Seller's net	$ 94,000

If a seller wants to net $100,000 from the property, the $100,000 would be 94 percent of the necessary gross sales price. To calculate the necessary sales price, the net amount would be divided by 0.94.

$$\frac{\$100,000}{0.94} = \$106,383$$

Six percent of $106,383 equals $6,383, when rounded to the nearest dollar.

Split Commission.   On larger properties brokerage fees are sometimes negotiated that give a higher rate of commission up to a certain base sales amount and a lower rate for any amount of sales price above the base amount. A flat fee plus a percentage might also be negotiated. For example, a commission of 6 percent on the first $100,000, plus 4 percent of any price in excess of $100,000, might be agreed to in listing a property. A sale for $640,000 would result in a commission of $27,600 under this arrangement:

Sales price			$640,000
Commission on first $100,000 @ 6%		$ 6,000	
Commission on price in excess of $100,000			
Sales price	$640,000		
Less: Base	100,000		
Excess	$540,000		
4% of excess is	× .04	21,600	
Total commission		$27,600	27,600
Seller's net			$612,400

Assuming that the owner wants to net $640,000 from a property, the desired selling price would be calculated as follows:

$$\frac{\text{Seller's net} + \$100,000 \times (.06 - .04)}{(1 - .04)} = \frac{\$640,000 + \$2,000}{.96} = \$668,750$$

Proof

Gross sales price		$668,750
Commission on first $100,000 @ 6%	$ 6,000	
Commission on price in excess of $100,000: $568,750 × 4%	22,750	
Total commission	$28,750	28,750
Seller's net		$640,000

Net Listing Commission. A net listing means that the broker gets anything above the asking price stipulated by an owner. Net listings are illegal in some states because they invite fraud. Thus, a sale of a property for $750,000 for which the owner expected $640,000 would be almost prima facie evidence of disloyalty by the broker. The duties of loyalty and of keeping a principal informed would require the broker to make an owner aware that $640,000 was too low an asking price. An owner would have a strong case for avoiding the payment of $110,000 commission on a $750,000 sale, which calculates to 14.7 percent rate, far above the more usual 5 to 7 percent rates.

Termination of the Agreement

A listing agreement may be terminated by action of the parties or by operation of the law. Actions of the parties that end the agreement include (1) mutual consent of the parties, (2) completion of the contract by sale, (3) expiration of the term of the contract, (4) revocation by the principal, and (5) revocation or abandonment by the agent. Operation of the law ends the agreement upon (1) destruction of the property, e.g., by fire, (2) death of the principal or agent, (3) insanity of principal or agent, and (4) bankruptcy of the principal or agent. If no time limit is specified in the contract, a listing agreement expires after a "reasonable time." A reasonable time might be three months for a one-family residence and from six months to a year for a large office building.

An agreement for a fixed period expires at the end of the period unless an extension is arranged. Some agreements contain a clause for automatic renewal or extension, meaning that the listing continues unless terminated by written notice. Automatic extensions are generally deemed to be unfair to an owner and are actually illegal in some states.

Broker Proof of Performance

A broker must perform according to the listing agreement to earn a commission. Generally, the broker's obligation is to produce a *ready, willing, and able* buyer. A purchaser acceptable to the seller or capable of meeting the seller's terms is such a buyer. The owner is not obligated to accept the buyer's offer even though the property is listed for sale. However, failure to complete a sale through fault of the owner does not cancel a commission. Such failure might result because of title defects, owner change of mind, or owner insisting on terms not included in listing agreement. While such situations happen rarely, a broker is entitled to a commission, whether or not the owner completes the sale to the aspiring purchaser.

An owner may include a *no-closing, no-commission* clause on a listing agreement. Such a clause means that unless the transaction results in a conveyance of title, no commission need be paid. Also, courts are increasingly saying that a broker is better able to judge the ability of a buyer to obtain financing than is an owner; therefore, a buyer is not ready, willing and able until adequate financing has been obtained.

SELECTING A BROKER

Experienced real estate investors often buy through one broker and sell through another. On the buying side, these investors know that some brokers bargain or counsel owners down rather than negotiate buyers up, which is likely to result in lower purchase prices. Other brokers work very hard to get the highest possible prices for their principals and, hence, provide a strong advantage to sellers. The higher price may more than pay the broker's commission. Care in selecting a broker is therefore prudent. The decision is too important to leave to chance or casually listing with a friend or relative.

The important considerations in selecting a broker are: (1) office and agent specialization, (2) office location and procedures, (3) firm's attitude and reputation, and (4) a track record evidenced by satisfied clients. Names of promising firms and agents may be obtained from fellow property owners. Also, names of firms that specialize in the type of property being listed may be obtained from classified ads and multiple-listing books. Given several firm names, a survey to collect the information necessary to make an informed decision is suggested. The first phase of the survey may be made by telephone. Later phases require personal contact.

Much background knowledge that is useful in the immediate selection as well as for long-term purposes may be obtained from a survey. Thus, while an investor may have one type of property in mind at the moment, another type may be of concern later on. Also, once a survey has been made, the broker selection process may be shortened in later situations.

Figure 29-3 provides useful questions to ask in making such a survey. The sequence goes from the general to the specific, from the firm to individual salespersons.

At some point during an investor's survey, it becomes apparent that the choice is really between two, three, or four firms. At this point the investor's concern should shift to selecting an agent, with an emphasis on specialization and performance. Suggested questions for a salesperson are given in Figure 29-4. Again, using a phone helps conserve time.

Eventually, the point is reached where the references of firms and agents still under consideration must be checked out. Visits to the firm offices for interviews with agents and sales managers become necessary. Agents who best measure up to the ideal agent concept might be invited to the property. Each agent under consideration might then be asked to research the market as to the value of the property, how long a sale is likely to take, and so on. An agent is likely to reveal a great deal about his or her professional competence in responding to this situation.

1. Does your firm specialize in any particular property type? If so, what type?
2. Does your firm specialize in any particular areas or locations? If so, which locations?
3. What properties of _____ type were sold by your firm in the last 12 months?
4. I'd like to contact some of the former owners of properties sold through your office. Would you give me the names of several?
5. How long has your office/firm been in operation?
6. During what hours does your office/firm operate?
7. Are your phones covered during off hours? If so, how?
8. What are your commission rates? Are they open to negotiation?
9. What listings do you currently have in _____ type of properties? What is their age? For how long are they?
10. Is your office affiliated with the Multiple Listing Service?
11. Where does your office rank in its sales of _____ type properties relative to other firms/offices in this area/community? (Firm preferably is among the leaders.)
12. Do you personally own any properties of _____ type? If so, which are they?
13. Does your firm have a continuing agreement with any financial institutions that might facilitate obtaining loans in times of tight money? If so, what institutions? With whom might I talk at these institutions?
14. Who are your leading salespersons for _____ type properties? Does anyone clearly stand out above the others?
15. Is there anything else about your firm that you would like me to know?

FIGURE 29–3

Investor Survey: Questions for Brokers or Sales Managers of Firms

The importance of achieving the widest possible exposure for your property cannot be emphasized enough when evaluating the agents' responses. The greater the exposure, the greater the likelihood of a quick sale. Reputation and track record of the agent also are extremely important.

1. Do you specialize in any particular type of property?
2. If so, in what type? In what locations?
3. How long have you specialized in these types of property?
4. What properties of this type have you sold in the past 12 months?
5. What are the names of the former owners of these sold properties? I'd like to contact them for reference purposes.
6. Are you full time in real estate sales?
7. How long have you been licensed?
8. To what real estate organizations do you belong?
9. What real estate courses have you taken in the last four years?
10. Do you have any real estate designations? If so, what are they?
11. What real estate publications do you usually read?
12. Where do you rank in sales in your company? In sales of this type of property in the area?
13. What listings of property do you currently have?
14. Do you own any investment property? If so, of what type?
15. Do you have any other comments or information that I should be aware of about yourself or your firm?

FIGURE 29–4

Investor Survey: Questions for Sales Agents

A real estate broker is a person who is engaged to negotiate the sale, purchase, lease, exchange, or financing of realty for a fee or commission. A broker operates according to the laws of agency, which means that the broker must be loyal and faithful to the principal and cannot legally profit from the arrangement except as agreed. A broker's effort on behalf of a principal must be diligent; the principal must give the broker a reasonable chance to accomplish the agreed-upon objective and cannot capriciously terminate the arrangement. The broker must have a contract of employment with a principal and bring about a completed transaction in order to earn a commission. A broker may not act for both parties in a transaction except with the knowledge of both.

Salespeople look to a broker as both principal and employer.

KEY CONCEPTS

Accountability   Responsibility for recordkeeping, money, and property.

Agency   A legal relationship created when one party, as an agent-broker, is authorized to act as the representative of another, as an owner-principal.

Agent   A person who represents another, a principal, by the latter's authority.

Disclosed principal   A principal known or identified to a third party by an agent.

Dual or divided agency   An agent that represents principals on opposite sides of a transaction; illegal except with knowledge and consent of both.

Fiduciary relationship   An arrangement calling for trust and faith between parties; the principal-agent or broker-seller relationship is a fiduciary one.

Independent contractor   One who agrees to act or work for another; an independent contractor is responsible for results but uses his or her own methods.

Listing agreement   A contract whereby a broker agrees to sell or lease property for an owner.

Loyalty   Legal requirement that an agent give priority to a principal's interest.

Middleman   A person bringing two parties together for a transaction.

Principal   A person who authorizes another to act for him or her in some undertaking; e.g., a seller who authorizes a broker to sell property.

Procuring cause   The broker who is primarily responsible for bringing about a transaction.

Ready, willing, and able buyer   A purchaser who meets all of a seller's terms, including the ability to finance the property.

Third party   A person negotiating or entering into an agreement with the agent of a principal.

Tort   A wrongful or damaging act against another for which legal action may be initiated.

Undisclosed principal   A principal who is secretly represented by an agent who appears to be acting in self-interest in transactions with a third party.

1. What is the law of agency?

2. What is a fiduciary relationship?

3. What duties does a principal owe an agent?

4. What duties does an agent owe a principal?

5. Identify and discuss from an owner's point of view at least four critical issues in listing a property.

6. List and discuss from an owner's point of view at least four important considerations in selecting a broker.

7. Identify and describe briefly at least four types of listing agreements; explain the use of each.

8. Outline and discuss the process suggested in this chapter for selecting a broker.

9. Selecting and using the right broker in selling real estate may result in a benefit greater than the amount of a commission. Do you agree? Discuss.

10. Are there any advantages, from an investor's point of view, in using a broker as a buyer's agent in acquiring property, even though a commission would be required? Explain.

1. A property sells for $320,000. Calculate the commission

   a. at 5 percent

   b. At a split rate of 6 percent on the first $100,000 and 4 percent of anything in excess of $100,000

2. An owner wants to net $85,000 from the sale of a residence. What selling price would apply, assuming that a 7 percent brokerage commission applies?

3. B, a broker, was hired by way of a listing agreement to sell A's house. B showed the property to C. However, before a sale could be arranged, the following occurred.

   a. A died. The executor later sold the house to C directly and refused to pay B a commission. B sued to collect a commission. What was the result?

   b. The house burned to the ground. A sold the lot and foundation to C shortly thereafter and refused to pay B a commission. B sued. What was the result?

   c. The listing expired. The next week, A sold the property to C and refused to pay a commission. B sued. What was the result?

   d. A rented the house to C during the last month of the listing agreement. The listing expired. B sued A for a commission, claiming to be the procuring cause for the lease. What was the result?

4. V contacted a real estate broker, A, to sell a ranch. No written listing agreement was made. Shortly thereafter, A mentioned V's desire to sell to I, another broker but not a business associate of A. I arranged a sale of the ranch. A now claims that a commission is owed based on procuring cause. Does V owe A a commission? Why or why not?

CHAPTER 30

BROKERAGE OPERATIONS AND PRACTICES

Chapter Outline

> *Nature magically suits a man to his fortunes, by making them the fruit of his character.*
>
> Ralph Waldo Emerson, *Conduct of Life: Fate*

Brokerage is the marketing part of the real estate business. Brokerage personnel provide a critical service as catalysts in the real estate market. Being a successful broker requires mastering such on-the-job skills as listing, selling, and self-management; a broker puts it all together.

In this chapter we provide an overview of the work performed by brokers, and the need they fulfill. The other brokerage functions—listing, sales, and advertising—are also discussed.

THE BROKERAGE FUNCTION

Brokerage is the bringing together of buyers and sellers in return for a commission (see Figure 30–1). A brokerage office typically serves as the place of exchange. Sales agents who work for the broker bring together the individual buyers and sellers. Generally, a brokerage office engages several sales agents. Thus, the broker needs to be both a manager and a negotiator to successfully market real estate on a continuing basis.

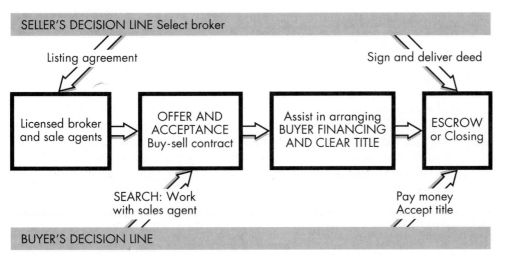

FIGURE 30–1
Brokerage and the Real Estate Transaction

Why Brokerage?

People do not pay large brokerage commissions without good reason. This raises the question, "Why is brokerage so widely used in real estate rather than other methods of marketing?" The reasons go back to the nature of real estate as an asset.

High value. A parcel of real estate generally has high value. It is just not feasible for someone to maintain an inventory of properties, as is done with cars, refrigerators, and other commodities; the cost would be too great.

Fixed, unique asset. Each parcel is unique in its location and improvements. A potential buyer would have to visit many properties to find the one that fits his or her specific need. And sellers would have to show each property many times until the right buyer came along. Brokers, as specialists in information, simplify a complex and difficult search problem for buyers and sellers, and thus make the market more efficient.

Financing needed. Because of it high value real estate usually needs to be financed. Brokers frequently assist buyers in arranging such financing.

The Broker as a Manager

A broker must first organize his or her own time. In addition, a broker with a large operation and a large staff must set up and establish organizational procedures for the employees. Attending to the details involved requires considerable managerial ability, attention to office procedures, and decision-making ability.

The Real Estate Office.   There are many kinds and sizes of real estate offices. A few specialize in distinct lines of work, but many of them attempt to transact all kinds of business. Larger offices, with separate departments comprised of an executive and various subordinates, are often found in major cities. Such firms often provide several or all of the following functions:

1. Appraising
2. Brokerage (property, mortgage, and exchange)
3. Counseling
4. Development and construction
5. Insurance
6. Management and leasing

The Real Estate Organization.   A real estate organization performs many different functions, but all are basically engaged in selling ownership equity, or space. The broker-manager must obtain business, retain and train personnel, and maintain the organization. A small office may consists of the broker-manager and one or more sales personnel; larger operations expand this organization. Naturally, the ambition of many sales agents is to work up to an executive position and possibly to establish their own office.

Following Through.   The broker is the person in the driver's seat in almost every organization. Sales and other office personnel attend to details, but the broker, through his or her organizational ability, must see to it that the details are taken care of for each transaction. The broker's skill and persistence in following through on matters of listing, finance, insurance, accounting, property management, and closings provide the key to customer satisfaction and to success.

The Broker as a Negotiator

The basic function in brokerage is negotiation between buyers and sellers. In day-to-day operations, listing a property at a reasonable asking price is as great a challenge as selling the property. The objective in either case is to persuade another person to make a major decision about value and property ownership. Working arrangements must be negotiated with office personnel on a continuing basis, as well as with other offices.

The basic qualifications for negotiations include being clean and neat in appearance, being reasonably well dressed, and conducting oneself with self-confidence. Tact, good judgment, and reasonable knowledge of property and laws are equally important. Important points of negotiating strategy that brokerage personnel should keep in mind as they seek to list or to sell property are shown in Figure 30-2.

THE LISTING PROCESS

A successful and continuing brokerage program must (1) obtain, (2) service, and (3) sell listings. The first two are discussed in this section; the third is discussed in the next.

Listings may be secured by brokers and sales personnel from many sources. The most usual sources are: (1) repeat business or referrals from satisfied customers; (2) friends and acquaintances—e.g., fellow members of clubs and organizations; (3) "for sale by owner" leads; (4) watching for expiring listings of competing brokers in the multiple-listing pool; (5) leads based on notices of births, deaths, marriages, promotions, or corporate transfers published in newspapers; (6) soliciting office drop-ins by owners desiring to sell; and (7) *canvassing,* or contacting property owners by telephone or in person without a prior appointment. Leads to a possible listing opportunity must be followed up promptly.

Obtaining the Listing

An owner must make at least the following four decisions when listing a property for sale:

1. The owner must decide that the advantages of listing with a broker are worth the brokerage fee or commission to be paid upon sale of the property.

2. The owner must decide that the advantages of listing with one particular broker—your firm—are greater than the advantages of listing with any other broker.

3. The owner must decide on the listing price.

4. The owner must decide on the length of time to be allowed to the broker to find a buyer.

FIGURE 30-2
Negotiations Strategy
for Brokerage Personnel

1. Do not offer a property without having looked at it personally. You cannot sell what you do not know. You cannot know improved real estate without having inspected it thoroughly.

2. Analyze the property; know enough so that you can answer almost any question about it. Get your thoughts down on paper because most people read better than they listen.

3. Do not offer a property without clearly having thought out your presentation.

4. Talk to prospects in their own language. Never talk down to them.

5. Always try to please a prospect. A prospect does not have to deal with a broker or salesperson, and will not if irritated.

6. A prospect will not buy or sell unless he or she thinks it is personally advantageous. A prospect must be convinced that there is some good reason to act.

7. Do not lie or misstate. Almost all prospects look for misstatements. You have lost a sale the instant a prospect detects that you are making misstatements.

8. Never argue. You may be right, but you are still likely to lose the sale.

9. Get the prospect to the property as soon as possible. If there is more than one prospect—for instance, a husband and wife—get them there together; do not speak to them separately.

10. Concentrate on a few prospects rather than working only a little with many prospects and closing no sales.

11. Speak with discretion. Give your client ample opportunity to ask questions. Know when to stop talking so as not to talk yourself out of a sale.

12. Use the telephone to save time and steps. But, bear in mind that if an issue is critical, a personal interview is better.

13. Never fail to submit an offer. It is not your function to turn down an offer for an owner. You cannot be absolutely sure of what a principal has in mind. Ridiculous offers are sometimes accepted.

14. Look for business at all times. Many listings are found while an agent is working on something else.

15. Most prospects are busy people. Do not waste their time.

16. Do not worry about competitors. You will get your share of business if you work intelligently and diligently.

17. Never assume anything. Overconfidence has lost many a sale.

Advantages of Listing. To an owner the main advantages of listing a property for sale are: (1) obtaining an objective negotiator, (2) professional assistance and service, (3) technical knowledge, and (4) broker cooperation.

A broker or sales agent can negotiate the sale without personal involvement. In any sale, and particularly in the sale of a home, a seller often has strong feelings about the property and its worth. These feelings make direct negotiations with a buyer very difficult. In addition, not all people are skilled negotiators. Many owners try to sell their own homes and fail because they are unable to negotiate effectively with potential buyers. Personal contact with owners often creates deep-rooted resistance in the prospect. Eventually, many owners give up and list their properties with brokers.

Owners also recognize that in selling properties brokers render professional assistance and service, like advice on how to prepare the property to get a higher price and a quicker sale, and advertising. Brokers screen out unqualified prospects, know how to show the property to its best advantage, and can be present when a prospect visits the property. Looking after a property if the owner is out-of-town or has moved to another community is another broker service.

Brokerage personnel generally have better technical knowledge than do owners. Brokers know the real estate market and financing better. A broker's knowledge of sources of mortgage money is particularly useful in times of tight money.

Another reason why owners engage brokers is that they can get better market exposure through broker cooperation; this is especially true of brokers who belong to multiple-listing services. Increasing the number of brokers and people who know about the property increases the likely sales price and shortens the time required for sale.

Deciding on the Broker.   Owners must decide whether or not the advantages of listing with one specific broker outweigh the advantages of listing with other brokers. The advantages of listing with a specific broker may be that broker's greater knowledge, better service, or more effective promotion and sales ability. A broker's reputation for professional, competent handling of listings helps greatly in obtaining listings. The broker's or sales agent's task in obtaining a listing is to convince the owner that the broker's firm can do a better job of selling the property than anyone else can.

The Listing Price.   It is important that a property be listed at a price not greatly in excess of its market value. Every owner wants to sell his or her property for as much as possible. At the same time, almost all owners recognize that they are limited by market competition as to how much they will actually realize from their property. Very few owners know the market value of their properties. Usually, if they do have a value in mind, it may be well above the property's market value. Prudent brokers will not spend much time or effort promoting a property that is listed at a price greatly in excess of its market value.

An experienced broker usually has a fair idea of the most probable selling price or market value of a property at the time the listing is obtained. Even so, professional brokerage people use the principles of valuation, explained in Chapters 9–12, to advise owners on reasonable listing prices for their properties. These brokers do not concur with an owner who says, "Let's list at my price; I can always come down." Rather, they make a strong effort to persuade the owner to list at a price at which a sale can be made, relying on the adage "A property well-listed is a property half-sold."

The Listing Term.   A listing agreement may be written to run from one day to one year or more. Brokers prefer that a single-family house listing run for a minimum of three or four months to allow time for a reasonable promotion and sales effort. Usually, the larger and more valuable the property, the longer is the desired listing time. Some multiple-listing boards have minimum listing periods.

Obtain Accurate Listing Information.   All information likely to help sell a property should be obtained when the property is listed. Negotiating the listing contract is a major opportunity for client contact, and leaving a good impression with an owner is important. Thorough inspection, accurate measurement, and full and complete disclosure of all important facts at the time of listing are excellent ways to impress an owner with one's professional competence. A listing form usually provides space for specific items, such as the following:

1. Lot dimensions (frontage and depth) and area
2. Building dimensions and area or volume
3. Number and sizes of rooms

4. Kind of construction

5. Age and condition of structures

6. Equipment data (heat, water, electricity, etc.)

7. Financing offered by owner

8. Neighborhood data

9. Zoning (very important for vacant land)

10. Tax data

Additional items should be noted if they pertain directly to the sale of the property.

Servicing the Listing

Owners select brokers more on the basis of their sales results and of service offered than for any other reason. A reputation for sales and service performance must be earned. Clear communication at the following times greatly helps to establish such a reputation.

Initial communication. The owner-seller should be specifically informed at the time of listing as to what services are to be provided, who will provide each service, and why the services are necessary.

Continuing communication. Owner-sellers should be advised as to what services are rendered and what results are to be expected. Personal contact, such as setting up the listed property to be shown and explaining the results of a showing, are particularly important.

Periodic review and recommendation. A listed property that is not sold within a reasonable time requires a discussion between the owner and the broker. The history of the listing and selling prices of comparable properties or houses should be reviewed. The broker or sales agent should have recommendations in mind before the review. This review typically takes place just before the expiration of the listing. If initial and continuing communications have been clear, and if all services have been performed, the owner should be receptive to extending the listing and following other suggestions.

SELLING THE LISTED PROPERTY

Successful selling of listed properties involves three essential steps: (1) prospecting, (2) presenting and negotiating, and (3) closing. A broker and any sales agent must continually sell themselves, as well as the property, throughout the sales process.

Prospecting

A broker's task is to sell properties once they have been listed. A sale cannot be made until someone is located who might be interested in the property. Locating potential buyers is called *prospecting*.

Several methods are used to locate prospects, the most widely used of which is advertising the property. Advertising is so important to locating prospects that the last section of this chapter is devoted to the classes, methods, and principles of advertising real estate.

While advertising is the most usual way to locate prospects, other methods are also used. A well-run brokerage office will maintain a file of properties wanted in addition to the properties listed for sale. Every time an inquiry is made for a property the office cannot supply, a memorandum of the details of the property desired should be noted. When a new listing comes into the office, it can be checked against the inquiry file.

The tenants in a building are another likely source of prospects, particularly for business properties. They usually do not want to move, but a new owner may wish to occupy their unit. The broker should interview the tenants in a building as soon as a property is listed. If none of the tenants are interested in buying, tenants in neighboring buildings should be canvassed. One of them may be persuaded to stop paying rent and become an owner.

Finally personal contacts are important and helpful in finding prospects. Friends who know that a broker is capable are likely to refer prospects. The same is true of old customers if they know that a broker is reliable and industrious. Brokers and sales agents are therefore wise to promote their listings among friends and old customers.

Presenting and Negotiating

Prospecting leads to negotiations, which begin once the initial contact has been made. The contact may be the result of an advertisement and come in by way of a telephone call or office drop-in.

A broker must take care to determine whether the prospect is serious or merely a "looker." An experienced salesperson can usually determine early in the interview whether or not the prospect is serious. Considerations such as urgency to move, newness to the community, or a recent birth in the family indicate a serious intent. Time should not be wasted on a looker.

The broker must be a keen student of human nature. The first contact with a prospect is often brief and the first impressions and analysis must be made in a few minutes. Older and more experienced brokers sometimes seem to have a sixth sense. In reality, it is merely the ability to judge the prospect quickly and with a minimum of error.

Some prospects harbor an inner fear of brokerage personnel. They fear that the broker's power of persuasion may lead them to a premature decision or put them in a disadvantageous position in the negotiations. Improved brokerage practices and ethics can put this fear to rest.

Almost all established brokers are conscious of the benefits that arise from satisfied customers and community good will. Thus, efforts are made to sell the customer what is needed and affordable. The broker tries to avoid allowing a customer to contract to purchase a home beyond his or her means. If nothing else, this could result in the customer failing to qualify for a mortgage loan. If the customer does get title and then later becomes unable to carry the property, that could also create ill will. Negotiations carried out in a spirit of service, not only win friends but aid in building a professional reputation that is essential to sound business growth and continued success for the broker.

Having determined what the customer needs and can afford, the salesperson next shows the property. The initial presentation is to a large extent oral, but it must always be borne in mind that most people learn more by seeing than by hearing. Ordinarily, the sales agent should tell his or her story simply and truthfully, without exaggeration.

Use of the prospect's language is important. Few prospects are familiar with real estate terms and some may be buying for the first time. The prospect should be taken out to the property as soon as possible, with full explanation of its advantages and disadvantages. A thorough knowledge of the property inspires confidence in the prospect.

Sales personnel may legally engage in *puffing,* which is making positive statements and opinions about a property without misrepresenting facts and without an intent to deceive. The intent, or course, is to induce a purchase. Misstating facts is misrepresentation and the basis of fraud. Also, making superficial or inaccurate statements may cost the sale and injure the reputation of the brokerage firm. A salesperson should describe structural or property limitations or faults in detail, but in perspective. Good points, especially those that fit the prospect's needs or wants, should be stressed with similar honesty.

It is usually helpful to have something in writing to show a prospect. This often takes the form of a *property brief,* which may be simple or complicated. If the property is an apartment house or office building, the brief may be a pamphlet of several pages that includes a description of the property, diagrams of the lot and the building, floor plans, elevation, information on available mass transit, and a detailed financial statement of operating expenses and income. If it is a one-family home, the property brief should diagram the lot and the house and include a photograph of the house; the financial statement is reduced to a statement of average monthly carrying charges. Almost all realty boards have a special form for this purpose. Placing the brief in the hands of the prospect during the interview gives him or her something to look at that will probably be absorbed more readily than the salesperson's words. Further, the prospect can study the property brief before making a decision.

A professional salesperson fits the presentation to the temperament of the prospect. In addition, the salesperson should seek out important facts about the prospect's occupation or business as early as possible in the negotiations. Approximate family income, marital status, number and ages of children, if any, civic and cultural interests, and where the prospect lived previously are all important items of information. With these facts in hand the presentation can be tailored to the prospect's situation. For example, if children are involved, the salesperson could say, "This is a safe, healthy place in which to bring up children," adding, if the children are of school age and the prospect is in the average income group, "The public schools are convenient and very good, and the trip to and from schools is safe."

Closing

Closing is the stage in the negotiations at which the prospect is finally persuaded to purchase a property; that is, when negotiations are brought to a conclusion. Much has been written on this subject, but as far as the salesperson is concerned, there are no set rules. Experience seems to be the best teacher.

Rarely does the psychological moment to close arrive during the first interview. But, the time may be right during a second visit to the property while the sales agent and the prospect are standing in the living room of the home that is of interest. More often, several interviews may be necessary; in any event, there comes a time when the sales agent must frankly and tactfully bring the prospect to a decision. The trend of negotiations will usually indicate when the time is ripe.

The sales agent can learn to judge when to try to close by noting when the prospect has made the following key buying decision: (1) recognition of the need for a new dwelling unit; (2) recognition of the unit most likely to fill the need; (3) acceptance, based on analysis, that the price is manageable; and (4) recognition that the time to decide is now. The sales agent, in continuing conversation with the prospect, must determine when the first three decisions have been made. Then, the sales agent's task is to persuade the prospect to make an offer to purchase the property.

ADVERTISING REAL ESTATE

Real estate prospects are usually found through advertising, although direct personal sales effort is needed to close the sale. Occasionally, a salesperson closes a sale in only one or two interviews, but even here advertising almost always preceded the effort. Advertising is an essential element to successful brokerage.

Classes of Advertising

Real estate advertising falls into three general classes: (1) name, (2) institutional, and (3) specific.

Name Advertising.   General or *name advertising* places the broker's name and business before the public; the purpose is to establish identity and location in the minds of potential clients or other brokers. When these people need real estate services, they are likely to remember the broker's advertisement. Name advertising is not intended to sell or lease a specific piece of property or to obtain a mortgage loan on a certain home.

Name advertising often takes the form of *professional cards* in local papers. Occasionally, general advertising is used to indicate a specific aspect of real estate in which a broker is engaged. Examples would be a small box advertisement reading, "**JOHN JONES,** Real Estate—Factory Sites" or "**HELEN SMITH,** Real Estate Mortgage Financing." Advertisements like these often appear in real estate trade journals. Sometimes, several offices advertise as having a common specialty. Their objective is to establish a name and an identity with other brokers. Some brokers advertise in national real estate magazines, seeking to inform brokers in other areas of their services.

Institutional Advertising.   Advertising to create good will and confidence in real estate organizations or groups is known as *institutional advertising.* Such advertising is carried out by the National Association of Realtors, by local real estate boards, and by other groups seeking to inspire interest in a district, a city, or a specialized area of real estate transactions, and to direct business to member firms. The general public is likely to have greater confidence in an individual or firm governed by or holding to a code of ethics and business rules designed to protect its clients, such as those of the National Association of Realtors.

Specific Advertising.   *Specific advertising* pertains to the promotion of a particular property. It generally takes the form of a classified ad, although it may be a sign or display. A news release is another way to get such information published. In any event, the purpose is to sell a specific piece of real estate, to secure a mortgage loan on a definite property, or to lease a particular location. The greatest individual effort is expended in direct or specific advertising.

Advertising Media

Many different types of advertising media can be employed by someone engaged in brokerage and sales work. However, we shall discuss the following general classes of advertising media:

1. Newspapers
2. Billboards, signs, and posters (mainly outdoor)
3. Direct mail, including pamphlets and circular letters
4. Miscellaneous

Most home buyers are motivated to purchase by newspapers. Also, most home buyers are motivated to use a broker. If this were not so, most brokers would go out of business. Still, a small percent of home buyers are motivated by friends and neighbors, open-house signs, billboards, and other advertising sources.

Advertising Principles

Advertising is absorbed primarily through the eye. Newspapers, billboards, signs, window displays, and direct-mail circulars must all produce a reaction when they are seen. Television and movie advertising are absorbed through the ears as well and, of course, radio ads rely only on the listener's ears. In any case, the purpose of advertising is to initiate a *chain of intended effects:* (1) attention, (2) interest, (3) desire, and (4) action; the acronym is called *AIDA*.

The first intended effect is to get attention. No matter how good the offered property may be, no matter how much care may have been taken in preparing the copy, no matter how important the message, unless the attention of the prospect is caught, the advertising is ineffective.

Second, the ad must arouse interest; the prospect's emotions or curiosity must be stimulated enough so that the entire message is read or heard. The copy, letter, or other advertising vehicle must be interesting and human.

Third, the ad must arouse desire. The desire for the property or service must be strong enough to cause the prospect to take the fourth step, action, to initiate contact with a sales agent. Once contact has been made, sales ability must take over.

Advertising Agencies

Many brokerage firms engage advertising agencies to handle their needs, particularly for major campaigns such as promoting a large development or the auction of valuable properties. However, the expense of an agency is far too great for the average property.

Real estate brokerage is fast becoming a part of the developing financial services industry, and it is changing from a business comprised of many small, local firms to one dominated by a few national, full-service firms. This change is due largely to recent advances in information processing, communications, and transportation. Wider use of computers, of phones, faxes, and other electronic communications, and of air travel have made national brokerage operations possible.

Increasingly, computers are used to store listing data on properties, as well as to do analyses and process everyday transactions. Information in one branch office is readily transmitted over phone lines to other offices and to national headquarters. Thus, when people move from one community to another, referrals are easily made. The branch office selling a property for an owner who is moving to another location is likely to have the trust and confidence of the owner. That office then merely notifies a branch office in the new community of the seller's needs; the trust carries over. Alternatively, the original office may provide the seller with a listing of homes for sale in the new community before the seller makes the trip to the new community.

In a comparable fashion, data banks of commercial and investment properties for sale in the entire country are now provided by some national brokerage firms. Thus, an investor may view available properties from a brokerage office in his or her home community.

Sales agents are likely to find it highly advantageous to affiliate with firms that have the latest computer and communications equipment and that also provide specialized training.

SUMMARY

The broker's role in marketing real estate is to establish a sales organization, and to bring together buyers and sellers or owners and users in the most efficient manner possible.

The principal steps in the real estate marketing process are: (1) listing, (2) prospecting, (3) negotiating, and (4) closing.

The four principles of real estate advertising are to attract attention, stimulate interest, arouse desire, and cause action. The action desired is for the prospect to contact a sales agent. Advertising media include newspapers, billboards, signs, posters, and direct-mail letters and pamphlets.

KEY CONCEPTS

AIDA Attention, Interest, Desire, and Action; the four principles of advertising.

Canvassing Contacting owners by telephone or in person without a prior appointment to obtain listings.

Closing Stage when negotiations are brought to a conclusion.

Institutional advertising Promotions to create good will and confidence in an organization or group.

Name advertising   Promotion to establish identity and location for a brokerage office in the minds of potential clients or customers.

Prospecting   Locating potential buyers for a property, for example, by advertising.

Puffing   Making positive statements to induce a purchase without misrepresenting facts and without an intent to deceive.

Specific advertising   Promotion of a particular property.

QUESTIONS FOR REVIEW AND DISCUSSION

1. Explain the broker's function as a manager and as a negotiator.
2. Identify at least three key decisions an owner must make in listing a property.
3. Explain the real estate sales process from the viewpoint of the salesperson.
4. What are the three main advertising media used by brokers?
5. What steps or decisions must be made in determining an appropriate asking price?
6. What does AIDA mean?
7. An owner wants to list a service station with a broker for $330,000, which is about $80,000 more than its market value. Should the broker accept the listing? If not, how might the broker best proceed? What about an interested buyer?
8. What advantages does selling through a broker offer an owner? What disadvantages? Should an owner always sell through a broker? Discuss.

CHAPTER 31

CONTRACTS FOR THE PURCHASE AND SALE OF REAL ESTATE

Chapter Outline

A verbal contract isn't worth the paper it's written on.
Popularly ascribed to Samuel Goldwyn, a movie executive

A *contract* is a voluntary and legally binding agreement between competent parties calling for them to do or not to do some legal act. A contract is also said to be a mutual set of promises to perform or not perform some legal act. In making a contract, the parties create for themselves a set of rights and duties that are interpreted and enforced according to the *law of contracts.* A contract is created when the parties indicate their intention by their words or actions.

An *expressed* or *explicit contract* is created if words, spoken or written, lead to the agreement. Thus, a lease reached by a student answering a landlord's ad offering an apartment for rent at $500 per month is an expressed contract. A contract for the purchase and sale of real estate is also an expressed contract.

An *implied contract* is reached when actions lead up to the agreement, as when I step into a cab. My entering the cab implies that I wish a ride for which I will pay; by allowing me into the cab, the driver implies that he will take me where I wish to go.

This chapter begins with a review of the essential elements of a legal contract. The emphasis then shifts to contracts for the sale of real property, with secondary emphasis on listing contracts and escrow agreements.

ESSENTIALS OF A VALID REAL ESTATE CONTRACT

Real estate contracts are subject to state statutes of frauds. Under the Statutes a contract for the sale or exchange of real estate must meet five criteria:

1. Legally competent parties
2. Bona fide offer and acceptance
3. Consideration
4. Legal object (including accurate property description)
5. Written and signed (some listing agreements are exceptions)

Legally Competent Parties

A *legally competent party* is a person qualified to enter into a binding contract. To begin with, that person must be of legal age, which is 18 years old in most states. A contract with a minor—a person under legal age—is *voidable,* meaning that it may be enforced or declared invalid, at the option of the party who is the minor. A legally competent person must not be under a mental handicap that makes for incompetency, such as being mentally retarded or insane.

Competence is also important when executors, administrators, trustees, people acting under a power of attorney, agents, and corporate officers are transacting real estate business. These persons have legal authority to perform their duties only to the extent that such rights and privileges are granted by legal instrument. For example, a corporation about to sell real estate must authorize its president or other officer, by resolution or bylaw, to execute the sales contract.

Offer and Acceptance

The entire purpose of a real estate contract is to bind the buyer and seller to do something at a future time. Written contracts are not needed to buy personal property that we pay for and take with us. But a real estate transaction is different. The seller claims ownership of the property, with good and marketable title, subject only to certain liens and encumbrances. None of these can be verified by a quick and simple examination of the property. The buyer must have the title searched and does not want to go to this expense unless the deal is relatively certain. The seller does not wish to remove the property from the market without a deposit and a commitment that binds the purchaser.

An offer and acceptance safeguards the interests of both parties. Each promises to do certain things in the future: the seller to give possession and title, the buyer to pay the price in accordance with specified terms.

A contract is not created unless there is mutual agreement. The offer and acceptance must therefore relate to a specific property. A mutual mistake or misunderstanding voids the contract; *void* means that the agreement is not binding on either of the parties; thus no contract was ever created.

Consideration

Consideration is the promise each party makes to the other or the price paid. It is what each party receives or gives up in the agreement. The amount paid for a property is consideration from a buyer. The conveying of title, evidenced by a deed, is consideration from a seller.

Consideration must be given by both parties for an agreement to be legally binding. In other words, the promise by one party must be offset by an undertaking of the other. Each must undertake an obligation. A promise, even if made in writing, is not binding on its maker if there is no offsetting consideration. For example, Able, seeing his good friend, Baker, says to him, "Baker, I will give you my car tomorrow." Baker cannot enforce the delivery of the car. But, if Able offers the car to Baker if Baker will cease to use tobacco for one week, and Baker accepts the offer, there is mutual consideration. And if Baker performs, delivery of the car can be enforced.

Legal Objective

An enforceable agreement must contemplate the attainment of an objective not expressly forbidden by law or contrary to public policy. An agreement for the sale of realty to be used expressly for an illegal purpose (e.g., gambling in a state which bars this activity) is therefore void and unenforceable.

Written and Signed

Real estate contracts are governed by the Statute of Frauds of the state in which the subject property is located. The purpose of the Statute of Frauds is to avoid possible perjured testimony and fraudulent proofs in transactions of consequence. Thus, oral testimony is not admitted into court to alter the terms of a written real estate agreement.

To be enforceable, real estate contracts must include the following:

1. Signature of buyer or buyers
2. Signature of any and all owners or sellers
3. Spouse's signature (necessary to release marital rights such as dower, homestead, or community property)
4. Proper written authority; i.e., power of attorney when an agent signs for a principal

The contract should cover all points of agreement between the parties, so that the provisions may be carried out without difficulty. A carelessly written contract may well give rise to disagreements, extended legal action, and much loss of time to all parties.

A real estate contract may be written up by the parties themselves or by their attorneys. Blank, printed-form contracts are widely available and are used because most transactions are similar in nature and standard provisions apply. There are, however, three problems in using blank printed forms: (1) What goes in the blanks? (2) Which clauses or provisions are not applicable and should be crossed out? (3) Which clauses or provisions, termed *riders,* need to be added?

The parties (usually the buyer and seller) or their attorneys may prepare an original contract or fill in the blanks on a printed form. If form contracts are used, the parties usually put their initials near any additions or deletions.

A broker or salesperson may assist in completing a form contract only to the extent allowed by state law. In most states, brokerage personnel are not allowed to prepare other legal documents, such as deeds and mortgages. Finally, they are forbidden by law to give legal advice.

The Uniform Commercial Code

Sellers, buyers, and brokers must decide whether the Uniform Commercial Code is applicable to the transaction. The *Uniform Commercial Code* (UCC) is a set of laws governing the sale, financing, and security of personal property in secured transactions. A *secured transaction* is one in which a borrower (or buyer) pledges personal property to a lender (or seller) as collateral for a loan, with title remaining in the lender until the loan is repaid. A secured transaction is often evidence by a financing statement that is filed in the public record as evidence of the lender's interest or claim. Thus, in a sale of realty, fixtures, growing crops, and standing timber have the possibility of being regarded as security for a personal loan and as part of the subject property in the transaction. A financing statement, if properly recorded, would take precedence over a purchase contract and any deed conveying title. A clear statement in the sales contract would reduce uncertainty as to intent.

REAL ESTATE SALES CONTRACT CHECKLIST

1. Date of contract.

2. Name and address of seller.

3. Is seller a citizen, of legal age, and competent?

4. Name of seller's spouse, and whether that person is of legal age.

5. Name and address of purchaser.

6. Is the property description adequate? (Legal descriptions are preferred.)

7. The purchase price.

   a. Amount to be paid on signing of contract.
   b. Amount to be paid on acceptance by seller.
   c. Amount to be paid on delivery of deed.
   d. Purchase-money mortgage, if any, and details thereof, including who is to draw it and who is to pay the expense thereof?

8. What kind of deed is to be delivered: full warranty, bargain and sale, special warranty, or quitclaim?

9. What agreement has been made with reference to any specific personal property (i.e., gas ranges, heaters, machinery, partitions, fixtures, coal, oil, wood, window shades, screens, carpets, rugs, hangings, or fireplace irons)?

10. Is purchaser to assume or to take the property subject to the mortgage loan?

11. Are any exceptions or reservations to be inserted?

12. Are any special clauses to be inserted?

13. Stipulations and agreements, if any, relative to tenancies and rights of persons in possession.

14. Is there compliance with all governmental regulations, such as zoning ordinances, building codes, sanitation laws, and the like?

15. Stipulations and agreements, if needed relative to the facts a survey would show: party walls, encroachments, easements, and so forth.

16. What items are to be adjusted for at closing of title?

17. Name of broker who brought about the sale, his or her address, the amount of the commission and who is to pay it, and whether or not a clause covering the foregoing facts is to be included.

18. Are any alterations or changes being made, or have they been made, in street lines, name, or grade?

19. Are condemnations or assessment proceedings contemplated or pending, or has an award been made?

20. Are there any covenants, restrictions, and consents affecting the title?

21. The place and date for the closing of title.

22. Is time of the essence in the contract?

23. Are any alterations to be made in the premises between the date of the contract and the date of closing?

24. Amount of fire and hazard insurance, payment of premium, and rights and obligations of parties in case of fire or damage to the premises from other causes during the contract period.

TYPES OF SALES CONTRACTS

The sales contract holds an agreement together while the details are worked out. Neither the buyer nor the seller has assurance that the other can perform when the contract is drawn up. Time is needed to verify ownership, conditions of title, and the accuracy of representations concerning the property. Also, time is needed to arrange financing and to work out the mechanics of closing. The buyer and seller want to avoid the effort and expense of preparing for a title closing without assurance that the other party is bound to the agreement.

A property transfer may be arranged without a formal contract. A deed, conveying title, could be exchanged directly for cash or other consideration. In practice, direct property transfers are most uncommon and are subject to many pitfalls, particularly from the buyer's viewpoint. The quantity and quality of an owner's interest in a property cannot be ascertained without a title search, which takes a certain minimum time. For example, Able conveys ownership of a house to Baker by warranty deed; in fact, Able is merely a tenant in the house. The only rights Baker gets are those of a tenant, because Baker cannot get rights that are greater than those possessed by Able, which in this case are those of a lessee. Of course, Baker might sue Able for damages and recovery of the money—if Able can be found.

Real estate buy-sell contracts take the forms of (1) an earnest money receipt, offer, and acceptance (for short-term transactions), (2) binder, (3) installment or land contract (for long-term transactions) and (4) options. Of these, the earnest money contract, which calls for a relatively immediate transfer of title, is the most common and most important.

Earnest Money Contract

An earnest money receipt, offer, and acceptance is a special-purpose form contract. Because of its wide use, the earnest money contract is taken up at length in the next section of this chapter.

The form contract gets its name from the general requirement that a cash payment, termed *earnest money,* is expected of buyers when an offer is made on real estate. Earnest money is an initial deposit of money, or other consideration, made to evidence good faith in entering the agreement. Failure to live up to the proposed contract means forfeiture of the deposit. Typically, from 5 to 10 percent of the offered price is put up as earnest money.

In almost all states earnest money paid to a broker must be held in a special trust or escrow account and not commingled with personal funds of the broker. A separate account is not needed for each earnest money deposit received, however; one account for all funds is sufficient. But complete and accurate accounting records for each deposit must be kept.

Binder

Some sales transactions are very involved and are not suited to a standard-form contract. Also, one of the parties may insist that the contract be drawn up by an attorney so that particular provisions may be included. In either case, time is needed to draw up a formal contract. In order to hold the transaction together until the detailed contract can be written up and agreed to by both buyer and seller, a binder is prepared.

A *binder* is a brief, written agreement to enter into a longer, written contract for the sale of real estate. The essential terms of the transaction and a brief description of the property are included, along with a statement about the intent of the parties. A binder is, therefore, a valid contract, meeting the requirements of the Statute of Frauds. It is prepared in duplicate, with the buyer and seller each getting a copy. An attorney may then be contacted to prepare the more involved contract. If a broker is involved, a small earnest money deposit may be made by the buyer, for which a receipt is given. Also, a statement concerning the amount of a commission and who pays it is usually included.

Installment Contract

An *installment contract,* widely termed a *land contract,* is a written agreement for the purchase of real estate. It calls for occupancy by the buyer, who makes payments over an extended time (two or more years), but with title remaining in the seller until the terms of the arrangement are satisfied. An installment contract is also known as a *contract for deed* or an *agreement of sale.*

An installment contract may be used when the purchaser does not have sufficient cash to make a down payment that is acceptable to the seller. If title is transferred on a "thin" down payment, and then the buyer defaults, the cost to the seller of regaining clear title may exceed the initial down payment. If the buyer is willing to pay the price in installments, a contract is drawn up specifying the amount and time of periodic payments. A land contract may also be used where a seller wishes to delay payment of taxes on capital gains realized in the sale. A completed installment land contract is shown in Figure 31-1.

Option

An *option* is created when an owner agrees to sell property at a stipulated price to a certain buyer within a specified time, without the buyer having to purchase. The tentative buyer pays a fee, or price, or gives some other consideration to obtain this right of purchase. An option is sometimes included as part of a lease; with the combination being called a lease option. An option contains all the terms of a sale (see Figure 31-2).

An option is used when a buyer is uncertain about whether or not to buy, but is willing to pay something to the owner for the right to buy. For example, the buyer may be trying to purchase two or three adjacent properties to assemble a larger property. Each owner gets paid for holding his or her property off the market for the agreed-upon time. If the last owner refuses to sell for a reasonable price, the buyer may not want to purchase any of the optioned parcels. In this instance, the buyer loses the amount of money paid for the options. Another common use of the option is to purchase a portion of a large tract for development, with the right to buy additional acreage if the development program on the first parcel goes well.

COMPONENTS OF AN EARNEST MONEY CONTRACT

Figure 31-3 shows a completed, standard-form earnest money receipt, offer, and acceptance contract. The form is divided into six parts, A-F, which follow the flow of a transaction as it develops.

CONTRACT—REAL ESTATE

THIS CONTRACT, *Made this* .... 31st .... *day of* .... February .... *, 19* 94 *, between*
.... Wendy Wells, Unit 77, Condominium Towers, Urbandale, Anystate ....
...., *hereinafter called the seller,*
and .... Gerald & Nancy Investor, 3278 Exotic Drive, Urbandale, Anystate 00000 ....
...., *hereinafter called the buyer,*

WITNESSETH: *That in consideration of the mutual covenants and agreements herein contained, the seller agrees to sell unto the buyer and the buyer agrees to purchase from the seller all of the following described lands and premises situated in* .... Rustic .... *County, State of* .... Anystate .... *, to-wit:*

Douglas Manor, 2001 Century Drive, Urbandale
(Lots 16 & 17, Block 3, Edgewood South Subdivision)

for the sum of .... Six Hundred Forty Thousand and no/100 .... *Dollars (* $ .... 640,000 .... *),*
hereinafter called the purchase price, on account of which .... Thirty two thousand and no/100
.... *Dollars (* $ .... 32,000 .... *) is paid on the execution hereof (the receipt of which is hereby acknowledged by the seller), and the remainder to be paid to the order of the seller at the times and in amounts as follows, to-wit:*

Equal installments of $7,402.40 on the first day of each month
for sixty (60) months, at the end of which the buyer is to arrange
financing for the remaining balance of five hundred thousand dollars
($500,000) from another source, for which title will be conveyed.

The true and actual consideration for this conveyance is $ .... *(Here comply with ORS 93.030.)*

....
....

All of the purchase price may be paid at any time; all of the deferred payments shall bear interest at the rate of .... one (1) .... *per-cent per month from* .... March 1st, 1994 .... *until paid; interest to be paid* .... monthly .... *and* * {*in addition to* / *to be included in*} *the minimum regular payments above required. Taxes on the premises for the current tax year shall be prorated between the parties hereto as of* .... this date .... *, 19* ....

The buyer warrants to and covenants with the seller that the real property described in this contract is (B)
* *(A) primarily for buyer's personal, family or household purposes,*
  (B) for an organization or (even if buyer is a natural person) is for business or commercial purposes.

The buyer shall be entitled to possession of the lands on .... 1 March .... *, 19* 94 *, and may retain such possession so long as buyer is not in default under the terms of this contract. The buyer agrees that at all times buyer will keep the premises and the buildings, now or hereafter erected thereon, in good condition and repair and will not suffer or permit any waste or strip thereof; that buyer will keep the premises free from construction and all other liens and save the seller harmless therefrom and reimburse seller for all costs and attorney's fees incurred by seller in defending against any such liens; that buyer will pay all taxes hereafter levied against the property, as well as all water rents, public charges and municipal liens which hereafter lawfully may be imposed upon the premises, all promptly before the same or any part thereof become past due; that at buyer's expense, buyer will insure and keep insured all buildings now or hereafter erected on the premises against loss or damage by fire (with extended coverage) in an amount not less than $* .... *in a company or companies satisfactory to the seller, specifically naming the seller as an additional insured, with loss payable first to the seller and then to the buyer as their respective interests may appear and all policies of insurance to be delivered to the seller as soon as insured. Now if the buyer shall fail to pay any such liens, costs, water rents, taxes or charges or to procure and pay for such insurance, the seller may do so and any payment so made shall be added to and become a part of the debt secured by this contract and shall bear interest at the rate aforesaid, without waiver, however, of any right arising to the seller for buyer's breach of contract.*

The seller has exhibited unto the buyer a title insurance policy insuring marketable title in and to the premises in the seller; seller's title has been examined by the buyer and is accepted and approved by buyer.

Contemporaneously herewith, the seller has executed a good and sufficient deed (the form of which hereby is approved by the buyer) conveying the above described real estate in fee simple unto the buyer, buyer's heirs and assigns, free and clear of encumbrances as of the date hereof, excepting the easements, building and other restrictions now of record, if any, and .... none other
.... *and has placed the deed, together with an executed copy of this contract and the title insurance policy mentioned above, in escrow with* .... Hifidelity Escrow Services, Urbandale .... *escrow agent, with instructions to deliver the deed, together with the fire and title insurance policies, to the order of the buyer, buyer's heirs and assigns, upon the payment of the purchase price and full compliance by the buyer with the terms of this agreement. The buyer agrees to pay the balance of the purchase price and the respective installments thereof, promptly at the times provided therefor, to the said escrow agent for the use and benefit of the seller. The escrow fee of the escrow agent shall be paid by the seller and buyer in equal shares; the collection charges of the agent shall be paid by the* .... buyer ....

(Continued on Reverse)

* **IMPORTANT NOTICE:** Delete, by lining out, whichever phrase and whichever warranty (A) or (B) is not applicable. If warranty (A) is applicable and if the seller is a creditor, as such word is defined in the Truth-in-Lending Act and Regulation Z, the seller MUST comply with the Act and Regulation by making required disclosures; for this purpose, use Stevens-Ness Form No. 1319 or equivalent.

FIGURE 31-1
An Installment Land Contract; a Land Contract

OPTION FOR PURCHASE OF REAL ESTATE

KNOW ALL MEN BY THESE PRESENTS, That _____ Wendy Wells, Unit 77, _____
Condominium Towers, Urbandale, Anystate 00000 _____, *as Seller, does hereby bargain, give and grant*
to ___ Owner paid by P.O. Tential _____
as Buyer, the sole, exclusive, and irrevocable right and option to purchase that certain real estate in the County of
___ Rustic _____, *State of* _____ Anystate _____, *more particularly described as follows:*

Douglas Manor, 2001 Century Drive
(Lots 16 &17, Block 3, Edgewood South Subdivision)

This option commences on _____, 19_____, *and expires at midnight on* _____,
19_____. *To exercise this option, Buyer shall notify Seller by written notice delivered to the Seller at* _____
_____
on or before the latter time.
The purchase price of said property, if purchased under this option, shall be $ ___ $700,000 _____. *The*
consideration given for this option is $ ___ $50,000 _____, *which amount shall/shall not (indicate which) be applied*
to the purchase price, should Buyer exercise this option.
Buyer's written notice to Seller shall be accompanied by a further payment of $ ___ $30,000 _____, *which*
payment shall be applied toward the purchase price. Upon execution of the contract or deed pursuant to the exercise
of this option, Buyer shall pay Seller the sum of $ ___ $30,000 _____. *The balance of the purchase price shall be paid*
as follows: $600,000 at closing which is to be held on or before December 31st, 1994

Should the Buyer elect to purchase said premises hereunder, the Buyer shall pay said consideration and deliver
all necessary documents to the Seller as hereinbefore specified within _____ *days of Buyer's election to purchase,*
and Seller shall furnish Buyer title insurance prepared by a reputable title insurance company insuring in the amount
of said purchase price good marketable title in the Seller free and clear of all encumbrances whatsoever except only as
hereinafter stated. The Seller shall forthwith convey said premises free of all encumbrances except _____
___ Easements of record filed as part of the subdivision _____
_____
_____
to the Buyer by good and sufficient deed with covenants of warranty, together with said title insurance. Buyer shall
have _____ *days after the delivery of said title insurance in which to examine same, and Seller is to have* _____
days after written notice of defects is delivered to Seller to remedy same. If the Seller is unable to so perform, Seller
shall thereafter immediately refund to the Buyer all sums previously paid pursuant to this option. If the Buyer does
not within said period elect to purchase said premises, then this agreement shall at the expiration of said period become
null and void, and the Seller shall retain to the Seller's own use and benefit all money paid hereunder.

Dated _____ July 4th _____, *19* 94 .   /s/ Wendy Wells

THE PROPERTY DESCRIBED IN THIS INSTRUMENT MAY NOT BE WITHIN A FIRE PROTECTION DISTRICT   _____
PROTECTING STRUCTURES. THE PROPERTY IS SUBJECT TO LAND USE LAWS AND REGULATIONS,
WHICH, IN FARM OR FOREST ZONES, MAY NOT AUTHORIZE CONSTRUCTION OR SITING OF A   _____
RESIDENCE AND WHICH LIMIT LAWSUITS AGAINST FARMING OR FOREST PRACTICES AS DEFINED
IN ORS 30.930 IN ALL ZONES. BEFORE SIGNING OR ACCEPTING THIS INSTRUMENT, THE PERSON   _____
ACQUIRING FEE TITLE TO THE PROPERTY SHOULD CHECK WITH THE APPROPRIATE CITY OR COUNTY
PLANNING DEPARTMENT TO VERIFY APPROVED USES AND EXISTENCE OF FIRE PROTECTION FOR   _____
STRUCTURES.

STATE OF OREGON, County of _____) ss.
This instrument was acknowledged before me on _____, 19_____,
by _____
This instrument was acknowledged before me on _____, 19_____,
by _____
as _____
of _____

_____
Notary Public for Oregon
My commission expires _____
The form of security agreement which shall be used to consummate this transaction shall be a _____

FIGURE 31–2
An Option to Purchase

EARNEST MONEY RECEIPT

City Urbandale , State Anystate , November 28 , 19 94 . 1

A. RECEIVED FROM Gerald and Nancy Investor, husband and wife 2

(hereinafter called "purchaser") the sum of Thirty-two thousand Dollars ($ 32,000.00) 3

in the form check as earnest money and in part payment for the purchase of the following described real estate situated in the City of Urbandale , 4
CASH, CHECK, DRAFT

County of Rustic , State of Anystate , to-wit; Douglas Manor, 2001 Century Drive 5

(Lots 16 & 17, Block 3, Edgewood South, Rustic County, Anystate) 6

which we have this day sold to said purchaser 7

for the sum of Six hundred fourty thousand Dollars ($ 640,000.00) 8

on the following terms, to-wit: The sum, hereinabove receipted for, of Thirty-two thousand Dollars ($ 32,000.00) 9

{ on owner's acceptance. (Strike whichever not applicable) 10

{ on , 19 as additional earnest money, the sum of Dollars ($) 11

Upon acceptance of title and delivery of { deed (Strike whichever not applicable) 12

{ contract, the sum of One hundred eight thousand Dollars ($ 108,000.00) 13

Balance of Dollars ($) 14

payable as follows: conditional on obtaining 15

mortgage loan for Five hundred thousand dollars ($500,000) or more, at ten (10) 16

percent interest or less, with a life of twenty five (25) years or more, with 17

monthly debt service; and no more than two points required to obtain financing 18

Also, conditional on closing in escrow, with escrow costs shared equally between 19

seller and buyer. 20

1. If this transaction includes dwelling units, purchaser and seller certify that a working smoke detector shall be installed in each such unit according to applicable law, prior to closing. 21
2. A title insurance policy from a reliable company insuring marketable title is to be furnished purchaser in due course at seller's expense; preliminary to closing, seller shall furnish purchaser a title 22
insurance company's preliminary title report showing its willingness to issue title insurance, which shall be conclusive evidence as to seller's record title. 23
3. It is agreed that if seller does not approve this sale within the period allowed broker below in which to secure seller's acceptance, or if the title to the said premises is not insurable or 24
marketable, or cannot be made so within thirty days after notice containing a written statement of defects is delivered to seller, the said earnest money shall be refunded. But if said sale 25
is approved by seller and title to the said premises is insurable or marketable and purchaser neglects or refuses to comply with any of said conditions within ten days after the said evidence 26
of title is furnished and to make payments promptly, as hereinabove set forth, then the earnest money herein receipted for and additional earnest money, if any, shall be forfeited and 27
disposed of as stated in Section F below and this contract thereupon shall be of no further binding effect. 28
4. The property is to be conveyed by good and sufficient deed free and clear of all liens and encumbrances except zoning ordinances, building and use restrictions, reservations in Federal 29
patents, easements of record and none other, Title is to be conveyed by a general warranty deed. 30
5. All irrigation, plumbing, ventilating, cooling and heating fixtures and equipment (including stoker and oil tanks but excluding fireplace fixtures and equipment), water heaters, light 31
fixtures, bulbs and lamps, bathroom fixtures, venetian blinds, drapery and curtain rods, window and door screens, storm doors and windows, attached floor coverings, attached television 32
antenna, all shrubs and trees and all fixtures except No exceptions; stoves and refrigerators, one in each unit, to be considered as fixtures 33
are to be left upon the premises as part of the property purchased. The following personal property is also included as a part of the property for said purchase price. 34
(Any personal property to be conveyed by separate bill of sale.) 35
6. Pro rates for current tax year, rents, interest, premiums for existing insurance and other matters shall be made as of the date of ☐ closing, date of ☒ possession. Date of closing is 36
, 19 . Date of possession is , 19 ; or as soon thereafter as existing laws and regulations will permit removal of tenants, if any. Any real property taxes, 37
interest or assessment thereon which is attributable to periods before closing, but the due date for payment of which has been deferred, shall be paid by ☒ purchaser ☐ seller. Encum- 38
brances to be discharged by seller may be paid at his option out of purchase money at date of closing. 39
7. THE PROPERTY DESCRIBED IN THIS INSTRUMENT MAY NOT BE WITHIN A FIRE PROTECTION DISTRICT PROTECTING STRUCTURES. THE PROPERTY IS SUBJECT TO LAND USE LAWS AND REGULATIONS, WHICH, IN 40
FARM OR FOREST ZONES, MAY NOT AUTHORIZE CONSTRUCTION OR SITING OF A RESIDENCE AND WHICH LIMIT LAWSUITS AGAINST FARMING OR FOREST PRACTICES AS DEFINED IN ORS 30.930 IN ALL ZONES. BEFORE 41
SIGNING OR ACCEPTING THIS INSTRUMENT, THE PERSON ACQUIRING FEE TITLE TO THE PROPERTY SHOULD CHECK WITH THE APPROPRIATE CITY OR COUNTY PLANNING DEPARTMENT TO VERIFY APPROVED USES 42
AND EXISTENCE OF FIRE PROTECTION FOR STRUCTURES. Seller may be required to provide purchaser with an "as is" disclaimer or a property disclosure statement. (Chapter 547, Oregon Laws 1993.) 43
8. Time is the essence of this contract. This contract is binding upon the heirs, executors, administrators, successors and assigns of purchaser and seller. However, the purchaser's rights herein are 44
not assignable without written consent of seller. In any suit or action brought on this contract, the losing party therein agrees to pay the prevailing party therein (1) the prevailing party's 45
reasonable attorney's fees in such suit or action, to be fixed by the trial court, and (2) on appeal, if any, similar fees in the appellate court, to be fixed by the appellate court. 46

Address 41 East Third, Urbandale, Anystate Evans Realty Co. ☐ Listing Broker 47
☒ Selling Broker 48

Phone 345-4321 By /s/ Harvey Hudelson, Sales Representative 49

B. AGREEMENT TO PURCHASE November 28 , 19 94 , 3:00 p. M. 50
51

I hereby agree to purchase the above described property in its present condition, for the price and on the terms set forth above and grant to said broker a period of two days here- 52
after to secure seller's acceptance hereof, during which period my offer shall not be subject to revocation. I acknowledge delivery of an executed copy of this earnest money receipt which I 53
have read and understood; said deed or contract to be in the name of Gerald I. and Nancy O. Investor, husband and wife 54

Address 3278 Exotic Drive, Urbandale /s/ Gerald I. Investor 55
Purchaser

Phone 686-3343 /s/ Nancy O. Investor Purchaser 56

C. PURCHASER'S AND SELLER'S AGREEMENT RE DEPOSIT OF EARNEST MONEY 57

The Earnest Money deposit in this transaction of $ 32,000.00 in the form stated above shall be deposited in the Client's Trust Account of the Broker indicated above until this offer is 58
accepted, whereupon the parties agree and direct that such , 19 . 59
funds be deposited (or retained) in the Client's Trust Account of Evans Realty Co. , the listing 60
broker. 61
62

/s/ Gerald I. Investor Purchaser /s/ Wendy Wells Seller 63

/s/ Nancy O. Investor Purchaser Seller 64

D. AGREEMENT TO SELL 65

November 28 , 19 94 , 8:30 p. M. 66
I hereby approve and accept the above sale for said price and on said terms and conditions and agree to consummate the same as stated. 67

Seller's Address Condominium Towers, Unit 77 /s/ Wendy Wells (widow) Seller 68

Urbandale, Anystate Phone 345-2020 Seller 69

E. Deliver promptly to purchaser, either manually or by registered mail, a copy hereof showing seller's acceptance. 70
Purchaser acknowledges receipt of the foregoing instrument bearing his signature and that of the seller Copy hereof showing seller's signed acceptance sent purchaser by registered mail to 71
showing acceptance. purchaser's above address. 72
Date Nov. 30, 1994 /s/ Nancy O. Investor Purchaser (return receipt requested) on , 19 . 73
Return receipt card received 74
Time 9:45 am /s/ Gerald I. Investor Purchaser and attached to broker's copy . , 19 . 75

F. SELLER'S CLOSING INSTRUCTIONS AND AGREEMENT WITH BROKER RE FORFEITED EARNEST MONEY November 29 , 19 94 . 76
77
I, the seller whose signature appears below, agree to pay to said broker a fee amounting to $ 27,600.00 for services rendered in this transaction and hereby grant to said broker 78
a lien on the proceeds of the seller to secure payment of said fee. In the event that the purchaser's deposit is forfeited pursuant to sub-paragraph 3, above, said forfeited deposit shall 79
be dispersed in accordance with the terms and conditions set forth in the listing agreement, or in the event it is not stated or there is no signed listing agreement, then in the following 80
manner: One third (1/3) to broker ($10,667) and Two-thirds (2/3) to seller ($21,333). 81
Seller acknowledges receipt of an executed copy of this contract, which seller has read and understands, bearing signatures of seller and purchaser named above. 82

Ivan Evans, Evans Realty Co. Listing Broker /s/ Wendy Wells Seller 83

By /s/ Harvey Hudelson, salesperson Seller 84

If this is a Co-op transaction between Listing and Selling 85
Broker, the commission is based on the following: Listing Broker %; Selling Broker %; Listing Broker's Initials Selling Broker's Initials . 86

NOTE: IF BLANK SPACES ARE INSUFFICIENT, USE S-N No. 810 "HANDY PAD", TO BE SEPARATELY SIGNED BY BUYER AND SELLER. FOR COUNTER-OFFER USE S-N No. 910.

BROKER'S COPY – FILE IN DEAL ENVELOPE

FIGURE 31–3
Earnest Money Receipt and Real Estate Contract

A. Earnest money receipt

B. Agreement to purchase

C. Buyer's and seller's agreement regarding earnest money deposit

D. Agreement to sell

E. Acknowledgment by buyer of seller's acceptance

F. Seller's closing instruction and agreement with broker regarding earnest money if forfeited

The form must meet the five essentials, discussed earlier, of a valid legal contract. It also automatically provides for the receipt of the earnest money put up by the buyer, and for a seller's agreement to pay a commission on accepting the offer. In addition, it specifies the type of deed to be used, the financing arrangements, and the closing date and place. In the following sections we identify and explain each of these elements.

Earnest Money Receipt

Before paying earnest money, a buyer wants the terms of the offer spelled out. Hence, the amount of consideration offered, the property description, the type of deed to be used, and the conditions related to financing are all stipulated in part A of the standard-form contract.

The first five lines include the purchaser's name, the amount of the deposit, and the description of the property. In this case, the purchasers are Gerald and Nancy Investor. The amount of the earnest money is $32,000. By signing at the bottom of part A, Harvey Hudelson, a sales representative of the Evans Realty Co., acknowledges getting $32,000 from the Investors, as evidenced by the opening words, "Received from."

Financing. The source of the money used to finance the purchase price follows the legal description. The price offered is $640,000. The earnest money deposit is $32,000. The minimum conditional loan is $500,000. This means that the Investors will have to come up with an additional $108,000 in equity funds to see the transaction through. The offer is conditional on getting the $500,000 loan at 9 percent interest or less, with a life of 25 years or more, and with monthly debt service. If any one of these conditions is not met, the buyer may withdraw from the transaction without penalty. On the other hand, if the seller can arrange financing that meets these conditions, the buyer must continue with the transaction.

Title Evidence and Deed. The first three paragraphs of the form pertain to title assurance and deed requirements. Paragraph 1 calls for a title insurance policy to be provided to the buyer at the seller's expense. Paragraph 2 says that the seller must provide marketable title within 30 days of written notice or the earnest money is to be refunded to the buyer. Also, if the seller does not accept the offer, the earnest money reverts to the buyer. If, however, the seller accepts and the buyer defaults, paragraph 2 says that the earnest money is to be forfeited by the buyer. Paragraph 3 specifies the type of deed and what kinds of loan are acceptable. Paragraph 4 defines the items that are included in the transaction as fixtures.

Prorations, Possession, and Assignment. Prorations of taxes, rents, interest, and so forth are spelled out in paragraph 5. Also, the condition in the offer (typed in)

says that the transaction must be closed in escrow, with the costs shared equally between buyer and seller.

Paragraph 6 calls for possession by the buyer on or before December 31, 1994. Prompt performance in accordance with the contract is required of the seller because the paragraph also states, "Time is of the essence." Finally, assignment of buyer's rights is allowed only with written consent of the seller. Assignment means a transfer of one's rights in a contract to another.

Agreement to Purchase

Part B contains an agreement to purchase the property "in its present condition" or "as is" for the price and under the conditions stated. By signing the contract, the Investors make an offer to buy under the terms outlined in part A, which may contain stipulations and contingency clauses to protect the prospective buyer. The binding words are, "We hereby agree to purchase and pay the price of $640,000." The offer is made at 3:00 P.M. on November 28, 1994. The two-day limitation means that an acceptance by the owner before 3:00 P.M. on November 30, would immediately create a binding contract. The offer may be withdrawn by the buyer without obligation anytime before it is accepted. An acceptance after the expiration time would really be an offer by the owner to sell under the specified terms and conditions.

The buyer is entitled to a copy of the offer immediately, as a record of the transaction.

Interim Handling of Earnest Money

The earnest money check must be cashed to protect the seller's and the broker's interests. Once cashed, what happens to the money? In part C of the contract, both the buyer and seller agree that the $32,000 earnest money is to be held in the broker's client trust account until the contract is fulfilled or otherwise terminated. If a buyer and seller enter into a contract without a broker, the contract is likely to require that the money be held by an escrow officer.

Agreement to Sell

Part D provides for the seller's acceptance of the offer to purchase at the price, terms, and conditions stipulated by the buyer. The seller may refuse to accept if the price and terms are not satisfactory. Or the seller may make a counteroffer. If no major change from the initial offer is involved, the counteroffer may be written in on the same form. A major change would necessitate a completely new contract. In this example, Wendy Wells, the owner, accepts the offer of the Investors at 8:30 p.m. on the day after the offer was initially made.

The contract is now complete and binding. The parties are competent; there is a bona fide offer and acceptance, with consideration by both; the object is legal, and both parties have signed. A copy is given to the seller as a record of the price and terms of the agreement. The buyer is entitled to a copy of the contract promptly after the seller signs it. Good brokerage practice requires that the buyer sign, acknowledging receipt of a copy of the contract, as shown in part E.

Forfeited Earnest Money

Part F shows the amount of the commission ($27,600) due the broker, Evan Realty, for negotiating the sale. However, if a forfeiture of earnest money occurs ($32,000), the split is to be one-third ($10,667) to the broker and two-thirds ($21,333) to the owner-seller. Forfeiture is prima facie evidence that the buyer is not ready, willing, and able to complete the transaction. The split gives the broker some payment for the effort and expenses incurred in arranging the transaction. In turn, the owner-seller is entitled to compensation as the principal party in the transaction and also for holding the property off the market.

By signing part F, the parties make the contract complete, even as to the commission to be paid by the owner to the broker, and also to the split in case of forfeiture. This completeness eliminates the need to refer back to the listing agreement in closing the sale. Needless to say, this signing of part F takes place at the same time that part D, the agreement to sell, is signed.

REMEDIES FOR NONPERFORMANCE

Failure of a buyer or a seller to perform on a contract is variously called *breach of contract, nonperformance,* or *default.* Remedies for failure to perform are available to both parties.

Buyer Remedies

A buyer has three alternative courses of action against a seller who is able but unwilling to fulfill a contract. First, the buyer may end the contract and recover the earnest money deposit, plus any reasonable expense incurred, such as for examination of the title. Second, the buyer may sue for specific performance—that is, require the seller to live up to the contract. Third, the buyer may sue the seller for damages. If a seller has acted in good faith but is unable to perform—for example, by inability to convey clear title—the buyer's recovery in a suit for damages is likely to be minimal. Some contracts contain a liquidated damages clause to be invoked on nonperformance. *Liquidated damages* is the money paid for nonperformance, as agreed by the parties when making up the contract.

Seller Remedies

A seller has five alternative courses of action against a buyer who is able but unwilling to fulfill a contract. First, the seller may rescind or cancel the contract and return the earnest money deposit and all other payments received from the buyer. This, of course, is not very probable. Second, the seller may cancel the contract and keep the earnest money deposit and all payments received from the buyer. Third, the seller may tender a valid deed to the buyer; which, if it were refused, would provide the basis for a suit for the purchase price. The deed must be offered to the buyer first to force the buyer to live up to the contract or to default. Fourth and fifth, the seller may sue the buyer for specific performance or for damages. Again, liquidated damages may be stipulated in the contract.

ESCROW ARRANGEMENTS

Escrow is the deposit of money, legal documents (deeds, mortgages, options, and the like), other valuables, and instructions with a neutral third party to be held until acts or conditions of a contract are performed or satisfied. Any contract may be placed in escrow. The parties to the contract make up the escrow agreement (separate from the contract that contains instructions for the escrow agent). The escrow agreement also states the duties and obligations of the parties to the contract and the overall requirements for completing the transaction. The escrow agent must perform his or her duties in a neutral or impartial manner. That is, the escrow agent must not be a party to the contract and must not be in a position to benefit in any way from the main contract, except for the escrow fee. Escrows are commonly used in the closing or settlement of a sale, an exchange, an installment sale, or a lease.

In a sale, the escrow agreement states all the terms to be performed by the seller and the buyer. The escrow holder is usually a title institution, an attorney, or a bank. Sometimes, at the signing of the escrow agreement, the buyer's cash and the seller's deed and the various other papers that are to be delivered by each are all turned over to the escrow holder who, when the title search has been completed, makes the adjustments, holds the title instruments, and remits the amount due to the seller. Other escrow agreements provide for initial payment of the deposit only and for the seller and buyer later to deliver the papers and the money needed to consummate the transaction. A completed escrow instructions form is shown in Figure 31–4.

The usual requirements of a buyer and seller in closing a sale of real estate in escrow are as follows.

The buyer provides:

1. The balance of the cash needed to close the transaction.
2. Mortgage papers, if a new mortgage is taken out.
3. Other papers or documents as needed to complete the transaction.

The seller provides:

1. Evidence of clear title (abstract, title insurance policy, or Torrens certificate). See Chapter 32.
2. A deed conveying title to the buyer.
3. Hazard insurance policies, as appropriate.
4. Statement from the holder of the existing mortgage specifying the amount of money needed to clear the mortgage.
5. Any other documents or instruments needed to clear title and to complete the transaction.

Instructions to the escrow agent contain authority to record the deed and the mortgage or deed of trust. When all conditions of the escrow agreement have been satisfied and clear title shows in the buyer's name, the escrow agent may disburse money as provided in the instructions.

The advantages of an escrow closing include the following:

1. Neither the buyer nor the seller need be present at the closing of title.

FORM No. 936
687 Stevens-Ness Law Publishing Co., Portland, Ore.

ESCROW INSTRUCTIONS

To: Hifidelity Escrow Services   Date .... December 1st, 1994 ....

221 N. Main

Urbandale, Anystate 00000

Re: Wendy Wells   Gerald & Nancy Investor
.... Seller .... Buyer ....

Gentlemen:

The following checked items are enclosed for your use in closing the above transaction:

1. (x) Earnest money receipt
2. (   ) Exchange agreement
3. (x) Deed showing subject property description
4. (x) Previous title insurance covering subject property
5. (x) Fire insurance policy covering subject property
6. (   ) List of personal property included in sale
7. (   ) Rental list
8. (   ) Earnest money note executed by buyer
9. (x) Our check in the amount of $32,000 ....earnest money paid
10. (   )
11. (   )
12. (   )
13. (   )
14. (   )

You are directed to:

a. (x) Pay Multiple Listing Bureau ....5.... % of the commission
b. (   ) Pay ....% of the commission to ....
c. (   ) Pay ....% of the commission to ....
d. (x) Pay all commission (less MLB, if any), to I.M. Evans, Realtor
e. (   ) Have .... prepare contract of sale
f. (x) Order title insurance from Hifidelity Title Co.
g. (x) Pro-rate taxes, fire insurance, if any, and make necessary adjustments as of closing date
          Start interest on contract/trust deed or mortgage as of ....
h. (x) split escrow fee evenly between buyer and seller.
i. (x) payoff existing 1st mortgage w/ 1st National Bank of Rustic Co. and record release.
j. (x) collect additional money from buyer as necessary to complete settlement.
k. (x) take account of and adjust other fees and charges as appropriate.

Please call undersigned and/or Harvey Hudelson .... should you need further information.

Very truly yours,

/s/ Ivan Evans
Evans Realty Co.
41 East Third
Urbandale, Anystate 00000

Receipt of above mentioned items and
instructions acknowledged.

By: /s/ Tom Barry

Telephone 345-4321

Form designed by
RUTH E. BEUTELL
MARION-POLK COUNTY ESCROW CO.
Salem, Oregon

FIGURE 31–4

Escrow Instructions

2. The seller receives no money until the title is searched, found marketable, and is in the name of the buyer.

3. The seller has assurance that if the title is found marketable, the contract will be carried out and payment will be forthcoming.

SUMMARY

A contract for the sale of real estate sets forth the price and terms of the transaction, a complete property description, and the obligations of the parties relative to the transaction. The purpose is to provide time to check and verify ownership, title conditions, accuracy of statements, and to allow sufficient time to arrange financing and title closing. The essentials of a valid contract are that there be (1) competent parties, (2) an offer and acceptance, (3) consideration, (4) legality of object, and (5) that the contract be in writing and signed by all parties.

Several types of contracts are in use. A binder acknowledges an earnest money deposit by the buyer and holds the deal together until a formal contract can be reached. A formal contract contains an agreement to sell and buy, a property description, a financial statement, the kind and form of deed to be executed, the closing time and place, and signatures of all the parties. An option is an owner's agreement to sell at a stipulated price for a specified time in return for a consideration from a potential buyer. An installment contract may be used when the purchaser does not have sufficient cash to make a downpayment acceptable to the seller.

KEY CONCEPTS

Binder   A short buy-sell contract that is used to hold a transaction together until a more formal contract can be signed.

Competent party   A person legally qualified to enter into binding contracts.

Consideration   Something of value, such as money, an act, or a promise, given or received as part of a contractual arrangement.

Contract   A legally binding agreement to do, or not do, a specific thing.

Earnest money   Money submitted with an offer to purchase as evidence of good faith.

Escrow   Depositing money, documents, and/or directions with a neutral third party to be held until contractual conditions are met.

Installment contract   An arrangement for purchasing and financing property in which the seller retains title while the buyer takes possession and makes payments over time; also called a land contract.

Liquidated damages   A monetary penalty provided for in a contract as compensation if the arrangement is not satisfactorily completed.

Option   The right to buy or lease a property at a stipulated price within a stated time.

Rider   An addition to a document, such as a contract, that is made part of the document by reference only.

Secured transaction The pledging of personal property as additional collateral for a loan or purchase of a property.

Uniform Commercial Code Laws governing the sale, financing, and security of personal property in commercial transactions.

Void contract A contract that is not legally binding or enforceable.

Voidable contract A contract that binds one of the parties but gives the other party the right to live up to the agreement or to withdraw.

QUESTIONS FOR REVIEW AND DISCUSSION

1. List and briefly explain the five essential elements of a real estate sales contract. Might additional items be important in making up the contract? If so, discuss the possibilities.

2. List and explain briefly the four types of real estate sales contracts, including the functions of each. How does a binder differ from a form contract?

3. In what ways is the Uniform Commercial Code of importance in real estate sales contracts?

4. List and explain at least three alternative remedies for the buyer and the seller upon nonperformance by the other.

5. Explain the nature and advantages of closing in escrow.

6. Is it legally possible to sell a property without a written contract?

7. May an owner and a buyer make up a valid real estate sales contract without a broker or an attorney?

8. Must fixtures be specifically mentioned in a sales contract? Is there any reason to do so?

9. Give at least four examples of persons not legally competent to make valid and binding contracts.

PROBLEMS

1. M enters into a written agreement to sell a tract of land to B. The boundaries are stated in the agreement. After the closing, with full payment to M, M discovers that the tract conveyed contained 10 acres rather than 5. M sues, contending there was no intention of selling 10 acres to B, that there was no meeting of the minds, and therefore that no contract existed. Can M get the land back? Why or why not?

2. R paid S $6,000 for a 90-day written option to buy S's farm. Thirty days later, a major highway improvement project is announced that will make the farm a prime location for a shopping center; the value increases tenfold. S refuses to convey title, claiming the consideration was insufficient. R sues. What is the result?

3. J agrees to sell a house to G for $110,000; a written contract is made up. Subsequently, J decides to keep the house and offers to return G's earnest money. G asks you what remedies are available. Explain the alternatives.

4. If J were agreeable to performing, and G were not, what remedies are open to J in problem 3 above?

CHAPTER 32

TITLE ASSURANCES AND TITLE TRANSFER

Chapter Outline

> *Property is necessary but it is not necessary that it should remain forever in the same hands.*
>
> Remy De Gourmont, French critic and novelist

Having title to property means holding the elements that make up legal ownership. A person about to pay a substantial amount of money for real estate wants the best possible title, usually called marketable title. Without marketable title, it will be very difficult to sell for market value at a later time. The desire for high-quality title is true even if ownership is obtained through inheritance or gift. Also lenders and lessees demand that an owner have marketable title to assure their position.

Marketable title means an ownership interest that is readily salable to a reasonable, intelligent, prudent, and interested buyer at market value. Ultimately, it means title of adequate quality for courts to require its acceptance by a purchaser following a buy-sell agreement. A marketable title assures minimum risk of loss in the event of an action at law as a result of superior claims.

In addition, a prudent buyer wants the deed through which title is received to include the best possible assurance of valid title from the *grantor,* the person conveying title. Finally, a buyer wants the public records to be as current and clear as possible so that mistakes in title search and analysis are avoided.

The purpose of this chapter is to explain how marketable title is assured and transferred. Attention is focused on the following critical concerns:

1. The tentative grantor must actually have an ownership interest in the property that can be conveyed. This means that the chain or history of ownership must run to the grantor.

2. The legal description must be accurate and complete.

3. Encumbrances against the property must neither preclude its use for the desired purposes nor hinder its reconveyance later.

4. Documentary evidence from experienced, competent, professional people must be provided so that the preceding conditions are satisfied. Adequate public records are a substantial part of the means by which documentary evidence is obtained.

5. The deed by which title is received gives the greatest possible assurances and protection to the recipient or *grantee.*

METHODS OF TRANSFERRING TITLE

Transfer of title to real estate from one person to another takes place in one of three general ways: (1) by public grant, (2) by private grant, which is a voluntary act of an owner, and (3) by action of law.

Public Grant

Originally public lands were transferred to states, corporations (primarily railroads), and individuals by *public grant.* This was how the West was opened up. Railroads were granted ownership to every other section for six miles on either side of any new line built. And, under homestead laws, title was granted to individuals or families after they had occupied a certain tract of land for several years and made certain improvements.

The federal government used patents to make the original public grants of ownership. A *patent* is a conveyance or grant of real estate from a government to a private citizen or corporation. Thus, most private ownership in the West traces back to the granting of a patent by the U.S. government. Subsequent conveyances of ownership by grantees must conform to the laws of the state in which the land is located. For all practical purposes, patents are no longer issued.

Private Grant

An owner may voluntarily transfer property (1) by sale or exchange for consideration, (2) by gift, and (3) by will. Technically, in some states a mortgage is also considered a voluntary title transfer; however, the owner retains the rights of possession and use, and the transfer is effectively only a lien on the title.

Transfer for Consideration. An owner may sell or otherwise agree to transfer any real property interest to another for consideration. A deed is used to actually convey the interest.

Transfer by Gift. An owner may transfer title by gift. The owner making the gift is termed a **donor;** the recipient is the **donee.** The transfer by gift is not void because of lack of consideration. A donee, however, cannot enforce any covenants against the donor because of the lack of consideration.

Transfer by Will. A will, legally termed "a last will and testament," is a written instrument directing the voluntary conveyance of property upon the death of its owner, and not before. An owner may write a will, or have one drawn up, at any time before death. And after making a will, an owner is free to draw up a new will, to sell, or to give the property away. The owner who makes a will is a *testator.* Someone who dies is termed a *decedent,* and if that person had a will they are said to have died *testate.*

The law requires certain formalities for the execution or carrying out of the will. The testator must be of legal age and mentally competent. The will must be written and signed. The will cannot cut off the rights of a surviving spouse. In many states, two witnesses who have no interest in the will must acknowledge the signing. Upon the testator's death, the will must be submitted to probate court to prove or establish that it is the last will and testament of the decedent. A probate court is a court that specializes in wills and, when necessary, administering estates. If no valid objection is raised, the will is accepted for probate and entered into the public record.

The person empowered to carry out the terms and provisions of the will is an *executor,* also called a personal representative in some states. If a will does not name an executor, the probate court will appoint one. The executor settles the affairs of the decedent, which may involve selling real property, perhaps to raise cash to pay debts of the decedent, or conveying property to designated persons, organizations, or causes. The giving of real property under a will is a *devise* and the recipient is a *devisee*. The giving of personal property under a will is a *bequest* or *legacy* and the recipient is a *legatee*. An executor's deed is used to convey title to real property in probating a will and settling an estate.

Actions of Law

There are six basic methods by which title to real estate may be transferred by actions of law: (1) transfer by descent, (2) transfer by lien enforcement, (3) transfer by adverse possession, (4) transfer by condemnation, (5) transfer by confiscation, and (6) transfer by erosion. Only transfer by descent necessarily occurs at the death of the owner.

Transfer by Descent. Transfer of ownership by *descent* comes about when an owner dies without a will, or *intestate*. Owned property passes to certain relatives, termed heirs or distributees, of the decedent according to specific state statutes of descent and distribution. The rights of the surviving spouse are always protected by dower, community property, or intestate share laws. In the absence of other surviving blood relatives of the decedent a surviving spouse usually gets the entire estate. Offspring, the lineal descendants of the deceased, share along with the spouse. If no offspring exist, parents of the decedent are next in line to inherit. Subsequent to parents come brothers and sisters, termed *collateral heirs*. If no heirs exist, the property goes to the state, by escheat.

The affairs of a decedent who dies intestate are settled by an administrator (in some states, a personal representative) who is appointed by a probate court. Generally, close relatives to the decedent are selected as administrators. The job of the administrator is essentially the same as that of an executor. Any real property sold is conveyed with an administrator's deed, which is exactly comparable to an executor's deed.

Transfer by Lien Enforcement. Failure of an owner to meet the obligations of a lien gives the creditor the right to enforce the lien. Thus, properties are sold as a result of mortgage default, unpaid taxes, unpaid assessments, or not meeting other lien obligations.

Transfer by Adverse Possession. Title may be seized or taken from an owner of record who fails to maintain possession and control of the premises under a process known as *adverse possession*. In a few states, this is called *title by prescription*. Title by adverse possession is particularly important in boundary disputes. Conditions for gaining title by adverse occupancy are generally that the possession must be:

1. Actual and open
2. Notorious
3. Exclusive of the true owner
4. Uninterrupted
5. Hostile to the interests of the true owner

6. Under written claim of title (or payment of taxes)

7. For a prescriptive period as required by law

Actual, open, and notorious means the land has been occupied and used just as a typical owner would use it. The true owner must not use the property at the same time; exclusiveness is lost if this is the case. And the use must not serve the interests of the true owner in some way. The prescriptive period varies from state to state, but it generally runs from 10 to 20 years, which is long enough that an attentive owner has ample opportunity to defeat the developing claim (see Figure 32–1). In some states the prescriptive period may be as short as five years where adverse possession is under *color of title*—meaning that the possessor believes that the title to the property is valid even though it is actually defective—and where the possessor pays the taxes.

Prescriptive title may be converted into marketable title by an occupant able to prove that all these conditions have been met, called an *action to quiet title*. Considerable proof is required of the claimant.

FIGURE 32–1
Time Required to Claim Title by Adverse Possession, by State

STATE	WITHOUT COLOR OF TITLE	WITH COLOR OF TITLE	STATE	WITHOUT COLOR OF TITLE	WITH COLOR OF TITLE
Alabama	20	10	Montana	—[a]	5
Alaska	10	7	Nebraska	10	10
Arizona	10	3	Nevada	—[a]	5
Arkansas	15	7	New Hampshire	20	20
California	—[a]	5	New Jersey	60	30
Colorado	18	7	New Mexico	10	10
Connecticut	15	15	New York	10	10
Delaware	20	20	North Carolina	30	21
Florida	—[a]	7	North Dakota	20	10
Georgia	20	7	Ohio	21	21
Hawaii	20	20	Oklahoma	15	15
Idaho	5	5	Oregon	10	10
Illinois	20	7	Pennsylvania	21	21
Indiana	—[a]	10	Rhode Island	10	10
Iowa	10	10	South Carolina	20	10
Kansas	15	15	South Dakota	20	10
Kentucky	15	7	Tennessee	20	7
Louisiana	30	10	Texas	25	5
Maine	20	20	Utah	—[a]	7
Maryland	20	20	Vermont	15	15
Massachusetts	20	20	Virginia	15	15
Michigan	15	10	Washington	10	7
Minnesota	15	15	West Virginia	10	10
Mississippi	10	10	Wisconsin	20	10
Missouri	10	10	Wyoming	10	10

[a] In these states, title may not be gained by adverse possession except under color of title, which includes payment of property taxes. Note that in some states special circumstances may reduce the prescriptive period.

Transfer by Condemnation. A governmental or quasi-governmental agency may acquire title to real estate, against the owner's will, for public uses or purposes under the right of eminent domain. Just compensation must be paid the owner.

Transfer by Confiscation. The taking of property by a government in time of war, without compensation, is confiscation. Traditionally, only property of enemies of the government is confiscated.

Transfer by Erosion. An owner gains *title by erosion* or *accretion* when additional soil is gradually brought to his or her property by natural causes, such as water or wind. The eroded soil must be deposited somewhere. However, the sudden breaking away of land from one owner and attachment to the land of another, as when a stream changes course, does not transfer ownership. Title may be gained by *reliction,* also termed *dereliction,* when waters gradually recede, leaving dry land; this, however, is not necessarily transfer of title.

TITLE EVIDENCE

Documentary proof, termed *title evidence,* must be developed for prospective owners before title is considered marketable and acceptable. Title evidence takes three basic forms: (1) an attorney's opinion or certification, (2) a title insurance policy, and (3) a Torrens certificate. The first two are based on a proper legal description, a proper chain of title, and a search of the public records. A *chain of title* is the succession of all previous owners, back to some acceptable starting point. A chain of title is a theoretical construct of all previous holders of title; it is not written and actions or claims of nonowners are not a part of it. An abstract of title differs from a chain of title. An *abstract of title* is a condensed, written history of all transactions affecting the ownership of a given property.

An abstract contains a listing of all documents bearing on quality of title, and often includes summaries of important segments of the documents. Thus, such items as mortgages, wills, liens, deeds, foreclosure proceedings, tax sales, and other matters of record are noted. The information is arranged in chronological order, without any judgments made concerning the rights of the parties involved. A properly prepared abstract indicates the records examined, the period covered, and a certification that all matters of record are included and indexed against the owners in the chain of title. A deed by itself is not evidence of title; it contains no proof concerning the kind or the conditions of the grantor's title.

Some interpretation and judgment are often necessary even after evidence of title is provided by one of the three forms. For example, certain easements or deed restrictions may or may not be acceptable to a buyer. Or, if an encroachment is suspected, a survey may have to be ordered because an encroachment would not necessarily be brought to light by any of the three forms.

Opinion or Certificate of Title

A *certification of title* or an opinion that title is good is rendered by an attorney or other qualified person based on an examination of specified public records (e.g., an abstract of title, or other sources of information). Historically, the search and opinion were made by an attorney, who made up an informal abstract of title for personal use. An attorney's opinion of title is used primarily in rural areas of the United States.

In recent decades abstracts of title have largely replaced the traditional attorney's opinion based on a search of public records. Abstract companies, using qualified abstractors and title analysts, specialize in producing abstracts based on records they maintain for the purpose. If flaws or encumbrances stand in the way of clear title, they are listed as exceptions. An abstract does not guarantee title. The attorney's interpretation is still required for title to be certified as good or to point out significant flaws and/or encumbrances.

In practice, title and abstract companies, attorneys, and other title analysts assume that a title is good or marketable at some early date. An irritating and expensive duplication of work is involved, nevertheless, in doing successive title examinations. And some meticulous attorneys want an examination carried back to an unreasonable date, as shown by the following tale.

In a legal transaction involving transfer of property in New Orleans, a firm of New York lawyers retained a New Orleans attorney to search the title and to perform other related duties. The New Orleans attorney sent his findings, which traced title back to 1803. The New York lawyers examined his opinion and wrote again to the New Orleans lawyer saying, in effect, that the opinion rendered was all very well, as far as it went, but that title prior to 1803 had not been satisfactorily documented.

The New Orleans attorney replied to the New York firm as follows:

I acknowledge your letter inquiring as to the state of the title of the Canal Street property prior to 1803. Please be advised that in 1803 the United States of America acquired the territory of Louisiana from the Republic of France by purchase. The Republic of France had acquired title from the Spanish Crown by conquest. The Spanish Crown had originally acquired title by virtue of the discoveries of one Christopher Columbus, sailor, who had been duly authorized to embark upon the voyage of discovery by Isabella, queen of Spain. Isabella, before granting such authority, had obtained the sanction of His Holiness, the Pope; the Pope is the Vicar on Earth of Jesus Christ; Jesus Christ is the Son and Heir Apparent of God. God made Louisiana.

Title Insurance Policy

Title insurance is protection against financial loss due to flaws, encumbrances, and other defects in the title that existed but were not known when the insurance policy was purchased. Therefore, title insurance is protection against events in the past rather than the future. The purchase of a policy simply shifts the risk of loss from a property owner or lender to the title insurance company. The premium or purchase price is paid only once, and the term is forever into the future. Title insurance, introduced in the late 1800s, currently provides ownership protection on more than half of all realty in the United States.

For several reasons new owners and distant lenders increasingly prefer title insurance to an attorney's certification of title as evidence of marketable title. To begin with, an attorney depends on an abstract, which may not disclose all possible defects of title. Further, an attorney's ability is uncertain. In either case, the purchaser or lender suffers rather than the attorney if a claim against the property is missed and subsequently proven. Recovering damages from an attorney for an error or omission is extremely difficult and costly. And recovering losses from a previous owner is often impossible because of death or change in location. With title insurance, defects such as these are automatically insured against, provided they are not listed as exceptions in the title policy. And claims of loss are usually settled promptly. Remote lenders prefer title insurance because the reputation and corporate integrity of title insurance companies mean quick and easy settlements should there be a problem.

From an owner's point of view the main limitation to title insurance is that the amount of coverage is fixed. Reimbursement is only to the face amount of the policy, even though improvements may have been added or land values increased sharply after the policy was issued.

The Insurance Contract.   Title insurance policies are usually made between the company and an owner (usually a new or purchasing owner), a lender, or a lessee. In return for the premium, the company contracts to reimburse or compensate against all loses due to title defects other than those listed as exceptions in the policy. However, as is typical of all insurance contracts, a loss must be shown in order to collect. The insurance company also agrees to pay legal expenses necessary to protect an owner against a title lawsuit.

The main items insured against are the following:

1. Flaws in the chain of title due to forged documents, improper delivery of a deed, incompetence or lack of capacity of a grantor, or lack of signature of a spouse.

2. Errors and omissions in the title search and examination due to negligence or fraud by a company employee, or due to improper indexing of public records.

3. Possible lack of acceptability of title to a subsequent intelligent, prudent buyer who may be unwilling to accept some minor encumbrance not listed as an exception in the title insurance policy; for example, a shared-driveway easement.

The following items may not be covered, unless extended coverage is obtained at some additional cost:

1. Defects disclosed by title examination and listed as exceptions to the policy.

2. Defects that a survey or physical inspection of the property would disclose. Examples are encroachments, rights of an adverse possessor, unrecorded easements or leases, uncertain or incorrect boundary lines, and lack of access.

3. Defects known to the insured although not listed as an exception. Examples are a recorded mortgage known to the insured but missed by the title analyst, and a violation of a covenant or condition.

4. Police power restrictions, which legally are not considered to make title unmarketable in any event.

5. Mechanic's liens not on record at the time the policy was issued.

6. Rights of parties in possession at the time of title transfer.

The coverage provided a mortgagee or lessee in a mortgagee's or lessee's policy is basically the same as the coverage provided an owner.

Obtaining Insurance. In a sales transaction, the seller or the broker usually arranges for a title company to provide the insurance that is to serve as evidence of clear title. The title company frequently issues a preliminary title or informational report. The report lists the owner of record, unreleased liens, easements, restrictions of record, and other apparent encumbrances, and it indicates clouds that are likely to require removal. It is the seller's obligation to remove serious encumbrances or *clouds on title* that block marketable title. After completing a reexamination of title, the title company issues a commitment to write a title policy.

The commitment (1) names all the parties involved, (2) gives the legal description of the property, (3) defines the interest or estate covered, and (4) lists terms and stipulations, including exceptions, of the policy. In a sale or refinancing, the policy is actually issued shortly after the closing, when all pertinent documents have been recorded.

Torrens Certificate

The *Torrens system* is a method of title registration in which clear title is established with a state agency, which later issues title certificates to owners as evidence of their claim. The Torrens system of title registration operates in a fashion very similar to that used by states for automobiles. Title is initially cleared and registered into the system on a voluntary basis, at which point a certificate of ownership that serves as proof of title is issued. Since sales, mortgages, and other claims against the property must be registered to be effective, the status of title may be determined at any time by checking with the registrar.

In theory, the Torrens system is ideal. But the high initial cost of registering a property in the system has worked against its wide acceptance. Also, some uncertainty about its operation exists, because the laws establishing Torrens registration vary from state to state. Hence, the Torrens system is not widely used.

DEEDS

A *deed* is a legal instrument that, when properly executed and delivered, conveys title to or ownership of an interest in realty from a grantor to a grantee. By definition and in accordance with the Statute of Frauds, a deed must be written. Proper execution means being signed by the grantor (or grantors), attested to by a witness or witnesses (in nearly every state), acknowledged by a notary public or other qualified officer, and, in some states, sealed. A seal is a particular sign or mark to indicate the formal execution and nature of the instrument.

The circumstances surrounding the conveyance of real property vary greatly from one transaction to another. Generally, a grantor prefers to minimize the quality of title conveyed, consistent with the transaction, to avoid future obligation or liability to the grantee. Consequently, deeds take many forms to reflect the kind and quality of conveyance intended.

Deeds are sometimes classed as statutory or nonstatutory. Statutory deeds are short forms of the deed in which any covenants or warranties mentioned are stipulated by law, as though written out in full. Nonstatutory deeds are usually written for special purposes or situations; thus only the covenants, warranties, and terms included in the deed apply. The main types of statutory deed are the general or full warranty, the limited warranty, and the quitclaim.

General Warranty Deed

A *general warranty deed* provides a grantee the most complete set of assurances of title possible from a grantor, and is therefore the one most preferred by a grantee. The grantor covenants (or warrants) a good title free of encumbrances, except as noted, which the grantee should be able to enjoy quietly, and that if necessary, the grantor will protect the grantee against other claimants. A grantee may not receive a full warranty deed unless it is provided for in the sales agreement.

Although not stated in the deed, a general warranty deed commits the grantor to several covenants that are binding on the grantor because of the deed's statutory basis. Thus, the grantor legally incurs a continuing future obligation when certain words, stipulated by state law, appear in the deed covenants. The statutes of each state must be examined to determine the exact stipulated words. Typically the stipulated words indicating a warranty of deed are "warrant generally" or "convey and warrant" (see Figure 32–2).

1. **Covenant of *Seizin.*** The grantor claims and warrants that he or she holds, or is seized with, ownership of the subject property and the right to convey it. If this covenant is breached or broken, the grantee may recover from the grantor any losses or expense up to the consideration paid for the property.

2. **Covenant Against Encumbrances.** The grantor claims and warrants that the property title is free of encumbrances, except as stated specifically in the deed. Thus, it is promised that there are no unmentioned liens, easements, or title restrictions. If an encumbrance does exist against the property, the grantee may recover any expenses incurred to remove it.

3. **Covenant of Quiet Enjoyment** The grantor claims and warrants that the grantee will be able to quietly enjoy or not be disturbed in the use of the premises because the title conveyed is good and superior to that of any third person. If the grantee, or any subsequent grantee, is dispossessed by a superior title predating the conveyance, the grantor is legally liable for any damages or losses incurred. Threats and claims of superior title by outsiders do not constitute a breach of this covenant.

4. **Covenant of Further Assurance.** The grantor warrants that any other instrument needed to make the title good will be obtained and delivered to the grantee. Under this covenant, if a faulty legal description were given in the deed, the grantor would be obligated to prepare a new deed, containing the correct legal description, for the grantee. Enforcement of this covenant is under a suit for specific performance rather than for damages.

5. **Covenant of Warranty of Title.** The grantor warrants forever the title to the premises, with monetary compensation to the grantee for any fault in the title, in whole or in part. This covenant is an absolute guarantee to the grantee of title and possession of the premises.

The first two covenants relate to the past and apply only at the time of conveyance. The last three relate to the future and run with the land.

WARRANTY DEED—STATUTORY FORM
INDIVIDUAL GRANTOR

NA

Wendy Wells (widow)
...., *Grantor,*

conveys and warrants to ....Gerald and Nancy Investor, husband and wife...

...., *Grantee, the following described real property free of encumbrances*

except as specifically set forth herein situated in ......Rustic.. *County, Oregon, to-wit:*

Lots 16 & 17, Edgewood South Subdivision

(IF SPACE INSUFFICIENT, CONTINUE DESCRIPTION ON REVERSE SIDE)

The property is free from encumbrances except

easements of record in subdivision plot

The true consideration for this conveyance is $ ......640,000...... *(Here comply with the requirements of ORS 93.030)*

Dated this ...15th... *day of* ......December......, *19*.94.   /s/ Wendy Wells

THIS INSTRUMENT WILL NOT ALLOW USE OF THE PROPERTY DESCRIBED IN THIS
INSTRUMENT IN VIOLATION OF APPLICABLE LAND USE LAWS AND REGULATIONS.
BEFORE SIGNING OR ACCEPTING THIS INSTRUMENT, THE PERSON ACQUIRING FEE
TITLE TO THE PROPERTY SHOULD CHECK WITH THE APPROPRIATE CITY OR COUNTY
PLANNING DEPARTMENT TO VERIFY APPROVED USES AND TO DETERMINE ANY
LIMITS ON LAWSUITS AGAINST FARMING OR FOREST PRACTICES AS DEFINED IN
ORS 30.930.

STATE OF OREGON, County of ......Rustic......................) *ss.*

This instrument was acknowledged before me on ...., *19*....,

by ..../s/ Alfred B. Culbertson..............................

Notary Public for Oregon
My commission expires ......December 31, 1995......

FIGURE 32–2
A General Warranty Deed (Statutory Form)

A warranty deed with covenants does not guarantee clear title. A grantor may be a complete fraud and plan to leave town immediately after collecting money from the sale. Or valid claims against the title may be outstanding even though not pressed by legal action. Therefore, evidence of clear title is desirable even with the use of a general warranty deed.

Limited Warranty Deed

A *limited warranty deed* is also known as a special warranty deed or a bargain and sale deed. From a layman's point of view the difference between the latter two terms is slight.

A *special warranty deed* contains a single covenant—a covenant against the grantor's acts—that title has not been impaired, except as noted, by any acts of the grantor. This means that the grantor has liability only if the grantee is disturbed by a claim arising from or due to some act of the grantor during his or her ownership. A special warranty deed may be considered to be similar to a quitclaim deed with a covenant. A special warranty deed gives a grantee much less protection than does a general warranty deed.

A *bargain and sale deed* gives slightly different assurances; the grantor asserts ownership, by implication, of an interest in the property and, unless stated, makes no other covenants or claims. The granting words are usually "grant, bargain, and sell," "grant and release," or simply "conveys." Thus, the grantee must demand or obtain good title evidence to be sure of receiving marketable title. Covenants against liens and other encumbrances may be inserted if agreeable to the grantor; the instrument is then called *a bargain and sale deed with covenants.*

Quitclaim Deed

A *quitclaim deed* conveys the rights of the grantor, if any, without any warranty, claim, or assertion of title. A quitclaim deed is the simplest form of deed and gives the grantee the least possible title protection. It conveys only an interest that a grantee *may* have when the deed is delivered. The operative words in a quitclaim deed are that (the grantor) "releases and quitclaims" (to the grantee). Title may be conveyed just as effectively and completely with a quitclaim deed as with a warranty deed, but the grantee receives no warranties. With a quitclaim the grantee has no recourse against the grantor if the title received is defective.

Quitclaim deeds are widely used to clear up clouds on title. For example, a quitclaim deed is used whenever an heir might have a very weak title claim. Or whenever a long-ago, common-law wife might have a dower claim. For a small consideration, the heir or "wife" gives up any claim held. A quitclaim deed to make right a legal description, names of parties, or some other error in a previously recorded deed is termed a *deed of confirmation* or a *deed of correction.* The obvious purpose is to clear up or correct the defect so that it does not become or continue to be a cloud on title. A quitclaim deed is shown in Figure 32–3.

Deeds of Trust and of Release

A deed conveying title to a third party (trustee) to be held as security for a debt owned a lender-beneficiary is know as a *deed of trust,* a *trust deed,* or a *trust deed in the nature of a mortgage.* A deed of trust is a nonstatutory deed. When the terms have been satisfied (the debt has been paid off), the trustee reconveys title to the former borrower on a *deed of release* or a *deed of reconveyance.* A deed of release is also used to lift or remove a claim from a dower, remainder, reversionary interest, or mortgage lien.

Miscellaneous Deeds

Many other deeds are used for special purposes or situations, sometimes by court order. For the most part, the name of the deed indicates the nature of the purpose or

QUITCLAIM DEED—STATUTORY FORM
INDIVIDUAL GRANTOR

Wendy Wells (widow) ...., Grantor,

releases and quitclaims to Gerald and Nancy Investor, husband and wife ...., *Grantee, all right, title and interest in and to the following described real property situated in* Rustic .... *County, Oregon, to-wit:*

Lots 16 & 17, Edgewood South subdivision

(IF SPACE INSUFFICIENT, CONTINUE DESCRIPTION ON REVERSE SIDE)

The true consideration for this conveyance is $ 640,000 .... *(Here comply with the requirements of ORS 93.030)*

Dated this 15th *day of* December ...., *19* 94

/s/ Wendy Wells

THIS INSTRUMENT WILL NOT ALLOW USE OF THE PROPERTY DESCRIBED IN THIS INSTRUMENT IN VIOLATION OF APPLICABLE LAND USE LAWS AND REGULATIONS. BEFORE SIGNING OR ACCEPTING THIS INSTRUMENT, THE PERSON ACQUIRING FEE TITLE TO THE PROPERTY SHOULD CHECK WITH THE APPROPRIATE CITY OR COUNTY PLANNING DEPARTMENT TO VERIFY APPROVED USES AND TO DETERMINE ANY LIMITS ON LAWSUITS AGAINST FARMING OR FOREST PRACTICES AS DEFINED IN ORS 30.930.

STATE OF OREGON, County of Rustic ....) ss.

This instrument was acknowledged before me on December 15th ...., *19* 94,

by ....

/s/ Alfred B. Culbertson

Notary Public for Oregon

My commission expires December 31, 1995

FIGURE 32–3
A Quitclaim Deed (Statutory Form)

situation. Fiduciaries, administrators, trustees, executors, and corporate officers do not wish to assume any greater future obligation than necessary when using these special-purpose deeds. Therefore, they include a covenant against the grantor's acts in such deeds by stating that they "have not done or suffered anything whereby the said premises have been encumbered in any way whatsoever." A quitclaim deed may serve as the vehicle for this covenant. In most cases, fiduciaries hold title only briefly and have no personal interest in the realty.

Administrator's Deed. An *administrator's deed* is a nonstatutory deed used to convey the realty of a person who died intestate to an heir or to a purchaser. The administrator executes the deed, which should recite the proceeding under which the court authorizes the sale or conveyance.

Executor's Deed. An *executor's deed* is used to convey title to realty owned by a person who died leaving a will to a devisee (heir) or to a purchaser if the property is sold. If more than one executor is designated in the will, all must sign the deed.

Deed of Cession. A *deed of cession* is a nonstatutory instrument to convey street rights of an abutting owner to a municipality. The purpose for the deed should be stated in the deed.

Committee's Deed. A *committee's deed* is a nonstatutory instrument to convey property of infants, mentally retarded persons, and other incompetents whose affairs are managed by a court-appointed committee. Authority from the court must precede any such conveyance.

Gift Deed. An instrument conveying title from a donor-grantor to a donee-grantee is a *gift deed.* The usual consideration is "love and affection." The grantee has no recourse against the grantor if title is defective because no monetary consideration was given by the grantee.

Guardian's Deed. A *guardian's deed* is an instrument used by a legal guardian to convey the realty interest of an infant or ward, with court permission. Full consideration should be cited because the guardian is a long-term fiduciary.

Referee's Deed in Foreclosure. An instrument used by an officer of the court to convey a mortgagor's title following a foreclosure sale is called a *referee's deed in foreclosure* or, in some areas, a *sheriff's deed.* The conditions surrounding the conveyance, including the price paid by the purchaser, should be cited in the deed.

Referee's Deed in Partition. Concurrent owners sometimes sue for partition, or splitting up, of jointly owned property. The instrument used following a partition judgment and sale is a *referee's deed in partition.* An officer of the court (the referee) conveys the interests with no other supporting covenants, of the former concurrent owners to purchasers.

Deed of Surrender. A *deed of surrender* is a nonstatutory instrument to convey a life estate to a remainderman or to convey a qualified fee estate to the holder of the reversionary interest.

ESSENTIALS OF A VALID DEED

A deed containing the following items will be valid in every state. Some states do not require the last two or three items.

1. Name of grantor with legal capacity to execute the deed.
2. Name and address of grantee, adequate for identification with reasonable certainty.
3. A granting clause or words of conveyance.

4. A description of the realty, and if less than a fee interest is involved, a statement of the interest being conveyed.

5. Proper execution; signature of the grantor, notarized, with witnesses and seal when required.

6. Voluntary delivery and acceptance.

7. A statement of some consideration.

8. *Habendum* clause.

Grantor and Grantee

The conveyance must be from a competent grantor to a grantee capable of holding title. The rules of contracts usually apply in determining whether a grantor is competent to convey title. The names of the grantor and the grantee should be followed by their addresses to aid in their identification. The status of the parties should also be clearly indicated, for example, "John Jones and Mary Jones, husband and wife," or "brother and sister."

A deed conveying corporation property should be supported by a resolution properly passed by the corporate board of directors. The deed can be signed only by a corporate officer deriving authority from the corporate board of directors by resolution. Finally, the corporate seal must be affixed to the deed.

Consideration

Consideration is anything of value given in a contractual agreement; for example, money, services, or love and affection. In most states, the consideration must be cited, which shifts the burden of proving lack of consideration to anyone attacking the conveyance. Dollar consideration is usually required; however, in a gift deed love and affect are sufficient. The full dollar amount of the consideration is usually not cited, except when the deed is executed by a fiduciary.

Words of Conveyance—The Granting Clause

The granting clause includes words of conveyance, such as "Convey and warrant," "Grant and release," "Grant, bargain and sell," "Releases and quitclaims," "Gives," or "Grants." The interest being conveyed, including appurtenances, should follow the granting clause. Only a present interest in realty can be conveyed; a deed to convey at some future time, for example, at the grantor's death, is invalid.

The *habendum,* "to have and to hold," clause indicates the estate being conveyed. If a habendum clause is included, the description of the interest cited should agree with the description in the granting clause. Title restrictions and other encumbrances are usually stated in the habendum clause.

Unique Description

A description must be used that identifies the property clearly and uniquely. Street addresses are often inadequate because ambiguity and uncertainty might result; thus, a legal description is preferred.

Proper Execution

Proper execution includes signatures, a seal, witnesses (in some states), and an acknowledgment of the signing before a notary public. Customarily, only the grantor or grantors sign a deed. If a mortgage is being assumed, the grantee must also sign, unless a collateral agreement is made.

The word seal printed or written after a grantor's signature is required in some states to indicate the formal nature of the deed. In conveying corporate realty, the signature of an authorized officer must be followed by the corporate seal. In some states the signatures of the witnesses to the signing are also required for proper execution.

An *acknowledgment* is a formal declaration, before a notary public or other authorized public official, by a person signing a legal document that the signing is a "free and voluntary act." A justice of the peace, a judge, or a commanding officer in one of the military services may also acknowledge a signature. An acknowledgment is required for recording in nearly every state. The public official is expected to require proper identification of parties involved in an acknowledgment. The purpose of the acknowledgment is to prevent the recording of forged instruments. A deed without an acknowledgment is not a satisfactory instrument for most conveyance purposes. Deeds should be recorded as soon as received to give notice to the world that the grantee's rights in the property have been received.

Delivery and Acceptance

The final requirement for a valid deed is delivery and acceptance. *Delivery* means that the grantor, by some act or statement, signifies intent for the deed to be effective. The grantor handing the deed to the grantee is the most obvious form of delivery. Similarly, the grantor's directing an attorney or an escrow officer to give a signed deed to the grantee also constitutes delivery. Delivery must take place while the grantor is alive. If several people share ownership of a property, for delivery to occur, all must sign and in some way indicate that the deed is to be effective.

The grantee must accept the deed for title to pass. *Acceptance* is agreeing to the terms of a deed. Since most people desire to own property, acceptance is ordinarily assumed. Thus, if a grantor records a deed conveying title to a grantee, the grantee must object and dissent immediately to avoid an acceptance.

Delivery is essential for a valid deed. A grantor handing a deed to a grantee is clearly delivery. But delivery takes other forms as well.

Example: Seller signs a deed naming Buyer as grantee. The deed is then handed to Buyer's attorney, with intent to immediately give ownership to Buyer. The attorney is an agent of the grantee; therefore the delivery is valid. (However, note that Seller handing a deed to his or her own lawyer, with a request that it be looked over IS NOT DELIVERY; in this case the lawyer is simply the seller-grantor's agent.)

Example: Seller signs a deed naming Buyer as grantee. The deed is then placed with the ABC Escrow Company, along with directions to deliver the deed to Buyer when certain monies are paid the Escrow Company by Buyer. This constitutes an escrow delivery, which is valid.

The rightful holder of title to realty claims all elements of legal ownership—rights of possession, control, enjoyment, and disposition, plus recourse to legal power to defend the title holdings. Only a written agreement for transfer of realty is enforceable, according to the Statute of Frauds.

Title to realty may be transferred voluntarily—by sale, by gift, or by will—or by an action of law, which is an involuntary transfer. Selling, leasing, placing a mortgage lien against the property, or making a gift of the property are all examples of voluntary transfer. Public sales caused by lien enforcement or loss of title through adverse possession are examples of involuntary transfer.

A title search is conducted to inspect public records in order to prepare an abstract of title. The abstract of title is a history of the title to the property. A qualified examiner then evaluates the abstract and renders an opinion or provides a certification of title for the client.

A person about to acquire title may also obtain title insurance, which protects against events that have already taken place and covers such losses up to a stipulated amount. The premium for the insurance is paid only once by each owner. Title insurance does not protect against defects and encumbrances discovered during examination of the records; these are listed as exceptions. The buyer may demand that the seller remove all exceptions except those that have been accepted in the sales contract.

The Torrens system is theoretically more accurate and efficient than the certification of title or title insurance. However, it has gained little acceptance in the United States.

The essential fact that a purchaser should bear in mind is that the seller must give a good and marketable title, free of all encumbrances except those stated in the contract. A general warranty deed offers the buyer the greatest amount of protection. It warrants that the grantor holds ownership of the property and has the right to convey the property; that the title is free of encumbrances, except as stated specifically in the deed; that the title is good and superior to that of any third person; that any other instrument needed to make the title good will be obtained and delivered to the grantee; and that the grantor warrants forever the title to the premises, with monetary compensation to the grantee for any fault in the title, in whole or in part. Other types of deed include the limited warranty deed, the quitclaim deed, deeds of trust and of release, and miscellaneous deeds.

KEY CONCEPTS

Abstract of title   A digest of all the recorded documents that pertain to the title to a given parcel of real estate.

Acceptance   Agreeing to all the terms of a contract.

Acknowledgment   A formal declaration that a contract was signed freely and voluntarily.

Adverse possession   Obtaining title to real estate by long-term, unauthorized occupancy, possibly under color of title.

Bargain and sale deed   A deed without covenants, except that it is implied that the grantor does have title.

Chain of title   The succession of previous owners back to the original source of title.

Deed   A written document that, when properly executed and delivered, conveys title to real estate.

Delivery   An act by a grantor showing intent to make a deed effective.

Devise   A transfer of real property ownership through a will.

Donee   Person receiving a gift.

Donor   Person giving a gift.

General warranty deed   A deed giving the greatest assurances to a grantee; including covenants of seizin, against encumbrances, of quiet enjoyment, of further assurance, and of title.

Grantee   Person receiving property rights in a deed.

Grantor   Person conveying property rights in a deed.

Intestate   To die without a last will and testament.

Legacy   Personal property given or received under a will.

Marketable title   Real property for which there is reasonable certainty as to who the owner is; title likely to be accepted by an interested, reasonable, prudent, intelligent buyer at market value.

Quitclaim deed   A legal instrument whereby a grantor conveys any interests held, but makes no claims, covenants, or warranties of ownership.

Reliction   Process of gradual increase in an owner's land due to a lowering of the water level: Sometimes called dereliction.

Special warranty deed   Deed containing only one warranty, which is against title defects caused by acts of the grantor.

Testate   To die having left a last will and testament.

Title evidence   Documentary proof of real property ownership.

Title insurance   Insurance against financial loss due to defects not listed in a title report or abstract.

Torrens system   State registration of real property ownership.

QUESTIONS FOR REVIEW AND DISCUSSION

1. Briefly define and explain the difference between the following methods of transferring title:

   a. Contract for consideration

   b. Gift

   c. Will

   d. Descent

   e. Adverse possession

   f. Lien enforcement

2. Explain the use of an attorney's opinion of title, including any advantages or disadvantages from a prospective owner's or lender's point of view.

3. What is an abstract of title? What is its use or purpose?

4. A property survey is sometimes required to validate title. What purpose does a survey serve?

5. Explain title insurance in detail, including any advantages or disadvantages for a potential owner's or lender's point of view.

6. Explain the nature of a general warranty deed, including five accompanying covenants or warranties.

7. What kind of deed would you prefer to use as a grantor of title? As a grantee? Why? How is the difference in attitude reconciled in practice?

8. Explain the nature and uses of the following deeds:

   a. Special warranty

   b. Bargain and sale

   c. Quitclaim

   d. Trust

9. List and explain at least five essentials of a valid deed.

10. Are deeds necessary? If not, what might be used instead?

11. Would extension of the Torrens system eliminate the need for deeds to convey title? Should the Torrens system be adopted nationwide? Discuss. What major obstacles would have to be overcome? What would be the probable effect on the cost of title transfer?

12. Title may be gained by adverse possession by occupying and using land for 20 years or longer in almost all states. Would not title by adverse possession, therefore, invalidate other claims of title that are more than 20 years old? Discuss.

PROBLEMS

1. A recently bought an older property and accepted a quitclaim deed and title insurance with typical coverage as sufficient assurance of ownership and quiet possession. Subsequently, the following situations arose. Indicate in each case whether A is protected against loss by the insurance.

   a. The grantor is a minor and now wants to rescind the conveyance.

   b. A contractor files a mechanic's lien against the property for repairing its roof after a storm three months prior to the sale.

   c. The property is zoned as single-family residential. A had believed it to be zoned two-family residential, meaning that the house could be divided into two dwelling units.

   d. A's garage, built 22 years ago, extends two feet onto a neighbor's lot.

2. There are 40 acres of unused land adjacent to B's farm. B fences and farms the land for more than 20 years. The county assessor, in turn, levies and collects taxes on the land from B. In actuality, the land is a portion of an 800-acre estate owned by C,

who lives in a neighboring state. C dies. Upon settling the estate, the executor discovers B's use of the 40 acres. The executor sues for back rent. What is the result?

3. H brings an abstract of title up to date for a house that is being sold to V. An attorney examines the abstract and certifies the title as marketable. Title is conveyed to V and the transaction is closed.

   a. After the closing, a forgery of an earlier deed is discovered, meaning that V did not have marketable title. V sues the attorney for negligence. What is the result?

   b. V also sues H, the grantor. What is the likely result if a quitclaim deed were used to convey title? A special warranty deed? A general warranty deed?

   c. Does V have a basis for a valid claim for damages against the abstract company?

4. W is negotiating with N about the sale of a bookstore W owns. N verbally offers $225,000 for the store and asks W to think it over.

   a. W, willing to accept, prepares and signs a deed and puts it in a desk drawer. That evening W has a heart attack and dies. Is there delivery?

   b. If W had given the signed deed to an escrow agent, would there have been delivery?

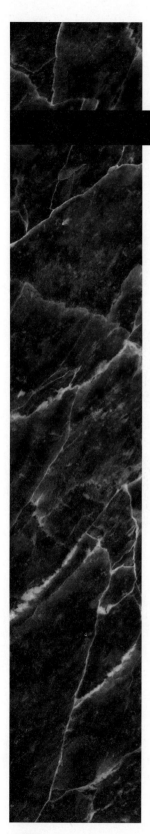

CHAPTER 33

TITLE CLOSING

Chapter Outline

Good deeds always have their rewards.
Anonymous.

A knowledge of closing procedures and adjustments is advantageous to a prospective buyer. With an understanding of the documents, costs, and procedures related to title closing, an investor will have a better idea of what is going on during these negotiations. And the need for certain documents or information becomes much more obvious. Further, a knowledge of closing procedures is absolutely essential for an agent or broker who is arranging financing or the closing itself.

The most common type of settlement is actually a double transaction: a title transfer and financing. The purpose of this chapter is to explain how the closing process works for a title transfer and financing transaction. In this process closing costs and various prorata adjustments may be substantial for the buyer, totaling between 3 and 8 percent of the property's value.

Other common title closings are: (1) a sale of property financed by an existing loan, (2) an exchange of two or more properties, (3) refinancing of a property under a continuing owner, and (4) sale of a leasehold. These types of closings are similar and, therefore, are not discussed separately.

PRELIMINARIES FOR CLOSINGS

Many details must be attended to between the signing of a sales contract and an actual closing. If an escrow closing is required, the details must be cleared through the escrow agent. Figure 33–1 lists some of the more usual documents and reports, who is responsible for preparing them, and who is responsible for having them prepared.

The entire escrow closing process, within which these items must be processed, is shown in Figure 33–2. Even if a closing is not in escrow, the same considerations or details must be handled by the broker, lender, or others to complete the transaction.

Survey and Inspection

A survey specifically identifies the property and may bring to light encroachments onto or from the property. Lenders increasingly demand property surveys to ensure that the legal description applies to the property being financed. Encroachments, if any, must be corrected by the seller before the closing can be completed.

If the property is an income property, a detailed property inspection is usually necessary prior to a closing to ascertain that conditions are as represented in the contract. The inspection verifies such matters as names of tenants, rents, space occupied, length of leases, and amount of security deposits. The inspection is also to make sure that no one in possession of any part of the premises has or claims any rights of

FIGURE 33-1

A Summary of the Title
Closing Documents

REPORT OR DOCUMENT	PREPARED BY	RESPONSIBLE PARTY
Property survey	Surveyor	Buyer
Property inspection	Buyer/buyer's agent	Buyer
Abstract of title, including title search	Abstract company	Seller
Preliminary title report	Title company	Seller
Title insurance policy	Title company	Seller
Deed	Attorney	Seller
Mortgage satisfaction, or deed of reconveyance for retired loan	Old lender	Seller
RESPA disclosure statement	Lender	Lender
Mortgage or trust deed	Lender	Lender
Promissory note	Lender	Lender

ownership or other interest in the property. The law is clear that possession gives public notice of an interest just as strongly as does a recorded instrument. An inspection should be made shortly before the closing in conjunction with the title search and analyses.

Title Search and Report.   Having the title searched and obtaining the title report are probably the most important requirements from the purchaser's viewpoint. The purpose of the search and report is for the purchaser to be sure that the seller's title is clear, or at least meets contract requirements. The seller usually provides title evidence in the form of a current abstract of title and a commitment for title insurance. If an abstract of title is provided, the buyer must obtain an opinion of title from an attorney. The title commitment or the title opinion sets forth liens, assessments, deed restrictions, and other encumbrances of record. The seller's title is subject to these limitations. The seller must remove any limitations that make the title unmarketable or otherwise do not meet the requirements of the sales contract.

Encumbrances: Acceptance or Removal

A marketable title must be delivered by the seller, except for encumbrances specifically excepted in the sales contract. Customarily, shortly after receipt of the title report or opinion, the purchaser notifies the seller of all encumbrances to be removed. The acceptability of encumbrances and other objections of title that show up on the title report or opinion must be settled between the buyer and seller prior to closing. If encumbrances or objections to title are acceptable or waived by the buyer and the new lender, these limitations need not be removed or "cured."

Typical encumbrances that must be removed are mortgage liens, tax liens, clouds on title because of improperly signed deeds, and unexpected easements, encroachments, or title restrictions. However, title restrictions and setback lines placed against the property by the developer are typically exempt.

A title report or opinion occasionally shows a title to be extremely unmarketable or clouded. After adequate opportunity has been given to the seller to remove the clouds and encumbrances, the buyer may reject such a title and rescind the sales contract. Upon rejection and rescission, the buyer is entitled to recover reasonable expenses incurred because of the seller's inability to perform according to the contract of sale.

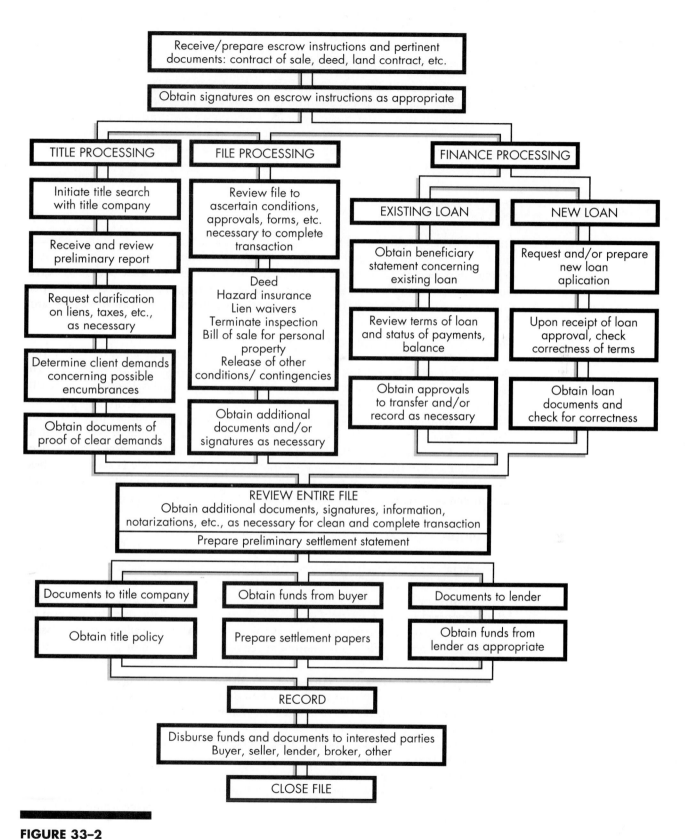

FIGURE 33–2
The Escrow Closing Process

Instruments to Be Delivered

The seller must sign and convey title either by a deed of the kind required by the sales contract or by one of higher quality. The new lender, in turn, provides a promissory note and a mortgage or trust deed to be signed by the buyer-borrower. If an existing loan is paid off as part of the closing, the old lender must sign and provide a mortgage satisfaction or deed of reconveyance. Finally the seller is often asked to sign an affidavit of title. If the sales contract calls for an escrow closing, all these instruments must be delivered to the escrow agent, along with escrow instructions.

ELEMENTS OF CLOSING COSTS

The main types of closing costs and adjustments include: (1) title assurance charges and legal fees, (2) loan-related charges and fees, (3) brokerage commissions and miscellaneous fees, and (4) buyer-seller adjustments. Typical buyer closing costs range from 3 to 8 percent, not including adjustments for property taxes and special assessments. Tax adjustments and special assessments may double these percentages.

Title Assurance Charges and Legal Fees

Buyers and lenders both want assurance that the title to the property has no hidden claims or liens filed against it. Therefore, a detailed search of various documents in the public record must be made to assure that such claims and liens do not exist. Title assurance evidence generally consists of an attorney's certification of title or of a title insurance policy.

Title assurance charges include costs for the search and examination of title and for title insurance. The costs of bringing the abstract of title up to date and of the title insurance itself is usually paid by the seller. A buyer may incur fees for legal counsel to examine the title evidence and to otherwise look after his or her interests throughout the transaction.

Incidental charges connected with title assurance include deed recording fees and escrow fees. Unless otherwise agreed, escrow charges are usually split evenly between the buyer and the seller. A buyer must pay to have the deed recorded, to give public notice of the conveyance.

Loan-Related Charges and Fees

Fees likely to be incurred when loan financing is used are as follows:

Lender's Service Charge. Loan origination fees, also called service charges, payable by a borrower typically amount to 1 to 2 percent of the amount borrowed. In essence, the charge covers the expense incurred in initiating a mortgage loan with a lending firm. Also, a seller may be required to pay a penalty for prepaying a loan. Thus, a seller prepaying a loan balance of $200,000 might be penalized a 1½ percent charge of $3,000.

Credit Report. A credit report showing a borrower's income, assets, outstanding debt, if any, and the borrower's credit history is required by almost all lending agencies. The charge is generally rather small.

CHECKLIST FOR CLOSING A REAL ESTATE SALE

At title closing, the seller should be prepared to do or have the following:[a]

1. Seller's copy of the contract.
2. Latest receipts for payments for taxes, utilities, and assessments.
3. Latest utility meter readings for water, gas, and electric.
4. Originals and certificates of all fire, liability, and other insurance policies.
5. Estoppel certificates from the holder of any mortgage loans that have been reduced, showing the loan balance, amounts due, and the date to which interest is paid.
6. Receipts for latest payment of interest on mortgage loans.
7. Any subordination agreements called for in the contract.
8. Satisfaction pieces of mechanic's liens, chattel mortgages, judgments, and mortgage loans that are to be paid at or before closing.
9. Statement with names of tenants, dates when rents are due, amounts of rents paid and unpaid, and assignment of unpaid rents.
10. Assignment of leases.
11. Letters to tenants directing payment of subsequent rents to purchaser.
12. Seller's last deed.
13. Affidavit of title.
14. Authority to execute deed if seller is acting through an agent.
15. Bill of sale for personal property included in the contract.
16. Any unrecorded instruments that affect the title, including extension agreements.
17. Deed and other instruments that the seller is to deliver or prepare.

At title closing, the purchaser should be prepared to do or have the following:[a]

1. Purchaser's copy of the contract.
2. Up-to-date abstract of title.
3. Up-to-date title report.
4. Examine deed to see that it conforms to the contract.
5. Compare property description.
6. See that deed is properly executed.
7. Have sufficient cash or certified checks to make required payments at the closing.
8. See that all liens that were to be removed have been.
9. Obtain names and other details concerning tenants and rents.
10. Obtain assignment of unpaid rents and assignment of leases.
11. Obtain and examine estoppel certificates for mortgage loans that have been reduced and are being taken over.
12. Obtain letters to tenants.
13. Obtain affidavit of title.
14. Obtain and examine (accept or reject) authority if the seller acts through an agent.
15. Obtain bill of sale for personal property included in the contract.
16. Examine survey.
17. Ascertain content and acceptability of title report relative to covenants, restrictions, and consents affecting the title or use of the property.
18. Ascertain amounts due, including any accrued interest, for unpaid utility and tax bills and assessments as of the closing date.
19. Arrange for adjustments as called for in the contract.
20. Examine purchase-money mortgage loan documents and execute same.
21. Have damage awards for public improvements, if any, assigned to the purchaser.
22. Obtain any unrecorded instruments affecting the title, including extension agreements.

[a] These items may be attended to by an escrow agent rather than by the seller and purchaser on an individual basis.

Recording Fee.   Recording fees for mortgages and loan-assumption documents are customarily paid by the purchaser. The seller pays for recording a mortgage satisfaction to meet the requirement of delivering title free and clear of encumbrances. These fees vary with the length of the documents and local recording customs.

Appraisal Fee.   An appraisal report is generally required when borrowed funds are used to purchase a property, with the cost paid by the purchaser.

Prepaid Interest.   Prepaid interest is customarily charged from date of settlement to the end of the month, when a new loan is obtained. The first regular payment of debt service then begins at the end of the first full month of ownership. This prepayment makes it unnecessary to compute interest for periods of less than one-month's time later on.

Hazard Insurance.   At closing, lenders require the purchaser-mortgagor to provide hazard insurance on the property. This insurance protects the lender against loss by fire, windstorm, and other specified hazards. If new insurance is obtained, the buyer usually pays the premium in advance.

Property Survey.   A property survey by a licensed land surveyor is often required by lenders, with the cost borne by the purchaser.

Commissions and Miscellaneous Charges

Brokerage commissions run from 4 to 7 percent of the sales price and are paid by the seller since the broker usually works as an agent of the seller. Of course, if the buyer employs the broker, the buyer pays the commission. Commissions on sales of lots and land may run up to 10 percent.

Other costs may be encountered in a title closing. Special handling costs or mailing charges incurred by the escrow agent will be assessed against the responsible party. Deed stamps, required by law in most states, are paid for by the seller. Some states require a documentary stamp on the promissory note, which is a tax on the intangible mortgage debt.

Buyer-Seller Adjustments

When an outstanding mortgage is assumed, an adjustment is made between the seller and the buyer, each bearing the interest costs for his or her time of ownership. Thus, an appropriate credit is given to the buyer for interest charges due up to and including the day of the settlement.

If the seller's insurance policy is taken over, an adjustment is necessary for prepaid premiums, representing the remaining term of the insurance being taken over. The buyer must also reimburse the seller for premiums in the reserve account, if they are taken over.

Real property taxes, if unpaid, constitute a lien prior to the mortgage lien. Therefore, lenders frequently require a reserve account from a borrower to be sure the money for the tax payments is available when the payments are due. If a reserve account is required, the estimated real property tax for the year is prorated on a monthly basis. The prorata amount is added to the payments due each month for loan interest, principal repayment, and hazard insurance. With a reserve account, the necessary adjustment must cover the amount the seller has in the account, plus any other tax adjustments agreed to by the buyer and the seller.

In addition to these costs and settlement charges, adjustments are made for accrued or prepaid rentals, if tenants are occupying the premises, and for any security deposits held by the seller. Finally, fuel or supplies on hand, or other items transferred from seller to buyer also call for appropriate adjustments.

CLOSING-STATEMENT ENTRIES AND PRORATIONS

A settlement statement is needed at a closing to satisfy all parties involved, particularly the buyer and the seller. The statement shows the amount of money the buyer must pay to get title and possession. The statement also tells how much the seller will net after paying the broker's commission and other expenses.

Prorations are necessary to divide closing costs and expenses proportionately between a buyer and a seller. The seller typically may have prepaid property taxes and hazard insurance, and may own reserve deposits, all of which require adjustments. The buyer wants these and similar items cleared at or before the closing. Also, if an existing mortgage is taken over by the buyer, adjustments for accrued interest to the date of closing are necessary. These adjustments are representative of the many that may be necessary at the closing.

General Rules of Prorating

The rules or customs applicable to prorations vary widely from state to state. In some states, closing rules and procedures have been established by realty boards or bar associations. The rules most generally applicable are as follows:

1. The seller is generally responsible for the day of the closing, which means that prorations are made to and including the day of closing. In the few states where the buyer is responsible for the day of closing, adjustments are made as of the day preceding the closing.

2. A year is presumed to have 360 days, with twelve 30-day months, for prorations of mortgage interest, real estate taxes, and insurance premiums. The actual number of days in a month may be used in prorations if specified in the sales contract.

3. Accrued real estate taxes that are not yet payable are prorated at the closing. If current taxes cannot be ascertained, the amount of the last tax bill is used in prorating.

4. Special assessment taxes are increasingly paid by the seller and are not prorated at the closing, unless the buyer agrees to assume with a proration.

5. Rents are usually prorated over the actual number of days in the month of the closing. The buyer agrees in a separate statement to collect any unpaid rents for current and previous periods and to forward the prorata share to the seller. (A buyer is advised against taking uncollected rents as an adjustment in the closing

statement because the buyer should not accept the responsibility for rents that the seller cannot collect.)

6. Tenants' security deposits for the last month's rent or to cover possible damages to the property must be transferred to the buyer without any offsetting adjustment. The deposits belong to the tenants and not to the seller. And, as the new owner, the buyer will be responsible for refunding these deposits at a later time. Prior tenant consent to such transfers may be necessary.

7. If closing is between wage payment dates, unpaid wages of employees working on the property are prorated, including amounts for social security and other fringe benefits.

8. Adjustments for chattels (personal property) are made according to local custom. No adjustment is required for fixtures. Unless otherwise stipulated in the sales contract, the following items are fixtures and a part of the real property: plumbing, heating, built-in appliances, oil tanks, water heaters, light fixtures, bathroom fixtures, blinds, shades, draperies and curtain rods, window and door screens, storm doors and windows, wall-to-wall carpeting, shrubs, bulbs, plants, and trees. Hall carpets, refrigerators, stoves, and washers and dryers are also usually regarded as fixtures in apartment buildings.

Closing-Statement Entries

Several items on a closing statement are direct entries and do not require adjustments between the buyer and the seller. These items are commonly called credits. A *credit* is an entry in a person's favor, as, for example, the balance in a bank account is in the depositor's favor. We also speak of giving credit to someone for doing us a favor or showing honesty or otherwise being financially trustworthy. A credit, as used here, is recognition to the buyer or seller for a contribution made to the transaction.

The obvious first entry on a closing statement is the sales price, which is credited to the seller. Crediting the seller with the sales price is recognition of the seller's contribution of the property to the transaction.

A direct credit at current market price is also given to the seller for fuel oil, cleaning supplies, and other items on hand that are taken over by the buyer. These items are over and above the sales price of the real estate and represent additional seller contributions to the transaction. In a similar vein, seller reserve deposits that are being taken over by the buyer are a credit entry to the seller. Reserve deposits are commonly assumed by a buyer who takes over an existing mortgage.

A buyer is credited in the closing statement with any earnest money deposit or down payment made. In addition, if the buyer takes over an existing mortgage, a credit is due to the buyer for the outstanding loan balance. A credit is also due to a buyer who gives a purchase-money mortgage to the seller as part of the sale price, in that the purchase-money mortgage creates a new obligation from the buyer to the seller.

Tenants' security deposits, if carried as an obligation of the property owner, must also be treated as a credit to the buyer. The buyer is relieving the seller of the obligation to repay the security deposits, which constitutes a contribution to the transaction. Alternatively, if the security deposits are carried in escrow accounts, the accounts may be transferred to the buyer's name, with no adjusting entry in the settlement statement.

Figure 33–3 is a summary of closing-statement entries. It lists the settlement statement items and indicates whether the credit entry goes to the buyer or the seller.

Prorata Calculations

Some items must be prorated between the buyer and seller rather than be directly credited to one or to the other. Prorating is necessary when the charge or payment covers an overlapping time period for which both the buyer and the seller are responsible. An *accrued expense* is an accumulated charge owed but not yet paid. A *prepaid expense* is a charge paid for in advance. Real estate taxes and accrued interest are examples of accrued expenses; rents collected in advance or prepaid hazard insurance are prepaid expenses.

Three distinct steps are involved in prorating:

1. Identify the item to be prorated (taxes, insurance premiums, etc.).
2. Determine whether the item is a prepaid or accrued expense.
3. Calculate the amount of the proration.

For example, a hazard insurance premium prepaid by the seller means that the seller is due a credit for the portion of the premium that covers the buyer's ownership period. Additionally the buyer eventually must pay all the real estate taxes due for the period, including the time for which the seller would be responsible. Thus, they become a credit entry to the buyer on the closing statement.

Prepaid Expense Prorations. The premium for hazard insurance is a typical adjustment of a prepaid expense. Hazard insurance premiums usually are prepaid for one, three, or five years, and as a matter of convenience a buyer frequently takes over the insurance coverage of a seller. First, a careful check is necessary to determine cor-

CREDITS TO BUYER	CREDITS TO SELLER
DIRECT ENTRY, NO PRORATION NECESSARY	
Earnest money and down payment	Sales price
Outstanding loan balance, if taken over by buyer	Fuel on hand (oil, gas, etc.) at current market price
New loans to finance purchase	Reserve deposits for taxes and hazard insurance, when taken over by buyer
Tenant security deposits	
PRORATION NECESSARY	
Accrued property taxes, seller's portion	Prepaid property taxes, buyer's portion
Accrued loan interest, seller's portion	Prepaid water and sewer charges, buyer's portion
Accrued employee wages, including vacation allowance, seller's portion	Prepaid hazard insurance, buyer's portion
Rents collected in advance by seller, buyer's portion	Uncollected rents, seller's portion

FIGURE 33–3
Closing-Statement Items

rectly the period for which a premium has been paid. Then, the number of years, months, and days for which the premium has been prepaid must be calculated. The following example illustrating the usual method of prorating prepaid insurance expense concerns a one-year prepayment.

Assume a seller's policy with an annual premium of $600 ($50 per month) that runs to August 15, 1995. The closing is on April 12, 1995. The buyer agrees to take over the seller's policy. What is the amount of the adjustment?

	YEARS	MONTHS	DAYS
Premium paid to 8/15/95	1995	8	15
Closing date 4/12/95	1995	4	12
Remaining coverage available	0	4	3

The end date of the prepaid period is compared with the closing date. Then, beginning with the Days column, the closing date is subtracted from the end date. In this example, 4 months and 3 days of premium are prepaid as of the closing date. At $50 per month, this means a credit of $205 to the seller ($50 × 4.1 months = $205.)

As a second, more complex example, assume a three-year premium of $5,400 for a policy that ends on November 12, 1996. Closing is assumed to take place on September 15, 1994.

	YEARS	MONTHS	DAYS
Premium paid to 11/12/96	1996	11	12
Closing date 9/15/94	1994	9	15
Future years, months, and days for which premium is prepaid	?	?	?

Again begin with the Days column. When the end date day (12) is less than the closing date day (15), a month must be borrowed from the Months column. This increases the end date day by 30, to 42. The 15 days left to the closing date may now be subtracted from 42, to give 27 future days for which a premium has been paid. Next, move to the Months column. The months in the closing date line (9) are now subtracted from the months in the end date line (now 10 because 1 was borrowed) to give one prepaid month. If the end date months were less than the closing date months, 1 year (12 months) would have to be borrowed from the Years column.

	YEARS	MONTHS	DAYS
		10	42
Premium paid to 11/12/96	1996	1̶1̶	1̶2̶
Closing date 9/15/94	1994	9	15
Future years, months, and days for which premium is prepaid	2	1	27

Finally, in the Years column, 1994 is subtracted from 1996 to give 2 future years for which the premium is paid. In total, the premium has been prepaid for 2 years, 1 month, 27 days.

The $5,400 premium breaks down to $1,800 per year, or $150 per month. Two years times $1,800 equals $3,600. One month at $150 per month equals $150. And 27 days or 0.9 month (27 days/30 days) at $150 per month gives $135. The total credit due the seller for the prepaid insurance premium is $3,885.

Prepayment credit for 2 years	$3,600
Prepayment for 1 month	150
Prepayment for 27 days	135
Total prepayment credit due seller	$3,885

Accrued Expense Prorations. Real property taxes and water and sewer charges are typical accrued expenses. To illustrate the proration of an accrued expense, assume that a water and sewer charge is payable at the end of each quarter. The quarterly charge is $45, or $0.50 a day. An accrual is needed for the portion of the quarter from April 1 to the date of closing, April 12. Thus, 12 of the 90 days in the quarter are chargeable to the seller. At $0.50 a day, this equals $6, or

$$\$45 \times \frac{12}{90} = \$6$$

Accrued interest on an assumed loan is calculated in a similar fashion. Assume a closing on April 12, with the seller paying off a $70,000 mortgage loan, plus accrued interest at 9 percent, compounded monthly. The accrued interest would be $210, calculated as follows:

$$9\% \div 12 = .0075 \text{ per month}$$
$$\$70,000 \times .0075 = \$525$$

$$\$525 \times \frac{12 \text{ days}}{30 \text{ days}} = \$210$$

ESCROW CLOSING

To illustrate escrow closing procedures and prorata calculations we will prepare a settlement worksheet. The calculations for the hazard insurance and water and sewer charges are shown above. The closing is handled by Hifidelity Escrow Services. The data are representative; some detail is omitted and round numbers are used for greater clarity.

A Case Problem

On March 7, 1995, a buyer made an earnest money deposit of $4,000 toward the purchase of a duplex for $100,000. On March 8, the owner agrees to sell. The sale was negotiated by Evans Realty Company. The parties subsequently agree to a closing date of April 12, 1995. Escrow closing costs are to be shared equally, as agreed in the contract. A 30-day month and a 360-day banker's year are customarily used for closing adjustments in the area.

The offer is conditional on the buyer obtaining a 30-year, monthly payment loan for $90,000 or more, at 10 percent interest or less. The Urbandale Savings and Loan agrees to make such a loan, with a 2 percent loan origination fee. Payments are to begin on June 1, so interest must be paid on the $90,000 to the end of April at the closing. There is an existing loan on the duplex of $70,000, with interest paid to the end of March 1995.

Details of the transaction requiring entries or buyer-seller adjustments are as follows:

A. Title Assurance Entries

1. The owner's title policy from the Hifidelity Title Company costs $360, which is payable by the seller. A lender title policy rider costs $110, payable by the buyer.

2. The escrow fee, by Hifidelity Escrow Services, is $176, to be shared equally by buyer and seller.

3. Recording fees are payable as follows: mortgage satisfaction—$4.00, by seller; deed—$4.00, by buyer; and new mortgage papers—$24.00, by buyer.

4. To prepare documents and to clear up some miscellaneous details, seller engaged Tangle & Webb, attorneys, who charged $120.

B. Financing Entries

5. Seller pays off existing loan of $70,000, along with accrued interest of $210.

6. Buyer gets new loan of $90,000 at 10 percent, compounded monthly, but must pay a 2 percent origination fee. Interest must be prepaid to the end of April at closing, so that the first full payment will be due on June 1.

7. To obtain the financing, the buyer incurred the following charges: attorney's fee for document preparation—$40.00; charge for credit report—$40.00; and appraisal fee—$240.

C. Miscellaneous Charges

8. Seller's brokerage commission at 6 percent is $6,000.

9. Seller lived in another state and shipped the deed and other materials for overnight delivery: charge is $14.00.

D. Buyer-Seller Adjustments

10. Sales price is $100,000; credit seller, debit buyer. Buyer made earnest money deposit with offer of $4,000.

11. Annual property taxes of $2,880 were prepaid to June 30 by seller.

12. Seller prepaid hazard insurance to August 15; policy is being taken over by buyer. Adjustment is $205, as calculated earlier.

13. Rents of $540 per unit were prepaid to the end of April.

14. Water and sewer charge accrued to April 12; quarterly charge is $45. The adjustment is $6 as calculated earlier.

Summary Statements. Figures 33–4 and 33–5 summarize the necessary adjustments and prorations for the data presented.

ITEM	DEBITS	CREDITS
Contract Sales Price	$100,000	
Title Assurance Entries		
Hifidelity Title Co.: lender's policy	110	
Recording fees: deed and mortgage	28	
Escrow fee (one half)	88	
Financing Entries		
New loan, Urbandale S&L		$ 90,000
New loan, interest to April 30	450	
New loan, origination fee at 2%	1,800	
Attorney, H Light: prepare documents	40	
Credit report: Rustic County Credit Bureau	40	
Appraisal report: A Measure	240	
Earnest money		4,000
Buyer-Seller Adjustments		
Tenant security deposits		900
Property taxes, prepaid to June 30	624	
Hazard insurance, prepaid to August 15	205	
Rents, prepaid to April 30		648
Accrued sewer and water charges		6
Subtotals	$103,625	$ 95,554
Balance required		8,071
Totals (must balance)	$103,625	$103,625

FIGURE 33–4
Buyer's Closing
Statement

TITLE CONVEYANCE

When all necessary payments are made, title is conveyed by delivery of a deed. In an escrow closing, title passes upon performance of all conditions in the escrow agreement, with the recording and delivery of the deed.

A grantor must be legally competent at the time of deed execution to convey title. Competency includes being of legal age and acting voluntarily and intentionally, with understanding. All rights of the grantor cease upon delivery of the deed. The settlement statement becomes the buyer's and seller's permanent record of the transaction.

REAL ESTATE SETTLEMENT PROCEDURES ACT (RESPA)

Figure 33–6 shows a completed Real Estate Settlement Procedures Act (RESPA) form for the transaction just discussed.

The Real Estate Settlement Procedures Act was designed as consumer protection legislation to shield homebuyers from unnecessarily high closing costs. Implementation has two ends: (1) to ensure that borrowers purchasing one- to four-unit residential properties are fully informed of closing costs, and (2) to reserve to

FIGURE 33–5

Seller's Closing
Statement

ITEM	DEBITS	CREDITS
Contract Sales Price		$100,000
Title Assurance Entries		
Hifidelity Title Co.: owner's policy	$360	
Recording fee: mortgage satisfaction	4	
Escrow fee (one half)	88	
Attorneys: Tangle & Webb	120	
Financing Entries		
Existing loan, pay off	70,000	
Existing loan, accrued interest	210	
Miscellaneous		
Commission: Evans Realty	6,000	
Federal Express: overnight delivery	14	
Buyer-Seller Adjustments		
Tenant security deposits	900	
Property taxes, prepaid to June 30		624
Hazard insurance, prepaid to August 15		205
Rents, prepaid to April 30	648	
Accrued sewer and water charges	6	
Subtotals	$78,350	$100,829
Balance required	22,479	
Totals (must balance)	$100,829	$100,829

borrowers the right to select the parties who provide services to the transaction, such as attorneys, appraisers, and title companies. RESPA also covers the financing and closing of individual condominium and cooperative units and mobile homes. The Act requires one settlement form to be used nationwide, and has, therefore, standardized closing practices across the United States.

The Act extends to lenders who invest more than $1 million per year in one- to four-family residential loans and to all federally related first mortgage loans. The Federal Reserve System directs implementation under Regulation X. Note that RESPA does not regulate or limit fees and does not require disclosure of the loan terms of the transaction, which is provided for in the Truth-in-Lending Act.

Under RESPA a lender has the following obligations to borrowers.

1. To supply an information booklet, *Settlement Costs and You: A HUD Guide for Homebuyers,* to anyone making a written loan application. The booklet explains the basics of settlement procedures, home financing, and the functions of the various parties in the sales transaction.

2. To supply a "good faith estimate" of the costs likely to be incurred in a closing for settlement services. The intent is to forewarn the buyer of the approximate amount of cash likely to be needed at closing.

3. To supply specific costs to the buyer "at or before" actual settlement. The buyer may waive this requirement. At the same time, the buyer is entitled to see the settlement charges that have been definitely determined, upon request, within one business day of closing.

FIGURE 33–6
Completed RESPA Form

A. Settlement Statement

U.S. Department of Housing and Urban Development

OMB No. 2502-0265

B. Type of Loan			
1. ☐ FHA 2. ☐ FmHA 3. ☒ Conv. Unins.	6. File Number	7. Loan Number	8. Mortgage Insurance Case Number
4. ☐ VA 5. ☐ Conv. Ins.			

C. Note: This form is furnished to give you a statement of actual settlement costs. Amounts paid to and by the settlement agent are shown. Items marked "(p.o.c.)" were paid outside the closing; they are shown here for information purposes and are not included in the totals.

D. Name and Address of Borrower	E. Name and Address of Seller	F. Name and Address of Lender
John Burgan 3278 Exotic Drive Urbandale 00000	Andrew Wright Condominium Towers, Unit 77 Urbandale 00000	Urbandale Savings & Loan Association

G. Property Location	H. Settlement Agent Hifidelity Escrow Services	
2001 Zigzag Avenue Urbandale 00000	Place of Settlement 221 N. Main, Urbandale 00000	I. Settlement Date 4/12/95

J. Summary of Borrower's Transaction		K. Summary of Seller's Transaction	
100. Gross Amount Due From Borrower		**400. Gross Amount Due To Seller**	
101. Contract sales price	100,000	401. Contract sales price	100,000
102. Personal property		402. Personal property	
103. Settlement charges to borrower (line 1400)	2,796	403.	
104. Property taxes to 6/30	624	404.	
105. H. Insurance 8/15	205	405.	
Adjustments for items paid by seller in advance		*Adjustments for items paid by seller in advance*	
106. City/town taxes to		406. City/town taxes to	
107. County taxes to		407. County taxes to	
108. Assessments to		408. Assessments to	
109.		409. Property taxes to 6/30	624
110.		410. H. Insurance 8/15	205
111.		411.	
112.		412.	
120. Gross Amount Due From Borrower	103,625	**420. Gross Amount Due To Seller**	100,829
200. Amounts Paid By or in Behalf of Borrower		**500. Reductions in Amount Due To Seller**	
201. Deposit or earnest money	4,000	501. Excess deposit (see instructions)	
202. Principal amount of new loan(s)	90,000	502. Settlement charges to seller (line 1400)	6,586
203. Existing loan(s) taken subject to		503. Existing loan(s) taken subject to	
204.		504. Payoff of first mortgage loan	70,000
205.		505. Payoff of second mortgage loan	
206.		506. Acc'd interest on loan	210
207.		507.	
208.		508.	
209.		509.	
Adjustments for items unpaid by seller		*Adjustments for items unpaid by seller*	
210. City/town taxes to		510. City/town taxes to	
211. County taxes to		511. County taxes to	
212. Assessments to		512. Assessments to	
213. Rents prepaid to 4/30	648	513. Rents prepaid to 4/30	648
214. Acc'd sewer & water charge	6	514. Acc'd sewer & water charges	6
215. Tenant security deposits	900	515. Tenant security deposits	900
216.		516.	
217.		517.	
218.		518.	
219.		519.	
220. Total Paid By/For Borrower	95,554	**520. Total Reduction Amount Due Seller**	78,350
300. Cash At Settlement From/To Borrower		**600. Cash At Settlement To/From Seller**	
301. Gross Amount due from borrower (line 120)	103,625	601. Gross amount due to Seller (line 420)	100,829
302. Less amounts paid by/for borrower (line 220) (	95,554)	602. Less reductions in amt. due seller (line 520) (	78,350)
303. Cash ☒ From ☐ To Borrower	8,071	603. Cash ☒ To ☐ From Seller	22,479

Previous Edition Is Obsolete

Great Lakes Business Forms, Inc.
Form No. 2384 (8702)

HUD 1 (3 86)
RESPA, HB 4305 2

Great Lakes Business Forms, Inc. ■
To Order Call: 1-800-530-9393 ☐ FAX 616-791-1131

FIGURE 33–6
(continued)

L. Settlement Charges

700. Total Sales/Broker's Commission based on price $ 100,000 @ 6 % = 6,000	Paid From Borrower's Funds at Settlement	Paid From Seller's Funds at Settlement
Division of Commission (line 700) as follows:		
701. $ 6,000 to Evans Realty Co.		
702. $ to		
703. Commission paid at Settlement		
704.		

800. Items Payable in Connection With Loan		
801. Loan Origination Fee 2 % $90,000		
802. Loan Discount %	1,800	
803. Appraisal Fee to A. Measure	240	
804. Credit Report to Rustic County Credit Bureau	40	
805. Lender's Inspection Fee		
806. Mortgage Insurance Application Fee to		
807. Assumption Fee		
808. Record Mortgage Satisfaction		4
809.		
810.		
811.		

900. Items Required By Lender To Be Paid in Advance		
901. Interest from 4/12 to 4/30 @$ /day	450	
902. Mortgage Insurance Premium for months to		
903. Hazard Insurance Premium for years to		
904. years to		
905.		

1000. Reserves Deposited With Lender		
1001. Hazard Insurance months @ $ per month		
1002. Mortgage Insurance months @ $ per month		
1003. City property taxes months @ $ per month		
1004. County property taxes months @ $ per month		
1005. Annual assessments months @ $ per month		
1006. months @ $ per month		
1007. months @ $ per month		
1008. months @ $ per month		

1100. Title Charges		
1101. Settlement or closing fee to Hifidelity Escrow Services	88	88
1102. Abstract or title search to		
1103. Title examination to		
1104. Title Insurance binder to		
1105. Document preparation to H. Light, Atty/Tange & Webb Attys.	40	120
1106. Notary fees to		
1107. Attorney's fees to		
(includes above items numbers:)		
1108. Title Insurance to Hifidelity Title Co.	110	360
(includes above items numbers:)		
1109. Lender's coverage $		
1110. Owner's coverage $		
1111. Federal Express; Overnight document delivered		14
1112.		
1113.		

1200. Government Recording and Transfer Charges		
1201. Recording fees: Deed $; Mortgage $; Releases $		
1202. City/county tax/stamps: Deed $; Mortgage $		
1203. State tax/stamps: Deed $; Mortgage $		
1204.		
1205.		

1300. Additional Settlement Charges		
1301. Survey to		
1302. Pest inspection to		
1303.		
1304.		
1305.		

1400. Total Settlement Charges (enter on lines 103, Section J and 502, Section K)	2,796	6,586

I have carefully reviewed the HUD-1 Settlement Statement and to the best of my knowledge and belief, it is a true and accurate statement of all receipts and disbursements made on my account or by me in this transaction. I further certify that I have received a copy of HUD-1 Settlement Statement.

_____   _____

Borrowers   Sellers

The HUD-1 Settlement Statement which I have prepared is a true and accurate account of this transaction. I have caused or will cause the funds to be disbursed in accordance with this statement.

_____   _____

Settlement Agent   Date

WARNING: It is a crime to knowingly make false statements to the United States on this or any other similar form. Penalties upon conviction can include a fine or imprisonment. For details see: Title 18 U.S. Code Section 1001 and Section 1010.

The seller, buyer, and other interested parties settle accounts at a closing. Attention must be given to many details before the closing if it is to go smoothly. These include a title search, a survey, a property inspection, an abstract and report of title, and a review of the documents involved. Also, agreement must be reached as to whether encumbrances are to be accepted by the buyer or removed by the seller.

Title passes at a closing upon delivery of the deed. In an escrow closing title passes when all conditions have been met.

The Real Estate Settlement Procedures Act places lenders at the heart of closing activity because it applies to almost all transactions involving new financing of one- to four-family homes. RESPA requires a standardized form for the disclosure of actual settlement costs at closing.

The main cost elements to a buyer in a closing are title insurance, property survey, closing fees, appraisal report, and property taxes. The RESPA settlement statement has effectively replaced the conventional buyer's and seller's closing statements.

KEY CONCEPTS

Accrued expense   A charge owed but not yet paid, such as property taxes or accrued interest.

Credit   A bookkeeping entry in a person's favor.

Prepaid expense   A charge paid in advance, such as rent or an insurance premium.

Prorate   Dividing ongoing expense and income items proportionately between a buyer and a seller in a closing statement.

QUESTIONS FOR REVIEW AND DISCUSSION

1. Explain the nature and importance of the following in the title closing process:
    a. Survey and inspection
    b. Title search and report
    c. Acceptance or removal of encumbrances
2. List and briefly explain four classes of costs and adjustments in a title closing.
3. List and explain four rules of prorating.
4. Identify two buyer and two seller closing statement entries that do not involve proration.
5. Name two buyer and two seller closing statement entries that involve proration and briefly discuss the nature of each.
6. All closings should be in escrow, by law. Discuss.
7. An escrow agent is apparently an agent of both the buyer and the seller. What are the implications of such a role? Discuss.

8. Discuss the advantages from a buyer's point of view and from a seller's of a closing being handled by each of the following:

   a. Attorney

   b. Lender

   c. Broker

   d. Escrow agent

PROBLEMS

1. Property taxes of $19,200 are payable for the current year. Closing is to be on November 10. Calculate the amount of the adjustment and indicate whether the buyer or seller gets the credit.

2. A one-year hazard insurance premium of $660 provides coverage to April 15 of next year. Calculate the amount of the adjustment for a November 10 closing and indicate whether the buyer or the seller gets the credit.

3. A building contractor listed a 4-unit apartment building for $160,000 that was to be completed for sale on October 15, 1994, with the Red Hot Realty Company. A commission rate of 5 percent on the first $100,000 and 3 percent on anything in excess of $100,000 was agreed upon in the listing contract. A buyer agreed to purchase the property for $150,000, with a stipulation for an escrow closing as of April 30, 1995. The offer was conditional upon getting a new first mortgage for $120,000 at an interest rate of 9 percent or less, compounded monthly, with amortization over 30 years. A loan at exactly these terms was obtained from the Ace Savings and Loan Association. A 10 percent earnest money deposit was submitted with the offer to purchase.

   An escrow agent was contracted to act as agent for the closing. Adjustments required of the escrow agent are as follows:

   1. Premium for title insurance, $300.

   2. The contractor's construction loan was for $100,000, at 12 percent, with interest payments of $1,000 being required on the last day of each month. The last payment was made on March 31, 1995.

   3. Taxes for 1995 are expected to be $3,000, a figure agreed to by both parties. Being new, the property was not taxed as a fully completed property in 1994.

   4. All four units are rented as follows.

      a. Lower 1: $400 per month paid for April on April 7, 1995

      b. Lower 2: $400 per month unpaid for April

      c. Upper 3: $450 per month unpaid for April

      d. Upper 4: $450 per month paid for April on April 2, 1995

   5. Escrow fee is one-half of 1 percent, all payable by the buyers because they insisted on an escrow closing.

   6. Some yard improvements are to be made later in the spring. All parties agree that $2,200, left in escrow, would ensure completion.

7. Fuel oil of 840 gallons is on hand at 90 cents per gallon.

8. Hazard insurance was prepaid for three years, with $1,080 premium paid to run from September 21, 1994.

9. A part-time custodian cares for the property for $8 per day. The expense has not been paid for April.

10. A mortgage satisfaction recording fee of $8 must be paid.

11. The legal fee for drawing up a deed to convey title is $50.

12. Cleaning supplies on hand, to be taken over by buyer, are valued at $210.

   a. Prepare a buyer's closing statement. (Additional amount to be paid by the buyer, including escrow fee, is $17,186.)

   b. Prepare a seller's closing statement. (Amount to be paid to the seller upon closing, after paying commission, is $42,618.)

TIME VALUE OF MONEY

In this appendix we present a brief discussion of the concept of the time value of money. Four elements are involved in calculating the time value of money: (1) a cash payment or a series of uniform payments, (2) a percentage rate, (3) a time period, and (4) a calculated value. Traditionally, factor tables are used for time and percentage to speed calculations.

The four elements have a fixed relationship, as expressed in the following equation:

Present value = Payment × Factor (i% interest rate, n periods)

In any application, if three of the elements are known, the fourth may be determined. It is the ability to determine unknown information that makes time value of money techniques so useful in the financial analysis of real estate.

Time value of money calculations can be done in one of two ways: by compounding or by discounting.

Compounding or Future Value

Money put into a savings account that earns interest grows. In technical terms, it compounds. Compounding means that one earns interest not only on the principal but also on the accrued interest. That is, the interest earned in period 1 is added to the principal; in period 2, interest is earned on the original principal and on the accumulated interest.

Let us look at one example that illustrates the concept. Consider an individual who deposits $100 in a savings account that pays 5 percent interest, compounded annually. What balance is in the account at the end of year 1? At the end of year 2? A simple calculation gives the answer:

$$
\begin{aligned}
\textit{EOY1 balance} &= \text{Deposit } (1 + \text{interest rate } (i)) \\
&= \text{Deposit } (1 + i) \\
&= \$100(1 + .05) \\
&= \$105
\end{aligned}
$$

Therefore, at the end of year 1, the account balance is $105. At the end of two years, the savings account is worth $110.25 because in year 2, interest at 5 percent is earned on the original deposit plus the accumulated interest from year 1: $5 is earned on the initial deposit of $100, and 25 cents is earned on the $5 of interest earned in the first year.

$$
\begin{aligned}
\textit{EOY2 balance} &= \text{Deposit } (1 + i)(1 + i) \\
&= \$100 (1 + .05)^2 \\
&= \$110.25
\end{aligned}
$$

Generalizing, the future value of a deposit at the end of n years may be calculated by the formula:

$$EOYn \text{ balance} = \text{Deposit} (1 + i)^n$$

where n is the number of years and i equals the interest rate.

The compounding of interest on $100 for 10 years at 10 percent is shown in Figure A–1. That interest is being earned on interest shows up clearly in the interest earned column. Note that the balance grows much faster at 10 percent than in our earlier example using 5 percent.

Two basic principles of compounding follow from these calculations: (1) the higher the interest rate, the faster the balance increases, and (2) the greater the number of periods, the larger the future balance.

Discounting or Present Value

Now assume you wish to have $1,000 on deposit at the end of two years. How much must you deposit now to have that balance? Again, assume an interest rate of 5 percent. Thus, the question is, "What deposit made today at 5 percent interest would grow to $1,000 two years from now?"

To calculate the future value of a cash deposit made today (a present value), we multiply the initial deposit by $(1 + i)^n$, where i equals the interest rate and n equals the number of periods. Here, we have a future balance and an interest rate. We can solve for the required initial deposit or present value by reversing the compounding process. Consequently, dividing the desired future payment by $(1 + i)^n$ will give us our desired result. In our example, if the payment were to be received at the end of year 1, it would have a present value of $952.38.

$$\text{Required deposit, } BOY1 = \frac{\text{Account balance, } EOY1}{(1 + i)^1}$$

$$= \frac{\$1,000}{1.05}$$

$$= \$952.38$$

FIGURE A–1

Ten Years of Compound Interest at 10 Percent on $100

YEAR	BALANCE, BEGINNING OF YEAR	INTEREST EARNED	BALANCE, END OF YEAR
1	$100.00	$10.00	$110.00
2	110.00	11.00	121.00
3	121.00	12.10	133.10
4	133.10	13.31	146.41
5	146.41	14.64	161.05
6	161.05	16.11	177.16
7	177.16	17.72	194.87
8	194.87	19.49	214.36
9	214.36	21.44	235.79
10	235.79	23.58	259.37

But, we are talking of two years. Repeating the calculation, we find the present value, or required deposit, for an account balance of $1,000 at the end of year 2 is $907.03.

$$\text{Required deposit, } BOY1 = \frac{\text{Desired } EOY2 \text{ balance}}{(1 + i)(1 + i)}$$

$$= \frac{\text{Desired } EOY2 \text{ balance}}{(1 + i)^2}$$

$$= \frac{\$1,000}{1.05^2}$$

$$= \frac{\$1,000}{1.1025}$$

$$= \$907.03$$

The general formula for finding the present value of a future payment to be received at the end of year n, discounted at rate i, is, therefore,

$$\text{Present value, } BOY1 = \frac{\text{Future payment, } EOY_n}{(1 + i)^n}$$

Figure A–2 shows the present value of $1,000, discounted at 10 percent, received at the end of years 1–10. Note that the required deposits are less at 10 percent than at 5 percent.

Two basic principles of discounting follow from these calculations: (1) the higher the discount rate, the smaller the present value of a future payment, and (2) the greater the number of discounting periods, the smaller the present value.

Time Value of Money Factors

Traditionally tables of precalculated factors or multipliers have been used to speed time value of money calculations. To illustrate the construction of a time value of money table, let us develop three factors by using a discount rate of 10 percent.

YEARS UNTIL $1,000 IS RECEIVED	REQUIRED DEPOSIT
1	$909.09
2	826.45
3	751.31
4	683.01
5	620.92
6	564.47
7	513.16
8	466.51
9	424.10
10	385.54

FIGURE A–2
Present Value of $1,000 Discounted at 10 Percent for 10 Years

Present Value of 1 (PV1) Factor. A *PV*1 factor converts a single payment to be received in the future into a present, lump-sum value. The general expression is:

$$PV1 \text{ factor} = \frac{1}{(1 + i)^n}$$

The *PV1* factor at 10 percent for two years is:

$$PV1 \text{ factor} = \frac{1}{(1 + .10)^2} = \frac{1}{1.21} = 0.826446.$$

Going back to the prior example and multiplying $1,000 by 0.826446 yields the deposit required to be made now in order to have $1,000 at the end of two years, assuming 10 percent interest and annual compounding.

The *PV*1 factor provides a means to calculate two other commonly used factors: the present value of an annuity (*PVAIF*) and the mortgage constant (*MC*), otherwise known as the principal recovery (*PR*) factor.

Present Value of an Annuity Interest Factor (PVAIF). Several *PV*1 factors may be used in a single problem, such as determining the discounted value of a mortgage or an annuity. Suppose we are to receive an annuity of $20 at the end of each of the next three years. Using a discount rate of 10 percent what is the present value of this series of payments? Using *PV*1 factors, we obtain an answer of $49.74.

TIME	EXPECTED PAYMENT		PV1 FACTOR		PRESENT VALUE
EOY1	$20	×	0.909091	=	$18.18
EOY2	$20	×	0.826446	=	16.53
EOY3	$20	×	0.751315	=	15.03
Total present value					$49.74

Given a *PV*1 table, we can calculate the present value of any series of future cash flows in a similar manner. However, when the future cash flows are equal, the procedure can be simplified. For one thing, we can add the factors and make up a table.

TIME	PV1 FACTOR
EOY1	0.909091
EOY2	0.826446
EOY3	0.751315
Total of factors	2.486852

The total of the *PV*1 factors for three years equals 2.486852. Multiplying 2.486852 by the $20 gives us $49.74. Thus, adding the *PV*1 factors for the desired number of years gives us a new, shortcut multiplier, termed the present value of an annuity interest factor (*PVAIF*). The PVAIF factor, used as a multiplier, converts a series of equal or level payments into a single, lump-sum present value.

A further example seems in order. Suppose that we wish to know the present value of a series of $20 payments to be received at the end of each of the next four years. The discount rate is 12 percent. Looking in the *PVAIF* column of the 12 percent annual table in the appendix, we obtain the factor, 3.037349. The present value equals $60.75, rounded.

$$\text{Present value} = \text{Payment} \times PVAIF \text{ factor (12\%, 4 years)}$$
$$= \$20 \times 3.037349$$
$$= \$60.75$$

Principal Recovery Factor

A principal recovery (*PR*) factor converts a present lump-sum amount into a series of future cash flows. Assume a lender makes a $40,000 fixed-rate loan at 10 percent to be repaid by equal end-of-year payments over four years. How much is each payment?

$$\text{Required payment} = \text{Present value} \times PR \text{ factor (10\%, 4 years)}$$
$$= \$40,000 \times 0.315471$$
$$= \$12,618.83 \text{ per year}$$

The *PR* factor allows us to calculate quickly the necessary payment of $12,618.83. A brief look at the amortization of the loan assures us that the arithmetic works out (see Figure A–3).

Principal Balance, BOY1		$40,000.00
Year 1 debt service	$12,618.83	
Less: Interest (10% × $40,000)	4,000.00	
Principal reduction	$8,618.83	−8,618.83
Principal Balance, BOY2		$31,381.17
Year 2 debt service	$12,618.83	
Less: Interest (10% × $31,381.17)	3,138.12	
Principal reduction	9,480.71	−9,480.71
Principal Balance, BOY3		$21,900.46
Year 3 debt service	$12,618.83	
Less: Interest (10% × $21,900.46)	2,190.05	
Principal reduction	10,428.78	−10,428.78
Principal Balance, BOY4		$11,471.68
Year 4 debt service	$12,618.83	
Less: Interest (10% × $11,471.68)	1,147.17	
Principal reduction	$11,471.66	$11,471.66
		$0.02[a]

FIGURE A–3
Amortization of a $40,000, 4-year, 10 Percent Loan with Annual Payments of $12,618.83

[a] Difference is due to rounding in the calculations.

Time Value of Money Tables

These time value of money tables show annual and monthly factors at the following interest rates:

6.00%	11.00%	20.00%
7.00%	12.00%	25.00%
8.00%	13.00%	30.00%
9.00%	14.00%	40.00%
10.00%	15.00%	50.00%

Symbols and Formulas for the Factors

	Annual interest rate = i $m = 12$ ANNUAL FACTORS		Number of years = n MONTHLY FACTORS	
	SYMBOL	FORMULA	SYMBOL	FORMULA
Future value of 1 factor	FV1	$(1 + i)^n$	MFV1	$(1 + i/m)^{n \times m}$
Future value of 1 per period factor	FV1/P (Table) FVAIF (Text)	$(FV1 - 1)/i$	MFV1/P (Table) MFVAIF (Text)	$(MFV1 - 1)(i/m)$
Sinking fund factor	Sff (Table) SFF (Text)	$i/(FV1 - 1)$	MSFF	$(i/m)/(MFV1 - 1)$
Present value of 1 factor	PV1	$1/FV1$	MPV1	$1/MFV1$
Present value of 1 per period factor	PV1/P (Table) PVAIF (Text)	$(1 - PV1)/i$	MPV1/P (Table) MPVAIF (Text)	$(1 - MPV1)(i/m)$
Principal recovery factor	PRF (Table) PR (Text)	$i/(PV1/P)$ (Table) PVAIF (Text)	MPRF (Table) MPR (Text)	$(i/m)/(MPV1/P)$ (Table) (i/m) (MPVAIF) (Text)

6.00% NOMINAL RATE

Annual Compounding

EFFECTIVE (ANNUAL) RATE = 6.00%

YEAR	Future Value of 1 FV1	Future Value of 1 per Period FV1/P	Sinking Fund Factor SFF	Present Value of 1 PV1	Present Value of 1 per Period PV1/P	Principal Recovery Factor PRF	YEAR
1	1.060000	1.000000	1.000000	0.943396	0.943396	1.060000	1
2	1.123600	2.060000	0.485437	0.889996	1.833393	0.545437	2
3	1.191016	3.183600	0.314110	0.839619	2.673012	0.374110	3
4	1.262477	4.374616	0.228591	0.792094	3.465106	0.288591	4
5	1.338226	5.637093	0.177396	0.747258	4.212364	0.237396	5
6	1.418519	6.975319	0.143363	0.704961	4.917324	0.203363	6
7	1.503630	8.393838	0.119135	0.665057	5.582381	0.179135	7
8	1.593848	9.897468	0.101036	0.627412	6.209794	0.161036	8
9	1.689479	11.491316	0.087022	0.591898	6.801692	0.147022	9
10	1.790848	13.180795	0.075868	0.558395	7.360087	0.135868	10
11	1.898299	14.971643	0.066793	0.526788	7.886875	0.126793	11
12	2.012196	16.869941	0.059277	0.496969	8.383844	0.119277	12
13	2.132928	18.882138	0.052960	0.468839	8.852683	0.112960	13
14	2.260904	21.015066	0.047585	0.442301	9.294984	0.107585	14
15	2.396558	23.275970	0.042963	0.417265	9.712249	0.102963	15
16	2.540352	25.672528	0.038952	0.393646	10.105895	0.098952	16
17	2.692773	28.212880	0.035445	0.371364	10.477260	0.095445	17
18	2.854339	30.905653	0.032357	0.350344	10.827603	0.092357	18
19	3.025600	33.759992	0.029621	0.330513	11.158116	0.089621	19
20	3.207135	36.785591	0.027185	0.311805	11.469921	0.087185	20

Monthly Compounding

EFFECTIVE (MONTHLY) RATE = 0.500000%

MONTH	MFV1	MFV1/P	MSSF	MPV1	MPV1/P	MPRf	MONTH
1	1.005000	1.000000	1.000000	0.995025	0.995025	1.005000	1
2	1.010025	2.005000	0.498753	0.990075	1.985099	0.503753	2
3	1.015075	3.015025	0.331672	0.985149	2.970248	0.336672	3
4	1.020151	4.030100	0.248133	0.980248	3.950496	0.253133	4
5	1.025251	5.050251	0.198010	0.975371	4.925866	0.203010	5
6	1.030378	6.075502	0.164595	0.970518	5.896384	0.169595	6
7	1.035529	7.105879	0.140729	0.965690	6.862074	0.145729	7

YEAR						
8	0.127829	7.822959	0.960885	0.122829	8.141409	1.040707
9	0.113907	8.779064	0.956105	0.108907	9.182116	1.045911
10	0.102771	9.730412	0.951348	0.097771	10.228026	1.051140
11	0.093659	10.677027	0.946615	0.088659	11.279167	1.056396

YEAR						
1	0.086066	11.618932	0.941905	0.081066	12.335562	1.061678
2	0.044321	22.562866	0.887186	0.039321	25.431955	1.127160
3	0.030422	32.871016	0.835645	0.025422	39.336105	1.196681
4	0.023485	42.580318	0.787098	0.018485	54.097832	1.270498
5	0.019333	51.725561	0.741372	0.014333	69.770031	1.348850
6	0.016573	60.339514	0.698302	0.011573	86.408856	1.432044
7	0.014609	68.453042	0.657735	0.009609	104.073927	1.520370
8	0.013141	76.095218	0.619524	0.008141	122.828542	1.614143
9	0.012006	83.293424	0.583533	0.007006	142.739900	1.713699
10	0.011102	90.073453	0.549633	0.006102	163.879347	1.819397
11	0.010367	96.459599	0.517702	0.005367	186.322629	1.931613
12	0.009759	102.474743	0.487626	0.004759	210.150163	2.050751
13	0.009247	108.140440	0.459298	0.004247	235.447328	2.177237
14	0.008812	113.476990	0.432615	0.003812	262.304766	2.311524
15	0.008439	118.503515	0.407482	0.003439	290.818712	2.454094
16	0.008114	123.238025	0.383810	0.003114	321.091337	2.605457
17	0.007831	127.697486	0.361513	0.002831	353.231110	2.766156
18	0.007582	131.897876	0.340511	0.002582	387.353194	2.936766
19	0.007361	135.854246	0.320729	0.002361	423.579854	3.117899
20	0.007164	139.580772	0.302096	0.002164	462.040895	3.310204
21	0.006989	143.090806	0.284546	0.001989	502.874129	3.514371
22	0.006831	146.396927	0.268015	0.001831	546.225867	3.731129
23	0.006688	149.510979	0.252445	0.001688	592.251446	3.961257
24	0.006560	152.444121	0.237779	0.001560	641.115782	4.205579
25	0.006443	155.206864	0.223966	0.001443	692.993962	4.464970
26	0.006337	157.809106	0.210954	0.001337	748.071876	4.740359
27	0.006240	160.260172	0.198669	0.001240	806.546875	5.032734
28	0.006151	162.568844	0.187156	0.001151	868.628484	5.343142
29	0.006070	164.743394	0.176283	0.001070	934.539150	5.672696
30	0.005996	166.791614	0.166042	0.000996	1004.515042	6.022575

7.00% NOMINAL RATE

Annual Compounding

EFFECTIVE (ANNUAL) RATE = 7.00%

YEAR	Future Value of 1 — FV1	Future Value of 1 per Period — FV1/P	Sinking Fund Factor — SFF	Present Value of 1 — PV1	Present Value of 1 per Period — PV1/P	Principal Recovery Factor — PRF	YEAR
1	1.070000	1.000000	1.000000	0.934579	0.934579	1.070000	1
2	1.144900	2.070000	0.483092	0.873439	1.808018	0.553092	2
3	1.225043	3.214900	0.311052	0.816298	2.624316	0.381052	3
4	1.310796	4.439943	0.225228	0.762895	3.387211	0.295228	4
5	1.402552	5.750539	0.173891	0.712986	4.100197	0.243891	5
6	1.500730	7.153291	0.139796	0.666342	4.766540	0.209796	6
7	1.605781	8.654021	0.115553	0.622750	5.389289	0.185553	7
8	1.718186	10.259803	0.097468	0.582009	5.971299	0.167468	8
9	1.838459	11.977989	0.083486	0.543934	6.515232	0.153486	9
10	1.967151	13.816448	0.072378	0.508349	7.023582	0.142378	10
11	2.104852	15.783599	0.063357	0.475093	7.498674	0.133357	11
12	2.252192	17.888451	0.055902	0.444012	7.942686	0.125902	12
13	2.409845	20.140643	0.049651	0.414964	8.357651	0.119651	13
14	2.578534	22.550488	0.044345	0.378817	8.745468	0.114345	14
15	2.759032	25.129022	0.039795	0.362446	9.107914	0.109795	15
16	2.952164	27.888054	0.035858	0.338735	9.446649	0.105858	16
17	3.158815	30.840217	0.032425	0.316574	9.763223	0.102425	17
18	3.379932	33.999033	0.029413	0.295864	10.059087	0.099413	18
19	3.616528	37.378965	0.026753	0.276508	10.335595	0.096753	19
20	3.869684	40.995492	0.024393	0.258419	10.594014	0.094393	20

Monthly Compounding

EFFECTIVE (MONTHLY) RATE = 0.583333%

MONTH	MFV1	MFV1/P	MSSF	MPV1	MPV1/P	MPRF	MONTH
1	1.005833	1.000000	1.000000	0.994200	0.994200	1.005833	1
2	1.011701	2.005833	0.498546	0.988435	1.982635	0.594379	2
3	1.017602	3.017534	0.331396	0.982702	2.965337	0.337230	3
4	1.023538	4.035136	0.247823	0.977003	3.942340	0.253656	4
5	1.029509	5.058675	0.197680	0.971337	4.913677	0.203514	5
6	1.035514	6.088184	0.164253	0.965704	5.879381	0.170086	6
7	1.041555	7.123698	0.140377	0.960103	6.839484	0.146210	7

YEAR						
8	1.047631	8.165253	0.122470	0.954535	7.794019	0.128304
9	1.053742	9.212883	0.108544	0.948999	8.743018	0.114377
10	1.059889	10.266625	0.097403	0.943495	9.686513	0.103236
11	1.066071	11.326514	0.088288	0.938024	10.624537	0.094122

YEAR						
1	1.072290	12.392585	0.080693	0.932583	11.557120	0.086527
2	1.149806	25.681032	0.038939	0.869712	22.335099	0.044773
3	1.232926	39.930101	0.025044	0.811079	32.386464	0.030877
4	1.322054	55.209236	0.018113	0.756399	41.760201	0.023946
5	1.417625	71.592902	0.013968	0.705405	50.501994	0.109801
6	1.520106	89.160944	0.011216	0.657849	58.654444	0.017049
7	1.629994	107.998981	0.009259	0.613499	66.257285	0.015093
8	1.747826	128.198821	0.007800	0.572139	73.347569	0.013634
9	1.874177	149.858909	0.006673	0.533568	79.959850	0.012506
10	2.009661	173.084807	0.005778	0.497596	86.126354	0.011611
11	2.154940	197.989707	0.005051	0.464050	91.877134	0.010884
12	2.310721	224.694985	0.004450	0.432765	97.240216	0.010284
13	2.477763	253.330789	0.003947	0.403590	102.241738	0.009781
14	2.656881	284.036677	0.003521	0.376381	106.906074	0.009354
15	2.848947	316.962297	0.003155	0.351007	111.255958	0.008988
16	3.054897	352.268112	0.002839	0.327343	115.312587	0.008672
17	3.275736	390.126188	0.002563	0.305275	119.095732	0.008397
18	3.512539	430.721027	0.002322	0.284694	122.623831	0.008155
19	3.766461	474.250470	0.002109	0.265501	125.914077	0.007942
20	4.038739	520.926660	0.001920	0.247602	128.982506	0.007753
21	4.330700	570.977075	0.001751	0.230910	131.844073	0.007585
22	4.643766	624.645640	0.001601	0.215342	134.512723	0.007434
23	4.979464	682.193909	0.001466	0.200825	137.001461	0.007299
24	5.339430	743.902347	0.001344	0.187285	139.322418	0.007178
25	5.725418	810.071693	0.001234	0.174660	141.486903	0.007068
26	6.139309	881.024427	0.001135	0.162885	143.505467	0.006968
27	6.583120	957.106339	0.001045	0.151904	145.387946	0.006878
28	7.059015	1038.688219	0.000963	0.141663	147.143515	0.006796
29	7.569311	1126.167659	0.000888	0.132112	148.780729	0.006721
30	8.116497	1219.970996	0.000820	0.123206	150.307568	0.006653

8.00% NOMINAL RATE

Annual Compounding

EFFECTIVE (ANNUAL) RATE = 8.00%

YEAR	Future Value of 1 (FV1)	Future Value of 1 per Period (FV1/P)	Sinking Fund Factor (SFF)	Present Value of 1 (PV1)	Present Value of 1 per Period (PV1/P)	Principal Recovery Factor (PRF)	YEAR
1	1.080000	1.000000	1.000000	0.925926	0.925926	1.080000	1
2	1.166400	2.080000	0.480769	0.857339	1.783265	0.560769	2
3	1.259712	3.246400	0.308034	0.793832	2.577097	0.388034	3
4	1.360489	4.506112	0.221921	0.735030	3.312127	0.301921	4
5	1.469328	5.866601	0.170456	0.680583	3.992710	0.250456	5
6	1.586874	7.335929	0.136315	0.630170	4.622880	0.216315	6
7	1.713824	8.922803	0.112072	0.583490	5.206370	0.192072	7
8	1.850930	10.636628	0.094015	0.540269	5.746639	0.174015	8
9	1.999005	12.487558	0.080080	0.500249	6.246888	0.160080	9
10	2.158925	14.486562	0.069029	0.463193	6.710081	0.149029	10
11	2.331639	16.645487	0.060076	0.428883	7.138964	0.140076	11
12	2.518170	18.977126	0.052695	0.397114	7.536078	0.132695	12
13	2.719624	21.495297	0.046522	0.367698	7.903776	0.126522	13
14	2.937194	24.214920	0.041297	0.340461	8.244237	0.121297	14
15	3.172169	27.152114	0.036830	0.315242	8.559479	0.116830	15
16	3.425943	30.324283	0.032977	0.291890	8.851369	0.112977	16
17	3.700018	33.750226	0.029629	0.270269	9.121638	0.109629	17
18	3.996019	37.450244	0.026702	0.250249	9.371887	0.106702	18
19	4.315701	41.446263	0.024128	0.231712	9.603599	0.104128	19
20	4.660957	45.761964	0.021852	0.214548	9.818147	0.101852	20

Monthly Compounding

EFFECTIVE (MONTHLY) RATE = 0.666667%

MONTH	MFV1	MFV1/P	MSSF	MPV1	MPV1/P	MPRF	MONTH
1	1.006667	1.000000	1.000000	0.993377	0.993377	1.006667	1
2	1.013378	2.006667	0.498339	0.986799	1.980176	0.505006	2
3	1.020134	3.020044	0.331121	0.980264	2.960440	0.337788	3
4	1.026935	4.040178	0.247514	0.973772	3.934212	0.254181	4
5	1.033781	5.067113	0.197351	0.967323	4.901535	0.204018	5
6	1.040673	6.100893	0.163910	0.960917	5.862452	0.170577	6
7	1.047610	7.141566	0.140025	0.954553	6.817005	0.146692	7

YEAR						
8	1.054595	8.189176	0.122112	0.948232	7.765237	0.128779
9	1.061625	9.243771	0.108181	0.941952	8.707189	0.114848
10	1.068703	10.305396	0.097037	0.935714	9.642903	0.103703
11	1.075827	11.374099	0.087919	0.929517	10.572420	0.094586

YEAR						
1	1.083000	12.449926	0.080322	0.923361	11.495782	0.086988
2	1.172888	25.933190	0.038561	0.852596	22.110544	0.045227
3	1.270237	40.535558	0.024670	0.787255	31.911806	0.031336
4	1.375666	56.349915	0.017746	0.726921	40.961913	0.024413
5	1.489846	73.476856	0.013610	0.671210	49.318443	0.020276
6	1.613502	92.025325	0.010867	0.619770	57.034522	0.017533
7	1.747422	112.113308	0.008920	0.572272	64.159261	0.015586
8	1.892457	133.868583	0.007470	0.528414	70.737970	0.014137
9	2.049530	157.429535	0.006352	0.487917	76.812497	0.013019
10	2.219640	182.946035	0.005466	0.450523	82.421481	0.012133
11	2.403869	210.580392	0.004749	0.415996	87.600600	0.011415
12	2.603389	240.508387	0.004158	0.384115	92.382800	0.010825
13	2.819469	272.920390	0.003664	0.354677	96.798498	0.010331
14	3.053484	308.022574	0.003247	0.327495	100.875784	0.009913
15	3.306921	346.038222	0.002890	0.302396	104.640592	0.009557
16	3.581394	387.209149	0.002583	0.279221	108.116871	0.009249
17	3.878648	431.797244	0.002316	0.257822	111.326733	0.008983
18	4.200574	480.086128	0.002083	0.238063	114.290596	0.008750
19	4.549220	532.382966	0.001878	0.219818	117.027313	0.008545
20	4.926803	589.020416	0.001698	0.202971	119.554292	0.008364
21	5.335725	650.358746	0.001538	0.187416	121.887606	0.008204
22	5.778588	716.788127	0.001395	0.173053	124.042099	0.008062
23	6.258207	788.731114	0.001268	0.159790	126.031475	0.007935
24	6.777636	866.645333	0.001154	0.147544	127.868388	0.007821
25	7.340176	951.026395	0.001051	0.136237	129.564523	0.007718
26	7.979407	1042.411042	0.000959	0.125796	131.130668	0.007626
27	8.609204	1141.380571	0.000876	0.116155	132.576786	0.007543
28	9.323763	1248.564521	0.000801	0.107253	133.912076	0.007468
29	10.097631	1364.644687	0.000733	0.099033	135.145031	0.007399
30	10.935730	1490.359449	0.000671	0.091443	136.283494	0.007338

9.00% NOMINAL RATE

Annual Compounding

EFFECTIVE (ANNUAL) RATE = 9.00%

YEAR	Future Value of 1 FV1	Future Value of 1 per Period FV1/P	Sinking Fund Factor SFF	Present Value of 1 PV1	Present Value of 1 per Period PV1/P	Principal Recovery Factor PRF	YEAR
1	1.090000	1.000000	1.000000	0.917431	0.917431	1.090000	1
2	1.188100	2.090000	0.478469	0.841680	1.759111	0.568469	2
3	1.295029	3.278100	0.305055	0.772183	2.531295	0.395055	3
4	1.411582	4.573129	0.218669	0.708425	3.239720	0.308669	4
5	1.538624	5.984711	0.167092	0.649931	3.889651	0.257092	5
6	1.677100	7.523335	0.132920	0.596267	4.485919	0.222920	6
7	1.828039	9.200435	0.108691	0.547034	5.032953	0.198691	7
8	1.992563	11.028474	0.090674	0.501866	5.534819	0.180674	8
9	2.171893	13.021036	0.076799	0.460428	5.995247	0.166799	9
10	2.367364	15.192930	0.065820	0.422411	6.417658	0.155820	10
11	2.580426	17.560293	0.056947	0.387533	6.805191	0.146947	11
12	2.812665	20.140720	0.049651	0.355535	7.160725	0.139651	12
13	3.065805	22.953385	0.043567	0.326179	7.486904	0.133567	13
14	3.341727	26.019189	0.038433	0.299246	7.786150	0.128433	14
15	3.642482	29.360916	0.034059	0.274538	8.060688	0.124059	15
16	3.970306	33.003399	0.030300	0.251870	8.312558	0.120300	16
17	4.327633	36.973705	0.027046	0.231073	8.543631	0.117046	17
18	4.717120	41.301338	0.024212	0.211994	8.755625	0.114212	18
19	5.141661	46.018458	0.021730	0.194490	8.950115	0.111730	19
20	5.604411	51.160120	0.019546	0.178431	9.128546	0.109546	20

Monthly Compounding

EFFECTIVE (MONTHLY) RATE = 0.750000%

MONTH	MFV1	MFV1/P	MSSF	MPV1	MPV1/P	MPRF	MONTH
1	1.007500	1.000000	1.000000	0.992556	0.992556	1.007500	1
2	1.015056	2.007500	0.498132	0.985167	1.977723	0.505632	2
3	1.022669	3.022556	0.330846	0.977833	2.955556	0.338346	3
4	1.030339	4.045225	0.247205	0.970554	3.926110	0.254705	4
5	1.038067	5.075565	0.197022	0.963329	4.889440	0.204522	5
6	1.045852	6.113631	0.163569	0.956158	5.845598	0.171069	6
7	1.053696	7.159484	0.139675	0.949040	6.794638	0.147175	7

YEAR						YEAR
8	1.061599	8.213180	0.121756	0.941975	7.736613	0.129256
9	1.069561	9.274779	0.107819	0.934963	8.671576	0.115319
10	1.077583	10.344339	0.096671	0.928003	9.599580	0.104171
11	1.085664	11.421922	0.087551	0.921095	10.520675	0.095051

YEAR						YEAR
1	1.093807	12.507586	0.079951	0.914238	11.434913	0.087451
2	1.196414	26.188471	0.038185	0.835831	21.889146	0.045685
3	1.308645	41.152716	0.024300	0.764149	31.446805	0.031800
4	1.431405	57.520711	0.017385	0.698614	40.184782	0.024885
5	1.565681	75.424137	0.013258	0.638700	48.173374	0.020758
6	1.712553	95.007028	0.010526	0.583924	55.476849	0.018026
7	1.873202	116.426928	0.008589	0.533845	62.153965	0.016089
8	2.048921	139.856164	0.007150	0.488062	68.258439	0.014650
9	2.241124	165.438223	0.006043	0.446205	73.839382	0.013543
10	2.451357	193.514277	0.005168	0.407937	78.941693	0.012668
11	2.681311	224.174837	0.004461	0.372952	83.606420	0.011961
12	2.932837	257.711570	0.003880	0.340967	87.871092	0.011380
13	3.207957	294.394279	0.003397	0.311725	91.770018	0.010897
14	3.508886	334.518079	0.002989	0.284991	95.334564	0.010489
15	3.838043	378.405769	0.002643	0.260549	98.593409	0.010143
16	4.198078	426.410427	0.002345	0.238204	101.572769	0.009845
17	4.591887	478.918252	0.002088	0.217775	104.296613	0.009588
18	5.022638	536.351674	0.001864	0.199099	106.786856	0.009364
19	5.493796	599.172747	0.001669	0.182024	109.063531	0.009169
20	6.009152	667.886870	0.001497	0.166413	111.144954	0.008997
21	6.572851	743.046852	0.001346	0.152141	113.047870	0.008846
22	7.189430	825.257358	0.001212	0.139093	114.787589	0.008712
23	7.863848	915.179777	0.001093	0.127164	116.378106	0.008593
24	8.601532	1013.537539	0.000987	0.116258	117.832218	0.008487
25	9.408415	1121.121937	0.000892	0.106288	119.161622	0.008392
26	10.290989	1238.798495	0.000807	0.097172	120.377014	0.008307
27	11.256354	1367.513924	0.000731	0.088639	121.488172	0.008231
28	12.312278	1508.303750	0.000663	0.081220	122.504035	0.008163
29	13.467255	1662.300631	0.000602	0.074254	123.432776	0.008102
30	14.730576	1830.743483	0.000546	0.067886	124.281866	0.008046

10.00% NOMINAL RATE

Annual Compounding

EFFECTIVE (ANNUAL) RATE = 10.00%

YEAR	Future Value of 1 FV1	Future Value of 1 per Period FV1/P	Sinking Fund Factor SFF	Present Value of 1 PV1	Present Value of 1 per Period PV1/P	Principal Recovery Factor PRF	YEAR
1	1.100000	1.000000	1.000000	0.909091	0.909091	1.100000	1
2	1.210000	2.100000	0.476190	0.826446	1.735537	0.576190	2
3	1.331000	3.310000	0.302115	0.751315	2.486852	0.402115	3
4	1.464100	4.641000	0.215471	0.683013	3.169865	0.315471	4
5	1.610510	6.105100	0.163797	0.620921	3.790787	0.263797	5
6	1.771561	7.715610	0.129607	0.564474	4.355261	0.229607	6
7	1.948717	9.487171	0.105405	0.513158	4.868419	0.205405	7
8	2.143589	11.435888	0.087444	0.466507	5.334926	0.187444	8
9	2.357948	13.579477	0.073641	0.424098	5.759024	0.173641	9
10	2.593742	15.937425	0.062745	0.385543	6.144567	0.162745	10
11	2.853117	18.531167	0.053963	0.350494	6.495061	0.153963	11
12	3.138428	21.384284	0.046763	0.318631	6.813692	0.146763	12
13	3.452271	24.522712	0.040779	0.289664	7.103356	0.140779	13
14	3.797498	27.974983	0.035746	0.263331	7.366687	0.135746	14
15	4.177248	31.772482	0.031474	0.239392	7.606080	0.131474	15
16	4.594973	35.949730	0.027817	0.217629	7.823709	0.127817	16
17	5.054470	40.544703	0.024664	0.197845	8.021553	0.124664	17
18	5.559917	45.599173	0.021930	0.179859	8.201412	0.121930	18
19	6.115909	51.159090	0.019547	0.163508	8.364920	0.119547	19
20	6.727500	57.274999	0.017460	0.148644	8.513564	0.117460	20

Monthly Compounding

EFFECTIVE (MONTHLY) RATE = 0.833333%

MONTH	MFV1	MFV1/P	MSSF	MPV1	MPV1/P	MPRF	MONTH
1	1.008333	1.000000	1.000000	0.991736	0.991736	1.008333	1
2	1.016736	2.008333	0.497925	0.983539	1.975275	0.506259	2
3	1.025209	3.025069	0.330571	0.975411	2.950686	0.338904	3
4	1.033752	4.050278	0.246897	0.967350	3.918036	0.255230	4
5	1.042367	5.084031	0.196694	0.959355	4.877391	0.205028	5
6	1.051053	6.126398	0.163228	0.951427	5.828817	0.171561	6

YEAR					
7	1.059812	7.177451	0.139325	0.943563	6.772381	0.147659
8	1.068644	8.237263	0.121400	0.935765	7.708146	0.129733
9	1.077549	9.305907	0.107459	0.928032	8.636178	0.115792
10	1.086529	10.383456	0.096307	0.920362	9.556540	0.104640
11	1.095583	11.469985	0.087184	0.912756	10.469296	0.095517

YEAR					
1	1.104713	12.565568	0.079583	0.905212	11.374508	0.087916
2	1.220391	26.446915	0.037812	0.819410	21.670855	0.046145
3	1.348182	41.781821	0.023934	0.741740	30.991236	0.032267
4	1.489354	58.722492	0.017029	0.671432	39.428160	0.025363
5	1.645309	77.437072	0.012914	0.607789	47.065369	0.021247
6	1.817594	98.111314	0.010193	0.550178	53.978665	0.018526
7	2.007920	120.950418	0.008268	0.498028	60.236667	0.016601
8	2.218176	146.181076	0.006841	0.450821	65.901488	0.015174
9	2.450448	174.053713	0.005745	0.408089	71.029355	0.014079
10	2.707041	204.844979	0.004882	0.369407	75.671163	0.013215
11	2.990504	238.860493	0.004187	0.334392	79.872986	0.012520
12	3.303649	276.437876	0.003617	0.302696	83.676528	0.011951
13	3.649584	317.950102	0.003145	0.274004	87.119542	0.011478
14	4.031743	363.809201	0.002749	0.248032	90.236201	0.011082
15	4.453920	414.470346	0.002413	0.224521	93.057439	0.010746
16	4.920303	470.436376	0.002126	0.203240	95.611259	0.010459
17	5.435523	532.262780	0.001879	0.183975	97.923008	0.010212
18	6.004693	600.563216	0.001665	0.166536	100.015633	0.009998
19	6.633463	676.015601	0.001479	0.150751	101.909902	0.009813
20	7.328074	759.368836	0.001317	0.136462	103.624619	0.009650
21	8.095419	851.450244	0.001174	0.123527	105.176801	0.009508
22	8.943115	953.173779	0.001049	0.111818	106.581856	0.009382
23	9.879576	1065.549097	0.000938	0.101219	107.853730	0.009272
24	10.914097	1189.691580	0.000841	0.091625	109.005054	0.009174
25	12.056945	1326.833403	0.000754	0.082940	110.047230	0.009087
26	13.319465	1478.335767	0.000676	0.075078	110.990629	0.009010
27	14.714187	1645.702407	0.000608	0.067962	111.844605	0.008941
28	16.254954	1830.594523	0.000546	0.061520	112.617635	0.008880
29	17.957060	2034.847258	0.000491	0.055688	113.317392	0.008825
30	19.837399	2260.487925	0.000442	0.050410	113.950820	0.008776

11.00% NOMINAL RATE

Annual Compounding

EFFECTIVE (ANNUAL) RATE = 11.00%

YEAR	Future Value of 1 — FV1	Future Value of 1 per Period — FV1/P	Sinking Fund Factor — SFF	Present Value of 1 — PV1	Present Value of 1 per Period — PV1/P	Principal Recovery Factor — PRF	YEAR
1	1.110000	1.000000	1.000000	0.900901	0.900901	1.110000	1
2	1.232100	2.110000	0.473934	0.811622	1.712523	0.583934	2
3	1.367631	3.342100	0.299213	0.731191	2.443715	0.409213	3
4	1.518070	4.709731	0.212326	0.658731	3.102446	0.322326	4
5	1.685058	6.227801	0.160570	0.593451	3.695897	0.270570	5
6	1.870415	7.912860	0.126377	0.534641	4.230538	0.236377	6
7	2.076160	9.783274	0.102215	0.481658	4.712196	0.212215	7
8	2.304538	11.859434	0.084321	0.433926	5.146123	0.194321	8
9	2.558037	14.163972	0.070602	0.390925	5.537048	0.180602	9
10	2.839421	16.722009	0.059801	0.352184	5.889232	0.169801	10
11	3.151757	19.561430	0.051121	0.317283	6.206515	0.161121	11
12	3.498451	22.713187	0.044027	0.285841	6.492356	0.154027	12
13	3.883280	26.211638	0.038151	0.257514	6.749870	0.148151	13
14	4.310441	30.094918	0.033228	0.231995	6.981865	0.143228	14
15	4.784589	34.405359	0.029065	0.209004	7.190870	0.139065	15
16	5.310894	39.189948	0.025517	0.188292	7.379162	0.135517	16
17	5.895093	44.500843	0.022471	0.169633	7.548794	0.132471	17
18	6.543553	50.395936	0.019843	0.152822	7.701617	0.129843	18
19	7.263344	56.939488	0.017563	0.137678	7.839294	0.127563	19
20	8.062312	64.202312	0.015576	0.124034	7.963328	0.125576	20

Monthly Compounding

EFFECTIVE (MONTHLY) RATE = 0.916667%

MONTH	MFV1	MFV1/P	MSSF	MPV1	MPV1/P	MPRF	MONTH
1	1.009167	1.000000	1.000000	0.990917	0.990917	1.009167	1
2	1.018417	2.009167	0.497719	0.981916	1.972832	0.506885	2
3	1.027753	3.027584	0.330296	0.972997	2.945829	0.339463	3
4	1.037174	4.055337	0.246589	0.964158	3.909987	0.255755	4
5	1.046681	5.092511	0.196367	0.955401	4.865388	0.205533	5
6	1.056276	6.139192	0.162888	0.946722	5.812110	0.172055	6
7	1.065958	7.195468	0.138976	0.938123	6.750233	0.148143	7

YEAR						
8	1.075730	8.261427	0.121044	0.929602	7.679835	0.130211
9	1.085591	9.337156	0.107099	0.921158	8.600992	0.116266
10	1.095542	10.422747	0.095944	0.912790	9.513783	0.105111
11	1.105584	11.518289	0.086818	0.904499	10.418282	0.095985

YEAR						
1	1.115719	12.623873	0.079215	0.896283	11.314565	0.088382
2	1.244829	26.708566	0.037441	0.803323	21.455619	0.046608
3	1.388879	42.423123	0.023572	0.720005	30.544874	0.032739
4	1.549598	59.956151	0.016679	0.645329	38.691421	0.025846
5	1.728916	79.518080	0.012576	0.578397	45.993034	0.021742
6	1.928984	101.343692	0.009867	0.518408	52.537346	0.019034
7	2.152204	125.694940	0.007956	0.464640	58.402903	0.017122
8	2.401254	152.864085	0.006542	0.416449	63.660103	0.015708
9	2.679124	183.177212	0.005459	0.373256	68.372043	0.014626
10	2.989150	216.998139	0.004608	0.334543	72.595275	0.013775
11	3.335051	254.732784	0.003926	0.299846	76.380487	0.013092
12	3.720979	296.834038	0.003369	0.268747	79.773109	0.012536
13	4.151566	343.807200	0.002909	0.240873	82.813859	0.012075
14	4.631980	396.216042	0.002524	0.215890	85.539231	0.011691
15	5.167988	454.689575	0.002199	0.193499	87.981937	0.011366
16	5.766021	519.929596	0.001923	0.173430	90.171293	0.011090
17	6.433259	592.719117	0.001687	0.155442	92.133576	0.010854
18	7.177708	673.931757	0.001484	0.139320	93.892337	0.010650
19	8.008304	764.542228	0.001308	0.124870	95.468685	0.010475
20	8.935015	865.638038	0.001155	0.111919	96.881539	0.010322
21	9.968965	978.432537	0.001022	0.100311	98.147856	0.010189
22	11.122562	1104.279485	0.000906	0.089907	99.282835	0.010072
23	12.409652	1244.689295	0.000803	0.080582	100.300098	0.009970
24	13.845682	1401.347165	0.000714	0.072225	101.211853	0.009880
25	15.447889	1576.133301	0.000634	0.064734	102.029044	0.009801
26	17.235500	1771.145485	0.000565	0.058020	102.761478	0.009731
27	19.229972	1988.724252	0.000503	0.052002	103.417947	0.009670
28	21.455242	2231.480981	0.000448	0.046609	104.006328	0.009615
29	23.938018	2502.329236	0.000400	0.041775	104.533685	0.009566
30	26.708098	2804.519736	0.000357	0.037442	105.006346	0.009523

12.00% NOMINAL RATE

Annual Compounding

EFFECTIVE (ANNUAL) RATE = 12.00%

YEAR	Future Value of 1 FV1	Future Value of 1 per Period FV1/P	Sinking Fund Factor SFF	Present Value of 1 PV1	Present Value of 1 per Period PV1/P	Principal Recovery Factor PRF	YEAR
1	1.120000	1.000000	1.000000	0.892857	0.892857	1.120000	1
2	1.254400	2.120000	0.471698	0.797194	1.690051	0.591698	2
3	1.404928	3.374400	0.296349	0.711780	2.401831	0.416349	3
4	1.573519	4.779328	0.209234	0.635518	3.037349	0.329234	4
5	1.762342	6.352847	0.157410	0.567427	3.604776	0.277410	5
6	1.973823	8.115189	0.123226	0.506631	4.111407	0.243226	6
7	2.210681	10.089012	0.099118	0.452349	4.563757	0.219118	7
8	2.475963	12.299693	0.081303	0.403883	4.967640	0.201303	8
9	2.773079	14.775656	0.067679	0.360610	5.328250	0.187679	9
10	3.105848	17.548735	0.056984	0.321973	5.650223	0.176984	10
11	3.478550	20.654583	0.048415	0.287476	5.937699	0.168415	11
12	3.895976	24.133133	0.041437	0.256675	6.194374	0.161437	12
13	4.363493	28.029109	0.035677	0.229174	6.423548	0.155677	13
14	4.887112	32.392602	0.030871	0.204620	6.628168	0.150871	14
15	5.473566	37.279715	0.026824	0.182696	6.810864	0.146824	15
16	6.130394	42.753280	0.023390	0.163122	6.973986	0.143390	16
17	6.866041	48.883674	0.020457	0.145644	7.119630	0.140457	17
18	7.689966	55.749715	0.017937	0.130040	7.249670	0.137937	18
19	8.612762	63.439681	0.015763	0.116107	7.365777	0.135763	19
20	9.646293	72.052442	0.013879	0.103667	7.469444	0.133879	20

Monthly Compounding

EFFECTIVE (MONTHLY) RATE = 1.000000%

MONTH	MFV1	MFV1/P	MSSF	MPV1	MPV1/P	MPRF	MONTH
1	1.010000	1.000000	1.000000	0.990099	0.990099	1.010000	1
2	1.020100	2.010000	0.497512	0.980296	1.970395	0.507512	2
3	1.030301	3.030100	0.330022	0.970590	2.940985	0.340022	3
4	1.040604	4.060401	0.246281	0.960980	3.901966	0.256281	4
5	1.051010	5.101005	0.196040	0.951466	4.853431	0.206040	5
6	1.061520	6.152015	0.162548	0.942045	5.795476	0.172548	6
7	1.072135	7.213535	0.138628	0.932718	6.728195	0.148628	7

YEAR						
8	0.130690	7.651678	0.923483	0.120690	8.285671	1.082857
9	0.116740	8.566018	0.914340	0.106740	9.368527	1.093685
10	0.105582	9.471305	0.905287	0.095582	10.462213	1.104622
11	0.096454	10.367628	0.896324	0.086454	11.566835	1.115668

YEAR						
1	0.088849	11.255077	0.887449	0.078849	12.682503	1.126825
2	0.047073	21.243387	0.787566	0.037073	26.973465	1.269735
3	0.033214	30.107505	0.698925	0.023214	43.076878	1.430769
4	0.026334	37.973959	0.620260	0.016334	61.222608	1.612226
5	0.022244	44.955038	0.550450	0.012244	81.669670	1.816697
6	0.019550	51.150391	0.488496	0.009550	104.709931	2.047099
7	0.017653	56.648453	0.433515	0.007653	130.672274	2.306723
8	0.016252	61.527703	0.384723	0.006253	159.927293	2.599273
9	0.015184	65.857790	0.341422	0.005184	192.892579	2.928926
10	0.014347	69.700522	0.302995	0.004347	230.038689	3.300387
11	0.013678	73.110752	0.268892	0.003678	271.895856	3.718959
12	0.013134	76.137157	0.238628	0.003134	319.061559	4.190616
13	0.012687	78.822939	0.211771	0.002687	372.209054	4.722091
14	0.012314	81.206434	0.187936	0.002314	432.096982	5.320970
15	0.012002	83.321664	0.166783	0.002002	499.580198	5.995802
16	0.011737	85.198824	0.148012	0.001737	575.621974	6.756220
17	0.011512	86.864707	0.131353	0.001512	661.307751	7.613078
18	0.011320	88.343095	0.116569	0.001320	757.860630	8.578606
19	0.011154	89.655089	0.103449	0.001154	866.658830	9.666588
20	0.011011	90.819416	0.091806	0.001011	989.255365	10.892554
21	0.010887	91.852698	0.081473	0.000887	1127.400210	12.274002
22	0.010779	92.769683	0.072303	0.000779	1283.065279	13.830653
23	0.010686	93.583461	0.064165	0.000686	1458.472574	15.584726
24	0.010604	94.305647	0.056944	0.000604	1656.125905	17.561259
25	0.010532	94.946551	0.050534	0.000532	1878.846626	19.788466
26	0.010470	95.515321	0.044847	0.000470	2129.813909	22.298139
27	0.010414	96.020075	0.039799	0.000414	2412.610125	25.126101
28	0.010366	96.468019	0.035320	0.000366	2731.271980	28.312720
29	0.010324	96.865546	0.031345	0.000324	3090.348134	31.903481
30	0.010286	97.218331	0.027817	0.000286	3494.964133	35.949641

13.00% NOMINAL RATE

Annual Compounding

EFFECTIVE (ANNUAL) RATE = 13.00%

YEAR	Future Value of 1 (FV1)	Future Value of 1 per Period (FV1/P)	Sinking Fund Factor (SFF)	Present Value of 1 (PV1)	Present Value of 1 per Period (PV1/P)	Principal Recovery Factor (PRF)	YEAR
1	1.130000	1.000000	1.000000	0.884956	0.884956	1.130000	1
2	1.276900	2.130000	0.469484	0.783147	1.668102	0.599484	2
3	1.442897	3.406900	0.293522	0.693050	2.361153	0.423522	3
4	1.630474	4.849797	0.206194	0.613319	2.974471	0.336194	4
5	1.842435	6.480271	0.154315	0.542760	3.517231	0.284315	5
6	2.081952	8.322706	0.120153	0.480319	3.997550	0.250153	6
7	2.352605	10.404658	0.096111	0.425061	4.422610	0.226111	7
8	2.658444	12.757263	0.078387	0.376160	4.798770	0.208387	8
9	3.004042	15.415707	0.064869	0.332885	5.131655	0.194869	9
10	3.394567	18.419749	0.054290	0.294588	5.426243	0.184290	10
11	3.835861	21.814317	0.045841	0.260698	5.686941	0.175841	11
12	4.334523	25.650178	0.038986	0.230706	5.917647	0.168986	12
13	4.898011	29.984701	0.033350	0.204165	6.121812	0.163350	13
14	5.534753	34.882712	0.028667	0.180677	6.302488	0.158667	14
15	6.254270	40.417464	0.024742	0.159891	6.462379	0.154742	15
16	7.067326	46.671735	0.021426	0.141496	6.603875	0.151426	16
17	7.986078	53.739060	0.018608	0.125218	6.729093	0.148608	17
18	9.024268	61.725138	0.016201	0.110812	6.839905	0.146201	18
19	10.197423	70.749406	0.014134	0.098064	6.937969	0.144134	19
20	11.523088	80.946829	0.012354	0.086782	7.024752	0.142354	20

Monthly Compounding

EFFECTIVE (MONTHLY RATE = 1.083333%

MONTH	MFV1	MFV1/P	MSSF	MPV1	MPV1/P	MPRF	MONTH
1	1.010833	1.000000	1.000000	0.989283	0.989283	1.010833	1
2	1.021784	2.010833	0.497306	0.978680	1.967963	0.508140	2
3	1.032853	3.032617	0.329748	0.968192	2.936155	0.340581	3
4	1.044043	4.065471	0.245974	0.957815	3.893970	0.256807	4
5	1.055353	5.109513	0.195713	0.947550	4.841520	0.206547	5
6	1.066786	6.164866	0.162210	0.937395	5.778915	0.173043	6
7	1.078343	7.231652	0.138281	0.927349	6.706264	0.149114	7

						YEAR
0.131170	7.623674	0.917410	0.120337	8.309995	1.090025	8
0.117216	8.531253	0.907578	0.106383	9.400020	1.101834	9
0.106055	9.429104	0.897851	0.095221	10.501854	1.113770	10
0.096924	10.317333	0.888229	0.086091	11.615624	1.125836	11

						YEAR
0.089317	11.196042	0.878710	0.078484	12.741460	1.138032	1
0.047542	21.034112	0.772130	0.036708	27.241655	1.295118	2
0.033694	29.678917	0.678478	0.022861	43.743348	1.473886	3
0.026827	37.275190	0.596185	0.015994	62.528811	1.677330	4
0.022753	43.950107	0.523874	0.011920	83.894449	1.908857	5
0.020074	49.815421	0.460333	0.009241	108.216068	2.172341	6
0.018192	54.969328	0.404499	0.007359	135.894861	2.472194	7
0.016807	59.498115	0.355437	0.005974	167.394225	2.813437	8
0.015754	63.477604	0.312326	0.004920	203.241525	3.201783	9
0.014931	66.974419	0.274444	0.004098	244.036917	3.643733	10
0.014276	70.047103	0.241156	0.003443	290.463399	4.146687	11
0.013746	72.747100	0.211906	0.002913	343.298242	4.719064	12
0.013312	75.119613	0.186204	0.002479	403.426010	5.370448	13
0.012953	77.204363	0.163619	0.002119	471.853363	6.111745	14
0.012652	79.036253	0.143774	0.001819	549.725914	6.955364	15
0.012400	80.645952	0.126336	0.001567	638.347406	7.915430	16
0.012186	82.060410	0.111012	0.001353	739.201542	9.008017	17
0.012004	83.303307	0.097548	0.001171	853.976825	10.251416	18
0.011849	84.395453	0.085716	0.001016	984.594826	11.666444	19
0.011716	85.355132	0.075319	0.000882	1133.242353	13.276792	20
0.011601	86.198412	0.066184	0.000768	1302.408067	15.109421	21
0.011502	86.939409	0.058156	0.000669	1494.924144	17.195012	22
0.011417	87.590531	0.051103	0.000583	1714.013694	19.568482	23
0.011343	88.162677	0.044904	0.000509	1963.344717	22.269568	24
0.011278	88.665428	0.039458	0.000445	2247.091520	25.343491	25
0.011222	89.107200	0.034672	0.000389	2570.004599	28.841716	26
0.011174	89.495389	0.030467	0.000340	2937.490172	32.822810	27
0.011131	89.836495	0.026771	0.000298	3355.700690	37.353424	28
0.011094	90.136227	0.023524	0.000261	3831.637843	42.509410	29
0.011062	90.399605	0.020671	0.000229	4373.269783	48.377089	30

14.00% NOMINAL RATE

Annual Compounding

YEAR	Future Value of 1 — FV1	Future Value of 1 per Period — FV1/P	Sinking Fund Factor — SFF	Present Value of 1 — PV1	Present Value of 1 per Period — PV1/P	Principal Recovery Factor — PRF	YEAR
			EFFECTIVE (ANNUAL) RATE = 14.00%				
1	1.140000	1.000000	1.000000	0.877193	0.877193	1.140000	1
2	1.299600	2.140000	0.467290	0.769468	1.646661	0.607290	2
3	1.481544	3.439600	0.290731	0.674972	2.321632	0.430731	3
4	1.688960	4.921144	0.203205	0.592080	2.913712	0.343205	4
5	1.925415	6.610104	0.151284	0.519369	3.433081	0.291284	5
6	2.194973	8.535519	0.117157	0.455587	3.888668	0.257157	6
7	2.502269	10.730491	0.093192	0.399637	4.288305	0.233192	7
8	2.852586	13.232760	0.075570	0.350559	4.638864	0.215570	8
9	3.251949	16.085347	0.062168	0.307508	4.946372	0.202168	9
10	3.707221	19.337295	0.051714	0.269744	5.216116	0.191714	10
11	4.226232	23.044516	0.043394	0.236617	5.452733	0.183394	11
12	4.817905	27.270749	0.036669	0.207559	5.660292	0.176669	12
13	5.492411	32.088654	0.031164	0.182069	5.842362	0.171164	13
14	6.261349	37.581065	0.026609	0.159710	6.002072	0.166609	14
15	7.137938	43.842414	0.022809	0.140096	6.142168	0.162809	15
16	8.137249	50.980352	0.019615	0.122892	6.265060	0.159615	16
17	9.276464	59.117601	0.016915	0.107800	6.372859	0.156915	17
18	10.575169	68.394066	0.014621	0.094561	6.467420	0.154621	18
19	12.055693	78.969235	0.012663	0.082948	6.550369	0.152663	19
20	13.743490	91.024928	0.010986	0.072762	6.623131	0.150986	20

Monthly Compounding

MONTH	MFV1	MFV1/P	MSSF	MPV1	MPV1/P	MPRF	MONTH
			EFFECTIVE (MONTHLY) RATE = 1.166667%				
1	1.011667	1.000000	1.000000	0.988468	0.988468	1.011667	1
2	1.023469	2.011667	0.497100	0.977069	1.965537	0.508767	2
3	1.035410	3.035136	0.329475	0.965801	2.931338	0.341141	3
4	1.047490	4.070546	0.245667	0.954663	3.886001	0.257334	4
5	1.059710	5.118036	0.195387	0.943654	4.829655	0.207054	5
6	1.072074	6.177746	0.161871	0.932772	5.762427	0.173538	6
7	1.084581	7.249820	0.137934	0.922015	6.684442	0.149601	7

YEAR						
8	0.131651	7.595824	0.911382	0.119985	8.334401	1.097235
9	0.117693	8.496696	0.900872	0.106026	9.431636	1.110036
10	0.106528	9.387178	0.890483	0.094462	10.541672	1.122986
11	0.097396	10.267392	0.880214	0.085729	11.664658	1.136088

YEAR						
1	0.089787	11.137455	0.870063	0.078120	12.800745	1.149342
2	0.048013	20.827743	0.757010	0.036346	27.513180	1.320987
3	0.034178	29.258904	0.658646	0.022511	44.422800	1.518266
4	0.027326	36.594546	0.573064	0.015660	63.857736	1.745007
5	0.023268	42.977016	0.498601	0.011602	86.195125	2.005610
6	0.020606	48.530168	0.433815	0.008939	111.868425	2.305132
7	0.018740	53.361760	0.377446	0.007073	141.375828	2.649385
8	0.017372	57.565549	0.328402	0.005705	175.289927	3.045049
9	0.016334	61.223111	0.285730	0.004667	214.268826	3.499803
10	0.015527	64.405420	0.248603	0.003860	259.068912	4.022471
11	0.014887	67.174230	0.216301	0.003220	310.559534	4.623195
12	0.014371	69.583269	0.188195	0.002705	369.739871	5.313632
13	0.013951	71.679284	0.163742	0.002284	437.758319	6.107180
14	0.013605	73.502950	0.142466	0.001938	515.934780	7.019239
15	0.013317	75.089654	0.123954	0.001651	605.786272	8.067507
16	0.013077	76.470187	0.107848	0.001410	709.056369	9.272324
17	0.012875	77.671337	0.093834	0.001208	827.749031	10.657072
18	0.012704	78.716413	0.081642	0.001037	964.167496	12.248621
19	0.012559	79.625696	0.071034	0.000892	1120.958972	14.077855
20	0.012435	80.416829	0.061804	0.000769	1301.166005	16.180270
21	0.012330	81.105164	0.053773	0.000663	1508.285522	18.596664
22	0.012239	81.704060	0.046786	0.000573	1746.336688	21.373928
23	0.012162	82.225136	0.040707	0.000495	2019.938898	24.565954
24	0.012095	82.678506	0.035417	0.000428	2334.401417	28.234683
25	0.012038	83.072966	0.030815	0.000371	2695.826407	32.451308
26	0.011988	83.416171	0.026811	0.000321	3111.227338	37.297652
27	0.011945	83.714781	0.023328	0.000279	3588.665088	42.867759
28	0.011908	83.974591	0.020296	0.000242	4137.404359	49.269718
29	0.011876	84.200641	0.017659	0.000210	4768.093467	56.627757
30	0.011849	84.397320	0.015365	0.000182	5492.970967	65.084661

15.00% NOMINAL RATE

Annual Compounding

EFFECTIVE (ANNUAL) RATE = 15.00%

YEAR	Future Value of 1 FV1	Future Value of 1 per Period FV1/P	Sinking Fund Factor SFF	Present Value of 1 PV1	Present Value of 1 per Period PV1/P	Principal Recovery Factor PRF	YEAR
1	1.150000	1.000000	1.000000	0.869565	0.869565	1.150000	1
2	1.322500	2.150000	0.465116	0.756144	1.625709	0.615116	2
3	1.520875	3.472500	0.287977	0.657516	2.283225	0.437977	3
4	1.749006	4.993375	0.200265	0.571753	2.854978	0.350265	4
5	2.011357	6.742381	0.148316	0.497177	3.352155	0.298316	5
6	2.313061	8.753738	0.114237	0.432328	3.784483	0.264237	6
7	2.660020	11.066799	0.090360	0.375937	4.160420	0.240360	7
8	3.059023	13.726819	0.072850	0.326902	4.487322	0.222850	8
9	3.517876	16.785842	0.059574	0.284262	4.771584	0.209574	9
10	4.045558	20.303718	0.049252	0.247185	5.018769	0.199252	10
11	4.652391	24.349276	0.041069	0.214943	5.233712	0.191069	11
12	5.350250	29.001667	0.034481	0.186907	5.420619	0.184481	12
13	6.152788	34.351917	0.029110	0.162528	5.583147	0.179110	13
14	7.075706	40.504705	0.024688	0.141329	5.724476	0.174688	14
15	8.137062	47.580411	0.021017	0.122894	5.847370	0.171017	15
16	9.357621	55.717472	0.017948	0.106865	5.954235	0.167948	16
17	10.761264	65.075093	0.015367	0.092926	6.047161	0.165367	17
18	12.375454	75.836357	0.013186	0.080805	6.127966	0.163186	18
19	14.231772	88.211811	0.011336	0.070265	6.198231	0.161336	19
20	16.366537	102.443583	0.009761	0.061100	6.259331	0.159761	20

Monthly Compounding

EFFECTIVE (MONTHLY) RATE = 1.250000%

MONTH	MFV1	MFV1/P	MSSF	MPV1	MPV1/P	MPRF	MONTH
1	1.012500	1.000000	1.000000	0.987654	0.987654	1.012500	1
2	1.025156	2.012500	0.496894	0.975461	1.963115	0.509394	2
3	1.037971	3.037656	0.329201	0.963418	2.926534	0.341701	3
4	1.050945	4.075627	0.245361	0.951524	3.878058	0.257861	4
5	1.064082	5.126572	0.195062	0.939777	4.817835	0.207562	5
6	1.077383	6.190654	0.161534	0.928175	5.746010	0.174034	6
7	1.090850	7.268038	0.137589	0.916716	6.662726	0.150089	7

YEAR						
8	0.132133	7.568124	0.905398	0.119633	8.358888	1.104486
9	0.118171	8.462345	0.894221	0.105671	9.463374	1.118292
10	0.107003	9.345526	0.883181	0.094503	10.581666	1.132271
11	0.097868	10.217803	0.872277	0.085368	11.713937	1.146424

YEAR						
1	0.090258	11.079312	0.861509	0.077758	12.860361	1.160755
2	0.048487	20.624235	0.742197	0.035987	27.788084	1.347351
3	0.034665	28.847267	0.639409	0.022165	45.115505	1.563944
4	0.027831	35.931481	0.550856	0.015331	65.228388	1.815355
5	0.023790	42.034592	0.474568	0.011290	88.574508	2.107181
6	0.021145	47.292474	0.408844	0.008645	115.673621	2.445920
7	0.019297	51.822185	0.352223	0.006797	147.129040	2.839113
8	0.017945	55.724570	0.303443	0.005445	183.641059	3.295513
9	0.016924	59.086509	0.261419	0.004424	226.022551	3.825282
10	0.016133	61.982847	0.225214	0.003633	275.217058	4.440213
11	0.015509	64.478068	0.194024	0.003009	332.319805	5.153998
12	0.015009	66.627722	0.167153	0.002509	398.602077	5.982526
13	0.014603	68.479668	0.144004	0.002103	475.539523	6.944244
14	0.014270	70.075134	0.124061	0.001770	564.845011	8.060563
15	0.013996	71.449643	0.106879	0.001496	668.506759	9.356334
16	0.013768	72.633794	0.092078	0.001268	788.832603	10.860408
17	0.013577	73.653950	0.079326	0.001077	928.501369	12.606267
18	0.013417	74.532823	0.068340	0.000917	1090.622520	14.632781
19	0.013282	75.289980	0.058875	0.000782	1278.805378	16.985067
20	0.013168	75.942278	0.050722	0.000668	1497.239481	19.715494
21	0.013071	76.504237	0.043697	0.000571	1750.787854	22.884848
22	0.012989	76.988370	0.037645	0.000489	2045.095272	26.563691
23	0.012919	77.405455	0.032432	0.000419	2386.713938	30.833924
24	0.012859	77.764777	0.027940	0.000359	2783.249347	35.790617
25	0.012808	78.074336	0.024071	0.000308	3243.529615	41.544120
26	0.012765	78.341024	0.020737	0.000265	3777.802015	48.222525
27	0.012727	78.570778	0.017865	0.000227	4397.961118	55.974514
28	0.012695	78.768713	0.015391	0.000195	5117.813598	64.972670
29	0.012668	78.939236	0.013260	0.000168	5953.385616	75.417320
30	0.012644	79.086142	0.011423	0.000144	6923.279611	87.540995

20.00% NOMINAL RATE

Annual Compounding

EFFECTIVE (ANNUAL) RATE = 20.00%

YEAR	Future Value of 1 (FV1)	Future Value of 1 per Period (FV1/P)	Sinking Fund Factor (SFF)	Present Value of 1 (PV1)	Present Value of 1 per Period (PV1/P)	Principal Recovery Factor (PRF)	YEAR
1	1.200000	1.000000	1.000000	0.833333	0.833333	1.200000	1
2	1.440000	2.200000	0.454545	0.694444	1.527778	0.654545	2
3	1.728000	0.640000	0.274725	0.578704	2.106481	0.474725	3
4	2.073600	5.368000	0.186289	0.482253	2.588735	0.386289	4
5	2.488320	7.441600	0.134380	0.401878	2.990612	0.334380	5
6	2.985984	9.929920	0.100706	0.334898	3.325510	0.300706	6
7	3.583181	12.915904	0.077424	0.279082	3.604592	0.277424	7
8	4.299817	16.499085	0.060609	0.232568	3.837160	0.260609	8
9	5.159780	20.798902	0.048079	0.193807	4.030967	0.248079	9
10	6.191736	25.958682	0.038523	0.161506	4.192472	0.238523	10
11	7.430084	32.150419	0.031104	0.134588	4.327060	0.231104	11
12	8.916100	39.580502	0.025265	0.112157	4.439217	0.225265	12
13	10.699321	48.496603	0.020620	0.093464	4.532681	0.220620	13
14	12.839185	59.195923	0.016893	0.077887	4.610567	0.216893	14
15	15.407022	72.035108	0.013882	0.064905	4.675473	0.213882	15
16	18.488426	87.442129	0.011436	0.054088	4.729561	0.211436	16
17	22.186111	105.930555	0.009440	0.045073	4.774634	0.209440	17
18	26.623333	128.116666	0.007805	0.037561	4.812195	0.207805	18
19	31.948000	154.740000	0.006462	0.031301	4.843496	0.206462	19
20	38.337600	186.688000	0.005357	0.026084	4.869580	0.205357	20

Monthly Compounding

EFFECTIVE (MONTHLY) RATE = 1.666667%

MONTH	MFV1	MFV1/P	MSSF	MPV1	MPV1/P	MPRF	MONTH
1	1.016667	1.000000	1.000000	0.983607	0.983607	1.016667	1
2	1.033611	2.016667	0.495868	0.967482	1.951088	0.512534	2

621

						YEAR
0.344506	2.902710	0.951622	0.327839	3.050278	1.050838	3
0.260503	3.838731	0.936021	0.243836	4.101116	1.068352	4
0.210110	4.759408	0.920677	0.193444	5.169468	1.086158	5
0.176523	5.664991	0.905583	0.159856	6.255625	1.104260	6
0.152538	6.555729	0.890738	0.135872	7.359886	1.122665	7
0.134556	7.431865	0.876136	0.117889	8.482551	1.141376	8
0.120574	8.293637	0.861773	0.103908	9.623926	1.160399	9
0.109394	9.141283	0.847645	0.092727	10.784325	1.179739	10
0.100250	9.975032	0.833749	0.083584	11.964064	1.199401	11

YEAR						
1	0.092635	10.795113	0.820081	0.075968	13.163465	1.219391
2	0.050896	19.647986	0.672534	0.034229	29.214877	1.486915
3	0.037164	26.908062	0.551532	0.020497	48.787826	1.813130
4	0.030430	32.861916	0.452301	0.013764	72.654905	2.210915
5	0.026494	37.744561	0.370924	0.009827	101.758208	2.695970
6	0.023953	41.748727	0.304188	0.007286	137.246517	3.287442
7	0.022206	45.032470	0.249459	0.005540	180.520645	4.008677
8	0.020953	47.725406	0.204577	0.004287	233.288730	4.888145
9	0.020027	49.933833	0.167769	0.003360	297.633662	5.960561
10	0.019326	51.744924	0.137585	0.002659	376.095300	7.268255
11	0.018786	53.230165	0.112831	0.002120	471.770720	8.862845
12	0.018366	54.448184	0.092530	0.001699	588.436476	10.807275
13	0.018035	55.447059	0.075882	0.001369	730.697658	13.178294
14	0.017773	56.266217	0.062230	0.001106	904.169675	16.069495
15	0.017563	56.937994	0.051033	0.000896	1115.699905	19.594998
16	0.017395	57.488906	0.041852	0.000728	1373.637983	23.893966
17	0.017259	57.940698	0.034322	0.000592	1688.165376	29.136090
18	0.017149	58.311205	0.028147	0.000483	2071.697274	35.528288
19	0.017060	58.615050	0.023082	0.000394	2539.372652	43.322878
20	0.016988	58.864229	0.018930	0.000322	3109.651838	52.827531

25.00% NOMINAL RATE

Annual Compounding

EFFECTIVE (ANNUAL) RATE = 25.00%

YEAR	Future Value of 1 — FV1	Future Value of 1 per Period — FV1/P	Sinking Fund Factor — SFF	Present Value of 1 — PV1	Present Value of 1 per Period — PV1/P	Principal Recovery Factor — PRF	YEAR
1	1.250000	1.000000	1.000000	0.800000	0.800000	1.250000	1
2	1.562500	2.250000	0.444444	0.640000	1.440000	0.694444	2
3	1.953125	3.812500	0.262295	0.512000	1.952000	0.512295	3
4	2.441406	5.765625	0.173442	0.409600	2.361600	0.423442	4
5	3.051758	8.207031	0.121847	0.327680	2.689280	0.371847	5
6	3.814697	11.258789	0.088819	0.262144	2.951424	0.338819	6
7	4.768372	15.073486	0.066342	0.209715	3.161139	0.316342	7
8	5.960464	19.841858	0.050399	0.167772	3.328911	0.300399	8
9	7.450581	25.802322	0.038756	0.134218	3.463129	0.288756	9
10	9.313226	33.252903	0.030073	0.107374	3.570503	0.280073	10
11	11.641532	42.566129	0.023493	0.085899	3.656403	0.273493	11
12	14.551915	54.207661	0.018448	0.068719	3.725122	0.268448	12
13	18.189894	68.759576	0.014543	0.054976	3.780098	0.264543	13
14	22.737368	86.949470	0.011501	0.043980	3.824078	0.261501	14
15	28.421709	109.686838	0.009117	0.035184	3.859263	0.259117	15
16	35.527137	138.108547	0.007241	0.028147	3.887410	0.257241	16
17	44.408921	173.635684	0.005759	0.022518	3.909928	0.255759	17
18	55.511151	218.044605	0.004586	0.018014	3.927942	0.254586	18
19	69.388939	273.555756	0.003656	0.014412	3.942354	0.253656	19
20	86.736174	342.944695	0.002916	0.011529	3.953883	0.252916	20

Monthly Compounding

EFFECTIVE (MONTHLY) RATE = 2.083333%

MONTH	MFV1	MFV1/P	MSSF	MPV1	MPV1/P	MPRF	MONTH
1	1.020833	1.000000	1.000000	0.979592	0.979592	1.020833	1
2	1.042101	2.020833	0.494845	0.959600	1.939192	0.515679	2
3	1.063811	3.062934	0.326484	0.940016	2.879208	0.347318	3

YEAR						
4	0.263155	3.800041	0.920832	0.242322	4.126745	1.085974
5	0.212672	4.702081	0.902040	0.191838	5.212719	1.108598
6	0.179028	5.585712	0.883631	0.158195	6.321317	1.131694
7	0.155007	6.451310	0.865598	0.134174	7.453011	1.155271
8	0.137001	7.299242	0.847932	0.116167	8.608283	1.179339
9	0.123003	8.129870	0.830628	0.102170	9.787622	1.203909
10	0.111812	8.943546	0.813676	0.090979	10.991531	1.228990
11	0.102663	9.740616	0.797070	0.081830	12.220521	1.254594

YEAR						
1	0.095044	10.521420	0.780804	0.074211	13.475115	1.280732
2	0.053372	18.736585	0.609654	0.032538	30.733120	1.640273
3	0.039760	25.151016	0.476021	0.018926	52.835991	2.100750
4	0.033157	30.159427	0.371679	0.012324	81.143837	2.690497
5	0.029351	34.070014	0.290208	0.008518	117.398588	3.445804
6	0.026937	37.123415	0.226596	0.006104	163.831191	4.413150
7	0.025312	39.507522	0.176927	0.004478	223.298892	5.652060
8	0.024173	41.369041	0.138145	0.003339	229.461053	7.238772
9	0.023352	42.822522	0.107864	0.002519	397.004337	9.270924
10	0.022749	43.957406	0.084221	0.001916	521.931099	11.873565
11	0.022300	44.843528	0.065760	0.001466	681.928746	15.206849
12	0.021961	45.535414	0.051346	0.001128	886.842783	19.475891
13	0.021703	46.075642	0.040091	0.000870	1149.282656	24.943389
14	0.021507	46.497454	0.031303	0.000673	1485.397684	31.945785
15	0.021355	46.826807	0.024442	0.000522	1915.870809	40.913975
16	0.021239	47.083966	0.019084	0.000405	2467.191327	52.399819
17	0.021148	47.284757	0.014901	0.000315	3173.284913	67.110102
18	0.021079	47.441536	0.011635	0.000245	4077.601254	85.950026
19	0.021024	47.563949	0.009084	0.000191	5235.787733	110.078911
20	0.020982	47.659530	0.007093	0.000149	6719.113709	140.981536

30.00% NOMINAL RATE

Annual Compounding

EFFECTIVE (ANNUAL) RATE = 30.00%

YEAR	Future Value of 1 FV1	Future Value of 1 per Period FV1/P	Sinking Fund Factor SFF	Present Value of 1 PV1	Present Value of 1 per Period PV1/P	Principal Recovery Factor PRF	YEAR
1	1.300000	1.000000	1.000000	0.769231	0.769231	1.300000	1
2	1.690000	2.300000	0.434783	0.591716	1.360947	0.734783	2
3	2.197000	3.990000	0.250627	0.455166	1.816113	0.550627	3
4	2.856100	6.187000	0.161629	0.350128	2.166241	0.461629	4
5	3.712930	9.043100	0.110582	0.269329	2.435570	0.410582	5
6	4.826809	12.756030	0.078394	0.207176	2.642746	0.378394	6
7	6.274852	17.582839	0.056874	0.159366	2.802112	0.356874	7
8	8.157307	23.857691	0.041915	0.122589	2.924702	0.341915	8
9	10.604499	32.014998	0.031235	0.094300	3.019001	0.331235	9
10	13.785849	42.619497	0.023463	0.072538	3.091539	0.323463	10
11	17.921604	56.405346	0.017729	0.055799	3.147338	0.317729	11
12	23.298085	74.326950	0.013454	0.042922	3.180260	0.313454	12
13	30.287511	97.625036	0.010243	0.033017	3.223277	0.310243	13
14	39.373764	127.912546	0.007818	0.025398	3.248675	0.307818	14
15	51.185893	167.286310	0.005978	0.019537	3.268211	0.305978	15
16	66.541661	218.472203	0.004577	0.015028	3.283239	0.304577	16
17	86.504159	285.013864	0.003509	0.011560	3.294800	0.303509	17
18	112.455407	371.518023	0.002692	0.008892	3.303692	0.302692	18
19	146.192029	483.973430	0.002066	0.006840	3.310532	0.302066	19
20	190.049638	630.165459	0.001587	0.005262	3.315794	0.301587	20

Monthly Compounding

EFFECTIVE (MONTHLY) RATE = 2.500000%

MONTH	MFV1	MFV1/P	MSSF	MPV1	MPV1/P	MPRF	MONTH
1	1.025000	1.000000	1.000000	0.975610	0.975610	1.025000	1
2	1.050625	2.025000	0.493827	0.951814	1.927424	0.518827	2

YEAR						
3	1.076891	3.075625	0.325137	0.928599	2.856024	0.350137
4	1.103813	4.152516	0.240818	0.905951	3.761974	0.265818
5	1.131408	5.256329	0.190247	0.883354	4.645828	0.215247
6	1.159693	6.387737	0.156550	0.862297	5.508125	0.181550
7	1.188686	7.547430	0.132495	0.841265	6.349391	0.157495
8	1.218403	8.736116	0.114467	0.820747	7.170137	0.139467
9	1.248863	9.954519	0.100457	0.800728	7.970866	0.125457
10	1.280085	11.203382	0.089259	0.781198	8.752064	0.114259
11	1.312087	12.483466	0.080106	0.762145	9.514209	0.105106

YEAR						
1	1.344889	13.795553	0.072487	0.743556	10.257765	0.097487
2	1.808726	32.349038	0.030913	0.552875	17.884986	0.055913
3	2.432535	57.301413	0.017452	0.411094	23.556251	0.042452
4	3.271490	90.859582	0.011006	0.305671	27.773154	0.036006
5	4.399790	135.991590	0.007353	0.227284	30.908656	0.032353
6	5.917228	196.689122	0.005084	0.168998	33.240078	0.030084
7	7.958014	278.320556	0.003593	0.125659	34.973620	0.028593
8	10.702644	388.105758	0.002577	0.093435	36.262606	0.027577
9	14.393866	535.754649	0.001867	0.069474	37.221039	0.026867
10	19.358150	734.325993	0.001362	0.051658	37.933687	0.026362
11	26.034559	1001.382375	0.000999	0.038410	38.463581	0.025999
12	35.013588	1360.543518	0.000735	0.028560	38.857586	0.025735
13	47.089383	1843.575325	0.000542	0.021236	39.150552	0.025542
14	63.329985	2493.199404	0.000401	0.015790	39.368388	0.025401
15	85.171789	3366.871568	0.000297	0.011741	39.530361	0.025297
16	114.546587	4541.863497	0.000220	0.008730	39.650797	0.025220
17	154.052425	6122.097012	0.000163	0.006491	39.740348	0.025163
18	207.183385	8247.335405	0.000121	0.004827	39.806934	0.025121
19	278.638619	11105.544769	0.000090	0.003589	39.856445	0.025090
20	274.747965	14949.518599	0.000067	0.002669	39.893259	0.025057

40.00% NOMINAL RATE

Annual Compounding

EFFECTIVE (ANNUAL) RATE = 40.00%

YEAR	Future Value of 1 FV1	Future Value of 1 per Period FV1/P	Sinking Fund Factor SFF	Present Value of 1 PV1	Present Value of 1 per Period PV1/P	Principal Recovery Factor PRF	YEAR
1	1.400000	1.000000	1.000000	0.714286	0.714286	1.400000	1
2	1.960000	2.400000	0.416667	0.510204	1.224490	0.816667	2
3	2.744000	4.360000	0.229358	0.364431	1.588921	0.629358	3
4	3.841600	7.104000	0.140766	0.260308	1.849229	0.540766	4
5	5.378240	10.945600	0.091361	0.185934	2.035164	0.491361	5
6	7.529536	16.323840	0.061260	0.132810	2.167974	0.461260	6
7	10.541350	23.853376	0.041923	0.094865	2.262839	0.441923	7
8	14.757891	34.394726	0.029074	0.067760	2.330599	0.429074	8
9	20.661047	49.152617	0.020345	0.048400	2.378999	0.420345	9
10	28.925465	69.813664	0.014324	0.034572	2.413571	0.414324	10
11	40.495652	98.739129	0.010128	0.024694	2.438265	0.410128	11
12	56.693912	139.234781	0.007182	0.017639	2.455904	0.407182	12
13	79.371477	195.928693	0.005104	0.012599	2.468503	0.405104	13
14	111.120068	275.300171	0.003632	0.008999	2.477502	0.403632	14
15	155.568096	386.420239	0.002588	0.006428	2.483930	0.402588	15
16	217.795334	541.988334	0.001845	0.004591	2.488521	0.401845	16
17	304.913467	759.783668	0.001316	0.003280	2.491801	0.401316	17
18	426.878854	1064.697136	0.000939	0.002343	2.494144	0.400939	18
19	597.630396	1491.575990	0.000670	0.001673	2.495817	0.400670	19
20	836.682554	2089.206386	0.000479	0.001195	2.497012	0.400479	20

Monthly Compounding

EFFECTIVE (MONTHLY) RATE = 3.333333%

MONTH	MFV1	MFV1/P	MSSF	MPV1	MPV1/P	MPRF	MONTH
1	1.033333	1.000000	1.000000	0.967742	0.967742	1.033333	1
2	1.067778	2.033333	0.491803	0.936524	1.904266	0.525137	2

YEAR						
3	1.103370	3.101111	0.322465	0.906314	2.810580	0.355798
4	1.140149	4.204481	0.237841	0.877078	3.687658	0.271175
5	1.178154	5.344631	0.187104	0.848785	4.536444	0.220437
6	1.217426	6.522785	0.153309	0.821405	5.357849	0.186642
7	1.258007	7.740211	0.129195	0.794908	6.152757	0.162529
8	1.299941	8.998218	0.111133	0.769266	6.922023	0.144466
9	1.343272	10.298159	0.097105	0.744451	7.666474	0.130438
10	1.388048	11.641431	0.085900	0.720436	8.386910	0.119233
11	1.434316	13.029479	0.076749	0.697196	9.084106	0.110082

YEAR						
1	1.482126	14.463795	0.069138	0.674706	9.758813	0.102471
2	2.196699	35.900968	0.027854	0.455229	16.343144	0.061188
3	3.255786	67.673570	0.014777	0.307146	20.785634	0.048110
4	4.825486	114.764586	0.008713	0.207233	23.783010	0.042047
5	7.151981	184.559427	0.005418	0.139821	25.805358	0.038752
6	10.600140	288.004211	0.003472	0.094338	27.169849	0.036806
7	15.710749	441.322465	0.002266	0.063651	28.090479	0.035599
8	23.285317	668.559511	0.001496	0.042946	28.711634	0.034829
9	34.511785	1005.353555	0.000995	0.028976	29.130732	0.034328
10	51.150831	1504.524930	0.000665	0.019550	29.413499	0.033998
11	75.812002	2244.360048	0.000446	0.013191	29.604284	0.033779
12	112.362976	3340.889274	0.000299	0.008900	29.733008	0.033633
13	166.536143	4966.084287	0.000201	0.006005	29.819859	0.033535
14	246.827629	7374.828867	0.000136	0.004051	29.878458	0.033469
15	365.829767	10944.893015	0.000091	0.002734	29.917995	0.033425
16	542.205989	16236.179658	0.000062	0.001844	29.944670	0.033395
17	803.617859	24078.535757	0.000042	0.001244	29.962669	0.033375
18	1191.063316	35701.899472	0.000028	0.000840	29.974812	0.033361
19	1765.306491	52929.194733	0.000019	0.000566	29.983006	0.033352
20	2616.407513	78462.225385	0.000013	0.000382	29.988534	0.033346

50.00% NOMINAL RATE

Annual Compounding

EFFECTIVE (ANNUAL) RATE = 50.00%

YEAR	Future Value of 1 FV 1	Future Value of 1 per Period FV1/P	Sinking Fund Factor SFF	Present Value of 1 PV1	Present Value of 1 per Period PV1/P	Principal Recovery Factor PRF	YEAR
1	1.50000	1.00000	1.000000	0.666667	0.666667	1.500000	1
2	2.25000	2.50000	0.400000	0.444444	1.111111	0.900000	2
3	3.37500	4.75000	0.210526	0.296296	1.407407	0.710526	3
4	5.06250	8.12500	0.123077	0.197531	1.604938	0.623077	4
5	7.59375	13.18750	0.075829	0.131687	1.736626	0.575829	5
6	11.39063	20.78125	0.048120	0.087791	1.824417	0.548120	6
7	17.08594	32.17188	0.031083	0.058528	1.882945	0.531083	7
8	25.62891	49.25781	0.020301	0.039018	1.921963	0.520301	8
9	38.44336	74.88672	0.013354	0.026012	1.947975	0.513354	9
10	57.66504	113.33008	0.008824	0.017342	1.965317	0.508824	10
11	86.49756	170.99512	0.005848	0.011561	1.976878	0.505848	11
12	129.74634	257.49268	0.003884	0.007707	1.984585	0.503884	12
13	194.61951	387.23901	0.002582	0.005138	1.989724	0.502582	13
14	291.92926	581.85852	0.001719	0.003425	1.993149	0.501719	14
15	437.89389	873.78778	0.001144	0.002284	1.995433	0.501144	15
16	656.84084	1311.68167	0.000762	0.001522	1.996955	0.500762	16
17	985.26125	1968.52251	0.000508	0.001015	1.997970	0.500508	17
18	1417.89188	2953.78376	0.000339	0.000677	1.998647	0.500339	18
19	2216.83782	4431.67564	0.000226	0.000451	1.999098	0.500226	19
20	3325.25676	6648.51346	0.000150	0.000301	1.999399	0.500150	20

Monthly Compounding

EFFECTIVE (MONTHLY) RATE = 4.166667%

MONTH	MFV1	MFV1/P	MSSF	MPV 1	MPV1/P	MPRF	MONTH
1	1.04167	1.00000	1.000000	0.960000	0.960000	1.041667	1
2	1.08507	2.04167	0.489796	0.921600	1.881600	0.531463	2

YEAR					
3	1.13028	3.12674	0.319822	0.884736	2.766336	0.361489
4	1.17738	4.25702	0.234906	0.849347	3.615683	0.276573
5	1.22643	5.43439	0.184013	0.815373	4.431055	0.225680
6	1.27753	6.66083	0.150132	0.782758	5.213813	0.191798
7	1.33076	7.93836	0.125971	0.75147	5.965261	0.167637
8	1.38621	9.26912	0.107885	0.721390	6.686650	0.149552
9	1.44397	10.65534	0.093850	0.692534	7.379184	0.135516
10	1.50414	12.09931	0.082649	0.664833	8.044017	0.124316
11	1.56681	13.60345	0.073511	0.638239	8.682256	0.115177

YEAR					
1	1.63209	15.17026	0.065918	0.612710	9.294966	0.107585
2	2.66373	39.92955	0.025044	0.375413	14.990082	0.066711
3	4.34746	80.33904	0.012447	0.230019	18.479535	0.054114
4	7.09546	146.29114	0.006836	0.140935	20.617557	0.048502
5	11.58047	253.93117	0.003938	0.086352	21.927544	0.045605
6	18.90041	429.60984	0.002328	0.052909	22.730186	0.043994
7	30.84725	716.33395	0.001396	0.032418	23.221973	0.043063
8	50.34561	1184.29470	0.000844	0.019863	23.523295	0.042511
9	82.16878	1948.05069	0.000513	0.012170	23.707918	0.042180
10	134.10718	3194.57236	0.000313	0.007457	23.821039	0.041980
11	218.87554	5229.01306	0.000191	0.004569	23.890349	0.041858
12	357.22549	8549.41179	0.000117	0.002799	23.932816	0.041784
13	583.02563	13968.61509	0.000072	0.001715	23.958835	0.041738
14	951.55271	22813.26498	0.000044	0.001051	23.974778	0.041711
15	1553.02359	37248.56618	0.000027	0.000644	23.984546	0.041694
16	2534.68069	60808.33658	0.000016	0.000395	23.990531	0.041683
17	4136.83748	99260.09961	0.000010	0.000242	23.994198	0.041677
18	6751.70819	162016.99645	0.000006	0.000148	23.996445	0.041673
19	11019.42332	264442.15957	0.000004	0.000091	23.997822	0.041670
20	17984.73614	431609.66734	0.000002	0.000056	23.998666	0.041669